THE ESSENTIAL GUIDE TO TV ON DVD

Author and critic Jo Berry has written about TV and film for numerous publications including the *Guardian*, *Radio Times*, *Empire*, *Eve* and *Maxim*. A contributor to the books *1001 Movies You Must See Before You Die* and *The Rough Guide To Cult TV*, among others, she is also the author of *The Ultimate DVD Easter Egg Guide*, *Chick Flicks* (with Angie Errigo) and *The Parents' Guide To Kids' Movies*.

THE ESSENTIAL GUIDE TO TV ON DVD

Jo BERRY

Copyright © Jo Berry 2008

The right of Duane Jo Berry to be identified as
the author of this work has been asserted by her in accordance with the
Copyright, Designs and Patents Act 1988.

First published in Great Britain in 2008 by
Orion Books
an imprint of the Orion Publishing Group Ltd
Orion House, 5 Upper St Martin's Lane,
London WC2H 9EA
An Hachette Livre UK Company

1 3 5 7 9 10 8 6 4 2

A CIP catalogue record for this book is available
from the British Library.

ISBN: 978 0 7528 8603 9

Printed in Great Britain by Clays Ltd, St Ives plc

The Orion Publishing Group's policy is to use papers that are natural,
renewable and recyclable and made from wood grown in sustainable forests.
The logging and manufacturing processes are expected to conform to the
environmental regulations of the country of origin.

Every effort has been made to fulfil requirements with regard to reproducing
copyright material. The author and publisher will be glad to rectify
any omissions at the earliest opportunity.

www.orionbooks.co.uk

For Steve and Danny
Thank you both for holding my heart in your hands.
And for Dad. 'I'm all clear' are my three favourite words of all time.

Huge thank yous to two people,
without whom this book would not have been possible:
Ndidi Nkagbu and Jana Stubniakova

CONTENTS

INTRODUCTION

I love TV. When it's really good it can make you laugh, make you cry, make you scratch your head, or maybe even surprise you. And when it's bad, it can make you turn it off and go and do something more interesting instead.

When I was a child there were just three TV channels in England, then four and now, thanks to satellite TV, Freeview and the internet, there are hundreds. Of course, much of what is shown is utter drivel, but there are many gems, some hidden on obscure cable channels, some shown late at night, and some winning huge audiences. And some of those shows aren't just great – they're collectable. Even before I started this book, my DVD shelves were brimming with classic TV series I just had to own on DVD, from *24* to *Flambards*, *Moonlighting* to *Arrested Development* and *Star Trek* to *The Office*. Now they're completely buckling under the strain, though my collection is nothing compared to the thousands of TV series on DVD you can find at your local store or DVD website.

This book, hopefully, will remind you of some classics you may have forgotten about, introduce you to lesser known series you may like and even warn you against spending your hard-earned cash on a bad show that somehow has been deemed fit to take up space on a DVD shop's shelf. Over the next pages you'll find series old and new, American, Australian, Irish and British, long and short-lived, black and white, and colour. And while I've tried to include as many series as possible, this is a guide to the best, worst, most memorable and just plain odd shows that you can buy – it's not a list of absolutely every TV show ever made that's on DVD. The reason? Well, if I'd included every TV DVD in existence, I'd still be writing this book as new series are released on DVD every day. I would also probably be square-eyed, divorced and have a son who thinks Mummy is physically soldered to her laptop. And you would be holding a book thicker than the British Isles Yellow Pages. Let's just hope I haven't missed out your favourite.

A quick note: just as new series come to DVD on a daily basis, so do some disappear from DVD into obscurity. For the purposes of this guide, I have made sure each TV DVD featured is readily available from at least one major supplier (HMV, Amazon.co.uk, Play.com, Zavvi) – if a series was issued on DVD but now is only available to buy second-hand (eg. the distributor has stopped making new discs), I have not included it.

Happy viewing!

Jo Berry
October 2008

COP SHOWS

THE GOOD, THE BAD AND THE TRIGGER-HAPPY

24 (2001–)

Starring Kiefer Sutherland, Mary Lynn Rajskub, Carlos Bernard

LA-based Counter Terrorism Unit member Jack Bauer (Sutherland) has very bad days. In a clever twist, each season of *24* follows Jack over the course of one such nightmare day, spread over 24 episodes (so each episode covers one hour of said day, in 'real time'). While this format has been criticised for never showing Jack peeing or having a snack, it's an incredibly effective device that pulls you in and has you on the edge of your seat for an entire season as a complicated terrorist-related plot unravels, twists, turns and confuses while poor hungry and possibly bladder-challenged Jack remains at its heart.

The first season had Jack being manipulated to shoot the presidential candidate, David Palmer (Dennis Haysbert) in order to save his own daughter (the kidnap-prone Kim, as played by Elisha Cuthbert), while subsequent plots have seen our hero trying to locate nuclear bombs, prevent viruses from being released, capture nefarious international bad guys and surprising turncoats, or save friends and family from hideous fates. No one is safe (as fans will know, many regular cast members have been shockingly bumped off, and Sutherland has himself hinted even Jack may get killed off at some point), and poor Jack has undergone graphic torture, drug addiction and even captivity by Chinese bad guys, all before lunch. It's heart-stopping stuff, anchored by a superb, believable performance from Sutherland as a man who is often on the edge or over it, mourning the loss of those close to him and questioning why in the hell he does the job in the first place. Other notable cast members include Rajskub, as dour computer whiz Chloe, Bernard, James Morrison, and Reiko Aylesworth as fellow CTU operatives Tony Almeida, Bill Buchanan, and Michelle Dessler, Penny Johnson as Sherry Palmer, and Gregory Itzin and Jean Smart as Charles and Martha Logan.

Season 1 and Season 5 are the best so far (Season 7, especially, was too far-fetched), but aside from a couple of awful plots for Kim Bauer (terrorised by a mountain lion!), none of the seasons are anything less than teeth-grindingly gripping.

 TV Trivia: So the cast look like events are all happening on the same day, they are required to have their hair cut every five days so it looks the same throughout a season.

BERGERAC (1981–1991)

Starring John Nettles, Terence Alexander

For anyone under the age of 60, this was an inexplicably successful British crime drama set on the wealthy island of Jersey. John Nettles (now better known for *another* detective series, *Midsomer Murders*) starred as detective sergeant Jim Bergerac (later Jim resigned and became a private eye), who shuffled along miserably solving crime in the 'exotic' Channel Island where the series was filmed on location (*Bergerac* marked a change for the BBC, who had previously spent little money on location filming for previous crime series). Joining him were Terence Alexander, Deborah Grant and various guest stars each week (who were obviously happy to fly to the location for a few days of filming and a short break) including Beryl Reid, Norman Wisdom and Liza Goddard.

The series ran for over 80 episodes, from 1981 until 1991, and Nettles became the face of Jersey tourism – quite surprising when Bergerac himself described his home thus: 'Jersey is an island. It's nine miles by five. And if you drive *very* slowly, you can take a whole hour to go right round it. But when you get back, there's still the same old restaurants and bars, discos and boutiques. Same sad faces waiting to be faced. Jersey is some kind of prison.'

TV Trivia: Martin Campbell, who directed some episodes of *Bergerac*, went on to helm the rather more exotic James Bond movies *Golden Eye* and *Casino Royale*.

BETWEEN THE LINES (1992–1994)

Starring Neil Pearson, Tom Georgeson, Siobhan Redmond

Set in the Complaints Investigation Bureau of the London Metropolitan police – the department which polices the police (usually known as Internal Affairs in the US, which, let's face it, sounds far sexier) – this grubby-looking (it's all set in mundane offices, shabby flats and grimy pubs) drama series had Tony Clark (Pearson), Harry Naylor (Georgeson) and Maureen O'Connell (Redmond) investigating bribery, corruption and other nasties amongst the police force for two series (for the third series, they were no longer at CIB, but working in the private sector).

Of course, they're not liked by the rest of the force and, as is always the case in cop shows, the characters all have their personal demons, too – Tony's marriage is crumbling and he has an unstable mistress, followed by a relationship with a married woman (Francesca Annis); Mo comes out as gay to her colleagues; Harry's wife is diagnosed with multiple sclerosis. It's dark, gripping stuff, and the best episodes include Series 1's 'Out Of The Game' and 'Lies And Damned Lies' and Series 2's 'Manslaughter' and 'Some Must Watch'. The third series is something of a disappointment, although it does have an explosive ending.

 TV Trivia: Pearson was appearing alongside Leonard Rossiter on stage in *Loot* the night Rossiter died.

BONES (2005–)

Starring Emily Deschanel, David Boreanaz, Michaela Conlin, TJ Thyne

Loosely based on Kathy Reichs' novels about forensic anthropologist Temperance Brennan (Deschanel), this series throws the bookwormy scientist – nicknamed 'Bones' because she can find out vital clues from skeletons – into a partnership with FBI man Seeley Booth (*Angel*'s Boreanaz). Together, they solve murders, catch bad guys, and identify long-dead corpses from their bone structure. Of course, in the tradition of most TV partnerships, they are an odd pairing – he's cocky and charming, and has ghosts from his former job as an Army Ranger; she's socially challenged, naive and has a tortured family history (parents abandoned her, and were wanted by the government for activist activities – her dad, played by Ryan O'Neal, pops up occasionally).

A drama with a nicely humorous vein – comedy often provided by Brennan's naivety about the world, and the office relationships between her fellow scientists, including the sultry Angela (Conlin), conspiracy theorist Jack (Thyne) and young boffin Zack (Eric Millegan) – this is a nice twist on the odd-couple-solving-crime genre (so far, there's been no romance between the pair, either) that boasts interesting stories, hi-tech sleuthing and a group of genuinely likeable characters. Great stuff.

 TV Trivia: Billy Gibbons of ZZ Top plays Angela's dad, while British thesp Stephen Fry has played Booth's shrink.

CAGNEY AND LACEY (1982–1988)

Starring Sharon Gless, Tyne Daly

At the time, a ground-breaking cop show for featuring two reasonably unglamorous women in the lead roles – let's face it, neither Cagney or Lacey looks like Angie Dickinson in *Police Woman* (sadly not on DVD) – this series focused as much on tough single gal Christine Cagney (Gless) and sensitive family woman Mary Beth Lacey's (Daly) home lives and relationships as it did on the crimes they were working on. Over the years, Cagney had to deal with her boozy dad and her own alcoholism, while Lacey had errant kids and wishy-washy husband Harvey (John Karlen) to put up with.

Originally a TV movie that starred Loretta Swit in the Gless role, the New York-set series was almost cancelled for low ratings in its first year but viewers wrote into the TV company to protest and the series returned, and was more successful, a year later. Throughout the series run, the crimes themselves aren't that thrilling (and when they chase down a criminal in heels and a restrictive skirt it borders on hilarious), it's the relationships between the women and the men in their lives that make this worth watching, and for the strong lead performances from Gless and Daly.

The series ended in 1988, but a series of TV movies reuniting the pair were made between 1994 and 1996.

TV Trivia: The first six episodes ever made didn't star Gless – the role of Cagney was played by Meg Foster. She was fired, however (apparently for looking too similar to Daly on screen),and it is only the Gless-starring episodes that are availaible on DVD.

CHiPS (1977–1983)

Starring Erik Estrada, Larry Wilcox, Robert Pine

The decade that brought us such cheesy TV as *The Love Boat* and *Charlie's Angels* also gave us the cheesiest show of them all – *CHiPs*. An 'action' show about two California highway patrolmen, hot-headed 'Ponch' (Estrada) and his by-the-book partner Jon Baker (Wilcox, who apparently didn't get on with his co-star in real life), who spend their days zipping up California's roads and freeways on their motorbikes, giving people speeding tickets, helping stranded motorists, giving aid at accident scenes and, bizarrely, solving murders, and intervening in hijackings. (A little more exciting than *Dixon of Dock Green* on his pushbike, then).

Aimed firmly at children – Ponch and Jon never once draw a gun or swear – this has lots of high speed chases, fun dialogue and easy-to-follow (okay, simple) plots. The performances aren't exactly Oscar-worthy – Estrada delivers more ham than a truck full of Danish Bacon – but for seventies kitsch, hilarious biker outfits and general silliness, it can't be beat.

TV Trivia: Real-life CHP officers don't ride in pairs – the teaming of Ponch and Jon was explained by having Jon be Ponch's training officer while he was on probation.

COLUMBO (1971–1978; 1989–2003)

Starring Peter Falk

One of the most memorable cops on TV, Columbo (Falk) was a dishevelled, mac-wearing detective who mumbled and looked more shifty than most of the criminals he was investigating. He seems too polite, and even a little slow, but his manner is what lulls the bad guys into a false sense of security, and causes them to be trapped by their own arrogance. We're not sure it would work in the real world, but on screen, Columbo's tactic of nicely asking a few questions, getting up to leave and then stopping, saying 'oh, just one more thing...' was usually all it took to get the killer to confess or reveal a slip-up in his diabolical plan.

The character – whose first name is never spoken – had originally appeared in a US TV series called *The Chevy Mystery Show*, as played by Bert Freed, but it is Falk who made the role his own from the first episode (actually a TV movie, *Prescription for Murder*). He's dishevelled, dogged and yet manipulative, and more than a match for the bad guys (Donald Pleasance, Janet Leigh and Leonard Nimoy were just some of the well-known actors playing criminals trying to outwit Columbo and they all failed, of course).

The series ran until 1978 and then a new series of TV movies were made between 1989 and 2003.

 TV Trivia: A spin-off series, *Mrs Columbo*, was made in 1979 with Kate Mulgrew, but was cancelled after 13 episodes.

THE COMMANDER (2003–2007)

Starring Amanda Burton, Matthew Marsh

Writer Lynda La Plante, who had created the memorable character Jane Tennison for *Prime Suspect*, delivered another strong female role for this series. Clare Blake (Burton) is commander of the Homicide division of the Metropolitan Police – all murders are reviewed by her department. With her team, which includes DCI Hedges (Marsh), she investigates crimes in the capital, often putting her own life in danger in the process.

Seven 'series' – they are actually pairs of 90-minute episodes telling one story each time – were made of this drama that has Blake dealing with a lover who may be a murderer, a stalker who is terrorising her, and the murder of a loved one. Burton is suitably tough and strong-willed in the lead, but while she gives a terrific performance, this is never quite as gripping or involving as La Plante's other dramas.

TV Trivia: Burton's first TV role was as yuppie wife Heather in the early years of *Brookside*.

CRACKER (1993–1996; 2006)

Starring Robbie Coltrane, Geraldine Somerville, Barbara Flynn

Anyone who thinks of Robbie Coltrane as a comic actor (or as Hagrid in the Harry Potter movies) should check out this powerful series in which he thunders across every scene as Dr Eddie 'Fitz' Fitzgerald, a forensic psychologist who aids the British police during difficult investigations. Fitz is eccentric, rude, arrogant, a gambler, a drunk – but he's also brilliant.

To say Coltrane gives a powerhouse performance in each of the feature-length episodes (often shown in two parts) of *Cracker* would be understating the case – he's mesmerising and delivers the sharp dialogue with glee. Whether Fitz is tracking a murderous couple in 'To Say I Love You' or questioning the murderer (Robert Carlyle) of a Pakistani shopkeeper, you'll be gripped almost as tightly as Fitz holds his forever smouldering cigarette. Only 10 episodes of this series were made.

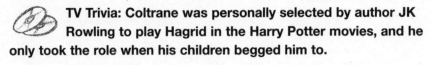 **TV Trivia: Coltrane was personally selected by author JK Rowling to play Hagrid in the Harry Potter movies, and he only took the role when his children begged him to.**

CRIMINAL MINDS (2005–)

Starring Thomas Gibson, Mandy Patinkin, Shemar Moore, Matthew Gray Gubler

An intelligent TV drama, *Criminal Minds* follows a team of profilers from the FBI's Behavioural Analysis Unit (BAU) as they unravel the psychology of the bad guys to find out whodunit. As the title suggests, the team are able to get inside the head of a villain to find out how they think, their motivations and what they're likely to do next thereby cracking the case. Jason Gideon (Patinkin) is the man in charge, accompanied by his standard issue sidekicks, including geeky genius Dr Spencer Reid (Gray Gubler) and special agent Derek Morgan (Moore) looking like he just stepped off the cover of Men's *Vogue*. Patinkin left the series unexpectedly at the end of Season 2 (he did a similar thing when he starred on *Chicago Hope*) leaving humourless suit Aaron Hotchner (Gibson) at the helm.

Television crime dramas are two a penny but, of course, some are better than others. Although *Criminal Minds* bears some resemblance to numerous shows, including *CSI* – a brilliant yet unfathomable investigator leading his trusty band of colleagues, all of whom are gorgeous, with at least one being some shade of brown – this is not necessarily a bad thing. This series takes a more disturbing approach to the genre. Intriguing cat and mouse games ensue as the profilers pit their wits against the most devious, depraved and highly intelligent murderers. Most episodes recall true-life cases, shown in brief flashes, which outline techniques used by serial killers to lure and assault their victims. These real cases lend some credence to the story being told. One of the more pretentious elements of this glossy show is the moment in each episode when one of the main characters drops a quote from a great philosopher, or in one case Yoda, making some insightful comment on the human psyche.

This is an entertaining, though pretty formulaic, show. Wise words from Aristotle are not going to elevate it to anything more than that.

 TV trivia: In the show's opening credits, mug shots of real-life serial killers and mass murderers are shown.

CSI: CRiME SCENE INVESTiGATiON (2000–)

Starring William Petersen, Marg Helgenberger, Gary Dourdan, George Eads

The highly successful *CSI* franchise began with this Las Vegas-based series charting the investigations of that city's Crime Scene Investigation division of the police department. The gambling capital of the world, looking like a latter day Sodom and Gomorrah, is the perfect backdrop for this seething murderous mass of humanity. In some ways the series is standard fodder – a body is discovered at the start of each episode and the team is dispatched to look for clues and find the culprit. The enigmatic and spookily insightful Gil Grissom (Petersen) leads his perky team of specialists to the crime scenes where the victims are splayed, usually in highly improbable circumstances. Forty-five minutes, numerous red herrings and a handful of monochrome flashbacks later, the perpetrator is unmasked.

The use of state-of-the-art technology to crack cases was new to TV crime dramas when *CSI* premiered, which probably accounts for the instant success of the show. The forensic world of blood spatters, bullet trajectories, fingerprints and DNA gave an interesting perspective to the crime-solving business. Although the emphasis is always on the case in hand, there are occasional glimpses into the team's personal lives, including the touching will-they-won't-they sexual undercurrent between Grissom and his co-worker Sara Sidle (Jorja Fox). Unfortunately, Sidle leaves the series in

Season 8, shortly after love blossoms between the two.

The slick production, which includes segments in each episode showing the scientists at work in the lab with some bangin' tunes laid over the top, certainly appealed to the MTV generation. A peculiar, but quite compelling, multi-episode arc in Season 7 about the miniature serial killer, who built tiny models of her crime scenes, sums up the quirkiness of this series.

 TV trivia: The popularity of *CSI* has been credited for a large surge of applications for courses in forensic science.

CSI: MiAMi (2002–)

Starring David Caruso, Emily Proctor, Adam Rodriguez, Khandi Alexander

Same format, different city. The forensic scientists of the Miami-Dade Police department deploy the same techniques to solve crimes in this first *CSI* spin-off. Lt. Horatio Caine (Caruso) leads his team of identikit investigators to one picture-perfect location after another – picture-perfect, that is, apart from the blood-spattered bodies spoiling the view. With Miami being so close to Cuba and the Caribbean, many of the crimes are drug-related but in this show, even the dealers and smugglers are glamorous.

Some critics have branded this incarnation of *CSI* as style over substance – certainly, it doesn't quite have the class and intelligence of the original. Caruso's Caine lacks the gravitas of William Petersen's Grissom. While Grissom is prepared to roll up his sleeves and poke around the dead bodies himself, Caine, on the other hand, seems content to waft around looking mysterious while his team go about the dirty business of gathering evidence. Miami's bad guys should fall about laughing at the sight of him fixing them with a watery stare before clamping on his sunglasses for dramatic effect. Perhaps it's unfair to compare the two shows – the producers chose a completely different city to create a completely different feel so it was never going to be the same. However, if you're looking for a fast paced, sexy cop show with the same views, watch *Miami Vice*, it does a better job. It's obvious why Florida is called the Sunshine State but episode after episode of blue skies, blue seas and impossibly good looking people does start to wear thin and the crime-solving aspect of the series is almost incidental.

This series is a poor relation of its Vegas-based stablemate – the only reasons to watch it are to perv at the cast and enjoy the scenery.

 TV trivia: Following the success of the original *CSI*, producers anticipated a string of copycat shows so decided to get in first with the Miami version of their own.

CSI: NY (2004–)

Starring Gary Sinise, Melinda Kanakaredes, Carmine Giovinazzo, Hill Harper

The Big Apple's incarnation of *CSI* started off on a sombre note with Season 1 focusing on Det. MacTaylor (Sinise) as he mourned the loss of his wife who was killed in the Twin Towers on 9/11. This storyline ran throughout the season and the dark, gritty cases presented in each episode reflected Taylor's melancholy state of mind. Cynical New York City, bathed in a grey wash, is the perfect backdrop for such bleak goings on and the suitably street-wise, smart-mouthed team of investigators are unfazed by even the most depraved cases. Subsequent seasons are less grim and conform more to the *CSI* standard with bizarre scenarios, numerous suspects, multiple motives and the last-minute twist at the end.

The *CSI* formula works better in the desolate urban landscape of New York than it does in sunny Miami but it is still quite different from the original. This is essentially a cop show underpinned by forensic science. There is less emphasis on hi-tech gadgetry, which was very much a feature of the original *CSI*, although the annoying music video/lab test sequences remain. Oscar-nominated Sinise, like Petersen, is a proper thespian and brings that authority to this role as the poker-faced, heroic lone wolf fighting through his pain to clean up the mean streets of New York. He almost manages to make the cheesy one-liners sound respectable.

If you've never seen any of the *CSI*s but you're partial to a sharp, glossy US crime drama, start with the original, skip Miami then move straight on to NY.

 TV trivia: Andy Garcia was originally offered the lead role. He declined, as did Ray Liotta.

DALZIEL AND PASCOE (1996–2007)

Starring Warren Clarke, Colin Buchanan

Another odd-couple cop show, this one set in the fictional Yorkshire town of Wetherton, pairs nose-picking, politically incorrect Andy Dalziel – pronounced Dee-el – (Clarke) with the rather more sensitive and intellectual Peter Pascoe (Buchanan). Based on the books by Reginald Hill, so far 12 series have been made, each featuring two-part feature-length episodes in which the pair investigate crimes such as a man possibly murdered by animal rights activists, the death of an entrepreneur whose widow (Cheri Lunghi) is an ex-lover of Dalziel's, and a sleepy village that seems to have a rather high death toll.

While some of the plots are based on Hill's books, many are original works. The stories are often punchy and enjoyable, and the teaming of Clarke and Buchanan works well with some nice dialogue between the pair. There's nothing here that's incredibly different from numerous other British cop series, but it's well made and features a few strong twists and turns in each season.

 TV Trivia: The characters of Dalziel and Pascoe first appeared in a 1993 TV serial called *A Pinch of Snuff*... played by comics Gareth Hale and Norman Pace.

DEMPSEY & MAKEPEACE (1985–1986)

Starring Michael Brandon, Glynis Barber, Ray Smith

In the mid-eighties, America had the slickness that was *Miami Vice*, and over in Blighty we had something a little more, erm, cheap, in the form of this daft London-set crime drama. Tough-talking (though not too tough, remember it was made for restrained British TV) New York cop James Dempsey (Brandon) is sent to work with an elite London police force (apparently a secret division of Scotland Yard), and teamed with Harriet 'Harry' Makepeace (Barber), a bit of posh totty who immediately irritates him. Of course, they don't get along but still fancy the pants off each other, so the series became less about the bad guys and more of a will they/won't they comedy drama as the pair traded sometimes witty barbs and double entendres.

Not as gritty as *The Sweeney* or *The Professionals*, this perhaps stayed around for three seasons because the tabloid-reading public loved the fact that co-stars Barber and Brandon became a real-life couple during filming. Brandon and Barber married in 1989, and had a son together in 1992. Awww.

 TV Trivia: Michael Brandon was previously married from 1976 to 1979 to the Bionic Woman herself, Lindsay Wagner.

DRAGNET (1951–1959)

Starring Jack Webb, Ben Alexander

Anyone under the age of 40 probably only remembers the dire Dan Aykroyd/Tom Hanks comic movie remake, but the *Dragnet* series which began in 1951 was far funnier in retrospect, although quite unintentionally. What had begun as a radio serial in 1949 was transferred to TV with Jack Webb as Sgt. Joe Friday (he also wrote and directed many of the episodes) spouting infamous phrases like 'all we know are the facts' ma'am' (everyone thinks he said 'just the facts, ma'am', but he never did), while each episode (allegedly based on real crimes and events, Webb offered $25 to any police officer submitting a story idea) ended with 'The story you have just seen is true. The names have been changed to protect the innocent.' It was the first US show to be broadcast on ITV, actually beginning the second day the channel was on air.

The series, which tried to be as authentic about police procedure as possible, ended in 1959, but returned a decade later as *Dragnet 67* with Webb returning as Friday and Harry Morgan starring as his partner, Officer Gannon. That show ran until 1970 and there was a failed attempt to resurrect the format in 1989 (unavailable on DVD) and again in 2003, with *Married With Children*'s Ed O'Neill as Friday and a cast that included *Desperate Housewives*' Eva Longoria. It was cancelled after 20 episodes.

 TV Trivia: One of the real-life police officers who submitted story ideas was a cop called Gene Roddenberry, who went on to create *Star Trek*.

HAMISH MACBETH (1995–1997)

Starring Robert Carlyle, Shirley Henderson, Ralph Riach

Based on characters from MC Beaton's mystery novels, Hamish Macbeth was a sweet little police detective drama, with Robert Carlyle in the lead role as local bobby Hamish, who, with the help of his West Highland Terrier, Wee Jock, keeps the peace and does everything in his power to not be promoted to a more high-pressure job. So laid back he's almost asleep, Hamish occasionally gets up the energy to lust after local journalist Isobel (Shirley Henderson) or chat to his best friend, TV John McIver (Ralph Riach), who has supernatural powers.

It's very sweet, and slightly surreal in places, while the gorgeous Scottish Highland locations must have done wonders for the Scottish Tourist Board. Carlyle, better known for playing tougher characters like Begbie in *Trainspotting* and Renard in the Bond movie *The World Is Not Enough*, is a treat in the title role, and all in all this is as warm and smooth as a dram of whiskey.

 TV Trivia: Shirley Henderson also appeared in *Trainspotting* along with Carlyle.

HAWAii FiVE-o (1968–1980)

Starring Jack Lord, James MacArthur, Kam Fong

One of the most famous TV theme tunes of all time by Morton Stevens launched this sunny detective show set, of course, in Hawaii. Five-0 is the name of a special police unit answerable to the governor, which investigates the most important crimes in the Hawaiian islands, from terrorism and kidnapping to murder and espionage. The men who work at Five-0 are bouffant-haired Det. Steve McGarrett (Lord), Danny Williams (MacArthur) – as in 'Book em, Dann-o', pipe-smoking Chin Ho Kelly (Fong), Hawaiian Kono (Zulu), and in some episodes, Ben Kokua (Al Harrington) and Duke Lukela (Herman Wedemeyer), while their chief adversary over the years is nasty Chinese agent Wo Fat (he's captured in the very last episode).

Packed with sixties references, from Vietnam to hippies, this is as kitsch and dated as a Hawaiian shirt, but enjoyably so. Lord was just right as the serious cop on the trail of some really bad guys, and there are some deliciously horrible baddies for him to chase, from Kevin McCarthy's murderer to the *Love Boat*'s Gavin McLeod as a slimy drug dealer.

 TV Trivia: *Hawaii Five-0* was the longest-running cop show on TV in the US until *Law and Order* took its crown.

HiLL STREET BLUES (1981–1987)

Starring Daniel J. Travanti, Bruce Weitz, Betty Thomas, Kiel Martin

More than two decades after it finished airing, US cop show *Hill Street Blues* remains one of the best police shows ever made for TV. Without this gritty, grimy series, it's unlikely later programmes such as *NYPD Blue* and *The Shield* would have seen the light of day. *Hill Street Blues* set the standard in true-to-life, almost cinematic series, and was the first cop show to feature continuous storylines rather than 'bad guy of the week' plots.

Centering around the Hill Street precinct in a city that is never mentioned but believed by fans to be Chicago, the series introduced us to a collection of truly memorable characters – Captain Frank Furillo (Travanti), his younger second wife, prosecutor Joyce Davenport (Veronica Hamel), and his ex, Fay (Barbara Bosson); Sergeant Phil Esterhaus (Michael Conrad), who sent the cops out each day with the words 'Let's be careful out there' (his replacement, Stan Jablonski, went for the more forthright 'Let's do it to them before they do it to us'); bumbling Andy Renko (Charles Haid) and his partner Bobby Hill (Michael Warren); smooth plain clothes detective JD La Rue (Martin) and his partner, Washington (Taurean Blaque); tough female cop Lucy (Thomas) and her pretty boy partner Joe (Ed Marinaro); and, of course, the almost feral, growling Belker (Weitz).

Over seven seasons, the characters' private lives mixed with their professional ones, and hard-hitting storylines were woven in alongside the day-to-day experiences as subjects such as racism, alcoholism, rape, gang wars and bribery were touched on. An unforgettable ensemble drama, this was best in the first four seasons (before the death of Conrad led to the character Esterhaus being killed off) becoming a little formulaic by the end.

TV Trivia: The characters of Hill and Renko were supposed to be killed off in the pilot episode, but the chemistry between actors Haid and Warren meant the producers kept them on as regular characters.

HOMiCiDE: LiFE oN THE STREET (1993–1999)

Starring Richard Belzer, Yaphet Kotto, Kyle Secor, Andre Braugher

Based on crime reporter David Simon's book *Homicide: A Year On The Killing Streets*, this series had an impressive pedigree – created by Barry Levinson (*Rain Man*), and writers Tom Fontana (*St Elsewhere*) and Paul Attanasio (*Quiz Show*), it featured episodes directed by Peter Medak (*The Krays*), Uli Edel (*Last Exit To Brooklyn*) and Kathryn Bigelow (*Point Break*) among others. While it was shunted around the late night schedules in the UK, in the US the series was critically acclaimed and embraced by fans of gritty, no-holds-barred cop dramas as one of the best ever.

Set in Baltimore, the series isn't packed with gun battles and car chases and instead focuses on the characters who deal with their depressing jobs by developing a sort of gallows humour. There's shift commander Al Giardello (Kotto), Detective Frank Pembleton (Braugher), John Much (Belzer, who also appeared in the same role in *Law and Order*), and rookie Bayliss (Secor) as well as Bolander (Ned Beatty) and Crosetti (Jon Polito). Often filmed using hand-held cameras to give the show an edgy and intense feel, the show also boasted a meticulous attention to police detail that makes it feel all the more authentic.

Best episodes – and there are many – include Season 4's 'Subway' in which Pemberton stays with the dying victim of a subway accident, Season 5's 'Prison Riot' and Season 3's 'The City That Bleeds', while actors who have lined up to appear in the show include Steve Buscemi, Edie Falco, James Earl Jones, and director John Waters.

TV Trivia: The character of Munch has not only cropped up on *Homicide* **and** *Law and Order*, **but also** *The X-Files, The Wire, Arrested Development* **and** *Sesame Street.*

THE INSPECTOR LYNLEY MYSTERIES (2001–2007)

Starring Nathaniel Parker, Sharon Small

Inspector Thomas Lynley is posher than your average cop – this policeman is the eighth Earl of Asherton and swans around in a vintage Bristol 410 car. He's dapper, old-fashioned, well-mannered, and there's a hint of tragedy about him, too (first, the woman he loves marries his best friend, then he marries an old friend only for their baby to die and their marriage to crumble). And of course, he's been paired with his polar opposite – working-class Barbara Havers (Small), a cop who has already been demoted for her fiery temper (she shot a flare gun at a colleague).

Five series have been made following the pair as they go about their jobs for Scotland Yard, investigating murders, missing persons and nefarious wrong-doings up and down the British Isles. They're all watchable, and the pairing of Parker and Small works well, but throughout you can't help but feel each story has been done before, and better, elsewhere. (And at least *Dempsey & Makepeace* had some, albeit unintentional, laughs.)

 TV Trivia: All the episodes from the first two series are based on the books by American author Elizabeth George.

INSPECTOR MORSE (1987–2000)

Starring John Thaw, Kevin Whately

TV's most popular inspector, as played by the marvellous John Thaw, began life, of course, in Colin Dexter's novels. Set primarily in and around Oxford, where there seems an alarming amount of crime for Morse to solve consid-ering it's always been seen as a quaint, middle-class university town, the series – and the novels – follow the crumpled Morse and his partner Lewis (Whately) as they solve a variety of similar mysteries.

On the page, Dexter had given Thaw a terrific character to work with – Morse is a beer-loving, intellectual snob with a penchant for deductive reasoning and an annoying habit of pointing out other people's grammatical mistakes – but in Thaw's hands he becomes even more, a flesh and blood, complex person who is brilliant but fallible, cynical yet likeable. Whately –

whose character is Welsh and older in the novel, and adapted to be Geordie for the TV show – is a good foil, too, but ultimately it is Thaw's show from beginning to end and he shines in one of his best roles, rising above the sometimes predictable plots that usually have the character fall for one of the women he's investigating, guessing whodunnit, then having Lewis save the day. Thirty three feature-length episodes were made, ending, like the novels, with Morse sadly dying (tragically, Thaw himself died two years later, in 2002).

A spin-off for Whately named *Lewis* began in 2006.

 TV Trivia: Morse's distinctive Jaguar was sold at auction in 2005 for more than £100,000.

KoJAK (1973–1978)

Starring Telly Savalas, Dan Frazer, Kevin Dobson

As lollipop-sucking, bald-headed police lieutenant Theo Kojak, Savalas became something of a seventies icon, complete with a TV catchphrase ('Who loves ya, baby?'). A no-nonsense cop determined to rid the New York streets of its worst scum, he works for Captain MacNeil (Frazer) and shares the beat with Detective Bobby Crocker (Dobson), his young partner, and Detective Stavros (George Savalas – Telly's real-life brother).

One of the first truly gritty cop shows that began life as a TV movie, each episode is filmed to look like a movie and make you feel you are on the sweaty streets with the suit-clad cop. It's fast-paced, well written, and packed with great performances – young actors who guest-starred in the show include Harvey Keitel, James Woods and John Ritter, while *Lethal Weapon*'s Richard Donner is one of the young directors behind the camera. A slice of classic Telly...

 TV Trivia: In the first season, Kojak smokes, but then Savalas gave up and the lollipop was his cigarette substitute during filming.

LAW & oRDER (1990–)

Starring Jerry Orbach, Sam Waterston

One of the most successful TV shows on US TV ever, *Law & Order* has been spun off into two other series: *Law & Order: Special Victims Unit* (1999 onwards) and *Law & Order: Criminal Intent* (2001 onwards), both of which are available on DVD. All three shows were created by Dick Wolf, and began with 1990's *Law & Order*, the drama series which follows a New York-based crime from two separate vantage points – the investigation by the police, and the subsequent court case.

It's a clever idea, since a lot of viewers who like police procedural shows like law shows, too, and it's made all the more gripping by the fact that many of the crimes featured are adapted from real headline-making ones. The cast is impressive, too – the members of the 27th Precinct Homicide Division represented by a cast that has included, over the years, Jeremy Sisto, Jerry Orbach, Chris Noth and Benjamin Bratt; while the prosecutors have included Linus Roache, Angie Harmon, Jill Hennessy and Sam Waterston. There are often a few coincidences the writers rely on to wrap up the plot (a girl isn't just raped, it has to be by someone linked to her mother for full dramatic effect) but, considering the show has been running for almost two decades, more often than not the stories are well written and tightly plotted and the actors are some of the best on TV.

If you've never seen the series before, the best season contained the episodes made in 1995 and 1996, featuring Bratt and Orbach (who died in 2005 shortly after filming a first episode of another spin-off, *Law & Order: Trial By Jury*) as partners and Waterston and Hennessy in the DA's office. One final quibble – shouldn't it actually be called Order & Law?

TV Trivia: Co-star Fred Dalton Thompson, who played one of the DA's for five years, is an US senator and declared himself a presidential candidate in 2007. He later stepped aside to support John McCain for president.

LiFE ON MARS (2006–2007)

Starring John Simm, Philip Glenister, Liz White

A truly clever spin on the conventional cop drama. After suffering a car crash in 2006, DCI Sam Tyler (Simm) wakes up to discover it's 1973. Is Sam in a coma? Is he hallucinating? Has he travelled back in time? He has no idea, but there are some strange happenings around him – he keeps hearing a beep in the background (a life-support machine?) and the case he ends up working on in the seventies has links to the one he was investigating in the 21st century. Meanwhile, he has to deal with life over 30 years ago, which means a world without mobile phones, computers or, it seems, rules, as his boss, Gene (Glenister) seems to thump everyone in sight and get away with it.

Deliciously surreal, *Life on Mars* expertly mixed the head-scratching puzzle of Sam's predicament with a fish-out-of-water setting and all the trappings of a cop show. Simm is fine as Sam, but Glenister is the one who steals the series as the morally dubious cop who'll plant evidence if it helps get his man. After two series, Sam's dilemma was nicely resolved (we won't reveal it here), and Glenister got his own spin-off, the eighties-set *Ashes to Ashes* (both series, of course, named after decade-relevant David Bowie songs), which is available on DVD.

 TV Trivia: When the series ended, the Ford Cortina used in the show was auctioned for Comic Relief.

McCLOUD (1970–1977)

Starring Dennis Weaver, JD Cannon, Terry Carter

Sam McCloud (Weaver) is a US Marshal from New Mexico who travels to New York City to find an escaped bad guy, then decides he likes life in the Big Apple (possibly because he fancies reporter Chris, as played by Diana Muldar). She convinces her cousin, who just happens to be the deputy police commissioner, to let McCloud stay and learn big city police procedures, and it's not long before our stetson-ed hero is catching murderers and drug dealers using his laid-back country approach as well as the NY skills he's picking up.

It's another fish-out-of-water story, nicely played by Weaver, but it's the attention to detail and action that keeps it interesting over three decades on. There's a good dollop of police procedure mixed in, and some quite believable plots that mix sleuthing and humour. The episodes were originally shown in the US as part of the NBC Mystery Movies banner that also launched *Columbo* (see review, p.5) and the Rock Hudson-starring *McMillan and Wife* (1971–1977), that's also on DVD.

 TV Trivia: Weaver was a committed environmentalist, and his home in New Mexico was constructed almost entirely out of recycled materials.

MIAMI VICE (1984–1989)

Starring Don Johnson, Philip Michael Hall, Edward James Olmos

A groundbreaking series from producer Michael Mann, who went on to direct such stylish films as *Manhunter*, *Heat* and *Collateral* (as well as a 2006 movie update of *Miami Vice* with Colin Farrell). On the surface, it's the story of two undercover cops, suave Sonny Crockett (Johnson, who brought designer stubble to an unsuspecting public) and Ricardo Tubbs (Thomas) who befriend Miami's drug dealers, murderers and pimps in order to catch them. But it was so much more than that. Like a big budget movie, it was backed by a thumping rock soundtrack of songs by artists including former Eagle

Glenn Frey, who also guest-starred in the show, Tina Turner and Chaka Khan (none used more effectively than the pilot episode's play of Phil Collins' 'In The Air Tonight' as Sonny speeds along a neon-lit Miami freeway) and also featured Jan Hammer's memorable 'Miami Vice Theme' and haunting 'Crockett's Theme'. And like a movie, the production values were slick, fast-paced and with eye-catching imagery unlike anything seen before on TV – these cops cruised around photogenic Miami in Ferraris (so the bad guys thought they were drug dealers, you see), drove speedboats, and most memorably of all, wore pastel designer suits with t-shirts (and no socks) that created something of a fashion.

Beginning with a feature-length episode in which New York cop Tubbs comes to Miami to track down the man who killed his brother and then becomes Crockett's permanent partner, the series ran for five seasons but Seasons 1 and 2 remain the best. Season 3 was grittier (causing fans to turn off), and by the time Crockett married a pop star (played by Sheena Easton) who was then gunned down on their wedding day in Season 4, it had dipped considerably in the ratings. Easton wasn't the only star to pop up on Miami's mean streets – Willie Nelson, Bruce Willis, Melanie Griffith, Jimmy Smits (as Crockett's original, and doomed, partner), Liam Neeson and Julia Roberts were among the actors who appeared in episodes.

 TV Trivia: The soundtrack LP was number one in the US album charts for 11 weeks, making it (at the time) the most successful TV soundtrack of all time.

MIDSOMER MURDERS (1997–)

Starring John Nettles, Daniel Casey

Another inexplicably successful detective series starring housewives' favourite John Nettles. He stars as DCI Tom Barnaby, who, along with Sergeant Gavin Troy (Casey), investigates murders in the regional community of Midsomer, seemingly the most crime-ridden county in the country.

The scenery may look nice but unfortunately this series is blander than a wishy-washy cup of tea, and just as appealing. It's a sort of mish-mash of *Inspector Morse*, *Dalziel and Pascoe* and numerous other shows it liberally borrows from without managing to copy those series' charm. One for people who love murder-mysteries and have seen every episode of everything else, or fans of John Nettles only.

 TV Trivia: For most episodes, Oxfordshire doubles for the fictional Midsomer.

MONK (2002–)

Starring Tony Shaloub, Traylor Howard, Ted Levine, Jason Grey-Stanford, Bitty Scram

Adrian Monk (Shaloub) was a detective with the San Francisco Police Department when his wife Trudy was killed by a car bomb. Her death caused him to suffer a nervous breakdown which, combined with his pre-existing obsessive compulsive disorder, led to him leaving the force and becoming a recluse. The series starts a few years later when Monk, with the help of his nurse Sharona Fleming (Schram), begins to work as a consultant for the police on hard to crack cases. Monk's many and varied neuroses, which include a fear of lifts, handshakes and different types of food touching on his plate, coupled with his pathological attention to detail, help him to spot the smallest of clues and thereby discover whodunit. In fact, the only case he is unable to solve is his wife's murder.

This quirky, offbeat series bears a resemblance to *Columbo* in that both detectives are deceptively dishevelled, in Monk's case the dishevelment is psychological, and bad guys underestimate them at their peril. Monk's former partner, Captain Leland Stottlemeyer (Levine) is constantly irritated by his friend's seemingly endless list of disorders and this annoyance is compounded by the recognition that the defective detective is, in many ways, far more insightful than himself. After Sharona decides to re-marry her ex husband and move to New Jersey in the third season, single mother Natalie Teeger (Howard) is drafted in as Monk's new assistant. This, together with the new theme tune in Season 2, initially caused great consternation and much blogging among die-hard fans. The series was never given a primetime slot in the UK and its BBC scheduling was always erratic, therefore it never attracted the larger audiences it surely would have otherwise. Nevertheless, it does have a dedicated following and, like *Columbo*, is bound to be repeated for many years to come.

 TV trivia: Queen Latifah was originally in the running for the role of Sharona Fleming.

MURPHY'S LAW (2003–)

Starring James Nesbitt

James Nesbitt comes over all grizzled and gloomy for this series as undercover cop Jimmy Murphy, based on the book by Colin Bateman. He's a tough-talking fellow with a dark past – in Northern Ireland, his family were taken hostage and he had to choose whether to carry a bomb and blow himself up in an army barracks, or see his daughter killed, a decision he has had to live with ever since. In case you hadn't guessed, this is not a happy copper.

While the first three series of this gritty drama comprised individual episodes, from Series 4 a single story was told over three episodes, and the tone of the action got even darker than before (if you look at the DVD covers for each series, Nesbitt goes from reasonably clean-shaved to bearded and almost psychopathic by the fourth series). It's actually the most recent series that have been the best – gritty, depressing even, but also tense – and Nesbitt plays Murphy as the most convincing cop on the edge since Kiefer Sutherland's Jack Bauer.

 TV Trivia: As well as writing novels, Bateman has also written four children's books including 2001's *Reservoir Pups*.

NEW TRICKS (2003–)

Starring Alun Armstrong, James Bolam, Dennis Waterman, Amanda Redman

A neat idea for a cop show – and a way of bringing back a few actors probably considered 'too old' for TV – this has Detective Superintendent Sandra Pullman (Redman) recruiting three retired police officers to solve long-forgotten, unsolved crimes. Sounds like a good idea, except the men she recruits are Jack Halford (Bolam), who is still mourning the death of his wife, the obsessive Brian Lane (Armstrong) and aging lothario Gerry Standing (Waterman) – all with their own problems as well as the ones that come with them trying to solve crimes the old-fashioned way for a police force that has gone hi-tech in their absence.

What makes this comedy drama work is the casting of Waterman, Bolam and Armstrong – three skilled comic and dramatic actors who have terrific chemistry on screen and get all the best dialogue. Redman is a great comic/serious foil for them, too, and whether the quartet are solving a suspenseful murder or doing something more ludicrous like digging up a dead dog, this is always a treat to watch.

 TV Trivia: Dennis Waterman's daughter, Hannah (best known for her role in *EastEnders*), plays Gerry's daughter Emily in a few episodes.

NYPD BLUE (1993–2005)

Starring Dennis Franz, Gordon Clapp, Bill Brochtrup, James McDaniel

NYPD Blue was the first real adult drama broadcast on a TV network to compete with the more gritty shows cropping up on cable channels at around the same time. The series was co-created by Steven Bochco, the man behind the equally excellent *Hill Street Blues*. *NYPD Blue* follows a group of hard-working, under-appreciated detectives from the 15th squad in Manhattan as they go about their crime-solving business on the mean streets of New York. Veteran detective Andy Sipowicz (Franz) battles the bottle and the bad guys while struggling with his personal life. Franz, the only actor to appear in all 261 episodes over the 12-year run of the show, was initially joined by David Caruso as his moralistic partner, Detective John Kelly. He was replaced in the second season by the suave Detective Bobby Simone (Jimmy Smits), who set hearts fluttering for the next 10 years. The focus was on a handful of characters who viewers got to know intimately over the years, instead of the large ensemble casts as seen in many previous shows.

Apart from the excellent writing, *NYPD* is noteworthy for featuring nudity and proper swear words. If the cursing didn't cause offence, the sight of Sipowicz's stodgy exposed arse would certainly be enough to put you off your dinner. The long, lingering shots of bare flesh could be a bit gratuitous at times but the gripping storylines and extensive development of these flawed characters meant that you cared what happened to them. It was racy stuff for TV viewers in the early nineties, even though it seems pretty tame now through our 21st-century jaded eyes. Nevertheless, lovers of classic US TV cop dramas should definitely have this series in their collection. Hopefully, all 12 seasons will be released on DVD eventually.

 TV Trivia: Most episodes take place over the course of a single day.

PoLiCE SquAD! (1982)

Starring Leslie Nielsen, Alex North, William Duell

The team behind *Airplane!* – Jim Abrahams, David and Jerry Zucker – were the men who created this spoof cop show for Leslie Nielsen. He plays bungling detective Frank Drebin – the character he would later play in three *Naked Gun* movies and although this didn't get high ratings and was cancelled after only six episodes, it has become something of a fan favourite on video and DVD since.

Packed with slapstick comedy, double entendres, deadpan gags ('Like a midget at a water fountain, I was going to have to stay on my toes') and Nielsen's smooth-as-treacle narration, the series follows Drebin as he goes undercover to solve various crimes, usually with the aid of a tip from Johnny the snitching shoe shine boy (Duell). While he thinks it's all deadly serious, it's completely silly for the viewing audience, and if you like deliciously dumb but well-meaning comedy (one running joke is the special guest star of the week is always killed in the opening credits), this has plenty of laughs.

 TV Trivia: In each episode, the voice over from Nielsen gives the episode a different title than the one that appears on the screen.

PRIME SUSPECT (1991–2006)

Starring Helen Mirren, Tom Bell, John Bowe

Written by Lynda La Plante, the character of DCI Jane Tennison remains her most famous creation, and also the most famous role for star Helen Mirren (until she played the Queen, that is). More than a police drama, this series had Tennison investigating crimes but also trying to survive in a male-dominated profession, coming up against sexism from her colleagues in the earlier episodes. Each *Prime Suspect* 'series' ran for between two and four episodes (aside from Series 4, which had four separate stories), with a series appearing about once a year until Mirren decided to retire from the role in 1997 (she returned to it in 2003 for *Prime Suspect 5*, and then again in 2006 for *Prime Suspect The Final Act*).

In each series, she is a powerhouse, whether her character is working with the vice squad, looking into the death of a rent boy, investigating the murder of a drug dealer or of a Bosnian refugee. Tennison is methodical, dogged, determined and, unsurprisingly, has a messy personal life, and Mirren brings her every mannerism to believable life, creating a tough but human character. The final series was a little disappointing, but every other series of this hard-hitting, tense, edge-of-the-seat drama is deserving of the many awards the series won.

 TV Trivia: The role was originally offered to Janet McTeer.

THE PROFESSIONALS (1977–1983)

Starring Lewis Collins, Martin Shaw, Gordon Jackson

The Yanks had Starsky and Hutch, and us Brits had Bodie and Doyle, two agents for CI5 who answer to George Cowley (Jackson). They're assigned to fight and prevent terrorism, so Cowley hand-picked his team of tough guys: Bodie (Collins) is the ex-SAS man and mercenary while Doyle (Shaw) is the slightly more level-headed ex-copper with the curly perm.

One of the most iconic shows for men and boys in the seventies, *The Professionals* mixed hard men with numerous scenes of squealing tyres, machismo and punch-ups. Rumour has it that Collins and Shaw weren't particularly friendly off set, which may have helped their performances as men flung together as partners with nothing in common, and they certainly seem grumpy with each other much of the time they are on screen. Unfortunately, it's not just the perms and flares that have dated – their male bravado doesn't exactly sit well in the more illuminated 21st century, but this is fairly gritty in places and worth a trip down memory lane. Note that one episode, 'Klansmen', about the Ku Klux Clan, has never been repeated since it was first shown in 1977 due to its racist overtones, but it is included on the DVD.

 TV Trivia: Anthony Andrews was originally cast as Bodie and filmed some footage before he was replaced by Collins.

REBUS (2000–2001; 2005–2007)

Starring Ken Stott, Claire Price, John Hannah

Based on Ian Rankin's bestselling crime thrillers, this series expertly brought the character of John Rebus to the screen. For the first season, it was John Hannah playing the title role and then, after a four year gap, the series returned to TV with Ken Stott playing the detective inspector solving crimes in and around Edinburgh. With DS Siobhan Clarke (Price) at his side, the battle-weary detective plods along, dealing with the criminal underworld as only he knows how.

Cancelled in 2008 when Stott announced he no longer wanted to play the role, Rebus falls into the category of 'gritty British cop show', of which there have been many. While Stott is suitably grizzled as the copper and the cases often nasty (a prostitute buried alive, head wrapped in cellophane, was a particularly icky find), this is no better or worse than other dramas of its ilk. Fans of the novels should take a look, though.

 TV Trivia: The Rebus books account for 10 per cent of all crime book sales in the UK.

A TOUCH OF FROST (1992–)

Starring David Jason, Bruce Alexander, John Lyons, James McKenna

Long-running drama inspired by the RD Wingfield 'Frost' books (reportedly, the author was not pleased with the TV version), this stars David Jason as DI 'Jack' William Frost, a veteran police officer in the fictional town of Denton, who uses unorthodox tactics to solve crimes others have been puzzling over. He's seemingly emotionless – in the first series, he calmly goes off to work while a carer looks after his dying wife – but with a burning desire for justice, just so long as he doesn't have to fill out any paperwork while he's trying to catch a killer. And later episodes show us he's vulnerable, too, and more affected by his wife's death than people think.

Unsurprisingly, this is Jason's show, and the actor most-loved for comic creations such as Del Boy, Pop Larkin and Granville shows he is equally adept at tougher fare. He's actually executive producer on the show, and despite this being a series about murder, he has insisted there must be minimal graphic violence, so don't expect a show that will send granny into a frenzy: in fact, this well mannered cop series is probably just her cup of tea.

 TV Trivia: David Jason's real name is David White, but he changed it when he discovered another David White was already registered with actors' union Equity.

WAKiNG THE DEAD (2000–)

Starring Trevor Eve, Sue Johnston, Claire Goose, Holly Aird

Like *Cold Case* (which isn't on DVD), this series has a group of cops investigating cases that have been filed away as unsolved. Led by Peter Boyd (Eve), an arrogant maverick with a dark past (his son went missing, aged 17, and Boyd has never found out whether he was murdered), the group include forensic psychologist Grace Foley (Johnston), Spencer Jordan (Will Johnson) and, in the first few seasons, DS Mel Silver (Goose) and pathologist Frankie Wharton (Aird).

Focusing as much on the characters' personal lives as the crimes they are investigating, this is a popular drama, if not exactly a desperately original one. Eve is suitably grizzled (why oh why has no one brought his engagingly silly 1979 detective series *Shoestring* out on DVD?) and the rest of the team have their own character quirks and backstories, but this lacks the punch of a series like *Without A Trace* or the wit of *New Tricks*.

 TV Trivia: Holly Aird was pregnant during the filming of Series 4, and her bump was hidden by bits of furniture or voluminous lab coats.

THE WIRE (2002–2008)

Starring Dominic West, Michael K. Williams, Frankie Faison, John Doman

A US police show that has deservedly won critical praise even if it hasn't garnered the audiences it should have in the UK. A searing look at the decay of one American city, Baltimore, which becomes more in depth with each season, the show focuses on a different facet each time, adding another layer to the city's underbelly: the cops and local drug trade in Season 1, the middle class and the unions at the docks in Season 2, local politics and drugs in Season 3, the school system in Season 4 (and how the neglected kids slipped through and ended up on the streets) and, in Season 5, the local newspaper is added into the mix.

Viewers are drawn into this gripping, complex scenario that has, at its heart, characters such as Detective James McNulty (West), who is at the heart of drug busts in the first season but finds himself sent to the waterfront by the second (where he can see for himself the decline of the working classes, up close and personal), and the storylines unspurl around him like the plotlines of a novel. Watching *The Wire* requires commitment – if you miss an episode you'll be lost – but watch just one and you will be hooked. Produced by HBO, the home of the equally acclaimed *The Sopranos*, this is actually better than the mobster show, and even more skilfully written and performed. Dense, dark and wonderful – a true TV masterpiece.

 TV Trivia: Acclaimed novelists Richard Price (*Clockers*), George Pelecanos (*Hard Revolution*) and Dennis Lehane (*Mystic River*) are among the show's writers.

WIRE IN THE BLOOD (2002–)

Starring Robson Green, Mark Letheren, Hermione Norris

We can almost forgive Robson Green his singing career on the basis of his strong performance in this series as troubled psychologist Tony Hill. He understands the criminal mind and can get into the mind of a killer, but of course that's not very good for him, especially as he's called to work on solving some of the grisliest murders imaginable with Detective Inspector Carol Jordan (Norris).

Starting with three feature-length episodes (originally each one shown in two parts), this series, based on characters from Val McDermid's novels, proved us Brits can deliver drama for TV that would work just as well on the big screen. While Green isn't exactly George Clooney in terms of star quality, he still brings a nice amount of depth to a conflicted character that's believable, and the teaming with Norris works well. She left after the third series of mini-movies and her character was replaced by DI Alex Fielding (Simone Lahbib), who doesn't have the same chemistry with Green, alas.

TV Trivia: The series title is also the title of a McDermid novel, but originated in TS Eliot's poem Burnt Norton.

WiTHOUT A TRACE (2002–)

Starring Anthony LaPaglia, Poppy Montgomery, Marianne Jean-Baptiste, Eric Close, Enrique Murciano

Led by gruff Jack Malone (LaPaglia), a group of FBI men and women work together from a New York office trying to track down missing persons in this often gripping drama. Each episode begins as a person mysteriously vanishes and fades out from the screen, and then Jack, Samantha Spade (Montgomery), Danny Taylor (Murciano), Martin Fitzgerald (Close), Vivian Johnson (Jean-Baptiste) and, from 2005, Elena Delgado (Roselyn Sanchez) have to piece together the person's last movements and work out why they have disappeared, and where they may be.

With the chance that the person in question may not be found, or may be found dead rather than alive, this is not as formulaic as it could be, and it is made more interesting thanks to the fact that the agents' own histories aren't revealed to us from the very first episode. In fact, when we meet Jack and his team we know very little about them and it takes a long time for secrets to unravel such as Jack's affair with a fellow agent and his crumbling marriage, Vivian's heart condition, Danny's chequered family history and Samantha's own fraught upbringing. Gripping stuff, well played by the cast – especially LaPaglia and Montgomery, both Australians playing Americans – this has included some moving as well as fascinating episodes, especially the first season two-parter 'Fall Out' that deals, on a personal level, with the impact of 9/11 on the citizens of New York.

TV Trivia: In real life, the FBI does not have a dedicated Missing Persons Unit like the one featured in the show.

10 TV DVDS EVERYONE SHOULD OWN

There are literally thousands of TV series available on DVD. We can't buy them all, but here are the 20 essential shows everyone should have in their DVD collection:

THE 10 BRITISH SERIES EVERYONE SHOULD OWN

1. The Singing Detective
2. The Blue Planet or Life on Earth
3. Porridge
4. The Old Grey Whistle Test
5. Bagpuss
6. The Office
7. Doctor Who (21st-century version, or series with Jon Pertwee or Tom Baker)
8. Pride and Prejudice
9. Brideshead Revisited
10. The World at War

THE 10 AMERICAN SERIES EVERYONE SHOULD OWN

1. Lost
2. Moonlighting
3. The Sopranos (Season 1) or The West Wing
4. The Simpsons (any season from 2 to 8)
5. The Twilight Zone (episodes from the original series)
6. Arrested Development
7. Hill St. Blues or St. Elsewhere
8. Seinfeld
9. The Wire
10. 24 (all seasons except Season 6)

BAD GUYS

A LOOK AT TV'S BAD GUYS AND GIRLS, CRIMINALS AND
PRISONERS.

BAD GIRLS (1999–2006)

Starring Linda Henry, Victoria Alcock, Kika Mirylees, Helen Fraser, Zoe Lucker

So popular that it has since been turned into a West End musical, *Bad Girls* is
a rather brash ITV drama focusing on the staff and inmates of a women's
prison. Originally to be called Jailbirds, the series ran for eight seasons,
depicting life in the fictitious HMP Larkhall where abortion, riots, stabbings
and drug abuse seem to be commonplace. And what a lovely bunch is
incarcerated there: among them, tough gangster's wife Yvonne Atkins
(Henry); Julie Johnston (Mirylees), an ex-prostitute inside for GBH; brothel
madam Virginia O'Kane (Kate O'Mara); swindler Phyl Oswyn (Stephanie
Beacham) and footballer's wife Tanya Tucker (Lucker reprising her role from
Footballers'Wives).

  More of a soap than a serious drama – although there are a few murders
and nasty bits that may disturb the faint of heart and the depictions of prison
life are apparently very true – *Bad Girls* became increasingly packed with
celebrity actors as the show progressed and the storylines became trashier.
Former *Emmerdale* actress Claire King, Amanda Donohoe, ex-Corrie actress
Amanda Barrie and ex-*EastEnders* Sid Owen and Nicola Stapleton all joined
the cast but it is the early episodes from the first two series that are the grittiest and most watchable.

 **TV Trivia: Oxford Prison was used for some of the filming, and
it was also a location for *A Fish Called Wanda*.**

BAND OF GOLD (1995–1997)

Starring Geraldine James, Cathy Tyson, Barbara Dickson, Samantha Morton

Kay Mellor, who also wrote the series *Fat Friends* and *Playing The Field*, scripted this grim look at the seedy world of prostitution in the north of England.
Running for three series, the drama followed a group of women who, for
various reasons, have ended up selling sex on the streets. There's Gina
(Ruth Gammell), a mother of three trying to keep a loan shark from the

door, who is brutally murdered in the first episode; young Tracy (an excellent Morton, who was just 18), who lives with a violent pimp; Anita (Dickson), who thinks her boyfriend may be killing prostitutes, including Gina; Carol (Tyson), who ends up on a psychiatric ward after attacking one of her clients, and Rose (James), who is trying to start afresh and leave her history as a prostitute behind.

An often gritty and explicit series – poor Samantha Morton, especially, seemed to spend most of the second season on her knees or with her bottom in the air – it didn't exactly thrill Bradford residents (most of the action takes place on the 'Lane', an area of the city notorious for prostitution). Murder, rape, child prostitution, drug abuse and dealing, loan sharks and Leeds gangsters were all depicted – cheery stuff, then. A more glamorous portrayal of British prostitution – *The Secret Diary of a Call Girl* (2007), with Billie Piper playing the sex worker Belle de Jour (on whose anonymous diaries the series is based) is available on DVD.

 TV Trivia: Writer Kay Mellor's earlier work includes the rather less controversial kids' TV series *Dramarama* and *Children's Ward*.

BANGKOK HILTON (1989)

Starring Nicole Kidman, Denholm Elliott, Hugo Weaving

Before she met Tom Cruise and became a tabloid headliner, Nicole Kidman gave a sterling performance in this drug-trafficking drama. She stars as Kat Stanton, a nice Aussie gal who is searching for the father (Elliott) she has never known. Her journey takes her from Australia to London to Bangkok, and it is there she meets a charming young man named Arkie, who, unbeknownst to her, drops some drugs in her luggage when she is due to leave Thailand. Of course, she is searched and then imprisoned in a notorious (fictional) jail dubbed Bangkok Hilton for drug smuggling, a crime that carries the death penalty.

It's basically a female version of *Midnight Express*, as Kidman endures various humiliations and hideous conditions while her newly discovered dad and her lawyer (Weaving) battle the Thai authorities in an attempt to get her freed. And despite the fact you'll figure out early on how it is all going to end, it's nonetheless edge-of-your-seat stuff, thanks to a flawless central performance from Kidman and great support from Elliott and Weaving.

 TV Trivia: Although everyone thinks of Nicole Kidman as Australian, she was actually born in Honolulu, Hawaii.

BUDGIE (1971–1972)

Starring Adam Faith, Iain Cuthbertson

Former British pop star Faith shone in the role of Ronald 'Budgie' Bird in this enjoyable British TV series. Budgie was a petty criminal – basically a cheeky Cockney chappie with a twinkle in his eye – whose scams usually failed, landing him in trouble with the police and also, more often than not, with Charlie Endell, a Glaswegian club owner with London underworld connections.

The series ran for two seasons (26 episodes) and benefited from some great guest actors including Derek Jacobi, Gordon Jackson, John Thaw and James Bolam. It's an enjoyable mixture of comedy and drama, with a great central turn from Faith and nice support from Lynn Dalby as Hazel, Budgie's long-suffering girlfriend and mother of his son, and John Rhys-Davies as the fabulously named Laughing Spam Fritter. A forerunner to *Minder* and *Only Fools And Horses*, this enjoyed a successful repeat run on TV in the eighties, but sadly no more episodes were made.

 TV Trivia: A spin-off series, *Charles Endell Esq*, starring Cuthbertson, was made in 1979 but only two episodes were ever broadcast.

THE COUNT OF MONTE CRISTO (1975)

Starring Richard Chamberlain, Kate Nelligan, Tony Curtis, Trevor Howard

There have been over 20 film and TV adaptations of Alexandre Dumas's classic tale, but the only TV versions available on DVD are the 1998 French mini-series with Gerard Depardieu – which is worthy, beautifully filmed and performed but, at 400 minutes, a bit long – and 1975's deliciously camp one, starring Richard Chamberlain as literature's most famous prisoner. Any series that casts Tony Curtis in a dastardly role is a must-see, and this flashy seventies take on the novel has all that and more (Trevor Howard! Donald Pleasance! Louis Jordan!).

The story is, of course, that of Edmond Dantes (Chamberlain, at the height of his TV popularity). Falsely accused by jealous friends, he is sentenced to spend the rest of his life at the island prison Chateau d'If. There, he makes friends with a fellow prisoner, the Abbe Faria (Howard), and the Abbe tells him of a great treasure hidden on an island only he knows about. So when the Abbe dies, Edmond escapes (disguised as the Abbe's corpse), goes in search of the treasure, and then returns with his new-found wealth to Paris in disguise, ready to exact his revenge on those who betrayed him. What a corking story! With romping dialogue such as 'I shall move like the Sword of the Lord with a terrible swiftness' and a wonderfully coiffed Chamberlain, complete with white-as-snow hair and distinguished beard (seemingly the full extent of his 'disguise'), this is so much silly fun it should come with its own whoopee cushion.

 TV Trivia: Richard Chamberlain played Jason Bourne in the original TV version of *The Bourne Identity*, made 14 years before the film starring Matt Damon.

CRIME. INC (1984)

A fascinating seven-part documentary, made by Thames Television in the eighties, *Crime, Inc* looked behind the scenes of organised crime – and the Mafia in particular – in America and Europe. It's a well-researched history of the crime families, featuring interviews, photographic evidence and original footage detailing the extortion, torture and secrecy that takes place as a matter of course.

Perfect viewing for anyone fascinated with the Mob, this has so much gritty inside information that it makes an episode of *The Sopranos* look like *The Brady Bunch*. Well paced, if slightly dated (many of the imprisoned mobsters interviewed have since died, and the position of the Mafia has altered since the formation of various violent gangs who have challenged its power), the best episodes include the first, 'All In The Family', and the fifth, 'The Mob At Work'.

 TV Trivia: One of the facts revealed in the documentary is that for many years, US police forces refused to admit the Mafia even existed.

DEXTER (2006–)
Starring Michael C. Hall, Julie Benz, Jennifer Carpenter

Dexter Morgan (Hall) is such a twisted bad guy, he makes Jack The Ripper look like Mary Poppins. During the day, Dexter works as a police forensics expert for the Miami police department, but after hours he has a rather disturbing hobby – he likes killing criminals he believes have escaped justice in particularly nasty ways (in the first episode, one unfortunate man gets sliced up with a chainsaw). Dexter knows he's a monster (albeit a very disciplined and meticulous one who has never been caught) with no interest in sex (he gets his kicks from dismemberment, it seems), and his odd life even leads him to choose the 'perfect' girlfriend, a physically and emotionally damaged woman (Benz), who's very happy that her man has no interest in getting her into bed.

Blackly humorous – Dexter gets annoyed when another serial killer starts carving up Miami ('I think he's trying to impress me,' Dexter muses, 'and it's working') – this is a love it or hate it show. There's a very present and very irritating voiceover from Hall, but if you can stand his comments (and some are darkly funny) and enjoy a show whose main character is pretty irredeemable, this does have some strong performances and a compelling, original plotline. Hall is perfectly cool and calculated as the serial killer of the title (some viewers may find that off-putting, as he never shows much emotion except joy when he is slicing and dicing a victim), while Benz – best known for her role as vampire Darla in *Buffy* and *Angel* – is both vulnerable and quietly tough as the woman with no clue about the secrets her boyfriend is hiding. Shudder.

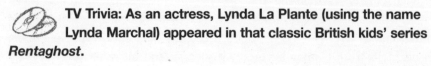 **TV Trivia: At one point, Dexter uses the pseudonym 'Patrick Bateman' – the name, of course, of the equally cold and calculating serial killer in Bret Easton Ellis' novel *American Psycho*.**

THE GOVERNOR (1995–1996)

Starring Janet McTeer, Paul Kynman

Another strong female role as written by Lynda La Plante (*Prime Suspect*). Janet McTeer is terrific as Helen Hewitt, a deputy governor at a female prison who, in the first episode, is asked to join an investigation into a prisoner's death and subsequent riot at a maximum security prison housing some of Britain's worst offenders. The prison has been partially burnt down by the riot but still houses over 80 prisoners, and when Helen is offered the job of governor there, she not only has to take on the task of being the youngest woman in charge of an all-male prison, she also has to discover whether the death at the jail was suicide or murder, and whether a cover-up has taken place.

Gritty stuff, indeed, as the series followed Helen settling in as governor while the prison was rebuilt, taking on new prisoners and tackling the old ones, trying to gain respect from her staff, and dealing with such problems as escapees, drug abuse, rape and violent attacks. A second series, *The Governor II*, continued the story and was even tougher than the first series.

TV Trivia: As an actress, Lynda La Plante (using the name Lynda Marchal) appeared in that classic British kids' series *Rentaghost*.

HUSTLE (2004 –)

Starring Robert Vaughn, Marc Warren, Adrian Lester, Robert Glenister

Think *Ocean's Eleven* for the small screen (and with fewer gorgeous men, alas!), and you have an idea of the premise of this show. Mickey (Lester) is fresh out of prison, and the former leader of a gang of conmen (and woman). Determined to pull off one more score before he retires, Mickey decides to get his gang back together: Danny Blue (Warren), a young guy wanting to learn from Mickey; old-timer Albert (Vaughn), a former Vegas conman; glamorous Stacie (Jaime Murray), who is also the group's 'banker'; fixer Ash (Glenister) and later newcomer Billy (Ashley Walters), who joined in Series Four following Mickey's departure for a con in Australia.

Fun rather than deadly serious, among the cons the team try to pull off is an attempt to sell the Hollywood sign, stealing the crown jewels and convincing the press that the Queen Mother died in the Blitz and a doppleganger pretended to be her for the next half-century. The show has been packed with amusing guest turns from actors including Mel Smith, Robert Wagner, Richard Chamberlain, Faye Ripley and Max Beesley. There are also a few neat tricks to keep the action moving – sometimes the actors talk directly to camera, or time stops so the actor can let the audience in on what's going on while the others in the scene remain frozen in time. While the series has suffered a little following the departure of the extremely engaging Lester (there are rumours he may return for later seasons), it's still an enjoyable weekly adventure.

 TV Trivia: Rumour has it that Clive Owen was originally offered the part of Mickey.

MINDER (1979–1994)

Starring George Cole, Dennis Waterman

One thing we Brits do well is create lovable rogues, and two of the best-loved ones of all time are, of course, Arthur Daley and his 'minder' Terry McCann. Daley (Cole) is the wheeler-dealer conman who hires ex-boxer and ex-con McCann (Waterman) to protect him from the other small-time crooks who populate South London's grimy streets. Both comedy and drama – the hilarious dialogue between the pair became one of the show's most popular aspects and was beefed up for later seasons – the series was known for its colourful language, both Cockney and 'mockney' (phrases made up for the show) to the point where the poshest people of the land tried to be cool by spouting dialogue such as 'getting a Ruby down your Gregory' (going out for a curry – Ruby Murray being slang for curry, and Gregory Peck slang for neck) or describing the missus as 'er indoors' and any money-making scheme as 'a nice little earner' (Daley's favourite phrase).

Each episode usually had Arthur (or 'Arfur' as everyone pronounced it) getting into some scrape due to greed, and the more honest and straightforward Terry getting him out of it, usually to his own cost. As the years progressed, Daley's schemes became more and more outrageous as he tried to make money and, hopefully, make a fool out of pursuing cop Det. Sgt Chisholm (Patrick Malahide) along the way. Subsequently it all got a bit silly and, by the time Waterman departed in 1991, it was almost unwatchable. Gary Webster joined the cast as Arthur's nephew, Ray, and things improved somewhat (the comedy remained but the plots were slightly more believable), with the final episode in which Arthur and Ray are arrested broadcast in 1994.

TV Trivia: *Minder* **was originally seen as a vehicle for Waterman, who was fresh from the success of** *The Sweeney***, with George Cole's Arthur Daley just a secondary character. But their chemistry on screen worked so well that Cole's role was expanded.**

MURDER IN MIND (2001–2003)

Starring Pauline Quirke, Gary Kemp, Dennis Waterman, Denise Van Outen

A neat twist on crime drama – this series of one-off psychological thrillers is seen from the killer's point of view. This means there are even some episodes where you have sympathy for the murderer, such as Rob Brydon's cuckolded husband, who decides to murder his wife's lover, although there are some pretty nasty characters, too, such as Jamie Theakston's city dealer, who decides to hire a contract killer (Adam Faith).

Each deliciously dark episode is a treat (the squeamish should probably avoid this series, though, as it is occasionally quite grim), and there is some terrific casting, too: Nicholas Lyndhurst is surprisingly creepy as the landlord from hell, while ex-EastEnder Michael Greco proves he's a decent actor as a man talked into murdering his lover's husband, while the supporting casts have included Diana Rigg, James McAvoy, Steve McFadden, Keith Allen and Gary Kemp. The best episodes include 'Memories', with Neil Pearson, in which a paediatric surgeon has recurring nightmares about a boy's death, and 'Passion', with Pauline Quirke wonderfully psychopathic as the supervisor obsessed with her boss to the point of murder. Unfortunately, the 1996 thriller *The Sculptress*, in which Quirke first proved how creepy she could be, isn't currently available on DVD.

TV Trivia: Series creator Anthony Horowitz is also the author of the Alex Rider schoolboy adventure novels (including *Stormbreaker*, which has been made into a movie).

OZ (1997-2003)

Starring Harold Perrineau, Terry Kinney, Lee Tergesen, Eamonn Walker

Right from the opening credits, where a succession of unidentified men are shown being tattooed, raped and executed (amongst other things), you know that *Oz* is not for the faint-hearted. The drama series is set in Oswald State Correctional Facility, which has an experimental unit called Emerald City where most of the stories unfold. In this tightly controlled environment, unit manager Tim McManus (Terry Kinney) tries to rehabilitate the inmates and help them see the error of their ways, although six seasons of rampant drug use, riots, murder and suicide make you admire his optimism.

The prisoners in Em City form into cliques based on ethnicity, religion, sexuality or other characteristics, with each of them vying for power and this calls for a large ensemble cast with numerous storylines ebbing and flowing throughout. Augustus Hill (Harold Perrineau) is a wheelchair-bound prisoner who acts as the narrator, expounding the theme of each episode and introducing new characters. One inmate, Tobias Beecher (Lee Tergesen), a lawyer, married with children, is incarcerated in the very first episode following a drink-driving incident in which a young girl was killed. His character is the 'everyman' we can relate to – one stupid mistake and he finds himself in this hellish place being abused and humiliated throughout the series in all kinds of unspeakable ways. There but for the grace of God...

Oz was the first hour-long drama produced by HBO, best known for series like *Sex and the City* and, later, *The Sopranos*. Despite the fact that it is set in a prison full of hardcore crims, the characters are complex and storylines are equally unpredictable. It's not a question of inmates bad/staff good, there are plenty of instances where it seems as though the wrong people are behind bars. The show doesn't pull any punches; it depicts prison life in all its sheer brutality and doesn't offer any simplistic solutions. There is no heavy moral standpoint either. Instead, *Oz* holds a mirror up to the US penal system and asks 'is this the answer?'

TV trivia: The arm that is being tattooed in the opening credits belongs to series creator Tom Fontana.

PRISON BREAK (2005–)

Starring Wentworth Miller, Dominic Purcell

A completely bonkers idea that somehow worked – for the first season, at least. Lincoln (Purcell) is sent to death row for a crime he swears he didn't commit – the murder of a political figure. His younger brother Michael (Miller) believes him – so much that he has the blueprints of the prison where Lincoln is incarcerated tattooed on his body, then commits a crime deliberately so he can be sent to the same jail in order to help Lincoln escape. Now *that's* brotherly love.

All of that preposterous plotting happens in the first episode, and then the series gets down to business, depicting life on the inside as Michael and Lincoln come up against gangs, nasty bad guys, murders, nastier bad guys and Michael's various attempts to match the marks on his body with the layout of the prison, while their pal Veronica (Robin Tunney) tries to unravel the conspiracy against Lincoln on the outside. By Season 2, as fans will know, the guys – along with some of the more memorable secondary characters – have managed to escape and are on the run, which changes the pace somewhat (one of the creators, Paul Scheuring, compared it to '*The Fugitive* x eight') as each tries to keep one step ahead of the law. By Season 3, some of the escapees are still at large, but with the creators realising they had strayed from the show's title, poor Michael is back in the slammer and may just have to try and break out again.

Elaborately plotted throughout, this – like *24* and *Lost* – remains a mystery to anyone who joins it part of the way through, but is a must-see every week for fans gripped by Lincoln and Michael's gritty adventures. Notable supporting performances come from Peter Stormare as a vicious con, John Abruzzi and Sarah Wayne Callies as Michael's love interest, Dr Sarah Tancredi.

 TV Trivia: Apparently, Michael's intricate tattoos would, in real life, take over 200 hours to do and would cost around $20,000.

PRISONER CELL BLOCK H (1979–1986)

Starring Val Lehman, Kerry Armstrong, Elspeth Ballantyne, Maggie Kirkpatrick

Known simply as *Prisoner* in its native Australia (in the UK, 'Cell Block H' was added to avoid confusion with *The Prisoner*), this notorious series from Grundy TV was essentially a soap opera set in a women's prison. It was created by Reg Watson, who had also been responsible for *Crossroads* and *Neighbours*. Like those shows, *Prisoner* was renowned for its wobbly acting and equally wobbly sets, but also for some of the radical subjects it tackled, including homosexuality, prison reform, physical abuse and rape.

Beginning with the arrival at Wentworth Detention Centre's maximum security wing of two new prisoners, Karen (Peta Toppano) and Lynn (Armstrong), the show followed – for almost 700 episodes – the lives of various prisoners and prison officers. It featured such iconic moments as the prison riot in which one inmate stabbed the prison psychiatrist to death, the escape of fan favourite Franky (and her being shot dead by a cop while on the run), the attempted escape of three of the girls during a pantomime performance of *Cinderella*, ex-prisoner Bea (Lehman) shooting her estranged husband just so she can be sent back inside, and the various machinations of Joan 'The Freak' Ferguson (Kirkpatrick), a prison officer more corrupt than most of her charges.

It's all a bit hysterical in places, but that's part of its charm, along with the believably rough-looking, unforgettable characters. Shown late night in the UK on ITV in the eighties and nineties, this has become something of a cult show amongst those who remember tuning in following an evening out, and it remains a classic (if not necessarily great) piece of Aussie TV.

TV Trivia: Following the success of *Prisoner*, Grundy Television produced an unsuccessful male version called *Punishment* in 1981 that was soon cancelled. It is most notable for an early performance from a young Mel Gibson.

THE SOPRANOS (1999–2007)

Starring James Gandolfini, Edie Falco, Michael Imperioli, Lorraine Bracco

The Sopranos quickly became a byword for quality TV drama. The series centres around New Jersey-based Mob boss, Tony Soprano (Gandolfini), as he struggles to meet the demands of his work and family life. Pressure mounts from a strained marriage, spoilt kids, power struggles, betrayals and constant attention from the Feds until he begins to suffer panic attacks and ends up seeking therapy from psychiatrist Dr Melfi (Lorraine Bracco) to help him deal with his unresolved issues. Considering the fact that his mother and uncle conspire to have him killed in the first season, it's understandable that he would be somewhat stressed. The show is darkly comic with plenty of adult content – strong language, sex, violence – but it also manages to be poignant without wandering into sentimental territory.

The series centres mainly on Tony and his family but there is also focus on other members of the New Jersey crew as well as the rival New York mob. There's Adriana, Tony's nephew Christopher's girlfriend, who unwittingly befriends an undercover FBI agent with tragic consequences. Vito, one of the

New Jersey captains, is finally outed in Season 6 when he is spotted strutting his leather-clad stuff in a gay club. With homosexuality in the Mob being the ultimate taboo, he is forced to go on the run which, again, leads to tragedy.

The Sopranos is often compared to popular gangster films, in particular *Goodfellas*, but although that movie is based on real people and true events, they both depict complex characters, rather than two dimensional wise-guy thugs, who we see develop as events unfold. Another reason for the comparison is that six of the regular cast members, including Lorraine Bracco, who was initially offered the role of Carmela, Tony's wife, appeared in *Goodfellas,* as did numerous other recurring cast members and guest stars. The controversial ending of the final episode raised a few eyebrows but, like the rest of the series, it kept viewers on the edge of their seats (see p.416 for more details).

 TV trivia: Ray Liotta, who starred as Henry Hill in *Goodfellas*, was the top choice to play Tony Soprano, but he turned it down, stating he did not want to commit to a television series.

WiDoWS (1983. 1985)

Starring Ann Mitchell, Eva Mottley, Maureen O'Farrell, Fiona Hendley

A cracking slice of eighties TV from *Prime Suspect* author Lynda La Plante, this is notable for being her first foray into the women/crime genre that she has been so successful at. When three armed robbers die while robbing a security van (it catches fire in a London tunnel), their widows – Dolly Rawlins (Mitchell), Shirley Miller (Hendley) and Linda Pirelli (O'Farrell) – uncover their deceased husbands' plans for the crime and decide to carry it out them- selves. You go, girls! Enlisting the help of a fourth woman, Bella O'Reilly (Mottley), the women get ready to pull off the heist. Problem is, the police and rival gangs are on their trail, as is someone altogether unexpected.

Six episodes of this tough, sassy series were made, and it proved so successful that a follow-up, *Widows 2*, followed in 1985 and followed the criminal women as they tried to hold onto their loot (unfortunately, it was less enjoyable or tightly paced as the series on which it was based). A disappointing third series, *She's Out*, which followed Dolly after she was released from prison, was made in 1995.

TV Trivia: An American version was made in 2002 with Mercedes Ruehl, Brooke Shields and Rosie Perez in the lead roles.

WiTHiN THESE WALLS (1974-1978)

Starring Googie Withers, Katharine Blake, Sarah Lawson

Credited with being the inspiration for Australian drama *Prisoner: Cell Block H* and later *Bad Girls*, *Within These Walls* was a ground-breaking British TV series set in a women's prison. Made by London Weekend Television, it focuses more on the prison warders than on the inmates, and in particular governor Faye Boswell (Withers). Set at the fictional Stonepark prison, the series followed Boswell as she attempted to improve the facilities and encourage her prisoners to improve their lives, often against the wishes of her staff, while also dealing with her own personal life outside the prison walls.

Over 70 episodes were made of the gritty series, and it hasn't dated, although fans of naff seventies TV may chuckle at some of the supporting cast which includes former kids' TV presenter Floella Benjamin, *Crossroads'* Kathy Staff, a rather awkward Simon MacCorkindale, *Birds of a Feather's* Linda Robson and comedienne Pamela Stephenson as a prison officer.

 TV Trivia: Googie Withers – real name Georgette – got her nickname from an Indian nurse when she was raised in Karachi. It means 'pigeon' in Hindi.

PRIVATE EYES AND SPIES

THERE ARE SOME CLASSIC SHOWS UNAVAILABLE ON DVD SUCH AS *CANNON*, *SHOESTRING*, *MIKE HAMMER*, AND, ERM, *SIMON & SIMON*, BUT HERE ARE SOME CRACKERS:

ALiAS (2001–2006)

Starring Jennifer Garner, Ron Rifkin, Victor Garber

One of the most complex serial dramas to confuse American TV audiences, *Alias* was, perhaps, too clever for its own good. A twisting, double-crossing, inventive plot meant that new viewers were too perplexed by the various intricacies to enjoy what was actually (if you watched from the very first episode and took notes) a rip-roaring spy thriller with a smart, ballsy lead in the form of Jennifer Garner.

She plays Sydney Bristow, a young spy, recruited out of college, who works for a branch of the CIA called SD-6... well, she thinks she does. Before the end of the first series, Sydney, who dons various colourful/skin-tight costumes in her work, discovers she has been lied to and SD-6 is actually part of something called The Alliance of Twelve, which is *against* the United States. So our Syd decides to offer her services to the *real* CIA, while remaining at SD-6 so she can spy on them and destroy them from the inside. If that sounds confusing, the series got even more so as Sydney entered into a complex friendship with one of her co-workers, Michael Vaughn (Michael Vartan), renewed her relationship with her spy dad (Garber), discovered her mother (Lena Olin) was a spy for the KGB, *and* learned her best friend/roommate had been killed and replaced by someone who looked like her. Phew.

Realising that even fans were getting a bit confused, producers simplified things in Season 3 (having Sydney return from supposed death after two years to discover everything had changed) and the series continued for another two years before eventually being cancelled due to low ratings. If you can follow what's going on, it's hugely rewarding, clever stuff from creator J.J. Abrams (a co-creator of another complex show, *Lost*), and, alongside Garner there are some terrific supporting performances, most notably from Rifkin (as Sydney's nemesis, Sloane), Garber, and a bevy of guest stars including Christian Slater, Quentin Tarantino, Roger Moore, Rutger Hauer and even Ricky Gervais.

TV Trivia: Ricky Gervais has admitted he can't watch himself on screen in *Alias* as he can't bear to see himself acting in a serious dramatic role.

THE AVENGERS (1961–1969): THE NEW AVENGERS (1976–1977)

Starring Patrick Macnee, Diana Rigg, Honor Blackman, Ian Hendry, Joanna Lumley, Gareth Hunt

The British spy series against which all others are measured, this late sixties show combined sex appeal, attitude, witty scripts, tongue-in-cheek humour and often bonkers plots – plus, of course, gorgeously snooty women in the form of Honor Blackman and later Diana Rigg. Patrick Macnee starred as dapper John Steed, an Eton-taught British intelligence agent, and in the first season he was joined by Dr David Keel (Hendry) as he solved crimes and despatched bad guys with his trusty umbrella. When Hendry left at the end of the first series, Mrs Catherine Gale, PhD (Blackman) helped Steed on various adventures, usually clad in tight leather ensembles and kicking ass in just as tough a manner as her male counterparts. Gale and Steed continued together until 1964 – Macnee and Blackman even entering the recording studio to sing the top five hit, 'Kinky Boots' – but when Blackman left at the end of Series Three, Rigg joined the cast as the infamously sultry Emma Peel. (Rigg left at the end of 1967 and was replaced by Linda Thorson as Tara King, but by then the series had taken a turn for the worse and it was eventually cancelled in 1969).

Best episodes include 'The House That Jack Built', in which Emma is held prisoner by a man intent on driving her insane, 'The Danger Makers' directed by *A Fish Called Wanda*'s Charles Crichton, in which Emma and Steed go undercover to infiltrate a strange organisation, 'Too Many Christmas Trees' from 1965 and 1964's 'Little Wonders' in which Catherine Gale and Steed actually kiss.

The series was resurrected in 1976 under the new name *The New Avengers*, with only Macnee as Steed returning. He was joined by Joanna Lumley as a pudding bowl-haired Purdey and Gareth Hunt as Mike Gambit. Fans of the original series quite rightly thought this new incarnation was below par, and even Macnee was reported to have been embarrassed by the end result (the second and final series was especially bad). All in all, the Diana Rigg episodes of *The Avengers* remain the best – and the eye-wincingly bad movie remake from 1998, with Ralph Fiennes as Steed and Uma Thurman as Emma Peel, should only be watched as a prime example of how *not* to remake a successful series for the big screen.

TV Trivia: *Avengers* stars Macnee, Rigg and Blackman have all appeared in Bond movies – Macnee was in *A View To A Kill*, Rigg married Bond in *On Her Majesty's Secret Service* and Honor Blackman was, of course, Pussy Galore in *Goldfinger*. New Avengers star Joanna Lumley also (briefly) appeared in *On Her Majesty's Secret Service* as 'the English Girl'.

BOON (1986–1992)

Starring Michael Elphick, David Daker, Neil Morrissey

This series made big stars of both Michael Elphick and Neil Morrissey… and also, alas, inflicted Jim Diamond's teeth-grindingly bad theme song 'Hi Ho Silver' on an unsuspecting nation.

Paunchy, rough-speaking ex-firemen Ken Boon (Elphick) and his pal Harry (Daker) set up a business together that is part-security service and part-private investigation company. A real rough diamond, Boon does the grunt work, beating up the bad guys, imagining himself as a modern-day Lone Ranger (hence the theme song) astride his beloved 'White Lightning' motorbike, while Harry looks after the business side – which includes the messenger company Texas Rangers – when he isn't trying to chum up to members of the local golf club. Later, Neil Morrissey was introduced as naive Rocky, a long-haired lad in a studded biker jacket, who first appears coming to Boon's rescue when he is cornered by a group of angry Hell's Angels – Rocky becomes a motorbike messenger and then later helps Boon crack some cases.

Like *Minder*, this series was essentially about a cheeky Cockney chappie with a good heart who finds himself in no end of scrapes, and Elphick was perfectly cast in the lead role. For the first three seasons, this was a slice of classic British telly – laughs, drama and even the occasional romance – but the final episodes weren't as crisp as the early ones. Elphick went on to appear in *EastEnders*, but died following a heart attack in 2002 at the age of only 55.

 TV Trivia: The series was loosely derived from the 1950s US show *Have Gun Will Travel*. The lead actor of that show was Richard Boone – which is where 'Boon's' name came from.

CADFAEL (1994–1996)

Starring Derek Jacobi, Michael Culver, Julian Firth

Possibly the most unusual idea for a detective series – not only is this set in the 12th century, but the investigator of the title is actually a Benedictine monk named Brother Cadfael (Jacobi). Based at Shrewsbury Abbey, former Crusade-fighter Cadfael is an experienced gardener and herbalist who would prefer to be pottering amongst his plants, but it seems Shrewsbury is a hotbed of medieval murder and Cadfael is the only resident who uses deductive reasoning to figure out whodunnit.

As based on the mysteries by Ellis Peters (aka Edith Pargeter), the Cadfael mysteries are entertaining romps as the spiritual monk solves crimes such as a novice being accused of murder, a priest suspiciously killed for his political leanings and the search for two missing children. Set during a fascinating piece of England's history, when the country was split between the warring rulers King Stephen and Empress Maud, each episode is a self-contained mystery (just over an hour long) and 13 were made.

 TV Trivia: Although set in rural England, the series was actually filmed in Hungary.

CALLAN (1967–1972)

Starring Edward Woodward, Russell Hunter

No one does hardened and grizzled quite like Edward Woodward and he's perfectly cast here.

Woodward stars, of course, as David Callan, a bad-tempered assassin for the government (the character first appeared in a TV play *A Magnum For Schneider* in early 1967). While James Bond-made spies always seem dashing, suave, attractive and teflon-coated so bullets never graze them, Callan was a different kind of guy, a tough killer living on the fringes of society who counts dirty thief (literally – he needs a wash) Lonely (Hunter) as his only friend. Working for a series of authority figures all named Hunter (Ronald Radd, Derek Bond and William Squire playing the different anonymous bosses), Callan did British Secret Intelligence's (aka 'The Section') bidding, be it capturing a former SS officer or killing a Russian spy, but he often wasn't very pleased about it.

Gritty and bleak and featuring a lead character with a questionable moral centre, this was a dark, fascinating series that boasted one of Woodward's best performances (and that's a compliment indeed, when you remember his impressive turns in *The Wicker Man*, *Becket* and *Young Winston*). After this series finished in 1972, the character lived on: Woodward appeared in a made-for-cinema feature, *Callan*, in 1974, and the character was resurrected again in an unfortunately-titled TV movie, *Wet Job*, in 1981. Of the two, only *Callan* is available on DVD.

TV Trivia: Some fans of the series believe that Woodward's character in *The Equalizer*, a conscience-stricken former spy named Robert McCall, is actually meant to be an aged Callan living in New York with a new identity.

THE CHAMPIONS (1968–1969)

Starring Stuart Damon, William Gaunt, Alexandra Bastedo

Part spy series and part superhero drama, *The Champions* was a fun ITV series about three agents for Nemesis who discover they have acquired superhuman powers after they crash land en route to a mission in Tibet and encounter a lost tribe with a magical touch. These powers – basically they're extra strong and a bit telepathic – come in handy when the agents foil various plots involving more everyday villainy and espionage.

Looking back, it's pretty kitsch, but there's fun to be had from this fantasy thriller as Craig Sterling (Damon), Richard Barrett (Gaunt) and token female Sharron Macready (Bastedo) romp around sixties Europe exchanging witty banter and occasionally beating up bad guys. The best episodes include the tense 'The Interrogation', 'The Experiment' and 'Shadow Of The Panther', an episode that co-starred Donald Sutherland.

 TV Trivia: The Nemesis building, meant to be in Geneva, is actually a council office building in Barnet, North London.

CHUCK (2007–)

Starring Zachary Levi, Yvonne Strahovski, Adam Baldwin

One of two new shows from *The OC*'s creator Josh Schwartz in 2007 (the other is the equally addictive *Gossip Girl*), this one is aimed more at a male audience. It centres around slacker Chuck (Levi). A smart guy who was kicked out of college for something he didn't do, he works at the local computer store and has a pretty dull existence... until he accidentally downloads critical government secrets straight into his brain. Now, with his head packed with incriminating evidence, plans and missions, he's caught between perky CIA agent Sarah Walker (Strahovski) and rival spy John Casey (Adam Baldwin) – who both want access to the many secrets stored in his noggin.

It's a fun show that is part drama, part action, part spy adventure and part spoof as Chuck attempts to help catch bad guys and foil treasonous plots while remaining an ordinary guy and keeping his super-brain secret from his well-meaning sister (Sarah Lancaster) and his rather irritating friend Morgan

(Joshua Gomez). It's a neat idea that works well, although we doubt real CIA agents would wander round in the skimpy outfits that agent Sarah sports in just about every episode.

 TV Trivia: Series creator Josh Schwartz created *The OC* when he was just 26, making him the youngest creator of an hour-long TV show in US history.

DANGER MAN (1960-1962, 1964-1966)

Starring Patrick McGoohan

This British spy series began life as half-hour episodes detailing the adventures of British Secret Service (and later NATO) agent John Drake (McGoohan), but after two years (39 episodes), the series was cancelled, only to be resurrected two years after that in a slightly revamped form – the episodes were now each one hour long and it was renamed 'Secret Agent' in the US (the original *Danger Man* hadn't been a hit there, but this newer version was). The story, however, remained the same: agent Drake, a sort of anti-James Bond (he doesn't chase girls or carry a pistol), travels the world working for the government as a secret agent, foiling assassination attempts, catching bad guys and preventing nasty political problems that could change the world as we know it.

Despite being over four decades old, this series remains gripping stuff even if some of the technology is a bit dated. Filmed in black and white (apart from the final two episodes), it looks terrific even when British locations are clearly doubling for European ones, while McGoohan gives a storming performance as the often arrogant and ruthless, witty agent of the title. The best episodes are the ones from the first two years, as the hour-long format from 1964 did dilute the crisp, succinct writing a little. But McGoohan's fab in every one.

 TV Trivia: The 1964 episode 'Colony Three', about a village from where visitors never return, is believed to be the inspiration for *The Prisoner*, the next series McGoohan was to star in.

DEPARTMENT S (1969-1970); JASON KING (1971-1972)

Starring Peter Wyngarde, Joel Fabiani, Rosemary Nichols

An enjoyably camp and gimmicky series that spun off into the even camper Jason King show, *Department S* was a branch of Interpol specially set up to investigate bizarre and supposedly unsolvable crimes. Hunky macho man Stewart Sullivan (Fabiani), international man of mystery (and novelist) Jason King (Wyngarde) and computer expert/eye candy Annabelle Hurst (Nichols) worked for Sir Curtis Sertese (Dennis Alaba Peters) and dealt with such cases as that of a woman found in a secret lavish compartment of a shipping tanker ('The Trojan Tanker'), two men found dead on a Spanish beach with a fake fish filled with money ('The Treasure Of The Costa Del Sol') and the girl who wakes up to discover the village she lives in is deserted and all the residents have disappeared ('The Pied Piper Of Hambledown').

Extremely silly, the series worked thanks to Wyngarde's bonkers character – author King often tried to solve a crime by wondering what his fictional creation, detective Mark Caine, would do, much to the annoyance of his companions – and even more mad appearance (his infamous handlebar moustache, cravats and bouffant hairdo) so it's hardly surprising that a *Department S* spin-off series focused on his character. *Jason King*, the series, began in 1971 and followed the dandyish character after he left the department and returned to his playboy lifestyle, only for British Intelligence to blackmail him into working for them (their leverage was that he had a large amount of unpaid taxes). It wasn't a great series – and ran for just 26 episodes – but as an example of seventies kitsch, it's a classic.

 TV Trivia: Kate O'Mara was originally offered the role of Annabelle until a producer decided she looked too exotic to play an English rose-type character.

DiCK SPANNER. P.I (1986)

Voice by Shane Rimmer

Back in the early days of late night and early morning TV in Britain, quirky shows that would never have been broadcast during daylight were given an airing in the wee hours. One of the oddest was this stop-motion animated series from *Thunderbirds* creator Gerry Anderson – a low-budget (and it certainly looked it) collection of six-minute long episodes made for Channel Four (it originally aired on their Sunday morning show Network 7, then later in the middle of the night) that told the story of a robot private eye named Dick. He lived in a parallel universe to our own, looked like he had been made by a five-year-old using cardboard and some sticky backed plastic, and over 22 shows tried to solve two cases: 'The Case Of The Human Cannonball' and 'The Case Of The Maltese Parrot'.

It's packed with tongue-in-cheek humour, and Rimmer delivers a great vocal turn as the square-jawed hero. Completely bonkers in places, and well deserving of the classification 'cult', the series is a must-see for fans of that other sarcastic and weird animated detective, *Duckman* (whose adventures, tragically, are as yet unavailable on DVD).

 TV Trivia: Canadian actor Shane Rimmer also provided a voice to various unseen characters in another Anderson production: *Space 1999.*

THE DRESDEN FILES (2007)

Starring Paul Blackthorne, Valerie Cruz

Based on the novels by Jim Butcher, *The Dresden Files* features a detective, Harry Dresden (Blackthorne) who has a 'gift'– he's a sorcerer. With the help of a Chicago cop (Cruz) who calls him in whenever she has a case that defies explanation, and the spirit of a mediaeval wizard (Terence Mann) he calls 'Bob', Dresden tries to solve cases that usually involve something not quite everyday. It could be a boy who is being pursued by a demon, or a murderer who can move from body to body – if something is going bump in the night, Dresden is your man.

Only 12 episodes of this adventure featuring the wisecracking (and, to be honest, rather annoyingly smarmy) detective/wizard were made by the Sci-Fi Channel and it's not hard to see why. Everything from Harry Potter to *The X-Files* is ripped off (Dresden's mum, for example, was a wizard who died an early death and left him with a protective charm and relationship issues), while the revelation that there is a council that presides over the supernatural and undead will remind many fantasy/sci-fi viewers of *Buffy* and *Angel*. That it's not the world's most original idea wouldn't be too much of a problem if the lead was likeable and the scripts punchy, but instead the storylines are a mess and Blackthorne's swagger comes off as just a tad less grating than fingernails on a chalkboard.

 TV Trivia: Blackthorne is actually from Shropshire in England and is an accomplished photographer.

GET SMART (1965–1970)

Starring Don Adams, Barbara Feldon

Former stand-up comic Don Adams will forever be associated with the role of Maxwell Smart, the secret agent he played in this delicious spoof of spy movies and series. Also known as Agent 86, Smart works for government agency CONTROL alongside beautiful partner Agent 99 (Feldon). The pair receive their dangerous assignments from The Chief, and they usually involve foiling a plan by the evil villians who make up the KAOS organisation.

A tongue-in-cheek parody of the James Bond films, among others, this was a delight thanks to splendid dialogue, huge doses of silliness, Adams' terrific performance as the bumbling Smart, and his pairing with Feldon, whose clever, slick Agent 99 (her real name is never revealed) was usually the one who had to save the day for him.

Written and created by Buck Henry and the comic genius Mel Brooks, this was often bonkers (Max's shoe was also a phone and it's always hilarious watching him answer it) and remains as funny now as when it was first broadcast in the sixties. A film version was made in 2008, starring Steve Carrell and Anne Hathaway.

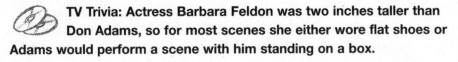 **TV Trivia: Actress Barbara Feldon was two inches taller than Don Adams, so for most scenes she either wore flat shoes or Adams would perform a scene with him standing on a box.**

HANNAY (1988–1989)

Starring Robert Powell, Christopher Scoular

Just 13 episodes (over two seasons) were made of this ITV series that was effectively a spin-off of 1978's film version of John Buchan's classic novel *The Thirty Nine Steps*. Powell reprised the role of Richard Hannay from the film, the mining engineer who became caught up in a conspiracy involving Prussian agents in the run-up to World War I. Some of the episodes were based on Buchan's other books to feature Hannay, and were all set in pre-war England.

Hannay's adventures included him investigating whether a valuable consignment of gold meant for Canada was actually placed aboard the ill-fated Titanic, a swashbucking story of priceless jewels and mistaken identity, and a romance with a woman who steals Hannay's heart but whom he suspects is a con-artist. It's all rip-roaring stuff, featuring duels, murders, espionage and British derring-do that, while not quite as gripping as *The Thirty Nine Steps*, is nonetheless entertaining fare (and Powell remains the best Hannay from both film and TV adaptations).

 TV Trivia: Robert Powell's wife is Barbara 'Babs' Lord, one of Pan's People (the *Top of the Pops* dancers in the 1970s).

THE HARDY BOYS AND NANCY DREW MYSTERIES (1977–1979)

Starring Parker Stevenson, Shaun Cassidy, Pamela Sue Martin

Young pre-teens of the seventies will remember these two series that were shown on alternate weeks. One week you would get a Nancy Drew mystery, the next it would be the Hardy Boys solving a crime (in the second season, the three sometimes got together to solve a mystery, then by Season 3 poor Nancy was dumped completely in favour of the allegedly cute boys). In the Hardy Boys stories, we got to meet sensible older brother Frank (Stevenson) and the more reckless Joe (teen heartthrob Cassidy, in real life the half-brother of pop star David), the sons of famous private investigator Fenton Hardy (Ed Gilbert). Each episode they miraculously stumbled upon something mysterious (though not too serious – this was aimed at kids) in their hometown of Bayport in a sort of Scooby Doo-style adventure, while in *The Nancy Drew Mysteries*, our eponymous heroine (*Dynasty*'s Martin) assisted her own dad, lawyer Carson Drew (William Schallert), in solving puzzling crimes, often with the help of her (female) cousin George.

Of course, for pubescent girls, the choice was between imagining what it would be like to solve crimes like kick-ass Nancy, and thinking what it would be like to kiss yummy, long-haired Joe Hardy (remember, this was the relatively innocent seventies, at least on TV). As adults, we may query the parenting of Mr Hardy and Mr Drew, who seem quite happy to put their offspring in the path of danger, but for young viewers this was an entertainingly camp slice of adventure at tea-time.

 TV Trivia: Shaun Cassidy is now a successful TV producer, who has made shows including *American Gothic* and *Cold Case*.

HART TO HART (1979–1984)

Starring Stefanie Powers, Robert Wagner, Lionel Stander

The familiar opening narration by gravel-voiced housekeeper Max (Stander) says it all: 'This is my boss, Jonathan Hart. A self-made millionaire. He's quite a guy. This is Mrs. H. She's gorgeous. She's one lady who knows how to take care of herself. By the way, my name is Max. I take care of both of them, which ain't easy; 'cause when they met… it was *murder!*' Yes, the loving, wealthy couple Jonathan (Wagner) and Jennifer Hart (Powers) have got bored counting their cash, so when they are not making googly eyes at each other or smooching (which happens *a lot*), they usually find themselves caught up in a mystery of some sort, be it murder, espionage or high-price theft.

The winning combination of Powers and Wagner made this daft show hugely enjoyable, while Stander as their housekeeper/chauffeur/cook (and, lest we forget, family dog Freeway) added to the fun. Created by Sidney Sheldon, who was best known for pulpy romance novels such as *Rage Of Angels* and *Master Of The Game*, this was just as much about a perfect married couple as it was about the mysteries they solved (usually while in dinner dress, hair perfectly coiffed even when they had tussled with a bad guy), and the leads made the relationship believable. Yes, it's camper than a field full of tents, but thanks to the casting and some rather fabulous eighties fashions, it's great fun, too. While the series finished in 1984, the Harts returned for a series of TV movies between 1993 and 1996 (as yet unavailable on DVD). And they still looked gorgeous.

 TV Trivia: Charlie, the dog that played Freeway, was rescued from a dog pound just days before shooting on the first series began. He became so popular, he even got to star in one episode 'Which Way, Freeway?'

HAZELL (1978-1980)

Starring Nicholas Ball, Desmond McNamara, Roddy McMillan

This series made by ITV followed the adventures of cockney private eye James Hazell (Ball) over 22 episodes. A sort of East End version of Philip Marlowe, complete with Hazell's wry narration, the series was a mixture of drama and humour that captured the feel of forties film noir while being firmly set in the seventies (check out Hazell's wide lapelled leather jacket – it was actually fashionable at the time).

As fans will remember, Hazell was an ex-copper, kicked off the force due to a drinking habit (like the best private eyes, he had a tumultuous private life: his missus had left him) who often butted heads with his former fellow policemen, including Inspector 'Choc' Minty (McMillan). It was Ball's charm and the cheeky chappy humour that carried the show, but after two seasons Hazell was cancelled and replaced by a similar – but more successful – mix of drama and cockney fun in the form of *Minder*. This is well worth a look, short-lived as it was, and keep an eye out for a young Michael Elphick ('Hazell And The Walking Blur'), Peter Mayhew (best known as Chewbacca in the *Star Wars* movies, he's in 'Hazell And The Big Sleep') and also Pamela Stephenson (Ball's wife at the time, she appears in 'Hazell Settles The Accounts') in supporting roles.

 TV Trivia: Former England football coach Terry Venables was a co-writer on the series.

HONEY WEST (1965–1966)

Starring Anne Francis, John Ericson, Irene Hervey

Originally the lead character in a series of mystery novels by Gloria and Skip Fickling, *Honey West* first appeared on TV in an episode of cop show *Burke's Law* and proved so popular that the character was spun off into her own series. Anne Francis starred as the slinky private eye, who had taken over her father's successful detective business after his death and now solved her own crimes but it was not the plots that this series was known for. Rather it was Francis's fetching wardrobe of leather jumpsuits and animal-print ensembles (oh, and she also had a pet ocelot) and undercover missions that required her to wear skimpy outfits that had people tuning in.

With the help of an exploding compact mirror, tear gas earrings and a radio hidden in her lipstick case, Honey was something of a feminine James Bond, with Sam Bolt (Ericson) as her Q, providing her with the gadgets when he wasn't eavesdropping on bad guys to solve a case. It was all a bit silly and ran for only one season, but for fans of shows like *The Avengers* (Honey could be a distant relative of the equally sultry Emma Peel), it was a treat.

 TV Trivia: When the sixties series *Burke's Law* was remade in 1994, Anne Francis returned to reprise her role of Honey for one episode.

IRONSIDE (1967–1975)

Starring Raymond Burr, Don Galloway

Terrific late-sixties cop/detective drama, this had deep-voiced Raymond Burr creating a TV icon as wheelchair-bound Robert T. Ironside. A chief of detectives shot by a sniper's bullet while on vacation, he returns to duty, crippled from the waist down, and runs his own special unit at San Francisco Police Headquarters, helping the cops with their most baffling cases. With the help of Detective Sergeant Ed Brown (Galloway), cop Eve Whitfield (Barbara Anderson) and former delinquent Mark Sanger (Don Mitchell), Ironside nearly always gets his man.

One of America's longest-running cop shows (199 episodes were made), the series boasted performances from actors including Harrison Ford, Bill Bixby, William Shatner, William Devane and Martin Sheen. The best episodes are from the first four years, before Barbara Anderson left in 1971.

 TV Trivia: Raymond Burr sustained painful injuries from all the time he spent acting in Ironside's wheelchair.

MAGNUM PI (1980–1988)

Starring Tom Selleck, John Hillerman, Roger E Mosley, Larry Manetti

Donald P. Bellasario and Glen A. Larson – creators (separately) of such hit shows as *Quantum Leap*, *Battlestar Galactica*, *Knight Rider* and *Buck Rogers in the 25th Century* – were the men behind this good-natured detective series that made a star of Tom Selleck. Previously a jobbing actor with a few roles in TV westerns and a slew of failed pilots behind him, Selleck shot to fame as the moustachioed, tight-shorts-wearing Thomas Magnum, a private detective who lives on a lavish Hawaiian estate belonging to the never seen Robin Masters. Supposedly Magnum is there to provide security, but in reality he just lives in Masters' guest house, drives his swish red Ferrari and annoys the hell out of the other resident, English housekeeper/major domo Higgins (Hillerman).

For eight years, former Navy SEAL Magnum solved amusing crimes, buddied around with his pals TC (Mosely) and Rick (Manetti), verbally sparred with Higgins, romanced the ladies and occasionally dealt with serious stories – later episodes show Thomas fell in love while stationed in Vietnam, and was married, but it ended tragically. At the end of the seventh season, the producers were told the show was not going to be renewed for another year, so they killed off Magnum in the final episode. However, due to an outcry from fans, the series was reinstated for one last season and the first episode of Season 8 showed that Magnum was only wounded from the supposedly fatal gunshot he had received at the end of the previous season.

The best and most fun episodes are from the earliest seasons (when Selleck's shorts were at their snuggest and his 'tache was at its fullest) before things got a bit repetitive, but fans of Frank Sinatra should seek out Season 7, Episode 18 ('Laura') in which Old Blue Eyes made his last major acting appearance before his death, as a retired cop chasing the men who murdered his granddaughter.

 TV Trivia: Tom Selleck was offered the role of Indiana Jones in *Raiders of the Lost Ark*, but had to turn it down due to his *Magnum* contract.

THE MAN FROM U.N.C.L.E. (1964–1968)

Starring Robert Vaughn, David McCallum

Based on an idea by Ian Fleming, *The Man from U.N.C.L.E* has some similarities to his most famous creation, James Bond. Napoleon Solo (Vaughn) and Illya Kuryakin (McCallum) are both suave, sophisticated spies ready to do anything to preserve world peace or seduce a beautiful lady – the main difference here is that their antics are played slightly more for laughs.

The pair worked for the United Network Command for Law Enforcement (the entrance to their offices was accessed through a door in a tailor's shop), and in the line of duty braved trained killer bees, hiccup gas and earthquake-creating devices on the orders of their boss, Alexander Waverly (Leo G. Carroll), while trying to capture mad scientists and various other megalomaniacs who believed they could rule the world and who were members of the nefarious group THRUSH. The first two seasons (Season 1 was black and white, the rest are in colour) are cracking and were so popular they spawned tons of merchandise from bubble gum to a collections of menswear in the US. However, following the success of the enjoyably silly *Batman*, the campness of U.N.C.L.E was increased in the third season and things became completely daft. Viewers stopped watching, and even though the show became more serious in the fourth season, no one tuned in and the series was cancelled. A spin-off, *The Girl From U.N.C.L.E*, was made in 1966 and starred Stefanie Powers, but it is not available on DVD.

 TV Trivia: Future *Star Trek* stars William Shatner and Leonard Nimoy appeared in the same Season 1 U.N.C.L.E episode: '*The Project Strigas Affair*'.

MAN IN A SUITCASE (1967–1968)

Starring Richard Bradford, Colin Blakeley

Poor CIA agent McGill (Bradford) has been falsely accused of treason and is now on the run with just a suitcase and gun for company. There's no way to clear himself, so he heads to Europe, earning his living as a private detective, zipping around town in a Hillman Imp and frequenting seedy London night-clubs in his spare time.

Thirty episodes were made of this cult sixties series, with Bradford suitably gruff as the chain-smoking, cynical American in London who suffers from a quick temper, and who likes to thump anyone who gets in his way. Known for its (at the time) strong violence, the show worked well thanks to the mix of action and Bradford's intense interpretation of a man who has lost everything including his own identity. Well worth a look, and take note: while his search for justice and bad guys took McGill to Manchester, Wales and even Africa, the majority of the series was filmed in and around Pinewood Studios.

 TV Trivia: Sound familiar? The theme tune for *Man in a Suitcase* was also used for Chris Evans' chat show *TFI Friday*.

MiSS MARPLE (1984–1992); MARPLE (2004–)

Starring Joan Hickson; Geraldine McEwan

Miss Jean Marple was a character who appeared in 12 of mystery writer Agatha Christie's novels – an elderly tweed-clad spinster who lives in the quaint English village of St Mary Mead, she often put down her knitting to solve crimes such as 'The Moving Finger', 'The Mirror Crack'd' and 'The Body In The Library'. Most of her adventures had already been made into films (with Margaret Rutherford and later Angela Lansbury in the Marple role) when the BBC decided to adapt the original novels in 1984, with Joan Hickson playing the prim amateur detective. The series' success no doubt inspired ITV to have a go, and in 2004 they began the series *Agatha Christie's Marple* (also known as *Marple*), with Geraldine McEwan in the lead.

Surprisingly the series are very different. The BBC's *Miss Marple* is a traditional adaptation of Christie's books, with Hickson giving a performance many think is a definitive one (she was 78 when she took on the role, close to the age *Miss Marple* is meant to be). It's handsome to look at, and each dramatisation is set in the late forties or early fifties, and expertly invokes the era as the sharp-minded Marple outwits the criminals and often puts the police to shame. ITV's *Marple,* on the other hand, is more controversial. The identity of the killer in the first episode is different from that in the novel on which it is based while – shock horror – affairs are added and there's even a bit of lesbianism thrown in for good measure. It also suffers from a surfeit of well-known faces in the supporting cast, ranging from Joanna Lumley, Simon Callow and Amanda Holden in the first series to Dawn French, Greta Scacchi and Martine McCutcheon in later episodes. All in all, if you want classic Christie mysteries, the BBC series is the best – and Hickson simply marvellous – while if you're looking for titillation and a more York Notes version of the stories, maybe the ITV adaptation is the one for you.

TV Trivia: Christie herself imagined Joan Hickson in the role of Marple after seeing Joan in a 1946 theatre production of *Appointment With Death*.

MiSSiON: IMPOSSiBLE (1966–1973)

Starring Greg Morris, Peter Lupus, Peter Graves, Barbara Bain, Martin Landau, Steven Hill

Boasting one of the most famous opening theme tunes of all time, *Mission: Impossible* also had one of the most famous intros: the hand striking a match that lights a fuse that burns across the screen as tempting hints of the action in the episode to come appear on screen. What more could you ask for? Well, in this superb spy series you also get inventive plots, fun gadgets, action, adventure, witty scripts and terrific performances.

Each week, the members of a secret branch of the US government, the IMF (Impossible Missions Force) were given an assignment. (In the first season, it was Dan Briggs, played by Hill, who received the orders via a recording, and when Hill left the cast the task went to Phelps, as played by Peter Graves). Then, the team would be assembled, the scheme would be planned, and the mission would involve rescuing political prisoners, thwarting evil plots and capturing nefarious dictators. For the first season, the group included gadget man Barney (Morris), muscleman Willy (Lupus), gorgeous Cinnamon (Bain) and magician Rollo (Landau, who was married to Bain at the time). Bain and Landau later left and were replaced by new characters, leaving Morris and Lupus as the only two actors to appear in every episode of the series. New additions to the cast in later seasons included Lesley Ann Warren, Sam Elliott and Lynda Day George.

The series was unsuccessfully revived in 1982, but, of course, there have been three popular movies since 1996 starring Tom Cruise that are inspired by the series.

 TV Trivia: Martin Landau was Gene Roddenberry's first choice to play Mr Spock on *Star Trek*. When Landau left *Mission Impossible*, it was Mr Spock – aka Leonard Nimoy – who replaced him.

THE MOD SQUAD (1968–1973)

Starring Peggy Lipton, Clarence Williams III, Michael Cole

A TV show about three drop-out kids who were recruited to work for the police as youthful undercover agents infiltrating the late sixties counter culture, The Mod Squad was a mix of relevant issues (the plots touched on draft dodgers, the My Lai massacre in Vietnam and a mix of grown-up criminals preying on Californian youth in one form or another) and sheer daftness, mainly thanks to the cheesy dialogue (which, of course, was 'groovy' at the time) and performances.

Each of the three members had a 'criminal' past: Pete (Cole), the son of wealthy parents, had stolen a car (shocking!), Julie (Lipton) ran away from home and was arrested for vagrancy (gasp!) and Linc (Williams), born and raised in Watts, was caught up in the riots there (okay, so that one *is* pretty serious). Captain Greer (Tige Andrews) was in charge of them as they tracked down bad guys in their Woody station wagon with only Linc's afro,

Pete's flares and roll-necks and Julie's chunky beads as weapons. A teen smash at the time (kids, in the US especially, picked up on the dialogue which mainly consisted of the words 'groovy' and 'solid'), the series was TV mogul Aaron Spelling's first big success and spawned a pile of merchandise from lunchboxes to comics, while star Peggy Lipton (who, following a virtual screen absence of over a decade went on to play cafe owner Norma in *Twin Peaks*) even released albums of her singing following her success on the show. If you enjoy this series, do note that an absolutely abominable movie, starring Giovanni Ribisi, Claire Danes and Omar Epps in the roles, that updated the action to the nineties, was made in 1999 and should be avoided at all costs.

 TV Trivia: Peggy Lipton was married to music producer Quincy Jones for 16 years.

MOONLiGHTiNG (1985–1989)

Starring Bruce Willis, Cybill Shepherd

A former model/actress best known as an ex-girlfriend of Elvis, and a bartender who had only a bit part in an episode of *Miami Vice* and a walk-on role in the Paul Newman drama *The Verdict* were the two actors chosen to star in this wonderfully quirky detective series that was part crime-solving, part comedy and part romance. She, of course, was Cybill Shepherd, and he was Bruce Willis, and together they created an on-screen chemistry that has rarely been captured since (interestingly, the pair were rumoured to hate each other in real life).

The story was simple: model Maddie Hayes (Shepherd) discovers her accountant has run off with all her money, leaving her a run-down detective agency that she had bought as an investment. Instead of selling it, she decides to make a go of the business, but that means she also has to take on the wiseguy private eye who runs it, David Addison (Willis). Together they try to solve some utterly bizarre cases, including one in which a man wants to find his son who is a contract killer, another where a woman wants to reunite with the ex-lover who threw acid in her face, and, oddest of all, the episode in which they work for a woman who says she is a leprechaun searching for the end of the rainbow.

If you can ignore Cybill's gigantic shoulder pads and blow-dried hairdo, this show hasn't aged badly at all. The first three seasons are punchy, funny and slick, and there are some superb stand-out episodes, including 'The Dream Sequence Always Rings Twice', filmed almost entirely in black and white as Maddie and David imagine themselves as ill-fated lovers at a nightclub in the forties; 'Big Man On Mulberry Street', in which Maddie learns about David's past – and ex-wife – when she follows him to New York; and, of course, 'I Am Curious… Maddie', the episode in which the pair finally revealed their true feelings for each other and 'did it'. Unfortunately, getting the couple together removed all the simmering sexual tension and sharp banter of the previous three seasons, and the show took a nosedive in series four as various reasons were given for David and Maddie not being together (Shepherd was also pregnant at the time so had to be written out of some episodes). Ratings dipped, and the series was cancelled at the end of series five (which was a slight improvement on Season 4). Enjoy the first three seasons (except the irritating episodes in which their assistant, Agnes Dipesto, took centre stage) and don't bother with the final two – they spoil what otherwise could have been the best TV show ever.

 TV Trivia: Over 3,000 men auditioned for the role of David. Legend has it that Bruce Willis was the very last actor to be seen.

MURDER SHE WROTE (1984–1996)
Starring Angela Lansbury

A phenomenally – if somewhat inexplicably – successful detective series with Angela Lansbury (formerly of *Bedknobs And Broomsticks* fame) as Jessica Fletcher, a frumpy, ageing mystery writer living in Cabot Cove, Maine, who is endlessly called upon to solve real crimes (if they weren't happening on her doorstep already). The rather preposterous (just how many murders can happen in one quaint town?) Miss Marple-style series (the show's title alludes to Agatha Christie's Marple mystery *Murder She Said*) began in 1984 and by 1994 was the longest running drama running on American TV at that time. It's pretty creaky stuff – eagle-eyed viewers will notice the harbour at Cabot Cove is actually the lake at Universal Studios LA where Jaws pops out of the water (sadly this never happens in an episode as it would have added some much-needed excitement) – that nonetheless earned Lansbury 12 Best Actress nominations at the Emmys and four Golden Globe awards.

George Clooney (Season 3, 'No Laughing Murder'), Tom Selleck (in his Magnum persona in the episode 'Magnum On Ice' from Season 3), Joaquin Phoenix (Season 1, 'We're Off To See The Wizard') and Courteney Cox (Season 3, 'Death Stalks The Big Top') were among the actors who appeared in episodes before they were famous, one of which, 'Dead Eye', co-starring Wayne Rogers, even attempted to solve the Kennedy assassination. While the series ended in 1996, a series of *Murder She Wrote* TV movies were made up until 2003.

TV Trivia: Jean Stapleton and Doris Day both turned the role of Jessica Fletcher down before it was offered to Lansbury.

PETER GUNN (1958–1961)

Starring Craig Stevens, Herschel Bernardi, Lola Albright

Blake Edwards, the director who gave us *10* and the *Pink Panther* movies, was the man behind this jaunty detective series that is often remembered for Henry Mancini's award-winning jazz score and opening theme tune. The music set the scene for this film noir-style series about suave detective Gunn (Stevens), a 1950s LA gumshoe who frequents the jazz bar Mother's when he isn't solving crime. With the glamorous Albright on hand as chanteuse/girl-friend Edie and Bernardi as police Lieutenant Jacoby, whom Gunn some-times works with, Gunn works the streets, dealing with lowlife scum and LA's underworld figures, while always looking cool.

Unlike modern-day detective dramas, episodes of *Peter Gunn* were only half an hour long, so the crime is sometimes solved a little too speedily in order to fit the resolution in before the end credits. But it looks incredibly stylish, and Stevens is perfect as the hard-boiled detective in this drama that's well worth checking out if you're a fan of *LA Confidential*-style crime mysteries.

 TV Trivia: Robert Altman, who made acclaimed movies like *The Player* and *Gosford Park*, was one of the episode directors of this show.

POIROT (1989–)

Starring David Suchet, Hugh Fraser

Agatha Christie's Belgian detective was memorably brought to life on screen by David Suchet in 1989, and his performance has been so successful that the series continues to be made with him in the lead role almost two decades on. Based on both Christie's novels and short stories, the episodes follow famous ex-policeman Hercule Poirot and his English sidekick, Captain Hastings (Fraser, providing a delicious slice of wit) as they solve crimes from their base in London.

Many of Christie's most well-known stories have been brought to TV, including *Evil Under The Sun*, *The Murder Of Roger Ackroyd* and *Death On The Nile* (*Murder On The Orient Express* and *Appointment With Death* will be available on DVD in 2009), and while the original stories were written over a long peri-od of time (1920 to the early 1970s), sensibly the producers have set all the mysteries in the 1930s, which adds a refined art deco feel to the proceedings. The era is beautifully realised in the sets, cars, costumes and architecture, and while some of the adaptations work better than others (*The Murder Of Roger Ackroyd* is particularly disappointing as it changes the infamous big twist of the novel), Suchet and Fraser – as well as supporting cast members Pauline Moran (as Poirot's secretary Felicity Lemon) and Philip Jackson (as Chief Inspector Japp) are all superb.

 TV Trivia: Suchet has to wear body padding to make himself appear more portly for the role of Poirot.

PUBLIC EYE (1965–1975)

Starring Alfred Burke, Ray Smith

One of the first British detective series to show London (and later, Birmingham and Brighton) at its seediest, *Public Eye* followed the exploits of gumshoe Frank Marker (Burke), who scraped a living as a private eye working for various scuzzy clients. Unlike the splashy shows of the eighties, this detective often *didn't* get his man, or a happy ending – something confirmed by the fact that one season ended with poor Frank being sent to jail for something he didn't do (later series would include John Grieve as Frank's probation officer following his release from prison).

Surprisingly bleak for the time – remember, this is the era of 'fun' mystery shows such as *The Mod Squad* and *The Avengers* – and featuring a very dour but principled central character ('Everywhere I look, there's dirt'), this was a very realistic and gritty detective series. Burke was perfectly cast in the lead role of a loner whose backstory was never truly revealed – a role the creators had originally envisioned for Donald Pleasance. Please note many of the early episodes (filmed in black and white, the series went colour in 1971) have been lost and only episodes from 1969 onwards are available on DVD.

 TV Trivia: Now 90 years old, Alfred Burke most recently appeared in 2002's *Harry Potter and the Chamber of Secrets*.

REILLY: ACE OF SPIES (1983)

Starring Sam Neill, Peter Egan, Ian Charleson, Leo McKern

A stormingly good drama loosely based on the true exploits of Sidney Reilly (aka Sigmund Rosenblum), who worked as a spy for Britain before, during and after World War I. Sam Neill stars as Reilly, and is supported by a cast that includes Tom Bell, Kenneth Cranham (as Lenin), David Burke (as Stalin) and David Suchet.

An epic 12-part mini-series, it began with cold, calculating Reilly's attempts to secure oil reserves for the British, and followed his exploits throughout Europe, ending with his tragic mission to overthrow Bolshevik authorities in Russia and install himself in a seat of power, while also encapsulating such historic events as the 1917 Russian Revolution and Stalin's rise to infamy. Beautifully filmed and expertly scripted – the heavier political stuff never gets dull – the only flaw in this excellent series is the rather odd casting of David Suchet as Oriental character Inspector Tsientin.

 TV Trivia: It is believed that author Ian Fleming used Sidney Reilly as inspiration for the character of James Bond.

REMINGTON STEELE (1982–1987)

Starring Pierce Brosnan, Stephanie Zimbalist, Doris Roberts

Private detective Laura Holt (Zimbalist) has a problem. In the world of private eyes, a woman just isn't taken seriously (this series was made in the less equality-minded eighties, remember), and when she starts her own detective agency she doesn't get any clients. But when Laura changes the name of the business from 'Laura Holt Investigations' to 'Remington Steele Investigations' and pretends she's working for the fictitious Mr Steele, suddenly business starts booming. Trouble is, many of her clients want to meet her non-existent boss – so it's very fortuitous when a dashing thief (Brosnan) comes along, finds out Laura's secret and assumes Remington Steele's identity. She doesn't know his real name, but soon Laura and 'Remington' are working together, exchanging witty banter and solving crimes.

Created by Glenn Gordon Caron, who went on to make another series about verbally sparring detectives (*Moonlighting*), this was originally planned to focus mainly on Laura's character, but Brosnan's suave interpretation of Remington was so popular, his role was beefed up and he became the star of the show. Urbane, good-looking and witty, Remington was the reason most people tuned in as he tried to solve crimes (usually comparing them to the plots of old movies as he was a film buff) and woo his employer. A mix of romantic comedy and mystery, this show really found its feet in the second and third series, and Season 4 is enjoyable as the 'will-they-won't-they' plot reached its peak. The series was cancelled at the end of that season, but was suddenly reinstated for a final (and rather limp) fifth series of just six episodes. They're only worth a look for completists who want to know whether the pair end up together or not.

TV Trivia: Pierce Brosnan was considered for the role of James Bond back in 1986, but lost the role to Timothy Dalton due to his contract on *Remington Steele*. He did, of course, finally get the role of Bond in 1996.

THE ROCKFORD FILES (1974–1980)
Starring James Garner, Noah Beery Jr.

The 1970s produced some of the best detective series on TV – *Banacek* and *Cannon* among them (sadly neither are on DVD in the UK) – but best of the bunch has to be this series starring the ever-charming James Garner as private eye Jim Rockford. Having already starred in a hit show (the western *Maverick*, again shockingly not on DVD), Garner donned the crumpled jacket and combed his seventies sideburns to give a terrific turn as a middle-aged, falsely accused ex-con scraping a living trying to solve crimes that often everyone else had given up on. Living in a trailer in Malibu, he took a considerable amount of punches while conning his way around town trying to find bad guys with the help of an ex-prison pal (Stuart Margolin) and wisecracks from his sceptical dad Rocky (Beery Jr.).

This was the first big success for producer Stephen J Cannell, who went on to make *The A-Team* and *Hunter*, and it's a treat – the fashions may have dated but Jim is as cool as he was three decades ago. A mix of car chases (Rockford had a rather eye-catching Pontiac Firebird), wit, action (usually poor Rockford getting punched) and sly looks from Garner mixed with some enjoyable crime-solving plots ensured the series ran for six years. Isaac Hayes, Rita Moreno, Sharon Gless, Lindsay Wagner and Tom Selleck were among the actors who appeared in episodes. Garner was unable to complete the final series due to illness, but he did return to the role in a series of 1990s TV movies.

 TV Trivia: James Garner received the Purple Heart honour after being wounded in the Korean War.

ROSEMARY AND THYME (2003–2006)
Starring Pam Ferris, Felicity Kendal

Rosemary Boxer (Kendal) and former police woman Laura Thyme (Ferris) have set up a gardening business together (called, naturally, Rosemary and Thyme), but while they should be spending their days pruning countryside trees, instead they often find themselves knee deep in mystery rather than mud. A tale of two very English ladies solving crime – a sort of Anglicised *Murder She Wrote* with added pruning shears – this was probably popular as it combined two very popular British pursuits: nosiness (as the gals spy on potential criminals) and gardening.

Unfortunately, a bit more wit would have made this series more enjoyable, as the rather ludicrous set-up is taken as seriously plausible rather than enjoyably daft. Ferris and Kendal are a treat, though, and a show that features two women of a certain age having fun while solving the occasional mystery should be celebrated (with a nice glass of sherry, of course).

 TV Trivia: One of the series' directors, Brian Farnham, dubbed the series 'Murder Most Floral'.

SHERLOCK HOLMES (1984–1994)

Starring Jeremy Brett, David Burke, Edward Hardwicke

Sir Arthur Conan Doyle's famous fictional detective – and resident, of course, of 221B Baker Street, London – is one of the most portrayed characters in the history of TV and film, with over 70 actors having played him. Perhaps the most definitive TV performance was actor Jeremy Brett's – he played Holmes on stage and also in numerous ITV adaptations of Doyle's stories, in series titled *The Adventures of Sherlock Holmes*, *The Memoirs of Sherlock Holmes*, *The Return of Sherlock Holmes*, and *The Casebook of Sherlock Holmes*.

Many fans of the novels rightly believe Brett's interpretation is the best, partly because he gives Holmes an arrogance mixed with the detective's renowned suaveness that makes him enjoyably irritating. With the help of Dr Watson (played first by Burke for 13 episodes, then Hardwicke), the complex, cocaine-addicted sleuth solves cases such as 'The Red-Headed League', 'The Hound of The Baskervilles' and 'The Last Vampyre', but the series focuses as much on Holmes and Watson's relationship as it does on the various mysteries, and that's what makes it such a treat. An earlier Sherlock Holmes series made in the US in 1954 with Ronald Howard as Holmes is available on DVD, as is a BBC box-set of their TV productions including *The Hound Of The Baskervilles* with Richard Roxburgh (2002), *The Case Of The Silk Stocking* with Rupert Everett (2004), and the older *A Study In Scarlet* with Peter Cushing (1968), which had a more Hammer Horror feel to it.

 TV Trivia: Jeremy Brett has also played Watson – in a stage adaptation of *The Crucifer of Blood*. Charlton Heston played Holmes.

THE SINGING DETECTIVE (1986)

Starring Michael Gambon, Joanne Whalley, Patrick Malahide

Writer Dennis Potter created some stunning scripts that have been adapted for film and television including *Pennies From Heaven* and *Brimstone And Treacle*, but it is *The Singing Detective* (and this TV version of it) that he is, quite rightly, best remembered and most acclaimed for. Directed by Jon Amiel (*Sommersby*, *Entrapment*), this seven-hour mini-series remains, two decades on, one of the most unusual and visually stunning pieces of TV to be made and broadcast on British TV.

Intricately plotted, and mixing autobiographical details of Potter's life with popular music from the thirties and forties, plus a film noir feel, the story focuses on miserable, rude, detective novelist Philip Marlow (Gambon, superbly gruff and leering). Bedridden and hospitalised with psoriatic arthropathy, a severe skin condition that also affects the joints that Potter himself suffered from, Marlow escapes from the pain into his imagination by envisioning one of his detective novels, *The Singing Detective*, with himself in the title role. So we see Marlow in this forties setting untangling a plot involving Nazis and a drowned woman, mixed with his present-day hospital care (tended to by nurse Whalley) that sheds light on the failings of the NHS. Interspersed with this are flashbacks to Marlow's childhood, including his mother's suicide and the experience of seeing his mother having sex with a neighbourhood man in the woods – a scene that enraged some sections of the press at the time. It's all beautifully realised as the layers of Marlow's life and imagination intermingle, causing his fictional characters to sometimes interact with those real people from his past, and sometimes to burst into song, lip-synching along to the forties tunes that make up the soundtrack. A masterpiece of storytelling and an unforgettable glimpse into one man's – Marlow's? Potter's? – mind.

TV Trivia: The 'flaky skin' that is seen on Gambon's body often took six hours to apply but it would only last for about two hours under the hot studio lights during filming.

WHAT TO DO WHEN THE STAR OF THE SHOW IS PREGNANT...

ADD iT TO THE PLOT:

ALiAS

Producers originally thought about using computer wizardry to superimpose Jennifer Garner's head onto another body when she announced she was pregnant, but in the end they worked her pregnancy into the storyline.

I LOVE LUCY

Lucille Ball and husband Desi Arnaz (who played her husband on screen) decided not to hide her pregnancy and made Lucy pregnant in the series – even though the word 'pregnant' couldn't be uttered on American TV at that time. When Lucy gave birth to Little Ricky on the show, a record 44 million viewers tuned in to the fake birth.

E·R·

When Ming-Na fell pregnant, producers decided to write it into the series. Her character, Deb, who was single, became pregnant and had to decide whether to put the baby up for adoption. When co-star Alex Kingston became pregnant, her character Dr Corday did, too.

FRiENDS

Lisa Kudrow's real-life pregnancy was written into the storyline – her character Phoebe agreed to carry her brother's triplets. It meant that Kudrow could not join her castmates when episodes were filmed in London, so Phoebe stayed in New York looking after Chandler and Joey's chick and duck when Ross went to the UK to marry Brit gal Emily.

ROSEANNE

When Roseanne Barr became pregnant, it was added to the plot of her eponymous sitcom, and her character, Roseanne Connor, gave birth to her fourth child, Jerry Garcia Connor.

ANGEL

When Charisma Carpenter (who plays Cordelia) became pregnant, it was written in – Cordy slept with Angel's son (to many fans' disgust), got pregnant, turned evil, and eventually gave birth to a woman (Jasmine) who sucked the life out of people and planned to take over the world. Nice.

HIDE IT:

FRASIER

As a pregnant Jane Leeves got bigger in real life, her character Daphne was seen snacking donuts and cream cakes and she was eventually sent to fat camp.

SEX AND THE CITY

Sarah Jessica Parker's character Carrie wore looser fashionable items to hide a bump and also spent less time walking and more time sitting to hide it.

THE COSBY SHOW

Phylicia Rashad, who played Bill Cosby's wife Clair Huxtable, had to hide behind potted plants and bags while she was pregnant.

SEINFELD

Since Julia-Louis Dreyfus' character Elaine didn't seem like mother material, her pregnancy was hidden by voluminous hippie-style dresses.

THE NANNY

(only available on US DVD): When Lauren Lane, who played CC, was pregnant, it was hidden but alluded to with jokes and visual gags (CC suddenly had the world's biggest handbags, etc).

FRIENDS

Courteney Cox became pregnant during the final season of *Friends*. However, because her character Monica, and husband Chandler, were adopting a baby as part of the plot, her pregnancy was hidden with loose tops rather than written in.

DESPERATE HOUSEWIVES

When Marcia Cross (aka Bree) became pregnant with twins, the show's directors hid her growing bump with conveniently placed plants and other household items. However, when Cross was prescribed bed rest and all her scenes for the third season hadn't yet been filmed, the writers caused Bree to have a small accident to explain why she spent the next few episodes in bed.

THE X-FILES

During Gillian Anderson's pregnancy, her character Scully was often pictured behind a desk or wearing more voluminous than usual suit jackets. Scully then mysteriously disappeared, only to return in hospital in a coma. She recovers – conveniently just after Anderson gave birth in real life.

LEAVE:

MELROSE PLACE

When actress Hunter Tylo told producers she was pregnant, she was fired (the actress found out shortly after being hired for the US soap, and never actually appeared in front of the cameras). She has since won a settlement of $5 million.

DIFF'RENT STROKES

(only available on US DVD): When teen actress Dana Plato, who played Kimberley, became pregnant, she was asked to leave the show as her TV character was supposed to be a virgin.

BRITISH SITCOMS

JUST ABOUT EVERY BRITISH SITCOM – AT LEAST FROM THE 1970S ONWARDS – IS AVAILABLE ON DVD, FROM COMEDIES THAT WERE FUNNY (AND HUGELY SUCCESSFUL) AT THE TIME BUT HAVE DATED HIDEOUSLY (*SOME MOTHERS DO 'AVE 'EM, DUTY FREE*) TO CULT SHOWS THAT HAVE GAINED A NEW FOLLOWING ON DISC (*SPACED*, REVIEWED ON P.87). WE CAN'T FEATURE THEM ALL AS THERE ARE ENOUGH TO FILL A WHOLE BOOK, SO HERE ARE SOME OF THE BESTSELLERS, CULT FAVOURITES AND MUST-HAVES...

ABSOLUTELY FABULOUS (1992–2004)

Starring Jennifer Saunders, Joanna Lumley, Julia Sawalha, June Whitfield

Loud, brash and fabulous (sweetie) comedy created by Dawn French and Jennifer Saunders in which Saunders plays the fashion-obsessed, self-obsessed Edina, who pals around with chain-smoking, man-hungry champagne-swilling Patsy – the pair coming across as middle-aged tarts, much to the horror of Edina's sweet-natured, studious daughter Saffy (Sawalha). Saunders, and especially Lumley, are just perfect as the oblivious, garishly dressed lushes, while June Whitfield as Edina's deadpan mother is inspired casting. By the final series it had gone so far over the top it was almost a parody of itself, but the first three series are still stiletto-heel-sharp comedy.

TV Trivia: Jane Horrocks originally auditioned for the role of Saffy, but Saunders expanded the role of ditsy personal assistant Bubbles for her instead.

'ALLO 'ALLO (1982–1992)

Starring Gorden Kaye, Carmen Silvera, Vicki Michelle

Incredibly daft, old-fashioned sitcom set in France during World War II. Cowardly Rene (Kaye) is the portly owner of a small café who is hiding his affairs from his wife Edith (Silvera) while trying to keep his Nazi officer customers happy – including homosexual tank driver Lt. Gruber (Guy Siner) – and secretly helping the French Resistance. Oh, and there are two English airmen hiding out in the café, too.

Written by David Croft, who also created *Dad's Army*, and *Are You Being*

Served?'s Jeremy Lloyd, this comedy often worked through repetition – each week, you knew Rene would end up in some sort of jam due to his dalliances or the manoeuvres of the Resistance (led by the comely Michelle, as played by Kirsten Cooke) – but it was worth tuning in to see what bumbling antics would get him through. Catchphrases like Michelle's hushed 'Listen very carefully, I shall say zis only once' and the various plotlines involving a painting of The Fallen Madonna (with the big boobies) became famous, and the broad Benny Hill-style humour was infectious. Sublimely British, with its mix of bawdy jokes, sexual double entendres and farce – and, dare we admit it, very funny.

 TV Trivia: 'Allo 'Allo was conceived by Lloyd as a spoof of the far more serious British series *Secret Army*.

ARE YOU BEING SERVED? (1972–1985)

Starring John Inman, Molly Sugden, Frank Thornton, Wendy Richard

Classic British comedy in the vein of the Carry On… movies, the humour in this ribald series is about as subtle as a brick to the head. Double entendres rule the day as the staff of Grace Brothers department store go about their daily routines. There's man-hungry Mrs Slocombe (Sugden), with her continually changing colourful hairdo's, who is forever talking about her pussy (cat); busty and rather dim-witted young salesgirl Miss Brahms (Richard), who works with her in the lingerie department; the camp Mr Humphries (Inman) with his catchphrase 'I'm free!' and his assistant, the cocky Mr Lucas (Trevor Bannister); and, peering down his nose at all he surveys, the head of the floor, the posh Captain Peacock (Thornton).

Avoid the last few years, when Bannister was replaced by Mike Berry as Mr Spooner and the cast look a bit weary, and also steer clear of the 1992 spin-off *Grace & Favour,* which had some of the characters reuniting to run a country hotel but forgetting to pack the laughs with them.

 TV Trivia: Wendy Richard's dog, which she named after her character Shirley Brahms, makes an appearance in an episode of *Grace & Favour*.

AS TIME GOES BY (1992–2005)

Starring Judi Dench, Geoffrey Palmer

Lovely romantic comedy – a sort of grey-haired update of *Just Good Friends* – has Judi Dench and Geoffrey Palmer as Jean and Lionel, who were lovers many years ago before he was due to be shipped off to Korea, when they lost touch over a lost letter. Their paths cross again when Lionel takes Judy (Moira Brooker) on a date only to discover she is the daughter of the woman he loved 38 years before, and Judy steps in to try and help Lionel and Jean rekindle their lost romance.

Beautifully played by Dench and Palmer, both playing characters who have got a bit cantankerous in the intervening years, this is both romantic and funny ('A man is sexually active as long as he gets one foot out of the wheel-chair. A woman passes 50 and her idea of sexual activity is supposed to be soaking her feet and listening to James Last') and ran for 65 episodes, plus a 2005 reunion special. Dench's previous romantic comedy, *A Fine Romance*, which she made with husband Michael Williams, is also available on DVD.

 TV Trivia: The photo of a young Jean and Lionel in the opening credits is actually of Dench's daughter Finty Williams and Palmer's son Charles.

BENIDORM (2007–)

Starring Johnny Vegas, Steve Pemberton, Kenny Ireland, Wendy Richard

A sitcom set at the all-inclusive Solana resort in Benidorm, this is a broad comedy (much in the same vein as eighties' sitcom *Duty Free* – also on DVD – although at least this one is filmed on location and not on a fake-looking set) about the various booze-swigging, red-skinned Brits who spend their two weeks of holiday soaking up the Spanish sunshine and trying to get a good deal for their euros. There's swinging pensioners Jacqueline (Janine Duvitski) and Donald (Ireland), who have been coming for over 20 years and never venture beyond the resort walls; Geoff (Vegas) and his mum Noreen (Elsie Kelly); Janice (Siobhan Finneran), husband Mick (Pemberton), their kids and Janice's nightmare mum Madge (Sheila Reid); and gay couple Gavin (Hugh Sachs) and Troy (Paul Bazely). Think *Carry on Abroad* updated for the 21st century and you get the idea.

 TV Trivia: The series is written by Derren Litten, co-writer of *The Catherine Tate Show*.

BLACKADDER (1983); BLACKADDER II (1986); BLACKADDER THE THIRD (1987); BLACKADDER GOES FORTH (1989)

Starring Rowan Atkinson, Tony Robinson

The character(s) of Blackadder remains comic Atkinson's best creation. We first meet him in the 14th century, as the nasty Prince Edmund, the Black Adder, in a dark comedy from Atkinson and Richard Curtis, but the show came into its own with the second series, in 1986, in which we meet one of his descendants, Lord Edmund Blackadder, in the court of Queen Elizabeth I (played as a petulant Queenie by Miranda Richardson). When his various schemes aren't blowing up in his face, poor Edmund has to deal with his stupid, enthusiastic pal Lord Percy (Tim McInerney) and his even dumber manservant Baldrick (Robinson). The following year, many of the cast and crew returned for *Blackadder The Third* – this time set in the 18th century, with a Blackadder as butler to the dim-witted Prince Regent (Hugh Laurie), while the fourth series was the most acclaimed of all, as the action was transplanted to the trenches of World War I and a final episode successfully managed to be funny and yet moving, too.

A show so clever, funny and wonderful it's impossible to summarise in a review, all four *Blackadder* series are witty, sarcastic and delicious (especially *Blackadder II* and *Blackadder Goes Forth*), thanks to the sharp writing and terrific performances from Atkinson, Robinson and the various costars that often pop up in more than one series – Hugh Laurie, Stephen Fry, Rik Mayall and McInerney.

 TV Trivia: The opening titles of *Blackadder II* are a parody of the opening credits of *I, Claudius*.

BRASS EYE (1997–2001)

Starring Chris Morris, Mark Heap, Kevin Eldon

A spoof of current affairs TV and the role of celebrities in the UK from Chris Morris, this became controversial when some real-life celebrities were duped into appearing, not realising they were not making a serious programme. Most notable was Noel Edmonds, hired to warn children about the drug 'cake', who, when he realised it was a spoof and not a real documentary at all, was rather unhappy – interesting when you think much of his career on radio and on TV had him duping other celebrities and giving them 'Gotchas' etc. Other episodes such as 'Sex' and the *Brass Eye* special, 'Paedogeddon', caused controversy at Channel 4 amid rumours that some episodes had to be edited before being broadcast. Only seven episodes were made, and each feature Morris' distinctive, snarky interviewing technique and sharp-as-a-razor humour.

 TV Trivia: The 'Paedophile' episode received over 2,000 complaints.

BREAD (1986–1991)

Starring Jean Boht, Melanie Hill, Peter Howitt, Nick Conway

Carla Lane comedy that did nothing positive for the image of Liverpudlians – here they are all depicted as con artists, layabouts and bolshy ne'er do wells. The Boswell family do their best to fiddle the state, including the DHSS, in this Thatcher's Britain-set comedy. Matriarch Nellie (Boht) keeps an eye on the family purse strings while her kids – the bouffant-haired, leather-jacketed Joey (Peter Howitt), wheeler dealer Jack (Victor McGuire), would-be poet Adrian (Jonathan Morris) and brassy Aveline (Gilly Cowman) – are expected to bring in their financial share by fair means or (usually) foul.

Criticised for depicting Liverpudlians as scroungers, it's very dated, loud and annoying, and populated with a group of characters you'd cross the street to avoid. Both Howitt and Cowman left the series midway, meaning their roles were recast and Graham Bickley and Melanie Hill took over but didn't manage to perk up the show.

 TV Trivia: Peter Howitt went on to direct movies including *Johnny English*, *Anti-Trust* and *Sliding Doors*.

BUTTERFLIES (1978–1983)

Starring Wendy Craig, Geoffrey Palmer, Bruce Montague, Nicholas Lyndhurst

Melancholy comedy that starred Wendy Craig as dissatisfied housewife and mother Ria, who contemplates embarking on an affair with the suave Leonard (Montague), whom she meets for chats on park benches, and struggles to remain faithful to her husband Ben (Palmer). Much of the comedy came from Ria's disastrous attempts at cooking in the kitchen, Ben's dour comments about it, and their two good-for-nothing kids, Adam (Lyndhurst) and Russell (Andrew Hall), whose old bangers litter up the family driveway. Sadder are the moments between Ria and Leonard, expertly written by Carla Lane, that truly depict the troubles, sense of loss and confusion that accompany middle age. Lovely stuff from the entire cast.

TV Trivia: A special reunion episode was made in 2000 for *Children In Need*, as Ria celebrates her 60th birthday and wonders if she should have done things differently.

THE COMIC STRIP PRESENTS... (1982–2000)

Starring Adrian Edmondson, Keith Allen, Peter Richardson, Jennifer Saunders, Dawn French, Rik Mayall, Nigel Planer

A series of self-contained spoof films mainly produced in the eighties, although a few have been made since 1990. The early ones are the best, from *Five Go Mad In Dorset*, a parody of the Famous Five books by Enid Blyton, the heavy metal rockumentary *Bad News Tour*, and *The Strike*, about a former Welsh miner (Alexei Sayle) who writes a hard-hitting film about his experience of the Miners Strike and then sees it turned into a glossy movie with Al Pacino (played by Richardson) as Arthur Scargill and Meryl Streep (played by Saunders) as his wife. At the time a great showcase for some of Britain's most popular alternative comics, now it all looks a little twee and dated.

 TV Trivia: The Comic Strip as a troupe first performed at the Comedy Store in London, and Jack Nicholson and Robin Williams were among those in the audience.

COUPLING (2000–2004)

Starring Jack Davenport, Gina Bellman, Ben Miles, Sarah Alexander

A comedy about sex and relationships that was a big success for the BBC, *Coupling* relied on being sexy and funny and more often than not succeeded. Written and produced by husband and wife team Steve Moffat and Sue Vertue, it's the story of six 30something friends shagging, laughing, dishing the dirt and trying to sort out their love lives. There's porn-addicted Steve (Davenport), who has split up with Jane (Bellman) and begun a relationship with Susan (Alexander), while Susan has recently been dumped by self-centered ladies man Patrick (Miles). He's now dating Sally (Kate Isitt), while Jeff (Richard Coyle) falls for a beautiful woman but can't chat her up. A hugely fun sitcom about sex, friends and more sex, this lasted 28 episodes.

 TV Trivia: An American version of the series was made in 2003 but was cancelled after just four episodes.

DAD'S ARMY (1968–1977)

Starring Arthur Lowe, John Le Mesurier, Clive Dunn, John Laurie, Ian Lavender

From the iconic opening credits, in which animated British flags see off the advancing Nazi ones, to the singalong theme song ('Who do you think you are kidding, Mr Hitler...', sung by Bud Flanagan) and quotable catchphrases ('Don't panic!' and 'Stupid boy!'), this WWII-set comedy remains a British sitcom to be treasured. It's certainly one of the best we ever made, and remains just as funny today as when it was first broadcast four decades ago (which is a good thing, since cable TV channels seem to repeat it daily).

As written by Jimmy Perry and David Croft, it is, of course, about the antics of the Walmington-On-Sea branch of the Home Guard, the men who contributed to the war effort by guarding the home front in case of possible German invasion. Led by pompous bank manager Captain Mainwaring (Lowe), this platoon is a particularly bumbling lot that includes mummy's boy Pike (Lavender), the posh Wilson (Le Mesurier), who is having an affair with Pike's mum, and the doddery butcher Lance Corporal Jones (Dunn). It mixed a feeling of nostalgia for a time when there was a real sense of British community, with terrific visual gags, ridiculous situations and an underlying mockery of the English class system and wartime manners. Classic British telly at its very best.

 TV Trivia: Creator Jimmy Perry had served with the Home Guard himself, in Watford.

THE FALL AND RISE OF REGINALD PERRIN (1976–1979)

Starring Leonard Rossiter, Pauline Yates, John Barron, Trevor Adams

After too many years working at Sunshine Desserts, Reginald Perrin (Rossiter) has a mid-life crisis, becoming more erratic until he eventually fakes his own death. After a few attempts at starting a different life, he returns in disguise, but his attempts to lead a simple life are thwarted when the business he and his wife start up turns out to be a success. A sublime mix of comedy and tragedy – most markedly shown as his nervous breakdown takes hold – this is both witty and poignant fare, expertly played by Rossiter. John Barron is more than a match as his boss, CJ, while Geoffrey Palmer (as Reggie's brother in law), Pauline Yates (as Elizabeth Perrin) and Sue Nicholls (as his frustrated secretary) are equally excellent. The first season remains the best.

 TV Trivia: David Nobbs, who wrote the series, apparently originally envisaged Ronnie Barker in the role.

FATHER TED (1995–1998)

Starring Dermot Morgan, Ardal O'Hanlon, Frank Kelly, Pauline McLynn

On remote Craggy Island, off the coast of Ireland, live three priests and their housekeeper in this infectious sitcom. There's Father Ted Crilly (Morgan), seemingly the most sensible of the bunch; young, naive and rather gormless Father Dougal McGuire (O'Hanlon); the aging, drunk and abusive Father Jack Hackett (Kelly) and their helper, Mrs Doyle (McLynn). From this quartet springs some of the best comedy in years, as Ted manages to offend his superiors in the Catholic Church on a regular basis, Jack swears at them ('Drink! Feck! Arse! Girls!') and poor Dougal blathers along while Mrs Doyle makes the tea. Only 25 episodes were made before Morgan's untimely death, and each is a classic – from 'The Passion Of St Tibulus', in which Ted and Dougal try to ban a blasphemous movie from being shown at the local picture house, to 'Speed 3', in which Dougal gets trapped in a runaway milk cart.

 TV Trivia: The character of Mrs Doyle is apparently based on creator Graham Linehan's mother.

FAWLTY TOWERS (1975–1979)

Starring John Cleese, Prunella Scales, Connie Booth

John Cleese's comic creation remains a classic, perhaps in part because only 12 episodes were ever made, making sure the show – unlike many other situation comedies – never had the chance to go stale. Originally, however, no one predicted its enduring success when it first aired on BBC2 in 1975: the first series only garnered three million viewers (which in the days when we only had three TV channels to choose from wasn't very impressive). But word of mouth grew and the show set in a fictional Torquay hotel became a favourite, thanks to Cleese's manic portrayal of hotel owner from hell Basil Fawlty, Scales' Sybil and, of course, Andrew Sachs' incompetent Spanish waiter/dogsbody/whipping boy Manuel. Every episode is hysterical, but if we had to choose one it would have to be 'The Germans', in which Basil seems incapable of not mentioning the war.

 TV Trivia: The building used to represent the hotel sadly burnt down in 1991.

GAViN AND STACEY (2007–)

Starring Joanna Page, Matthew Horne, Ruth Jones, James Corden

Ruth Jones and James Corden, who also co-star, created this romantic comedy that deservedly became a cult hit in 2007 following the first series being shown on BBC Three. Billericay bloke Gavin (Horne) and Stacey (Page), who lives in South Wales, have been phone buddies for months when they finally agree to meet, bringing along her friend Nessa (Jones) and his friend Smithy (Corden) for support. The pair is in love but the reason it won't run smoothly is down to their friends and family, from Gavin's excitable mother Pam (Alison Steadman) to Stacey's Uncle Bryn (Rob Brydon), who gives her a rape alarm for her first date. Packed with wonderfully realised characters, this is a love story for the 21st century that is well worth seeking out.

 TV Trivia: A US version is going to be made, with the American Gavin coming from New Jersey and Stacey from South Carolina.

THE GOOD LiFE (1975–1978)

Starring Richard Briers, Felicity Kendal, Penelope Keith, Paul Eddington

Classic British sitcom that has Tom (Briers) and Barbara Good (Kendal) dropping out of the rat race to run a self-sufficient home and farm garden in Surbiton – much to the annoyance of posh neighbour Margot Leadbetter (Keith) and her hen-pecked husband Jerry (Eddington). While Kendal became something of a sex symbol in her dungarees (it *was* the seventies) and Briers looked strangely foxy in a turtleneck, it was the pairing of Keith and Eddington that often stole the show, especially in the classic episode when snobby Margot, in wellies co-ordinated to match her outfit, lands smack in the mud much to everyone else's amusement. It should be a cheap laugh, but in the hands of the talented cast, it's brilliant.

 TV Trivia: The final episode was recorded in front of HRH Queen Elizabeth II and Prince Philip.

GOODNiGHT SWEETHEART (1993–1999)

Starring Nicholas Lyndhurst, Victor McGuire, Elizabeth Carling, Emma Amos, Dervla Kirwan

A sweet-natured comedy fantasy from Laurence Marks and Maurice Gran (*Birds of a Feather*), this sitcom followed the adventures of mild-mannered TV repairman Gary Sparrow (Lyndhurst). Married to Yvonne (Michelle Holmes, and then from Series 4, Amos), Gary finds a time portal that transports him back to the war-torn London of the 1940s. There he meets the lovely bar-maid Phoebe (Kirwan, followed by Carling from Series 4) and starts to lead a double life, flitting between his present day missus and his new love in the past. Cleverly plotted – Gary passes himself off in the forties as a spy, which explains his absences, and as a songwriter (the songs he claims to have writ-ten are ones he knows from the future) – this featured a winning cast, includ-ing McGuire as Ron, the only person who knows Gary's secret.

 TV Trivia: Most of the episodes are named after popular songs such as 'In The Mood' and 'Someone To Watch Over Me'.

HI-DE-HI! (1980–1988)

Starring Paul Shane, Ruth Madoc, Su Pollard, Jeffrey Holland

A series from the pens of Jimmy Perry and David Croft set at a fictional 1950s holiday camp called Maplins, this mixed farce with social class comedy as posh Jeffrey Fairbrother (Simon Cadell), a Cambridge professor, is hired to run the camp and its staff. That includes shifty comic Ted (Shane), his dim-witted sidekick Spike (Holland), snooty dance instructors Barry and Yvonne (Barry Howard and Diane Holland), senior staff member Gladys Pugh (Madoc) and ditsy chalet maid Peggy (Pollard), who really wants to become a Yellowcoat (one of the entertainment staff).

As subtle as a custard pie in the face, the series relied on bawdy humour and slapstick, plus a feeling of nostalgia for times past. Awww.

 TV Trivia: Perry himself had worked as a Butlins' Red Coat after the war.

I'M ALAN PARTRIDGE (1997–2002)

Starring Steve Coogan, Felicity Montagu, Phil Cornwell

Steve Coogan and Armando Iannucci's comic creation, the patterned-jumper wearing, banality-spouting radio and TV presenter (as played by Coogan) who could have been based on any number of Radio 2 DJs, first came to our screens in the cult series *The Day Today* and then 1994's spoof chat show series *Knowing Me Knowing You* With Alan Partridge (also available on DVD). This fol-low-up, beginning three years later, has the ageing Alan – not exactly in favour with TV bosses after his chat show ended with a guest being shot –

resorting to making a living on Radio Norwich, while spending his off-hours at the local Travel Tavern at the side of the M11 or harassing his put-upon assistant Lynn (Montagu).

Superbly scripted by Coogan, Iannucci and Peter Baynham, and featuring great performances from Coogan, Montagu and Cornwell (as Dave), this is one of the best TV comic characters of recent years – Alan's so awful he's almost lovable.

 TV Trivia: Coogan briefly resurrected the character of Alan for a 2005 Comic Relief sketch in which he interviewed a grown-up Milky Bar Kid (played by Simon Pegg).

THE INBETWEENERS (2008)

Starring Simon Bird, Joe Thomas, James Buckley, Blake Harrison

The Inbetweeners are a group of sixth-form school kids who are inbetween – not cool enough to be really popular and not geeky enough to be considered nerds. This cult sitcom for satellite channel E4 follows a handful of these kids as they negotiate the halls of a fictional south London comprehensive: Will (Bird), who has just transferred from a private school and is subsequently bullied by the other pupils, and his new friends Simon (Thomas), Jay (Buckley) and Neil (Harrison). Whether they're bunking off, planning a trip to Thorpe Park theme park or preparing for a school prom, this is fun stuff as the boys get into scrapes but never get into any real trouble.

 TV Trivia: Simon Bird and Joe Thomas had previously performed together on stage as part of Cambridge Footlights.

IT AIN'T HALF HOT MUM (1974–1981)

Starring Windsor Davies, Melvyn Hayes, Don Estelle

David Croft and Jimmy Perry – who also made *Dad's Army* and *Hi-De-Hi* – were the pair behind this much-loved comedy set during World War II. It focuses on the members of a Royal Artillery concert party, stationed in India (and later Burma) to provide entertainment for the troops. Led by gruff Sergeant Major Williams (Davies), barking orders and despairing of his charges on a regular basis, the entertainers include nervous Bombardier 'Gloria' Beaumont (Hayes), the foppish Gunner 'La-di-dah' Graham (John Clegg), and chubby and timid Lofty Sugden (Estelle). Best known for Davies' catchphrases of 'Shuuuuttt Uuuupppp', the politically incorrect 'You is a bunch of pooftahs', and the opening song ('Meet the gang, cause the boys are here, The boys to entertain you...'), this has dated quite badly, from the obviously fake set (it was filmed in Norwich and Sussex, with added plastic palm trees) to the dodgy stereotypes of Indians. But if you can get past that, there's a certain English charm to the whole thing, thanks to the cheesy gags, camp comedy and the career-making performances of Davies, Estelle and Hayes.

 TV Trivia: Co-stars Don Estelle and Windsor Davies teamed up in 1975 to record the song 'Whispering Grass', which went to number one in the UK.

JEEVES AND WOOSTER (1990–1993)

Starring Stephen Fry, Hugh Laurie

Based on the novels by PG Wodehouse, this series starred Laurie as the impeccably turned out charmer Bertie Wooster, who's a bit of a twit and gets into numerous scrapes, and Fry as his valet and saviour, Jeeves. Packed with pithy dialogue and bon mots, this looks like a period drama thanks to lush locations at various stately manors, but was hilarious at every turn thanks to Wodehouse's characters (plus writer Clive Exton's scripts) and the actors who played them. Laurie is perfect as the well-meaning buffoon Wooster, and while Fry is a little too young to play the valet, he is perfect at delivering the intelligent dialogue that whizzes over his employer's head.

TV Trivia: Laurie was cast in the role of Perry White for the 2006 movie *Superman Returns* but was replaced by Frank Langella due to filming schedule conflicts with his hit series *House*.

JUST GOOD FRIENDS (1983–1986)

Starring Paul Nicholas, Jan Francis

Nicholas is cheeky chappie Vince Pinner, who left the posh Penny Warrender (Francis) at the altar years before in this romantic comedy. They meet again five years later, and decide to try and be friends though it is obvious Vince wants to rekindle the relationship, while Penny's parents are less than impressed that the pair are seeing each other again (Penny's mother refers to Vince as 'Thing'). A tragi-comedy that enchanted thanks to the on-screen chemistry of the two leads and spot-on casting for their parents (Sylvia Kay and John Ringham as the Warrenders, Ann Lynn and Shaun Curry as the down-to-earth Pinners), this is one of the few shows in which the will-they-won't-they worked. That was mainly due to creator John Sullivan, who gave both of them believable self-doubt and conflicts rather than stretching the romance out for no reason. Three series were made, and a Christmas special in 1986 that ended the love story on a high note.

 TV Trivia: This was theatre actor/singer Paul Nicholas' first major TV role.

KEEPING UP APPEARANCES (1990–1995)

Starring Patricia Routledge, Clive Swift, Judy Cornwell, Geoffrey Hughes, Josephine Tewson

Enjoyably creaky sitcom that has Routledge stealing the show as social-climber Hyacinth Bucket (pronounced 'bouquet'), who puts on numerous airs and graces in her attempts to be accepted as part of the poshest end of society, even though one of her sisters has done better than her and the other two are loud and working class. Hyacinth's house is the type of place where afternoon tea comes on a silver tray and not a crumb ends up on the carpet, much to the consternation of her nervous neighbour Elizabeth (Tewson), who always seems to make a mess in Hyacinth's presence, and Hyacinth's poor husband Richard (Swift) is often on the receiving end of her ire as well. Quintissentially English.

 TV Trivia: Hyacinth and Richard's adult son is called Sheridan, but he is never seen in the series.

LAST OF THE SUMMER WINE (1973–)

Starring Bill Owen, Peter Sallis, Michael Bates

The longest-running comedy series in the world, this gentle show has even boasted a prequel (*First Of The Summer Wine*). A mix of light-hearted philosophy and broad slapstick (never better than in the episode when they hurtle down-hill in a tin bath), the country-set series brought us the lovable characters of ageing friends Compo (Owen), Clegg (Sallis), Cyril (Bates) and, of course, wrinkled-stockinged Nora Batty (Kathy Staff), the object of Compo's affections. The cast has, understandably, changed over the years – Bates had to leave due to ill health, and was replaced by Brian Wilde as Foggy, then Wilde himself left in 1985 (he returned five years later), and Michael Aldridge was brought in to play Seymour. Sadly, Bill Owen died in 1999, but his own son Tom was added to the cast to play Compo's long-lost son.

 TV Trivia: It was announced in 1996 that this is Her Majesty Queen Elizabeth II's favourite series.

THE LEAGUE OF GENTLEMEN (1999–2002)

Starring Mark Gatiss, Steve Pemberton, Reece Shearsmith

British comedy at its most bizarre, this is so strange, twisted and macabre it makes *Twin Peaks* look like an episode of *Crossroads*. Obsessively adored by fans, and treated with puzzlement by those who don't get its dark and quirky humour, it's set in the fictional town of Royston Vasey (town motto: You'll Never Leave) and features such odd characters as serial killers Edward and Tubbs, the local shopowners with a dislike for strangers, butcher Hilary Briss, vet Matthew Chinery (who 'accidentally' slaughters animals in his care) and Barbara Dixon, the local cab driver halfway through a male to female sex change. Based on a stage show that rose to prominence at the Edinburgh Fringe Festival, *The League of Gentlemen* is written by Gatiss, Pemberton, Shearsmith and Jeremy Dyson.

 TV Trivia: Stage comic Roy 'Chubby' Brown's real name is Royston Vasey.

MEN BEHAVING BADLY (1992–1999)

Starring Neil Morrissey, Martin Clunes, Caroline Quentin, Leslie Ash

Gary (Clunes) and Tony (Morrissey) are two slovenly, beer-swilling lads (*Loaded* readers, we presume) who share a flat and a general dislike of hard work. Tony lusts after Deborah (Ash) who lives upstairs, while Gary is in a relationship with the very long-suffering nurse Dorothy (Quentin). Written by Simon Nye, this enjoyable laddish sitcom made stars of Clunes, Quentin and Morrissey (who wasn't cast in the first few episodes – Gary shared the place with Dermot, as played by Harry Enfield) and, while most people laughed *at* the boys' antics, we have a feeling a few blokes were actually inspired by them.

 TV Trivia: In 2007, Ash was awarded a record £5 million against the hospital where she contracted the MSSA superbug.

THE MIGHTY BOOSH (2004–)

Starring Noel Fielding, Julian Barratt, Michael Fielding

Originally a stage show and then a radio series, *The Mighty Boosh* is created by Fielding and Barratt, who also star as sixties throwback Vince and vain jazzman Howard. It's a mad new wave comedy – produced by Steve Coogan's Baby

Cow Productions – that has the pair going on a series of adventures that combine surreal humour with comic fantasy as they go about their jobs as zoo keepers with the help of zoo kiosk worker and occasional mystic Naboo, and Bollo the talking ape. Yes, it's as weird and strange as it sounds, and something of a cult show for anyone looking for something a bit odder than the average comedy. It won NME/Shockwaves award for Best Comedy in both 2007 and 2008.

 TV Trivia: The show's title is apparently a comment Noel heard about his brother Michael's hair.

MR BEAN (1990–1995)
Starring Rowan Atkinson

Following the comic sophistication of the *Blackadder* series, Rowan Atkinson went for rather simpler humour in this series, which he also co-created with Richard Curtis. His character, Mr Bean, is a bumbling idiot who could be related to *Some Mothers Do 'Ave 'Em*'s Frank Spencer – except he is far more irritating. Bean, in tweed jacket and nylon trousers, is a grown man who has trouble completing the simplest tasks as if he were a toddler, and his adventures are played out without the character saying anything. Packed with the best of Atkinson's physical comedy, the slapstick series ran for 16 episodes and was also spun-off into two teeth-gnashingly awful movies. Far better is the kids' animated series based on the character of Bean that ran for 26 episodes in 2002.

 TV Trivia: The most successful episode of *Bean*, 'The Trouble With Mister Bean', garnered an audience of over 18 million viewers in the UK.

MY FAMILY (2000–)
Starring Robert Lindsay, Zoe Wanamaker

Phenomenally successful comedy that's a 21st-century twist on *Butterflies* – the dad here (Lindsay) is also a dentist named Ben, who is often frustrated by his kids – Janey (Daniela Denby-Ashe), slacker Nick (Kris Marshall, who left in 2005) and the youngest, Michael (Gabriel Thomson). It's extremely mainstream and rather predictable, but thanks to a sharp script and pitch-perfect performances from Lindsay and Wanamaker as his spiky-haired, often irritated wife, this plods along quite nicely and is a pleasant distraction rather than a side-splitting one.

TV Trivia: Kris Marshall reportedly asked for his character to be killed off, but the producers refused.

THE OFFICE (2001–2003)

Starring Ricky Gervais, Martin Freeman, Mackenzie Crook

A stroke of comic genius from creators Ricky Gervais and Stephen Merchant, who met while working at Xfm Radio and devised a 'mockumentary' about an office led by the sort of annoying twerp (who thinks he's funny but just isn't) whom we have all worked for at one time or another. Set in the fictitious Slough paper merchants, Wernham Hogg, *The Office*'s first series was shown in 2001 and introduced us to slimy, innappropriate regional manager David Brent (Gervais, who had never acted before but is creepily brilliant), whose mantra is 'I'm a friend first, boss second and entertainer third', Tim (Freeman), the office dreamer who clearly wishes he was somewhere else, Dawn the receptionist (Lucy Davis) and wannabe soldier/office suck up Gareth (the ghoulish-faced Crook). Made without a laugh track and featuring those moments so embarrassing you almost have to hide your eyes, it's surely the best British TV comedy in years. Only 12 episodes and a Christmas special which tied up loose ends, were made.

 TV Trivia: The series is the biggest selling non-movie DVD in the UK.

ONE FOOT IN THE GRAVE (1990–2000)

Starring Richard Wilson, Annette Crosbie

You either loved or hated Victor Meldrew, the obstinate, opinionated retired man at the centre of this long-running sitcom. With his trademark phrase 'I don't *believe* it!', usually uttered when another piece of bad luck befell him, Victor (Wilson) grumped his way through life, fighting with the neighbours and battling what he sees as the trials of modern life, while his long-suffering wife Margaret (Crosbie) looked on. On the surface this was an everyday suburban sitcom but it actually had a nice vein of black humour running through it, although some viewers complained at storylines that included a dead cat being found in the Meldrew freezer. The final episode actually had writer David Renwick killing the character of Victor off in a downbeat episode that Wilson applauded as he didn't want to be eternally typecast.

TV Trivia: Bill Cosby starred in a US TV show, *Cosby*, from 1996–2000, that was loosely based on *One Foot in The Grave*.

ONLY FOOLS AND HORSES (1981–2003)

Starring David Jason, Nicholas Lyndhurst, Roger Lloyd-Pack

So many people love this sitcom that it carried on for over 20 years, putting the Trotter brothers in increasingly outlandish situations as the years went by, while the catchphrase ('You plonker!') became recognised by all. As everyone knows, the brothers are older schemer Del Boy (Jason) and younger dreamer Rodney (Lyndhurst), a pair of dodgy market traders who drive around in a Reliant Regal van and live in a high-rise tower block (Nelson Mandela House) in Peckham. Many of the episodes had a nice sampling of slapstick comedy along with the well-written John Sullivan dialogue, especially in the episode 'Yuppy Love' when Del falls through an open bar, and the incompetent duo smashing a valuable chandelier in 'A Touch of Glass'.

A spin-off, *The Green Green Grass*, featuring characters Boycie and Marlene, began in 2005.

 TV Trivia: Over a dozen of the iconic vans were used in filming the series.

OPEN ALL HOURS (1976–1985)

Starring Ronnie Barker, David Jason, Lynda Baron

Lovely comedy in the same vein as *Last of the Summer Wine*, this boasted the terrific casting of Barker and Jason in the lead roles. Barker is the stuttering, tight-fisted Yorkshire shopkeeper Albert Arkwright, who harbours deep feelings for Nurse Gladys Emanuel (Baron) across the street, while Jason stars as his hapless nephew Grenville who works with him in the shop. Both Jason and Barker not only work brilliantly together, but deliver wonderfully endearing characters in this classic series that ran for just 25 episodes.

 TV Trivia: An American version was made called *Open All Night* with George Dzundza that only lasted three episodes.

PEEP SHOW (2003–)

Starring Robert Webb, David Mitchell

Mark (Mitchell) and Jeremy (Webb) are two ordinary roommates whose innermost thoughts we, the audience, get to hear, while – thanks to cameras mounted on their heads – we also get to see things from their perspectives, too. Mark has a stable life and boring office job, with the only distraction being co-worker Sophie whom he is in love with, while Jeremy's life is a bit more chaotic – an unemployed musician, he spends his time sleeping in and lusting after the neighbour when he isn't practising arson or sleeping with his friend's mother. Rude and crude, this isn't as funny as it thinks it is, but there are some hilarious moments thanks to the sharp writing and comic timing of Mitchell and Webb.

 TV Trivia: Before he was famous, David Mitchell had a job working in the cloakroom on the set of *TFI Friday*.

PHOENIX NIGHTS (2001–2002)

Starring Peter Kay, Dave Spikey, Janice Connolly

Featuring characters that originally appeared in comic Peter Kay's 2000 series *That Peter Kay Thing*, *Phoenix Nights* is a rib-tickling sitcom set in and around a Bolton working men's club. The owner of the Phoenix Club is wheelchair bound Brian Potter (Kay) – it's his third club after the first one flooded and the second burnt down. His ambition is to make the club the most popular in town, beating his arch-enemy Den, who runs The Banana Grove. Things never go that well, however, from the theft of the bingo machine on opening night to a Right Said Fred tribute band breaking into all the cars outside the club. It's terrific stuff, with Kay not only playing Brian but also three other characters including the bouncer Max who, along with Patrick McGuinness's character Paddy, was spun off into the series *Max & Paddy's Road To Nowhere*.

 TV Trivia: Kay was taught metalwork at school by Steve Coogan's dad.

PORRIDGE (1974–1977)

Starring Ronnie Barker, Richard Beckinsale

One of Britain's best-loved comedies, and deservedly so, this introduced us to lovable rogue Norman Stanley Fletcher (Barker) who, as we learn in the opening credits, is a 'habitual criminal who accepts arrest as an occupational hazard' and who has been sentenced to five years at Slade Prison. There, the quick-witted con shares a cell with young criminal Lennie Godber (the marvellous Beckinsale), whom he both teases and protects like a son, and the pair spend their jail time concocting schemes that usually annoy the prison officers – in particular Mr Mackay (Fulton Mackay).

Written by comedy maestros Dick Clement and Ian La Frenais, the series ran for just 20 episodes, but each one is a charmer (and, apparently, was essential viewing for real prisoners who found it a hoot). It was followed by a movie in 1979 and the 1978 spin-off comedy *Going Straight,* in which Fletcher tries life on the outside (available on DVD, it lasted just six episodes, and featured guest appearances from Beckinsale and Nicholas Lyndhurst as Fletcher's son).

 TV Trivia: Barker had originally played the character of Fletcher in *Seven of One*, a 1973 series in which he played a different character in each episode. The episode featuring Fletch is called 'Prisoner and Escort' and follows him as he is being transferred to Slade by prison officers including Mr Mackay.

RiPPiNG YARNS (1977–1979)

Starring Michael Palin, Charles McKeown, David Griffin

Former Monty Python comics Michael Palin and Terry Jones conceived this series, a collection of parodies of stories favoured by pre-war schoolboys. The series began with 'Tomkinson's Schooldays', in which Palin plays both the headmaster and the new boy at a school in 1912, and other episodes included 'Escape From Stalag Luft 112B', a parody of *The Great Escape* and a yarn about an explorer, 'Across The Andes By Frog'. They're all deliciously silly and Python-esque, and rib-ticklingly enjoyable – shame only nine episodes were made.

 TV Trivia: The introductions in the first series are a parody of Orson Welles' sherry adverts of the 1970s.

RiSiNG DAMP (1974–1978)

Starring Leonard Rossiter, Richard Beckinsale, Don Warrington, Frances De La Tour

Hilarious seventies sitcom with Rossiter perfectly cast as the smarmy land-lord Rigsby, who manages to be miserly, vain, creepy and yet somehow lov-able as he terrorises the two young men sharing a bedsit, Philip (Warrington) and Alan (Beckinsale) and pursues the unfortunate spinster Miss Jones (De La Tour) who lives upstairs. One of the best sitcoms ever made, this is so good, thanks to the smart interaction between the characters that it is still funny three decades after it was first shown, and a real sense of what it is like to be English (depressing, but somehow good, too). Beckinsale, who tragically died in 1979, filmed this at the same time he made the series *Porridge*.

 TV Trivia: The series was based on a play in which the main character was called Rooksby. The name of the character was changed when a Mr Rooksby threatened legal action.

THE ROYLE FAMILY (1998–2006)

Starring Caroline Aherne, Ricky Tomlinson, Sue Johnston, Ralf Little, Craig Cash

Cash and Aherne created this funny show about a working-class family named the Royles. All the action takes place in the house of unemployed Jim Royle (Tomlinson) and wife Barbara (Johnston), where they live with daughter Denise (Aherne) and son Antony (Little) until Denise marries Dave (Cash). At first this seems like just a depiction of a particularly hideous family, who exclaim saying 'My arse!' and 'Shite!' at regular intervals and barely move from the TV, but it's actually much more than that, as the audience becomes involved in their stories, whether it is Denise planning her wedding, or sitting petrified in the family bathroom with her dad when she goes into labour. It's all so realistic, from the cups of tea brought to the living room, to Barbara announcing there won't be sausages for tea after all, as they have gone past their sell-by date, that the viewer feels they're part of the family joke, joining them as they settle down for another night in front of the telly.

TV Trivia: Sue Johnston and Ricky Tomlinson have played husband and wife before, as Bobby and Sheila Grant in *Brookside*.

SHAMELESS (2004–)

Starring David Threlfall, Rebecca Ryan, Maggie O'Neill

Comedy set on the fictional Chatsworth Estate in Manchester, *Shameless* was created by Paul Abbott and is apparently based on his own experiences of growing up in Burnley. The Gallagher family are an interesting, and dysfunctional lot, led by unemployed dad Frank (Threlfall), who has eight children – Fiona, Lip, Ian, Carl, Debbie, Liam, Nigel and Delia. Part comedy and part drama, the series began with Fiona falling for Steve (Anne Marie Duff and

James McAvoy, who married in real life), and Frank dealing with his lesbian ex-wife, and errant kids, while later plot twists include a shooting, someone being buried under a patio, a kidnapping and even a severed hand. It's pretty bonkers and has got more so as the show has progressed.

 TV Trivia: The role of Frank went to Sean Gallagher, who shot some scenes before it was decided he was too young for the role and Threlfall was given the part.

SPACED (1999–2001)

Starring Simon Pegg, Jessica Stevenson, Nick Frost

Before they made the movies *Shaun of the Dead* and *Hot Fuzz*, writer/actor Simon Pegg and director Edgar Wright collaborated on this deservedly cult comedy series. Strangers Tim (Pegg) and Daisy (Stevenson) have to pretend to be a couple to rent a room in the house of alcoholic landlady Marsha. There they meet the troubled artist Brian, while Daisy has to get used to Tim's war-obsessed pal Mike (Frost) and life with slacker Tim, who still hankers after his old girlfriend and hates her new boyfriend Duane with a passion. Packed with parodies of TV and movies including the *Star Wars* films, *The Shining*, *The A-Team* and *Scooby Doo*, it's brilliantly silly, and fans of Shaun... should definitely check out Episode 3 ('Art') in which Tim, having played Resident Evil all night, taken speed and eaten some Twiglets, finds the combination leaves him imagining everyone around him is a zombie. Utterly brilliant.

 TV Trivia: In the final episode during a scene down the pub, one of the band members performing is Simon Pegg's dad.

TO THE MANOR BORN (1979–1981)

Starring Penelope Keith, Peter Bowles, Angela Thorne

Wonderfully English comedy about the veh veh posh Audrey Fforbes Hamilton (Keith) who, following her husband's death, realises she has to sell the family home, Grantleigh Manor, and move into the small lodge at the edge of the manor grounds. To her horror, Richard De Vere (Bowles), who buys the manor, isn't aristocracy, but is new money (shock horror) – the owner of a big supermarket chain. How simply awful. Of course, while Audrey doesn't welcome Richard with open arms, the pair slowly begin to form a friendship while we, the viewers, know they are reluctantly falling in love (as does his mother and her best friend Marjory). It's all very sweet and lovely, enlivened by some sharp sparring dialogue between the two perfectly cast leads. The cast were reunited in 2007 for a one-off Christmas special.

 TV Trivia: The series began life as a radio play in 1968, with Penelope Keith.

THE VICAR OF DIBLEY (1994–2007)

Starring Dawn French, James Fleet, Emma Chambers

Likeable, sweet-natured comedy from Richard Curtis about a female vicar, chocoholic Geraldine Granger (French) who stirs things up a bit when she comes to an eccentric but conservative village. The locals are expecting a doddery old male vicar and instead get, in Geraldine's own words, 'a babe with a bob cut and a magnificent bosom'. Meanwhile, she has to deal with the very dim verger Alice (Chambers), pompous councillor David (Gary Waldhorn) and Hugo (Fleet) his hesitant son (who loves Alice), farmer Owen (Roger Lloyd Pack), dreadful cook Letitia (Liz Smith) and rambling Jim Trott (Trevor Peacock). Hugely popular, guest stars have included Sting and wife Trudi Styler, Kylie Minogue, Johnny Depp and Sarah Ferguson.

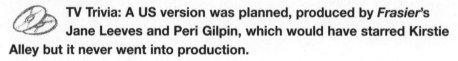 **TV Trivia: A US version was planned, produced by *Frasier*'s Jane Leeves and Peri Gilpin, which would have starred Kirstie Alley but it never went into production.**

YES MINISTER (1980–1984); YES PRIME MINISTER (1986–1987)

Starring Paul Eddington, Nigel Hawthorne, Derek Fowlds

Superb political comedy from writers Antony Jay and Jonathan Lynn, this satire took us behind closed doors in Whitehall as bungling MP Jim Hacker (Eddington) attempts to affect changes are usually thwarted by his Permanent Secretary Sir Humphrey Appleby (Hawthorne). Much of the comedy comes from the ministers believing they are running the country, when in fact it is the civil servants, such as Sir Humphrey, who have the upper hand. By the time Hacker becomes prime minister, however, he has become a more accomplished statesman and is aware of Humphrey's machinations, which brings new life to the sharp comedy.

 TV Trivia: Apparently this was the favourite TV show at the time of Prime Minister Margaret Thatcher.

THE YOUNG ONES (1982–1984)

Starring Adrian Edmondson, Rik Mayall, Nigel Planer, Christopher Ryan

The show that spoofed yet somehow epitomised youth in Thatcher's Britain, *The Young Ones* is the best remembered 'alternative comedy' show from the early eighties. Loud, manic, and often surreal, the series was about four students sharing a flat so hideous you could almost smell it – Vyvyan (Edmonson), the punk; Rick (Mayall), the spotty, nerdy one with a fondness for Cliff Richard; Mike (Ryan), the older, 'cool' one; and, of course, Neil (Planer), the long-haired dim-witted hippy. Through 12 episodes the quartet rampaged across the screen, thrilling teen viewers of the time and baffling anyone over the age of 20. It all looks a bit worn at the edges now, but back in the eighties it was side-splittingly funny.

 TV Trivia: Each week, a band performed so the show could be classed as 'light entertainment' because the BBC had no money left in their sitcom budget.

AMERICAN SITCOMS

MANY CLASSIC AMERICAN COMEDIES AREN'T AVAILABLE ON DVD HERE, INCLUDING *THE HONEYMOONERS*, *MURPHY BROWN*, *ALL IN THE FAMILY*, *RHODA*, *LEAVE IT TO BEAVER*, *THE MARY TYLER MOORE SHOW* AND THE MORE RECENT *THE DAILY SHOW*. BUT YOU CAN CONSOLE YOURSELF WITH THESE...

30 ROCK (2006–)

Starring Tina Fey, Alec Baldwin, Tracy Morgan, Jane Krakowski, Jack McBrayer

Two shows started in 2006 that were set behind the scenes of a (fictional) live TV series: the excellent but soon-cancelled drama *Studio 60 on the Sunset Strip* (see review, p. 368) and this slick, often hilarious comedy from creator and star Tina Fey (a comedienne well known in the US for her role on *Saturday Night Live*). She plays Liz Lemon, the head writer of a comedy sketch show who has to deal with her insecure writers, a vain lead actress (Krakowski), a new, unpredictable star of the show (Morgan, playing a character called Tracy Jordan) and, most frustrating of all, a new boss who has no experience of running a TV show. That boss is the arrogant Jack Donaghy, superbly played by Alec Baldwin, who would steal the entire series from the other stars if it wasn't for another actor – McBrayer – as nerdy, overly enthusiastic employee Kenneth.

 TV Trivia: Tina Fey's husband Jeff Richmond composes all the music for the show.

ARRESTED DEVELOPMENT (2003–2006)

Starring Jason Bateman, Portia De Rossi, Will Arnett, Michael Cera, David Cross, Jeffrey Tambor

Quite simply, one of the funniest shows ever. The Bluth family redefine the word 'dysfunctional', so son Michael (Bateman) is less than impressed when he has to take over the family's home and business affairs when his dad George (Tambor) is imprisoned for fraud. While trying to raise his teenage son, George-Michael (Cera), who has a secret crush on his own cousin, Maeby (Alia Shawkat), Michael has to rein in his twin sister Lindsay's (De Rossi) excessive spending, endure his brother Gob's (Arnett) failed magician tricks and bad ideas, deal with his spoilt mother (Jessica Walter) and babied younger brother Buster (Tony Hale). And then there's Lindsay's husband Tobias (Cross), who is a 'never-nude' (he wears denim shorts under his clothes because he has a phobia about being naked).

Shot like a documentary and narrated by producer Ron Howard, this is brilliantly scripted, sharply played and, at times deliciously bonkers.

 TV Trivia: Jason Bateman's actress sister Justine appeared in one episode entitled 'Family Ties'– the name of the hit sitcom she was in with Michael J. Fox in the 1980s.

BoSoM BuDDiES (1980–1982)

Starring Tom Hanks, Peter Scolari, Wendie Jo Sperber

While we can't laugh at George Clooney's early role in the sitcom *E/R*, or Sandra Bullock as Tess in the TV spin-off of *Working Girl*, the DVD gods, in their infinite wisdom, have seen fit to allow us to snigger (mainly unintentionally) at one of Oscar-winner Tom Hanks' earliest roles – as a cross-dressing advertising executive in this eighties comedy. The premise is supremely daft – pals Henry (Scolari) and Kip (Hanks) are having trouble finding somewhere to live, so their friend Amy (Sperber) suggests they try her building. Trouble is, it's women-only, so the boys have to dress up as women (Hildegard and Buffy) to rent the room. While the novelty of seeing a curly-haired, very youthful (he was 24) Hanks in drag (and bad drag, at that) is quite funny, and there's nice chemistry between the two leads, this really is a one-joke series that isn't a patch on *Some Like It Hot* (which it borrows from), and has dated rather badly. Only for Hanks completists.

 TV Trivia: Billy Joel's song 'My Life' was the original theme tune, but the song has been replaced for the DVD release as he refused to allow it to be reused.

CARoLiNE iN THE CiTY (1995–1999)

Starring Lea Thompson, Malcolm Gets, Eric Lutes

Inexplicably successful (in the US, anyway) comedy with *Back To The Future* star Thompson as cartoonist Caroline Duffy. She writes a comic strip called 'Caroline in the City' that is based on her own messy life with various failed relationships and unresolved ones, including old boyfriend Del (Lutes) and friend Richard (Gets), whose on/off feelings for Caroline dragged on for the show's entire run (it was never resolved as the fourth season ended on a cliffhanger and then the series was cancelled). Like *Suddenly Susan* and older series such as *The Mary Tyler Moore Show* and *Rhonda*, it's all about a single woman trying to find her way in the big city (in this case, Manhattan), but Caroline is so bloody needy, grating and whining you can see why no men want to go anywhere near her.

 TV Trivia: The character of Caroline was first introduced in an episode of *Friends* ('The One With The Baby On The Bus').

CHEERS (1982–1993)

Starring Ted Danson, Rhea Pearlman, George Wendt, John Ratzenberger, Shelley Long, Kirstie Alley

One of America's most-successful and long-running sitcoms, *Cheers* was considered a flop when it began, coming bottom in the ratings for the first season. Set in a Boston bar run by alcoholic ex-baseball player Sam Malone (Danson), the series followed ladies man Sam's many flirtations as he served drinks to a rag-tag group of regulars including Norm (Wendt), know-it-all postman Cliff (Ratzenberger), and from 1984, posh psychiatrist Frasier (Kelsey Grammer, whose character got his own spin-off). Helping Sam dole out the beer was Coach (Nicholas Colasanto), the very fertile waitress Carla (Pearlman) and the object of Sam's affection, prissy waitress Diane (Long). Sadly Colasanto died in 1985 and Long decided to leave the cast in 1987, but the loss of these two major cast members didn't affect the show – Woody Harrelson was brought in as lovable, dim-witted bartender Woody, while Kirstie Alley joined the cast as the new boss of the bar after Long left. This pithy ensemble series from James Burrows, Glen Charles and Les Charles ran for 11 award-winning seasons, and best episodes include Season 5's 'The Proposal', Season 6's 'The Last Angry Mailman' and Season 2's 'Homicidal Ham', while notable guest stars over the years have included John Cleese, Emma Thompson and Tom Berenger.

 TV Trivia: While the inside of the bar is a set, the outside is the Bull and Finch Pub in Boston.

THE COSBY SHOW (1984–1992)

Starring Bill Cosby, Phylicia Rashad, Malcolm Jamal Warner, Lisa Bonet

Comedian Bill Cosby was already an established name on TV in the US when this series debuted, but it was this show about an upper middle-class African-

American family living in Brooklyn that catapulted him to megastardom. He starred as Cliff Huxtable – voted the Greatest TV Dad of All Time in a 2004 TV guide survey – a doctor with a loving wife (Rashad) and a group of kids ranging from daughter-at-college Sondra (Sabrina Le Beauf) to irresponsible only son Theo (Warner). While the series wasn't a hit straight away – it was up against the number one show of the time, *Magnum PI* – it soon became a must-see show and has been credited with not only paving the way for other comedies that focused on African-Americans (*In Living Color*, *The Fresh Prince of Bel Air*) but also for being one of the first truly successful sitcoms to be based on a stand-up comic's act (*Roseanne*, *Seinfeld* etc soon followed suit). Cosby, who had creative control, wanted the show to be educational as well as funny, and while there are quite a few belly-laughs to be had over the years, there is also a moralising tone that can get a bit grating if you're not a huge Cosby fan.

A spin-off with Lisa Bonet, called *A Different World*, is not currently available on DVD.

 TV Trivia: Whitney Houston was second choice to play Cliff's eldest daughter Sondra.

CURB YOUR ENTHUSIASM (2000–)

Starring Larry David, Cheryl Hines, Jeff Garlin

Larry David, one of the creators of *Seinfeld*, takes centre stage this time for a show about himself. It's an exaggerated version of him, of course (we hope), in which the writer/producer/actor portrays himself as one of the most irritating people you are ever likely to meet. He's rude, thoughtless, blunt, angry and seems to spend his whole life with his foot in his mouth or getting himself into scrapes such as hiring a tourettes-afflicted chef when he opens a restaurant with a friend, or telling a blind man that the girlfriend he thinks is a model is actually ugly. Mainly improvised – the cast have a rough outline of the episode's plot and go from there – this is consistently brilliant, hilariously funny and very clever, thanks to the superb David and his cast, that also includes Hines as David's long-suffering wife and Garlin as Jeff Greene, one of his few friends.

 TV Trivia: In the pilot episode, Larry and Cheryl had children (who weren't seen) but they have none in all the other episodes.

CYBILL (1995–1998)

Starring Cybill Shepherd, Christine Baranski, Alicia Witt

Moonlighting star Cybill Shepherd got her own sitcom in 1995, playing an actress named Cybill (now, there's a stretch) – but not a very successful one. Cybill Sheridan (the character's name) is struggling to have a Hollywood career, mainly in commercials and B-movies, but the series mostly focuses on her relationships with headstrong daughter Zoe (Witt) and married daughter Rachel (DeeDee Pfeiffer), her two ex-husbands, Ira (Alan Rosenberg) and Jeff (Tom Wopat), and her friendship with rich and deliciously bitchy Maryann (Baranski, who steals the entire series away from Cybill). Sharply written, this only lasted four seasons – rumour has it there were many behind-the-scenes disagreements between the cast and crew, while Shepherd herself claimed the TV network was not thrilled with the series' feminist tones.

 TV Trivia: Cybill is named after her grandfather, Cy, and her father, Bill.

THE DICK VAN DYKE SHOW (1961–1966)

Starring Dick Van Dyke, Mary Tyler Moore

Created by comic actor and director Carl Reiner, who was originally also going to star in it (when the show was named *Head Of The Family*) until the network decided to cast Van Dyke, this series was a sitcom about a family man who makes a living as a TV writer. Rob Petrie (Van Dyke) is married to Laura (Moore), and commutes each day to his job in Manhattan as the head writer on a top TV show. Along with his fellow writers, Sally (Rose Marie) and Buddy (Morey Amsterdam), they have fun with their bosses, Mel Cooley (Richard Deacon) and the show's star, Alan Brady (Reiner). And if nothing much funny has happened at work, Rob is bound to come home to find zany antics courtesy of his wife and son Ritchie or the neighbours. Moore and Van Dyke have great chemistry, and each episode is packed with physical gags, one-liners and sharp insults that everyone delivers with glee. An American classic – shame Moore's own series, *The Mary Tyler Moore Show*, isn't on DVD, too.

TV Trivia: Mary Tyler Moore insisted on her character wearing capri pants, rather than skirts, as she said all her friends who were housewives and mothers wore trousers. Thanks to Mary wearing them on TV, capri pants became a fashion bestseller in the US.

DREAM ON (1990–1996)

Starring Brian Benben, Wendie Malick, Michael McKean

An odd premise that probably wouldn't have been made if the risk-taking TV channel HBO didn't exist, *Dream On* was a cult comedy about dreamer Martin Tupper (Benben), who's divorced and on the lookout for love, and whose dreams and thoughts are depicted using scenes from classic old movies and TV shows. Renowned at the time for its sexual references and female nudity (cable channel HBO later, of course, brought us the even more risque *Sex and the City*), the male-oriented series was created by David Crane and Marta Kauffman of *Friends* fame, along with director John Landis (*Trading Places*, *The Blues Brothers*), and boasts some super-sharp writing and very clever use of vintage black and white clips that often say what Martin himself can't. The affable Benben manages to make a slightly annoying man really likeable, while comedy veteran Malick (best known in the UK for her appearances in *Frasier*) is a treat as his ex-wife Judith, too. Best episodes include the second season ones where Martin is involved in the making of a biography of Judith's new husband Richard, where he falls for the actress playing Judith (Mimi Rogers), while some of the guest stars who appear in the show include Tippi Hedren as Judith's mother, Scott Bakula and musician Warren Zevon.

 TV Trivia: When this aired on a non-cable channel in the US, all the nudity and cursing had to be edited out.

DUE SOUTH (1994–1996)

Starring Paul Gross, David Marciano, Catherine Bruhier

A Canadian/American co-production, *Due South* was created by Paul Haggis, the writer/director of Oscar-winning movie *Crash*. It's the story of a Canadian Mountie named Benton Fraser (Gross), who travels to Chicago with his half-wolf, half-dog, Diefenbaker (who is deaf but can read lips) to find his father's killer, discovers it was a fellow Mountie who killed him, and then finds he's unable to return to his old job because of his accusations. Instead, Benton gets a job with the Chicago Police Department, much to the annoyance of Ray Vecchio (Marciano), the detective he is partnered with. Part cop show and part comedy, this combines the much used 'fish-out-of-water' plot with some completely bonkers storylines and Fraser's almost superhuman detective ability (he sniffs a rat to deduce what brand of barbecue ribs it had been eating to solve a crime).

TV Trivia: Most of the characters in the first season were named after famous Canadians, including dog Diefenbaker, who is named after Canada's prime minister from 1957–1963.

ENTOURAGE (2004–)

Starring Kevin Connolly, Adrian Grenier, Kevin Dillon, Jeremy Piven, Jerry Ferrara

Terrific, sharply written Hollywood series about an up-and-coming movie star and the gang of childhood friends he keeps around him that was inspired by executive producer Mark Wahlberg's own experiences. Vincent Chase (Grenier) is a star, complete with slithering snake-like agent Ari (the superb Piven), Beverly Hills pad, fawning women and a group of friends to share it all with: Eric (Connolly) who acts as Vince's manager; Vince's older brother Johnny 'Drama' Chase (Dillon), a wannabe actor who never made it big; and Turtle (Ferrara), who comes along for the ride. While Piven steals every scene as the pushy agent ('Let's hug it out, bitch!' has become a fan-favourite catchphrase), all the cast are excellent, and the numerous guest stars playing themselves (Mandy Moore, James Cameron, Ed Burns, Gary Busey) makes this something like Robert Altman's *The Player* for the small screen. A must for movie fans.

TV trivia: Piven's character is based on a real-life agent, Ari Emanuel.

EVERYBODY LOVES RAYMOND (1996–2005)

Starring Ray Romano, Patricia Heaton, Doris Roberts, Brad Garrett, Peter Boyle

Multiple award-winning family sitcom that has sportswriter Ray (Romano), his long-suffering wife Debra (Heaton) and kids living across the street in Long Island to his parents. And what parents they are – Ray's mother, Marie, thinks Debra isn't good enough for him and interferes at every available opportunity, while father Frank comes over to avoid his nagging wife and watch sports. And then there's Ray's policeman older brother Robert (Garrett) who has moved back home with his parents, despite the fact he gets annoyed at everything they do, especially when they favour golden boy Raymond over him. While it sounds like pretty standard sitcom fare, this comedy hits the right tickle-bone thanks to some sharp casting, especially Roberts, Boyle and Garrett as Ray's horrendous parents and downtrodden sibling.

TV Trivia: In real life, Ray Romano has a brother who is a police officer in the NYPD, just like his fictional brother Robert.

FAMILY TIES (1982–1989)

Starring Michael J. Fox, Michael Gross, Meredith Baxter

The sitcom that made Michael J. Fox a star, and something of a pre-pubescent girls' pin-up, this had a simple enough premise: sixties left-wing political activists/hippies Steven (Gross) and Elyse Keaton (Baxter) have to come to terms with the fact that they are now raising a family of rather more conservative offspring. There's the rather underachieving Mallory (Justine Bateman, sister of *Arrested Development*'s Jason), the young and precocious Jennifer (Tina Yothers) and, most horrifying of all, oldest son Alex (Fox), a suit-wearing member of the Young Republicans. Just where did Steven and Elyse go wrong? Sharply written and slickly performed, this family comedy was a huge US hit and still raises a smile even if Alex's politics are very dated – and watch out for a young Tom Hanks in some episodes as Elyse's ne'er do well brother, Ned.

 TV Trivia: Fox met his future real-life wife, Tracy Pollan, on the show – she played his first serious girlfriend, Ellen.

FRIENDS (1994–2004)

Starring Matthew Perry, Courteney Cox, Jennifer Aniston, Lisa Kudrow, David Schwimmer, Matt Le Blanc

In 1994, the US TV channel NBC launched two successful new shows on Thursday nights, the hospital drama *ER* and the long-running, much imitated sitcom *Friends*. Centering around six pals – obsessive Monica (Cox), flighty Phoebe (Kudrow), rich girl Rachel (Aniston), Monica's nerdy brother Ross (Schwimmer), his sharp-witted college roommate Chandler (Perry) and Chandler's ladies man flatmate Joey (Le Blanc) who congregate at coffee house Central Perk, never seem to go to work yet can afford nice Manhattan apartments – the series from creators David Crane and Martha Kauffman was sharply written, cleverly conceived and, most important of all, really funny. It soon became must-see TV as women copied Aniston's hairstyle, everyone wondered whether Ross and Rachel would end up together (he'd had a crush on her since high school) and celebrities from Bruce Willis to Brad Pitt and Julia Roberts lined up to make guest appearances.

Running for 10 seasons, the first couple are still the sharpest, but there is fun to be had in each season, from Chandler and Monica's secret romance to the revelation that every man has had the same Princess Leia gold bikini fantasy (we knew it!).

TV Trivia: When the series started, each member of the cast got $22,500 per episode. By the time the series finished, they each were getting over $1 million an episode.

THE GOLDEN GIRLS (1985–1992)

Starring Bea Arthur, Betty White, Rue McClanahan, Estelle Getty

Who would have thought one of the biggest sitcom successes of the eighties in the US would be a comedy about four elderly women living together? That was the premise of *The Golden Girls:* a quartet of previously married women sharing a home in Florida, bickering, trying to find men to end their days with, and generally rubbing each other up the wrong way. There's Southern Belle Blanche (McClanahan), who is very popular with the local men in the area; deep-voiced widow Dorothy (Arthur); Dorothy's sharp-tongued mother Sophia (Getty); and the naive Rose (White). It shouldn't be enjoyable to anyone under the age of 80, but somehow this silver-haired comedy worked, thanks to the chemistry between the women and the often razor-sharped scripts.

Avoid the 1992 spin-off series *The Golden Palace* (thankfully not on DVD but occasionally repeated on TV), in which Rose, Blanche and Sophia opened a hotel after Dorothy left to get married – it's awful, and is only of note for an early career role for *Ocean's Eleven*'s Don Cheadle.

 TV Trivia: Getty is actually over a year younger than Arthur, who played her daughter.

GREEN ACRES (1965–1971)

Starring Eddie Albert, Eva Gabor, Tom Lester, Frank Cady

Utterly bonkers soap/sitcom that was surreal, strange and completely addictive. Eddie Albert plays normal guy Oliver Wendell Douglas, who decides to leave the rat race of New York City and buy a farm in the odd town of Hooterville, much to the horror of his socialite wife, Lisa (Gabor). On the surface, the place looks okay, but Oliver soon discovers the locals are a bit weird, including the Ziffel family that treat pet pig Arnold like a son (he even gets to watch TV and loves Westerns). Three decades before *Twin Peaks*, this remains one of the quirkiest shows made for TV, with its chickens that lay square eggs, oddball locals and characters who addressed the audience directly. If you enjoy one episode, you'll soon be hooked.

 TV Trivia: The first pig to play Arnold was male, but all subsequent pigs playing the role were female.

HOW I MET YOUR MOTHER (2005–)

Starring Josh Radnor, Jason Segel, Cobie Smulders, Alyson Hannigan, Neil Patrick Harris

The closest a sitcom about twenty-something pals has come to filling the void left by *Friends*, this is a warm, fun comedy that's a big hit in the US but has sadly been relegated to satellite/cable TV in the UK. In the future (2029 to be exact), a dad (voiced by Bob Saget) tells his disinterested kids they should settle down for a long story – the tale of how he met their mother. Then the action flashes back to our present day as Ted (Radnor) begins his search for the perfect woman with the help and hindrance of best pal Marshall (Segel), Marshall's fiancée Lily (*Buffy The Vampire Slayer*'s Hannigan) and womanising Barney (Harris, best known as Doogie Howser). Could Ted's future-kids mom be Robin (Smulders), a TV reporter who becomes his pal and later, girlfriend (we soon learn it isn't her, as future-Ted refers to her as Aunt Robin). Like *Friends*, it's an ensemble comedy about relationships and being twentysomething and at sea with life. It's actually funnier, though, thanks to a punchy script and two knockout performances from supporting cast members Hannigan (who showed her comedic skills in the *American Pie* movies) and Harris, who steals every single scene he's in as the guy who thinks he's a love god to all women. You'll become a fan before the end of the first episode, and be addicted by the time Britney Spears pops up for a cameo in two of 2008's episodes.

 TV Trivia: Alyson Hannigan babysat narrator Bob Saget's kids when she was a teenager.

I LOVE LUCY (1951–1957)

Starring Lucille Ball, Desi Arnaz

It's over half a century since the last episode of *I Love Lucy* was made, but this sitcom has stood the test of time and remains one of the best ever, thanks in the main to a pitch-perfect performance from Lucille Ball as Lucy Ricardo, the ditzy wife of long-suffering bandleader Ricky (Arnaz, Ball's real-life husband at the time). Watch 'Lucy Does A TV Commercial' (in which she gets even sillier than usual as she gets drunk on the product 'vitameatavegamin'), 'Job-Switching' (in which Lucy and pal Ethel get jobs in a candy factory) or 'LA At Last' (in which celebrity-seeker Lucy heads to LA and meets, among others, William Holden) and you will see a master of physical comedy at work as Ball grimaces, prat-falls, giggles and delights. Arnaz is a terrific foil as he gets increasingly exasperated at his wife's oddball antics, while William Frawley and Vivian Vance both shine as the couple's friends, Fred and Ethel Mertz. A true classic.

 TV Trivia: Lucille Ball's real-life pregnancy was incorporated into the show as Lucy got pregnant and had Little Ricky. However, in the fifties, you couldn't say 'pregnant' on US TV, so Lucy had to describe her condition as 'expectant'.

JOEY (2004–2006)

Starring Matt LeBlanc, Paulo Costanzo, Drea De Matteo

It sounded so good on paper – a spin-off from *Friends*, one of the US's most successful sitcoms of all time. It worked when *Frasier* was launched from *Cheers*, so surely this was going to be a huge hit? Er, no. Taking the least fully fleshed out character from the New York sitcom – slightly stupid, failed actor Joey Tribbiani (LeBlanc) – and transferring him to LA where he moves in with his 20-year-old nephew (Costanzo) across a courtyard from Joey's sister Gina (De Matteo) on a very obviously fake set was bad enough. Then having poor LeBlanc, almost 40 years old, still chasing skirts and fluffing auditions just seemed very sad. Cast and production changes in Season 2 didn't make things any better.

 TV Trivia: For Season 2, 22 episodes were made but only 14 were ever shown on US TV.

KING OF QUEENS (1998–2007)

Starring Kevin James, Leah Rimini, Jerry Stiller

Comedian Kevin James stars as delivery man Doug in this sitcom – an average guy living an average life, with a pretty wife named Carrie (Rimini) and just one problem: his father-in-law Arthur (Stiller) lives in their basement. It's an affable enough comedy, which was surprisingly successful in the US despite being nothing special. Most episodes are about Doug wanting to watch his big screen TV or hang with the guys rather than spend time at home, and while James is an enjoyable buffoon to watch, and Rimini a good foil, both are overshadowed by Stiller (father of actor Ben), who gets all the best lines ('Paris. I haven't been back there since we liberated her in '44. The City Of Lights knew peace once more. I also got the clap, but that's a another story for another time') and delivers each one with glee. One to watch only when you've exhausted every episode of *Married With Children*.

TV Trivia: In the episode 'Shrink Wrap', Jerry Stiller's son Ben appeared as Arthur's father in flashback scenes.

THE LARRY SANDERS SHOW (1992–1998)

Starring Garry Shandling, Jeffrey Tambor, Rip Torn, Penny Johnson, Janeane Garofalo

An hilarious, deliciously ruthless look behind the scenes of a fictional late night talk show (that looks very similar to *The Tonight Show with Jay Leno* or *Late Show With David Letterman*), this cult series was shown in the middle of the night in the UK meaning that many people missed a treat. Stand-up comic Shandling, one of the show's creators, is eye-wateringly funny as the bundle of ego and neuroses that is talkshow host Larry Sanders, and the episodes highlighted his off-air antics with the (fictional) show's producer, Arti (Torn), Larry's open-mouth-and-insert-foot sidekick, Hank 'Hey Now!' Kingsley (Tambor), and the backstage writers (played, over the years, by comic talents including Garofalo, Wallace Langham and Jeremy Piven).

During the series, over 180 celebrities appeared as themselves – usually as guests on Larry's show – most memorably David Duchovny, who has a crush on Larry (a joke that was carried into *The X-Files* – Shandling appeared in one episode with a crush on Duchovny's character Mulder), Alec and Daniel Baldwin ('The List') and Henry Winkler ('Hank's Sex Tape'). Genius.

 TV Trivia: Most of the cast of *Seinfeld* guested on the show – partly because both series were filmed at the same studios.

MARRIED WITH CHILDREN (1987–1997)

Starring Ed O'Neill, Christina Applegate, Katey Sagal

Al Bundy (O'Neill) is a pig. He's rude to his wife Peg (Sagal), lusts after anything in a skirt, thinks he is god's gift to women, spends the best part of his day coming up with ways to avoid work (he's a shoe salesman) and his kids, and thinks a day well spent is one on the toilet with the sports section and a beer. Simply put, he makes Homer Simpson look like Noel Coward. And Al is the hilarious centre of this comedy in which everyone should be unlikeable – daughter Kelly is dumb and promiscuous, son Bud is dysfunctional and only dog Bud seems remotely normal – but is actually lovable in a twisted way. Packed with scathing one liners ('Ah, Peg. You're here. Damn. There I was dreaming you ran off with the dwarf down at the bookstore, and I was living in sin with a Playboy centerfold and her eight friends who could speak but chose not to'), and focusing on a group of people in a rundown house who love/hate each other, this makes you laugh from the opening credits (to the tune of Frank Sinatra singing 'Love And Marriage') to the end of each dumb episode. Even the worst episodes (those in the final two seasons) will make you giggle at the horror that is Al at least once.

 TV Trivia: Ed O'Neill only found out the series was cancelled when he was on holiday and a couple nearby told him after reading it in a newspaper.

MY NAME IS EARL (2005–)

Starring Jason Lee, Ethan Suplee, Jaime Pressly, Eddie Steeples

A terrific comedy that boasts a truly original premise: life's loser Earl Hickey (Lee) wins $100,000 on the lottery... then gets hit by a car. Realising in his hospital bed that the accident is some sort of karma he's received for all the bad things he's done in his life, Earl makes a list of all those bad deeds (more than 250 of them) and decides to make good on every one – and maybe if he finishes apologising and setting right everything on the list he'll finally be able to enjoy his winnings. Aided by his brother Randy (Suplee), most episodes have Earl preparing to cross off a bad deed from his list, but with a trailer trash ex-wife Joy (Pressly) hanging around, it's not always that easy. Wryly funny rather than rib-ticklingly silly, this is goofy stuff that has rightly been compared to the Coen Brothers' movie *Raising Arizona* – and if you like that, you should definitely make a point to catch an episode of Earl.

TV Trivia: Jason Lee and Ethan Suplee appeared together in Kevin Smith's movie *Mallrats*, and a few references to characters/places from Smith's films have appeared in the show.

THE OFFICE: AN AMERICAN WORKPLACE (2005–)

Starring Steve Carrell, Rainn Wilson, John Krasinski, Jenna Fischer

Ricky Gervais and Stephen Merchant's British mockumentary about life in an ordinary office was transplanted to the US with surprisingly effective results. Michael Scott (Carrell) is the self-important office manager of the Dunder Mifflin paper supply company in Scranton, Pennsylvania. He shares the office with co-workers Dwight (Wilson), the office suck-up and Jim (Krasinski) and receptionist Pam (Fischer). Other than the first episode, which had the same script as the British series, this has been completely independent of the original version, and that actually works in its favour as the scripts have been tailored to suit the cast's talents. Carrell's manager is more aware that he is irritating than Gervais's was, Dwight is more Machiavellian than his British counterpart, and some of the humour is more silly and less dour. Well worth a look, this honours the spirit of Gervais and Merchant's creation without trying to copy it.

 TV Trivia: There are a few homages to the British version in the show – the office is at 1725 Slough Road (the British series is set in Slough) and Michael has a Union Jack flag on his desk.

THE PHIL SILVERS SHOW (1955–1959)

Starring Phil Silvers, Paul Ford, Maurice Gosfield

Rightly regarded by many as one of the best sitcoms ever made, this starred comic Silvers as Sergeant Ernest Bilko, the enterprising army officer stuck out at the motor pool in Fort Baxter, a remote post in Kansas. Determined to make the most of this dire situation by running every money-making scheme he could come up with, Bilko ran card games, shirked his duties, memorably housed a horse at the motor pool, fiddled his taxes, feigned illness and even impersonated a Naval officer in a bid to earn some more cash. With Colonel Hall (Ford) as anti-hero Bilko's weary foil, and Barbella (Harvey Lembeck), Henshaw (Allan Melvin) and Doberman (Gosfield) as the soldiers Bilko often ropes into his schemes, this series romped along as a funny vehicle for Silvers' routines and slapstick, with writers including the legendary Neil Simon providing many of the scripted laughs.

A wonderful slice of fifties humour that ran for over 140 episodes, it's a tribute to the quick-witted, genius comic talent that was Phil Silvers.

TV Trivia: Creator Nat Hilken was allegedly paid a year's salary to spend time with Silvers and then go off and develop the show.

ROSEANNE (1988–1997)

Starring Roseanne Barr, John Goodman, Sara Gilbert, Laurie Metcalf

Comedienne Roseanne Barr took aspects of her own life as a working-class mum and turned it into this hugely successful sitcom. She plays Roseanne Conner, who, along with blue collar husband Dan (the wonderful Goodman), try to raise their family of three kids and stay above the poverty line. The first few seasons are the best (and watch out for a young George

Clooney as Roseanne's boss in the first season, and *Buffy* creator Joss Whedon as one of the show's writers), although the later ones should be commended for some of the subjects they tackled, including unplanned pregnancy, domestic abuse (Roseanne's sister Jackie, played by Metcalf, is beaten by a boyfriend), teenage love (Roseanne's sulky daughter Darlene's romance with David, who eventually moves into the Connor home) and gay relationships (Roseanne's boss in later series, Leon – played by comic Martin Mull – has a civil partnership, while Roseanne herself memorably shares a kiss with guest star Mariel Hemingway).

Avoid the head-scratching final season, in which the family become millionaires having won the lottery, and the finale which revealed the family hadn't won the prize, Dan had died of a heart attack, and the events of the previous season were part of a fictional book Roseanne was writing.

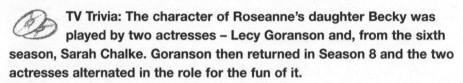 **TV Trivia: The character of Roseanne's daughter Becky was played by two actresses – Lecy Goranson and, from the sixth season, Sarah Chalke. Goranson then returned in Season 8 and the two actresses alternated in the role for the fun of it.**

SEINFELD (1990–1998)

Starring Jerry Seinfeld, Jason Alexander, Julia-Louis Dreyfus, Michael Richards

Phenomenally successful in the US but more of a cult hit in the UK due to the BBC's erratic scheduling (often in the early hours), *Seinfeld* is, famously, the show about nothing. In the early seasons, stand-up comic Jerry Seinfeld (and creator, along with Larry David) introduced and ended the episode with a slice of his stage comedy, while each episode followed New Yorker Jerry – sort of playing himself – and his neurotic friends, George (Alexander), Elaine (Dreyfus) and neighbour Kramer – as they traversed the minefield that is Manhattan. There are too many great lines to mention here, but if you have never seen an episode, the best ones to give you a sense of what this brilliant show is about would be Season 2's 'The Chinese Restaurant' (in which the entire show is set in a restaurant as the group queue for a table); Season 7's 'The Soup Nazi' (in which Jerry deals with an obsessive and rude soup stall vendor); 'The Sponge' (in which Elaine discovers her favourite contraceptive is being discontinued so she has to decide which of her dates are 'sponge-worthy'); 'The Invitations' (in which George's fiancée becomes a victim of his stinginess); and of course, Season 4's legendary episode 'The Contest' (buy this one just to find out what it is all about).

TV Trivia: The exterior used for the restaurant/diner where they all eat is Tom's at West 112th Street and Broadway in Manhattan. It is also known for the Suzanne Vega song it inspired, 'Tom's Diner'.

SEX AND THE CITY (1998–2004)

Starring Sarah Jessica Parker, Cynthia Nixon, Kristin Davis, Kim Cattrall, Chris Noth

Based on Candace Bushnell's bestseller of the same name that began as a newspaper column, *Sex and The City* became something of a female phenomenon, turning Parker into a major style icon and introducing women who usually shop at Primark and drink white wine to words such as 'Manolo' (as in Blahnik shoes) and 'Cosmopolitan' (as in the cocktail). Carrie (Parker) is the thirtysomething gal about town writing about her sexual experiences, while prissy Charlotte (Davis), workaholic Miranda (Nixon) and the very sexually active Samantha (Cattrall) share their own failed romances, bad and good sex and passion for fashion with her.

A comedy/drama renowned for being sexually frank – not many series have women openly discussing anal sex, group sex, or whether it's obligatory to kiss a man after he's performed oral sex on you – this was eyebrow-raising, convention-bursting stuff throughout, packed with the latest fashions from designers clamouring to be featured on the show. Although by the final season the girls were beginning to look a tad old to be wearing some of the more inventive creations, it remained pretty sharp in the script department, and the four leading ladies were terrific throughout. While the final episode resolved many of the relationships, a movie was released in summer 2008 to add another chapter to the tale.

TV Trivia: Sarah Jessica Parker was the only actress in the show to stipulate no full nudity, which is why she's always partially covered whereas the other actresses have all appeared naked.

TAXI (1978–1983)

Starring Judd Hirsch, Danny DeVito, Marilu Henner, Christopher Lloyd, Tony Danza

An almost legendary American sitcom, set in the dingy staff room of a New York City taxicab company, *Taxi* has rightly been acclaimed as one of the best comedies of the 1980s. It made stars of comic actors Danny DeVito (as diminutive, rude boss Louie), Tony Danza (dim-witted cabbie Tony), Judd Hirsch (as the worldly wise Alex) and Marilu Henner (as Elaine), while introducing the unique comedy styles of Christopher Lloyd (best known as Doc in *Back to the Future*) and Andy Kaufman (who played immigrant Latka) to the general viewing public. Pithy, smart and often very funny, the series was created by James Burrows and Glen and Les Charles, who went onto create *Cheers*, another wonderful ensemble show.

 TV Trivia: In the opening credits, a cab is driven over the Queensboro Bridge in New York. You can't see the driver, but it is Tony Danza.

TWO AND A HALF MEN

Starring Charlie Sheen, Jon Cryer, Angus T Jones

Affable US sitcom with Charlie Sheen as wealthy layabout jingle writer Charlie, whose straight-laced brother Alan (Cryer) and his 10-year-old son Jake (Jones) move into his beach house, cramping his love life and rather laidback lifestyle. It's like a 21st century version of *The Odd Couple* – Charlie is chilled and messy, Alan's a tensed-up, shy divorcé – that works well thanks to the comic skills of the three leads (the chubby Jones is a terrific match for the grown-ups around him) and a deliciously bitchy turn from Holland Taylor as the men's domineering mother, Evelyn. For some episodes, Melanie Lynskey (of *Heavenly Creatures* fame) crops up as the neighbour who stalks Charlie, while Sheen's former *Spin City* co-star Heather Locklear, and his real-life (ex) wife Denise Richards have also appeared in episodes. Cute rather than eye-wateringly funny.

 TV Trivia: Blythe Danner was originally going to play Charlie and Alan's mother, but had to drop out at the last minute.

WILL & GRACE (1998–2006)

Starring Debra Messing, Eric McCormack, Megan Mullally, Sean Hayes

A good example of a show where the secondary characters were much more interesting than the two leads. While *Will & Grace* should be commended for featuring gay characters in major rather than 'token' roles, after the first couple of years of this sub-*Friends* sitcom there's not much else to recommend it as Messing seems to do a Lucille Ball impersonation as the neurotic Grace and her gay roommate (and ex-boyfriend), lawyer Will (McCormack) is scripted as increasingly whiny and needy. Better are sharp-tongued rich bitch Karen (Mullally) and Will's over-the-top pal Jack (Hayes), Shelley Morrison as

Karen's sarcastic maid/friend Rosario, and in the occasional guest-starring role, Debbie Reynolds as Grace's theatrical mother and Harry Connick Jr and Woody Harrelson as two of Grace's most memorable beaux. In later seasons, this relied heavily on recruiting big name celebs to cameo (Demi Moore, Madonna, Cher among them) – the only one worth catching is Kevin Bacon's hilarious performance as himself which ends with him and Will dancing to 'Footloose' (Season 5's 'Bacon & Eggs').

 TV Trivia: Nicolette Sheridan and Yasmin Bleeth were both considered for the role of Grace.

40 SKETCH SHOWS

1) 3 NON BLONDES (2003)

Ninia Benjamin, Tamika Empson and Jocelyn Jee Esien traverse the high streets of the UK, performing sketches to hidden cameras in this funny but short-lived BBC series.

2) 8 OUT OF 10 CATS (2005–)

Comedy panel show based on opinion polls, hosted by the grating Jimmy Carr. Guests have included Alan Carr, David Walliams and Vic Reeves.

3) ARMSTRONG AND MILLER/THE ARMSTRONG AND MILLER SHOW (1997–2001; 2007–)

Alexander Armstrong and Ben Miller's show features such sharp sketches as the WW2 airmen talking like 21st-century chavs, and Rog (Miller), who is oblivious to his wife's affair with a neighbour (Armstrong).

4) BADLY DUBBED PORN (2005–)

The title says it all – this is clips of bad soft-porn with a dubbed over comedy soundtrack. Unfortunately, the porn itself is funny enough so the added commentary is almost redundant.

5) BALLS OF STEEL (2005–)

Mark Dolan presents this show that has special guests perform stunts to test other people's nerves (eg The Bunny Boiler, in which Thaila Zucchi flirts with a man in front of his girlfriend to see what she'll do).

6) THE BENNY HILL SHOW (1969–1989)

Broadcast in more than 140 countries, this is the classic saucy English comedy, featuring silly sketches, girls in sexy outfits, double entendres galore and slapstick.

7) BiG TRAiN (1998–2002)

Surreal show from *Father Ted* creators Arthur Matthews and Graham Linehan that featured then-unknown stars including Catherine Tate and Simon Pegg.

8) A BiT OF FRY AND LAURiE (1989–1995)

Before Hugh Laurie became a sexpot with a Yank accent on *House*, he co-starred (and was very witty, to boot) with the droll Stephen Fry in this dapper comedy.

9) THE CATHERiNE TATE SHOW (2004–2007)

Comedienne Tate's best known for the bolshy teenage character Lauren ('Am I bovvvered?') but the show also included The Aga Saga Woman, foul-mouthed granny 'Nan' Taylor and the camp Derek Faye.

10) DA ALi G SHOW (2000, 2003)

Sacha Baron Cohen's three characters – Ali G, Borat and Bruno – interviewed unsuspecting celebrities and politicians. You knew Ali G's 15 minutes had run out when Richard Madeley pretended to be him.

11) DAVE ALLEN (1971–1979; 1981–1990)

'May your god go with you', said Irish comic Allen at the end of each show as he knocked back his trademark whiskey. Some shows featured sketches as well as stand-up (except Allen sat down)…

12) THE DAY TODAY (1994)

Spoof current affairs show of just six episodes featuring Chris Morris and Patrick Marber. Also featured Steve Coogan's first appearances as character Alan Partridge.

13) DEF COMEDY JAM (1992–1997; 2006–)

Chris Rock, David Chappelle, and Jamie Foxx are just some of the African-American stand-ups who have performed on this show from hip-hop's Russell Simmons.

14) DENNIS PENNIS (1995–1997)

The scourge of celebrities, Pennis was the carrot-haired creation of comedian Paul Kaye, who cornered the stars and asked them things like (to Steve Martin) 'Why aren't you funny anymore?'

15) THE FAST SHOW (1994–1997. 2000)

Paul Whitehouse, Charlie Higson, Simon Day and pals created such memorable characters as Ron Manager, Ted and Ralph, Swiss Toni and the 'Suits you' tailors that Johnny Depp asked to appear in their final show.

16) FRENCH AND SAUNDERS (1987–2007)

Comediennes Dawn French and Jennifer Saunders spoofed movies, pop stars and popular culture in six series over two decades.

17) THE FRIDAY NIGHT PROJECT (2005–)

Alan Carr and Justin Lee Collins are joined by a celebrity host who helps with sketches, a game show involving the audience, and also answers questions.

18) GOODNESS GRACIOUS ME (1998–2001)

Originally on Radio 4, this often hilarious series starred Sanjeev Bhaskar, Meera Syal, Kulvinder Ghir and Nina Wadia in a series of sketches often poking fun at Asian and British culture.

19) HARRY ENFIELD (1990; 1994; 2000)

Kevin the teenager, naff DJs Smashy and Nicey, and slobs Wayne and Waynetta were introduced in Enfield's first TV sketch show.

20) THE KENNY EVERETT TELEVISION SHOW (1978–1988)

Known as *The Kenny Everett Video Show* until 1981 when it switched from ITV to BBC, Kenny brought us punk Sid Snot, Frenchman Marcel Wave and busty but bearded Cupid – as well as 'raunchy' dance troupe Hot Gossip.

21) THE KIDS IN THE HALL (1988–1994)

Surreal Canadian sketch show that ran for over 100 episodes and featured Chicken Lady, monologues from the cast and the controversial 'Dr Seuss's Bible' in which the crucifixion was told in the style of kids' author Dr Seuss.

22) LITTLE BRITAIN (2003–2006)

Hugely successful show from David Walliams and Matt Lucas that got a tad repetitive by the final series. Quintessentially British characters included Andy and Lou, virtually incomprehensible teen Vicky Pollard, Dafydd the only gay in the village, and the head of slimming club Fat Fighters.

23) LITTLE MISS JOCELYN (2006–)

Jocelyn Jee Eisen plays all the major characters in this sketch show that features Jiffy the Nigerian parking attendant, Florence the voodoo-practising nurse and North London schoolgirl Sharonisha.

24) MOCK THE WEEK (2005–)

A topical panel show along the lines of *Have I Got News For You* but with impressions and improvisations about newsworthy topics.

25) MONTY PYTHON'S FLYING CIRCUS (1969–1974)

Simply the best/most surreal sketch show ever, with, of course, Michael Palin, Eric Idle, John Cleese, Terry Jones, Graham Chapman and Terry Gilliam's distinctive animation. The Dead Parrot sketch is still one of the funniest moments ever committed to film.

26) THE MORECAMBE AND WISE SHOW (1968–1983)

Classic, wonderful, timeless comedy from Eric Morecambe and Ernie Wise that featured a host of seventies stars as guests. Their performance of making breakfast to 'The Stripper' is eye-wateringly funny and utterly unforgettable.

27) NOT THE NINE O'CLOCK NEWS

It has dated terribly, but this 'alternative comedy' sketch show is worth a look for early performances from Rowan Atkinson, Griff Rhys Jones, Mel Smith and comedienne-turned-psychologist Pamela Stephenson (aka Mrs Billy Connolly).

28) PETER COOK AND DUDLEY MOORE (1965–1987)

Pete and Dud's tremendous pairing began with *Not Only... But Also* and they reunited several times for TV in the seventies and eighties.

29) REEVES AND MORTIMER (1990–1999)

Vic Reeves and Bob Mortimer brought their surreal and inventive comedy to a series of shows including *Vic Reeves' Big Night Out* and *The Smell Of Reeves and Mortimer*, and *Shooting Stars*.

30) SATURDAY NIGHT LIVE/SNL (1975–)

Long-running US live stand-up/sketch show that brought comedians including John Belushi, Dan Aykroyd, Will Ferrell, Mike Myers, Bill Murray, Eddie Murphy and Adam Sandler into the public eye. Best in the early years, but still a must see.

31) SATURDAY LIVE (1985–1987)

Lame British attempt to copy the hugely successful US show *Saturday Night Live*, this featured great comedians such as Hugh Laurie, Adrian Edmondson, Harry Enfield, Rik Mayall and pals but never had the energy of the US version. Plus Ben Elton was on it.

32) SMACK THE PONY (1999–2003)

Fiona Allen, Sally Phillips and Doon Mackichan were the main players in this funny female-heavy sketch show.

33) SPITTING IMAGE (1984–1996)

Puppets spoofed the personalities, politicians and news of the day for this weekly satire– when it worked, it was superb, and when it didn't we got the Chicken Song.

34) THAT MITCHELL AND WEBB LOOK (2006–)

BAFTA-winning show featuring sketches such as the two party planners, Numberwang (a spoof of complicated quiz shows) and snooker commentators Ted and Peter.

35) TITTYBANGBANG (2005)

Derivative, bad taste sketch show with Lucy Montgomery and Debbie Chazen among others. Not worth bothering with.

36) THE TOMMY COOPER SHOW (1968–1980)

Fez-wearing comedian whose trademark was performing magic tricks on stage that went wrong. (In actual fact, he was an accomplished magician and member of the Magic Circle.)

37) TRIGGER HAPPY TV (2000–2002)

Hidden camera TV show with Dom Joly that featured surreal sketches and deliciously bonkers moments, such as the man in a Friday the 13th horror mask who washes his bloody outfit in the launderette.

38) THE TWO RONNIES (1971–1987)

Ronnie Barker and Ronnie Corbett delivered one of the best British sketch shows of all time – who can forget the Phantom Raspberry Blower (written by Spike Milligan), Four Candles (the original script of this sold for £50,000 in 2007) and, of course, their sign off: 'It's goodnight from me,' says Corbett, 'and it's goodnight from him,' says Barker.

39) VICTORIA WOOD AS SEEN ON TV (1985–1987)

With Julie Walters on board, Wood created such memorable sketches as Acorn Antiques and doddery daytime presenters Margery & Joan.

40) WHOSE LINE IS IT ANYWAY? (1988–1998)

Comics including John Sessions, Ryan Stiles, Josie Lawrence, Tony Slattery and Sandi Toksvig competed against each other in this fast-moving improvisation stand-up show presented by Clive Anderson.

ADULT ANIMATION

CARTOONS AIMED AT GROWN-UPS – SADLY, THE BEST OF THE BUNCH (DUCKMAN) IS NOT AVAILABLE ON DVD...

2DTV (2001–)

Voices by Dave Lamb, Kate O'Sullivan, Lewis Macleod, Enn Reitel

An animated *Spitting Image* of sorts, *2DTV* describes itself aptly as the world's first topical animated sketch show. Using a mix of traditional animation and newer computer techniques to allow for speedier production, the British series of half-hour episodes comments on breaking news stories – an impressive feat when you realise this means over half the show has to be animated from scratch in a week to remain up-to-date. Everyone from the Beckhams to Bush has been lampooned in the five series that have been made for ITV so far, and the humour is fast and furious, thanks to the input of producer Giles Pilbrow (whose writing credits include *Have I Got News For You*, *Spitting Image* and *Mock The Week*) and a team that includes writer Georgia Pritchett (*Smack The Pony*) and director Tim Searle (*Coogan's Run*, *Big Train*).

The show has, as you'd expect, had its moments of notoriety – in 2003, an advert for the video and DVD compilation *The Best Of 2DTV* was banned because it showed George Bush taking the video out of its box and putting it in a toaster – apparently the BACC (the Broadcasting Advertising Clearance Centre, the industry watchdog) believed this inferred Bush was endorsing the products, and that it would not be allowed without his permission. After a media furore, the decision was overturned.

TV Trivia: *2DTV* created the controversial music video for George Michael's 'Shoot The Dog', which depicted Tony Blair as Bush's lapdog and had George in bed with Cherie Blair, and also designed the Bush and Blair inflatables for the singer's 2007 concert tour.

AMERICAN DAD (2005–)

Voices by Seth McFarlane, Wendy Schaal, Rachael McFarlane

Seth McFarlane's follow-up to *Family Guy* attempts to be more of a political satire, but in the end is just a weak copy of his first series. American dad Stan Smith is a conservative CIA agent trying to save the world from terrorism.

He believes in true Americans, and if you're not patriotic, you're probably the enemy in his eyes. Surprisingly, Stan has a doting wife, and two kids – geeky Steve and liberal daughter Hayley – and two other houseguests, Klaus, a fish with the brain of a German skier (thanks to a CIA experiment), and a space alien in hiding named Roger who once saved Stan's life at Area 51 in Roswell.

While there are some good ideas in the series, it just isn't funny enough and some episodes fall completely flat. The better ones include 'Homeland Insecurity', in which Stan, suspecting new neighbours are terrorists, arrests them and keeps them in his back yard, and 'Not Particularly Desperate Housewives', in which Stan's wife Francine joins a secretive women's group.

 TV Trivia: Seth McFarlane was given voice training by a 90-year-old couple who used to train Frank Sinatra.

BEAVIS AND BUTT-HEAD (1993–1997)

Voices by Mike Judge, Tracy Grandstaff

Mike Judge, who also made the cult movie *Office Space*, created this series for MTV, which featured two dumb and crude teenage boys, Beavis (the blond, grunting one) and his pal Butt-head (the squinty-eyed one with braces). Each episode featured pop videos that the pair laughed at and talked over, as well as their various adventures, which were usually confined to their rubbish-strewn couch. When they're not insulting each other or thinking about sex, they are sniggering at everyone else, especially 'right-on' hippy teacher David van Driessen, or trying to avoid ex-marine Coach Bradley Buzzcut and Principal McVicker, who is so stressed by the duo that he stammers, shakes and is occasionally incontinent.

It's incredibly silly, and the sort of bad taste programming that had shocked parents snatching the remote controls from their kids – and then secretly laughing at the show after the children had gone to bed. The duo's antics did come in for some criticism (especially when they literally started playing with fire on the show), and eventually MTV added a disclaimer at the beginning of each episode which said: 'Beavis and Butt-head are not role models. They're not even human, they're cartoons. Some of the things they do could cause a person to get hurt, expelled, arrested… possibly deported. To put it another way, don't try this at home.'

Best of all were the episodes in which Beavis, spaced out on too much sugar, would become 'The Great Cornholio' and start spouting ridiculous phrases like 'I need TP for my bunghole' (much funnier than it sounds, honest), or when they would simply headbang in front of the TV like a couple of bonkers teenagers (which is, of course, what they are).

The series spawned a funny movie in 1997, *Beavis and Butt-Head Do America*, which is also available on DVD. *Daria*, the MTV series about one of Beavis and Butt-head's few friends, is unavailable on DVD in the UK.

 TV Trivia: The logo for Burger World, where the pair work, is simply the McDonald's 'M' upside down.

FAMILY GUY (1999–)

Voices by Seth MacFarlane, Alex Borstein, Seth Green, Mila Kunis

Often compared unfavourably with *The Simpsons* (usually by disgruntled Simpsons fans), creator MacFarlane's *Family Guy* developed such a cult following that when it was cancelled in 2002 (for an unprecedented second time), it was surprisingly revived for US TV three years later thanks to an online fan petition and huge sales when the first series was released on DVD.

The 'family guy' of the title is Peter Griffin (MacFarlane), an overweight, lazy, politically incorrect dufus who is lucky enough to have a reasonably forgiving wife in Lois (yes, that does sound like *The Simpsons*, but bear with it, it's far sillier and cruder, in a good way). They have three kids – dopey, pudgy teen Chris (Green); angst-ridden, spec-wearing Meg (Kunis); and baby Stewie (MacFarlane again), a kid with an upper-crust English accent who is secretly a genius intent on killing his own mother because he believes she is stifling his plans to take over the world. Also living with them is Brian, a talking – and smart – dog who is Peter's Martini-swigging best friend. Far ruder than any Simpsons episode (one episode featured a talking vagina, for starters), this is often far funnier, too. Stewie's world domination machinations are a scream, but there is also much fun to be had in Brian's affectations, sharp pop culture references, the sharp scripts and visual gags.

Best episodes include Season 2's 'Death Is A Bitch', in which the Grim Reaper twists his ankle so Peter has to take over his job dispatching people to the next world; 'Road To Rhode Island', in which Brian and Stewie end up singing and dancing on a cross-country trip; Season 3's 'Emission Impossible', where Stewie panics when he hears his parents may be having another baby; and Season 4's 'Sibling Rivalry', in which Stewie discovers he has a rival sibling following an accident Peter has at the sperm bank. Give it a try – it's hilarious…

 TV Trivia: Stewie's voice is based on Rex Harrison's in *My Fair Lady*.

FUTURAMA (1999-2003)

Voices by Billy West, Katey Sagal, John DiMaggio

Matt Groening's follow-up to the phenomenon that was and is *The Simpsons* may not have shared its success (it ran for only five seasons), but it does have the same sly humour, bright animation and surrealism (and is also deliciously ruder than the more family-friendly Simpson clan).

In 1999, pizza delivery boy Fry accidentally falls into a cryogenic machine and is frozen for 1,000 years, waking at the end of the 30th century. Things are quite different in the future – many former US presidents are still active in politics, even though they are now just heads in glass jars, for example – but with the help of a batty, ageing professor (who is also one of Fry's descendants), a foul-mouthed, alcoholic robot named Bender (his catchphrase: 'bite my shiny metal ass') and one-eyed ship's captain Leela he begins to adapt to his new, but often bizarrely similar surroundings. Packed with in-jokes, pop culture gags and witty asides, this show revels in its geekiness, and – while there are some jokes that don't translate that well outside the US – packs in enough laughs to satisfy everyone, not just sci-fi fans. Best episodes include 'A Flight To Remember', that includes a great parody of *Titanic*; the *Armageddon* spoof 'A Big Piece Of Garbage'; 'Xmas Story', featuring a scary Robot Santa; and 'Parasites Lost', in which Fry eats a dodgy sandwich packed with parasites that cause him to become much more intelligent.

 TV Trivia: Some of the show's sound effects are archived ones used in series such as *Star Trek* and *The Jetsons*.

KING OF THE HILL (1997–)

Voices by Mike Judge, Kathy Najimy, Brittany Murphy

Following the success of *Beavis and Butt-head*, Mike Judge went on to create this tamer series about life in American suburbia that's just like a regular sitcom – except, of course, that it's animated. Hank Hill is the redneck dad of the piece, a resident of fictional Arlen, Texas who sells propane gas, loves a beer, sports and a barbecue, and has a wife (substitute teacher Peggy), a son (Bobby) and a blowsy niece named Luanne also living under his roof. Hank wants a quiet life, but in each episode he rarely gets it.

Popular in the US where audiences immediately understand the caricature of Hank being a repressed Southerner, this has only a small cult following in the UK, but it is worth a look for some fun moments as Hank hangs out with his friends, including Dale, a paranoid conspiracy theorist who thinks everyone is out to get him yet doesn't notice his own wife cheating on him, and Boomhauer, a guy popular with the ladies, despite his Texan drawl making anything he says pretty unintelligible.

 TV Trivia: Before he worked in TV, creator (and physics scholar) Mike Judge worked on the electronics of F18 fighter jets.

MONKEY DUST (2003–2005)

Voices by Morwenna Banks, Frances Barber, Peter Dickson, Simon Greenall

The sinister theme music from the band Eels sets the tone – this British animated series from Shaun Pye and Harry Thompson is dark and bleakly humorous, rather than laugh-out-loud funny. Comprised of a series of sketches – with some characters such as Ivan Dobsky, the 'Meat-Safe Murderer' (so named because he allegedly killed a typist at a meat locker), returning each episode – the show has touched on such diverse subjects as paedophilia, Nazis, cannibalism at a wife-swapping party and suicide, while taking stabs at more obvious targets such as reality TV (there is a spoof here called 'People On The Toilet'.)

Highly offensive (at least to *Daily Mail* readers), yet at the same time absurdly funny, it's surprising that a show featuring Geoff the first-time cottager and a group of bumbling terrorists from West Bromwich even made it onto mainstream TV (it was first shown on BBC3, then later repeated on terrestrial BBC). A twisted portrayal of Britain today, it's certainly not for the faint-hearted, but if you want a cynical, if occasionally obvious, look at the world after dark, this could be for you.

 TV Trivia: David Baddiel, actress Morwenna Banks' partner in real life, appears as himself in the series.

MTV'S AEON FLUX (1995)

Voices by Denise Poirer, John Rafter Lee

Aeon Flux began as a series of shorts shown created by Korean animator Peter Chung for MTV in which the character died at the end of every episode – it was then expanded into longer episodes (in which she usually lived), and eventually made into a live action movie with Charlize Theron. A mix of Japanese-style animation and graphic comic images, the series tells of the adventures of Aeon Flux, an ass-kicking gal who works as a deadly double agent, killing, seducing or maiming anyone who gets in her way.

A sort of S&M Barbie, Aeon Flux says very little, but the images of her fighting a dystopian future filled with weird creatures and, in particular, a bad guy who wants to rule the world, are pretty strong (especially if you are a teenage boy admiring her rather scanty battle outfits). It's like an animated version of *The Matrix*, populated with cool but unlikeable characters, a sense of impending doom and some intriguing storylines. Cool.

 TV Trivia: Peter Chung also directed the opening title sequence for the kids' show *Rugrats*.

THE REN AND STIMPY SHOW (1991–1996)

Voices by John Kricfalusi, Billy West, Cheryl Chase

Toilet humour is the order of the day for this cartoon – actually made for kids' channel Nickelodeon – about a hyperactive, skinny chihuahua named Ren (with a Peter Lorre-style voice provided by creator Kricfalusi until he left the show, and later West) and a dumb, chubby cat named Stimpy (West), whose adventures usually involve farting, spitting, bringing up hairballs and vomiting. It's rude and weird, as anything can happen to this undynamic duo, and it usually does – from travelling into space to meeting a superhero named Toastman, whose head is the same shape as a slice of bread.

It's freaky stuff that offended some: one episode, 'Man's Best Friend', was banned from Nickelodeon due to its violence, while parental groups in the US complained that Ren continually abused Stimpy, but it also amused many with its rapid jokes, jerky animation, bonkers characters and silly moments such as the 'Happy Happy Joy Joy' song. Deliciously twisted, if you like that sort of thing.

 TV Trivia: 'The Hanging Song' from the episode 'Out West' has been edited out of the UK DVD because it presents hanging someone as comical and trivial.

THE SIMPSONS (1989–)

Voices by Dan Castellaneta, Julie Kavner, Nancy Cartwright, Yeardley Smith, Hank Azaria, Harry Shearer

Originally a series of short, animated clips that were used as fillers in 1987's *The Tracy Ullman Show*, *The Simpsons* as we know it today first hit the screens in 1989, when the unsuspecting world was properly introduced to the yellow family led by Homer and Marge, along with their kids, under-achiever Bart, bright spark Lisa and baby Maggie. A clever mix of fun stories, sharp one-liners, wry observations and movie and television parodies aimed at both adults and children, over the years the series has been criticised for the way it portrays an all-American family (George Bush Snr. was particularly offended) and also complimented for it (certainly luminaries such as Paul McCartney, Tony Blair and Elizabeth Taylor all seem to approve, as they have all lent their voices to the show).

Now a part of the world's popular culture (Homer's catchphrase 'D'oh!' even appeared in the *Oxford Dictionary*) that has spawned a hit movie and hit song ('Do The Bartman'), the series created by Matt Groening boasts more than 18 seasons of half-hour shows, and a cast of characters that spans out to include many more than just the Simpson family. Fan favourites include Comic Book Guy; Sideshow Bob, Krusty The Clown's ex-sidekick who is intent on killing Bart (Bob is voiced by *Frasier*'s Kelsey Grammer, and when one episode featured Bob's brother Cecil, the voice was provided by Grammer's *Frasier* sibling David Hyde Pierce); evil Mr Burns and his sycophantic assistant Smithers; Kwik-E-Mart shop owner Apu and Bart's ex-soldier headmaster, Principal Skinner.

With so many to choose from, it's almost impossible to recommend the best episodes, but things really hit their stride from Season 3 onwards (in very early episodes the characters are less yellow and some of the voices are different, which makes them less enjoyable if you're used to the Simpsons as they are now), while many fans think that the last few years have been slightly less successful. All of the 'Treehouse Of Horror' episodes (broadcast each year in the US around Halloween) have deliciously bizarre moments, and any episode with Sideshow Bob is worth a look, along with classics like 'Marge Vs The Monorail' (Season 4, guest voice Leonard Nimoy), Cape Feare (Season 5 – who knew Sideshow Bob being hit by brooms could be so funny?) and the Bond parody 'You Only Move Twice' (Season 8).

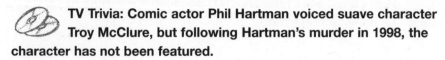 **TV Trivia: Comic actor Phil Hartman voiced suave character Troy McClure, but following Hartman's murder in 1998, the character has not been featured.**

SOUTH PARK (1997–)

Voices by Trey Parker, Matt Stone, Isaac Hayes

Parker and Stone's animated TV series scored such a success that their anarchic show became a movie (1999's *South Park: Bigger, Longer and Uncut*) long before *The Simpsons* did. Rude and fantastically crude, the primitively animated series follows the misfortunes of four eight-year-old kids – Cartman,

Kyle, Stan and Kenny – who live in the mountain town of South Park. Kyle and Stan are the reasonably sensible ones, so it is Cartman (angry, fat and foul-mouthed) and anorak-wearing Kenny (who, for the first few series, is killed off in nearly every episode to the cry of 'Oh my god, they killed Kenny!') who steal the show, along with characters such as teacher Mr Garrison, Big Gay Al, Mr Hankey the Christmas Poo, wise and sexy Chef (voiced by soul singer Hayes), Satan (who is gay) and his best pal, Saddam Hussein. New characters have also been added in recent years, including Towelie (a talking towel often seen smoking dope), sweet little Butters, Token Black and wheelchair-bound (except he isn't, really) Timmy.

The early episodes are the funniest and most enjoyably vulgar, especially 'Cartman Gets An Anal Probe', which is pretty self-explanatory, and 'Mecha Streisand', in which a robot monster Barbra Streisand terrorises the towns-people. Many of the episodes parody celebrities and current events, and particularly sharp ones include 'The Passion of The Jew' (a spoof of Mel Gibson's *The Passion of The Christ*) and 'It's Christmas in Canada', depicting the capture of Saddam Hussein. Another funny animated show featuring a Satan character, *God, The Devil and Bob*, is unfortunately not available on DVD at the present time.

 TV Trivia: Isaac Hayes, who sadly died in 2008, reportedly quit the role of Chef in 2006 due to the way his religion, Scientology, was portrayed.

CHILDREN

JUST ABOUT EVERY CURRENT SHOW LOVED BY KIDS – FROM *LAZYTOWN* TO *SPONGEBOB SQUAREPANTS* AND *SHAUN THE SHEEP* TO *DORA THE EXPLORER* – IS AVAILABLE ON DVD AND TO LIST THEM WOULD BE TO TAKE OVER THIS BOOK. AND WE'D RATHER SPEND THE TIME REMEMBERING THOSE CLASSIC SHOWS FROM OUR OWN CHILDHOODS, ANYWAY...

Note: Only the 21st-century versions of classics *Noddy*, *Rupert Bear* and *Andy Pandy* are available, so sadly they can't be included here.

THE ADVENTURES OF BLACK BEAUTY (1972–1974)

Anna Sewell's classic story of the beautiful, black thoroughbred horse that wins the heart of many was the basis (in the loosest sense) for this series set in 19th-century England. Brought into the Gordon household by father James, Beauty is soon 'adopted' by his children Vicky (Judi Bowker), Jenny (Stacy Dorning) and Kevin (Roderick Shaw), who take the horse on various adventures that usually involve scrapes where only the horse can save the day. So sweet and girly, the DVD should come wrapped in a big pink bow.

 TV Trivia: Author Sewell was reportedly only paid £40 when *Black Beauty* **was published.**

BAGPUSS (1974)

'Once upon a time, not so long ago, there was a little girl and her name was Emily, and she had a shop. It was rather an unusual shop because it didn't sell anything. You see, everything in that shop window was a thing that somebody had once lost, and Emily had found, and brought home to Bagpuss.' So began each episode of this delightful series, in which cloth cat Bagpuss and the other creatures in the shop – a wooden bookend that looked like a woodpecker, mice carved on the side of a mouse organ – would come to life (and the action would change from sepia to colour stop-motion animation) to see what new lost item had been placed on the window for the owner to collect. Delightfully nostalgic, this adorable series remains much loved. Only 13 episodes were made.

 TV Trivia: Creator Peter Firmin's daughter played Emily.

BARNEY (1992–)

Barney is the dopey-voiced purple dinosaur you either think has kitsch charm and a sweet message for toddlers ('I love you, you love me…' etc), or is deeply creepy and, in the words of one website user: 'an evil, brain-sucking alien'. Numerous enjoyably sadistic website games have demonstrated various ways that Barney (aka 'the purple anti-Christ') can be stopped, but while grown-ups debate his merits, tots still worship the bumbling creature. Oh well.

 TV Trivia: The man in the purple dinosaur suit is actor David Joyner, who has also appeared on the more adult series *ER*, 24 and *House*.

THE BASIL BRUSH SHOW (1968–1980)

Forget the new 2002 version in which Basil seems to have been given a new nose as well as more PC-personality, and revel in the old highlights you can get on DVD that feature the cheeky, dirty-laughing, bad-joke-telling fox at his very best. Packed with puns (typical joke: 'What do you call a man with a shark on his head? An ambulance – and quick!'), the hand-puppet-hosted show was a mix of sketches and silliness, with Rodney Bewes, Roy North and Derek Fowlds among the human presenters trying (and deliciously failing) to rein in the chaos. Boom boom!

 TV Trivia: Basil appeared in a French and Saunders spoof of Harry Potter in 2003, as Dobby the house elf.

BOD (1975)

Dad's Army star John Le Mesurier narrated this very basic little animated show about a simply-drawn, bald-headed boy named Bod, his Aunt Flo, Frank the Postman, Farmer Barleymow and PC Copper. Based on the books by Joanna and Michael Cole, the series of 13 episodes featured music by Derek Griffiths (best known, of course, for his appearances on *Playschool*) and is best-remembered for the opening line 'Here comes Bod…' and that chirpy flute theme tune.

 TV Trivia: Bod was called Gus in the French version of the series.

THE BORROWERS (1992)

Forget the 1995 film, this TV series is the best version of Mary Norton's much-loved stories about the family of tiny six-inch high people who live in the nooks and crannies of human homes and borrow all they need to survive. Ian Holm is simply superb as dad Pod Clock, and there's nice support from Penelope Wilton as over-protective mum Homily, Rebecca Callard as rebellious daughter Arietty and Paul Cross as George, the human boy who discovers them. The miniature effects are terrific, too.

 TV Trivia: Keep your eyes peeled for a young Ben Chaplin (*The Thin Red Line, Game On*) as Ditchley.

THE BOX OF DELIGHTS (1984)

John Masefield's children's novel gets the lavish BBC treatment, as young boy Kay (Devin Stanfield) gets drawn into a strange world after meeting immortal wanderer Cole Hawkins (Patrick Troughton). Together, they have to keep the Box of Delights from falling into the hands of a bunch of evil wolves disguised as clerics, led by the nefarious Abner Brown (Robert Stephens).

 TV Trivia: Julian Sands has a small role as a Greek soldier.

BUTTON MOON (1980–1988)

Very simple puppet show for toddlers, *Button Moon* followed the adventures of Mr Spoon, who travels to Button Moon in each episode in his homemade (from a plastic funnel and baked bean tin) rocket ship, and has a little adventure there with his wife Mrs Spoon, their daughter, Tina Teaspoon and her pal Eggbert. Sweet but forgettable – the best bit was the theme tune sung by ex-*Doctor Who* Peter Davison and his then-wife Sandra Dickinson.

 TV Trivia: A Button Moon stage show successfully toured the UK in the late eighties.

CAMBERWICK GREEN (1966); TRUMPTON (1967); CHIGLEY (1969)

Brian Cant narrated these much-loved stop-motion animated series that began with *Camberwick Green*. Each episode began with a music box that opened to reveal the character who would be the focus of that episode, be it villager Dr Mopp, town gossip Mrs Honeyman or windmill owner Windy Miller. *Trumpton* followed, with each instalment beginning with the town hall clock and then later featuring the firemen being called out ('Pugh! Pugh! Barney McGrew! Cuthbert! Dibble! Grub!'), though never to an actual fire. Finally, there was the less memorable *Chigley*, which often featured Windy Miller or the *Trumpton* firecrew in cameo appearances.

 TV Trivia: Windy Miller and his pals have found a new career advertising Quaker Oats. Charlie Higson narrates the adverts.

CAPTAIN PUGWASH (1957–1975)

Crudely animated but fun little show about a pirate ship and its crew, Captain Pugwash is often remembered for the urban myth that arose about the names of the characters. People were convinced the show featured characters named Seaman Staines and Master Bates, but, funny as that is, it's not true. Instead the Captain sailed the high seas on his ship (the *Black Pig*) with pirates Barnabas and Willy, cabin boy Tom and Master Mate. Never mind, it was still funny.

 TV Trivia: Pugwash began life as a comic strip in the first issue of *The Eagle* in 1950 and later in the *Radio Times*.

CATWEAZLE (1970–1971)

Created by Richard Carpenter, who was also behind kids TV shows *Dick Turpin* and *The Ghosts of Motley Hall*, Catweazle was the odd story of a rather bonkers (and creepy looking) 11th-century wizard (Geoffrey Bayldon) who travels through time and ends up in 1970. He's hidden by a young boy and spends the episodes marvelling at modern magics such as 'electrickery' while attempting to find a way home. Broadly comic, this was either viewed as great fun by kids at the time or as something utterly scary and evil (by this one).

 TV Trivia: Carpenter saw the name Catweazle written on a gatepost in the Sussex countryside and it made him think of a magician and led to the creation of the series.

CHAMPION THE WONDER HORSE (1955–1956)

A black-and-white western adventure for kids, this series told of the friendship between the rather wonderful wild stallion Champion and 12-year-old boy Ricky (Barry Curtis) in the American South-West of the 1880s. Ricky seemed to spend the entire time getting himself into trouble, but good old Champion always came to the rescue along with Ricky's German Shepherd Rebel.

TV Trivia: There were four horses that played Champion over the years in the series and the Gene Autry movies that started it all off. One of them has his hoofprints cemented outside Mann's Chinese Theater in Hollywood.

'CHARLEY SAYS...' (1973)

Over 300 live and animated public information short films – many warning children about the dangers of crossing the roads and speaking to strangers, etc – have been collected together on DVD, including Alvin Stardust telling us to 'be smart, be safe', Jon Pertwee extolling the virtues of the Green Cross Code and, most memorably of all, the minute-long ones in which animated cat Charley warned us not to play with matches, and never to go off without telling Mummy where you were going (it was a simpler time...)

 TV Trivia: One of the segments, 'Lonely Water' (about the dangers of drowning), was voted one of the scariest things ever shown on TV.

CHILDREN OF THE STONES (1977)

An almost legendarily creepy TV series. Adam Brake (Gareth Thomas) and his son Matthew (Peter Demin) go to the village of Milbury to study the 4,000-year-old stone circle around it. However, it seems the stones may be an ancient power that has entralled the village – a power that the creepy Mr Henrick (Iain Cuthbertson) may be trying to tap into... Scary stuff from the producer of the equally enjoyable *Into the Labyrinth* (recently released on DVD).

 TV Trivia: The stone circle used in the series is around the village of Avebury in Wiltshire.

CHOCKY (1984); CHOCKY'S CHILDREN (1985) CHOCKY'S CHALLENGE (1986)

Based on John Wyndham's novel *The Day of the Triffids*, *Chocky* was the terrific sci-fi story about Matthew (Andrew Ellams) who is befriended by an extraterrestrial mind wanting to find out about life on Earth. Surprisingly sinister for children's TV, the three series followed Matthew as Chocky infinitely expanding his knowledge and powerful groups tried to find out what was going on.

TV Trivia: Star Ellams never acted on screen again and is now an economics professor.

CHORLTON AND THE WHEELIES (1976–1979)

If you think *The Magic Roundabout* (which, sadly, isn't on DVD) was psychedelic, check out this bizarre TV series about the Wheelies, who live in Wheelie World, and are miserable because the evil witch Fenella has cast a spell on them. Luckily the Wheelies (who, naturally, are little potato-like creatures on wheels) find an egg that hatches out Chorlton, a happiness dragon who makes everything better by foiling Fenella's latest plan by the end of each episode. Exceedingly irritating unless you're stoned.

 TV Trivia: The series was co-written by Brian Trueman, who played the voice of Stiletto in *Danger Mouse*.

THE CHRONICLES OF NARNIA (1988–1990)

A well thought-out BBC production, *The Chronicles of Narnia* covered four of CS Lewis's popular books – *The Lion, The Witch and The Wardrobe*; *Prince Caspian*; *The Voyage of the Dawn Treader* and *The Silver Chair*. They are, of course, the stories of Peter, Susan, Edmund and Lucy, who find the entrance to the world of Narnia hidden at the back of a wardrobe, and discover a world of flying horses, talking fauns, a majestic lion and an evil snow queen. While not as flashy as the recent 2005 movie, these series are enjoyable to watch and feature a cast including Barbara Kellerman, Samuel West, Warwick Davies and Tom Baker.

 TV Trivia: The other three books in Lewis' series were not filmed as they were deemed too expensive.

THE CLANGERS (1969–1974)

Hugely tiresome series about the long-nosed, knitted Clangers who live beneath the surface of a planet making irritating flute-like noises at each other. In the narration they were described as gentle mouse-like creatures, and each gratingly whimsical episode involved them doing things like eating blue string pudding or getting soup from the Soup Dragon. Created by Oliver Postgate and Peter Firmin, who also made the much nicer *Bagpuss* (reviewed on p.122) and *Noggin the Nog* (which isn't currently on DVD).

 TV Trivia: Narrator Postgate also provided narration for *Noggin The Nog*, *Bagpuss* and *Ivor the Engine*.

DANGER MOUSE (1981–1992)

'He's the greatest, he's fantastic, wherever there is danger he'll be there...'
So began the theme song for one of the funniest animated kids shows ever
made. Danger Mouse was the British super agent with an eyepatch who saves
the world from various dastardly criminals with the help of his trusty but
rather timid sidekick, hamster Penfold. A spoof of James Bond-style adventures, this was hilarious for all ages and benefited from terrific vocal
performances of David Jason as DM and Terry Scott as Penfold.

 **TV Trivia: Count Duckula, which became a popular series for
kids, originally appeared on this show.**

DARK SEASON (1991)

Russell T. Davies – who went on to revamp *Doctor Who* for the 21st century –
was the creator of this cracking six-episode sci-fi series that also marked one
of Kate Winslet's first major roles. Marcie (Victoria Lambert), Reet
(Winslet) and Thomas (Ben Chandler) notice strange goings-on at their
school that seem to originate with the creepy Mr Eldritch (Grant Parsons).
Seems he has a plan to rule the world and only the three kids can stop him...

 **TV Trivia: Winslet's first appearance on TV was in an episode
of *Casualty*.**

DICK TURPIN (1979–1982)

Richard O'Sullivan – best known, of course, as star of *Man About The House* –
got serious (well, sort of) for the 18th-century swashbuckling adventures of
legendary highwayman Dick Turpin. With the help of young Swiftnick
(Michael Deeks), Dick robbed the rich, occasionally gave to the poor and also
helped the occasional damsel while trying to find ways to irritate the baddie
of the piece – Sir John Glutton (Christopher Benjamin). It's about as historically
accurate as a fairy story, but that doesn't mean it isn't heaps of fun.

 **TV Trivia: One of the series' writer/directors was Charles
Crichton, best known for directing *The Lavender Hill Mob* and
A Fish Called Wanda.**

DO NOT ADJUST YOUR SET (1967–1969)

Before *Monty Python*, there was this children's TV series featuring Eric Idle,
Michael Palin and Terry Jones, who shared the screen alongside David Jason,

Denise Coffey and the Bonzo Dog Doo-Dah Band. There were parodies of grown-up shows (and, gasp, even a sketch with a naked Eric Idle) but this was aimed at kids, which is apparent in some of the infectious, childish humour and slapstick. Regular sketches included ones featuring the bowler-hatted Captain Fantastic (Jason) and animated segments from another Python member, Terry Gilliam.

 TV Trivia: Elton John named his album 'Captain Fantastic' after the character in the series.

DOCTOR SNUGGLES (1979)

An animated adventure from Germany (although it was written and created by Brit Jeffrey O'Kelly), dubbed into English with Peter Ustinov providing some of the voices. Dr Snuggles is a kind and gentle fellow, who lives at the edge of a wood and can communicate with anything, including the animal friends who take him on various adventures around the world. Memorable characters in this sweet little series included the robot Mathilda Junkbottom, housekeeper Miss Nettles and Knobby the mouse, while Snuggles' inventions included the Dreamy Boom Boom rocket and the Multi-Whereabouts Machine.

 TV Trivia: *Hitchhiker's Guide to the Galaxy* author Douglas Adams wrote one of the episodes.

DOGTANIAN (1981)

Or, to give this series its correct name: 'D'Artacan y los tres mosqueperros'. Alexandre Dumas' famous Musketeer, D'Artagnian, gets a canine makeover for this Spanish/Japanese production as Dogtanian and his three doggy pals try to protect the French royal family from evil Cardinal Richlieu's schemes. Twenty-six half-hour episodes of this simple but funny cartoon were made and are available on DVD.

 TV Trivia: Cam Clarke provided Dogtanian's voice – he also voiced two of the Teenage Mutant Ninja Turtles.

FINGERBOBS (1972)

Unfortunately, it's just an urban myth that Oscar-winner Jeremy Irons appeared on *Fingerbobs* (he actually pranced around with toddlers on another kids' show, *Play Away*, that sadly isn't on DVD) – instead it was Rick Jones as

Yoffy who wore various coloured gloves and a paper finger puppet to represent mouse Fingermouse, Gulliver the seagull, Scampi the, erm, scampi, and other characters including Flash the tortoise. Cute if you're under five.

 TV Trivia: Jones was also a regular presenter of *Play School* and *Play Away*.

THE FLUMPS (1976)

A group of furry creatures that basically looked like fluffy tennis balls with big eyes, the Flumps were Grandpa Flump (complete with cloth cap), Mother and Father Flump and kids Posie, Perkin and Pootle. It was all incredibly cute and sweet, as the mini-flumps learned important lessons about life from their mum while Grandpa dozed and dad did DIY, but only 13 episodes were made.

 TV Trivia: The Flumps were made of papier mache covered in fur, while their legs and arms were metal covered with chamois leather.

THE GHOSTS OF MOTLEY HALL (1976-1978)

A children's comedy about the ghosts that haunt the 16th-century mansion Motley Hall. There's pompous Sir George Uproar (Freddie Jones), 18th-century fop Fanny Uproar (Nicholas le Provost), Bodkin the jester (Arthur English), Matt the stable boy (Sean Flanagan) and the White Lady (Sheila Steafel), who all haunt the house and scare the living daylights out of poor Mr Gudgin (Peter Sallis), the estate agent trying to sell it. The effects are hilariously bad, but the humour is often rib-ticklingly silly.

 TV Trivia: Arthur English was a painter and decorator until 1949, when he auditioned to be a comic at the Windmill Theatre in London.

GRANGE HILL (1978-2008)

A groundbreaking show in its depiction of life at a London comprehensive. Any child of the seventies and eighties (definitely the series' golden age) will probably still have a favourite pupil or teacher from Phil Redmond's sharp school-set show, be it from the earliest cast that featured ruffian Tucker Jenkins (Todd Carty), Trisha Yates (Michelle Herbert), with her permanent scowl and wind-defying flicked-back hair, and decidedly unfit-looking sports teacher

'Bullet' Baxter (Michael Cronin). The storyline featuring Zammo's (Lee MacDonald) drug abuse made newspaper headlines, the introduction of a gay teacher in 1992 was handled skilfully, and the series has also focused on teen suicide and rape – it was originally aimed at teenagers but in recent years became less hard-hitting and more humorous as it moved from BBC1 to CBBC, whose target audience is children under 12.

 TV Trivia: The late Anthony Minghella, the Oscar-winning director of *The English Patient*, was a former script editor for *Grange Hill*.

H R PUFNSTUF (1969)

The name of this quirky show was possibly the least weird thing about it. Young Jimmy (*Oliver!*'s Jack Wild) and his magic flute, Freddie, who can talk, are captured by the evil Witchiepoo (Billie Hayes), who wants Freddie for herself. Luckily they are rescued by dragon Pufnstuf (Lennie Weinrib), who lives on an enchanted isle where everything (including the books, houses etc) are alive. A bizarre mix of songs, scares and silliness, this has to be seen to be believed!

 TV Trivia: The creators of the show successfully sued McDonald's for copyright infringement, noting similarities in the characters of Mayor McCheese and Big Mac to the character of Pufnstuf.

HECTOR'S HOUSE (1965)

French-made puppet series (dubbed into English by the BBC) called *La Maison De Toutou*. Hector the dog and Zsazsa the cat live in a house with a beautiful garden, while Kiki the frog often pops in through her hole in the wall. In each episode poor Hector is tricked by his friends to teach him a lesson, but he never seems to mind. Affable fare for toddlers.

 TV Trivia: Denise Bryer provided the voice of Kiki. She has also been the voice of Noddy and Zelda in *Terrahawks*.

THE HERBS (1968)

Created by *Paddington Bear*'s Michael Bond, *The Herbs* was a lovely TV series (especially if you were a vegetarian) about a group of herbs (played by stop-motion animated puppets) who lived in the garden of Sir Basil and Lady Rosemary. There was Dill the dog, Sage the owl, Aunt Mint, Tarragon the dragon and, of course, Parsley the lion, who got his own spin-off series (1970's *The Adventures of Parsley*). Just as cute as you remember it.

 TV Trivia: Michael Bond was originally a BBC cameraman on series like *Blue Peter* before he created *Paddington* in 1958.

IVOR THE ENGINE (1975–1977)

A black and white series about a small steam engine named Ivor was first shown on British TV in 1958, but it is the version in which the original animation was coloured in that's available on DVD. While not as bright or action-packed (actually, nothing much happens at all) as that other famous show about an engine (see *Thomas the Tank Engine* review, p.140), Ivor was nonetheless a cute animated tale about the Welsh railway line, run by Jones the Steam, along which Ivor puffed along (with a dragon living in his engine). Toot toot!

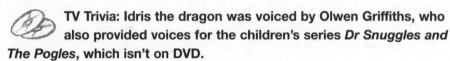 **TV Trivia: Idris the dragon was voiced by Olwen Griffiths, who also provided voices for the children's series *Dr Snuggles and The Pogles*, which isn't on DVD.**

JACKANORY (1965–1996; 2006–)

More than 3,000 episodes of this classic BBC series have been made, sadly only some of the more modern are available on DVD. Created to encourage kids to read, the format was simple – an actor in an armchair reading from a novel or folk tale, sometimes with illustrations mixed in to spice things up. Everyone from Tom Baker to Judi Dench, and Ian McKellen to Prince Charles have read out stories (HRH reading his own book, *The Old Man of Lochnagar*), while Kenneth Williams, Bernard Cribbins and author John Grant each appeared over 50 times each.

 TV Trivia: Alan Bennett's reading of *The House at Pooh Corner* was the final one to be broadcast before the series was cancelled in 1996.

JAMIE AND THE MAGIC TORCH (1976–1979)

The seventies were just as psychedelic as the sixties, if children's TV is to be believed. In this animated show, young Jamie would shine his magic torch on his bedroom floor, a hole would appear and he and his shaggy sheepdog Wordsworth would tumble along a helter-skelter into Cuckoo Land, where they would meet such characters as Mr Boo in his flying submarine, Strumpers Plunkett and Nutmeg the rag doll. Completely nuts, with a rocking theme tune...

 TV Trivia: Tim Brooke-Taylor of *The Goodies* sang the theme tune.

LASSIE (1997)

The most famous dog in the world has been the subject of numerous movies and TV series, including the classic 1954 black and white series and this 1997 update. The stories are much the same, just with more modern surroundings – lovely collie Lassie is taken in by young Timmy and together they have lots of adventures, usually with Lassie saving the boy and the day before the end credits. Not as good as the original, but it'll do.

 TV Trivia: Even though Lassie is a girl, she was always played by male dogs, partly because they don't go 'on heat', but also because it was thought the bigger male dogs looked more impressive on film.

THE LITTLEST HOBO (1979–1985)

Originally a series from 1963–1965, *The Littlest Hobo* was revived in 1979 for a series that ran for six years. The hobo of the title is a German Shepherd dog who wanders from town to town and always finds someone down on their luck or in trouble that he can help (sort of like a four-footed Incredible Hulk). Utterly adorable if you love canines, this also featured the weepy theme tune that began 'There's a voice that keeps on calling me / Down the road, that's where I'll always be...' (Sniff). For the more Western-theme dog series, *The Adventures of Rin Tin Tin*, see page 195.

 TV Trivia: The dog is never given a name in the series, but in real life the dog that played him was called London.

MARY, MUNGO AND MIDGE (1969)

They sound like a sixties pop band from Liverpool, but Mary, Mungo and Midge were in fact three animated characters – a little girl and her dog Mungo and mouse Midge. The trio lived in a tower block and in each episode they would go down in the lift to start their adventure in the town (nowadays, of course, their negligent parents would be reported to the police).

Newsreader Richard Baker narrated for each of the thirteen 15-minute episodes that were made for the BBC.

 TV Trivia: The theme music was written by Johnny Pearson, who also wrote the theme for *All Creatures Great and Small* and ITN's *News at Ten*.

MICHAEL BENTINE'S POTTY TIME (1973–1980)

Former Goon Bentine brought his wonderfully zany humour to children's TV, writing the episodes and doing the voices for this hilarious show about the Potty people: squat little puppets who gave us a potted history of Britain and literary works such as *The Scarlet Pimpernel*. It was quite clever stuff, featuring a potty-sized Sherlock Holmes and Dr Watson one week and a Great Escape spoof, in which British potty soldiers try to escape a Colditz-like POW camp, another.

 TV Trivia: Bentine was offered the role of Dr Who after Jon Pertwee left the series.

MR BENN (1971–1972)

Some would suggest you need to have ingested an illegal substance to truly appreciate the oddness of this animated kids series. In each episode, bowler hat-wearing Mr Benn would leave his house on Festive Road and enter a strange costume shop, try on an outfit and emerge from the fitting room in a different time and place – becoming, perhaps, a cowboy, an astronaut or a pirate, before the shopkeeper appeared to take him back to the shop. Only 13 episodes were made, but each one is a trippy treasure.

 TV Trivia: Festive Road was based on Festing Road in Putney, south London.

MOOMINS (1977–1982, 1990–1992)

Originally twee characters in a set of children's books and comics by Finnish writer Tove Jansson, the Moomins found their way onto TV as early as 1969 in Scandinavia. The versions British kids know are the 1977 Polish one and the 1990s Japanese one, both of which have the wide-eyed creatures – Moominmamma, Moominpappa, Too-ticky, and pals – embarking on a series of pretty dull adventures. We don't get it; we just want to punch them…

 TV Trivia: There is a Moomin World theme park in Naantali, Finland.

MUFFIN THE MULE (1946–1955)

Performed live from Alexandra Palace from 1946–1952 (from then on it was pre-recorded), *Muffin the Mule* was created by Annette Mills, and it was she who presented the series and sang the songs including, of course, the theme 'Here comes Muffin, Muffin the mule...' Ann Hogarth wrote the stories that Mills told the children and also manipulated the puppets – as well as Muffin, there was Sally the Seal, Peregrine the Penguin, kittens Prudence and Primrose and Poppy the Parrot. An animated version of *Muffin the Mule*, made in 2005, is available on DVD but the original black and white puppet show remains the best.

 TV Trivia: Annette Mills was the sister of Sir John Mills.

PADDINGTON (1975–1986)

School-day tea-times for over a decade were signalled by this cute series created by animation company FilmFair and based on the hugely popular Michael Bond books about the polite, marmalade sandwich-loving bear from Peru who went to live with the Brown family at 32 Windsor Gardens. (He was named Paddington, of course, because that was the station where the family first found him.) The show was quirky to look at – the backgrounds were sparsely drawn in black and white, while the characters were drawn and coloured in, and Paddington was the only 3D puppet – and, with the narration of the wonderful Michael Hordern, captured the warmth and cheekiness of the original stories.

 TV Trivia: There is a bronze statue of Paddington at Paddington Station, at the base of an escalator.

PINGU (1986–)

It's easy to see why kids love this series of five-minute episodes from Switzerland – Pingu the penguin is a cheeky little sod who thinks nothing of peeing everywhere when the mood takes him (one concerned parent wrote that he's a 'terrible influence on children', no less). He gets angry, jealous, petulant – exactly like a human toddler – but he does usually learn his lesson before the episode is over. In 1989, *Baywatch*'s David Hasselhoff released a single called 'Pingu Dance', based on the show. Scary.

 TV Trivia: The honking sounds Pingu and his fellow penguins make is, apparently, called Pinguish.

THE PINK PANTHER SHOW (1969–1976, 1978–1979)

Also known as *The New Pink Panther Show* and then *The All New Pink Panther Show*, this animated series featured the pink cat-like creature originally created for the opening titles of the *Pink Panther* movies starring Peter Sellers. Each episode, he would outwit some foe, and his adventures would be mixed with other cartoon shorts featuring such characters as the ant and the aardvark, Misterjaws, the near-sighted shark and dimwitted bird Crazylegs Crane. A newer version (unavailable on DVD, thank goodness) in 1993 had the formerly silent Panther actually speaking (voiced by Matt Frewer).

 TV Trivia: In the opening titles, theme music author Henry Mancini is seated in the theatre.

PIPKINS (1973–1981)

A quirky, much-loved puppet TV show featuring Pig, Topov the monkey, Tortoise, Hartley Hare and Octavia the ostrich, this series featured the characters going out into the world to teach children about important things such as going to school and visiting the dentist. Very funny in places, especially when the loud Hartley Hare was about, this was also groundbreaking in its casting of black presenters (Wayne Lareya) as early as 1974.

 TV Trivia: George Woodbridge, who played puppetmaker Inigo Pipkins, died during the second series and, unusually, the death of his character was explained to the young viewers.

POSTMAN PAT (1981–1996; 2004–)

Possibly the only TV show to make being a postman seem (almost) cool, stop-motion animated series *Postman Pat* followed the gentle adventures of mailman Pat Clifton, who delivers the post in the village of Greendale with his black and white cat Jess by his side. Aimed at toddlers, it's sweet, inoffensive stuff as Pat helps the villagers with the problem of the day. A newer version of the series, with the addition of an Asian family, a 4x4-driving vet, and other 'modern' twists (including a jazzed-up version of the theme tune, sung by narrator Ken Barrie) began in 2004.

 TV Trivia: After the first eight episodes, the Royal Mail gave the series-makers permission to use their logo on Pat's van.

PRESS GANG (1989–1993)

Julia Sawalha, Lucy Benjamin, Sadie Frost and Dexter Fletcher were among the young actors who starred in this drama about a group of kids working on the children's newspaper 'Junior Gazette'. Ground-breaking at the time, the series tackled such serious subjects as teen suicide, sexual abuse, and drug addiction, but also featured a nice ironic sense of humour that endeared it to kids.

 TV Trivia: Headmaster Bill Moffat came up with the idea for the series and his son Steven, also a teacher, wrote it.

RAINBOW (1972–1992)

An entertaining show with human presenters (Geoffrey Hayes being the best known) and a group of cheeky puppets, the huge teddy bear-like Bungle, the slow-talking, shy pink hippo George and, of course, the wide-mouthed wise ass that was Zippy. There was singing (in later years, courtesy of permanently chipper Rod, Jane and Freddy), little documentaries about kids' lives and animated segments – much in the same vein as the US's *Sesame Street*. But they never had a character as teeth-gratingly annoying as Zippy...

 TV Trivia: To this day, no-one knows quite what animal Zippy was meant to be.

RENTAGHOST (1976–1984)

A fun teatime comedy, *Rentaghost* followed the antics of ghosts who were hired out to the public by Harold and Ethel Meaker. There was Timothy Claypole, the ghost of a court jester; Hazel McWitch, a Scottish witch; Nadia Popov, a Dutch ghost who disappeared every time she sneezed (which was often, as she suffered from hay fever); stuffy Victorian gentleman Hubert Davenport and the original (newly deceased) founder of Rentaghost, Fred Mumford. Very funny in the first few years, this got a bit worn at the edges by the eighties, when established cast members left and new characters were introduced.

 TV Trivia: Prime Suspect author Lynda La Plante played witch Tamara Novek under her stage name, Lynda Marchal.

ROBIN HOOD (2006–)

If you like your Robin Hood swashbuckling and dashing, this gritty new BBC series is not for you. It's all a bit irritatingly modern; despite being set in medieval times, the cast are kitted out in hoodies, T-shirts and desert boots – and there's a subtext commenting on modern politics that runs through the series. Jonas Armstrong isn't bad as Robin, but Richard Armitage steals the show as baddie Guy of Gisbourne, while Keith Allen chews the scenery as the Sheriff of Nottingham. Traditionalists should instead seek out the classic 1955–1960 series *The Adventures of Robin Hood* with Richard Greene.

 TV Trivia: When the first series was being filmed in Budapest, some of the tapes were stolen and thieves demanded £1 million for their return.

ROBIN OF SHERWOOD (1984–1986)

Yes, we know adults liked this Robin Hood drama too, but it was boys who tuned in for the arrow fights and punch-ups and girls who watched for dashing Robin (played by dark-haired Michael Praed in the first two series, then by blond Jason Connery). More mystical than most Robin Hood series (backed by a spooky Clannad theme tune), the show featured a forest spirit to guide Robin in the form of Herne the Hunter, as well as his traditional gang of merry men, including Will Scarlet (Ray Winstone), Friar Tuck (Phil Rose) and Little John (Clive Mantle). Cracking adventure telly, with great bad guys in the form of Nikolas Grace and Robert Addie.

 TV Trivia: Jenny Seagrove was the original choice for Maid Marian before Judi Trott won the role.

ROOBARB (1974)

Only 30 episodes were made of this series, best remembered for its characteristic 'wobbly' animation. Narrated by Richard Briers, each episode followed the adventures of enthusiastic green dog Roobarb and the rather more cynical Custard the pink cat. With the catchy theme tune by Johnny Hawksworth, the sweet series soon became cult viewing just before the BBC evening news and has been oft repeated over the years. A new, but faithful, version of the series – *Roobarb And Custard Too* – began in 2005.

 TV Trivia: The animators used marker pens to animate the characters and get that distinctive 'wobble'.

THE SECRET GARDEN (1975)

One of many versions of Frances Hodgson Burnett's much loved story about a young orphaned girl named Mary who is sent to live with her uncle on his estate in the Yorkshire moors. It is there she finds a secret overgrown garden and later discovers hidden in the house a cousin she never knew existed. It's not a bad adaptation, although the garden itself was disappointingly built on a set, but the 1993 film of the book is much better.

 TV Trivia: A letter written to the *New York Times* after Frances Hodgson Burnett's death claimed the inspiration for the secret garden was a rose garden at Great Maytham Hall in Kent.

SKIPPY THE BUSH KANGAROO (1966)

The Aussie alternative to *Lassie*, Skippy the kangaroo always came to the rescue when bush ranger Matt (Ed Deveraux) or his son Sonny (Garry Pankhurst) and his pals got into trouble. Whether they were tangling with rustlers or escaped convicts, the series is best remembered for the jaunty theme song, the often visible hands of the crew pushing the poor kangaroo into a scene, and the tut-tut exchanges Skippy had with his boy owner that seemed to explain the entire plot.

TV Trivia: The clicking noises Skippy made aren't made by real kangaroos.

SOOTY (1968–1993)

The yellow and black teddy bear hand-puppet named Sooty first appeared – with human Harry Corbett – on TV in 1952. He didn't speak (he just whispered in Harry's ear) but he immediately enchanted kids with his magic wand ('Izzy, wizzy, let's get busy!') and cheeky antics, along with his pals, dog Sweep and panda Soo. When Harry retired, son Matthew took over and later picked Richard Cadell and Liana Bridges to replace him as Sooty's pal. Later series were known as *The Sooty Show* and *Sooty & Co.*

TV Trivia: The makers of *Sooty* were criticised for allowing Sooty to hit character PC Nab over the head with a toy hammer as it was deemed to be anti-police.

THOMAS THE TANK ENGINE & FRIENDS (1984–)

Also known as *Thomas & Friends*, this long-running series is based on the books and characters created by the Reverend W. Audry for his son Christopher. Using miniature trains and sets to depict the island of Sodor (which looks like a slice of 1920s Cornwall complete with beach, castle, lighthouse and mountain), the episodes tell the stories of cheeky blue train Thomas and his friends, including Harold the helicopter and Bertie the bus. For the first 13 episodes, former Beatle Ringo Starr provided the narration and the action looked a little ropey, but when the series returned in the nineties it was slicker, with a theme tune, flashier animation, and even special effects. Michael Angelis provided the narration.

 TV Trivia: Pierce Brosnan is taking over the narration of the series because his children loved the books so much.

THUNDERBIRDS (1965–1966)

Filmed in 'Supermarionation' (puppets whose strings you could see, basically) by creator Gerry Anderson, *Thunderbirds* captured the imagination of British kids who tuned in to watch avidly the adventures of International Rescue, a secret organisation dedicated to saving lives set up by wealthy ex-astronaut Jeff Tracy. Using hi-tech Thunderbirds craft, his five sons blast off to the rescue, while Lady Penelope and her chauffeur Parker speed around on terra firma. Cracking stuff, and its predecessors, *Fireball XL5*, *Supercar* and *Stingray*, and the later *UFO* and *Captain Scarlet* from Anderson are also available on DVD (as is Anderson's human/puppet cop/sci-fi show *Space Precinct*, but that is best left on the shelf).

 TV Trivia: Lady Penelope's home is modelled on Stourhead House in Wiltshire.

TIMESLIP (1970–1971)

Teenagers Simon (Spencer Banks) and Liz (Cheryl Burfield) stumble across a strange noise near a military base, and the next thing they know they have fallen through a barrier and also tumbled through time. Over 26 episodes, the pair travel backwards and forwards in time and to alternative realities, each time encountering the creepy Commander Traynor (Dennis Quilley) in various different guises. Cracking stuff from writer Ruth Boswell, who also contributed to *The Tomorrow People*.

TV Trivia: Some episodes were filmed in black and white, due to a technicians' strike at ITV.

TISWAS (1974–1982)

ITV's Saturday morning show for nearly a decade, *Tiswas* (Today Is Saturday, Wear A Smile) was sillier than BBC's alternative *Multi-Coloured Swap Shop* as Chris Tarrant, Sally James, Lenny Henry and Bob Carolgees (with puppet Spit the Dog) threw custard pies at the audience, doused them in water (The Bucket of Water Song becoming a chart hit) and had the Phantom Flan Flinger cover them in goo. Best of… DVDs are available.

 TV Trivia: Sally James gave up TV after *Tiswas* to raise her son.

THE TOMORROW PEOPLE (1973–1979)

Remembered for its creaky sets and awful special effects, *The Tomorrow People* told the story of a group of children who discovered in adolescence that they had special powers of telepathy, teleportation (which they managed by touching special belt buckles, and called 'jaunting') and telekinesis, which came in handy when they had to fight nasty extra terrestrials. Camp rather than scary, this show is hideously dated (the clothes! the hair!) but it's still fun. A new version was made in 1992 but wasn't as enjoyable as the original. It is available on DVD.

 TV Trivia: Actor Nicholas Young got the role of John by repeatedly sending the producers his CV and photograph while he had a part-time job at his agent's office.

TRANSFORMERS (1984–1988)

First came the fiddly Japanese toys, then came this cartoon based on the robots that could transform into other vehicles and animals. According to the series, these robots were aliens split into two different factions – the evil Decepticons and the nicer Autobots – who had lain dormat on Earth for centuries before popping up to do battle in the 1980s. One for boys who love toys, this is incomprehensible to anyone over the age of 14, but boasts flashy action for fans.

 TV Trivia: The first ever Transformer to appear in the series is Wheeljack.

THE WALTONS (1972–1981)

The saga of the Walton family is often compared to that other family drama *The Little House on the Prairie* (see review, p.201), which is set in the 19th century while *The Waltons* has the depression of the 1930s as its backdrop. It's a bit grimmer, too, as the large family endure various hardships over the years as seen through the eyes of son John-Boy (Richard Thomas), an aspiring novelist (and, dare we add, annoying little sod).

Best remembered for the scene which ended almost every episode of all the family members saying goodnight to each other, this is missable sugary-sweet fare. (Another reason to avoid: in a speech about American values, George Bush said he wanted American families to be 'more like The Waltons and less like The Simpsons.' Boo.)

 TV Trivia: The Walton house was actually a set on the Warner Brothers lot in Burbank that has also been used in the series Gilmore Girls.

WILLO THE WISP (1981)

If you were a kid in the early eighties you either loved this odd little animated series narrated/voiced by Kenneth Williams or more likely found it a bit weird and creepy. Willo the Wisp was the puff of smoke who narrated the tales about the residents of Doyley Wood – Arthur the caterpillar, Mavis the chubby fairy, dopey dog The Moog, The Beast (a prince transformed into a bumbling hulk) and Evil Edna, a sort of walking TV set with witchy powers. It was all very strange in an annoying sort of way, and a new 2005 version was no better – and, horror of horrors, to keep up with modern times Edna is now a widescreen TV!

 TV Trivia: In his diaries, Kenneth Williams wrote that he hated the show and thought it would fail.

THE WIND IN THE WILLOWS (1983, 2006)

Two TV versions of Kenneth Grahame's classic story are available on DVD, the stop-motion animated series from 1983 featuring the voices of David Jason (Toad), Michael Hordern (Badger) and Ian Carmichael (Rat) and the flashy new version featuring actors playing the animal roles (Matt Lucas is Toad, Mark Gattis is Ratty and Bob Hoskins is Badger). While the new version is charming, we still have a soft spot for the eighties one, in which, of course, things start to go wrong when Toad becomes obsessed with his new car and ends up in jail for reckless driving...

TV Trivia: Kenneth Grahame wrote the stories to amuse his young son.

THE WOMBLES (1973–1975)

Forget the late 1990s version (in which, shock horror, our cuddly friends have gained such hi-tech items as a helicopter) and instead fondly remember the wonderful Bernard Cribbins-narrated series about the Wombles of Wimbledon Common, who 'make the most of the things that we find, the things that the everyday folk leave behind' (presumably the newer version should have them making interesting things from discarded needles and condoms). Every child of the seventies had a favourite Womble – muscular Tomsk, lazy Orinoco, bossy Bungo, studious Wellington – but, let's face it, every one of those stop-motion animated figures was utterly adorable – even strict Uncle Bulgaria.

 TV Trivia: Creator Elisabeth Beresford got the name for her creatures when her children said 'Wombledon Common' while they were out walking on Wimbledon Common in London.

WORZEL GUMMIDGE (1979–1981, 1986–1989)

One of our favourite Doctor Whos, Jon Pertwee, created another iconic character for this love-it or (more likely) hate-it series. Worzel, the walking, talking scarecrow with interchangeable heads (he had a 'singing head' for example, which he put on when he wanted to warble), lived in Ten Acre Field and got up to various mischievous antics that the two children he befriended, John and Sue, usually had to get him out of. He had his own teeth-gnashingly annoying language (Worzelese), loved the snobby doll Aunt Sally (played by Una Stubbs) and ended up down under for an eighties New Zealand spin-off.

 TV Trivia: Worzel's first appearance was on the radio, before World War II on *Children's Hour*.

HANNA BARBERA FUN

WILLIAM HANNA AND JOSEPH BARBERA PRODUCED SOME OF TV'S MOST SUCCESSFUL CARTOONS IN THE SIXTIES, SEVENTIES AND EIGHTIES. SADLY SOME – *HUCKLEBERRY HOUND*, *YOGI BEAR*, *MAGILLA GORILLA*, *THE JETSONS* AND *JONNY QUEST* AMONG THEM – ARE ONLY AVAILABLE ON DVD IN THE US, BUT BRITS CAN ENJOY THESE:

THE FLINTSTONES (1960–1966)

Yabba-dabba-doo! Everyone loves the prehistoric adventures of dopey Fred Flintstone, his long-suffering wife Wilma, pal Barney Rubble and Barney's wife Betty (not forgetting kids Pebble and Bam-Bam, and Dino the pet dinosaur who flattened Fred at the beginning of each episode). Set in the stone-age town of Bedrock, this animated sitcom was much loved for all the little touches, from the cars powered by feet to the woolly mammoth that doubled as a vacuum cleaner, and the prehistoric puns littered throughout. Still as fun four decades on from when it was first broadcast – without this show, *The Simpsons* would never have existed.

HONG KONG PHOOEY (1974–1976)

Hilarious cartoon about the mild-mannered police station janitor (a dog) who has an alter ego – crime-fighting, karate-chopping Hong Kong Phooey (voiced by Scatman Crothers). Any kid who watched this will remember Rosemary, the telephone operator, Phooey's method of changing from everyday guy to hero (running into a filing cabinet), the Phooeymobile, and his sidekick, cat Spot, who is really the one who helps Hong Kong Phooey out of the jams he gets himself into. Just brilliant.

SCOOBY DOO (1969–)

Beginning with *Scooby Doo, Where Are You?*, the quivering mutt and his pals – the Mystery Inc gang – have appeared in a series of TV shows in various incarnations. The most familiar versions feature crime-solving teens Daphne (the one with glasses and a pudding-bowl haircut), blond 'hunk' Fred, pretty Velma and the perpetually terrified Shaggy along with, of course, pet dog Scooby Doo. The plots are pretty predictable (the bad guy usually has a disguise ripped off in the finale) but the double act of Shaggy and Scooby remains a treat. Avoid the later episodes with Scooby's annoying nephew Scrappy Doo.

TOP CAT (1961–1962)

The comic adventures of a group of New York alley cats, led by Top Cat ('TC'), and featuring members Spook, Benny the Ball, Brain, Choo Choo and Fancy-Fancy. In each episode they usually ran up against dim-witted cop Officer Dibble, who tried to catch out the cats as they tried another illegal way of making money. Only 30 episodes were made, but each one is a treat.

WACKY RACES (1968–1970)

A sort of animated version of *The Cannonball Run*, this series featured 11 racing cars pitted against each other, trying to win the title of World's Wackiest Racer. Among the competitors were Penelope Pitstop in her pink car, the cavemen The Slag Brothers in their Bouldermobile, the Ant Hill Mob, a group of gangsters in a 1920s car and, of course, the nefarious Dick Dastardly and his canine sidekick Muttley, whose every cheating plan backfires. Silly and rather repetitive, but fun.

THE GENIUS OF JIM HENSON

ONE OF THE WORLD'S MOST FAMOUS PUPPETEERS, JIM HENSON, WHO SADLY DIED IN 1990, AGED 54, WILL ALWAYS BE REMEMBERED FOR HIS SUPERB SEVENTIES CHILDREN'S SHOWS *THE MUPPETS* AND *SESAME STREET*, AS WELL AS FOR THEIR SPIN-OFF MOVIES (MANY OF WHICH ARE AVAILABLE ON DVD). SADLY, SOME SHOWS FROM HENSON AND THE CREATURE WORKSHOP HE HELPED CREATE, INCLUDING *DINOSAURS*, ARE CURRENTLY NOT AVAILABLE ON DVD IN THE UK, WHILE THE CARTOON SPIN-OFF *MUPPET BABIES* IS ONLY AVAILABLE ON VHS TAPE. FANS SHOULD NOTE THE WORKSHOP ALSO CREATED PUPPETS FOR THE SCI-FI SERIES *FARSCAPE*, WHICH IS REVIEWED ON P.216.

BEAR IN THE BIG BLUE HOUSE (1997–)

Bear (Noel McNeal in a huge bear suit) is a cuddly big bear who, you guessed it, lives in a big blue house, along with Tutter the mouse, Treelo the lemur, Ojo the bear cub and Pip and Pop the otters (all puppets). Each episode has a different topic, whether it is a nervous Tutter's first day at mouse school, or how the group get covered in dirt but learn about the magic of bath time (there's even a potty-training episode that's a great aid for stressed parents). Soulful, R&B-style songs are dotted throughout, while each episode ends with Bear going up to the attic balcony to tell his friend Luna (the moon, as voiced by Lynn Thigpen) about his day and what everyone has learnt. Terrific stuff for tots who'll squeal with delight when Bear does his Bear Cha-cha-cha.

ELMO'S WORLD (1997–)

Elmo is a cute red monster who speaks about himself in the third person (which some parents may not like) and who was originally introduced as a new toddler-friendly character on *Sesame Street*. That led to the spin-off series *Elmo's World*, in which the innocent muppet learns about a different subject per episode (eg School, Dinosaurs, Weather), often with the help of neighbour Mr Noodle (Michael Jeter, who sadly died in 2003) and his brother, Mr Noodle (Bill Irwin). It's sweet stuff, but inevitably led to a much-demanded toy, the Tickle Me Elmo, which most grown-ups want to throttle.

FRAGGLE ROCK (1983–1987)

Delightful puppet series that ran for 96 episodes about creatures that live in a secret underground world. Doc and his dog Sprocket have a hole in their wall and behind it live a civilization of carefree furry creatures called the Fraggles. They share their Fraggle Rock home with the teeny builders Doozers and the giant Gorgs, while one Fraggle – Uncle Matt – explores Outer Space (the human world) and sends postcards back to the Fraggles about the Silly Creatures (humans, of course) he encounters.

An animated version of the show was made in 1987 but is not available on DVD, while *Fraggle Rock: The Movie* is to be released in cinemas in 2009.

THE HOOBS (2000–)

Created by Henson's company, *The Hoobs* features four alien creatures – Iver, Tula, Roma and Groove – who have travelled from Hoobland to Earth to discover things about us and record them in their Hoobopaedia. In each episode, there is usually a song, a question posed to children (whom the Hoobs call 'tiddly peeps'), an animated story and the answer to the episode's theme.

MOPATOP'S SHOP (1999–2000)

Another toddler show, this one is set in a magical store where you can get anything at all: perhaps a rainbow, a bee's knee or a friend. Mopatop and his assistant Puppyduck introduce children to shapes and musical sounds with the help of other characters including the deliveryman Lamont (a sloth), DIY expert Odd Job Gerald (a rabbit) and Moosey Mouse and his family. Over 200 bite-size episodes were made in conjunction with Carlton TV and were broadcast during ITV's CITV kids' slot.

THE MUPPET SHOW (1976–1981)

If there was an award for the greatest family TV show ever, *The Muppet Show* would deserve to win it. Much more than a children's show – adults quite rightly loved it too – this provided laughs, songs and some of the most memorable TV moments featuring just about every star from the 1970s you can think of. Each episode, the Muppets (including Kermit the Frog, his amour Miss Piggy, Animal, Gonzo, Fozzie Bear, Rolf the dog, Swedish chef, Scooter and sourpuss critics Statler and Waldorf) attempted to put on their variety show with the help of a star guest. John Cleese, Liza Minelli, Peter Sellers,

Steve Martin, Elton John, Gene Kelly, Mark Hamill (at the height of *Star Wars* mania) and Bob Hope are just some of the mega-watt stars who appeared.

SESAME STREET (1969–)

The classic kids TV show that teaches tots their alphabet and numbers has been airing in the US – and in many countries around the world – for almost 40 years. Puppets Bert and Ernie, Cookie Monster, Big Bird, Oscar The Grouch, The Count, Grover and Kermit (who all reside in Sesame Street, along with a handful of lucky humans) are familiar the world over, while stars have lined up to make their own appearances on the most famous street in the world. Liam Neeson, Haley Joel Osment, James Blunt and Natalie Portman are just some of the more recent stars to appear on the show that also launched the spin-off for toddlers, *Elmo's World* (see review, p.146). Adored by both adults and kids, the show has won over 100 Emmy awards, and also boasted the first regular deaf character – Linda (Linda Bove) – on American television. And here's a deliciously daft fact to leave you with – in one episode, Cookie Monster revealed that, before he tried cookies, his real name was Sid.

THE STORYTELLER (1988)

Only nine episodes were made of this series in which an old storyteller (John Hurt) and his dog (voiced by Jim Henson's son, Brian) delivered a tale to bewitch – or possibly terrify – children (this was not one for very young viewers). One episode is the story of the storyteller himself, another the tale of a Hussar who gambles with devils and manages to trap Death before realising a world without the grim reaper could be a strange place indeed. Actors including Sean Bean, Jonathan Pryce and Miranda Richardson star.

TEENAGERS

RAGING HORMONES, YOUNG LOVE AND OTHER TEENAGE TRAUMAS...

21 JUMP STREET (1987–1991)

Starring Johnny Depp, Peter DeLuise, Holly Robinson

Before he became a movie star, Johnny Depp was something of a teen idol in the US as the star of this cop show. Created by Stephen J. Cannell, one of the seventies and eighties' most successful producers thanks to TV shows like *Hunter*, *The A-Team* and *The Rockford Files*, *21 Jump Street* was the story of a group of very young-looking police officers hired to form a special unit to tackle youth crime by going undercover in schools as students. The team were made up of baby-faced Officer Tom Hanson (Depp), jokey Doug Penhall (DeLuise, one of comedian Dom DeLuise's sons), token sassy girl Judy Hoffs (Robinson), martial arts expert H.T. Ioki (Dustin Nguyen) and grown-up leader Captain Jenko (Frederic Forrest). Forrest only appeared in the first six episodes, however, and was replaced by Stephen Williams as Captain Fuller for the rest of the show's run.

The programme ran for five years in the US (in Britain, ITV showed the occasional episode, very late at night), and tackled subjects such as drug dealing in schools, teen rape, drunk driving, gay bashing, racism and steroid abuse – sometimes successfully, sometimes in a rather annoyingly moralising fashion. Aside from some nice buddy chemistry between Depp and DeLuise, it was all pretty daft stuff, and by the third season, it's obvious on screen that Depp had grown increasingly uncomfortable in his role, both as teen pin-up and cop who ratted on school kids. A new cast member – Richard Grieco as Booker – was added in Season 3 as a potential replacement for Depp (who left during Season 4), but he was instead given a spin-off show named *Booker*, which lasted for 22 episodes (it's not available on UK DVD but you're not missing anything). The final season featured new characters Anthony McCann (Michael Bendetti) and Doug's brother Joey (Michael DeLuise), but by then even the most ardent fans had given up watching.

Now best enjoyed by Johnny Depp fans (he does look extremely cute and is very funny in the first two seasons), this is also worth a look to spot some of the up-and-coming actors who appeared in the series including

Brad Pitt, Sherilyn Fenn (who was engaged to Depp at the time), Jason Priestley, Bridget Fonda and Vince Vaughn.

 TV Trivia: Holly Robinson sang the theme song 'Jump', while Depp and DeLuise provided back-up vocals.

BEVERLY HILLS 90210 (1990–2000)

Starring Jason Priestley, Tori Spelling, Luke Perry, Shannen Doherty

This teen drama ran for an astonishing 10 years and 292 episodes, charting the loves, lives and day-to-day traumas of a group of teens living in Los Angeles' swankiest suburb. Created by Aaron Spelling of *The Love Boat* fame (could this be why his daughter Tori was cast as one of the leads – surely not!), the series began with Minneapolis twins Brandon (Priestly) and Brenda (Doherty) transferring to West Beverly High and learning they really weren't in Hicksville anymore. The students drive Porsches, get nose jobs during summer vacation and spend their evenings hanging out at the dullest-looking local diner, the Peach Pit (where Brandon eventually finds gainful employment), and it's not long before the cool kids – bitchy Kelly (Jennie Garth), jock Steve (Ian Ziering), dumb Donna (Spelling) and bad boy Dylan (Perry) – are letting the new kids on the (very expensive) block hang out with them.

At the time, the show was quite unusual in the way it covered 'tough' subjects like drugs, teen pregnancy and social issues like alcoholism and AIDS, and for the first few years it was an enjoyably glossy soap in which the girls were pretty and the boys looked good in swimming trunks. Behind the scenes, things weren't always so cute – the cast and crew reportedly grew tired of Doherty's diva-like ways, and so Brenda was shipped off to London at the end of Season 4 to be replaced by old family friend (never before mentioned, of course) Valerie Malone (Tiffani Thiessen) from Season 5. By that point, the show was on the wane and turned to ridiculous plot twists (Dylan falls for the daughter of the man who killed his dad, and she is shot and killed the day after they marry), rock star performances (the Peach Pit is now open in the evening and has bands perform) and tangled relationships to keep remaining viewers hooked. It went out with a whimper (Donna and her on-off beau David finally tie the knot), but should still be credited with influencing future teen shows such as *Dawson's Creek* and *The O.C.* A new version, with Garth and Doherty in guest roles, began in late 2008.

 TV Trivia: Luke Perry was a very un-teenage 25 years old when he started playing Dylan – in fact, only Tori Spelling and Jennie Garth were still in their teens when filming began.

DAWSON'S CREEK (1998–2003)

Starring James Van Der Beek, Katie Holmes, Joshua Jackson, Michelle Williams

Created by writer Kevin Williamson (who also wrote *Scream*), *Dawson's Creek* was a teen TV show with a difference. Set in the fictional Massachusetts town of Capeside (the series was actually filmed in Wilmington, North Carolina), it featured elaborate vocabulary (causing detractors to proclaim teens didn't really talk so intelligently), much grown-up soul searching by the characters, a nice dose of wit and realism, a pop soundtrack (including the theme 'I Don't Want To Wait' by Paula Cole) and four strong central performances.

In the first series, the story was primarily focused around Dawson Leery (Van Der Beek), a ponderous boy who dreams of becoming the next Steven Spielberg. Across the creek from his house lives Joey Potter (Holmes), his childhood friend who harbours secret feelings for him, while Dawson's best (male) friend is Pacey (Jackson), a wisecracking low achiever. Into this mix comes new girl Jen (Williams), a sexy New York teen (her first appearance is shown in slow motion) sent to live with her grandmother in an attempt to quell her wayward ways.

In five seasons, these four had romance, fallings out and various life changes as the series followed them from age 15 to their college years. Dawson falls for Joey and their on/off relationship twists and turns throughout (especially as he first dates Jen and then Joey falls for Pacey), while Pacey's relationship with a foxy teacher in Season 1 won both criticism and praise. In Season 2, new characters Jack (Keir Smith) and sister Andie (Meredith Monroe) were added and manic depression, homosexuality (Jack is outed), first sex and peer pressure were among the subjects tackled. Most fans agree that those two seasons, and Season 3 (in which Pacey and Dawson fall out over Joey) are the best. Season 4 has some good moments and gives more screen time to Jackson, Williams and Holmes (the programme makers finally realising Dawson was the least interesting and most whiny character on the show), but sadly Season 5 (in which the group go off to college/jobs and spend most of the time apart) and Season 6 are a mess. Watch the first four seasons then skip those and return for the special two-part finale (written by Williamson, who left the series at the end of Season 2), which resolves all the romances and relationships.

 TV Trivia: The necklace Dawson wears in every episode was made by James Van Der Beek's mother.

DEAD LiKE ME (2003-2004)

Starring Ellen Muth, Mandy Patinkin, Callum Blue

College dropout George (Muth) doesn't particularly like her life. And when she is hit and killed by the toilet seat of the re-entering Mir Space Station, she discovers she's not too fond of death, either. It seems George's job in the afterlife is to be a Grim Reaper, under the tutelage of boss Rube (Patinkin), who also manages George's fellow undead workers, Betty (Rebecca Gayheart), Roxy (Jasmine Guy) and Mason (Blue). They can all communicate with the living, and be seen by them (though they appear differently than in their previous human form, meaning George can pop back to visit her mother without her mum having a clue who she is), and their job is to gather souls (but they're not paid — to make money, the reapers either get a day job or steal money off the recently deceased). Each reaper has to gather so many souls before they can move on to the next level of afterlife, but none of them know how many souls that is.

Only two seasons of this quirky show were made, but both were packed with levity and melancholy at the same time. Crisply written by a team led by creator Bryan Fuller (later a producer on the sci-fi hit *Heroes*), the series also focused on those left behind, from George's divorced parents to Rube's daughter, but the best scenes were between the main characters, especially Roxy, who was strangled in 1982 with leg-warmers (!) and the mysterious Londoner Mason.

 TV Trivia: Creator Bryan Fuller loosely based the idea for this series on Piers Anthony's novel *On a Pale Horse*.

DEGRASSi JUNiOR HiGH (1987-1991)

Starring Stefan Brogren, Amanda Stepto, Neil Hope

In 1979, a Canadian children's series named *The Kids of Degrassi Street* was made, and was successful enough in its native country that it lasted seven years. The show wasn't well known outside of Canada, but its follow-up, *Degrassi Junior High*, became a hit in the US and was subsequently shown on BBC1 here. It focused on a group of teenage students experiencing sex, drugs, rock and roll (and accompanying problems such as teen pregnancy) for the first time, and won acclaim for its realistic and often gritty portrayal of teenage life.

While it does look a bit dated now (just check out the haircuts and eye-wincingly awful eighties fashion), the shows themes remain current, and the performances are terrific, especially when you consider most of the cast were the age they were playing (unlike, say, *Beverly Hills 90210* — apparently inspired by Degrassi — in which most of the cast were twentysomethings playing younger).

Often funny, always thought-provoking, it remains one of the best teen TV shows ever made and is well worth seeking out on DVD. The adventures of the Degrassi students continued in *Degrassi High* (1989–1991), the TV movie *Degrassi: School's Out* (1992) and *Degrassi: The Next Generation* (2001–), but none of these are currently available on disc.

 TV Trivia: *Clerks* director Kevin Smith loved the show so much, he appeared in five episodes of *Degrassi: The Next Generation* as himself.

FAME (1982–1987)

Starring Debbie Allen, Lee Curreri, Valerie Landsburg

A spin-off of the hugely successful 1980 movie musical, *Fame* the series began in 1982 and told the story of a group of students who just want to dance/sing/act/play music at the High School Of Performing Arts in New York. Many of the characters were taken from the film and transplanted to the small screen (with some of the movie's actors continuing their roles, too), including dance teacher Lydia Grant (Debbie Allen), dancer Leroy (Gene Anthony Ray) and music geek Bruno (Lee Curreri), while Carlo Imperato (as comedian Danny), Valerie Landsburg (as dowdy Doris), cellist Julie (Lori Singer), and Erica Gimpel (taking over from the movie's Irene Cara as singer/dancer Coco) rounded out the cast.

The plot each week was often similar to the old Mickey Rooney 'let's put on a show' idea (so that the episode could feature at least one song and dance number) but there was a good dollop of moralising thrown in with the two-stepping as the kids learnt about life, competitiveness and not starving themselves to fit into a skimpy leotard. It all looks terribly twee now, but at the time the show was so successful it spawned a handful of soundtrack albums (including songs like 'Desdemona', an R&B re-working of the story of Othello, 'High Fidelity', and 'Starmaker') and stage tours featuring the cast.

Landsburg, Imperato, Singer (who is a trained cellist) and Erica Gimpel continue to work on stage and on TV, while Curreri is a successful music producer. Gene Anthony Ray, at one point a real-life student at the school featured in the series, died in 2003 following a stroke.

 TV Trivia: While the movie *Fame* was filmed in New York, the series was made in Los Angeles with just a few exterior Manhattan shots dropped in.

THE FRESH PRINCE OF BEL AIR (1990–1996)

Starring Will Smith, Alfonso Ribeiro, James Avery

Will Smith was already known as a likeable rap star, the Fresh Prince, when this terrific series was created with him in mind. He plays a kid named Will Smith(!), whose mother, worried about his rough and tough Philadelphia surroundings, sends him to live with his aunt, uncle and cousins at a fancy mansion in Bel Air, California. Of course, he's there to learn how to be a good boy, but the posh Banks family also learns a thing or two from their earthier relative in this fish-out-of-water tale. While much of the plot revolves around Will and his adapting to his new environment, the comedy worked so well (and lasted for six seasons) because all the characters were interesting and entertaining, from Will's square and stuffy, Tom Jones-loving cousin Carlton (Ribeiro) to spoiled Hillary (Karyn Parsons) and British butler Geoffrey (Joseph Marcell, who delivers his lines with sarcastic zeal).

The first three seasons were a treat, but things took a downturn by the fourth, when Carlton and Will move into the family poolhouse and attend college, and later get jobs and talk marriage (not to each other, of course). Many fans attribute the show's slow demise also to the removal of Janet Hubert-Whitten, who played Will's aunt Vivian, but who was replaced by another actress, Daphne Maxwell Reid, from Season 4, after a falling out with Smith (by then an executive producer on the series).

At its best, though, this was a smart, snappy comedy that tackled African–American issues and other topics such as alcohol abuse, peer pressure, absent parents and racial stereotypes without over-moralising.

TV Trivia: The cab driver who drops Will off at the Banks home in the opening credits is played by Quincy Jones, who was the show's executive producer.

GILMORE GIRLS (2000–2007)

Starring Lauren Graham, Alexis Bledel

The Gilmore girls of the title are mother Lorelai (Graham) and her teenage daughter Rory (Bledel), who live together in Stars Hollow, Connecticut. There is only 16 years between them, and as the show begins, Lorelai is still estranged from her own parents who weren't too impressed when their 16-year-old daughter got pregnant. That situation changes, however, when Lorelai needs money to send Rory to a posh private school that should help her on the road to Harvard, and she strikes a deal with her mother: both

Rory and Lorelai have to go to dinner with Lorelai's parents every Friday so they can finally get to know their granddaughter. As Lorelai tries to reconnect with her family, Rory has her own problems including raging hormones, a cute new boy in town and a school full of pupils who aren't very friendly to outsiders. To confuse matters, her mother begins a relationship with one of her teachers, and also has a puzzling relationship with local diner owner Luke.

Yes, it's very girly stuff, full of hurt feelings, emotional trauma and misunderstandings, but it also has a snappy script and some nice performances from the leads. While not as universally enjoyable as the similar *Everwood* (sadly as yet unavailable on DVD in the UK), there are laughs to be had in the show's seven seasons if you can stomach the treacle that goes with them.

 TV Trivia: Both *The OC*'s Adam Brody and *One Tree Hill*'s Chad Michael Murray had recurring roles in *Gilmore Girls* before they became teen stars.

GoSSiP GiRL (2007–)

Starring Blake Lively, Leighton Meester, Penn Badgley, Chace Crawford, Ed Westwick

One of the most talked about TV shows of 2007 is also one of the most addictive – a sort of cross between *The OC* and *Cruel Intentions* with a bit of *Sex and the City* thrown in for good measure. Set among the elite and privileged of New York's Upper East Side, the series focuses on the dysfunctional moneyed kids (and their equally confused parents) who attend a posh private school and whose antics are reported online by the anonymous blogger 'Gossip Girl' (voiced by *Veronica Mars*' Kristen Bell). All their lives are changed when former queen bee Serena van der Woodsen (Lively) returns to school after mysteriously disappearing for a year – bitchy Blair (Meester) had taken Serena's place as top-girl in her absence and doesn't want to return the crown; Blair's boyfriend Nate (Crawford) has a secret of his own about Serena and why she went away; Nate's nefarious pal Chuck (Westwick) is just enjoying the scandal of it all; and Dan (Badgley), the regular guy, may finally get a chance with the girl who never noticed him before.

Like *The OC* (which GG's Josh Schwartz also created), *Gossip Girl* works well because it focuses on the equally complicated lives of the grown-ups as well as the kids (Nate's dad has financial problems, while Dan's former rock star dad is separated from his mum and also has a connection with Serena's posh mother), and also boasts a razor-sharp script that details the machinations and rivalries of the privileged few. However, it's the fashions that the girls and women sport that have granted *Gossip Girl* space in top fashion magazines, as the wealthy characters swan around in jaw-dropping ensembles the rest of us can only fantasise about.

 TV Trivia: The series is based on a set of teen novels from author Cecily Von Ziegesar.

HAPPY DAYS (1974–1984)

Starring Ron Howard, Henry Winkler, Marion Ross, Tom Bosley

Happy Days was the series that made the fifties look cooler, and somehow naffer at the same time, than they actually were. A half-hour comedy based in Milwaukee, the series introduced us to the Cunningham family – homemaker Marion (Ross) and husband Howard (Bosley), their kids Richie (Howard) and Joanie (Erin Moran), and ladies man/biker Arthur 'Fonzie/The Fonz' Fonzarelli, who lived above their garage. Teenager Richie's problems were mainly due to his awkwardness with girls and his bumbling pals Ralph Malph (Don Most) and 'Potsie' Weber (Anson Williams), but he could always turn to the leather jacket and jeans-clad Fonz for advice, because, hey, he was cooool.

A classic that, because it was set in the past to begin with, hasn't seemed to age, *Happy Days* made a star of Winkler (in a role that The Monkees' Mickey Dolenz reportedly also auditioned for), made the members of the Cunningham family household names, and made the Cunningham house and Arnold's Drive-In the place everyone wanted to be. While it was very formulaic – there's usually a life lesson to be learnt, in between Fonz clicking his fingers to get the ladies to come running, and Richie doing something dumb – it had a great deal of charm, and nice performances from the cast that in later years also included Scott Baio as Fonzie's cousin Chachi (a spin-off series in which Chachi and girlfriend Joanie left town to form a band only lasted 17 episodes and isn't on DVD).

The series also spawned two other hit shows – the missable *Laverne & Shirley* (not on UK DVD) and daft *Mork and Mindy* (see Sci-Fi, p.225) – and boasts an impressive number of the cast who have gone onto even better things. Comic actor Robin Williams debuted his character Mork on the show before becoming one of the world's biggest box office stars in the nineties, while Howard is an Academy Award-winning director (*A Beautiful Mind*), Winkler is a successful director and producer (*The Sure Thing*, *MacGyver*), and Williams also directs popular TV shows including *Charmed* and *Sabrina: The Teenage Witch*. Meanwhile, Tom Bosley went on to star in *The Father Dowling Mysteries* and Marion Ross regularly appears on TV in roles as varied as Spongebob's Grandma in *Spongebob Squarepants* and as Kitty's mother in law in *That '70s Show*.

TV Trivia: In the opening episode of Season 5, Fonzie jumps over a shark (still in his leather jacket, of course) while water-skiing. Considered the moment when *Happy Days* started to go badly downhill, the phrase 'jump the shark' has since been used to describe the instant that any show has a severe drop in quality.

HiGH SCHOOL MUSiCAL (2006–)

Starring Zac Efron, Vanessa Anne Hudgens

A TV movie from director Kenny Ortega (previously the choreographer for *Dirty Dancing*), this is a squeaky clean *Fame* for the 21st century. Anyone over the age of 14 will think it's awful, but young teens, especially girls, love the story of cute kids Troy and Gabriella who try out for their high school musical, annoying the pair who usually win the lead roles in the process. Packed with toe-tapping tunes and dance numbers, including the enjoyably cheesy 'Status Quo', sung in the school cafeteria, this has been a phenomenal success for Disney, who made it for their cable TV channel and tapped into the 'tweenie' audience of girls looking for something super sweet (instead of kissing in a romantic moment, the two leads burst into a smoochie song) so well that the TV film has already spawned two more made-for-TV movies and has become one of the biggest selling TV movies ever on DVD.

And that's not all: there is also a one-off TV show in which the stars of the movies teach viewers the moves to the biggest dance numbers in the film (*High School Musical Dance-Along*), the soundtrack to the first movie, *High School Musical The Concert* (on CD and DVD) and even spin-offs such as Top Trumps cards, a DVD game, novelisations, dolls and sheet music for kids wanting to recreate the inoffensive poppiness at home. You have been warned.

TV Trivia: *High School Musical* was just the film's working title, but when no one could think of anything better, they kept it.

HOLLYOAKS (1995–)

Starring Nick Pickard, Andree Bernard, Jeremy Edwards

Brookside creator Phil Redmond had already had some TV experience dealing with teenage issues as the producer of *Grange Hill*, but with this show he injected a lot more sex and soap opera into the lives of a group of teenage friends leaving school and college and venturing out into the world of work. Set in a fictional suburb of Chester unsurprisingly called Hollyoaks, the series has grown from one episode a week in 1995 to its current five episodes a week in the UK.

Over the years, the show has tackled themes including teen pregnancy, abortion, male rape, homosexuality and drug abuse, while a series of 'late night' specials and made-for-DVD dramas have featured the most controversial plot lines of all. In between the serious stuff, it's often pretty ridiculous (an escaped rapist turns mass murderer is just one of the more eyebrow-raising ones) and badly acted, although the reputation for poor performances hasn't hindered some of the cast's CVs as the show has helped launch the careers of actors such as Gary Lucy, Jeremy Edwards, Will Mellor and Jodi Albert.

The series underwent a major revamp in 2007, with many cast changes and a new theme and opening credits aimed at appealing to an older audience. It is only the late-night episodes that are available on DVD.

 TV Trivia: *Hollyoaks* was the only soap to be nominated in every category at the 2007 British Soap Awards.

HOME AND AWAY (1988–)

Starring Simon Bossell, Dannii Minogue, Kate Ritchie, Melissa George

If you were a teenager at the beginning of the 1990s, chances are you were either a *Neighbours* fan (see review, p.173) or a *Home and Away* devotee. The other soap imported from Australia, the more sun-soaked H&A is set in Summer Bay and originally focused on Pippa and Tom Fletcher's foster home and the kids they raised, but later broadened to include all the residents of the coastal resort.

In the 20 years it has been on air, there have been romances, weddings, deaths, betrayals, bad perms and more Aussie stereotypes than you could shake a boomerang at. There have been early appearances from well-known actors, too, including Naomi Watts, *nip/tuck*'s Julian McMahon, *Emmerdale*'s Emily Symons, *Wedding Crashers*' Isla Fisher, Guy Pearce (who was also in *Neighbours*) and Heath Ledger. So far, two compilation DVDs, 'Romance' and 'Weddings' have been released, and a spin-off episode entitled 'Home and Away: Secrets and the City', featuring characters from the series.

TV Trivia: *Home and Away* actors Dannii Minogue and Julian McMahon were briefly married, and he appears in her music video for the song 'This Is It'.

THE MONKEES (1966–1968)

Starring Mickey Dolenz, Davy Jones, Peter Tork, Michael Nesmith

It only ran for 58 episodes, but *The Monkees* can be credited with changing television forever: before this show, nothing was made for TV that was specifically aimed at a teenage audience. A comedy show about the misadventures of a struggling pop band, the idea was originally presented by producer Bob Rafelson to TV executives as far back as 1965, but it wasn't until the success of The Beatles' movie *A Hard Day's Night* that the potential for a show about four bumbling young guys was realised, and an ad was placed in industry newspaper *Variety* looking for possible members (it was rumoured that convicted murderer Charles Manson auditioned for the Monkees, but it's not true – he was in prison at the time the auditions were held).

Former jockey Jones, ex-child actor Dolenz and struggling folk singers Nesmith and Tork were picked as the four goofy guys who spend each episode dealing with ludicrous but terrific comic situations (including being kidnapped, visiting a haunted mansion and escaping a mad scientist) in between musical numbers such as 'Last Train to Clarksville', and the classic 'Daydream Believer'. While the four didn't actually play any of the instruments you see them with on screen for the first two series, by the time their third (bestselling) album was released, they both sung and played on it in between performing for a sell-out tour.

The series ended in 1968 and the four members went their separate ways as a musical group in 1970, though they reformed for an album in 1996. Dolenz has continued to act and direct (he was also the producer of kids TV series *Metal Mickey*), Jones and Tork both continue to perform, and Nesmith (who is quite well off, since his mother invented Liquid Paper, the US version of Tipp-ex) has a successful career as a novelist, recording artist and producer.

 TV Trivia: Davy Jones made his TV debut when he was 15 in an episode of *Coronation Street*.

MY SO-CALLED LIFE (1994)

Starring Claire Danes, Jared Leto, Bess Armstrong

This US TV series only ran for 19 episodes, but it launched the careers of Claire Danes and Jared Leto, and over a decade later is still considered one of the best teen series ever made (fans bombarded TV production company ABC with begging letters to stop the show being cancelled, unfortunately to no avail).

Created by *thirtysomething* writer Winnie Holzman, the series introduced us to 15-year-old Angela Chase (Danes, in a role originally earmarked for Alicia Silverstone), who is going through the usual adolescent crises. She doesn't like school, she's becoming a stranger to her parents, she's in love with handsome hunk Jordan (Leto) and unaware how much geeky Brian is in love with her.

Smartly scripted ('My parents keep asking how school was. It's like saying, "How was that drive-by shooting?" You don't care how it *was*, you're lucky to get out alive.') and just a touch downbeat, the series effectively deals with the bitter realities of growing up, from drug problems to unrequited love, to feelings of inadequacy and not fitting in. Shame it wasn't given a chance to get to adulthood.

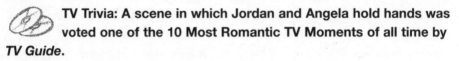 **TV Trivia: A scene in which Jordan and Angela hold hands was voted one of the 10 Most Romantic TV Moments of all time by** *TV Guide.*

NEiGHBOURS (1985–)

Starring Kylie Minogue, Jason Donovan, Stefan Dennis, Alan Dale

The series renowned for producing pop stars (Jason Donovan, Natalie Imbruglia, Holly Valance, Delta Goodrem and the phenomenally successful Kylie) and early roles for up-and-coming Aussie actors including Russell Crowe and Guy Pearce, *Neighbours* began life as a five-days-a-week soap opera on Australian TV about a group of middle-class people living in a cul-de-sac called Ramsay Street. Originally a flop in Oz, the series became hugely popular outside the country when it was shown in the UK at lunchtime and at teatime, appealing to mums and the teenagers who should have been doing their homework. It is now enjoyed by over 30 million viewers throughout the world and is Australia's longest-running soap.

Set in the fictional town of Erinsborough (an almost-anagram of 'neighbours'), the series originally focused on the Robinsons, led by dad Jim (Dale) who had a businessman son named Paul (Dennis) and bleach blond 'hunk' Scott (Donovan), and their less well-to-do neighbours, the Ramsays – led by Madge (Anne Charleston). Producers soon realised they were gaining a young audience so mainly focused on the teens in the show, and it paid off – viewing reached a peak in the late eighties as the teen relationship between Scott and tomboy Charlene (Minogue) turned into marriage and gave *Neighbours* one of its most-viewed episodes.

It has had many successes since as racier subjects were tackled in recent years such as incest, prostitution, contraception and lesbianism. And over the years, families and cast members have left the street (some, like Stefan

Dennis, have since returned), the sets still wobble when they slam doors and the scripts have got increasingly bizarre – including bomb plots, blackmail and even a character returning from the dead – but fans remain faithful to this daft but somewhat addictive drama.

Because there have been thousands of episodes, only a 'Best Of' DVD has been released. Called 'Defining Moments', it features a few births as well as the weddings of Scott and Charlene, Des and Daphne, and Beth and Brad among others, and a selection of deaths including Madge's and Jim's.

TV Trivia: Working on *Neighbours* didn't do Alan Dale any harm: the former milkman has since become a fixture of US dramas, with starring roles in *The OC* (as Caleb, Kirstin's dad), *Lost* (as the villainous Charles Widmore), *24* (as the Vice-President) and *Ugly Betty* (as millionaire Bradford Meade).

ONE TREE HILL (2003–)

Starring Chad Michael Murray, James Lafferty, Hilarie Burton, Sophia Bush, Bethany Joy Lenz

A teen soap opera that owes a great debt to *Dawson's Creek* (with a bit of *Rich Man Poor Man* thrown in), this revolves around hunky Lucas Scott (Murray, who appeared as Joey's boyfriend in Series 5 of *Dawson's Creek*), a high school teen raised by single mom Karen (Moira Kelly). Karen was dumped by her high school sweetheart Dan (Paul Johansson) when she was pregnant, while he went on to marry Deb (Barbara Alyn Woods) and have a son, Nathan (Lafferty), who was given all the luxuries Lucas didn't have. The boys, close in age, attend the same school in the small town of Tree Hill, and come to blows when Lucas joins the school basketball team (Nathan, of course, is the star player).

There are subplots involving girls – Lucas's best friend Haley (Lenz) ends up dating Nathan, and Lucas finds himself torn between Peyton (Burton) and Brooke (Bush) and ends up being awful to both of them – but the first series mainly concerned itself with basketball and the boys' rivalry, and Dan's obsession with Nathan's successes. Oddly, aside from Dan/Deb/Karen, there are very few parents around – Peyton's mother is dead and her father works away, Brooke's are rarely mentioned nor are Haley's, and Nathan gets himself emancipated to escape his dad – so these teens seem to be rather grown up for their supposed ages, living in apartments, getting married and starting up businesses in between cheerleader and basketball practice.

Thanks to nice performances from the cast (aside from Johansson, who delivers an over-the-top performance as dad-from-hell Dan, and becomes a pantomime villain by Season 3), this is enjoyably daft stuff, made all the more so for the behind-the-scenes goings on that had fans transfixed: Murray and Bush fell in love in real life and were married, only to divorce months later... just as their characters hooked up on screen and they had to perform love scenes!

Important note – Episode 16 of Season 3 featured a Columbine-style shooting in the school and was not broadcast on British TV but is available on the series DVD. Viewers should note it is quite upsetting.

TV Trivia: The series was originally going to be a TV movie called Ravens (the name of the school's basketball team) but it was decided that there were enough plot ideas for it to be made into a series.

THE OC (2003–2007)

Starring Benjamin Mackenzie, Mischa Barton, Adam Brody, Rachel Bilson

Another teen drama in the *Dawson's Creek* mode (teen relationships, hip soundtrack, adult soap plots and cool parents), this time set in the sunny and wealthy community of Newport Beach in California's Orange County (the 'OC' of the title).

When teen Ryan (Mackenzie), from the decidedly rougher area of Chino, is arrested with his older brother, a do-gooder lawyer named Sandy (Peter Gallagher) decides to take Ryan back to his home to show the kid a better life. So cool dude Ryan ends up in the OC, living with Sandy's wife Kirsten (Kelly Rowan) and geeky son Seth (Brody), much to the annoyance of snobby neighbour Julie Cooper (Melinda Clarke), who is worried Ryan will corrupt her designer-clothes-wearing daughter Marissa's (Barton) life with his bad boy ways. And that's just the first episode.

A huge hit in its first year thanks to the fun plots (which usually culminated in fisticuffs or Ryan staring broodily off into the distance) and the cast's model good looks, this got more preposterous (if that's possible) during the second and third seasons as new characters were introduced (including a scheming woman Kirsten meets in a rehab centre who tries to con everyone out of their money) and old ones (such as Sandy) had complete changes in personality. The third season ended with a bang as one character was killed (we won't reveal who, here, but it was the least convincing actor among the cast members – phew!) and things thankfully picked up as the show reverted to its witty roots for the fourth and final season.

TV Trivia: The pool at the Cohen house is apparently only four feet deep, so when there are scenes in the water the cast are performing on their knees.

THE PARTRIDGE FAMILY (1970–1974)

Starring David Cassidy, Shirley Jones, Susan Dey, Danny Bonaduce

Following the death of her husband, Shirley Partridge (Jones) is struggling to support her five children. The kids dream of making it big in the music business, and spend time singing in the basement – teen Keith (Cassidy, Jones' real-life stepson) can write songs, sister Laurie (Dey) can sing and play keyboard, ten-year-old Danny (Bonaduce) is on bass and is also quite deft as a mini-businessman, while Chris and Tracy are good on drums and percussion. It turns out Mom can sing too – hang on, could a family band be a way of making ends meet?

With producer Reuben (Dave Madden) on board, it's not long before the family have bundled into their colourful school bus to perform catchy, innocent pop across the country in this series that was decidedly more sassy (for its time, at least) than the squeaky-clean *Brady Bunch*. Storylines included Danny getting involved with the Mob, the self-absorbed Keith regularly having girl trouble, and Mom dating again, which unsurprisingly doesn't sit well with her brood.

Originally it was only Jones who was expected to sing (the rest of the vocals to be provided by young session musicians), but producers then discovered Cassidy's vocal talent – and his popularity with teenage girls. Soon the show was a phenomenon, not only on TV but in record stores, as albums of the songs (including 'I Think I Love You' and the theme 'C'Mon Get Happy') featured in the show were released to great success (everyone knew Jones and Cassidy were the only cast members providing their own voices). Cassidy went on to have a hugely successful solo singing career and became less interested in being seen on TV as clean-cut Keith (he even posed nude in *Rolling Stone* to show his, erm, harder side), and left at the end of Season 4. The ratings had been declining and an attempt to bring in a new singing cutie, Ricky (Ricky Segall) for the fourth season was unsuccessful, so the series was then cancelled.

An animated series, set in the future, called *Partridge Family 2200 AD* was made in 1974 with little involvement from the original Partridges.

TV Trivia: Jeremy Gelbwaks, who played little Chris in the first series, was replaced by another actor for Season 2 because he reportedly had behavioural problems that included biting one of his co-stars.

PARTY OF FIVE (1994–2000)

Starring Matthew Fox, Neve Campbell, Scott Wolf

How's this for a depressing premise: five siblings, ranging in age from twentysomething Charlie (Fox) to baby Owen, are left orphaned when their parents are killed by a drunk driver. Prepare to have tissues at the ready as things don't get much cheerier than that for the Salingers in this superb drama that follows them in the years after their parents' death as they struggle to grow up and look after each other (they have handily been left the family house and business in the will). Charlie, as the only adult, has to give up his dream of being an architect to work in the family restaurant, although he doesn't take much responsibility in the home, leaving 16-year-old brother Bailey (Wolf) to be the one who has to pay bills and hire nannies for little Owen. Meanwhile teen sister Julia (Campbell) thinks this is a perfect time to rebel and precocious 11-year-old Claudia discovers everyone is too busy with their own problems (which include cancer, drug use, failed relationships and alcoholism) to notice her. And if they can't keep it together, there is always the threat of social services intervening and separating the family.

Different from just about every other teen show, this is about kids who realise they only have each other and no one else can help them, and thanks to terrific casting, it largely works, and appeals to a much wider audience than it was originally aimed at. Fox (now best known for his lead role in *Lost*) is perfect as the unshaven and unkempt ladies man (and also gives the show some very nice grown up appeal), while Wolf is the wholesome-looking one of the bunch whose hormones are exploding (in the first series he falls for a virgin who won't have sex, then an on-the-edge gal who will). Campbell, now known for the *Scream* movies, is a little whiny as Julia but still occasionally charms, while Chabert is spot-on as the youngest member (if you don't count baby Owen, who doesn't get a speaking part until later). As well as launching these actors' careers, the show also featured Jennifer Love Hewitt (as Bailey's on/off love from Series 2) and Jeremy London (as a love interest for Julia). It finished in 2000 with an episode that (finally) gave fans a happy ending.

TV Trivia: Cast member Campbell is a trained ballerina and appeared in the Toronto stage version of *Phantom of the Opera* before she was cast in *Party of Five*.

ROSWELL (1999–2002)

Starring Shiri Appleby, Jason Behr, Katherine Heigl, Brendan Fehr

A cracking science-fiction series aimed at teens and set at that most infamous of places, the town of Roswell, New Mexico, supposed setting of a secret US Army base that houses a crashed UFO. It is there that teens Liz Parker (Appleby) and Maria DeLuca (Majandra Delfino) live and work (at the alien-themed Crashdown cafe), and where they meet three kids who are not all they seem. For Max (Behr), his sister Isabel (*Grey's Anatomy*'s Heigl) and their pal Michael (Fehr) are part human, part alien, and for their whole lives no one has known their secret except them. But when Max magically heals Liz after a Crashdown customer shoots her, she and Maria are drawn into their world, bound to keep their secret. And it's a scary place to be – forever worried their true identities will be discovered, these kids face scary FBI men, even scarier fellow human/aliens, and numerous risks in their everyday lives (as well as some bubbling-over hormones, too).

When rumours abounded in the US that the series would be cancelled after only one season, ardent fans sent miniature bottles of Tabasco sauce (a favourite drink/meal among the alien teens) to the TV channel in an attempt to save the show. The series continued for two more seasons – many fans aren't keen on Season 2, as Max and Liz are no longer together and one major character, Alex (Colin Hanks) was written out due to his burgeoning real-life film career – but it ended in a way that should keep most viewers happy.

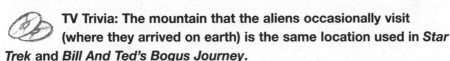 **TV Trivia: The mountain that the aliens occasionally visit (where they arrived on earth) is the same location used in *Star Trek* and *Bill And Ted's Bogus Journey*.**

SABRINA THE TEENAGE WITCH (1996–2003)

Starring Melissa Joan Hart, Caroline Rhea, Beth Broderick, Nate Richert

Based on the Archie Comics character of the same name (also the source for the short-lived 1971 animated TV series), this sweet teen sitcom starred Hart as teenager Sabrina, who just happens to be a witch. She lives with her two aunts (also witches), Zelda (Broderick) and Hilda (Rhea) and Salem (voiced by Nick Bakay), a warlock who has been turned into a cat for his various misdeeds. The plot was simple – Sabrina leads a normal teenage life, with none of her mortal friends knowing her secret, but each episode something crops up to cause Sabrina to use her magical powers.

For the first four seasons it's all very squeaky clean – Sabrina does have a boyfriend, Harvey (Richert), but hand-holding seems about the peak of their physical relationship – and it doesn't get much raunchier for the final three seasons as Sabrina leaves her aunt's home to go to college, but it's cute, *Clueless*-style stuff with a winning central performance from Hart, who had already had a hit show prior to this when she was just 15 (*Clarissa Explains It All*). Stealing the show from her, however, is Nick Bakay as the voice of the wise-cracking cat, while the puss himself is a regular black cat (that was apparently impossible to train) and a rather unconvincing fake one that adds to the comedy value.

 TV Trivia: Three of Hart's siblings (she has six) appeared in the series, with younger sister Emily playing Sabrina's cousin Amanda.

SAVED BY THE BELL (1989–1993)

Starring Mark-Paul Gosselaar, Tiffani Thiessen, Elizabeth Berkley, Dustin Diamond

Before she stripped and lap-danced her way to infamy in the movie *Showgirls*, Elizabeth Berkley was one of the stars in this teeth-gnashingly dreadful sitcom set at Bayside High School. Initially centering on egotistic Zack (Gosselaar, who talked directly to the camera in early episodes – an annoying technique dropped for later series), the show followed him and his pals, brainy Jessie (Berkley), 'hunky' Slater (Mario Lopez), ditzy Lisa (Lark Voorhies), popular girl Kelly (Thiessen) and nerd Screech (Diamond) as they got into various scrapes on perhaps the cheapest and creakiest-looking set since *Crossroads*.

Shown on Saturday mornings in the US, it became something of a cult show to twentysomething viewers wanting something banal and badly acted to watch while munching their cornflakes, and was enough of a success to warrant four series of the show, plus two spin-off TV movies, and two subsequent series, *Saved By The Bell: The College Years* (in which everyone bar Berkley and Voorhies returned for the 18 episodes that were made) and *Saved By The Bell: The New Class*, which inexplicably ran for seven seasons and featured a new group of pupils at the school (Dennis Haskins, who played the principal in the original series returned, along with Diamond's Screech, now the principal's assistant). Neither of the series, which both began in 1993, are available on UK DVD (thank goodness).

TV Trivia: Then-unknown actors Tori Spelling, and *Starship Troopers* co-stars Denise Richards and Casper Van Dien all appeared in the series in guest roles.

THE SECRET LIFE OF US (2001–2005)

Starring Claudia Karvan, Samuel Johnson, Deborah Mailman

This Australian TV series ran for four years (although only three series were shown in the UK but all are available on DVD) and revolves around a group of friends living in an apartment block in a beachside suburb of Melbourne. There's Kelly, who is having an affair with her married boss as the series begins; flatmates Evan and Alex, a female doctor; actors (and couple) Miranda and Richie; Alex's best friend Gabrielle and her fiancé Jason, who kicks off the first episode by cheating on his betrothed with Alex. Nice.

An enjoyable tangle of relationships (there is a running storyline featuring a mutual but unexplored attraction between Alex and Evan) mixed with everyday dramas and comedy and an Australian rock soundtrack, the series won much critical acclaim in its first two years but suffered a downturn in both viewership and praise by the third series, as old characters were removed and new, less appealing ones drafted in. (Only Kelly, and another original character, Simon, remained by Series 4).

 TV Trivia: Cast member Joel Edgerton (who played Will in the series) appeared as 'Uncle' Owen Lars in Star Wars Episode II and Episode III.

SKINS (2007–)

Starring Nicholas Hoult, Joseph Dempsie, April Pearson

Blimey! The awkward little kid who starred alongside Hugh Grant in *About A Boy* sure has grown up, as evidenced in this raunchy look at British teens from the makers of *Shameless* that features some very adult content. Over nine one-hour episodes (a second series is currently being shown), these kids love, cheat, betray, do drugs and shag around, especially Tony (Hoult), the arrogant ladies' man whose manipulative antics and thrill-seeking ways have alienated most of his friends, except for the lovable Sid, despite Tony continually taking advantage of his friendship. Throw in an unstable anorexic with suicidal tendencies, a conflicted Muslim, a sex-mad boy in love with his teacher and a gay kid in love with his best friend, and you have an explosive cocktail of trashy but addictive viewing.

Teens who watched the Bristol-set show scoffed that it was unrealistic (well, how many 18-year-olds do you know whose parents give them £1,000 to do with what they wanted while Mum was away?), while parents watching the teens in search of sex, cheap thrills and spliffs prayed that it was.

Packed with stereotypical characters (the party animal, the nerd, etc) and contrived situations, it's also (rightly) been accused of being over-hyped and rather smug – but, bizarrely, that's part of its X-rated charm.

 TV Trivia: British TV channel E4 struck a landmark deal with myspace.com that meant the first episode of *Skins* was broadcast on the website before it was shown on TV.

SUGAR RUSH (2005–)

Starring Olivia Hallinan, Leonora Crichlow, Sara Stewart

Journalist Julie Burchill's novel about a teenage lesbian and her relationship with girls and her own family works better on screen than it did on the page. Kim (Hallinan) is 15, gay, in love with her best (straight) friend Sugar (Crichlow), and stuck at home with her dysfunctional folks – or, as she puts it: 'I'm a 15-year-old queer virgin and my mum's a whore, and she's so scared I'll tell my dad she's trying to be my best friend.'

Surprisingly funny and sweet for a show dubbed as 'controversial' when it first aired, this is packed with sharp dialogue (perhaps sharper than the average teen would actually mutter) and works well, thanks to the central relationship between sweet Kim and the tougher Sugar, who seems to be working her way towards sexually satisfying the male population of Brighton single-handed. There are a few clichéd characters, of course (mainly the grown-ups) but this is, in the main, an enjoyable, occasionally raunchy depiction of what it is like to be a sexually frustrated teenager in the 21st century.

 TV Trivia: Julie Burchill claims the original *Sugar Rush* novel only took her around ten afternoons to write.

THAT 70'S SHOW (1998–2006)

Starring Topher Grace, Ashton Kutcher, Mila Kunis, Laura Prepon

Relegated to cable channels and late night TV in the UK (there was also a terrible UK version called *Days Like These* that disappeared without a trace within a few episodes), this sitcom about teenagers in the 1970s was a deserved hit in the US. Eric (Grace) lives with his parents, Kitty (Debra Jo Rupp) and Red (Kurtwood Smith) and hangs out in his basement with fellow schoolkids Donna (Prepon), anti-establishment doper Hyde (Danny Masterson), foreign kid Fez (Wilmer Valderrama), dumber-than-dumb Kelso (Kutcher) and Kelso's irritating girlfriend Jackie (Kunis).

A fun seventies flashback for grown-ups and a witty sitcom for teens, this worked best thanks to the performances of Rupp and Smith as the parents (Don Stark, as dufus next door Bob, is also hilarious) who get all the best lines (Red's mainly consist of calling son Eric a 'dumbass' in a variety of ways). There's teen romance and the accompanying drama, of course, as Eric realises Donna is more than just the girl next door, and Kelso and Jackie break up and make up, but things got more convoluted in later seasons as new characters were brought in to replace Grace and Kutcher as their film careers took off in real life (Grace co-starred in *Spider-Man 3*, while Kutcher has made movies including *Just Married* and *The Guardian*).

 TV Trivia: Fez's name stands for Foreign Exchange Student. Throughout the series we never learn exactly where he is from.

THE WONDER YEARS (1988–1993)

Starring Fred Savage, Dan Lauria, Danica McKellar

One of the best US TV shows of the late eighties, *The Wonder Years* followed young Kevin Arnold (Savage) as he grew up in the years 1968 to 1973, with a voiceover from Daniel Stern as the adult Kevin reflecting back on his youth. As well as the expected family dramas: Kevin is tormented by older brother Wayne (Jason Hervey), his mum (Alley Mills) is frustrated being a housewife and his dad (Lauria) is easily annoyed and seldom happy – there's tentative romance in the form of Kevin's neighbour Winnie Cooper (McKellar), and a backdrop of social upheaval due to the series' late sixties setting.

Boasting a pitch-perfect recreation of America during this time – from the clothes to the hairstyles, attitudes and music (one of the reasons only some of the episodes are available on DVD is that it's too expensive to secure the DVD music rights for some of the other episodes) – this appealed to adults yearning a dose of nostalgia as well as teens more interested in the relationships, fights and make-ups between Kevin, Winnie, Wayne, hippie sister Karen and Kevin's best friend, nerdy Paul (played by Josh Saviano, and not a young Marilyn Manson as some websites would lead you to believe). The show finished with an episode that featured an epilogue set eight years later and revealed what happened to grown-up Kevin, his family and friends.

TV Trivia: The character of Winnie took a background role for one season because actress Danica McKellar had experienced a growth spurt and was too tall to play alongside Fred Savage (she was brought to the forefront again when Savage had himself grown a bit taller).

SUPERHEROES AND ACTION HEROES

TOUGH GUYS, GOOD GUYS AND BAD GUYS WITH SUPERHUMAN POWERS... BUT ALAS, NO *AUTOMAN*, *STREETHAWK* OR *MAN FROM ATLANTIS*...

THE ADVENTURES OF YOUNG INDIANA JONES (1992–1999)
Starring Sean Patrick Flanery

Originally titled *The Young Indiana Jones Chronicles* when it was a weekly series in the early nineties of 45-minute episodes, the name was changed for a series of 1999 TV movies featuring the younger version of Harrison Ford's much-loved movie character, and it is that title that has been used for the DVD releases of both the episodes (now re-edited into feature-length episodes) and TV movies. Sean Patrick Flanery is the young Indy (while Corey Carrier plays him as a little boy), who grows up to be an archaeologist and professor, but here is a teenager who manages to have adventures wherever he goes, and usually ends up meeting an important historical character in the process, from T.E. Lawrence (aka *Lawrence Of Arabia*) to Pablo Picasso, Franz Kafka and Thomas Edison.

The collections cover episodes from 1908 to the 1920s, and feature guest stars including Catherine Zeta Jones, Daniel Craig, Elizabeth Hurley and Timothy Spall. They also boast accompanying well-researched documentaries, tying in Indy's adventures with the real-life events he encounters, so there's some really fascinating education stuff along with the rip-roaring adventures.

With George Lucas overseeing the entire project, it's just as slick, funny, enjoyable and exciting as the classic movies, and – of course – was released at the end of 2007/early 2008 just in time to get us all in the mood for 2008's fourth cinema Indiana Jones adventure, *Indiana Jones And The Kingdom Of The Crystal Skull*.

TV trivia: George Lucas plotted a whole *Indiana Jones* time line, from 1910 up to when we meet him in *Raiders of the Lost Ark*, including who Indy would meet in the intervening years. It's said he had up to 70 plots for the TV series planned, but only 31 were made.

THE A-TEAM (1983–1987)

Starring George Peppard, Dirk Benedict, Mr T, Dwight Schultz

An outrageously preposterous action series that was a phenomenal success for its first couple of years on air, *The A-Team* captured the hearts of boys big and small from the moment the intro music ('dah dah dah, da-da-daah') started and the narrator told us the background to the series: 'In 1972 a crack commando unit was sent to prison by a military court for a crime they didn't commit. These men promptly escaped from a maximum security stockade to the Los Angeles underground. Today, still wanted by the government, they survive as soldiers of fortune. If you have a problem, if no one else can help, and if you can find them, maybe you can hire... *the A-Team.*'

The team were, of course, cigar-chomping leader (and occasional B-movie extra) 'Hannibal' Smith (Peppard), engineer/muscleman B.A Baracus (Mr T), who was terrified of flying and had to be sedated in just about every episode, smooth-talking trickster 'Face' Peck (Benedict) and 'Howling Mad' Murdock, a former pilot now sequestered in a mental institution until the boys spring him out. Each week, they would get in their distinctive black van and help someone who couldn't go to the cops, by pulling scams, tricking bad guys, having a few shootouts (in which, miraculously, no one ever seemed to die, possibly because the series had a huge children's following) and usually build some amazing tank/weapon/escape vehicle using a couple of paper clips and an old tyre. And all before the army (led by Lance LeGault's Colonel Decker) turned up to bungle another arrest of the Team. Of course, it was all very formulaic, (catchphrases like 'I love it when a plan comes together' ended up being in every episode), and by the third series had begun to look somewhat worn around the edges. Fans knew it had truly gone all wrong when eighties pop star Boy George turned up in a 1986 episode, 'Cowboy George', playing himself... badly.

TV Trivia: The crime the gang 'didn't commit' was a robbery of the Bank of Hanoi. They had been instructed to do it by their senior commander, but when he was murdered there was no evidence the team had been acting under orders.

ADAM ADAMANT LIVES! (1966)

Starring Gerald Harper, Juliet Harmer

It only ran for 29 episodes (over two series), but this bonkers British show – produced by Doctor Who's Verity Lambert, no less – is memorable, firstly for the daft plot: Edwardian adventurer Adam Adamant (Harper) is frozen by his enemy The Face in 1902, only for him to accidentally defrost in 1966. Of course, life in the swinging sixties is a bit bewildering for our hero, but he soon comes to terms with his environment with the help of Georgina Jones (Harmer), and together they fight crime using his turn-of-the-century sword-fighting skills.

Camper than *The Avengers*, this also boasts some episodes directed by Ridley Scott (best known for his acclaimed movies such as *Blade Runner*, *Alien* and *Gladiator*), and scripts by *Avengers'* writers Brian Clemens and Tony Williamson. It's not desperately original once Adam is solving a crime, but the premise is a treat (and, perhaps, an inspiration for *Austin Powers*). Sadly some of the episodes were lost by the BBC, but all the remaining ones – including the entire first series bar one episode– are available on DVD.

 TV Trivia: One episode, 'D For Destruction', was thought missing until it was discovered in 2003 in a mislabelled film can.

AIRWOLF (1984–1986)

Starring Jan Michael Vincent, Alex Cord, Ernest Borgnine

Vincent, who had become something of a pin-up following his role in the mini-series *The Winds of War*, took on the lead hero role for this action series devised by Donald Bellisario (*Magnum PI*) about a man and his flying machine. Vietnam vet Stringfellow Hawke (great name) is something of a brooding loner following the loss of his brother (missing in action), living in a remote area with only an owl and his cello for company. That is, until the US government gives him a call after a super hi-tech helicopter called Airwolf is stolen. They think Hawke is the man to retrieve it, and he agrees in return for help in finding his brother. When the men in suits let him down, Hawke does the sensible thing and nicks the 'copter for himself, hiding it away in a cave. Unable to find it, the government lets him keep it on the understanding that Hawke uses it to perform covert missions on their behalf with the help of his pal, Dominic Santini (Borgnine) and under the instruction of white-suited agent Archangel (Cord).

The helicopter is the star of the show, thanks to some whizzy technological gadgets and neat flying stunts, though Vincent does a pretty nice turn as the sullen loner who really just wants to be left in peace. The first two seasons are an entertaining mix of sometimes moralising plots, action, humour and sadness that was surprisingly dark for a show that appealed to children, but things took a bit of a nosedive, plot-wise, in Season 3, and the show was cancelled (there were also rumours that Vincent's alcoholism affected production). A fourth season featuring a new cast was made in 1987, with Barry Van Dyke starring as Hawke's formerly missing brother, but was made on a much smaller budget and was cancelled after 24 episodes. *Blue Thunder*, the other series featuring a hi-tech flying machine, is only available on DVD in the US.

 TV Trivia: Watch out for *Beverly Hills 90210*'s Shannen Doherty in the early episode 'Bite of The Jackal' as a little girl who stows away on Airwolf.

BATMAN (1966–1968)

Starring Adam West, Burt Ward

1966's *Batman* only lasted two years, but thanks to its campy nature, over the top performances from Adam West (as Batman and his millionaire alter-ego Bruce Wayne) and Burt Ward (as sidekick Robin, who was also Wayne's teenage ward Dick Grayson) and scheduling during children's TV, it became a huge hit and a camp classic that remains a favourite to this day.

The dynamic duo, as they were known, lived in a comic book world of bright colours, wacky camera angles and exaggerated action scenes punctuated with words like 'zap!', 'pow!' and 'smash!' flashing across the screen. It also helped that the villians were so much fun, be it Burgess Meredith (later Rocky's trainer in *Rocky*) as The Penguin, Frank Gorshin as The Riddler, Cesar Romero as The Joker and, of course, Julie Newmar (and later, Eartha Kitt and Lee Merriweather) as slinky sexpot Catwoman, who was surely too sexy for children's TV. (Other notable guest stars included Otto Preminger, Tallulah Bankhead and Liberace.)

While many Batman fans think it's far too camp and silly, Batman creator Bob Kane commented that the show's popularity actually saved the comic books series from being cancelled (once the TV show ended, it's interesting to note that the comic books got much darker, perhaps giving inspiration for Tim Burton's dark 1989 movie *Batman* and subsequent movie versions). The series also features arguably the most recognisable Batmobile – a customised 1955 Lincoln Futura, designed by George Barris who also designed the cars for the Munsters – which was criticised by the National Safety Council of the US for not having seat belts. (In later episodes, Batman and Robin are seen buckling up before driving off to save the day.)

 TV Trivia: During the first season, Burt Ward was paid just $350 a week.

BATMAN: THE ANiMATED SERiES (1992–1995)

Voices by Kevin Conroy, Bob Hastings, Loren Lester

Also known as The Adventures of Batman and Robin, this animated version of Bob Kane's comic book creation is darker than the camp sixties live action series, and features a very square-jawed caped crusader battling the various bad guys that roam Gotham City. Considered by fans to be the definitive version of the Batman story, this deliciously bleak adaptation works really well in animated form, allowing the illustrators to create truly menacing bad guys as well as giving Batman wings that don't come courtesy of CGI.

Numerous episodes were made, including 'Two-Face', which examines the psychology behind Harvey Dent's split personality, 'Beware The Grey Ghost', in which Batman teams up with his own childhood hero, the Grey Ghost (as voiced by sixties Batman Adam West) and 'The Man Who Killed Batman', an episode in which the man in the cape dies, much to the distress of his arch-enemy The Joker, who wishes he had killed Batman himself.

Although aimed at children, this is gripping stuff for adults as the lone hero deals with his grief over the loss of his parents by fighting crime, and is a must for fans of the original comics. As well as over 80 thirty-minute episodes, various spin-off feature length TV movies have been made including *Batman: The Mask of the Phantasm* (1993) and *Batman Beyond: The Movie* (1999).

 TV Trivia: The voice of The Joker is provided by Mark Hamill, best known, of course, for his role as Luke Skywalker in the original three *Star Wars* **movies. He also provides voices for the animated series** *Robot Chicken*, *Spawn* **and** *Avatar*.

BAYWATCH (1989–2001)

Starring David Hasselhoff, Pamela Anderson, Yasmin Bleeth, Gena Lee Nolin, Carmen Electra

It's hard to believe now, but Baywatch — which ran for an impressive nine seasons despite having only about six episodes' worth of plots — was cancelled after its first season due to low ratings. Star Hasselhoff believed it had potential, though, so he invested his own money and got other financial backers involved (including British TV channel LWT) to bring it back, and it went on to be such a success it even spawned a spin-off, Baywatch Nights (unavailable on DVD, possibly because it was so awful) and the TV movie Baywatch: Hawaiian Reunion.

While it is best known now for launching the centrefold careers of its curvaceous actresses (many of whom went on to pose for *Playboy* and other men's magazines), *Baywatch* did, in the early days at least, have something of a plot. Mitch Buchannon (Hasselhoff), a veteran lifeguard and ex-Navy SEAL, watches over the younger lifeguards that come and go while also raising his son, Hobie (originally played by cutie Brandon Call and later by the more whiny Jeremy Jackson). He also saves drowning swimmers and solves crimes that occur near his beach in Santa Monica and... oh, forget it. Males of all ages didn't tune in to watch Hasselhoff fighting crime (that's what reruns of *Knight Rider* are for), they tuned in for the slow-motion scenes (which became longer and more frequent as the show progressed) of tanned Pamela Anderson, Carmen Electra and pouting pals as they ran along the beach in their straining red swimming cossies, floatation device tucked under their toned arms (surely they didn't need one, as they had two bouncing up and down already...).

Badly acted, incredibly silly – over the years, plots twists included a sea monster, a psycho fisherman, evil gold prospectors and a nuclear bomb – but strangely absorbing, *Baywatch* lost many of its cast members in later years (speculation has it they left when old plots were regurgitated), with only Hasselhoff remaining until the series end. In 1999, the plan was to relocate filming to Sydney, Australia, but local residents objected. Eventually Hawaii was chosen as a location for the final series and the name of the show was changed to *Baywatch Hawaii* for the final two seasons.

 TV Trivia: *Baywatch* has been credited with being the most watched show internationally of all time, with 1.1 billion viewers – at one point the show was broadcast on every continent except Antarctica.

THE BiONiC WOMAN (1976–1978)

Starring Lindsay Wagner, Richard Anderson

Following the huge success of *The Six Million Dollar Man* (see review, p.186), the creators came up with this equally enjoyably (though slightly dafter) spin-off about another crime fighter with robotic body bits and pieces. When her parachute fails to open, Jaime Sommers' (Wagner) body is pretty squished, but, yes, there are people who do have the power and the capability to rebuild her. She gets a new ear (with, of course, super hearing), a super-strength arm, and two super-speedy bionic legs, which comes in very handy when she is pursuing bad guys for the OSI (Office of Scientific Investigation). Jaime was actually even more special than the sum of her bionic parts – her character (the girlfriend of *Six Million Dollar Man* Steve Austin) had actually died in an episode of *Six Million Dollar Man*, her body having rejected the bionic bits, only for the next season's opener to reveal she was actually in a coma (good thing they hadn't cremated her). When she awakes, she has amnesia and doesn't remember Steve (and a weird blood clot means that if she does remember him, she'll have blinding headaches!), making it nice and easy for the producers to explain how Jaime gets on with life as a bionic woman without pining for her former fiancé (the pair were brought back together for a series of spin-off movies, though).

The series was very similar to *The Six Million Dollar Man*, boasted some of the same cast (Anderson as Jaime's boss Oscar Goldman and Martin E. Brooks as Dr Rudy Wells), and there were often episodes that 'crossed-over': for example, the three-episode 'Kill Oscar' from Season 2 – the first and third episodes of the story were for *The Bionic Woman*, whereas the middle episode was actually an episode of *The Six Million Dollar Man*. Sadly, because of those similarities, it was cancelled in the same year (1978) as Lee Majors' series, but not before a bionic dog, Maximillian, was added to the cast.

A new, improved *Bionic Woman* was launched on TV in 2007, with ex-*EastEnder* Michelle Ryan in the role of Jaime. Unfortunately, the series was cancelled after just a few episodes, but those that were made are available on DVD.

 TV Trivia: In the spin-off movie, *Bionic Showdown* (1989), a young Sandra Bullock starred as the Bionic Girl.

CHARLIE'S ANGELS (1976–1981)

Starring Farrah Fawcett, Jaclyn Smith, Kate Jackson, Cheryl Ladd

Back in the seventies, everyone had their favourite angel. If you were a little girl, you chose which angel – the sensible one with the dark bob, the busty blonde or the pouty brunette – you wanted to be in the playground, while little boys (and big ones) had their own favourite angels, too (a poster of Farrah Fawcett in a cossie became one of the bestselling posters of all time). Devised by Aaron Spelling, *Charlie's Angels* was, as the opening credits said, about 'three little girls who went to the police academy and they were each assigned very hazardous duties. But I took them away from all that, and now they work for me. My name is Charlie.' Charlie, of course, was never seen – the voice was provided by *Dynasty*'s John Forsythe – but the girls took their instructions from him in each episode and then went off and kicked butt wherever they were needed, with the help of Charlie's employee, Bosley (David Doyle).

For the first season, the angels were Jill Munroe (Fawcett), Kelly Garrett

(Smith) and Sabrina Duncan (Jackson), but following Fawcett's departure, Cheryl Ladd was brought in as Jill's little sister, Kris. Later, Shelley Hack and Tanya Roberts joined the cast following Ladd and Jackson's exits, leaving Smith as the only star to remain for the entire five years. Originally dubbed 'jiggle TV' by the American press, due to the angels' outfits when they went undercover to help someone (for some reason, undercover situations usually involved them wearing bikinis or maid outfits), the series actually boasted some pretty serious episodes as well as the campy ones most people remember, including 'Angels In Chains', featuring a young Kim Basinger, and 'Angel On My Mind', in which Kris loses her memory after witnessing a murder and can't be found by her fellow angels.

 TV Trivia: Michelle Pfeiffer is rumoured have auditioned for the role of one of Charlie's Angels early in her career.

THE DUKES OF HAZZARD (1979–1985)

Starring Tom Wopat, John Schneider, Catherine Bach, Denver Pyle

With that catchy country theme song ('Just the good ole' boys, Never meanin' no harm, Beats all you never saw, been in trouble with the law since the day they was born...'), numerous car chases and smashes, funny scripts and Catherine Bach in the shortest denim shorts ever, this series was loved by boys and men of all ages. The Dukes, of course, were Bo (Schneider) and Luke (Wopat), two cousins who live with another cousin, Daisy (Bach) and Uncle Jesse (Pyle) on a farm in Georgia. The boys are good guys who always seem to be in trouble as they speed through the arid countryside in their 1969 Dodge Charger car, The General Lee, usually trying to outrun obese Boss Hogg (Sorrell Booke) and the corrupt nincompoop sheriff, Roscoe P. Coltrane (James Best).

Boys everywhere banged their heads trying to emulate the Dukes as they eschewed car doors and instead used the windows of the General Lee to get in and out, and one imagines more than a few cars in the late seventies were dented by young drivers wanting to send their Austin Maestro flying through the sky (perhaps not the best idea – during production, over 200 cars were smashed). A dumb, fun piece of entertainment that managed to have a moral centre in between the car crashes, *The Dukes of Hazzard* ran for seven seasons.

Two spin-off TV movies were made (1997's *Reunion!* and 2000's *Hazzard in Hollywood*) but they are not available on DVD. In 2005, the Dukes hit the big screen with *The Dukes of Hazzard* which is now available on DVD. A further movie, *Dukes of Hazzard: The Beginning*, that follows Bo and Luke as teenagers, was made in 2007 and is on DVD – but don't bother, it's terrible.

TV Trivia: Over half of the fan mail sent to the show was addressed to the General Lee.

THE FALL GUY (1981–1986)

Starring Lee Majors, Douglas Barr, Heather Thomas

Majors had already proved he was one of the best TV action heroes of the seventies in *The Six Million Dollar Man*, and in the eighties he followed that up with this fun adventure about a movie stuntman named Colt Seavers, who worked as a bounty hunter when he wasn't filming. With the help and often hindrance of his cousin, Howie (Barr), and blonde totty Jody (Thomas), Seavers got into various scrapes both on set and on the trail of bad guys he was tracking down for bail bond agent Big Jack (Jo Ann Pflug).

Packed with car chases, explosions, fisticuffs, guns, gals and daredevil stunts, the testosterone-fuelled series was created by Glen A. Larson, who also made *Knight Rider*, *Magnum PI* and *BJ and the Bear* (the last, sadly not on DVD). A must for fans of *Hooper*, *Smokey and the Bandit* and their ilk, this is inoffensive, highly entertaining stuff that may not win prizes for clever scripts or deeply thought-out acting, but gets the gold star for sheer adrenalin adventure. Lou Rawls, James Coburn, Heather Locklear and Majors' ex, Farrah Fawcett, were among the guest stars during the show's 100-plus episodes.

TV Trivia: Majors also sang the theme song, 'The Unknown Stuntman', which featured lyrics such as 'I might jump an open drawbridge, or Tarzan from a vine, 'Cause I'm the Unknown Stuntman that makes Eastwood look so fine.'

FANTASTIC FOUR (1994–1996)

Voices by Beau Weaver, Brian Austin Green, Lori Alan

Reed Richards, Sue and Johnny Storm and Ben Grimm take a trip on a new space shuttle, only for them to be bombarded by radiation. Back on earth, they discover they have been transformed – Sue can become invisible, Reed (rather arrogantly calling himself Mr Fantastic) is all stretchy, Johnny (The Human Torch) can burst into flames and Ben has come over all rock-like, so the poor man gets the name 'The Thing'. Together they fight crime as The Fantastic Four.

Unfortunately, like the live action movie that was to come later, the crime fighters in this animated series aren't that fantastic, despite being based on comic book characters created by Stan Lee. The Thing, bless him, is little more than comic relief, while Mr Fantastic is a know-it-all, Sue/Invisible Woman is a bit wet and The Human Torch just runs around being annoying and shouting 'Flame on!' at every possible opportunity (oh, to have a fire extinguisher handy). It's all pretty dull with some very basic animation, although things do perk up slightly in the second season. Missable stuff, though.

 TV Trivia: Brian Austin Green, who voiced the Human Torch in the first series, is better known as sweet-faced David in *Beverly Hills 90210*.

THE FUGITIVE (1963–1967)

Starring David Janssen, Barry Morse

Loosely based on a real-life case (the Sam Sheppard case in the 1950s that has been the subject of TV movies and documentaries), The Fugitive, is, of course, the edge-of-the-seat series that followed Richard Kimble (Janssen), a doctor wrongly accused of murdering his wife, as he escaped custody and tried to stay one step ahead of the law as he also attempted to prove his innocence. He says that when he got home, he saw a one-armed man fleeing the scene, but no one believes him, although Philip Gerard (Morse), the relentless cop determined to bring Kimble back to justice does, over the course of the episodes, begin to wonder whether Kimble may just be telling the truth. Each week, Kimble would be moving on to another place to find this mysterious man, and on his travels he would often, anonymously, come to the aid of someone using his medical training. For 120 episodes he ran, until the final two-part episode *The Judgement* which, when it was broadcast in the US, was watched by 30 million viewers (about 70 per cent of the TV audience). Tense, clever, and anchored by a mesmerising central performance from Janssen, it's still terrific four decades later and inspired both the 1993 Harrison Ford movie, and a TV remake in 2000 with Tim Daly that was less successful.

 TV Trivia: Originally, the possible murderer was going to have red hair, but the producers decided it would be more distinctive to have a man with one arm.

THE INCREDIBLE HULK (1978–1982)

Starring Bill Bixby, Lou Ferrigno

Hollywood may try and remake it with splashy CGI effects and a mega-budget, but to anyone who grew up in the 1970s, there is only one Hulk, and that is former Mr Universe Lou Ferrigno. Based on the *Marvel* comic (in which the lead character is named Bruce, not David), the story is, of course, about mild-mannered scientist David Banner (Bixby) and his hulking alter-ego. Bereft at the death of his wife and his inability to save her, he's dosed up on gamma radiation that was part of his experiment to harness a human being's true power, and has discovered it has a nasty side-effect: whenever he gets angry ('Don't make me angry. You wouldn't like me when I'm angry'), Banner turns into a huge, green, grunting beast (Ferrigno). To make matters worse, the Hulk has been falsely accused of murder, leading Banner to run from town to town, trying to find a cure for his rage while also attempting to clear the big green guy's name.

It's all preposterous, of course – especially Banner's transformation into Hulk, which involves some green light effects and lashings of emerald make-up, but no explanation as to how Banner's shirt rips during his expansion but his trousers only fray below the knee (surely his fly would pop open due to its straining, at least). But silliness like that is part of the fun as the lone man with a terrible secret roams from town to town, helping people by letting his inner green guy out. Forget the plots – tune in for the grunting, the seventies effects and a really nice central performance from the late Bixby, who sadly died in 1993 aged 59, of prostate cancer.

As well as the series, there were three spin-off movies that are all available on DVD – *The Incredible Hulk Returns* (1988), *The Trial of the Incredible Hulk* (1989) and *The Death of the Incredible Hulk* (1990), the last two of which Bixby directed.

 TV Trivia: Richard Kiel (aka 'Jaws' from the Bond movies, and Arnold Schwarzenegger were both considered for the role of Hulk.

THE INCREDIBLE HULK (1996–1997)

Voices by Neal McDonough, Lou Ferrigno, Matt Frewer, Mark Hamill

An animated series based on the big green *Marvel* comic character, this only lasted for 21 half-hour episodes. As well as reminding viewers of the Hulk's back story – Dr Banner's misuse of gamma radiation causes him to turn into a big muscular hulk whenever he gets angry – the series introduced characters including The Leader (Frewer), who wants the Hulk power for himself, and his henchmen The Gargoyle (Hamill) and The Abomination.

The animation is colourful and the action comes thick and fast in most episodes, while the first season remained true to the spirit of the original comics. Unfortunately things took a turn for the worse in the second season with the introduction of She-hulk, who spends far too much time quipping and not enough time kicking butt. Two other animated versions have been made – a lighter cartoon series in 1982 that is also known as *The All New Incredible Hulk*, and 1966's *Hulk*, with Max Ferguson as the voice of the Hulk, but neither is available on DVD.

 TV Trivia: Hulk creator Stan Lee provides the voice of She-Hulk's father in one episode, 'Down Memory Lane'.

JUSTICE LEAGUE (2001–2006)

Voices by Kevin Conroy, George Newbern

Known as *Justice League Unlimited* from its third season, this cartoon series is based on the comic book, *Justice League of America*, that brought together superheroes Batman, Superman, Wonder Woman, The Green Lantern, The Flash, Martian Manhunter and Hawkgirl (in the original comics, the final member was Aquaman, but it was felt another female was needed for the series). Together they fight crime and various bad guys such as Lex Luthor, a super-intelligent ape called Gorilla Grodd, Arthurian legend Morgan le Fay, Darkseid and The Joker.

The idea of bringing all these superheroes together had been explored once before on TV with the naff seventies kiddie cartoon *Superfriends* (only available on US DVD) but this is much more adult-friendly fare, boasting some witty scripts, decent plots, impressive animation, and even some flirtation between Wonder Woman and The Flash. A must for comic book fans.

TV Trivia: Fan favourite Tim Daly, who voiced Superman for the animated Superman series (see review, p.192), was unable to reprise his role here due to filming commitments, so the role was offered to George Newbern, who is best known for his guest role as Danny in the series *Friends*.

KNIGHT RIDER (1982–1986)

Starring David Hasselhoff, Edward Mulhare

One of those eighties series that sounds daft on paper, but somehow worked both as a children's TV series and a grown up one, too. The story was set out in the series pilot – cop Michael Long is shot and left for dead during an investigation. Then along comes millionaire Wilton Knight (whom we briefly see in the pilot as played by Richard Basehart), who gives Michael a new face and a new name: Michael Knight (Hasselhoff). Wilton wants Michael – with the help of posh associate Devon Miles (Mulhare) – to wage a war against those criminals who operate above the law, and he gives him a nice little gadget to aid his quest: KITT (as voiced by William Daniels), the Knight Industries Two Thousand, a souped-up Pontiac Trans Am car with a flashing red light at the front and the ability to go at great speeds. Oh, and KITT has an onboard computer that can talk with Michael, and it drives itself, too.

At the time, the technology (both real and imagined) featured in the show was really novel, whereas nowadays, when you think of onboard car computers, sat nav and even the Austin Maestro that told you to put your seatbelts on, it doesn't seem that far-fetched at all. One could argue that the car's acting was better than Hasselhoff's (certainly, Daniels has more expression in his voice than our Dave has in his whole body), but this kitsch but watchable show was really about a lone, brooding vigilante in impossibly tight jeans who thankfully didn't say that much, and a car that everyone coveted.

The best series was the first one, which included the episode 'Trust Doesn't Rust' with KITT's evil twin car, KARR, while Season 2 has some of the worst episodes of all, including one in which Michael gets amnesia 'Knightmares', another with his evil twin Garthe 'Goliath, Goliath Returns' and – shudder – the episode 'Let It Be Me', in which Michael has to go undercover as the lead singer of a rock band (giving wannabe pop star Hasselhoff a chance to stretch his vocal chords).

A future-set, and incredibly awful, TV movie reuniting the cast, *Knight Rider 2000*, was made in 1991 and is available on DVD. There was also a movie loosely based on the series called *Knight Rider 2010* that doesn't feature any of the original cast, and a short-lived spin-off series, *Team Knight Rider*, in 1997, but neither is thankfully on DVD.

 TV Trivia: The line spoken at the beginning of every episode was: 'Knight Rider. A shadowy flight into the dangerous world of a man...who does not exist.'

MACGYVER (1985–1992)

Starring Richard Dean Anderson, Dana Elcar

You can imagine someone in a bar once said: 'I know, let's make a series like *The A-Team*... but with just one guy!' and the end result was this testosterone-fuelled series that became something of a hit with ladies of a certain age due to its star, Richard Dean Anderson (Homer Simpson's unattractive sisters-in-law, Patty and Selma, are so obsessed with him that they actually kidnap their rugged hero in an episode of *The Simpsons*, with Anderson supplying his character's voice). The premise was certainly similar – hero rights wrongs with nothing but a pen knife and his quick wits – with a few tweaks: MacGyver doesn't carry a gun due to his deeply felt principles, and he's a scientific whiz, which comes in handy when he has to make an intricate gizmo that will save the good guy and hamper the bad guy, all at the touch of a button… or stops a chemical leak with some chocolate bars (yes, really).

Boasting one of the worst mullets on TV, Anderson isn't exactly god's gift to acting, nor does the surprisingly limited action make up for his lack of different facial expressions. Instead, this is best watched as a nostalgia piece for those kids (and mums) who thought Anderson was cool two decades ago, rather than by anyone actually looking for a fast-paced slice of entertainment. Two TV movies, *MacGyver: Lost Treasure of Atlantis* and *Trail to Doomsday*, were made after the series finished in 1994, and a pilot episode for a TV series, *Young MacGyver* in 2003 – none are available on DVD.

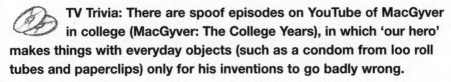 **TV Trivia: There are spoof episodes on YouTube of MacGyver in college (MacGyver: The College Years), in which 'our hero' makes things with everyday objects (such as a condom from loo roll tubes and paperclips) only for his inventions to go badly wrong.**

MiGHTY MORPHiN POWER RANGERS (1993–1996)

Starring Austin St John, Amy Jo Johnson, Thuy Trang, Steve Cardenas

Possibly the oddest kids' show to become a big hit, the *Power Rangers* was a strange mish-mash of American and Japanese ideas. The action sequences were taken from a Japanese series named *Kyoryu Sentai Zyuranger* featuring Japanese actors and some bad dubbing, and then the non-action sequences were filmed in the US using American actors – it worked, simply because the Power Rangers wore biker helmets, so audiences (supposedly) wouldn't notice that each role was played by two people. The story was this: an evil witch named Rita Repulsa has been released from 10,000 years of confinement, and has headed to earth with an army of Space Aliens. A wise man named Zordon decides the only hope for Earth is to find five teenagers to defend the planet, and gives them snazzy bold-coloured biker outfits and helmets in order to fight Rita (the five become six when former bad kid Tommy joins the power rangers). Upon yelling 'It's morphin' time!', the gang would hold their power morphers (a rather naff gadget that looked like it had been made out of sticky-backed plastic and some cardboard) and chant out the name of the creature that gave them their powers, then the battle (usually a rather badly play-acted kicking fest) would commence.

Badly acted, badly dubbed, badly written, and packed with awful special-effects, this series made about as much sense as building a cooker out of chocolate. Kids loved it, but for anyone above the age (mental or physical) of 13, the show's appeal remains an utter mystery. A contender for the worst TV series ever made.

 TV Trivia: Although the yellow power ranger is a girl, she wears trousers because in the original Japanese series, the yellow ranger was a man (whereas the pink power ranger is a woman in both countries, so her outfit includes a skirt).

MONKEY (1978–1980)

Starring Masaaki Sakai, Masako Natsume

Known as *Saiyuki* in its native Japan, this series was dubbed into English and broadcast on BBC TV in 1979 (although the final 13 episodes were not translated until the DVD release in 2002). Based on the Chinese novel *Journey to the West*, it was filmed in Mongolia and Northern China but with Japanese actors, and the tongue-in-cheek dubbed dialogue was then written by David Weir for British audiences. Monkey is an arrogant king who is imprisoned under a mountain to learn humility. When he is released, he embarks on a pilgrimage to find holy scrolls with the priest Tripitaka, along with a water monster named Sandy and a pig spirit named Pigsy who help Monkey whenever bad creatures attack them along the way.

Something of a cult phenomenon, especially in Australia, *Monkey* has a certain charm, thanks to Weir's anglicised scripts, the wonky acting and even wonkier effects. Backed by a horrendous disco-style soundtrack, including, of course, the unforgettable theme 'Monkey Magic', this is one of those series that you can't actually believe was ever made until you see it for yourself.

TV Trivia: Masaaki Sakai is a former Japanese pop star.

THE PERSUADERS (1971–1972)

Starring Roger Moore, Tony Curtis

Those sideburns! Those ties! Those dashing polo necks! It must be *The Persuaders*! Deliciously daft, this early seventies series followed the adventures of two wealthy international playboys, Lord Brett Sinclair (Moore) and American Danny Wilde (Curtis). Brought together by Judge Fulton (Laurence Naismith), he gives them the option of going to jail for their frivolous ways, or teaming up to solve the crimes that the government can't figure out. Of course, the two are complete opposites – Sinclair is from old, inherited money, and has a touch of class; Wilde is a brash self-made million-aire – and they spend as much time arguing as they do foiling assassination attempts and bringing criminals to justice.

Fans of *The Saint* (see below) will love this jolly series that's part buddy show and part crime-solving adventure. Curtis and Moore (who here shows the dashing hero style that later won him the role of James Bond) had terrific onscreen chemistry – clearly, neither took their roles too seriously, which makes it all the more fun – and the episodes are packed with lovely ladies, fast cars and those memorable seventies fashions. Sadly, only 24 episodes were made.

> **TV Trivia: Brett Sinclair's car had the licence plate 'BS 1' — this wasn't produced especially for the show, it was actually a licence plate on loan from circus master Billy Smart, Jr.**

THE SAINT (1962–1969)/RETURN OF THE SAINT (1978–1979)
Starring Roger Moore, Ivor Dean

Ah, the sixties – a time when Britain really was cool, thanks to James Bond, The Beatles and a young Roger Moore zipping through the countryside in his white Volvo P1800 (licence plate, ST 1) as Simon Templar, aka The Saint. In 71 black and white and then 42 colour episodes, his Brylcreemed hair shone, the ladies swooned and the international man of mystery usually saved the day.

Based on the books by Leslie Charteris, some of which had already been adapted for radio and the big screen, the series focused on Simon as he fought injustice (and in one daft instance, attempted to catch the Loch Ness monster) while often pocketing the loot of any rich bad guy who crossed his path (well, how else could he fund his jetset lifestyle?)

While the series has dated, there's still immense fun to be had watching Moore in a variety of get-ups (Simon likes disguises), dodging Inspector Teal (Dean) who doesn't think Templar should be above the law, while the distinctive theme and the halo that appears around Moore's head in each episode still raises a smile. The early black and white episodes are the best – including 'The Arrow of God', co-starring Honor Blackman, and 'Judith', with Julie Christie. The dashing Saint was resurrected for a new TV series in 1979 – *The Return of the Saint* – with Ian Ogilvy taking over the role of Simon, now in a Jaguar XJS. Boasting a bigger budget than the original series, 'Return' featured exotic locations, 'babes' including Kate O'Mara, Rula Lenska and Britt Ekland, and a slightly campy sense of humour, but is best remembered for the fab seventies opening titles and not for Ogilvy's rather wooden acting.

The entire series (24 episodes) is available on DVD. In 1989 a series of made for TV movies were produced with Simon Dutton in the lead role, but these are currently not available on DVD.

 TV Trivia: 19 actors have played Simon Templar on big and small screen and the radio, including George Sanders, Vincent Price and Val Kilmer.

THE SIX MILLION DOLLAR MAN (1973–1978)

Starring Lee Majors, Richard Anderson, Martin E Brooks

'Steve Austin: astronaut. A man barely alive. We can rebuild him. We have the technology. We can make him better than he was. Better…stronger…faster.' So began this cracking series that soon had children mimicking high-speed running in the playground – when they weren't playing with their Steve Austin action figure (complete with magnifying eye you could look through and peel-back skin so you could see the 'bionics'), eating from their *Six Million Dollar Man* lunchbox or reading the spin-off comic book.

As the introduction suggested, Steve Austin (Majors) was an astronaut before an accident left him mushed up beyond all recognition. The government decides to rebuild him, giving him bionic legs that helped him run at super speed and jump tall buildings, a bionic arm (the right one) with a crushing grip, and a robotic left eye that could see great distances – all for the bargain price of $6 million. Of course, they weren't just doing this to save his life – Austin was then put to work as a secret agent under the watchful eye of Oscar Goldman (Anderson) and doctor Rudi Wells (Brooks) investigating everything from terrorists and mad scientists to, erm, Bigfoot.

Loosely based on Martin Caidin's novel *Cyborg*, the series became so popular with children that the level of violence was turned down early on. It also spawned a spin-off series, *The Bionic Woman* (see review, p.190), after the Jaime Sommers character (Lindsay Wagner) appeared in an episode as Austin's former girlfriend, only for her to get squished doing a parachute jump from a plane (this, of course, led to her being made bionic). Due to various plot twists, the couple could not be together – possibly because she had her own TV series! – but after both series ended, there were three 'reunion' movies that eventually brought Jaime and Steve back together, and in the sappy but enjoyably awful *Bionic Ever After?* they were finally married. Awww. (Unfortunately, the spin-off movies are not available on DVD.)

 TV Trivia: Towards the end of the series, Majors grew a moustache. Fans didn't like it so he shaved it off, but not before some merchandise had been produced with him sporting facial hair.

SPIDER-MAN: THE ANIMATED SERIES (2003)

Voices by Neil Patrick Harris, Lisa Loeb, Ian Ziering

There have been a few versions of Spider-Man made for TV, including the camp 1967 animated adventure, a 1981 animated series, 1978's hilariously daft live action *The Amazing Spider-Man* (with bouffant-haired Nicholas Hammond as Peter Parker and some of the dodgiest special-effects you are ever likely to see on TV) and the mid-nineties cartoon series that boasted star voices including Hank Azaria, Martin Landau and Malcolm Dowell. While a few episodes of that series occasionally turn up on DVD, the most easily obtainable is, unsurprisingly, the most recent adaptation of Spider-Man, 2003's animated series that ran for just 13 episodes.

Created by using computer animation but made to look like a traditional animated series, this Spider-Man is brought up to date (our hero and his pals all have mobile phones, etc) but the story background remains the same: student Peter (Harris) is bitten by a spider that gives him the power to shoot webs from his fingers and climb tall buildings, so he makes a snazzy red and blue costume and saves the day once in a while, his face hidden behind a mask so even Peter's best friend Mary Jane (singer Lisa Loeb) doesn't know his secret. It's pretty standard stuff that never gets really exciting, and one can't help but wonder whether this animated version saw the light of day simply to cash in on the successful *Spider-Man* movies out at the cinema at the same time.

 TV Trivia: *Spider-Man* creator Stan Lee also created *The Fantastic Four* and *The Incredible Hulk*.

TEENAGE MUTANT NINJA TURTLES (1987-1996)

Voices by Rob Paulsen, Cam Clarke, Barry Gordon

Based on a 1984 comic book, the Teenage Mutant Ninja Turtles first came to TV in 1987 as an animated series, before later being made into a series of live action movies in the early nineties (a newer, edgier animated series began in 2003, too, followed by the computer animated movie *TMNT* in 2007). The turtles of the title are four teenage turtles (each with colour-coded masks so you can work out who is who) who have mutated thanks to some nasty goo, and now live in the Manhattan sewers where they train to be ninjas by their rat sensei, Splinter, and dine on their favourite food, pizza. As kids of the eighties remember, the turtles have distinctive Italian names and characters – Leonardo (the serious leader), Raphael (the bad boy), Donatello (the smart one) and Michelangelo (the fun one). The four are sometimes helped by

Casey Jones, a vigilante crime fighter, while their arch nemesis is Shredder.

The fun action series became phenomenally successful, although some parents worried that the ninja fighting was too violent for younger viewers, causing the British broadcast of the show to originally be renamed Teenage Mutant HERO Turtles, as the word 'ninja' was deemed too threatening – and soon Teenage Mutant Ninja Turtle action figures, lunch boxes, clothes and games were lining toyshop shelves. Unsurprisingly, the Turtles' phrases and language ('Turtle Power!' 'Cowabunga!') became de rigeur in the playground, and the fact that parents looked on disapprovingly made it even cooler.

 TV Trivia: In later episodes, Michelangelo's weapon of choice, the nunchaku, was replaced with a special turtle hook as nunchakus were outlawed in many countries where the series was shown.

THE WATER MARGIN (1976–1978)

Starring Atsuo Nakamura, Kei Sato

Before *Monkey* (see review p.184), there was *The Water Margin*, a Japanese series based on a Chinese folk tale that was dubbed into English (with scripts by David Weir) and with Burt Kwouk narrating the anglicised version. Twenty-six episodes were made, each telling the story of a group of 108 renegades, led by Lin Chung, who roam the land fighting bad guys and restoring honour.

Packed with pretty decent martial arts scenes and action set pieces, this is less silly than the more popular *Monkey*, and worth a look for fans of big screen adventures such as *Crouching Tiger Hidden Dragon*.

TV Trivia: The book on which this series is based is considered one of the four great classical novels of Chinese literature.

WONDER WOMAN (1976–1979)

Starring Lynda Carter, Lyle Waggoner

Men of a certain age will probably remember this series for curvy Carter's star-spangled costume (a tiny strapless swimsuit-like number which looked like it would fall down every time she did her Wonder Woman twirl), while little girls of the seventies loved it for a more innocent reason – Diana Prince (Carter) was a nice lady who transformed into a girly superhero. Cool!

Originally (for the first series at least) set during World War II (as was the comic, first written in 1941, in which the character first appeared), the story begins as Colonel Trevor (Waggoner) washes up on the secret Amazonian Paradise Island. He's nursed back to health by Princess Diana, and she then accompanies him back to Man's World (better known as Washington DC) under the alias Diana Prince and uses her superpowers to dispatch evil Nazis – with the help of her invisible plane, truth-getting lasso and bullet-deflecting bracelets. For the second season – by which time the production had switched from one US TV company, ABC, to CBS (the title was changed to *The New Adventures Of Wonder Woman*) – the action was brought forward to the present day: Steve (Waggoner again), the son of original Colonel Trevor, is in a plane crash near the Bermuda Triangle, and is saved by the ageless Diana. She decides to head back into the world in an even skimpier costume to kick some more ass in a series of rib-ticklingly silly adventures.

While all three seasons are campy and kitsch, it's the second season that is the treat, whether you're sniggering at the ropey 'special effects' for Wonder Woman's invisible plane (erm, how does she see the controls to fly it?), grinning as you spot Carter's stunt double (who looks suspiciously man-like), or rolling around in hysterics at the plots – choose from evil toys and a robotic Wonder Woman double ('The Deadly Toys'), mad scientists creating volcanoes ('The Man Who Made Volcanoes') or that old favourite: missing people near the Bermuda Triangle ('The Bermuda Triangle Crisis').

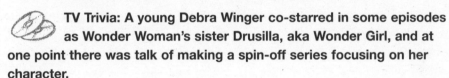 **TV Trivia: A young Debra Winger co-starred in some episodes as Wonder Woman's sister Drusilla, aka Wonder Girl, and at one point there was talk of making a spin-off series focusing on her character.**

X-MEN: EVOLUTION (2000)

Voices by Kirby Morrow, Venus Terzo, Brad Swaile

An animated *X-Men* series was first made in 1992, but it is only this reworking of the X-Men story that is available on DVD. As fans of the movies and comics will know, mutants live among us on Earth, hiding their ability to do cool things such as read minds, move objects or burn things with their eyes. Kindly Professor Xavier has brought some of these people together to a special school, to train them to use their abilities for good, while bad guy Magneto has gathered his own army of not-so-nice mutants ready to wage war. The difference here is that the mutants aren't grown ups – they are cool teens who are dealing with the usual pubescent angst as well as their burgeoning powers.

Unfortunately, this tweaking of the X-Men legend turns it into *Grange Hill* (except without the spotty faces and bad teeth). Too much time is spent on kids stuff, and not enough on zapping bad guy ass, and the end result is a tedious bore that only perks up when 'true' X-Men like Storm or Wolverine are featured.

 TV Trivia: Kirby Morrow, who voices Cyclops, began his career as a stand-up comedian.

OH, SUPERMAN

SUPERMAN FIRST CAME TO TV AS AN ANIMATED SERIAL IN THE FORTIES. THIS IS NOT ON DVD AND NEITHER IS THE SIXTIES ANIMATED *SUPERMAN*, WHICH BEGAN IN 1966 AND INTRODUCED SUPERBOY TO THE VIEWING PUBLIC. THERE WAS ALSO A SHORT-LIVED 1988 ANIMATED SERIES THAT'S NOT AVAILABLE ON DVD. IN 1988, SUPERBOY RETURNED IN LIVE-ACTION FORM, TELLING THE STORY OF OUR SUPERHERO'S TIME IN COLLEGE (AS PLAYED BY JOHN HAYMES NEWTON AND THEN GERARD CHRISTOPHER – ALAS, ONLY AVAILABLE ON US DVD). AND HERE ARE THE SUPERMAN INCARNATIONS YOU CAN GET ON DISC…

SMALLVILLE (2001–)

Starring Tom Welling, Kristin Kreuk, Michael Rosenbaum

Movies and comics touched on the early years of the Superman legend, but this series – aimed initially at teens – is wholly focused on Clark Kent's teenage life, before he headed off to Metropolis to save the world, romance Lois Lane (who appears from Season 4) and write hard-hitting news stories. Former model Tom Welling is the young Clark, who lives with mom Martha (Annette O'Toole, who played Lana Lang in the movie *Superman III*) and pop Jonathan (former Duke of Hazzard John Schneider) on their farm in the rural town of Smallville. Across the fields is his childhood pal (and secret crush) Lana (Kristin Kreuk), who was affected in her own way when a certain super-baby dropped from the sky during a meteor storm that killed her parents. While at school, Clark has pals Chloe (Allison Mack) and Pete (Sam Jones III), neither of whom know his super-secret. While each week featured a new foe (often locals affected by the toxic kryptonite, dubbed 'freaks of the week' by fans), the most interesting character is bad-guy-in-the-making Lex Luthor (Michael Rosenbaum). Exiled from Metropolis to Smallville by his father (John Glover), the bald-headed Lex (thanks again to that meteor shower) starts off as a nice guy who befriends Clark after the teenager saves his life, so viewers get to anticipate his descent into mad and bad-ness.

The first season was a good start (although there were a few too many 'freak' shows and not enough plot development for the recurring characters), but things picked up considerably by Season 2. Must-see episodes include 'Exile' (Season 3), in which Clark embarks on a Metropolis crime spree having been infected by mood-changing red kryptonite, and the 100th episode, 'Reckoning' (Season 5), a weepie in which Clark loses someone close to him.

 TV Trivia: The mansion used for Lex Luthor's home is the same one seen in the X-Men movie *X2*.

SUPERMAN (1996–2000)

Voices by Tim Daly, Dana Delaney, Joely Fisher

This enjoyable animated TV series was made following the success of *Batman: The Animated Series*. TV actor Tim Daly provided the voice of the chisel-jawed Man Of Steel, who saves Metropolis from various bad guys including Metallo (Malcolm McDowell), The Parasite (*Blade Runner* actor Brion James), Livewire (Lori Petty), The Toyman (Bud Cort), Bizarro (also voiced by Daly) and Darkseid (cult sci-fi actor Michael Ironside).

The series began with a three-part story (shown in the US as one long 90-minute episode) called 'The Last Son Of Krypton', which focused on Superman's arrival on Earth and transformation from mild-mannered Clark Kent into superhero, while later episodes featured guest appearances from other superheroes, including Batman (Superman was often shown before or after an animated Batman episode and titled 'The New Batman/Superman Adventures'), Supergirl, The Green Lantern, The Flash and Aquaman.

Aimed at teens and grown-ups, the series also featured vocal performances from stars including Jennifer Jason Leigh, Michael York, Brian Cox and Mark Hamill.

 TV Trivia: Real-life husband and wife Mike Farrell and Shelley Fabares voice Clark's parents, Jonathan and Martha Kent.

ADVENTURES OF SUPERMAN (1952–1958)

Starring George Reeves, Phyllis Coates, Noel Neil

'Faster than a speeding bullet! More powerful than a locomotive! Able to leap tall buildings at a single bound! Superman – strange visitor from another planet who came to Earth with powers and abilities far beyond those of mortal men! Superman – who can change the course of mighty rivers, bend steel in his bare hands, and who, disguised as Clark Kent, mild-mannered reporter for a great metropolitan newspaper, fights a never-ending battle for truth, justice, and the American way!' So began each episode of the first TV series featuring the comic book superhero. Originally in black and white (the series went colour from the third season), the half-hour episodes starred George Reeves (reportedly being paid a princely $200 an episode) as the Man of Steel, with Phyllis Coates as Lois (she was later replaced by Noel Neil).

Known for creaky effects (for some of the flying scenes, Reeves lay on a board with clouds projected alongside him, later a more effective spring-board technique was used) and often daft dialogue, this became camper as the years went by (fans prefer the grittier, earlier episodes). Cancelled after just over 100 episodes, any hopes that it would be revived by the scores of child fans were dashed in June 1959 when star Reeves was found shot dead at his home. Ruled a suicide, though many people believe he was murdered, his death contributed to the supposed 'curse of Superman' that conspiracy theorists believe contributed to the fates of Superman film star Christopher Reeve and others who have worked on Superman projects.

TV Trivia: When the series was being filmed in black and white, Superman's costume was actually brown, grey and white to give the right colour on screen.

LoiS AND CLARK – THE NEW ADVENTURES OF SUPERMAN (1993–1997)

Starring Dean Cain, Teri Hatcher, Lane Smith

Superman got sexy with this fun nineties interpretation of the comic book that follows Clark Kent/Superman (Cain) as he arrives in Metropolis, gets a job as a reporter on the *Daily Planet* and is teamed with hotshot journalist Lois Lane (Hatcher). Instantly, of course, Clark gets all gooey-eyed in her presence, despite the distraction of voluptuous office worker Cat (Tracy Scoggins), but it takes three seasons for Lois to notice his brooding sensitivity and rippling muscles (plus, she's distracted herself by a crush on Superman – whom she doesn't realise is Clark – and an infatuation with businessman Lex Luthor, seedily played by John Shea).

More of a romantic soap opera than a superhero show, this series hit its stride in Season 2 – space-wasting character Cat was eliminated, newspaper editor Perry White (Lane Smith) was given more to do, and Season 1's bland Jimmy Olsen (Michael Landes) was replaced by Justin Whalin, who became something of a pre-teen heartthrob (rumour has it that dark-haired Landes was canned as producers thought he looked too much like a junior version of Dean Cain). The potential romance between L&C perked up, too, as the pair shared their first kiss in 'Lucky Leon' and Lois briefly realised that Clark was Superman in the superb time-travelling episode 'Tempus Fugitive' that features the first appearance of Lane Davies' deliciously sarcastic bad guy Tempus. From Season 3, Lois knows exactly who Clark is (and he's proposed marriage, too), but the path to true love doesn't run too smoothly when you factor in the arrival of bad guys from Krypton. Of course, the duo do finally get it together, and go up the altar, in the fourth season, but this is about the same time things get unbearably sappy as the former sparring partners spend far too much time going mushy over each other and far too little exchanging the witty barbs that made the show such a treat. The series was cancelled at the end of the fourth season and went out on a truly treacly note – after discovering Clark's super-sperm is too super for them to conceive, the pair opened the door of their house to find a baby outside and a note saying he was theirs. Who wrote the note, we will never know...

 TV Trivia: Phyllis Coates, who plays Lois's mother in a few episodes, was the original Lois Lane in *Adventures of Superman*.

WESTERNS

SADDLE UP! SADLY, SOME OF THE BEST-LOVED SERIES ARE NOT AVAILABLE ON UK DVD AT PRESENT, INCLUDING *MAVERICK*, *GUNSMOKE*, *LARAMIE*, *HAVE GUN WILL TRAVEL* AND *RAWHIDE*...

THE ADVENTURES OF RIN TIN TIN (1954–1959)
Starring Jim L. Brown, Lee Aaker

The 1950s were a good time if you were a four-footed actor: there was Trigger, Roy Rogers' trusty horse; Lassie, everyone's favourite collie, *The Lone Ranger*'s Silver, *The Cisco Kid*'s Diablo, and, of course, German Shepherd Rin Tin Tin. As played by three dogs, this gorgeous mutt roamed the Old West, and specifically the fort where Lieutenant Rip Masters (Brown), bumbling Sergeant Biff O'Hara (Joe Sawyer) and little boy Rusty (Aaker) – who had the honorary title Corporal Rusty and was an orphan after his parents were killed by Indians – resided. It was Rusty who cared for Rin Tin Tin and knew his faithful dog would save the day from bad guys (usually by sinking his teeth into their flesh... good dog!).

Rougher and tougher than Lassie, Rin Tin Tin was a rip-roaring adventure for kids that's just as much fun now as it was back then, especially for canine fans.

 TV Trivia: The original Rin Tin Tin was a puppy rescued by an American serviceman stationed in Europe during World War I.

ALIAS SMITH AND JONES (1971–1973)
Starring Ben Murphy, Pete Duel, Roger Davis

Glen A Larson, the man behind successes like *Magnum PI* and *Knight Rider*, was also the creator of this popular seventies series. A comedy western, it's the story of two outlaws, Hannibal Heyes (Duel) and Kid Curry (Murphy), who are given amnesty by the law providing they manage to stay out of trouble for a year and don't tell any folks who they really are. So they adopt the aliases Smith and Jones and try to live a normal life, despite being wanted men with a $20,000 bounty on their heads.

Set at the time the old West was changing – cars replacing horses, telephones taking the place of the rather slower telegraphs – this was a sprightly series that worked, thanks to the chemistry between the two leads and an often-sparking script. Beginning with a TV movie-length pilot episode (which isn't that great), the series romped along for a year before tragedy struck. Pete Duel committed suicide on 31 December 1971, during production of a second series. Instead of closing down production, Roger Davis, who had narrated the first season, stepped into Duel's role for the show's remaining 17 episodes until the entire series was cancelled in 1973.

 TV Trivia: Roger Davis's first wife was Charlie's Angel Jaclyn Smith.

THE BIG VALLEY (1965–1969)

Starring Lee Majors, Linda Evans, Barbara Stanwyck

A soap opera with a Western setting, *The Big Valley* followed the adventures and relationships of the Barkley family, led by widow Victoria (Stanwyck), who keeps a close eye on her brood of three sons and a daughter while running their large ranch in the San Joaquin Valley of the 1870s. She's got her work cut out for her – Jarrod (Richard Long) is a dashing lawyer; Nick (Peter Breck), is the hot-tempered ranch-hand; younger Eugene (Charles Briles) gets into various scrapes and there is also tight blue-jean-wearing Audra (*Dynasty*'s Evans) to worry about. Oh, and there's also brooding Heath (Majors), who pops up claiming to be the late Daddy Barkley's illegitimate son.

Deliciously melodramatic – as well as a bastard son stirring things up, there's shootings, kidnappings, misunderstandings and doomed romances – this arrived on American TV at a time when most Westerns were winding down due to falling ratings, but its mix of adventure and more girlie elements such as strong female characters and good-looking leading men (the good guy, the bad boy and the misunderstood one – a man for all tastes!) made it a reasonably-sized hit among women and an entertaining romp for everyone.

 TV Trivia: Charles Briles' character Eugene was sent off to college after the first season because Briles had been drafted in real life to join the US Army.

BONANZA (1959–1973)

Starring Lorne Greene, Dan Blocker, Michael Landon

One of the best-loved Western series ever made, and understandably so, *Bonanza* didn't start off as a successful show and only found its audience after it was moved from Saturday to Sunday nights in the US – its ratings then ballooned, and by 1961 it had become the number one show. It is, of course, the saga of the Cartwright family, who live on the ranch named Ponderosa. There's the daddy, Ben (Greene), and his three sons (each by different wives, all of whom have died) – Adam (Pernell Roberts), the sturdy, soft-hearted Hoss (Blocker) and the young, handsome one (and fan favourite), Little Joe (Landon). Together with their Chinese cook, the men run the ranch, care for the land, befriend their neighbours and occasionally have a romance – although, since this show was really about the boys, women rarely lasted more than an episode or two before succumbing to a nasty disease or accident that would leave their Cartwright amour in mourning.

Other cast members were added as the series progressed – including Mitch Vogel as orphaned Jamie, whom Ben adopted and Tim Matheson as ranch hand Griff – while major cast member Roberts left in 1965 following a contractual dispute. The series was dealt its worst blow in 1972 when Blocker died following surgery, and it was written into the plot that Hoss had died. Unfortunately by this point, the series ratings had dipped and *Bonanza* was cancelled the following year.

A trio of missable TV movies, following the next generation of the Cartwright clan (and starring Landon's son, Michael Jr), were made – *Bonanza The Next Generation* (1988), *Bonanza The Return* (1993), *Bonanza Under Attack* (1995) – but are not available on DVD. A prequel TV series, *Ponderosa*, was made in 2001 but is also not available.

TV Trivia: Before Bonanza, Lorne Greene was known as the 'voice of Canada', for his voiceover and announcing work in his native land. He went on to record several albums of spoken word songs in character as Ben Cartwright.

THE CISCO KID (1950–1956)

Starring Duncan Renaldo, Leo Carrillo

Similar in theme to the better-known *The Lone Ranger*, *The Cisco Kid* was another story about a man righting wrongs and doing good in the West (in this case, close to the Mexican border). Originally created as a comic book character by O Henry, the Cisco Kid (Spanish-born Renaldo) rode his horse Diablo on his adventures and was accompanied by the dependable Pancho and his steed, worryingly named Loco.

The character had already been heard on the radio and seen on the big screen in the forties – first with Cesar Romero in the lead role, then with Renaldo and later Gilbert Roland – before Renaldo saddled up his steed for TV. This version was firmly aimed at older kids rather than grown-ups, so the emphasis is on comedy and light plots rather than gritty depictions of the old west. It's not exactly stood the test of time, but it's a sweet adventure that's notable for boasting one of the first lead Hispanic characters on American TV.

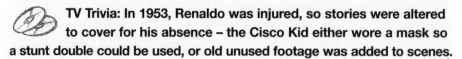 **TV Trivia: In 1953, Renaldo was injured, so stories were altered to cover for his absence – the Cisco Kid either wore a mask so a stunt double could be used, or old unused footage was added to scenes.**

DANIEL BOONE (1964–1970)

Starring Fess Parker, Ed Ames, Patricia Blair

An old-fashioned adventure series about frontiersman Boone (Parker, who had made his name in the 1950s series of Disney TV movies about Davy Crockett), best known for his raccoon-skin hat. Set before and during the Revolutionary War, the show followed Daniel in his encounters with the pesky British (be warned, we don't come off well) and friendlier relationships with local folk and the Native Americans – including Boone's well-educated sidekick Mingo (Ames) – who are finding their land threatened due to the advancement of the frontier.

For a show that began in the mid-sixties, this handles the racial stereotypes and the politically incorrectness of the time period surprisingly well. Not all of the Indians are nice (some are pretty nasty), but then the invading white guys aren't portrayed nicely either, and there's a lovely episode from the second series in which a former African–American slave is stealing, not so that he can buy himself the right to become a free man in America, but so that he can pay for his passage back to Africa. Of course, the 40-year-old series has dated in places (check out Blair's more 1960s than 1860s hairdo), but it is worth a look for some of the then-young actors who crop up in guest roles: Kurt Russell, Leslie Nielsen and *Alien*'s Veronica Cartwright (as Boone's daughter) among them.

 TV Trivia: Fess Parker is an impressive 6 ft 5 in tall.

DEADWOOD (2004–2006)

Starring Timothy Olyphant, Ian McShane, John Hawkes, Molly Parker

This ground-breaking show from *NYPD Blue* creator David Milch was not like any Western you had seen before – there's not a cattle rustler or barn dance in sight and no one ever says 'aw shucks'. Instead, *Deadwood* was based on a real fledgling town in Dakota and many of the characters in the show were depictions of historical figures. Former lawman Seth Bullock (Olyphant), Wyatt Earp and gunslinger Wild Bill Hickok all make an appearance, while fans of Doris Day's saccharine sweet portrayal of Calamity Jane should be prepared – here, Jane is a hard-drinking, potty-mouthed version of the legendary gal (brilliantly played by Robin Weigert).

Set in the late 19th century, Deadwood is a small, rag tag community of cut throats seeking to make their fortune after gold is discovered in them thar hills. Al Swearengen (McShane) is the devious, manipulative and charismatic owner of the town's biggest saloon, The Gem, where every kink and perversion is catered for. He is the lord and master of all he surveys but as outside forces gradually drag Deadwood kicking and screaming from being a small gold mining camp into something resembling a civilised town, Swearengen gradually loses his influence. By the end of the final season, Big Al is literally brought to his knees by a Rupert Murdochesque mining magnate which, rather frustratingly, hints at exciting developments to come. *Deadwood*'s realism was the main draw – you could practically smell the sweat and manure through the screen. All the characters were engaging, as was the dialogue, and the plot lines kept you riveted. Wild Bill Hickok, one of the central characters as the show started, was shot and killed during a poker game in Episode 4, which might be a historically accurate depiction of his demise but certainly not what you would expect from a TV drama.

Despite the show's foul language, misogyny, racism and all-round general nastiness, it received critical acclaim but was cancelled after only three seasons because each episode was rumoured to cost $5 million to make. This premature cancellation does leave the series looking somewhat truncated but it's the only criticism of an otherwise stellar series.

 TV trivia: It has been reported that the 'F' word was used a total of 2,980 times in the series. Forty-three of those were in the first episode.

iNTo THE WEST (2005)

Starring Matthew Settle, Josh Brolin, Tonantzin Carmelo, Gary Busey, Skeet Ulrich

Executive produced by Steven Spielberg, this lavish 12-hour mini-series follows the fortunes (and misfortunes) of two very different families who become entwined in the early 19th century. In 1825, the Virginian family the Wheelers head west for a new life, while members of the Dakota tribe try to come to terms with the new settlers. Their stories become united when Jacob Wheeler (Settle) has a series of adventures – including one with a bear – that lead him to Thunder Heart Woman (Carmelo), whom he weds. Their family eventually heads back to Virginia, while other members of the Wheeler clan head to California by wagon train, a perilous journey that many settlers did not survive.

Spanning generations over 65 years, the series touches on historical events such as the Gold Rush and culminates with the massacre at Wounded Knee. It's quite confusing, though, as members of the Wheeler family, and Thunder Heart Woman's family, come and go, and at different points in their lives are played by different actors (adding to the confusion). It's all terribly politically correct (our hero saves lovely Native American woman from nasty white man, etc), too, and – despite encompassing a whole lot of history – surprisingly tedious.

Best watched for the yummy scenery and the impressive cast, which also includes Tom Berenger, Keri Russell, Sean Astin and Balthazar Getty.

 TV Trivia: A Mescalero Apache family sued the production after their daughter's hair was cut without their permission for her role in the series.

KUNG FU (1972–1975)

Starring David Carradine, Radames Pera, Keye Luke

While many classic Western series aren't available on Region 2 DVD (including, sadly, *Gunsmoke*, *High Chaparral*, *The Virginian*, *Laramie*, *Have Gun Will Travel* and *The Wild, Wild West*), happily this cheesy favourite is available, as is a 1986 follow-up TV movie (however, the 1993–1997 series *Kung Fu: The Legend Continues*, is not). As fans of kitsch seventies TV will know, *Kung Fu* is the story of Kwai Chang Caine (Carradine, in a role Bruce Lee was originally considered for), a Shaolin monk who flees to America after killing the Chinese emperor's nephew (he did deserve it, though). Kwai roams the Wild West in search of his brother, dodging bounty hunters after the price on his head and kung fu-kicking some major butt when he isn't remembering the teachings of his former master, Po (Luke) who, of course, called him 'Grasshopper'.

Oozing with Eastern philosophies mixed with Western brawn, the best episodes include the Emmy award-winning 'An Eye For An Eye' and 'Alethea' (co-starring Jodie Foster) from Season 1, while you may also want to seek out 'Crossties' (Season 2), featuring a young Harrison Ford, 'The Spirit Helper' (Season 2), with Don Johnson and 'A Small Beheading' (Season 3) with William Shatner.

 TV Trivia: David Carradine's younger brother, Keith, played Kwai in the flashbacks to when he was a teenager.

LITTLE HOUSE ON THE PRAIRIE (1974–1983)

Starring Michael Landon, Melissa Gilbert, Melissa Sue Anderson

Awwww. If you sat a kitten in a bowl of treacle it wouldn't be as sweet as this classic family series, based on the beloved Laura Ingalls Wilder autobiographical novels set in the West of the late 1800s. Wise, kind Charles Ingalls (Landon) and calm, loving wife Caroline (Karen Grassle) raise their three daughters – Mary (Anderson), Laura (Gilbert) and Carrie (played by twins Lindsay and Sidney Greenbush) and later some adopted children, too – in a little house near the town of Walnut Grove in Minnesota. Over nine seasons, the family loved, laughed and lost, as Laura grows up, attends the local school house and eventually falls in love, Mary slowly loses her sight, and everyone has lots of hugs and well-meaning moments in between gold rushes, hostage situations, tragic fires, and the like.

A delightful – and sometimes heart-achingly sad – look at family life on the frontier, this gorgeously melancholy series benefited from terrific performances from Gilbert, Anderson and most notably Michael Landon, who also wrote and directed many of the episodes. The early seasons – when Laura and Mary are still young school kids – are the best, as the family settle into their life on the prairie and get to know the neighbours (including the deliciously haughty Harriet Oleson (Scottie MacGregor) and her hideous daughter Nellie, as played by Alison Arngrim), although sentimentalists will also want to seek out Episodes 1 and 2 of Season 7, when Laura marries her Almanzo; and Season 6's well acted but upsetting 'May We Make Them Proud'.

Since the series ended in 1983, two TV movies (*Look Back To Yesterday*; *Bless All The Dear Children*) continuing the saga have been made and also a new Disney mini-series (featuring new actors in the roles) in 2005, but they are not available on DVD in the UK. There were also two TV movies (*Beyond the Prairie* Part 1 and 2) purporting to be the true story of Laura Ingalls Wilder, but they have largely been ignored by fans.

 TV Trivia: Melissa Gilbert was the youngest person to receive a star on the Hollywood Walk of Fame, celebrating her role in the series.

THE LONE RANGER (1949–1957)

Starring Clayton Moore, Jay Silverheels

'A fiery horse with the speed of light, a cloud of dust and a hearty "Hi-yo Silver" – the Lone Ranger! With his faithful Indian companion, Tonto, the daring and resourceful masked rider of the plains led the fight for law and order in the early West. Return with us now to those thrilling days of yesteryear. The Lone Ranger rides again!' So began each episode of this classic series as the mysterious masked gunslinger (Moore) rode the plains with his sidekick Tonto (Silverheels), came to the rescue of damsels and good guys in distress, then rode off again in a cloud of dusk before the hero's identity could be revealed (he was a former Texas Ranger, the only survivor of an ambush by the Hole In The Wall gang).

Half a century on, it all looks decidedly creaky – and Moore is terrifically uncomfortable on his steed – while the dialogue is almost wincingly bad. But that's part of this innocent series' charm that boasted a hero who never killed anyone, he only winged them with his silver bullets. Watch out for episodes made in 1951 and 1952 – you'll notice the Lone Ranger's voice is a bit different than before. That's when Moore left the series (reputedly in a salary dispute) and a new actor, John Hart, was hired to wear the mask. Series creator George Trendle didn't think anyone would notice, but fans did, and Moore was reinstated in 1954. In 1966, an animated series was made about The Lone Ranger, but it is not available on DVD in the UK.

 TV Trivia: *The Lone Ranger* actually began as a radio series in 1933.

LONESOME DOVE (1989)

Starring Robert Duvall, Tommy Lee Jones, Danny Glover, Anjelica Huston, Diane Lane

Larry McMurty's Pulitzer Prize-winning, epic novel was made into a classic, sprawling mini-series featuring an all-star cast. Set in the late 19th century, it's the story of two retired Texas Rangers, Woodrow Call and Gus McCrae, who are content to spend their lives in the Texas town of Lonesome Dove until they hear of a unique opportunity – the chance of a better life cattle ranching in Montana. Joined by other townspeople, the pair embark on the 3,000 mile, perilous cattle drive – there's cattle rustlers, horse thieves, angry tribes and a killer in them there hills – to the state, with Gus hoping to meet up with his former sweetheart Clara (Huston) in Nebraska and rekindle their romance along the way.

A sweeping drama that beautifully realises the spirit of the Old West, this is gripping stuff, magnificent to look at and boasting superb performances from Jones and Duvall, as well as terrific support from Glover, Huston, Robert Urich (as Jake Spoon, the man who suggests the Montana adventure), Rick Schroder, Diane Lane, Chris Cooper and Steve Buscemi. A slightly inferior (and unofficial) 1993 sequel, *Return To Lonesome Dove* (with Barbara Hershey taking over Huston's role and Jon Voight taking over Jones's) was made, followed by the disappointing *Streets of Laredo* in 1995 (with James Garner now starring as Call, alongside Sissy Spacek and Sam Shepard) and the fun prequel *Dead Man's Walk* in 1996, which starred Jonny Lee Miller as young Call and David Arquette as Gus. All are available on DVD, but the *Lonesome Dove* spin-off series, made in 1994, and its follow-up, 1995's *Lonesome Dove: The Outlaw Years*, are only available on US DVD.

 TV Trivia: McMurty's novel began life as a 1971 movie script that he later expanded. He originally wanted John Wayne to play Call and James Stewart to play Gus.

THE MAGNIFICENT SEVEN (1998–2000)

Starring Michael Biehn, Eric Close, Dale Midkiff

Another attempt to resurrect the TV Western in the nineties with a group of pretty young boys (see *The Young Riders*, p.205), *The Magnificent Seven* includes episodes directed by Christopher Cain of *Young Guns* fame and is something of a TV series remake of the classic 1960 John Sturges movie. It's basically an excuse for lots of male actors to wave guns around, spit tobacco, occasionally growl and throw back shots of whiskey, and the cast certainly look like they are having fun while they are doing it.

Biehn and Close are Chris Larabee and Vin Tanner, two of the most impeccably coiffed men you're likely to find in the Old West (did they have conditioner and hairspray in those days – we think not) who ride into town, save an ex-slave from a lynching and then are hired to assemble a bunch of men to protect the local people and the nearby Seminole tribe. None of them are exactly up to the Steve McQueen, Yul Brynner et al posse (or, for that matter, anyone from Kurosawa's original *Seven Samurai* movie that started it all), but Kurtwood Smith is well cast as the nasty Confederate colonel, and there is nice support from Ron Perlman and Robert Vaughn.

One for the kids, really, especially those too young to watch either of the movies upon which this dusty romp is based.

TV Trivia: The series was going to be cancelled after one season, but fans emailed executives and raised money for an ad campaign to beg for the series renewal.

WAGON TRAIN (1957–1965)

Starring Frank McGrath, Ward Bond, Terry Wilson, Robert Fuller

Nearly 300 episodes were made of this enjoyable saga that followed a group of pioneers heading for California from Missouri in a train of wagons – yet in all that time they never actually make it to their destination. Led by wagon master Seth Adams (Bond, who sadly died on location in 1960) and later Christopher Hale (from Season 4 onwards), the recurring cast also included Robert Horton as hunky scout Flint McCullough, ex-stuntmen Terry Wilson and Frank McGrath as Bill and Charlie, and in later years, Robert Fuller as scout Coop and Michael Burns as young Barnaby West, who joined the train looking for his father.

Each episode of the series (filmed in black and white until 1963, then in colour) focused on one passenger on the 'train' (sort of like *The Love Boat*, but with less water) and attracted a host of big names and up-and-coming actors including Jack Lord and James Caan ('Echo Pass', Season 8) Ernest Borgnine and Leonard Nimoy ('The Estaban Zamora Story', Season 3), Bette Davis ('The Elizabeth McQueeney Story', Season 3) and Lee Marvin ('The Jose Morales Story', Season 4). The enjoyably hokey 1976 series *Oregon Trail*, a similarly themed adventure starring Rod Taylor and Blair Brown, is unfortunately not available on DVD.

 TV Trivia: Watch out for John Wayne in the fourth season episode, 'The Colter Craven Story', directed by the legendary John Ford, both of whom were friends with Ward Bond.

WANTED DEAD OR ALIVE (1958–1961)

Starring Steve McQueen

The b&w series that made Steve McQueen a star (his biggest role prior to this had been in the B-movie *The Blob*) as brooding anti-hero Josh Randall. He's a late 19th century bounty hunter who rides off in pursuit of bad guys with a sawn-off shotgun that he calls his 'mare's leg' at his side. Of course, he was a tough guy with a heart of gold who would often donate his fees to the needy or come to the aid of one of his targets if he thought he had been wrongly accused.

Over 90 half-hour episodes were made, boasting some rather hokey dialogue and ropey effects, but each episode is still a (somewhat dated) treat for Western fans and a must for those who, quite rightly, drool over McQueen. The series finished in 1961 – rumour has it that McQueen grew more diffi-cult on set in the final year of the show, as he was desperate for it to be cancelled so he could continue his film career. A feature film, *Wanted: Dead or Alive*, was made in 1987, set in the present day, and starring Rutger Hauer as Nick Randall, the great-grandson of McQueen's character in the series.

 TV Trivia: The series was actually a spin-off from an episode of *Trackdown* (unavailable on DVD) that McQueen starred in with Robert Culp.

THE WEST (1996)

Narrated by Peter Coyote

A superb eight-part documentary series made for American TV and produced by acclaimed documentary maker Ken Burns, who is best known for 1990's *The Civil War* (see review, p.289). For five years, Burns and his fellow filmmaker Steven Ives, travelled the American West, photographing the scenery, interviewing the people, and piecing together the history of the land west of the Mississippi River. Beginning with an episode focusing on the people of the area prior to 1806, the Comanches, the Hidastas, the Kiowa, and other tribes, the series follows the story as the land was discovered by other nations, and eventually invaded by peoples coming from the east who wanted to populate the seemingly untamable land and search for its gold.

Spanning the centuries up to 1917 (the year of the death of Buffalo Bill Cody and also America's entry into World War I), this is a sprawling, fascinating look at a slice of America's history, and also a well-balanced one, as it takes in the opinions and history of Native Americans, Mexicans, Chinese and other peoples who made their way into the West. Well-known characters are featured, including explorers Lewis and Clark, writer Mark Twain, President Theodore Roosevelt and infamous General Custer, but many lesser known people who shaped the history of the 'wild west' are featured, too. Simply magnificent.

 TV Trivia: During filming, the crew flew over 100,000 miles, completed over 250 hours of filming, and interviewed over 70 people.

THE YOUNG RIDERS (1989–1992)

Starring Josh Brolin, Stephen Baldwin, Ty Miller

With a similar idea to the movie *Young Guns*, this series followed a group of young horseback riders in the days before the American Civil War who make their living working for the mail delivery service, the Pony Express. There's the Kid (Miller); short-tempered James Butler Hickok (Brolin), who would later become better known as Wild Bill; impulsive William Cody (Baldwin), later known, of course, as Buffalo Bill; Lou McCloud (Yvonne Suhor), a young woman dressed as a man so she can join the group; half-Indian Running Back Cross (Gregg Rainwater) and, last but not least, Ike (Travis Fine), who can't speak but communicates with signs to his pals. While they should be delivering the mail, these boys want to do good so also deliver the occasional ass-whuppin' to anyone who deserves it, and they help the local US Marshal (Brett Cullen), when things get sticky, too. Bless them.

It's an entertaining Western series that benefits from Brolin's fun performance as Hickok and its overall sense of rip-roaring adventure. Students of the history will be irked by the show's historical inaccuracy – Pony Express riders rode alone for 75 miles, handing over the mail to the next rider and then heading back in a sort of relay, whereas these guys seem to spend all their time together – but if you're looking for a few brawls and shoot-outs rather than a history lesson, this is a fun diversion.

 TV Trivia: One of the directors of the series was actor James Brolin – star Josh Brolin's dad.

SCI-FI

SADLY, SOME OF THE LESSER KNOWN BUT VERY WATCHABLE SCI-FI SERIES AREN'T AVAILABLE ON DVD, INCLUDING THE *LOGAN'S RUN* SERIES FROM THE SEVENTIES, THE UNINTENTIONALLY FUNNY *THE TRIPODS* (ALTHOUGH IT WILL GET A BELATED RELEASE IN 2009), AND 1996'S *DARK SKIES*. FOR MORE SCIENCE FICTION, SEE TEENAGERS, P.149–169 AND CHILDREN, P.122–143.

THE 4400 (2004–2007)

Starring Joel Gretsch, Jacqueline McKenzie, Bill Campbell, Patrick Flueger

The title of this series refers to the number of people who suddenly appear in a ball of light several years, and in some cases decades, after they mysteriously disappeared. All of them look exactly as they did when they vanished and none of them can recall what has happened to them. Naturally, this attracts a lot of attention and it doesn't take long for Homeland Security to get involved, especially when some of the returnees begin to display supernatural abilities such as telepathy and enhanced strength. Alien interference is suspected, but by the end of Season 1 it is revealed that the group was taken by humans from the future and returned in order to prevent some kind of catastrophic event.

The show was originally intended to be a five-part mini-series but it proved to be so popular that new episodes were commissioned. As a result, the mystery of whether aliens were behind it all was answered early on. Once extra-terrestrial involvement was excluded, however, the series then became about groups of people trying to survive in extreme and unknown circumstances. As the series continues, new factions evolve, some of whom want to create separate communities for returnees where they can live in peace without being regarded as freaks while others have darker motives which gradually unfold. With the increasingly nervous agents in hot pursuit, the series has an 'X-Filian' quality with lots of shady goings on and few conclusive answers, keeping you on the edge of your seat. Unfortunately, a fifth season was not forthcoming, leading die-hard fans to start a petition calling for the show's return. Watch this space.

TV trivia: Billy Campbell, the actor who plays Jordan Collier, the charismatic, self proclaimed leader of the returnees, took most of Season 3 off to sail around the world.

ALIEN NATION (1989–1990)

Starring Eric Pierpoint, Gary Graham

A spin-off of the movie of the same name, *Alien Nation* imagined what life would be like in the present day if aliens lived among us. When a flying saucer crashes in the desert, the inhabitants turn out to be intelligent, strong alien slaves who are controlled by Overseers. Dubbed 'Newcomers', the aliens are assimilated into society, and the series focuses on one in particular – cop George Francisco (Pierpoint), who is teamed with a human partner, Matthew Sykes (Graham), who, of course, doesn't want to work with poor George. They're different, they grudgingly fight crime together, but George has to fight prejudice against the aliens alone. Gee, do you think this is a thinly veiled racism allegory?

Cancelled due to budget problems (one assumes the Fox network that made it didn't want to waste any more money on it) after just one series, this was a cheaper, shabbily written cousin to the 1988 movie, which wasn't that great in the first place (and at least that had James Caan in the cast). Only worth watching for the fun alien make-up effects, the daft names the Newcomers are given (Virginia Hamm, etc) and the scenes in which they get drunk on sour milk. Otherwise utterly missable.

 TV Trivia: The opening credits feature 'alien' lyrics – they are actually the names of producer Kenneth Johnson's family sung backwards.

ANDROMEDA (2000–2005)

Starring Kevin Sorbo, Lisa Ryder, Lexa Doig

Based on notes written by *Star Trek* creator Gene Roddenberry back in 1976 (Roddenberry died nine years before this series aired), *Andromeda* also shares similarities with two Roddenberry TV movies, 1973's *Genesis II* and 1974's *Planet Earth*. In the future, Dylan Hunt (*Hercules'* Sorbo) is the captain of spaceship *Andromeda Ascendent* (whose central computer appears in the form of the beautiful Andromeda, played by Doig). Following a series of complicated events, he and his crew are frozen in time and only defrosted 300-odd years later when they are discovered by a salvage ship. The Commonwealth that the crew knew is now under the control of nasty Nietzcheans, so Hunt and his team in their skimpy outfits (doesn't anyone have a cardi in space?) decide to fight to try and regain control of the three galaxies that have descended into barbarism.

It's all done quite well – nice effects, okay performances, reasonable plots, but there is something about *Andromeda* that just reminds you of better shows that have gone before and since, including, of course, *Star Trek* (this series is closest to *Voyager* and *Deep Space Nine*), *Battlestar Galactica* and *Firefly*.

If there's nothing else on TV, it's amiable enough, but not worth making much effort to see. And if you do end up enjoying it, be warned that the fifth and final season is pretty dire – the crew end up on a planet called Seefra but have seemingly left all the good plots up on the *Andromeda*.

 TV Trivia: Roddenberry's notes were also used to create the series Earth: Final Conflict (see review, p.233)

BABYLON 5 (1994–1998)

Starring Claudia Christian, Bruce Boxleitner, Michael O'Hare

Planned as a five-season 'epic video novel' by creator J. Michael Straczynski, *Babylon 5* begins in the year 2258, ten years after the Earth/Minbari war. Commander Sinclair (O'Hare) and, from Season 2, Commander Sheridan (Boxleitner), is in control of a space station named Babylon 5 (Babylons 1 to 3 were sabotaged and destroyed while Babylon 4 vanished without trace), where he has to keep the peace with the various interstellar travellers – mainly made up for humans, Minbari, Narn, Centauri and Vorlons – who pass by the station that the commander deems is the 'last, best, hope for peace'.

Unfairly criticised for being similar to *Star Trek: Deep Space Nine* (although *Babylon 5* was written before that series aired), this is a complex drama featuring conflict between alien nations, comments on war, peace, religion and social standing as well as more personal elements such as the inclusion of an alcoholic character, security chief Michael Garibaldi (Jerry Doyle) and sci-fi elements such as evil aliens, dangerous other-worldly technology and funny looking creatures from places no one can pronounce. The characters are all well-rounded and the story cleverly developed (Straczynski even wrote plans for each character's exit, in case an actor wanted to leave the show before the five seasons were done), and there are even some cool space battles to enjoy too. While you have to watch the first season to understand what's going on, the best episodes are in the second, third and fourth seasons. A spin-off series, *Crusade*, with Gary Cole, ran for 13 episodes, and there are also a series of direct-to-DVD movies (a box set featuring all these and the original series is available to fans prepared to part with £200).

 TV Trivia: The series is reported to have cost $90 million for the 110 episodes that were made.

BATTLESTAR GALACTICA (1978–1979; 2004–)

Starring Dirk Benedict, Richard Hatch, Lorne Greene (1978 version); Edward James Olmos, Mary McDonnell, Katee Sackhoff (2004 version)

An enjoyably cheesy sci-fi adventure that was TV's answer to *Star Wars*, the original *Battlestar Galactica* told the story of how, in another galaxy, humans were at war with an alien cyborg race, the Cylons (who look like their costumes have been made from a biker's helmet and kitchen foil). A treaty is about to be signed to finally end hundreds of years of battles, but it turns out it was all a ruse by those nasty Cylons, who come along and almost obliterate the human race. Luckily, one remaining human warship, the Galactica, remains, and the survivors follow Commander Adama (Greene) and his crew (including hot-shot pilots Apollo and Starbuck) on a quest to find the one planet that will apparently keep them safe – Earth.

Focusing mainly on the adventures of ladies' man Starbuck (Benedict) and the more earnest Apollo (Hatch), the 1978 series was jolly good fun rather than serious sci-fi, packed with lots of blasting through space and fist-fights, and while some of the acting was as wooden as the sets (yes, Richard Hatch, we mean you), Benedict's charming cockiness and John Colicos as the nasty Baltar more than made up for it. Kitsch it certainly was, so when it was announced that a 21st-century version of the series was going to be made, no one expected *Battlestar Galactica* version two to be quite the kick-ass show it has become. The basic plot is the same – here Olmos plays Adama, leading his crew towards Earth – but it's much darker, faster, slicker – and the Cylons here are very, very, creepy. Some of them can take human form, and one even seduces Helo, one of the crew of *Galactica*, in an attempt to produce a cylon/human hybrid. And did we mention Starbuck (Sackhoff) is now a woman?

Packed with superb acting, well-developed characters, fast-paced plots and solid special effects, this Galactica is one of the few examples of a remake that is miles better than the original.

 TV Trivia: In 1980, a series, *Galactica 1980*, was made in which the crew do arrive on Earth and have to protect us from the Cylons. It was cancelled after 10 episodes.

BLAKE'S 7 (1978–1981)

Starring Gareth Thomas, Paul Darrow, Jacqueline Pearce

Bleak, grown-up science fiction from the creator of the Daleks, Terry Nation, the BBC's *Blake's 7* is set in a future where the earth and other planets are ruled by the Terran Federation. Roj Blake (Thomas) is a freedom fighter who has been sent to a penal colony on a remote planet, but escapes, taking control of a spacecraft called the Liberator with other prisoners. He wants to fight against the regime, but his crewmates, who are petty criminals, smugglers and killers, aren't so bothered about saving the world. Among them is computer genius Kerr Davon (Darrow), a psychopath who may or may not have a conscience, computer Zen and former thief Vila.

A cult hit, *Blake's 7* was much darker fate than you'd expect from the Beeb, presenting a dystopian future of brainwashing, pacification (with food that has been drugged) and loss of free will, while also never shying away from bumping off a regular, and well-liked character if the plot demanded it. Described by *Nation* as 'the Dirty Dozen in space', the episodes often featured a battle of wills between the idealistic Blake and the charismatic, yet sinister Avon (Darrow perfectly capturing the character). In fact, while Blake could be perceived as the 'hero', it was Avon who became the fan favourite, along with the ruthless Commander Servalan (Pearce). Well written, tightly paced and featuring fascinating characters, the series only ran for four seasons, and, frustratingly for fans, it ended on a whopper of a cliffhanger.

 TV Trivia: Parents of children who loved the series complained to the BBC when it ended, as many of their offspring's favourite characters were killed off in the finale.

BUCK ROGERS IN THE 25TH CENTURY (1979–81)

Starring Gil Gerard, Erin Gray, Tim O'Connor, Thom Christopher

The seventies produced some of the best sci-fi of all time (*Star Wars*, *Close Encounters Of The Third Kind*) but also some of the most kitsch, like this jolly adventure series from Glen A. Larson (Battlestar Galactica) starring pudding bowl-haired Gil Gerard as Buck, the 20th-century astronaut who is caught in a freak accident that causes his spacecraft to hurtle through space before returning to earth... 500 years later. Once he gets there, he discovers that there's been a nuclear war and quite a few technological advances while he was away, including the invention of mechanoids like Dr Theopolis and cute/irritating (depending on your point of view) little Twiki. Oh, and there are some nasty aliens called the Draconians, too, who have the rather sultry Princess Ardala (Pamela Hensley) as their leader.

Mainly remembered fondly by men who were pubescent boys at the time it was first broadcast – check out Buck's pal Wilma Deering's (Gray) all-in-one lycra bodysuit and Ardala's various skimpy ensembles and you'll see why – this was meant to be fun, rather than serious sci-fi, which is obvious when you realise the voice of Twiki was provided by none other than Mel Blanc, the voice of Bugs Bunny. Everyone plays it very tongue-in-cheek, with Gerard as the seventies stud who flirts with the ladies when he isn't kicking alien butt, while the rest of the cast try and deliver some awful dialogue without laughing. The first season, in which Buck adjusts to life in the future, was the best, as the second had him, Wilma and the ever-present trashcan that was Twiki travelling around in a starship to find the lost tribes of earth, while also introducing the ridiculous bird-headed character that was Hawk (Christopher).

 TV Trivia: Props from Larson's other sci-fi series, *Battlestar Galactica*, were also used in this series.

CHARLiE JADE (2005–)

Starring Jeffrey Pierce, Michael Filipowich

A Canadian/South African co-production, this series is science fiction mixed with detective drama – set in not one, but three parallel universes. Detective Charlie Jade (Pierce) lives in a world run by greedy corporations, including the sinister Vex-Cor. While on an investigation, he finds himself at a secret desert facility that explodes, propelling Jade from his universe (Alphaverse) to a parallel universe (Betaverse) that's more like earth as we know it. It's there he finds out there is a third, idyllic universe (Gammaverse) and meets someone called '01 Boxer' (Filipowich), the son of the head of Vex-Cor and the only human who can travel at will between the three universes.

Shot on location in South Africa, this is a clever science-fiction show that has gathered a small but very devoted following among fans who compare it to *Blade Runner* (certainly the Alphaverse looks like something Ridley Scott concocted). It has an underlying theme of terrorism – the initial explosion that sent Charlie across universes was due to terrorists trying to sabotage a plan to establish a link between the Alphaverse and Gammaverse so water could be drained from the Gammaverse and delivered to the Alphaverse by Vex-Cor – and conspiracy, and plots that are often complex. If you have enough time to devote to this twisting tale, it's very rewarding, and fascinating to look at, too, thanks to the Cape Town locations and device of colouring each universe differently (Betaverse is very blue, for example, while the nicer Gammerverse has warmer, redder tones).

 TV Trivia: Fans believe the series has not been bought for transmission in the US due to the inclusion of a 'sympathetic' terrorist character. It has, however, become popular in America on internet sites such as Youtube.

CRIME TRAVELLER (1997)

Starring Michael French, Chloe Annett, Sue Johnston

The BBC clearly doesn't know what to do with actors once they leave *EastEnders* (usually letting them go over to ITV for big wadges of cash, as Ross Kemp did), which maybe explains why Michael French – aka David Wickes from the dreary soap – ended up in this pile of tosh. He plays detective Jess Slade, who is teamed with Holly Turner (Annett). It just so happens her dad was an inventor who left her a time machine before he vanished (possibly to another dimension, maybe down the pub), so she and Jeff use the gizmo to pop back and forth in time to solve crimes. Of course, the machine is a prototype, and completely unreliable, so our Mulder and Scully-esque heroes are never quite sure where they will end up.

An eight-part mini-series, *Crime Traveller* has quite a clever premise, blending cop show and time travel, and there are some nice ideas explored in the plots (Jeff pursuing a suspect that turns out to be him from another time travelling jaunt from the future, etc). Unfortunately, the makers were saddled with a small budget and a rather wooden cast (except for Johnston as Jeff's superior), so despite the input of writer Anthony Horowitz (Poirot), it never really engaged as much as it could have.

 TV Trivia: Michael French was originally tipped to be the lead in a nineties version of *Blake's 7*, which never materialised.

DARK ANGEL (2000–2002)

Starring Jessica Alba, Michael Weatherly, John Savage

James Cameron – the director behind *Aliens*, *The Terminator* and, of course, *Titanic* – was the brains behind this cool and complex sci-fi series set in the year 2019. A few years before, a group of genetically enhanced superhuman children escaped from a scary lab project. One of them, now grown up, is Max (Alba), and in the future where the world has almost collapsed, she exists as part of an underground street life in Seattle so she is not found by the government agents searching for her and others of her kind. When she's not trying to make a living as a courier, she does a little burglary, and it's while she is breaking into a swish high-rise apartment that she first encounters cyber journalist Logan (Weatherly). If she agrees to help him, he says he'll help her piece together the shattered memories of her past and find her fellow escapees – if any of them are still alive.

All of the above happens in the first episode, and things get far more complicated from there on, which is probably why this series wasn't the success everyone was expecting. You have to be on your toes to keep up with the show's mythology, and the answers to Max's questions are very slow in coming, which is also a bit frustrating (even more annoying is the fact that the series was cancelled abruptly, so ends on an unresolved cliffhanger). Alba, only 19 when the show began, is terrific in the lead and Savage is nicely cast as the series' bad guy, but throughout you can't help thinking this would have been so much better with a tighter script that would have perhaps made it a sci-fi version of *Buffy The Vampire Slayer*.

 TV Trivia: Jessica and co-star Michael Weatherly were engaged to be married during filming of the series, but have since broken up.

THE DAY OF THE TRIFFIDS (1981)

Starring John Duttine, Jo Payton, Maurice Colbourne

Already a camp movie from 1962 with Howard Keel, John Wyndham's classic sci-fi novel was made into a series by the BBC in 1981. Over six episodes, the story unfolded of an alien invasion that begins with the arrival of a bright comet that blinds everyone. Bill Masen (Duttine), whose eyes were bandaged at the time so missed the light show, is one of the only people who can see, and with a group of other sighted people he soon discovers that giant plants called Triffids that have been penned in fields on earth since a previous attack, can walk (sort of), communicate with each other... and kill humans with their sting before eating them. And it looks like they want to take over the world.

Early scenes of blind people calling out for help on London's streets are quite powerful, but once you see the Triffids clearly, it all descends into silliness. They are tall, at least, and the memorable music from Christopher Gunning plus the clicking noises they emit make them seem sinister, but once the Triffids move, you'll start to giggle at what are essentially venomous bits of waddling orange rubber. Saving it from complete disaster are some strong politicial comments in between the daft effects – the Triffids weren't eradicated when they first arrived as they are a source of fuel so it's all our own fault, etc – the impressive scenes of a crumbling society and some more shocking moments, such as when Emma (Payton), who can see, goes to the aid of a blind man only to be captured, beaten and forced to be a sighted slave for him.

 TV Trivia: Triffids were displayed at the Natural History Museum as part of an exhibition about carnivorous plants.

DOCTOR WHO (1963–1989; 2005–)

Starring William Hartnell, Tom Baker, Jon Pertwee, Peter Davison

It began in 1963 – a science-fiction adventure for the BBC packed with cheap props and wobbly sets that became a landmark cult favourite, running for over 25 years. Even people who have never watched an episode know who the Doctor was – a time traveller (a Time Lord from the planet Gallifrey) who zipped about in the Tardis, which resembled a police phone box – and can recognise his most famous foes, the Cybermen and, of course, the Daleks (impressively, for aliens who can't even go up stairs, they have their own entry in the *Oxford English Dictionary*).

The longest-running science fiction series in the world began in black and white with William Hartnell as the mysterious man at the controls of the Tardis. Broadcast at kids' tea-time (originally 5.15 pm), it was devised to appeal to both kids and adults with its mild scares (try telling a child at the time they were mild, though, as many a sixties kid was traumatised yet gripped), low-budget effects, clever scripts and action.

Hartnell was followed by Patrick Troughton (instead of dying, the Doctor regenerates but returns in different human form, you see). Then came Jon Pertwee, many viewers' favourite, although during his tenure, Mary Whitehouse complained the show was too frightening and gory for children and should be banned. Following Pertwee's departure we got Tom Baker's bonkers performance (complete with bulging eyes and long woolly scarf), Peter Davison's cricket-jumper clad doctor, and the ill-advised casting of Sylvester McCoy (playing it so twee that Timmy Mallet would have been a more serious choice) as the final incarnation before the series was cancelled in 1989.

Of course, as grown-ups and a whole new generation of kids know, the story doesn't end there. This time-travelling, interfering, cryptic character – who, over the years was partnered by a series of companions including much-loved robotic dog K-9 – was resurrected, first in a TV movie with Paul McGann, and then again, in 2005, with writer Russell T. Davies bringing the Doctor Who legend wittily, slickly and addictively up to date. First, he cast the dark, brooding Christopher Eccleston as the ninth Doctor and teamed him with sparky Billie Piper as Rose, and then added another dimension when David Tennant took over as the current time traveller after Eccelston's 13 episodes. It's slick, cool, sometimes scary, and – as it has always been – fun, clever and fast-paced. If you've never seen an episode, treat yourself to the post-2005 incarnations of the Doctor for a 21st-century slice of sci-fi, then indulge in the best of past series, such as the episodes featuring Pertwee and Baker that deal with Doctor Who's most memorable foes, the Daleks, Davros and the Master. The new series has spawned the more adult *Torchwood* (see p.243) and the kid-friendly *Sarah Jane Adventures*.

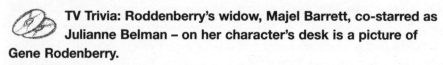 **TV Trivia: Some of the earliest *Doctor Who* episodes were erased or went missing. Episodes 1 and 4 of 1968's 'The Invasion' are among them, and the BBC commissioned an animated reconstruction available on DVD for fans.**

EARTH: FINAL CONFLICT (1997–2002)

Starring Kevin Kilner, Von Flores, Robert Leeschock, Leni Parker

Like the series *Andromeda*, this sci-fi show was based on notes left behind by the late Gene 'Star Trek' Roddenberry – in fact, one of the writers claims it grew from a brief note Roddenberry had written on the back of a napkin. Originally named *Battleground: Earth* until producers decided the title was too similar to Scientologist L. Ron Hubbard's *Battlefield: Earth*, the series introduces the Taleons, an alien species that comes to earth claiming they wish to share their knowledge with humans (yeah, right). Luckily, some people are suspicious of the Taleons' motives, including William Boone (Kilner), who appears to be working with the Taleons as an interspecies liaison, but is in fact on a mission to find out the extra terrestrials' true motives.

It's all a bit silly, featuring some very dodgy-looking aliens, but at least Season 1 boasted a decent conspiracy and some nice twists and turns. By Season 2, all that was abandoned for more hysterical plots, poor Boone was killed off, and an alien/human hybrid named Liam (Leeshock) took over trying to find out the Taleons' secrets, but by then, no viewers cared.

TV Trivia: Roddenberry's widow, Majel Barrett, co-starred as Julianne Belman – on her character's desk is a picture of Gene Rodenberry.

FARSCAPE (1999–2004)

Starring Claudia Black, Ben Browder, Lani Tupu

Widely considered to be one of the best science-fiction shows of recent years, *Farscape* was created by The Jim Henson Company (Henson, of course, being the man behind *Sesame Street* and *The Muppets*). A freak accident catapults 20th-century astronaut John Crichton (Browder) across a thousand galaxies and crashes onto an alien battlefield. Soon he's captured and taken aboard a living ship named *Moya*, a former prison ship where the prisoners – Luxan warrior Ka D'Argo, Delvian priestess Pa'u Zotoh and Hynerian Dominar Rygel XVI – are now running the place. Brought on board is Peacekeeper (the military) Aeryn Sun (Black), and in hot pursuit is Bialar Crais (Tupu), who believes Crichton's crash killed his brother. And that's just the first episode.

Packed with smart characterisation and terrific performances, *Farscape* is a superb space adventure brimming over with wit as Crichton tries to adapt his 20th-century pop culture ways to this strange place. There's betrayal, tragedy and obsession in the plot – poor Crichton going a bit bonkers as he tries to work out how the hell to get back home – along with twists such as a twin Crichton and an interstellar pregnancy, plus the bonus of two central characters being played by sophisticated animatronic puppets: Rygel (voiced by Jonathan Hardy) and Pilot (voiced by Tupu). The series was unexpectedly cancelled in 2002, but thanks to fan intervention, a mini-series called *Farscape: The Peacekeeper Wars* was made in 2004 to end the adventure, while webisodes have continued the story.

TV Trivia: The series was originally conceived by Brian Henson (son of Jim) and Rockne S O'Bannon (who came up with the idea for *Alien Nation*) as a show called *Space Chase*.

FIREFLY (2002–2003)

Starring Nathan Fillion, Gina Torres, Alan Tudyk, Adam Baldwin

A Western in space, this series from *Buffy The Vampire Slayer* creator Joss Whedon and *Angel*'s Tim Minear was clever, funny, unusual... and swiftly cancelled when no one tuned in. What on earth were you all watching that was better than this fabulous show? Set 500 years in the future, it followed sarcastic Captain Mal Reynolds (Fillion – a 21st-century Harrison Ford), a former galactic war veteran, as he travelled through space in the battered transport craft *Serenity*, taking on legal transport jobs or illegal ones (smuggling, for example) under the nose of the galaxy's creepy new rulers, the Alliance. On board with him is Zoe (Torres), the first-mate, her pilot husband Wash (Tudyk), ex-combat soldier Jayne (Baldwin), mechanic Kaylee (Jewel Staite), a 'companion' (space talk for hooker) named Inara (Morena Baccarin), and some passengers they have picked up – preacher Shepard Book (Ron Glass), medical man Simon (Sean Maher), and his near-catatonic sister River (Summer Glau), who has many secrets to hide and whose presence may endanger the rest of the ship.

Perhaps the Western-style language, battered costumes and old sharpshooters the characters carry, mixed with science fiction ideas and even some Chinese dialogue (in the future, you see, everyone can speak English and Chinese) was just too odd for people to get – although Whedon took the idea, gave it a little revamp (toning down some of the heavier Western references) and made the movie *Serenity* with the same cast to much acclaim. It's certainly innovative, perhaps an idea before its time, but with slick dialogue, winning performances, and a devil-may-care attitude (much like Mal's) throughout, this ill-fated series is really well worth seeking out, enjoying and revisiting again and again. It really is that good.

 TV Trivia: Astronaut Steven Swanson took the *Firefly* series on DVD with him to watch when he boarded space shuttle Atlantis for its June 2007 mission.

FRANK HERBERT'S DUNE (2000)

Starring William Hurt, Alec Newman, Saskia Reeves

In 1984, director David Lynch bravely tackled Frank Herbert's epic space saga *Dune*, with the end result best remembered as an expensive, confusing but stylish cinematic flop that featured a young Kyle Maclachlan in the lead and Sting, with flame-orange hair, in nothing but a pair of metal Y-fronts. Sixteen years later, writer/director John Harrison turned the story into a big budget mini-series and had more success, partly because the six-hour length allowed the story to unfold at a more manageable pace.

It's a complex tale of political machinations, religious beliefs, mythology and a spice called melange that is produced by nasty giant sandworms. At the centre of it all is Duke Leto Artreides (Hurt), sent to run the desert planet Arrakis (also known as Dune) against the wishes of the present ruler, Baron Harkonnen (Ian McNeice), and Leto's family – Lady Jessica (Reeves) and their clairvoyant son Paul (Newman), whom a desert tribe believe is the great redeemer that has been prophesised to come to them. While it keeps closer to the original book than the Lynch version, Harrison takes some liberties with the story (bumping up one character from observer to potential love interest for Paul). Unfortunately, it's also occasionally lacking in the acting department – Hurt is almost comatose and Newman just isn't strong enough as Paul – and the scenery just isn't as eye-popping as the 1984 film. The mini-series was followed by 2003's *Children Of Dune*, which Harrison also wrote (based on Herbert's sequel *Dune Messiah* and part of the third book, *Children of Dune*), which picks up the story with Paul, now known as Muad'Dib, ruling Arrakis but facing a revolution that only his son, Leto (James McAvoy) may be able to prevent.

Also starring Steven Berkhoff and Susan Sarandon, it's more soap operatic than the first series, but enjoyable for McAvoy's gripping performance.

TV Trivia: Alice Krige took over the role of Jessica for *Children of Dune* because Saskia Reeves was pregnant and unable to play the part.

THE HiTCHHiKER'S GUiDE TO THE GALAXY (1981)

Starring Simon Jones, David Dixon, Sandra Dickinson, Mark Wing-Davey

Originally an innovative 1970s radio show, *The Hitchhiker's Guide to the Galaxy* became an equally ground-breaking TV programme when it was first broadcast by the BBC in 1981. Based on an idea by Douglas Adams (and later spun off into books, T-shirts, games and the like), the comic story begins with a bang as average man Arthur Dent (Simon Jones) is told by his friend Ford Prefect (David Dixon) that the earth (and Dent's house) is about to be destroyed to make way for a hyperspace express route. Prefect, it transpires, is actually an alien spending time on earth to research a new edition of *The Hitchhiker's Guide to the Galaxy* (the book voiced by Peter Jones), and he convinces Dent to catch a lift on a passing Vogon spacecraft so they can both avoid the impending disaster.

That, of course, is just the beginning of their adventures that are packed with strange creatures, novel language and bizarre moments as they travel the universe with only the book to guide them ('Space is big. REALLY big. You just won't believe how vastly, hugely, mind-bogglingly big it is. I mean, you may think it's a long way down the street to the chemist, but that's just peanuts to space...')

Only six episodes of the cult classic were made, but each one is a gem as we are introduced to such characters as Zaphod Beelblebrox (Wing-Davey), Marvin the paranoid android (Stephen Moore) and Slartibartfast (Richard Vernon) and finally learn the answer to life, the universe and everything (it's '42', of course). The effects are pretty dreadful – such as Zaphod's animatronic second head and the Vogon creatures – but that's part of its very English charm.

TV Trivia: Author Douglas Adams appears in cameo roles in some of the episodes, including a scene in which a naked man walks into the sea (the actor who was meant to do it had called in sick that day).

HYPERDRIVE (2006–2007)

Starring Nick Frost, Kevin Eldon, Miranda Hart

It's the year 2151, and the crew of the spaceship *Camden Lock* are on a mission to convince alien governments to relocate their businesses to Britain. Of course, since this is a comedy, the crew – led by Captain Henderson (Frost) – are a bumbling bunch who never quite succeed in their tasks and usually get themselves into life-threatening situations with the ETs they do encounter.

Sci-fi comedy fans (and especially those who loved *Red Dwarf*) hated this series, and it was cancelled after 12 episodes. It's actually not bad – it's just not that funny or memorable, despite having the usually hilarious Frost (*Hot Fuzz*, *Shaun of the Dead*) on board. The supporting cast are competent, too – Kevin Eldon as psychopathic York, Miranda Hart as Teal and Dan Antopolski as Jeffers among them – but it's ultimately forgettable and missable even though the second season was a slight improvement on the first.

 TV Trivia: Frost wasn't an actor before his best friend/flatmate cast him in the series *Spaced* – he was a waiter and cook.

THE INVADERS (1967–1968)

Starring Roy Thinnes, Kent Smith

Tired after a hard day, David Vincent (Thinnes) is resting in his car when he sees an unidentified flying object in the sky. Investigating further, David discovers aliens are coming to our planet to invade it, but no one believes him because the aliens have taken on human form, and when they die their bodies burn, leaving no evidence they were ever there. Everyone thinks David is a crank, but he travels across the US, trying to figure out what the aliens are up to while also trying to warn people of their existence.

A fun sci-fi adventure from Quinn Martin, the producer of *The Fugitive*, this was very like that series in the way David ran from town to town, although he's trying to run from something far more sinister than the cops who are after Richard Kimble. After a while the episodes are a bit same-y – David gets to a place, pursues an alien, then heads off to the next town – but Vincent gives a great performance as the man no one believes, and there is nice support in later episodes from Smith as the industrialist who does believe him. A mini-series update, in which Thinnes returned in his role as David, who is now an old man handing the fight over to someone new (played by Scott Bakula) was made in 1995 but is not available on DVD.

TV Trivia: Throughout the series, you never see the aliens in their true form.

INVASION (2005–2006)

Starring William Fichtner, Eddie Cibrian, Kari Matchett

One of three mainstream sci-fi series to debut in autumn 2005 and then be cancelled by 2006 – the others were *Surface* (see review p.239) and *Threshold* (unavailable on DVD) – *Invasion* was co-written by Shaun Cassidy, who had also had a hand in the superb series *American Gothic* (see p.252). This series, alas, was much slower to get going (one of its major problems) as a hurricane hits the coast of Florida and strange things begin to occur. Park ranger Russell (Cibrian) isn't convinced even though his daughter says she saw hundreds of lights on the water during the storm, but then he begins to suspect something odd is going on when his ex-wife Mariel (Matchett) is found naked in the water with no memory of how she got there. Mariel's husband, the rather suspicious Sheriff Tom Underlay (Fichtner) wants the whole area quarantined, Russell's new brother-in-law Dave (Tyler Labine) is sure something otherworldly is going on (especially after he finds a weird skeleton) and there's a deadly flu virus on the way.

It all could have been quite fun if the script hadn't moved the plot along with the speed of a squashed snail. It's obvious to anyone who has ever caught a glimpse of a sci-fi movie in their life that something alien/hybrid or body-snatchy is going on in the Florida town, but it takes over half a season for 'our hero' (the rather wooden Cibrian) to find anything useful out. By the time he does you'll be too bored to care.

TV Trivia: The first episode of *Invasion* was first shown just weeks after the devastating Hurricane Katrina, so adverts featuring the plot's hurricane were toned down out of respect.

KINVIG (1981)

Starring Tony Haygarth, Patsy Rowlands, Prunella Gee, Colin Jeavons

Nigel Kneale, the creator of *Quatermass*, was the man behind this short-lived sci-fi comedy series – rumour has it the idea came to him after he visited a sci-fi convention packed with ardent fans. It's the story of Des Kinvig (Haygarth), who leads an ordinary, rather dull life, running an electrical repair shop and enduring the constant fussing of his wife Netta (Rowlands). All that changes, however, when one night he stumbles across an alien spaceship and encounters aliens Loom, Bat and Sagga, who tell him their leader is actually one of his customers, Miss Griffin (Gee).

It's quirky stuff as Des convinces his layabout pal Jim (Jeavons) that there is extraterrestrial life on earth and the pair of them then start to see alien happenings in everyday occurances, while Des's daydreams (or is it reality?) also lead him to believe he is a hero and Miss Griffin is his scantily clad other-worldly lover. The question of whether Des has been abducted or whether it is all in his mind was never resolved as the series was cancelled after just seven episodes. Worth a look, nonetheless.

 TV Trivia: Patsy Rowlands is best known for her roles as various long-suffering wives in 10 of the Carry On movies.

LEXX (1997–2002)

Starring Brian Downey, Michael McManus, Xenia Seeberg

The busty babe falling out of her bra on the DVD cover will give you more than a hint of what this show is about – yes, it's shagging in space! A Canadian/German production, *Lexx* quickly gained a reputation for being a mad sci-fi sex farce, about a crew of misfits who trawl the galaxy in a living ship named *Lexx* (it's supposed to be based on a dragonfly but some have commented that it is more X-rated in appearance – you decide). There's nerdy pilot Stanley Tweedle (Downey), love slave Xev (Seeberg) – originally called Zev and played by another actress in early episodes, reanimated assassin Kai (McManus) and lovesick robot head 790 (he lost his body in an unfortunate accident). Apparently they are on the lookout for food and other people, but really their explorations are of the naked kind.

Cheap and cheerful, the series divided sci-fi fans into those who thought it was so bad it was good, and those who decided it was so bad it was, well, bad. The latter is really true as the cast – clearly chosen for their cup-sizes (the women) or ability to raise one eyebrow at a time (the men) – either overact with the gusto of porn stars or appear so wooden they become part of the scenery. A shame, because some of the plot is almost (but not quite) clever. In some countries the series was known by another title – *Tales from a Parallel Universe* – but whatever you call it, it's still the same nonsense.

TV Trivia: No one is sure whether *Lexx* is male or female (although the ship does become pregnant in one episode) – in Germany, the ship is voiced by a female actress, whereas in English, the voice is male.

THE LONE GUNMEN (2001)

Starring Bruce Harwood, Tom Braidwood, Dean Haglund

A spin-off from the hugely successful *The X-Files* may have seemed like a good idea, but this series – focusing on the three computer-hacking, nerdy conspiracy geeks/journalists Agent Mulder sometimes went to for advice – only lasted 14 episodes, possibly because the central characters weren't that appealing. It was like a geeky version of *Mission: Impossible*, but with laughs, as Byers (Harwood), Frohike (Braidwood) and Langly (Haglund) went on missions to uncover the truth about things while Jimmy Bond (Stephen Snedden) was the benefactor who provided their funding.

Since the trio were social misfits, the creators obviously decided they needed someone a bit more appealing added to the cast in the form of character Yves Adele Harlow (Zuleika Robinson), whose name and the various aliases she uses are all anagrams of Lee Harvey Oswald. If you start watching the series, be prepared never to learn what exactly she is up to, as the series was cancelled before Yves' motives were unveiled. It's all pretty silly stuff packed with bad jokes, puking, peeing and slapstick moments that will probably turn off fans of the far more serious series that spawned it. And surely *X-Files* aficionados are the only viewers who might even care who the Lone Gunmen are anyway.

 TV Trivia: The pilot episode, broadcast in March 2001, included a scene in which someone attempts to crash a plane into New York's World Trade Center.

LOST IN SPACE (1965–1968)

Starring Guy Williams, June Lockhart, Mark Goddard, Marta Kristen, Jonathan Harris

This classic sci-fi family series was originally entitled *Space Family Robinson*, so you can easily guess the plot: the family Robinson blasted off into space in 1997 aboard the *Jupiter 2* spaceship, their five-year mission to colonise a planet in the Alpha Centauri planetary system. Unfortunately, Dr Zachary Smith (the wonderfully droll Harris) sabotaged the ship's controls, programming it for a crash landing in deep space, then got stuck on the ship as it took off. When the family – led by dad John (Williams) and mum Maureen (Lockhart) – wake from the suspended animation they were in for the journey, they discover they are stranded on an unknown planet with Smith sabotaging their every effort to get home.

For three seasons, the family (also including daughters Judy and Penny, son

Will, pilot Don West and the family robot), and Smith travelled from planet to planet, encountering various alien life forms while trying to find a way home. Their adventures – all of which are funny (even when they aren't meant to be) and as camp as a field of tents – abandon scientific accuracy and instead go for fun, fun, fun as the wobbly robot whirrs around saying 'Danger, Will Robinson, danger!', Dr Smith spends far too much time with young Will for it to be considered decent, and the crew encounter such weird entities as hillbilly space travellers, bubble creatures, and, of course, Debbie the Bloop (a chimp in costume). It's stupid, silly (surely the only way the family would 'colonise' the planet would be if the siblings started shagging each other to breed more kids... ew) and extremely cheesy, but that's all part of its tin foil charm. The first two seasons were marginally more serious, than the last – watch Season 3's episode 'The Great Vegetable Rebellion', in which the Robinsons are captured by a giant carrot and Smith is turned into a stick of celery – and you'll see how bonkers it got.

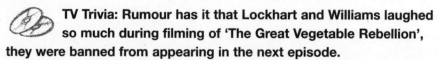 **TV Trivia: Rumour has it that Lockhart and Williams laughed so much during filming of 'The Great Vegetable Rebellion', they were banned from appearing in the next episode.**

MiLLENNiUM (1996–1999)

Starring Lance Henriksen, Brittany Tiplady, Terry O'Quinn

Frank Black (Henriksen), loving husband and father, worked for the FBI's behavioural science unit until he had a nervous breakdown, due to his unique and uncomfortable talent of being able to see into the mind and soul of serial killers. So now he works part-time for the mysterious Millennium Group, tracking down various evil people in what, at least for the first season, became a grim thriller about the evil that men do. However, by Season 2, the show's direction changed: the Millenium Group were now revealed not as the crime-busting group we thought they were, but an ancient sect preparing for various forms of weirdness – including a predicted plague – come the new century. And if that wasn't confusing enough, a third season completely ignored a previous cliffhanger, changed what the Group was again and caused much head-scratching among fans.

Created by Chris Carter of *The X-Files*, this series was dark, apocalyptic and often gripping, even if it is different, season to season (part of the reason was that Carter was less involved in Season 2, then returned for Season 3). Henriksen – probably best known for his role in *Aliens* – is fascinating to watch as Frank Black (the same name, incidentally, as the lead singer of the cult band The Pixies), and the supporting cast of *Lost*'s Terry O'Quinn and

Megan Gallagher (as Frank's wife) are also pitch-perfect. It's odd, uneven, occasionally ordinary and sometimes very extraordinary – one can only imagine what would have happened had there been a Season 4.

 TV Trivia: William Hurt was originally considered for the role of Frank.

MORK AND MINDY (1978–1982)

Starring Robin Williams, Pam Dawber, Conrad Janis

Sci-fi aficionados will probably shudder when they see that this naff comedy series, which ran for four seasons, is included in the sci-fi section, but since it does focus around an alien, here it stays. The alien, of course, is Mork from the planet Ork – a character who first appeared, bizarrely, in an episode of *Happy Days* – as played by stand-up comic Robin Williams. It was the role that made him famous, years before *Good Morning Vietnam* or *Mrs Doubtfire*, and the role of an alien new to earth and how he interacts with our human ways was well mixed with Williams' brand of zany, rapid-fire humour, even if he had to tone it down a lot for television and adopt an annoying catchphrase ('nanoo, nanoo').

The sitcom plot is simple: Mork has been sent down to earth to observe humans and report back to his boss, the unseen Orson (Ralph James). Luckily for Mork, he's not here on earth (Boulder, Colorado, to be precise) for long before he is befriended by average gal Mindy (Dawber), who takes him in and is the 'straight man' to Mork's wild and crazy antics as he gets used to the oddities of earth. Aimed at families, each episode usually ended with Mork reporting back to Orson on a valuable lesson learned while he was with Mindy or her dad, Fred (Janis). Aside from the fact Mork was an alien, it was pretty standard fare (there's a nosy neighbour, Mr Bickley, and most of the humour is built around Mork's misunderstandings of the English language so he could just as easily have come from France instead of Ork) that was funny enough until a romance between Mork and Mindy was added in, and the pair ended up with a child, Mearth from Earth (Jonathan Winters), who aged backwards, so started as a middle-aged man.

The first series is the best; just make sure you avoid the episodes featuring Mork's mentally unhinged (and very annoying) pal, Exidor (Robert Donner). Sadly, our favourite alien on earth comedy, *ALF*, isn't on DVD in the UK.

 TV Trivia: Creator Garry Marshall hired Robin Williams after he came to the audition and, when offered a seat, sat upside down on it. Marshall later commented that Williams got the part because he was the only alien who came to audition.

MUTANT X (2001-2004)

Starring John Shea, Victoria Pratt, Tom McCamus

Genetic mutants created as part of a secret government project are released into the general population. One of the scientists who created them, Adam Kane (Shea, best known as Lex Luthor in *Lois and Clark*), decides to help the mutants, while another Eckhart (who looks like Andy Warhol), wants to get hold of them and use them for his own ends. Adam forms a group of mutants – Mutant X – to try and help those that are still out there, being hunted by Eckhart. Could this be an X-Men rip-off, perchance? 20th Century Fox, who owned the film rights for X-Men certainly thought so, as they sued the creators of this series and demanded aspects of the show be changed that were similar, such as the use of mutant nicknames and similar logos. Bizarre when you consider that Mutant X and X-Men are both based on comics from the same team – Marvel.

With the team made up of *FHM* covergirl types such as cat-like Shalimar Fox (Pratt) and psychic Emma DeLauro (Lauren Lee Smith) and a couple of token pretty boys, electricity-projecting Brennan (Victor Webster) and Jesse (ex-model Forbes March), who can change his molecular structure to walk through walls, this is heavy on the cleavage and dumb action, so clearly aimed at teenage boys who only leave the house to venture to the nearest PlayStation/Nintendo games store. But they would think it's a hackneyed rip-off, too, while anyone over the age of seven will wince at the dreadful dialogue and wooden performances. Awful.

TV Trivia: In another legal case, Marvel was sued by Tribune Entertainment (who distributed the series) for $100 million for fraud, stating Marvel had encouraged them to promote the connection between Mutant X and X-Men.

ODYSSEY 5 (2002-2004)

Starring Peter Weller, Sebastian Roche, Christopher Gorham, Leslie Silva

Despite the title, this series has nothing to do with the popular sci-fi show *Babylon 5* – the five in the title refers to five crew members of a shuttle – Commander Chuck Taggart (Weller), his son Neil (Gorham), geneticist Kurt Mendel (Roche), journalist Sarah (Silva) and pilot Angela (Tamara Craig Thomas). After witnessing the destruction of Earth from their space shuttle Odyssey, the group of astronauts are sent back in time by a friendly alien called The Seeker so they can find out who destroyed the planet, and also set things right so it won't happen again. Oh, and – here's that five from the title again – they only have five years in which to do it.

Created by Manny Coto, who later worked on *24* and *Enterprise*, this has some nice conspiracy theories and interesting ideas, such as the crew returning to Earth with the knowledge of what is going to happen in their lives – Sarah knows her young son will die of cancer, but no one believes her as, at this point in history it is too early to diagnose, while Neil finds himself back on Earth as a teenager but knowing he is 22 and more worldly-wise – but ultimately the characters aren't as engaging as on some other sci-fi shows. The series was cancelled after just one season, but the writers knew in advance so were able to bring the adventure to some sort of slightly rushed conclusion.

 TV Trivia: Peter Weller is a huge jazz fan and is in a jazz band with fellow actor Jeff Goldblum (they starred in *The Adventures of Buckaroo Banzai Across The 8th Dimension* together).

THE OUTER LIMITS (1963–1965)

Starring Vic Perrin

Like the more famous *The Twilight Zone*, *The Outer Limits* was an anthology series, but with more of an emphasis on science fiction and stomach-tightening scares than the fantasy/mystery episodes that TZ sometimes boasted. 'There is nothing wrong with your television set. Do not attempt to adjust the picture,' said a voice as each hour-long episode began, and children (who probably shouldn't have been watching) hid behind sofas knowing something creepy was coming. Many of the stories dealt with science gone wrong, alien invaders and time travel screw-ups – classic episodes include the creepy 'Architects Of Fear'; 'Demon With A Glass Hand', with Robert Culp; 'The Man Who Was Never Born', in which hideous mutant from the future Martin Landau sacrifices himself for a better tomorrow; and 'The Zanti Misfits', featuring ant-like creatures with human faces. Actors who appeared in the series (often in their TV debuts) included Martin Sheen, Edward Asner, William Shatner, David McCallum, Donald Pleasance, Leonard Nimoy and Adam West.

A new version of the series was made in 1995 that ran until 2002. Among the guest cast were young actors Ryan Reynolds, Joshua Jackson, Kirsten Dunst, Spandau Ballet's Martin Kemp and *The OC*'s Kelly Rowan. While it's not as good as the original, it's not bad either, and is available on DVD.

 TV Trivia: The 1995 remake of *The Outer Limits* lasted longer than the original series (seven years while the original ran for just two).

PLANET OF THE APES (1974)

Starring James Naughton, Ron Harper

First there was the marvellous Charlton Heston-starring movie in 1968 based on Pierre Boulle's novel, and a series of sequels, *Beneath The Planet of The Apes* (1970), *Escape From The Planet of The Apes* (1971), *Conquest of The Planet of The Apes* (1972) and *Battle For The Planet Of The Apes* (1973). Then came this series loosely based on the first movie, set on the future Earth of 3085 where humans are slaves to ape rulers. Astronauts Burke (Naughton) and Virdon (Harper), on a NASA mission from 1980, crash land there, and are befriended by renegade ape Galen (McDowall, who had played ape Cornelius in the original films), who hides out the human fugitives while nasty ape General Urko attempts to track them down.

Only 14 episodes were made before the series was cancelled, and it's not hard to see why. While McDowall gets top billing, his character is mainly in the background, seemingly just there to serve as a reminder of his nice guy roles in the previous Apes movies. Any strong plot twists, such as the discovery of a vault holding mankind's history and secrets, are abandoned and forgotten by episode end, rather than expanded on, and it's safe to say that neither Harper nor Naughton are a patch (physically or performance-wise) on Charlton Heston, whose delivery of the line 'You maniacs! You blew it up! Ah, damn you! God damn you all to hell!' remains one of the most memorable in sci-fi cinema history.

One for completists only. A follow-up series, *Return to the Planet of the Apes*, was made in 1975 but isn't on DVD.

 TV Trivia: The astronauts' spaceship seen in the first episode is the same plywood model used in the *Planet of the Apes* movie.

QUANTUM LEAP (1989–1993)

Starring Scott Bakula, Dean Stockwell

Scientist Sam Beckett (Bakula) believes that he has devised a machine that can allow people to time travel within their own lifetime. Pressured to prove his theory, Sam steps into the device (the Accelerator) himself to test it out – and vanishes. In fact, he has 'leaped' – travelled into the past and assumed someone else's identity (when Sam looks in the mirror he sees the other man's face). The only person who can contact Sam, by appearing in hologram form, is Al (Stockwell), who with the help of a handheld computer named Ziggy tries to figure out what has happened. It seems Sam is destined to leap from one body to another – usually once he has resolved something in a person's life, he leaps again to another time and place and person – with the hope that one day he'll leap back into his own body in the present day.

Devised by Donald P Bellasario (*Magnum PI*), this is a cracking sci-fi adventure in which we follow Sam from one odd situation to the next. Each episode ends when he solves a dilemma and leaps again, then the next episode picks up from that leap as Sam has to work out where the hell he is, who he is this time, and what he is doing there, and each leap leads him to a year since he was born. Over the show's five seasons, this device had Sam leaping into the body of a black chauffeur to a wealthy white woman in the Deep South of 1955 ('The Color Of Truth'), a buxom secretary (yes, he can leap into women's bodies, too) who is being sexually harassed in 1961 ('What Price Gloria?'), and even into the body of Lee Harvey Oswald ('Lee Harvey Oswald'). One of the most heart-rending episodes had Sam leaping into the body of a young retarded man named Jimmy in 1964 ('Jimmy') – the episode was so popular that the character returned for three more episodes.

While the final season wasn't quite up to the previous four, this remains a lovely family sci-fi series that ended with a clever episode that left you wanting more.

 TV Trivia: At the end of each episode as he leaps, Sam usually says 'Oh boy' – a line Bakula apparently ad-libbed in an early episode.

THE QUATERMASS EXPERIMENT; QUATERMASS II; QUATERMASS AND THE PIT (1953; 1955; 1958–1959)

Starring Reginald Tate, Isabel Dean, John Robinson, Andre Morrell

A groundbreaking series created by Nigel Kneale, 1953's *The Quatermass Experiment* was a six-episode, black and white series that was broadcast live. Professor Quatermass (Tate) and his team of scientists have launched a rocket into space with three astronauts on board but something goes wrong inflight and the rocket crashlands into a house on Wimbledon Common. Only one astronaut emerges – Victor Carroon (Duncan Lamont) – and there is no trace of the other two. To make matters worse, Victor's wife had told him to 'take care and don't forget to bring something back' before he went on the trip… could the something he brought back be alien?

Spine-tinglingly atmospheric, *The Quatermass Experiment* was made even more so by the fact that the climactic showdown took place in Westminster Abbey, where less than three months before the broadcast, millions had seen Queen Elizabeth's coronation take place. Compulsory viewing for most of

Britain – and a 'watercooler' show before we had watercoolers – the gripping, tense and downright scary series was followed by *Quatermass II* in 1955 with John Robinson taking over the role of Quatermass because Tate had fallen ill during rehearsals (he died in the August). This second series focused on an alien invasion of Earth, while the third series, the completely cracking 1958's *Quatermass and The Pit*, followed the professor as a building excavation first uncovers a skull and then what looks like it could be a spaceship. For this series, Andre Morell took on the role of Quatermass.

All three series are terrific, but the first and final ones remain the best of the bunch. The 1979 *Quatermass* series (known by fans as 'Quatermass 4') is no longer available on DVD while a 'live' 2005 version of *The Quatermass Experiment* with Jason Flemyng is available, but not a patch on the original.

 TV Trivia: Nigel Kneale got the name 'Quatermass' by picking it from a London phone directory.

RED DWARF (1988–1999)

Starring Craig Charles, Chris Barrie, Danny John Jules, Robert Llewellyn

An often hilarious, quirky comedy from the BBC that began in 1988, *Red Dwarf* is the name of a shabby-looking mining ship hurtling through space. The crew are all dead thanks to a radiation leak, except soup machine repairman Dave Lister (Craig Charles), who has been in suspended animation for the three million years since the accident occurred. Now awake, he's not doomed to float through space completely alone, however, as he's joined by the holographic image of his irritating dead roommate Arnold Rimmer (Chris Barrie), the ship's cat, Cat, who has evolved into a more human lifeform (Danny John Jules), Holly, the ship's onboard computer (Norman Lovett, for Series 1, 2, 7 and 8, and Hattie Hayridge for Series 3 to 6), and from the third series, robot Kryten (Robert Llewellyn).

Sharpest in the earlier series, this was a mix of sharp and dumber-than-dumb comedy from creators Rob Grant and Doug Naylor that gained much of its humour from the odd couple relationship between prissy hologram Rimmer and the almost feral Lister (whose favourite curseword was the enjoyable 'smeg'). In Series 7, Rimmer went off to a parallel universe and Lister's former girlfriend, Kochanski (Clare Grogan in early episodes, then Chloe Annett from Series 7), is found in another parallel universe and joins the crew – from here the comedy was less successful and many fans of the earlier seasons tuned out.

Throughout, many of the episodes nodded their hats to classic sci-fi moments, and fans should check out episodes such as 'Polymorph' from

Series 3, which parodies *Alien*, and 'Meltdown' from Series 4, which is a homage to *Westworld*.

 TV Trivia: An American version was also planned and a pilot was filmed with Frasier's Jane Leeves as Holly, but the series was never made.

SEAQUEST DSV (1993-1996)

Starring Roy Scheider, Ted Raimi, Jonathan Brandis, Don Franklin

A fishy sci-fi series, set in the mid-21st century, has us humans colonising the oceans and even having an organisation – the UEO – to police it. Former member Nathan Bridger (Scheider) is called back into service (he's been brooding on an island, grieving for his late wife) when someone attempts to hijack the undersea vessel *Seaquest DSV* – his mission to assume command of it, since he designed the thing in the first place. With Commander John Ford (Franklin) at his side and a crew that includes a talking dolphin, a teen genius (Brandis), and later a genetically engineered lifeform named Dagwood (Peter DeLuise), and telepathic Dr Wendy Smith (Rosalind Allen), Bridger trawls the ocean blue on the lookout for anything fishy.

For the first series, this was interminably dull and all a bit worthy and new agey, but in response to poor viewing figures, the creators added alien life, lost civilisations and mystical elements from the second season. Things picked up a bit, but this never really got very exciting and was cancelled after Season 3.

All in all, it's a poor underwater rip-off of *Star Trek: The Next Generation* – and after a few meandering episodes, you'll find yourself hoping Schneider's toothy co-star from *Jaws* (and we don't mean Richard Dreyfuss) pops up to snack on some of the characters just for some light relief.

 TV Trivia: Steven Spielberg is one of the executive producers.

SLIDERS (1995-2000)

Starring Jerry O'Connell, Kari Wuhrer, John Rhys-Davies

Like the similar *Quantum Leap*, *Sliders* starts with an accident. Physics student Quinn Mallory (O'Connell) is trying to develop an anti-gravity device when – oops! – he accidentally creates a portal that leads to a parallel universe: it's the same time and place but a different version of Earth. Taking along his professor, Maximillian Arturro (Rhys-Davies), his pal Wade (Sabrina Lloyd) and innocent bystander Rembrandt (Cleavant Derricks, the only cast member to appear in every season), he decides to explore, only to discover the device that should bring them back is – oops again! – broken, so they are destined to 'slide' to and from different alternate realities, hoping one trip will lead them home.

It's a clever idea that allows lots of nice plot twists as the group go to an Earth without penicillin that is gripped by plague, one where America is still a British colony because the Civil War never happened (ha!), or another where it is men who get pregnant instead of women.

While each individual episode has good ideas (even if some are rip-offs from *The X-Files* and various sci-fi and horror movies), there isn't the ongoing character development viewers are used to in series like *Buffy* or *Lost*, and when finally an ongoing story is introduced – the pursuit of brain-eating, morphing and sliding baddie Rickman (played by, among others, Roger Daltrey) – it's too little, too late.

TV Trivia: Sharp-eyed viewers will notice less impressive effects from Season 4 onwards. This is because the TV channel making the show switched from Fox to the Sci-Fi Channel, which had a smaller budget.

SPACE 1999 (1975–1977)

Starring Martin Landau, Barbara Bain, Nick Tate

A thoroughly enjoyable series from Gerry Anderson of *Thunderbirds* fame, set in a futuristic 1999, this reportedly cost over £3 million to make, an astronomical figure at the time, and also the most (in 1975) that had ever been spent on a British TV series.

Moonbase Alpha is a scientific research colony that gets blasted out of Earth's orbit and travels through the galaxy, unable to return home – and, of course, the crew encounter strange aliens and planets while they drift. Onboard are Commander John Koenig (Landau), Dr Helena Russell (Bain), scientific advisor Professor Victor Bergman (Barry Morse) who has a robotic heart, and in the second season, shape-changing Maya (Catherine Schell) with her fetching pointy sideburns. The first season was quite serious stuff, although none other than Isaac Asimov criticised its scientific accuracy, but American producer Fred Freiberger was brought in for the second season to make it more action and humour-oriented for US audiences (Anderson reportedly described Freiberger's changes as 'awful').

Unsurprisingly, many British fans tuned out, and the series was cancelled. Watch out for actors including Joan Collins, Peter Cushing, Christopher Lee and Leo McKern in guest roles.

TV Trivia: Co-stars Barbara Bain and Martin Landau were husband and wife from 1957 until they divorced in 1993.

STAR TREK (1966–1969)

Starring William Shatner, Leonard Nimoy, DeForest Kelley, Nichelle Nichols

One of the longest-running science-fiction franchises in television history began with this groundbreaking series. Set in the 23rd century, *Star Trek* charts the adventures of the starship Enterprise and her crew, led by Captain James T. Kirk (Shatner), as they explore the galaxy. However, Gene Roddenberry, *Star Trek*'s creator, never intended to make a straightforward science-fiction show. Instead, he wanted the series to reflect and comment on American society as it was in the sixties. The multi-racial, mixed gender crew of the Enterprise contrasted with the racial segregation that existed in parts of the country, and Roddenberry also included a half-human, half-Vulcan first officer, Mr Spock (Leonard Nimoy), to show that not only will racism not exist in the 23rd century, but humans will also be working in harmony with aliens under the banner of the United Federation of Planets, a sort of futuristic United Nations.

Roddenberry had a constant battle with the network in his attempts to push boundaries. Communications officer Lt Uhura (Nichelle Nichols) was one of the first major black characters on an American TV series, and one episode, 'Plato's Stepchildren', is often quoted as showing television's first inter-racial kiss between a black and a white character. (Captain Kirk and Lt. Uhura are forced to smooch by evil aliens with telekinetic powers – executives at NBC felt that this was the only way that the 'kiss' could happen without angering TV stations in the deep south). Also, at the time when the feminist movement was beginning and Roddenberry wanted to show female crew as strong and authoritative, they were decked out in dresses so short they'd make a Pussycat Doll blush.

Not every episode makes a social commentary – Joan Collins guests in the critically acclaimed episode 'The City on the Edge of Forever' in which her character, Edith, with whom Captain Kirk has a brief romance after he is transported back to New York during the Great Depression era, has to die in order for the normal time line to be restored. 'The Trouble With Tribbles' is another stand-out episode in which the *Enterprise* becomes overrun with cute, but highly prolific, little creatures.

The series wasn't a hit when it first aired, perhaps viewers at the time felt it was too revolutionary. But over 40 years and countless re-runs later, audiences have finally come to appreciate Roddenberry's vision.

TV trivia: When NBC was promoting Star Trek in magazines, all shots of Spock's pointed eyebrows and ears were air-brushed out of the pictures because the network thought that no one would watch the show due to Spock's resemblance to the Devil.

STAR TREK: DEEP SPACE NINE (1993–1999)

Starring Avery Brooks, Rene Auberjonois, Nana Visitor, Alexander Siddig

The third instalment of the *Star Trek* franchise is set on a space station rather than a starship. The series began in 1993, airing alongside the final season of *The Next Generation* with both shows being set in the same time frame. Deep Space Nine (DS9) had been built by the Cardassians, a barbaric, warmongering race, who abandoned the station after their brutal persecution of the peace loving Bajorans came to an end. A Starfleet crew, led by Commander Benjamin Sisko (Brooks) is invited by the Bajoran government to help restore the station. The crew is composed of the usual *Star Trek* mix of genders races and species, and there's even a *Star Wars* cantina-style bar for them to hang out in which gave the make up department a chance to get creative with rubber and paint. A newly discovered wormhole leading to the mysterious Gamma Quadrant means a whole host of weird and wonderful aliens can rock up to the station saving Starfleet the trouble of having to go where no man has gone before in order to meet them.

Unlike the two previous Treks, where a story was generally done within a single episode, *DS9* featured longer story arcs sometimes spanning several episodes or even seasons. The series was also darker than viewers were used to. Storylines focused on conflict, terrorism and oppression as the evil Dominion, who rule the Gamma Quadrant, waged war on the Federation and its allies while the Cardassian occupation of Bajora echoes the Holocaust. Season 1's penultimate episode, 'Duet', is often sited as one of the best episodes of any *Star Trek* series. In it, an injured Cardassian brought aboard the space station turns out to be a war criminal, and Kira Nerys (Visitor), Sisko's Bajoran second in command, struggles with her feelings while she interrogates the defiant prisoner. Of all the spin offs, *DS9* is the most dramatic and therefore most accessible series for those who don't necessarily think of themselves as fans of science fiction, let alone *Star Trek*.

TV trivia: Malcolm McDowell once said he'd like to appear on *DS9*, but only if his nephew, Alexander Siddig, chief medical officer, Julian Bashir, would direct the episode. Alas, scheduling conflicts meant it was not to be.

STAR TREK: ENTERPRISE (2001–2005)

Starring Scott Bakula, Jolene Blalock, Connor Trinneer, Dominic Keating

The final offering from the *Star Trek* stable is a prequel set about a hundred years before the original series and ten years before the founding of the Federation. Although the premise of the series is standard fodder – a crew sets out in a starship Enterprise to explore space, encountering aliens and learning about humanity along the way – the fact that this series is set at the *beginning* of the *Star Trek* story when the technology was new and the crew a bit green makes for an interesting history lesson. The origins of many familiar concepts, such as the Prime Directive, the Federation's rules of cultural interference, are explained in this series. The crew, commanded by square-jawed, handsome, all-American Captain Jonathan Archer (*Quantum Leap*'s Bakula) is mostly human, seeing as few other alien species had been encountered at that point. In Season 3, as ratings fell, the voyage of discovery becomes a deadly mission after an alien race launches an attack on Earth.

Unfortunately, the early *Star Trek* novelty wore off pretty quickly and the more dramatic storylines weren't enough to lure viewers back. Although the show's focus on the three main characters, Archer, chief engineer Charles Tucker (Trinneer) and first officer T'Pol (Jolene Blalock), harked back to the original series, by now viewers were used to the more inclusive, ensemble casts of later shows so this became another bone of contention. At the same time there were other science-fiction shows doing good business and *Star Trek: Enterprise* just couldn't compete. *Enterprise* eventually ran out of steam after a four-year run although the *Star Trek* franchise still exists in movie form. Not surprisingly, the next big screen offering will also be a prequel.

TV trivia: The first name of Captain Archer was initially to have been Jeffrey. British fans pointed out the link to the disgraced politician Jeffrey Archer after learning of the name over the Internet leading to the producers changing it.

STAR TREK: THE NEXT GENERATION (1987–1994)

Starring Patrick Stewart, Jonathan Frakes, Brent Spiner, LeVar Burton

Although *The Next Generation* (TNG) hit US screens nearly 20 years after the original *Star Trek* series ended, early shows had none of the confidence or charm of its predecessor. Season 1 looked a bit ropey with stilted acting, unnatural dialogue and far from engaging stories. Set in the 24th century, about 80 years after the first incarnation, TNG featured a new crew and a new Enterprise but with the same mission of exploration, study and diplomacy as the previous starship. Captain Jean-Luc Picard (Patrick Stewart) is at the helm supported by, amongst others, first officer William Riker (Jonathan Frakes), Data (Brent Spiner), the android chief operations officer, and chief engineer Geordi La Forge (LeVar Burton). The Klingons, formerly mortal enemies of The Federation, are now allies, hence the Klingon security officer Worf (Michael Dorn). New technology was also unveiled in Season 1, most notably the holodeck, a room in which virtual reality worlds could be created. As the characters and relationships developed, storylines improved and became more challenging. New alien villains were introduced such as the duplicitous Ferengi and seemingly indestructible Borg, the latter being the antagonists in some of the best episodes including the Season 3 cliffhanger finale, 'The Best of Both Worlds: Part 1'.

The original Trek was made at a time of great upheaval in American society (the beginnings of the feminist and civil rights movements and the lead up to the war in Vietnam) so these were the issues the show would comment on. By the late eighties, when 'greed was good', the focus of TNG turned inwards, looking instead at humanity, what it means to be human and how we are all connected. Storylines now embraced all the main crew members, unlike the original series which mainly concentrated on Kirk and his inner circle. Data, although superior to humans in many ways, like Pinocchio, yearned to be a real boy and many episodes examined the human condition through his yellow eyes.

One of the most incongruous inclusions was the presence of a counsellor as a regular fixture on the ship's bridge. At a time when self-examination through therapy was all the rage, having an empath on board to psych out the bad guys while helping the crew stay sane probably made sense. But did she need to be on the bridge? After a shaky start, and despite the death of Star Trek's creator, Gene Roddenberry, in 1991, the show's popularity became such that another spin-off, Deep Space Nine, was created which aired alongside TNG as the series drew to a close.

TV trivia: A follow-up series to the original series was considered in 1977. It was to be called Star Trek 2 and feature a second mission for the original cast. It was cancelled before production but two of the scripts for this series were re-written as episodes for TNG — 'The Child' and 'Devil's Due'.

STAR TREK: VOYAGER (1995–2001)

Starring Kate Mulgrew, Robert Beltran, Tim Russ, Roxann Dawson

The *Star Trek* production line was in full swing in the nineties. A year after *The Next Generation* had ended and with *DS9* still pulling decent ratings, *Voyager* was launched, bringing a couple of new elements to the continuing Trek saga. For the first time the crew had a woman at the helm, the formidable Captain Kathryn Janeway (Mulgrew). Also, instead of a starship on a mission of exploration or a crew based on a space station, the USS *Voyager*, having been accidentally transported thousands of light years away from Federation space, is faced with a 75-year journey home. The *Voyager* crew is joined by the band of Maquis rebels they had been chasing before being catapulted into the Delta Quadrant. The Maquis, a rag-tag group of freedom fighters, some of whom had been Starfleet officers, felt abandoned by the Federation as part of its peace treaty to end the war with Cardassia, and had since been a thorn in both sides. Naturally, there is tension as both crews learn to work together aboard the starship.

The initial hostility between the integrated crew members provided a rich source of storylines. However, as things settled down, the series turned into a bit of a Trek soap opera with much inter-crew coupling and standard battling of mean aliens. *Voyager* divided both fans and critics – the main characters could have been more engaging and the villains just weren't villainous enough. There were some decent story arcs, but overall it was simply too formulaic. It wasn't until Season 4 when the Borg were draughted in as the main baddies that things started to pick up. The introduction of Seven of Nine (Jeri Ryan), the catsuit-clad Borg drone rescued by the *Voyager* crew, is credited with saving the series from possible cancellation as the sexy character sparked a revival in ratings.

 TV trivia: King Abdullah of Jordan, a die-hard Trekkie, made a cameo appearance in a Season 2 episode of *Voyager* while he was still a prince. However, he couldn't speak any lines because he wasn't a member of the Screen Actors' Guild.

STARGATE SG-1 (1997–2007)

Starring Richard Dean Anderson, Michael Shanks, Amanda Tapping, Christopher Judge

Egyptian mythology meets science-fiction fantasy meets *Top Gun* in this gung-ho series that starts one year after the events of the 1994 movie of the same name. The Stargate, a handy piece of alien technology which connects to other such devices scattered around the universe, is now ensconced in a secret US military base called Stargate Command. The gates have been used by alien system lords who cast themselves as gods, known as the Goa'uld, to travel through space and conquer many worlds. Our intrepid team of heroes, led by wise-cracking Col. Jack O'Neill (Anderson), are able to pass through the gates to explore the galaxy and find new ways to fend off the Goa'uld and other enemies before they can reach Earth. Obligatory tottie, Cpt. Samantha Carter (Tapping), is second in command on team SG-1 while archaeologist Daniel Jackson (Shanks) and Teal'c (Judge), an alien warrior who joined the humans in a bid to free his people, add a bit of quirkiness to the mix.

The series ran continuously for ten years engendering the same kind of fervent fanaticism as *Star Trek* before it. Unlike Trek, which had a diplomatic approach to spreading goodwill and understanding across the universe, Stargate *SG-1* could have been called The War on Terror in Space. Col. O'Neill is very much a meat and potatoes military man whose trigger finger is somewhat quicker than his tongue. Of course, there are many inward-looking moments throughout the series touching on social issues and examining the human psyche. There are also some pretty good battle scenes.

All in all, *Stargate SG-1* is rollicking good fun with the right mix of tongue-in-cheek comedy, action and adventure.

 TV trivia: *Stargate SG-1* is the only television series currently endorsed and supported by the United States armed forces.

STARGATE ATLANTIS (2004–)

Starring Joe Flanigan, Torri Higginson, Rachel Luttrel, David Hewlett

Every successful series inevitably spawns a spin-off and *Stargate Atlantis* became the first, of probably many, when it premiered in 2004. The series follows the adventures of a Stargate team that travels to the lost city of Atlantis, in a galaxy far, far away. The team consists of military and science personnel from around the world, like an interstellar United Nations expedition, the aim of which is to uncover the secrets of the mysterious city built millions of years ago by ancient beings. Once they arrive, however, they discover that the city has been abandoned for thousands of years with no power source and no means to get home. As if that wasn't bad enough, they also have to fend off the Wraith, an evil, life-force sucking species which has developed a taste for yummy humans.

The main difference between this series and the original *Stargate SG-1* is the fact that the Atlantis crew is stranded in another galaxy; the whole 'can't get home' thing adds an interesting dimension. Despite the fact that the leader of the Atlantis team is a civilian diplomat, the emphasis is still on the shoot-'em-up tendencies of *SG-1*. Again there are evil aliens trying to reach Earth and cause all manner of havoc and mayhem although the flashing-eyed, deep voiced Goa'uld seem tame compared to the vampiric, dreadlocked Wraith. Seasons 1 to 3 were not as polished as *Stargate SG-1* – stories were bland and predictable and the potential creepiness of the Wraith was never fully explored. Season 4, however, is much darker and the return of Cpt. Samantha Carter from *Stargate SG-1* as a regular cast member means it manages to combine the best of both Stargate worlds.

 TV trivia: Originally, all of the Wraith males featured on the series were played by one actor.

SURFACE (2005–2006)

Starring Lake Bell, Jay R. Ferguson, Carter Jenkins

This programme, which lasted only one season before it was cancelled due to low ratings, is about the possibility of extra-terrestrial life on Earth that's hiding beneath the surface of the water. Marine biologist/single mum Laura (Bell) is in the perfect position to find out – she's trundling around in a submarine looking at the underwater eco-system when she spots something big and green floating around. She thinks it's just going to be some sort of fishy creature no one's given a name to yet, but suspicious-looking military types soon pop up to quiz her. Meanwhile a diver (Ferguson) thinks he's seen something weird, too, that may have eaten his brother, and a kid down the street finds a mysterious egg thingy and (duh!) drops it in his mother's fish tank only for the thing to hatch and scurry out when no one's looking.

Sci-fi fans will notice plot points from just about every sci-fi film from *Close Encounters* to *The Abyss* with a bit of *Jaws* thrown in, as the characters slowly begin to realise there are some sea creatures out there who may be interested in turning humans into monster munchies. While it is very derivative, it has some nice performances from the cast and, had someone like Steven Spielberg been at the reins, one can't help thinking this could have been a cracking sci-fi series.

 TV Trivia: The series was originally called *Fathom*, and much of the early promotional material and merchandise still carried that title, even when it had been changed to *Surface*.

SURVIVORS (1975-1977)

Starring Lucy Fleming, Ian McCulloch, Carolyn Seymour

Everyone loves a good post-apocalyptic story, especially if there is a nasty plague thrown in, and this one's a cracker, for the first season at least. Created by Terry Nation – the man behind those *Doctor Who* baddies, the Daleks – each episode began by showing us how the world got into a very sorry state. A masked scientist accidentally breaks a test tube (containing an icky virus, of course) and then there is footage of people falling ill and we learn that over 90 per cent of the population has died. The series focuses on how the remaining people survive in a broken down society, including Abby (Seymour), who is desperately searching for her young son Peter, whom she's convinced has survived.

Unfortunately, Nation's gripping but depressing vision of a post-apocalyptic Britain was changed when he left the project after the first series, and the final two series (which launched with a fire that killed off some of the regulars) focused more on how people were getting things back to normal again (snore). The first season is well worth a look, though.

 TV Trivia: Watch out for a young June Brown (of *EastEnders* fame) as well as *Blue Peter*'s Peter Duncan and Denis Lawson (*Star Wars*).

TAKEN (2002)

Starring Dakota Fanning, Joel Gretsch, Steve Burton, Eric Close

Produced by Steven Spielberg, this ten-episode, 840-minute long series won an Emmy for best mini-series. It's a saga that covers three families over three generations, and their roles in the history of supposed alien abductions. The story begins with World War II pilot Russell Keys (Burton), whose plane is set to crash when he and his crew encounter strange blue lights on the horizon, then find themselves safely on the ground with no recollection of how they got there. Only later, as each of his fellow crew members mysteriously dies, does Russell realise there may be some alien connection, and he dedicates his life to finding out what happened, while realising he may be powerless to prevent his own child from being abducted. Then there is Owen Crawford (Gretsch), who connives his way into Roswell following the UFO crash of 1947, and becomes involved in the subsequent cover-up, with long-reaching results for his family, and Sally Clarke, who believes she has had a (very) close encounter with a man named John (Close) who may not have been human – and then has a child named Jacob (Anton Yelchin) with special powers...

Told from the point of view of Russell's 10-year-old great-granddaughter, Allie Keys (Fanning), this is quite slow in places but covers much ground from the forties, through the first UFO sightings of the fifties, the fascination with aliens in the seventies (in part, of course, thanks to Spielberg's own movies such as *Close Encounters Of The Third Kind*) and up to the present. There are nasty abductions along the way, grim-looking army men involved in cover-ups and just about every other conspiracy theory, but it is very, very, VERY long, and the voice-over from a preteen doesn't help things (although her blathering-on will all become clear by the final episode, of course). One for alien abduction conspiracy fans, and Spielberg aficionados, this series boasted Tobe Hooper (*Texas Chainsaw Massacre*) and *24*'s Bryan Spicer among its directors.

TV Trivia: The abduction and UFO stories in the series are based on accounts from real-life people who believe they were abducted or witnessed UFOs in the sky.

TERMiNATOR: THE SARAH CONNOR CHRONiCLES (2008–)

Starring Lena Headey, Thomas Dekker, Summer Glau

Cracking science-fiction adventure, co-written by the writer/director of the first two Terminator movies, James Cameron. Picking up after the events of the second film (conveniently avoiding the mess that was *Terminator 3*), the series joins Sarah Connor (Headey) and her son John (Dekker) as they continue to live with the knowledge that one day machines will take over the world, and John will grow up to be the leader of the resistance against them. Like *Terminator 2*, the action begins in the nineties, but is cleverly brought up to date when the pair encounter a 'good' Terminator named Cameron (Glau), sent from the future to protect John, who propels all three of them a few years into the future to avoid capture and then to focus on preventing the birth of Skynet, the computer technology that brings about man's destruction. If you never saw *The Terminator* or *Terminator 2: Judgment Day*, this will all be a bit head-scratching (but if you haven't seen those classic movies, why would you want to watch this anyway?), but if you remember the movies even just a little, there is enough reference to past events to jog your memory. Headey is less muscle-bound and chisel-jawed than Linda Hamilton, who played the Sarah role in the movies, but brings her own sense of toughness to the role, and Dekker is fine as John, though with not quite as much presence as Edward Furlong had in the movie version. It's Summer Glau as terminator

Cameron who steals the show and, over the first season's nine episodes (it was such a short season due to the 2007/2008 Hollywood writers' strike), it's her stunning features and fascinating performance that will keep you glued. Brian Austin Green, of *Beverly Hills 90210*, is terrific later in the season as a friend of future-John, and Garbage singer Shirley Manson has been tipped to be added to Season 2's cast.

 TV Trivia: Cameron was so named as a tribute to *Terminator* creator James Cameron.

THIRD ROCK FROM THE SUN (1996–2001)

Starring John Lithgow, French Stewart, Kristen Johnston, Jane Curtin, Joseph Gordon-Levitt

Twenty years after alien-on-earth comedy *Mork and Mindy* came this similarly themed sitcom about a group of aliens sent to Earth to learn about its population. Posing as a human family led by Dick Solomon (Lithgow), the team is made up of a military advisor who on Earth is Dick's sister Sally (Johnston), an intelligence expert who is in the form of Dick's teenage son Tommy (Levitt) and a transmitter/receiver who is now known as Harry (Stewart). The odd quartet end up in Rutherford, Ohio, and while Dick gets a job at the local college and becomes smitten with Dr Mary Albright (Curtin), Sally spends her time getting used to having human breasts ('Hmm, they seem to have greater power when they collide') and pursuing bumbling cop Don Orville (Wayne Knight), Tommy suffers the frustrations of human adolescence and Harry... well, Harry is awkward, bewildered, scared and hilarious as the fourth member who only came along for the ride.

Cleverly written, this is often hysterically funny and benefits from a skilled comic cast that also includes Elmarie Wendel as the floozy neighbour and Simbi Khali as Albright's suspicious assistant. You know something is funny when other comedians guest appear in a show – Roseanne Barr, Elaine Stritch, Phil Hartman and John Cleese among them – and other hilarious guest performances include Cindy Crawford and Angie Everhart as just two of a group of gorgeous Venusian women who want to take over the world ('36! 24! 36! Dick!') and William Shatner as the family's link to their home planet – the Big Giant Head.

 TV Trivia: The teenage boy, Leon, who annoys Dick in nearly every lesson he teaches is played by Lithgow's own son, Ian Lithgow.

TORCHWOOD (2006–)

Starring John Barrowman, Eve Myles, Burn Gorman, Naoko Mori, James Masters

A bonkers spin-off from *Doctor Who* aimed at adult audiences, *Torchwood* (an anagram of Doctor Who) follows the investigations of the seemingly ageless Captain Jack Harkness (Barrowman), a character who had originally appeared in the Russell T. Davies revamped *Doctor Who*, and his team as they track down nasty aliens. Apparently Torchwood (an organisation mentioned in *Doctor Who* as well) was formed by Queen Victoria to battle hostile supernatural and extraterrestrial threats to our nation, and now Captain Jack is in charge and based in a hidden lair in Cardiff (where the series is filmed) along with medical expert Owen (Gorman), techie Toshiko Sato (Mori), major domo Ianto Jones (Gareth David Lloyd) and new recruit, ex-copper Gwen Cooper (Myles).

With tongue firmly in cheek, this witty, silly and even raunchy show romps along in 50-minute episodes and features such situations as the team investigating a sex-addicted alien (we said this wasn't for kids), helping the passengers of a 1950s plane who arrive in the present day due to a time rift, or getting stuck in the past in a forties dance hall. While some of the special effects are a bit dodgy, there's sex and violence throughout (yes!), some delicious darkness to the plots and a neat touch of campness, too.

In the second series, former *Buffy The Vampire Slayer* star Masters joined the cast on a semi-regular basis as another time traveller like Jack, who has shared an intimate relationship with our bisexual hero (who, in turn, has got his eye on both Gwen and Ianto). You certainly won't get all this shagging on even the 21st-century version of *Doctor Who*…

 TV Trivia: Barrowman, who is gay, was reportedly turned down for the role of Will in *Will and Grace* for 'not being gay enough'.

THE TWILIGHT ZONE (1959–1964)

Starring Rod Serling

This legendary sci-fi/fantasy/horror/mystery series deserves its reputation as one of the best series ever made for TV – even the bad episodes (and there aren't many) are incredibly watchable. Created by Rod Serling, who also introduced the infamous opening narration ('You're travelling through another dimension, a dimension not only of sight and sound but of mind. A journey into a wondrous land whose boundaries are that of imagination.

That's the signpost up ahead – your next stop, the Twilight Zone!'), the series was an anthology of half-hour (and later hour-long) stories, some scary, some head-scratching and some thought-provoking, which captivated TV audiences for five years.

Among the most memorable are 'The Eye Of The Beholder' (Season 2), in which a woman awaits the outcome of surgery performed by the state to make her 'normal'; 'To Serve Man', in which a linguist and his team attempt to translate a book belonging to an alien race that has come to Earth (Season 3); one of a few scary plane rides in the series, 'Nightmare At 20,000 Feet' with William Shatner (Season 5); 'A Kind Of Stopwatch', in which a man is given a watch that can stop time (Season 5); and the scary 'Living Doll' (Season 5).

In 1985, a new *Twilight Zone* series was launched, with episodes helmed by renowned directors including Wes Craven, Jim McBride, Peter Medak, Joe Dante and Atom Egoyan and written by Stephen King, Harlan Ellison and Ray Bradbury. Some episodes were remakes of original Zone stories that weren't good enough the first time around, some episodes are terrific, and some are truly terrible. There are guest appearances from weighty names such as Bruce Willis, Morgan Freeman, Helen Mirren and Janet Leigh. The series was cancelled after three seasons, but there was yet another version made in 2002, with Forest Whitaker as the narrator, which lasted 44 episodes. It's the worst of the bunch – stick with the original and best.

 TV Trivia: Legend has it that the TV company CBS would have preferred Orson Welles to narrate the series, but decided he was too expensive.

V – THE MiNi-SERiES (1983) /V – THE FiNAL BATTLE (1984)

Starring Marc Singer, Jane Badler, Faye Grant, Michael Ironside, Robert Englund

Remember the spaceships that appear hovering all over earth in the blockbuster movie *Independence Day*? More than a decade before, similar images (made with matt paintings rather than computer-generated effects) chilled TV viewers to the bone as they kicked off this absolutely cracking series about aliens coming to Earth. Originally shown as two mini-series that followed directly on from each other (*V* and *V – The Final Battle*), *V* began with those ships hanging over Earth's major cities and a delegation of 'Visitors' (aliens) coming down to greet us and offer their hand in friendship. They look human, they act human, and they seem friendly enough, but a few people are suspicious of their motives, including cameraman Mike Donovan (Singer) and medical student Julie Parrish (Grant). It's not long before they discover the Visitors, led by 'John' (Richard Heard) and the vixen-like 'Diana' (Badler), aren't that human at all – they eat live birds and rats and their human faces are just masks hiding hideous reptile creatures underneath (gasp!)

So begins a battle between the invading Visitors and the human resistance fighters who are trying to discover what the aliens are really after, as it certainly isn't friendship. Do they want to turn people into monster munchies? Why are some humans collaborating with them (in one of the many parallels with Nazi Europe)? And, dear god, what is that hideous green thingy that teenager Robin (Blair Tefkin) gives birth to after she has sex with one of the Visitors? (Anyone who saw this series when it was first broadcast probably still gets the shivers remembering Robin's delivery – first a nice cute human baby was born, followed by an alien hybrid that turns to the camera and hisses).

More than two decades on, it's still skin-crawlingly awful, while the series itself stands the test of time in terms of tension and special effects. Some of the dialogue is cringe-making, and Singer's more wooden than an oak door in places, but this is still top-notch stuff, not to be missed, especially for a typically gruff performance from the always terrific Ironside. A spin-off, *V – The Series* was made in 1984 and picked up the plot a year after the miniseries left off. Many of the cast returned but the series was cancelled after one season, ending on an infuriating cliffhanger.

 TV Trivia: The character of Robin was originally to be played by actress Dominique Dunne (daughter of writer Dominic Dunne). Tragically, she was strangled one evening while rehearsing for the series by her ex-boyfriend, and she died four days later.

THE X-FILES (1993–2002)

Starring David Duchovny, Gillian Anderson, Mitch Pileggi

One of the most popular cult TV shows of all time, *The X-Files* mixed detective sleuthing with science fiction and became must-see TV for much of its nine-year run. Beginning in 1993, the series became a phenomenon as it created a fictional world of government conspiracies, secret organisations and strange happenings to be investigated by FBI agents Fox Mulder (Duchovny) and Dana Scully (Anderson). They are assigned to the 'X-Files' – weird cases no one else in the FBI wants to look into. He believes (partly because he thinks his own sister was abducted by aliens) and she doesn't (she's a practical doctor who utilises her scientific knowledge for cases), but over the years as the pair encounter shady government men (the Cigarette Smoking Man, otherwise known as Cancer Man), 'deep throat' informants with creepy stories to tell and frightening and unexplainable events, even the sceptical Scully has to admit there's something out there that goes bump (or possibly screech) in the night.

Created by Chris Carter, this clever series mixed humour (much of it biting sarcasm) with real chills and intricate conspiracies that will delight anyone who has ever wondered whether the alien at Roswell was real or is convinced the governments of the world know more about extra-terrestrial life out there than they are letting on. Some episodes are silly, some are intricate and gripping, and some are downright bloody scary ('Squeeze' from Season 1, Season 3's two-parter 'Nisei' and '731' and Season 4's 'Home', which was considered so unsettling that Fox TV in the US refused to repeat the episode after its first broadcast). Carter also cleverly introduced an X-Files mythology that rewarded regular viewers – ongoing plot devices such as the alien black oil, virus-carrying bees, Agent X, Scully's disappearance and subsequent pregnancy (in real life, Anderson became pregnant and was excused from some of the second season), Mulder's sister, alien bounty hunters and more.

Sometimes it's hard to follow it all – and a theatrically-released movie in 1998 added to the puzzle rather than solved it – but the mix of wit, scares, paranormal plotlines and Duchovny and Anderson's onscreen chemistry make it worth all the head-scratching moments. Later seasons aren't as good as the first six, and changes were made that weren't wholly successful in later years. Duchovny left before Season 8 (aside from a few guest appearances) and Robert Patrick, as Agent Doggett, was brought in to work with Scully, while Annabeth Gish as Reyes was added to the cast for a disappointing Season 9. A second X-Files movie, *I Want to Believe*, was released in August 2008.

 TV Trivia: William B. Davis, who plays Cigarette Smoking Man, is a non smoker, so the cigarettes he uses on camera are herbal.

STRANGE BUT TRUE...

THERE HAVE BEEN SOME VERY ODD SHOWS BROADCAST ON TV OVER THE YEARS. SADLY NONE OF THESE SHOWS ARE ON DVD IN THE UK. BUT THEY REALLY DID EXIST...

ALF (1986–1990)

(available on US DVD)

As any teenager of the 1980s could tell you, ALF stands for Alien Life Form – and that form is a crass, 229-year-old furry wise-guy who crashes on Earth and takes up residence with your average suburban American family. A kids sitcom with a puppet as its central character who wants to eat the family cat, this shouldn't work but it does, thanks to Paul Fusco's great vocal skills as ALF and a snappy script ('putting humans in charge of the Earth is the cosmic equivalent of letting Eddie Murphy direct').

COP ROCK (1990)

Steven Bochco, producer of such hits as *Hill Street Blues*, *LA Law* and *Murder One*, here stumbled with his bizarre idea for a series – a gritty cop show in which the characters burst into song. Junkies sang a rap song as they were arrested, a judge and jury did gospel during a trial, and there was usually a lavish song and dance number before the end of each episode. One of the most expensive shows to make at the time (well over $1 million an episode), this was doomed from the start and only 11 episodes were made. Bonkers.

DAViD CASSiDY: MAN UNDERCOVER (1978)

Yes, *that* David Cassidy. The former teen pin-up went all gritty and grown-up for this series about a twentysomething cop with the LA police department and his adventures undercover. Nine episodes were made of the show, which was originally a spin-off from an episode of *Police Story*, and then – following some terrible reviews – Cassidy was retired from the force.

DINOSAURS (1991–1994)

(on US DVD)

Jim Henson's Creature Workshop, who created *The Muppets* and *Sesame Street*, were behind this sitcom about a male chauvinist father, his wife, two teenage kids and baby son – who just happen to be dinosaurs. They talk, they go to work, they have fridges and TVs – yes, this isn't a children's show, it's a comedy about your average working-class family. And pretty funny it was in places, too, although one could argue that it was really just a reworking of *The Flintstones* or *The Honeymooners* with animatronic puppets.

DOOGIE HOWSER. MD (1989–1993)

(on US DVD)

Steven Bochco (*Hill Street Blues*) and David E. Kelly (*Ally McBeal*) were the brains behind this odd comedy drama. Doogie (Neil Patrick Harris) suffers through all the usual teenage problems, like getting a girlfriend and sneaking off to parties, but he has to fit them in around his day job... as a doctor. You see, 16-year-old Doogie just happens to be a boy genius who has already got his medical degree and is now a practising physician at a major hospital. A ludicrous concept, this actually works quite well if you can suspend your disbelief at the plot and and put your fingers in your ears during the cheesy theme tune.

DUCKMAN: PRIVATE DICK/FAMILY MAN (1994–1997)

(on US DVD)

A truly genius adult cartoon about a rude, ignorant, foul-mouthed duck named Duckman (voiced by *Seinfeld*'s Jason Alexander) who attempts to solve crimes with the help of his far more reliable sidekick, Cornfed (Gregg Berger). Ice-T, Tim Curry, Joe Mantegna and John Astin were among the actors who supplied their voices for some of the 70 episodes that were made by Klasky-Csupo (also creators of *Rugrats* and *The Wild Thornberries*).

HERMAN'S HEAD (1991–1994)

A sitcom with a difference: whenever central character Herman had a thought, the action shifted from his day-to-day life to an attic-like room that represented his brain, and the four people inside who personified his anxiety, intellect, sensitivity and lust. Essentially the show was just half an hour of watching four freaks fight in a room, which probably explains why it only ran for three seasons.

MANiMAL (1983)

Jonathan Chase (Simon MacCorkindale) isn't your average crime fighter – he has learnt the tricks of transformation from his father and knows the secret that 'divides man from animal, animal from man'. In other words, he can change from a posh professor into a hawk or a black panther whenever he feels like it. Utterly preposterous, this lasted just eight episodes (with many of the special effects shots of Chase's 'transformations' being used again and again to save money) and is deservedly considered one of the worst TV shows of all time.

SMALL WONDER (1985–1989)

A completely freaky family sitcom. Ted (Dick Christie) builds a robot named Vickie (Tiffany Brissette) and, with the help of his wife and kids, starts to pretend Vickie is a real girl and that she's his daughter. Oh dear, what if the neighbours find out the truth? Will they turn little, annoying sprite Vickie into scrap metal? Please?

HORROR, FANTASY AND LEGEND

THINGS THAT GO BUMP IN THE NIGHT, FANTASTICAL CREATURES AND WARRIOR BABES...

THE ADDAMS FAMILY (1964–1966)

Starring Carolyn Jones, John Astin, Jackie Coogan, Ted Cassidy

This famous comedy launched on US TV within a few weeks of *The Munsters*, and both shows only aired for two seasons before ending in 1966. Based on the Charles Addams' cartoon, The Addams Family is a loving group that just happens to be a little ghoulish – dad Gomez (Astin) is suave, if slightly manic; wife Morticia (Jones) raises man-eating plants; son Pugsley likes blowing things up; gothic daughter Wednesday has a headless doll and a fearsome collection of spiders; Uncle Fester (former child star Coogan) has a wicked sense of humour – and they are all served by butler Lurch (Cassidy), a hulk of a monster with a sensitive soul.

Sometimes this played like any other family sitcom, as misunderstandings took place and were resolved by the end of the episode, but in the most part this delicious black and white series had a quirky twist as neighbours or local bureaucrats learned first hand the strange practices that took place in the Addams mansion. Smartly acted with a very funny script, this series may have been ahead of its time in terms of its humour, ironic performances and Jones's blatant sexiness (not exactly commonplace on TV at the time), but that probably explains why it is still such a hysterical treat today. An animated version was made in 1973 (with a young Jodie Foster providing the voice of Pugsley), followed by another cartoon attempt in 1992 and an updated live-action version in 1998 – none of these are available on DVD.

 TV Trivia: Gomez and Morticia have been credited with being the first married couple on an American TV show to have an implied sex life.

ALFRED HITCHCOCK PRESENTS (1955–1962)

Starring Alfred Hitchcock

Master of suspense Hitchcock presented this anthology series of deliciously chilling short stories, introducing and concluding each one with a message from Hitch featuring his own brand of quirky humour. Filmed in black and white, and featuring a who's who of actors that includes Claude Rains, Walter Matthau, Charles Bronson, Steve McQueen, Peter Lorre, and Alfred's wife Patricia, the show included episodes based on tales by Ray Bradbury, Robert Bloch, Roald Dahl and A.A. Milne among others.

Each episode was half an hour long (the final three seasons featured hour-long episodes and were renamed *The Alfred Hitchcock Hour*), and includes such classics as 'Back For Christmas', in which a man tired of his nagging wife starts digging her grave in their basement; 'Breakdown', with Joseph Cotton as a man paralysed behind the wheel of his car after an accident who is powerless to stop vandals stripping the car and rescuers taking their time because they think he is dead; and the suspenseful 'Poison', written by Roald Dahl about a plantation owner who wakes to discover a very poisonous snake snoozing across his chest.

In 1985, a new series, also called *Alfred Hitchcock Presents*, was produced with many of the stories from the fifties series remade in colour. Each featured Hitchcock's original introductions. The series ran until 1989 but is currently unavailable on DVD.

TV Trivia: In the US, the show's sponsors were concerned if an episode featured someone seemingly getting away with a crime, so Hitchcock's closing monologues for those episodes had to hint that justice was eventually served.

AMAZING STORIES (1985–1987)

Starring Charlie Sheen, Kevin Costner

Steven Spielberg was the man behind this collection of spooky half-hour stories that ran for four seasons in the mid-eighties, and was loosely based on the forties and fifties magazine of the same name. As well as writing and directing some of the episodes himself, he also recruited an impressive collection of people behind the scenes, including director Phil Joanou (best known for his groundbreaking U2 music videos), *Gremlins* director Joe Dante, *Forrest Gump*'s Robert Zemeckis, actor/director Paul Bartel, and Lesli Linka Glatter, who has gone on to direct episodes of *ER*, *Twin Peaks* and *The West Wing*.

The cast are even more impressive – Kevin Costner and Kiefer Sutherland in the taut World War II drama 'The Mission'; Sam Waterston, as directed by Martin Scorsese no less, in the creepy 'Mirror Mirror'; Patrick Swayze as a murderer on death row with a special gift in 'Life On Death Row; and Harvey Keitel, directed by Clint Eastwood, in 'Vanessa In The Garden', to name just a few.

Like many anthology series, not every episode is successful (the lame 'The Sitter' and the soppy 'Grandpa's Ghost' spring to mind), but this is well worth seeking out for the phenomenal talent involved and also for a special treat – the second season featured the episode 'Family Dog' – an animated tale thought up by Tim Burton and directed by Brad Bird who went on to make *The Incredibles*.

 TV Trivia: Creator Spielberg actually started his career in TV, directing episodes of *Columbo* and Rod Serling's anthology series *Night Gallery*.

AMERICAN GOTHIC (1995–1996)

Starring Gary Cole, Lucas Black, Sarah Paulson

A truly creepy TV series created by Shaun Cassidy (the ex-actor who also produced *Invasion*), this ran for only 22 episodes but has developed (and deserves) something of a cult following. Set in the small South Carolina town of Trinity, the drama focuses on young Caleb Temple (the superb Black, who also starred in *Slingblade* as a child and went on to movies like *Jarhead* as an adult). He's become of special interest to the town's sinister sheriff, Lucas Buck (Cole), who is actually Caleb's father and a man determined to bring the boy over to evil, while on the side of good is Caleb's dead sister Merlyn (Paulson), who appears to him as an angel, and the rather more real Dr Crower (Jake Weber), a newcomer to town, and Caleb's cousin Gail (Paige Turco), who has arrived to protect him from harm.

It's eerie stuff that was obviously too unique, clever and downright skin-crawlingly creepy to find a proper TV audience (part of the problem in the US was that some episodes were shown out of order, unsurprisingly confusing viewers). Cole is utterly convincing as the lawman who knows everyone's needs and desires and exploits them, while Black shines as the little boy torn between good and bad. There are plenty of shocks to be had in the series, as well as ghoulishly witty moments, and the drama is so tautly written you will spend the whole time tensed up on the sofa, willing it to all end while also praying that it never does. (The only good news is that the series' writers knew the show was being cancelled so were able to write a pleasing finale).

TV Trivia: The series was filmed in Wilmington, North Carolina, which later became the location for *Dawson's Creek*.

ANGEL (1999–2004)

Starring David Boreanaz, Charisma Carpenter

A superb, slightly more adult spin-off of the cult hit *Buffy The Vampire Slayer* (see review on p.255), *Angel* followed the eponymous vampire with a soul (Boreanaz) as he made a new home in Los Angeles and opened a detective agency of sorts – a business designed to help people with supernatural problems that also spends much of its time locking horns with a sinister law firm named Wolfram & Hart.

Of course, Angel has problems of his own, too. In the first series he is still trying to get over his love affair with Buffy, and a cross-over episode (Season 1, Episode 8) in which she travels to LA just as Angel finds a way to become human (thanks to some demon goo in his bloodstream) remains one of the saddest episodes of fantasy TV you're likely to come across.

In the first series, Angel is joined in his quest to save humanity from things that go bump in the night by former Sunnydale cheerleader Cordelia (Carpenter), and part-demon Doyle (Glenn Quinn), who is cursed with visions that help Angel know who to help. Quinn, however, left part-way through the first series (thanks to a kiss, Cordelia inherits his visions), and new cast members were added including ex-*Buffy* character Wesley (Alexis Denisof), vampire-killer Gunn (J August Richards), demon Lorne (Andy Hallet) who can read thoughts when people sing, and Winnifred 'Fred' Burkle (Amy Acker), who is rescued from an alternate universe by the team and then joins them in their mission.

For the final season, James Marster's character Spike from *Buffy* also joined the show. Other *Buffy* cast members, including Eliza Dushku's Faith and Seth Green's Oz, also made the occasional appearance. (There was also the addition of Angel's son, Connor, as played by Vincent Karthesier, but most fans hated him and tend to pretend those episodes didn't happen).

The best episodes include the aforementioned 'I Will Remember You', Season 2's 'Are You Now or Have You Ever Been', and 'Reunion', Season 3's 'Lullaby' and Season 5's hilarious 'Smile Time', in which Angel turns into a puppet.

TV Trivia: Watch out for *Buffy* creator Joss Whedon as Lorne's brother Numfar in the episode 'Through The Looking Glass' – he's the one dancing in the background.

BEASTS (1976)

Starring Pauline Quirke, Martin Shaw, Simon MacCorkindale

Six episodes were made for ITV regional company ATV of this anthology series. Writer Nigel Kneale, who previously worked on programmes including *The Quatermass Experiment* for the BBC, was the creator behind this compendium of episodes, all loosely linked by the idea of man's relationship with animals. Despite the low budgets involved, these are quite creepy tales, from 'Baby', in which a pregnant wife discovers a cursed mummified creature in the walls of her new home, to 'During Barty's Party', in which a couple are under siege from an army of rats around their rural home which the viewer can only hear and not see (trust us, the sound effects are skin-crawling enough).

There are some less effective episodes – most notably 'Special Offer', about an almost laughably unscary ghost in a supermarket, and the dull 'What Big Eyes' – and the 'action' could be considered slow by today's standards, but the best of these mini-dramas remain atmospheric and menacing, especially if you watch them with the lights off.

 TV Trivia: Rumour has it that creator Kneale was asked to write episodes of *Dr Who* and *The X-Files*, but turned both requests down.

BEWITCHED (1964–1972)

Starring Elizabeth Montgomery, Agnes Moorehead, Dick York, Dick Sargent

Over 250 episodes (the first 74 in black and white) were made of this witchy comedy that begins when newlywed Darrin (York) discovers his blushing bride Samantha (Montgomery) is also a sorceress. With one twitch of her nose she can conjure up all kinds of chaos for her poor hubby, and madness usually ensues as she tries to hide her magical skills from us mere mortals. To complicate matters further, Darrin has also inherited mother-in-law Endora (Moorehead), who refers to her new son as 'whats-his-name' and delights in using her witchcraft to cause him trouble.

Witchiness aside, Darrin and Samantha could be your average, cute sixties sitcom couple, and in fact it's the supporting characters who often supply the best laughs – Moorehead is fabulous as the interfering mother from hell, David White is enjoyably oblivious as Darrin's co-worker/pal Larry and Sandra Gould and Alice Pearce are both a treat in the role of busybody neighbour Gladys (Gould took over the role in 1966 following Pearce's death). Sadly, Dick York – who was a deserved fan favourite as Darrin – had to leave the series in 1969 due to severe back problems and Dick Sargent, who had auditioned back in 1964, took on the role (no explanation of the 'new Darrin' was added to the plot).

A spin-off series following the antics of Samantha and Darrin's now grown-up daughter, Tabitha, was made in 1977, with Lisa Hartman in the lead role. It was cancelled after 11 episodes. Fans of magical comedies should note that *I Dream of Jeannie* is currently unavailable on DVD in the UK, and the children's comedy *Mr Merlin* is not available on DVD at all.

 TV Trivia: Special furniture was made and used on the set to help Dick York support his bad back in later episodes.

BLADE: THE SERIES (2006)

Starring Sticky Fingaz, Jill Wagner

A spin-off from the movie trilogy that starred Wesley Snipes, *Blade* follows the adventures of a half human/half vampire as he battles against fanged enemies. Beginning with a feature-length pilot, 'Blade: House Of Chthon', the series – which ran for 12 episodes before being cancelled due to low ratings – stays reasonably true to the movies, thanks to the input of the movies' writer David Goyer. Snipes, of course, didn't appear in the TV version, so his role is taken over by rapper Sticky Fingaz (who has also appeared in *The Shield* and the movie *Dead Presidents*). Joining Blade on his mission to save the world from nasty bloodsuckers is Krista Starr (Wagner), who is searching for the truth behind her brother's murder.

Produced for the US TV channel Spike, which is aimed at laddish men, this is just an excuse for lots of noise and in fact it's all a bit dull in the plot department in comparison to that other vampire-with-a-mission series, *Angel*. Wagner is amiable as the one woman to stick around, and there's also sidekick Shen (Nelson Lee), but all in all this is forgettable stuff without any teeth.

 TV Trivia: While the series may have flopped, the movies have made more than $400 million worldwide.

BUFFY THE VAMPIRE SLAYER (1997–2003)

Starring Sarah Michelle Gellar, Anthony Stewart Head, David Boreanaz

One of the most original TV series to come out of the US in the nineties, *Buffy The Vampire Slayer* told the story of a teenage girl named Buffy (Sarah Michelle Gellar) who was selected to be 'the chosen one' – a slayer of the vampires and demons who seem in endless supply in her Californian home of Sunnydale.

Cleverly realised by creator Joss Whedon as a show about a teenager that garnered a grown-up, cult audience, and wittily performed by a strong cast that included Head as Buffy's watcher, Giles, Alyson Hannigan as witchy Willow, Nicholas Brendon as Xander and James Marsters as punk-haired vampire Spike, the series followed Buffy as she dealt with the usual teen angst problems of school work, dating and fitting in, but turned the conventional ideas on their heads (Buffy's true love, Angel, is a two centuries' old reformed vampire, for example, which poses a whole new set of romantic problems).

As well as single episodes in which Buffy fought an other-worldy creature who had aimlessly wandered into (or had been resurrected in) Sunnydale, each season had it's own 'big Bad' (as fans came to call them) – a scarier than usual bad guy who took a whole series to defeat. For example, in Season 1, it was the extremely creepy vampire Master, in Season 2 it was vampire lovers Drusilla (Juliet Landau) and Spike and their surprising accomplice, while Season 3 featured the town's sinister new mayor (a superb performance from Harry Groener), working with ex-slayer Faith (Eliza Dushku). Most shocking of all, however, was who the bad guy turned out to be in Season 6 (we won't spoil it here).

By the time the 'Buffyverse' (as fans dub the Buffy universe) ended after seven series of wit, scares and sharp plotting (the only duff episode being the odd Season 4 finale 'Restless'), our heroine had died twice, gained a sister (Michelle Trachtenberg's annoying Dawn), lost a lover and a mother and saved the world at least three times. The best episodes include 'Angel' (Season 1, Episode 7); from Season 2, 'Halloween' (Episode 6) and 'Surprise' (Episode 13); the funny 'Band Candy' (Episode 6), clever 'Dopplegangland' (Episode 16) and 'Earshot' (Episode 18), and heartbreaking 'The Prom' (Episode 20) from Season 3, the almost dialogue-free 'Hush' (Episode 10) from Season 4 and the ground-breaking musical episode 'Once More…With Feeling' (Season 6, Episode 7). New fans should also note that when Angel (Boreanaz) left in Season 3, he went to the spin-off series *Angel* (see review above), and it is worth watching the first series of *Angel* at the same time as the fourth series of *Buffy* as some of the episodes cross-over between the shows.

 TV Trivia: The school used for Sunnydale High School is the same one used for West Beverly High in *Beverly Hills 90210*.

CARNiVALE (2003–2005)

Starring Nick Stahl, Clancy Brown, Clea DuVall

This Emmy award-winning drama is often confusingly surreal – set in the 1930s, it follows a young fugitive, Ben Hawkins (Stahl), as he finds refuge with a travelling carnival. It seems Hawkins has visions and can also heal people, which means he fits in quite nicely with the oddball band of travellers that includes a catatonic, telepathic fortune-teller and a blind psychic. There's also another man having similar dreams, Brother Justin (Brown), a preacher whipping up religious fervour out west, and after about 10 long, moodily-lit, plotless episodes, it seems that Justin and Ben may be fighting for good and evil – though who knows which one of them is the good guy and who is the bad.

There are lots of shots of grubby carnival people, a real sense of the time and place, memorable visuals (a woman who stole a coin from church suddenly has hundreds flying from her mouth) and dark moments as well as hints that all the characters are part of something much bigger. There's some interesting mythology as the show entered its second season, too, but ultimately it's just too darn slow and burdened with a too-frustrating plot to really draw you in. Ultimately, a missed opportunity.

Viewers should note that the show was abruptly cancelled at the end of Season 2, leaving many plot points unresolved.

 TV Trivia: When the series was cancelled by HBO, the network received over 50,000 emails from disappointed fans in one weekend.

CENTURY FALLS (1993)

Starring Catherine Sanderson

Russell T. Davies – the man credited with revitalising *Doctor Who* for the 21st century – wrote this six-part series about teenager Tess Harper (Sanderson), who moves with her pregnant mother to an isolated village called Century Falls. The town doesn't have any other children living there, except twins Ben and Carey Naismith, who have some mystical talents and know some of the secrets of the town. Things get creepier still when Tess learns that something sinister happened 40 years ago when the temple burnt down, and history could be ready to repeat itself with Tess and her mum at the centre of the action. What does it all mean? Why are there no children in the village? What do the Harkness sisters want? And who or what is Century?

Surprisingly chilling for something that was originally shown at children's teatime, this relies mainly on some taut dialogue rather than lots of action, and puts atmospheric locations such as Langthwaite, Fawcett Hall, Richmond and Muker in Yorkshire to good use.

 TV Trivia: Mary Wimbush, who plays Esme Harness in the series, is best known as the voice of Julia Pargetter in the radio serial ***The Archers.***

CHARMED (1998–2006)

Starring Holly Marie Combs, Alyssa Milano, Brian Krause, Rose McGowan, Shannen Doherty

When Phoebe Halliwell (Milano) moves back into her grandmother's San Francisco home to live with her two sisters, Prue (Doherty) and Piper (Combs), she finds a book of witchcraft and, naturally, decides to recite one of the incantations. This unleashes the three sisters' previously dormant witchy powers – Prue can move things with her mind, Phoebe has premonitions and Piper can freeze time – and they soon discover their mission is to protect themselves and others from demons and sorcerers with the help of 'whitelighter' (a other-worldly protector) Leo (Krause), while trying not to reveal their witch origins to mortals.

This Aaron Spelling-produced series – sort of *Buffy* to the power of three, mixed with *Charlie's Angels* and *The Craft* – was slow to hit its stride (the first season mainly concentrates on the girls getting used to their powers), but once various mythologies were introduced, including the Halliwell's own history, and the arrival of Cole (Julian McMahon) as a love interest for Phoebe who just happens to be a demon in disguise, things picked up considerably. After rumours of a falling out with the other female members of the cast, Shannen Doherty's character Prue was killed off at the end of Season 3, and in Season 4 the remaining sisters discover they have another sister, Paige, as played by Rose McGowan. Often funny and certainly never too serious, *Charmed* continued for eight seasons, with Seasons 3 and 4 the most enjoyable. Budget cuts in later series are sadly obvious, from demons who look much more human to the absence of Krause in Season 8. Best episodes include 'Once Upon A Time' (Season 3, Episode 3), 'All Hell Breaks Loose' (Season 3, Episode 22) and 'Witch Way Now?' (Season 4, Episode 22).

 TV Trivia: *Charmed* is, to date, the longest-running US TV series to feature all-female lead actors.

DARK SHADOWS (1966–1971)

Starring Jonathan Frid, Grayson Hall

A gothic daytime soap opera, this began without any mention of spookiness at all (the first mention of ghosts didn't occur until six months after the series was first broadcast). Instead, it starts innocently enough as Victoria Winters arrives at Collinwood mansion to work as a governess to David Collins, only to discover that there are strange goings-on within the stone walls – David's father Roger is convinced someone is trying to kill him, and Burke Devlin, with whom he has feuded, returns to town.

During the first 200 episodes, spooky things began to occur, from ghosts revealing secrets to an immortal phoenix returning for her son, but fans of the series note Episode 193 as the one in which *Dark Shadows* first deserved its cult status, as fan favourite, vampire Barnabas Collins (Frid), was introduced. The ground-breaking series ran for over 1,200 episodes, and during that time vampires, witches, warlocks and werewolves strolled the town of Collinsport and provided one of the most unusual daytime soaps ever made.

 TV Trivia: In the earlier episodes, the word 'vampire' was never used – instead Barnabas was described as either undead or not alive. It wasn't until over 400 episodes into the series that the word 'vampire' was finally spoken.

DINOTOPIA (2002–2003)

Starring David Thewlis, Wentworth Miller, Tyron Leitso

Beginning with a six-hour mini-series based on James Gurney's books, *Dinotopia* – as directed by *Demolition Man*'s Marco Brambilla – starts with the story of two teenage brothers, Karl (Leitso) and David (*Prison Break*'s Miller), who crash-land with their father on an uncharted island. The boys survive and begin to explore the island, only to discover it is populated both by humans (the first person they meet is eccentric Brit Cyrus, as played by Thewlis) and dinosaurs. Catching a lift on a brachiosaur with friendly Marion (Katie Carr), the boys head for Waterfall City and it is there they discover they can't ever leave, thanks to a dangerous reef that encircles the island. Never mind, at least they have friendly talking dino Zippeau (voiced by Lee Evans) to chat to.

A phenomenally expensive mini-series (thanks mainly to the massive and impressive European set that was created for the show and the equally cool CGI creatures) that didn't gain very good ratings, *Dinotopia* was spun into a series but only six episodes were shown in the US, though 13 were made.

A new cast was brought on board, including *Dempsey and Makepeace*'s Michael Brandon, but the problems that dogged the mini-series – lack of interesting plot, and a dull script, mainly – remained.

 TV Trivia: While the mini-series featured various locations including Brazil, Egypt and Thailand, the series was filmed in Hungary with an almost entirely Hungarian-speaking crew.

FREDDY'S NiGHTMARES (1988–1990)

Starring Robert Englund

Just over 40 episodes were made of this anthology horror series that was very loosely based on Wes Craven's *A Nightmare on Elm Street* movies. His bad guy from that film, Freddy Kreuger (Englund, who was also a series consultant), is the host who introduces each episode and occasionally pops up in a story to wreak some havoc. (The pilot episode focuses entirely on Freddy, telling the story of his trial and subsequent death, while a few subsequent episodes expand on his story). Each of the stories – often two per episode – is set in the same fictitious town (Springwood, Ohio) as the Elm Street movies, and includes a tale where the devil hosts a game show and another where a woman has to dig up her dead husband because he was buried with a winning lottery ticket in his pocket.

Tobe Hooper, Dwight Little and *Masters of Horror* creator Mick Garris were among the directors, while eagle-eyed viewers should look out for Brad Pitt in an early role as Rick in 'Black Tickets' (Episode 14) and former Bond George Lazenby as a doctor in 'The End Of The World' (Episode 12). Fans of the movies hated the show for its mix of bad jokes and tedious plots, while parents and TV watchdogs criticised it for the high levels of gore, violence and other general nastiness.

 TV Trivia: Another spin-off series, *A Nightmare On Elm Street: Real Nightmares* (2005) in which 'contestants' had to face their fears was hosted by Freddy Kreuger. It's unavailable on DVD and only six episodes were filmed.

GHOST WHiSPERER (2005–)

Starring Jennifer Love Hewitt, David Conrad, Aisha Tyler

A spookier – and sillier – version of *Touched By An Angel* (which is only available on US DVD), this drama has Jennifer Love Hewitt – usually in some flimsy outfit or other – as a young newlywed who is able to speak to ghosts and help them resolve things on Earth so they can have a nice afterlife. Trouble is, the ghosts often don't remember what happened to them, which means Melinda (Hewitt) has to do a bit of sleuthing to discover their unfinished business (an activity that understandably annoys/scares the relatives as they learn their dearly departed hasn't exactly, erm, departed).

With the help of her friend Andrea (Tyler) and the knowledge of her very understanding hubby (Conrad), Melinda calms spirits so they can cross over, be it the wife who doesn't want her husband remarrying or the man who is convinced his brother murdered him. It's often incredibly mushy stuff (try and hold back the tears as a six-year-old boy searches for his mummy, not realising she's dead) that mainly appeals to viewers who want a good sniffle or male Hewitt fans wanting yet another lingering look at her in a low-cut/see through top. Shame about her bad haircut, though.

TV Trivia: Think the Grandview town square looks familiar? That's because it is built on the Universal Studios lot in Hollywood, and is the same one used for the _Back to the Future_ movies.

HAMMER HOUSE OF HORROR (1980)

Starring Diana Dors, Simon MacCorkindale, Gareth Hunt

Produced by Britain's legendary low-budget horror film studios, Hammer, this anthology series gathered together a host of well-known TV and film faces including Leigh Lawson, Brian Cox, Peter Cushing, Dinah Sheridan, Denholm Elliott and Christopher Cazenove. Each of the 13 one-hour episodes was broadcast at 9 pm on ITV, and had a surprising amount of erotica and scary bits for a show on so early in the evening.

If you were a child at the time, the episode you'll remember is 'The House That Bled to Death', as it was the first shown. (After watching this one, most children were then forbidden to watch the rest of the series once their parents realised how adult it was). It's the story of a young couple and their daughter who move into a house where a man once killed his wife. Soon creepy things start happening, and then the gore really kicks in – could anyone who saw it forget the scene at a children's party in the house where blood suddenly sprays all over the guests from a pipe. Yuck.

Other notable episodes include 'The Silent Scream', in which master of horror Peter Cushing plays a Nazi concentration camp survivor who befriends an ex-con (Brian Cox) for sinister reasons; 'Children Of The Full Moon', in which couple Tom and Sarah meet the odd Mrs Ardoy (Dors) and her children when they get lost, and then things going bump in the night cause Sarah to suddenly have a hankering for raw meat; and the often comic 'The Thirteenth Reunion', in which a female journalist investigates a slimming club that boasts remarkable results.

The dialogue may be cheesy, the fashions and cars are definitely dated, and the gore and sex scenes are sometimes hilarious, but this remains an unique slice of British TV history that nonetheless delivers a few decent scares.

TV Trivia: The house in the title was Hampden House in Buckinghamshire, which Hammer Films bought for the series production. It can now be hired for weddings.

HERCULES: THE LEGENDARY JOURNEYS (1995-1999)
Starring Kevin Sorbo, Michael Hurst

Former model Kevin Sorbo flexed his biceps and squeezed his muscular frame into skintight leather trousers and an itty bitty top for this action series based (very loosely) on the legend of half-god Hercules. The mortal son of Zeus, Herc decides to give up the immortality he has earned and instead wanders the land fighting human and supernatural evil with the help of pal Iolaus (Hurst) following the murder of Hercules' family.

Beginning with a series of TV movies in 1994 (including *Hercules and The Lost Kingdom* and *Hercules in the Underworld*), the episodes mainly focused on Hercules and Iolaus saving villages from that week's evil – be it a local warlord or something far nastier cooked up by a nefarious god. (In the earlier episodes, this was often Hera, Zeus's wife, who isn't particularly fond of our musclebound hero since he reminds her of her husband's infidelity with a mortal.) Other main villains include god of war Ares (Kevin Smith), and this is also the show in which Xena: Warrior Princess (see review, p277) made her first sword-toting appearance.

Produced by Sam 'Evil Dead' Raimi, the series also featured *Evil Dead* star Bruce Campbell in a recurring role as Autolycus. An animated spin-off, *Hercules And Xena: The Battle For Mount Olympus*, is only available on US DVD.

TV Trivia: Kevin Sorbo was second choice for the role of Clark Kent in *Lois & Clark: The New Adventures of Superman*, but he lost out to fellow muscleman Dean Cain.

HEX (2004–2005)

Starring Christina Cole, Jemima Rooper, Jamie Davis

Described at the time it was broadcast as a show in a similar vein to *Buffy The Vampire Slayer*, the British gothic series *Hex* is the story of Cassie (Cole), a blonde student. She's discovered some voodoo trinkets in a hidden compartment at her English boarding school, and they awaken her own powers as a witch, which may come in handy since her lesbian best friend Thelma (Rooper) has been sacrificed to an evil being and is now a ghost, and the man with his eye on Cassie is the mysterious Azazeal (Michael Fassbender), the leader of a group of demonic fallen angels. A new character, Ella (Laura Pyper), was introduced after the first series of six episodes.

Eighteen episodes of the show – which, as well as *Buffy*, owes something of a debt to Stephen King's *Carrie* – were made by Sky TV. The best episodes to check out include 'Death Takes a Mother'; the first episode, 'The Story Begins'; and the finale ' The Showdown'. While aimed at teens (check out the rock soundtrack, featuring Garbage, Blur and Gorillaz), parents should note that the show included quite a lot of sex, drugs and even a bit of human sacrifice!

 TV Trivia: Director Andy Goddard also helmed episodes of the
***Doctor Who* spin-off *Torchwood*.**

HIGHLANDER: THE ANIMATED SERIES (1994)

Voices by Miklos Perlus, Lawrence Bayne

Unfortunately, the live action spin-off of the *Highlander* movies that starred Adrian Paul and aired from 1992 to 1998 is currently only available on Region 1 (USA) DVD. British fans of the Immortals legend will have to content themselves with the Canadian animated series that tells the story of Quentin MacLeod, the last of the MacLeods, a Highlander whose job it is to rid the world of evil Kortan. Forty 24-minute episodes of his adventures were made, beginning as immortal warrior Don Vincente Ramirez visits Quentin as a young boy and starts to train him for the ultimate fight between good and evil.

Set in Highlander's universe before the movie *Highlander: Endgame*, this is a fun, animated adventure for kids who like Japanese-style cartoons, but there's probably not enough to hold the interest here of anyone over the age of 14. The final *Highlander* TV series, the live action *Highlander: The Raven*, is, like the Adrian Paul series, only available on US DVD.

 TV Trivia: The series was edited into a 77-minute movie called
***Highlander: The Adventure Begins* in 1994.**

THE HUNGER (1997–2000)

Starring David Bowie, Eric Roberts

Fourteen years after the movie was released, director Tony Scott resurrected his modern-day vampire tale for this TV drama. It's all a bit silly but looks very stylish, thanks to direction from a handful of slick directors including Tony's nephew Jake Scott (son of Ridley) and *Highlander* director Russell Mulcahy.

Focusing more on the 'sensual' desire for blood and sex rather than the horror side of being fangy, this series played like a '15' certificate view of erotica (lots of glimpses of flesh through wispy curtains), with each half-hour episode telling a different story in the style of anthology series like *Masters Of Horror*.

Most interesting now is the cast, featuring now well-established names such as Daniel Craig (as a muscular handyman in the episode 'Menage à Trois'), Giovanni Ribisi (as a wounded drifter seeking help in 'Sanctuary') and Balthazar Getty (as an American visiting an odd London fetish club in 'The Swords'). Other cast members include Timothy Spall, former British 'wild child' Amanda De Cadenet and Eric Roberts.

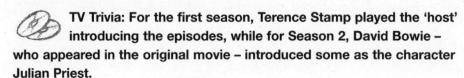 **TV Trivia: For the first season, Terence Stamp played the 'host' introducing the episodes, while for Season 2, David Bowie – who appeared in the original movie – introduced some as the character Julian Priest.**

KOLCHAK THE NIGHT STALKER (1974–1975)

Starring Darren McGavin, Simon Oakland

Beginning with a 1972 TV movie, *The Night Stalker*, in which McGavin's Kolchak was on the trail of a Las Vegas vampire, this series follows the newspaper reporter as he investigates strange and supernatural happenings on the streets of Chicago. Of course, his boss, editor Tony Vincenzo (Oakland) thinks Kolchak is nuts, even when he delivers evidence that there really is a vampire/werewolf or Satan himself on the loose. In his crumpled suit and dodgy hat, Kolchak has become something of a cult anti-hero (a sort of Mulder for the seventies), beloved by fans of this kitschy series that only ran for 20 episodes.

The best episodes include 'The Ripper', 'The Spanish Moss Murders' and 'The Zombie', and even the dafter episodes – like 'The Devil's Platform', featuring a rather laughable and cuddly demonic dog – are enjoyably silly. By the final few episodes, the plots had become a bit tired – poor Kolchak never quite wins the day or proves there really is something out there that goes bump in the night – but the witty scripts and McGavin's downtrodden performance make this well worth a look.

 TV Trivia: Actor Richard Kiel – aka 'Jaws' in James Bond – appears in two different episodes as different monsters.

THE LOST ROOM (2006)

Starring Peter Krause, Julianna Margulies, Kevin Pollak

A clever little mini-series that ran over three nights when it was broadcast, this stars *Six Feet Under*'s Peter Krause as Detective Joe Miller, a cop who comes across a special key and then discovers there's a whole host of odd people who are after it. It's because, of course, the key is no ordinary key – it opens any door and on the other side is an empty motel room in some sort of weird parallel universe. Apparently, since 1961 the room has housed various strange objects – including a bus ticket that can teleport its owner and a comb that can briefly stop time – but it is only when his own daughter (Elle Fanning) becomes trapped in the room that Miller begins to investigate, with the help and often hindrance of some very eccentric characters.

Only a true sci-fi/horror nerd will figure out what on earth (or is it hell?) is going on before the protagonist does, and that's part of the fun of this drama – the plot device of the unusual objects means the story could literally go anywhere. The actual, almost mundane, resolution is a bit of a disappointment, then, and one can't help wondering whether this could have worked better as a long-running series that never had a finale. Never mind – it sure is entertaining while it lasts.

 TV Trivia: One of the main writers, Christopher Leone, is better known as a visual effects artist on movies like *James And The Giant Peach*, *The X Files* and *Romeo + Juliet*.

THE LOST WORLD (2001)

Starring Bob Hoskins, James Fox

There have been numerous screen versions of Arthur Conan Doyle's novel, including a 1999 Canadian/Australian TV series that ran for 66 episodes, and a version of the story performed live on stage (and taped for TV) featuring *Star Trek* stars Leonard Nimoy and John De Lancie ('Q' from *Next Generation*). One of the most impressive, in terms of production, writing and cast, is this BBC/US TV version, filmed in New Zealand, which stars Bob Hoskins, James Fox and Matthew Rhys.

Written by Conan Doyle in 1912, *The Lost World* is the story of Professor George Challenger (Hoskins), who is convinced dinosaurs still roam a tiny part of the earth – a remote plateau in the deepest Amazon. Mounting an expedition to prove it, he travels with scientist Leo Summerlee (Fox), explorer Lord John Roxton (Tom Ward) and reporter Edward Malone (Matthew Rhys). Joining them from a jungle mission are missionary Reverend Theo Kerr (Peter Falk) and his niece, Agnes (two characters not in the original novel). With the help of an old map, the group undertakes a perilous journey through the wilds and not only discovers dinosaurs, but also an Indian tribe and some grumpy manlike apes. It's a terrific romp filled with great creature effects and a cast that deliver their lines with relish.

 TV Trivia: The dinosaur effects were created by the same team who made the factual series *Walking with Dinosaurs*.

MASTERS OF HORROR (2005–)

Starring Steven Weber, Henry Thomas, Lori Petty, Meat Loaf

A clever idea from creator Mick Garris (best known for his directing duties on Stephen King TV adaptations like *Desperation*, *The Shining* and *The Stand*), this cable TV series has amassed an impressive collection of horror writers and directors to create a fascinating but pretty uneven horror anthology series. Stuart Gordon, Dario Argento, Tobe Hooper, John Carpenter, Joe Dante and John Landis are among the directors, while the writers include Richard Christian Matheson (an acclaimed TV writer, he's also the son of author Richard Matheson) and horrormeister Clive Barker.

Each one-hour episode is like a mini-movie, from Gordon's 'Dreams In The Witchhouse', based on the HP *Lovecraft* story, to Garris's 'Chocolate', in which Henry Thomas discovers he is psychically linked to someone he has never met. In the main, they're all more silly than scary but the better ones worth seeking out are: Joe Dante's 'The Screwfly Solution', Larry Cohen's 'Pick Me Up' and Dario Argento's 'Jenifer'.

TV Trivia: Takeshi Miike's episode 'Imprint', with explicit scenes of torture, was considered too extreme to be shown on US TV but is available on the DVD release.

MEDIUM (2005–)

Starring Patricia Arquette, Jake Weber

An hourly drama from *Moonlighting* creator Glenn Gordon Caron, this has a similar premise to *Ghost Whisperer* (except star Arquette wears more clothes than Whisperer's Jennifer Love Hewitt).

Allison DuBois (Arquette) is a suburban mother of three who has a special gift: she can see dead people, communicate with them and can sometimes see the future. Which comes in handy during her day job, interning at the District Attorney's office – she can find evidence others have missed and use her supernatural powers to tell if a suspect is lying or not.

Usually mixing a criminal investigation with personal problems in Allison's own life – she doesn't spend enough time with her kids, her daughters may have inherited her 'gift', hubby isn't always understanding about it all – each episode kicks off with Allison having a dream that hints of what is to come. It's a successful formula (*Medium* was one of the surprise US TV hits of 2005) with an interesting twist – there is a real Allison DuBois on whom this is based, she's a psychic and medium well known for helping out law enforcement and aiding jury selection.

 TV Trivia: Arquette's real-life husband Thomas Jane has appeared in two episodes of *Medium*, as Allison's (dead) old flame Clay...

THE MUNSTERS (1964–1966)

Starring Fred Gwynne, Al Lewis, Yvonne De Carlo

The other spooky TV family (see *The Addams Family*, p.250), *The Munsters* were less ghoulish and more silly, as led by the mildly simple-minded Frankenstein monster lookalike Herman (Gwynne). Married to the devoted Lily (De Carlo), Herman works for the local morticians, and spends his home time bumbling around a house that is also home to werewolf son Eddie (Butch Patrick), potion-concocting Grandpa (Lewis), a descendant of Dracula, and Marilyn (originally played by Beverly Owen, and later by Pat Priest), Herman and Lily's more normal-looking niece.

Reuniting *Car 54 Where Are You?* stars Gwynne and Lewis, this benefited from strong chemistry between the cast but the jokes have faded over time and the show often looks dated, thanks to wobbly effects and occasionally groaningly awful dialogue.

A new version of the series, *The Munsters Today* (also known as *The New*

Munsters), in which the family wake up in the eighties having been in suspended animation for two decades, ran for three years from 1988. A TV movie, *Here Come The Munsters*, was made in 1995, and a Christmas special was made in 1996 (none featuring the original cast). None of these are available on DVD.

 TV Trivia: In an American magazine survey, Herman Munster was voted the 19th Greatest TV Dad Of All Time.

NEVERWHERE (1996)

Starring Gary Bakewell, Laura Fraser

Made by the BBC, this cult three-hour mini-series is created by graphic novelist/writer Neil Gaiman, and features a soundtrack by Brian Eno. It's strange stuff, with some very dodgy special effects, which begins with ordinary bloke Richard (Bakewell) finding a bleeding girl lying on the street in front of him. No one else seems bothered, so he scoops her up and carries her home to clean her up. The trouble is, when Richard wakes the next morning it seems he no longer exists – no one, including his fiancée, recognises him, and he finds himself dragged into London Below, an alternative London beneath the city streets that is home to many including the Angel Islington (Peter Capaldi) and where all manner of demons, magic and mysteriousness lurk. With Door (Fraser), the girl he rescued, as a guide, he has to travel this odd world looking for a way out.

Packed with London in-jokes, this has some witty and creepy moments but suffers from the fact it was cheaply filmed on video (Gaiman has himself noted that it doesn't look that great, especially because a filming technique they expected to be added later, wasn't). The cast are all entertaining, but stealing the show are Hywel Bennett and Clive Russell as the creepy assassins Mr Croup and Mr Vandemar. If the wobbliest bits of *Doctor Who* never bothered you, this is well worth checking out. A novel by Gaiman that expanded the story was written following the making of the series.

 TV Trivia: Gaiman's pal, comedian Lenny Henry, was the co-creator of this series.

NIGHT GALLERY (1970–1973)

Starring Rod Serling, Larry Watson

A supernatural series from the creator of *The Twilight Zone* (see Sci-Fi, p.243) in which each episode featured at least two separate stories, introduced by

Sterling himself. Every story was illustrated by a painting in the 'night gallery', a piece of art made by artists at Universal Studios where the show was made. Unfortunately, more effort was often put into the art than into the story, and some of these one-hour anthologies are pretty awful.

Among the highlights are 'Eyes', in which a wealthy blind woman (Joan Crawford) pays to have a healthy man's eyes transplanted into her head; 'The Little Black Bag', in which a former doctor finds a medical kit with the power to prevent all diseases; and 'They're Tearing Down Tim Riley's Bar'. But viewers be warned: there are some utterly terrible episodes, too, some of which are bad copies of *Twilight Zone* episodes and others, like 'A Matter Of Semantics' (in which Cesar Romero's Dracula visits a blood bank), which are so overacted they're beyond funny.

 TV Trivia: A young Steven Spielberg directed two stories, including the first season's 'Eyes'.

POINT PLEASANT (2005)

Starring Grant Show, Elisabeth Harnois, Dina Meyer

Buffy the Vampire Slayer producer Marti Noxon was one of the people behind this supernatural drama that was cancelled after just 13 episodes. Despite an interesting premise – Satan's daughter lives among us – the series was bogged down with dire dialogue, soap opera plots and diabolical acting, lacked both the wit and scariness of *Buffy*, and suffered from a slew of unlikeable characters. Oops.

The plot is this: teenage gal Christina (Harnois) has the Devil (literally) for a dad. But he's rather busy, so she spends most of her time in boarding schools until she falls off a boat on a school trip and washes up on the New Jersey shores of Point Pleasant, where she is rescued by cute Jesse (Sam Page). She decides to stay in town and look for her long-lost mother at just the same time that her inherited-from-dad powers start to emerge, but will the townspeople even notice, as they are too busy bed-hopping and bitching even to spot the sinister bloke (Show) who has just bought up half the town with his previously-dead girlfriend. Hmmm.

Neither soap nor horror nor teen drama, this can only be described as a big disappointment.

 TV Trivia: The real Point Pleasant – actually a mile from the coast – is the birthplace of actress Kirsten Dunst.

POLTERGEIST THE LEGACY (1996–1999)

Starring Derek De Lint, Martin Cummins

Although this series has 'Poltergeist' in the title, it has very little to do with the Steven Spielberg/Tobe Hooper horror movie of the same name. Instead, this is about 'the Legacy', people who belong to a secret group sworn to protect the innocent from the forces of darkness using their paranormal skills. Among them are the mysterious Derek (De Lint); a priest, Father Callaghan (Patrick Fitzgerald); psychiatrist Doctor Corrigan (Helen Shaver) and her daughter Kat (Alexandra Purvis) and ex-Navy SEAL tough guy Nick (Cummins), and each week they get together in an isolated mansion to sort out problems such as creepy cult leaders and resurrected Ancient Egyptian princesses.

As it was made for cable, it is slightly raunchier and bloodier than a mainstream TV horror show, but falls down in its special effects, which look a bit ropey compared to later series that benefited from CGI. There are quite a few scares to be had, though, and this is worth catching if you are a horror fan.

Fans of movie-to-TV spin-offs should note that there was also a *Friday The 13th: The Series*, and a *Tales from the Crypt* one but neither is currently available on DVD.

 TV Trivia: In the only crossover with the *Poltergeist* movies, diminutive actress Zelda Rubenstein (who played Tangina in the film) appears as a different character in one episode, 'The Reckoning', of the series.

PRIMEVAL (2007–)

Starring Douglas Henshall, Lucy Brown, Andrew Lee Potts

ITV delivered a cracking fantasy/sci-fi drama in 2007, in which a group of crack scientists led by Nick Cutter (Henshall) are hired by the government to investigate a series of dinosaur sightings. It seems the pesky prehistoric blighters have been popping up all over the place, from giant spiders in the London Underground tunnels to something called a gorgonopsid in the Forest of Dean. The creatures are coming through rips in time, and with the help of assistant Stephen (James Murray), zoologist Abby (Hannah Spearitt) and paleontologist Connor (Potts), Nick has to work out what is going on, and also whether the current events have anything to do with his wife's mysterious disappearance eight years before.

With effects from the team who made *Walking with Dinosaurs* (the series creators, Tim Haines and Adrian Hodges also worked with them on *The Lost*

World, see review p. 265), nice performances from the cast, and a sharp script, this is an enjoyable romp that should appeal to fans of *Doctor Who* and *Torchwood*. At the time of writing, a second series has been made.

 TV Trivia: Check out Connor's laptop – all the images are from other Impossible Pictures productions, including 2005's *Walking with Monsters.*

PUSHING DAISIES (2007–)

Starring Lee Pace, Anna Friel, Chi McBride, Kristin Chenoweth

One of the quirkiest shows to be aired as a mainstream comedy drama, this series should appeal to fans of Tim Burton's *Big Fish* and the series *Dead Like Me* (also created by *Pushing Daisies*' Bryan Fuller). As Jim Dale's velvet-voiced narrator tells us, young Ned (Pace) discovers at an early age that he's not quite like other people: he can bring the dead back to life with a single touch. Trouble is, if he touches that person again, they'll die forever, and if he leaves the resurrected alive for more than one minute, some other unfortunate person in the vicinity will drop down dead to take his place. As an adult, Ned has put his talent to good use, however, by running a pie shop where he makes tarts bursting with the yummiest fruit (thanks to his magic touch), and by reviving murder victims for long enough to find out who killed them so a detective (McBride) – the only one who knows Ned's secret – can solve the crime and collect the reward for them both. To complicate his life further, Ned discovers his childhood sweetheart, Chuck (Friel), has just been killed and when he resurrects her he decides to keep her alive, even though he knows the two of them will never be able to touch. Awww.

With oddball supporting characters such as Chuck's batty aunts (played by Swoosie Kurtz and Ellen Greene) and Ned's cute but nosey employee Olive (Chenoweth), this has some charmingly bonkers moments and nice touches, but suffers from the almost continual voice-over that seems to have been written just to drive home how kooky the whole set-up is in case you hadn't already noticed. Luckily the sweet performance from Pace makes this worth tuning in to, and it will be interesting to see how the writers manage with the Ned-and-Chuck no-touching rule as the show progresses.

TV Trivia: In the UK, only eight of the first season's nine episodes were shown, as there was no room in the schedule for all the episodes to air. It was later shown on ITV's website after fans complained.

RANDALL AND HOPKIRK (DECEASED) (1969–1971, 2000–2001)

Starring Mike Pratt, Kenneth Cope (original) Vic Reeves, Bob Mortimer (remake)

Jeff Randall (Pratt) and Marty Hopkirk (Cope) are private detectives with a twist – Marty is dead. Killed in a hit-and-run, he comes back as a ghost to solve his own murder but in doing so misses his chance to go up to heaven. Instead, he is destined to remain on earth in his spectral form (which includes a rather natty white suit), helping Jeff solve cases (Jeff being the only one who can see Marty).

A quirky British detective show (in the US it was renamed *My Partner the Ghost*) that has become a cult fave, this mixed ghostly jokes with sixties mod campness (and check out the miniskirts and PVC boots on most of the female castmembers) that you'll either love or hate. It has dated terribly, but there are some laughs to be had in the 26 episodes that were made.

In 2000, comic double act Vic Reeves and Bob Mortimer revisited the format, with Reeves taking on the ghostly role and Mortimer playing his often-annoyed partner. Emilia Fox added some glamour to the proceedings as Jeannie, Hopkirk's widow, while Tom Baker played the new character of Wyvern, a sort of heavenly guide for Marty. The writers of the new show included *League of Gentlemen* writer Mark Gatiss and *The Fast Show*'s Charlie Higson and Paul Whitehouse. Thirteen episodes were made, and the supporting cast is an impressive who's who of British TV, including Hugh Laurie, David Tennant, Charles Dance, Peter Bowles and Hywel Bennett.

Unfortunately, that other famous ghostly TV comedy, *The Ghost and Mrs Muir*, is unavailable on DVD. (For kids' comedies like *The Ghosts of Motley Hall* and *Rentaghost*, please see pages 130–137).

 TV Trivia: The original series was produced by Monty Berman, who also worked on classic sixties series *The Saint* and *The Champions*.

RELIC HUNTER (1999–2002)

Starring Tia Carrere, Christien Anholt

A sort of cut-price *Tomb Raider* or *Indiana Jones* with cleavage, *Relic Hunter* starred the buxom Carrere as university professor (stop sniggering) Sydney who travelled the globe searching for lost artefacts with the help of Brit assistant Nigel (Anholt), which she then returned to museums or the families that the trinkets originally belonged to. Such adventures usually involved lots of ass-kicking (good thing Syd's a black belt) as there was always someone else after the treasure, too, and a surprising number of people get killed in the pursuit, though the authorities rarely seem bothered.

The duo and their helpers, including pouty secretary Karen (Tanja Reichert) in the final season, searched for such varied items as Al Capone's diamond-encrusted gun, the remains of a 400-years-dead nun, a cursed Aztec doll and Pandora's Box, but alas, never discovered a decent script. It's fun, nonetheless, and mainly an excuse for Carrere to run around looking sweaty in tight tops.

 TV Trivia: Despite the exotic settings of the series, it was mainly filmed in Toronto, Canada.

REVELATIONS (2005)

Starring Bill Pullman, Natascha McElhone

The premise for this mini-series certainly sounds bonkers: just before the apocalpyse, a physicist named Massey (Pullman) teams up with a nun (!) to try and avert the end of the world. Written by David Seltzer (author of *The Omen*), it just gets stranger from there – Massey is seeking revenge for the ritualistic murder of his daughter, the odd couple (think Mulder and Scully but with crucifixes) get tips from a brain-dead girl who may be hearing directly from God – as religious beliefs are mixed in with a bit of regular human gore.

Could a baby, the second coming of Christ, have been born? And does that mean some poor pregnant woman is about to give birth to the anti-Christ? Numerous other questions pop up – some which are never answered – as nun and sceptic dodge bad guys and nuts with guns while trying to find the truth. The plot is stretched a bit over six hours, and Pullman isn't given enough to do, but fans of religious-themed thrillers will find much to enjoy as the battle for good and evil begins on earth.

 TV Trivia: Fans of camp British TV should keep an eye out for Cardinal La Veigh – played by Christopher Biggins!

THE STONE TAPE (1972)

Starring Michael Bryant, Jane Asher

Written by Nigel Kneale, who also scripted the various *Quatermass* series, this one-off TV drama tells the story of a team of scientists, led by Peter Brock (Bryant), who are trying to develop a new recording medium that is better than tape. Basing their operations in an old gothic mansion (uh-oh), it's soon obvious they are not alone: computer programmer Jill (Asher) senses a presence, and the group find stone steps that seem to lead nowhere hidden behind some wooden panelling. Then Jill sees the apparition of a Victorian maid, and Peter decides this is all too exciting and the team should investigate the weirdness around them. It seems that the stone walls can 'play back' events from the past, but when the group start playing around, you just know it's not going to end well.

Originally aired on the BBC on Christmas Day, this spooky drama has garnered quite a cult following, bolstered by its inclusion in Channel Four's '100 Scariest Moments' list. It has dated considerably in terms of production values, but the performances are terrific if you don't mind a bit of hamming towards the end, and Kneale's story is deliciously supernatural and a nice twist on the traditional haunted house story.

 TV Trivia: Star Jane Asher was no stranger to Kneale's writings – she was just nine when she played a little girl in the first Quatermass TV series, *The Quatermass Xperiment*.

SUPERNATURAL (2005–)

Starring Jensen Ackles, Jared Padalecki

When brothers Sam and Dean Winchester were little boys, they saw their mother die pinned to the ceiling, enveloped in flames thanks to a demon. Their father John raises them to fight supernatural forces, but Sam (Padalecki) moves away to college and washes his hands of the family business. When Dad goes missing during his long quest to find out what killed his wife, Dean (Ackles) turns to Sam for help, but he only agrees to search for him when his own girlfriend is murdered by the same demon. The brothers set off across country to find their father, using his evidence and diaries to try and locate him, while helping people affected by supernatural events along the way.

That's the set-up for this enjoyable drama/adventure series, created for the WB channel in the US that had also broadcast horror series *Buffy*, *Charmed* and *Angel*. The creatures/events/general spookiness the boys encounter is often based on real urban legends and myths, such as the Hook Man, the Woman in White and a killer truck, adding to the creepiness created by dark sets, moody music and the two leads' overall broodiness. There's also a biting script ('I'm not gonna die in a hospital where the nurses aren't even hot') that should appeal to *Buffy* fans, along with the growing fascinating back history to the boys' quest, which reveals Sam may have some hidden supernatural talents of his own.

TV Trivia: *Supernatural* **was one of the first series to have its episodes broadcast online the day after an episode was shown on US TV.**

TALES OF THE UNEXPECTED (1979–1988)

Starring Roald Dahl

Author Dahl's stories of the weird and wonderful were used (along with tales scripted by other writers in later series) for this ITV/Anglia anthology series that was hugely popular in the late seventies and early eighties. One reason for this – apart from the often witty tales themselves – was the all-star cast of actors who popped up to appear in episodes: Joan Collins, John Mills, Joss Ackland, John Alderton, Susan George, Janet Leigh, John Gielgud and Derek Jacobi among them.

Often a distorted and sometimes grotesque look at human nature, Dahl's collection owed much to the format used in *Alfred Hitchcock Presents* — Dahl acting as master of ceremonies as Hitch had done (Dahl doing the job for the first two seasons, not the later years, however) – unsurprisingly, perhaps, when you remember Dahl had himself contributed stories to that hit US series.

In fact, some of Dahl's stories that were successfully made for *Alfred Hitchcock Presents*, including 'Poison', were remade for this series, but unfortunately they suffer in comparison to their US counterparts. This is mainly due to the hammy acting that the show became known for – while it makes some episodes enjoyably silly and kitsch, when you watch how Hitchcock interpreted Dahl's stories, you realise how much scarier they could have been. Nonetheless, some of them are worth a look: 'Georgy Porgy', in which a young vicar is tormented by memories of his mother (Collins) and the resemblance a woman of his parish has to her; 'The Sound Machine', in which a scientist's sound amplifier picks up the tormented screams of plants as they are picked and 'Man From The South', the story of a bet between a gentleman (Jose Ferrer) and an American sailor (Michael Ontkean) – if the sailor can light his lighter 10 times in a row, he wins the gent's Jaguar. But if he loses, he has to sacrifice the little finger from his left hand. In all, 112 episodes were made.

TV Trivia: The famous theme to the series was composed by Ron Grainer, who also wrote the themes for *Doctor Who* **and** *The Prisoner*.

TRU CALLING (2003–2005)

Starring Eliza Dushku, Jason Priestley

Following her role as rogue slayer Faith in *Buffy the Vampire Slayer*, Dushku was offered her own series, playing university graduate Tru in this supernatural drama. Taking a job in the city morgue, Tru discovers she has a special ability: she can relive the previous day and change what happens, which comes in handy as she tries to help the corpses in the morgue who sit up and tell her they wrongly ended up dead. Why these people can only send her back one day is never explained, and the only reason Tru is helping them seems to be as some sort of penance for not being able to save her own mother's murder when she was a little girl. Hmmm.

It's pretty formulaic and rather disappointing stuff – sort of *Groundhog Day* with corpses, with the body-of-the-week storyline mixed with a sub-plot featuring one of Tru's friends and relations, her brother with a gambling problem and coke-addicted sister among them. The series did pick up with the introduction of Priestley's character Jack part way through Season 1: a mysterious guy who gets a job at the morgue and for some reason doesn't want Tru to help the dearly departed, but the show was unexpectedly cancelled six episodes into Season 2. The best episodes are Episode 14, in which Tru learns more about her mother's murder and Jack first appears, and Episode 20, the first season finale.

 TV Trivia: Dushku turned down an offer to revisit her *Buffy* character Faith in a spin-off series, choosing to appear in this show instead.

TWIN PEAKS (1990–1991)

Starring Michael Ontkean, Kyle MacLachlan

One of the strangest (in a wonderful way) shows ever to appear on TV, *Twin Peaks* was the brainchild of film director David Lynch (*Dune*, *Wild at Heart*) and co-producer Mark Frost (who had previously worked on *Hill Street Blues*). Ostensibly about the investigation into the murder of young Laura Palmer in a small town in north-west America, this was actually – much like Lynch's *Blue Velvet* – more about the secret and strange things hidden beneath the surface of the place, with some sex, violence, otherworldly spookiness, betrayal and doughnuts thrown in.

The characters – especially cherry pie-loving FBI Agent Dale Cooper (MacLachlan), Laura's vampy schoolmate Audrey (Sherilyn Fenn), the sinister

'Bob' (Frank Silva) and the 'log lady' – soon become cult favourites, along with the quotable dialogue ('Diane, I'm holding in my hand a box of chocolate bunnies') and general weirdness that went along with each episode. For fans, who killed Laura Palmer was as important as 'Who shot JR?', and even when the question was answered, Lynch managed to keep viewers hooked to see what other creepiness would befall Cooper and local Sheriff Truman (Ontkean).

The series only ran for a total of 30 episodes (including the feature-length pilot), but each was packed with trademark Lynch moments, from the surreal dream sequences featuring the dancing man who talks backwards to the continual hints that every suburbia hides weirdness behind the lace curtains.

Series one is superb in setting up the storylines and characters of the show, as well as the Laura Palmer mystery. Series two was not as successful – Lynch and Frost were forced by the TV company to reveal who killed Laura by the middle of the series, causing ratings to dive, and the show ended on a cliffhanger as Agent Cooper faced his past and his ex-partner, Windom Earle (Kenneth Welsh), who is searching for the sinister Black Lodge. A movie prequel, *Twin Peaks: Fire Walk With Me* was released in cinemas in 1992.

TV Trivia: Frank Silva was actually a prop master and set decorator for David Lynch, but while working on *Twin Peaks* Lynch accidentally filmed his reflection during an early scene and decided the long-haired technician would be perfect for the role of bogeyman Bob.

XENA: WARRIOR PRINCESS (1995–2001)

Starring Lucy Lawless, Renee O'Connnor

The sword-wielding warrior babe Xena (Lawless) made her first appearance in an episode of *Hercules: The Legendary Journeys* as a bad girl turned good who helped the muscular hero, before getting her own adventure series in 1995. Clad in what looks like a leather wonderbra, the warrior woman wanders into a village she once destroyed and, learning the locals are being threatened by thugs, despatches them in a gruesome manner before befriending a young farm girl, Gabrielle (O'Connor), who fancies seeing the sights as Xena's travelling companion. Soon the pair are roaming the land, battling with various mythic creatures and maiming just about anyone else who crosses their path.

Produced by *Spider-Man / Evil Dead* director Sam Raimi (his brother, Ted, appears in some episodes) and filmed in luscious New Zealand, this is tongue-in-cheek stuff, clearly aimed at hormonal boys after a bit of cleavage alongside their sword-play and Greek legends. There's a bit of lesbian tension thrown in for good measure between the two main gals and some very camp humour and slapstick that turned *Xena* into a love-it or hate-it sort of show. However, it has been attributed with blazing the trail for a new group of TV action heroines that may otherwise have never been given airtime, including *Buffy*, *Dark Angel's* Max and Sydney from *Alias*.

 TV Trivia: In Season 5, Xena became mysteriously pregnant to coincide with star Lawless's own pregnancy.

STEPHEN KING: HORROR MASTER

STEPHEN KING ADAPTATIONS

He's the master of horror, whose novels and short stories have been made into hit movies such as *Misery*, *Carrie*, *Dolores Claiborne* and *The Shawshank Redemption*. And those which haven't made it to the big screen, but instead were adapted into TV movies and TV mini-series, are reviewed here, although fans should note that some of King's work, including his TV series *Stephen King's Golden Years*, are only available on US DVD.

THE DEAD ZONE (2002–)

Starring Anthony Michael Hall, Chris Bruno, Nicole De Boer

Based on the King novel that had already been made into a movie in 1983 (starring Christopher Walken), this has former Brat Packer Hall as Johnny, a teacher who spends six years in a coma following an accident. When he finally wakes he discovers his fiancée has married someone else and has a son, and he has gained psychic powers that allow him to see into the life of anyone he touches, something he soon realises can be both a blessing and a curse.

While the movie and the book had a definitive end (Johnny realises a politician could bring about the apocalypse and has to decide whether to risk everything to prevent that), this is an ongoing and often gripping drama that mixes one-off stories (Johnny realises an ice hockey player will have a heart attack on the ice and has to stop him playing, etc) with continuing threads such as Johnny's relationship with his ex-fiancée, the media's interest in him, and the suspicious circumstances surrounding his mother's death while he was in the coma. Even the book and movie's climax is included in the plot, as politician Greg Stillson (Sean Patrick Flanery) is introduced at the end of the first season when he shakes Johnny's hand, an action that reveals one day he may become president and lead the nation towards nuclear holocaust (as of Season 6, his character is still on the loose). Terrific stuff.

 TV Trivia: Hall's *Breakfast Club* co-star Ally Sheedy appeared in the Season 2 episode 'Playing God'.

DESPERATION (2006)

Starring Tom Skerritt, Steven Weber, Annabeth Gish

When Peter and Mary Jackson are pulled off the road for no reason, arrested and taken to the town of Desperation by scary police officer Collie Entragian (Ron Perlman), they soon realise something decidedly spooky is going on. They're thrown together with a group of strangers that include an author (Skerritt), his pal Steve (Weber) and the Carver family, and discover that Desperation is a ghost town in which Entragian rules, especially since he is possessed by an ancient spirit called Tak who has a taste for yummy human bodies. The group decide to escape, only for little boy David Carver (Shane Haboucha) – who receives messages from God – to tell them they must stay and fight Tak and trap him forever underground.

One of King's more average stories becomes an average TV movie, filled with so-so performances, cheap special effects and only a few thrills. Unsurprisingly, following the critical drubbing this adaptation received, *The Regulators* – a 'mirror' book featuring some of the same characters, written by King under his pseudonym Richard Bachman – has yet to be made into a movie for cinema or TV.

 TV Trivia: The character Steve mentions growing up in Arnette, Texas, which is the same fictional town Stu in *The Stand* was from.

IT (1990)

Starring Harry Anderson, Dennis Christopher, Richard Masur, John Ritter

If clowns give you the creeps, this horror mini-series will have you quaking behind the sofa, and if they don't bother you, they will once you have watched this. Every 30 years, a nasty creature known as 'It' – who appears in the form of Pennywise the clown (Tim Curry) – feeds on the children of Derry in Maine. Despite being petrified, seven kids are able to defeat 'It', but 30 years later Mike (the only one of the seven to remain living in Derry) realises the scary monster is back and responsible for a series of child murders, so he calls on his friends to remember the pact they made three decades before – that if 'It' returned, they would come back to defeat it once more.

While this isn't as skin-crawlingly nasty as the novel (the scariest bits probably wouldn't be deemed suitable for TV), there are some shuddery moments thanks to Tim Curry, all cackles and googly eyes, as 'It'. The other grown-up actors don't get much to do except try and remain serious during the sillier moments, but there are nice performances by their younger counterparts, especially a young Seth Green (best known, of course, as Oz in *Buffy the Vampire Slayer*).

 TV Trivia: Apparently, Tim Curry's performance as Pennywise was so creepy, many of the cast avoided him during filming.

KiNGDOM HOSPiTAL (2004)

Starring Andrew McCarthy, Diane Ladd, Jack Coleman

In 1994, *Dogme* director Lars Von Trier made a TV mini-series for Danish TV called *Riget* (aka *The Kingdom*), about a haunted hospital. A decade later, Stephen King adapted the idea for American television, and expanded it to 13 episodes (he wrote a plot outline for a second season, but due to falling ratings for the original episodes, it was never made).

The 'New Kingdom' hospital is the setting for the story – it is built on the remains of another hospital that burnt down and has an uncomfortable history involving the death of a young girl who now haunts the corridors. It's this hospital where patient Peter Rickman (Coleman) is taken, comatose, after he is hit by a car, and in his sleeping state he learns about the hospital's creepy past and the equally unusual present day goings-on.

It's all rather odd stuff, with the building populated by quirky characters including an arrogant neurosurgeon (Bruce Davidson) and McCarthy's odd Dr Hook, as well as patients such as Diane Ladd's psychic, who is determined to discover the truth about the building. And did we mention the weird anteater-type creature that roams the halls, too? Over the 13 slow-moving and rather confusing episodes, their weird adventures are played out, baffling viewers and enthralling them at the same time, thanks to stunning set design and a *Twin Peaks*-style blend of quirkiness and shivers.

 TV Trivia: In writing Peter's accident, King used his own experiences of being hit by a car while out jogging in 1999.

THE LANGOLiERS (1995)

Starring Patricia Wettig, Dean Stockwell, David Morse

A TV movie (originally broadcast in two parts) based on one of King's short stories, this starts off in typically creepy Stephen King fashion: on a Boston-bound night flight, 10 passengers wake up to discover all the other people on board have disappeared, including the crew. First, they have to try and land the plane (scary enough, but don't worry as one of them is a trained pilot) and then, once on the ground, they discover everything around them is the same as it was in the air – no people, no sound, no signs of life. That is, until they hear ominous munching noises and realise they may not be as alone as they think...

Unfortunately, the effects here aren't very impressive (even the shots of the plane are ropey) and the creatures – the langoliers – aren't much cop, either. The action is stretched over three hours when it could have taken place in half that (cue lots of talking and dazed expressions among the survivors as they realise their predicament has something to do with time travel) and a good idea gets lost in amongst some very bad acting. Disappointing stuff.

 TV Trivia: Watch out for King himself in a brief cameo performance as a businessman quizzing Craig Toomey (Bronson Pinchot).

NiGHTMARES AND DREAMSCAPES (2006)

Starring William Hurt, William H. Macy, Tom Berenger

A television series of eight episodes, each one based on a short story, most from Stephen King's *Nightmares and Dreamscapes* collection ('Battleground' is actually from his *Night Shift* book). Among the best episodes are 'Battleground', in which William Hurt has to battle a group of surprisingly resilient toy soldiers; 'Umney's Last Case', in which a bereaved author (Macy) decides to change places with the 1930s detective he has created on the page; 'The Road Virus Heads North', with Tom Berenger as an author who can't seem to rid himself of a creepy painting; and the silly but enjoyable 'You Know They've Got One Hell Of A Band', the story of a couple who get lost on a road trip and stumble across Rock 'n' Roll Heaven, where Elvis is king, Janis Joplin is a waitress... and the price of admission is your soul.

The best episode of all is 'The End Of The Whole Mess' (the delicious sci-fi plot is too good to be spoiled here), while the one to avoid, especially by Londoners, is 'Crouch End', a cheap-looking horror about a tourist couple who take a taxi to the London suburb of the title only to find it is deserted except for a few creepy-looking kids and some strange creatures that won't let them leave. Apart from the story being utterly dumb, the location doesn't look anything like the real leafy area of the capital (the series was actually filmed in Melbourne, Australia).

 TV Trivia: The 'Battleground' episode doesn't actually feature any dialogue at all as Hurt takes on the mini-bad guys.

ROSE RED (2002)

Starring Nancy Travis, Matt Keeslar, David Dukes

A few years before this mini-series was made, Stephen King was in discussion with director Steven Spielberg, who wanted to make the scariest haunted house movie ever made. Unfortunately, by the time King was able to write it (he had suffered a debilitating accident in 1999 that prevented him writing for a time), Spielberg had moved onto other projects, so King's idea was turned into this drama instead. Of course, because it was made for TV, it just couldn't be as scary as something made for the cinema screen, and in fact, this comes off as silly rather than spine-tingling as a group of people with psychic powers, led by researcher Dr Joyce Reardon (Travis) decide to spend the weekend in a notorious haunted house that keeps adding to itself and changing shape in between offing the odious intruders.

Horror fans will notice nods to King's own *Carrie* and *The Shining*, and references are made to Shirley Jackson's *The Haunting of Hill House* as well, but unfortunately *Rose Red* doesn't match up to any of the horror classics it mentions. With some pretty poor acting, it's fairly doomed from the beginning, and gets worse as everyone runs around sets filled with crashing windows and ridiculous-looking ghosts, looking confused rather than petrified.

A 'prequel' of sorts, *The Diary of Ellen Rimbauer* (2003), is available on DVD and follows the story of the woman who haunts the Red Rose house, and is based on the *Rose Red* companion book that was written by King's associate, Ridley Pearson.

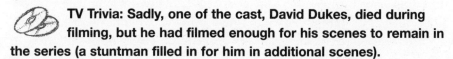 **TV Trivia: Sadly, one of the cast, David Dukes, died during filming, but he had filmed enough for his scenes to remain in the series (a stuntman filled in for him in additional scenes).**

SALEM'S LOT (1981)

Starring David Soul, James Mason, Lance Kerwin

People often assume this version of King's vampire novel was made for the cinema, as it was directed by Tobe Hooper (best known for *The Texas Chainsaw Massacre*), but in fact it started out as a three-hour mini-series – although it was later cut to 107 minutes for a cinema release in the UK (the full-length version is the one available on DVD).

The story begins as author Ben Mears (Soul) returns to his hometown of Jeruslaem's Lot to research the Marsten house, a creepy building on a hill that is rumoured to be haunted. A stranger named Mr Straker (Mason) has bought the house, along with his unseen partner Mr Barlow (who, when he is revealed, looks like Nosferatu), and just as they arrive, townspeople start dying from mysterious afflictions (though horror aficionados will probably spot the fang marks on their necks).

It's truly creepy stuff, especially the scene where young vampire Danny appears from a cloud of mist at friend Mark's window, entreating 'Open the window, Mark' while flashing his fangs, and the gothic horror climax, in which Ben realises the only way to free the town of vampires, is to kill the head one in his sleep. It's one of the better adaptations of a King book, and one that will make the hairs on the back of your neck stand up long after the series has finished. A sequel of sorts, *Return to Salem's Lot*, was made in 1987 but is not available on DVD.

 TV Trivia: Two of King's short stories are linked to *Salem's Lot* – 'Jerusalem's Lot' takes place in the 19th century and reveals some of the town's spooky history, while 'One For The Road' is set in a neighbouring town and features a vampire attack.

SALEM'S LOT: THE MiNi-SERIES (2004)

Starring Rob Lowe, James Cromwell, Donald Sutherland, Rutger Hauer

A second mini-series to be based on King's novel (see review, above). This one is actually less out-and-out scary, and also deviates more from the original source material – fans were particularly annoyed with the changes in Father Callahan (Cromwell): in the novel, his faith deserts him, whereas here he becomes chief vampire Barlow's new servant, voluntarily drinking the fanged one's blood, which isn't very priestly of him. The main story, of course, remains the same, with Rob Lowe taking up the role of the author who returns to his home town only to find that the local haunted house is now being inhabited by a mysterious newcomer (Sutherland) and his blood-sucking pal (Hauer).

It's quite suspenseful stuff, and director Mikael Solomon (who also directed two of King's *Nightmares and Dreamscapes* series) approaches the story from a different angle than the first adaptation, bringing in more about the townsfolk's own secrets and Ben's guilt about an event from his childhood. There's a classy cast on board, too, from Sutherland and Cromwell to Andre Braugher as the local teacher and Dan Byrd as the young kid Mark, who is almost as tortured as Ben. Well worth seeing, even if you are a fan of the 1981 version.

 TV Trivia: Co-stars Sutherland and Hauer have appeared on screen together before – as Buffy's watcher Merrick and

vampire Lothos respectively, in the movie version of *Buffy the Vampire Slayer*.

THE SHINING (1997)

Starring Steven Weber, Rebecca De Mornay, Courtland Mead

Not the Jack Nicholson-starring 1980 movie, of course, but a 1997 mini-series based on King's famous haunted hotel novel. Steven Weber stars as Jack Torrance, a recovering alcoholic and aspiring writer who moves his wife (De Mornay) and young son Danny (Mead) to a remote Colorado mountain hotel when he accepts a job as caretaker of the building during the winter months when the hotel is closed. Unfortunately, Danny has a psychic talent (called 'shining') that causes him to sense things, including the other inhabitants of the hotel – a collection of ghosts that feed off his power and twist his father's mind until Jack becomes convinced he has to kill his own wife and son.

A six-hour mini-series based on King's own screenplay, this is much more faithful to the original book than the Stanley Kubrick movie was, which should satisfy fans who hated the 1980 film's ending and missed elements such as Danny's invisible friend Tony (reinstated here) and the topiary animals that move when Danny looks at them (something Kubrick was unable to do in 1980, pre-computer generated animation). It's surprisingly effective, and often creepy, and actually benefits from Weber's 'ordinary guy' casting – as in the book Jack is a man struggling with alcoholism who finally goes over the edge at the Overlook Hotel over a period of months, whereas Mr Nicholson played it as if Jack was barking before he even got there. The series deservedly won two Emmys for sound and make-up and was also nominated for best mini-series.

Horror aficionados should watch out for some cameos – King plays the hotel's ghostly band leader, while *Evil Dead* director Sam Raimi also has a blink-and-you'll-miss-him role.

 TV Trivia: The Stanley Hotel, which was used for the Overlook Hotel, is also the hotel that originally inspired Stephen King to write the book when he stayed there.

SOMETIMES THEY COME BACK (1991)

Starring Tim Matheson, Brooke Adams

A TV movie based on one of King's short stories from the collection *Night Shift*, this terrible little film has surprisingly spawned two sequels – *Sometimes*

They Come Back... Again (1996), featuring Hilary Swank, and *Sometimes They Come Back... For More* (1999). The premise of the first movie is simple: Jim (Matheson) moves back to his hometown to work as a teacher, despite the fact his brother was murdered there a few decades before. He was killed in a train tunnel by a group of teenage thugs who then got squashed by the train, and now Jim finds his new pupils are dying – and each one is replaced by the ghost of one of the teens who killed his beloved brother!

It's a tedious mix of flashbacks and present-day 'chills' that are about as scary as watching an episode of *Noddy*, and Matheson wanders about the film looking dazed, perhaps wondering what happened to his film career post-*Animal House*. Very disappointing stuff – and King fans should note that the sequels are not based on King stories: the first is a reworking of this movie, but with more gore (it was made for video, not TV) while the second, set in Antarctica, doesn't seem to bear any resemblance to King's work at all.

 TV Trivia: Star Matheson, while still acting, is also a producer and director on the drama series *Cold Case*.

THE STAND (1994)

Starring Gary Sinise, Molly Ringwald, Rob Lowe

This is not only the best TV adaptation of a King novel (not surprising when you consider King wrote the teleplay himself), it is also one of the best TV mini-series ever made. A man-made virus that the army should have kept under wraps is leaked out, and millions die from the plague it creates. Some, however, are immune and survive only to be haunted by dreams – dreams of an old woman named Mother Abigail (Ruby Dee), who believes in God and calls for people to gather in Boulder, Colorado, and nightmares of Randall Flagg (Jamey Sheridan), a devil-like man who haunts the good people and commands the less law-abiding survivors to do his bidding in Las Vegas. It's a classic tale of good against evil, mixed with the story of a group of people struggling to survive without electricity, communications, or any idea of what could happen when a battle between the two factions begins.

One of King's weightiest novels, this deserved the mini-series treatment (it's six hours long) – King had once tried to cut the book down into a movie screenplay but realised it was an impossible task. Instead, we get a well-paced, fascinating story that mixes Biblical elements with fantasy and horror, but still has time to focus on the characters of the survivors, from pregnant Frannie (Ringwald) and her neighbour, Harold (Corin Nemec) who has a scary crush on her, to bemused Texan survivor Stu (Sinise), egotistical musician Larry (Adam Storke), deaf mute Nick (Lowe) and retarded man Tom

Cullen (Bill Fagerbakke). Stealing the show, however, is Sheridan, as the red-eyed, all powerful cowboy personification of all that is evil. Shudder.

 TV Trivia: Bill Fagerbakke, who plays Tom, is also the voice of Patrick Star the starfish in *Spongebob Squarepants*.

STORM OF THE CENTURY (1999)

Starring Tim Daly, Colm Feore

A six-hour mini-series that could have been half the length, this is based on a script King wrote for TV, which was then made into a novel after it was broadcast. Mike Anderson (Daly) is the part-time cop for a small Maine village that is experiencing a scary storm. As the wind blows in, so does mysterious stranger Andre Linoge (Feore), and it's not long before residents start dropping like flies whenever Linoge twirls his cane. He seems to know everyone's darkest secret, and Anderson knows the best plan to stop the mayhem would be to get rid of Linoge, to which the devil-in-disguise replies (in a letter written in blood, naturally): 'Give me what I want and I'll go away.' But what does he want?

Atmospheric to begin with, this suffers from being overly long and drawn-out. By the time you discover what it is Linoge wants, you probably won't care, but it is worth fast-forwarding to the dramatic finale nonetheless, as Feore – despite a rather odd accent – delivers a few delicious chills before the end credits roll.

 TV Trivia: Storm... is set in the same small town as King's *Dolores Claiborne* (keep your eyes peeled for a mention of her in the series).

THE TOMMYKNOCKERS (1993)

Starring Jimmy Smits, Marg Helgenberger, John Ashton

King's silliest novel becomes an entertainingly daft mini-series that boasts an eclectic cast, including former porn star Traci Lords, *Blade Runner*'s Joanna Cassidy and *Moonlighting*'s Allyce Beasley. They play just some of the residents of the small town of Haven, which – unbeknownst to them – has an alien spaceship buried in the local woods. Unfortunately, inquisitive Bobby (Helgenberger) unearths it, and the green glow of the UFO soon has the townspeople experiencing odd phenomenon, from telepathy to the ability to build quirky gizmos. Of course, it's not long before things start getting a bit more sinister as the locals fall under the control of the ship and decide to start digging it up, with only alcoholic poet Gard (Smits) realising this may not be such a good idea. (He's got a metal plate in his head that stops the aliens from controlling his mind like everyone else.)

The effects here look pretty cheesy (the green glow emanating from the ship looks like a disco light), and the ones at the series' finale are downright laughable, but the cast do their best to portray scared and confused while running around the woods and a New Zealand town that is supposedly doubling for a New England one. One for King completists only, perhaps.

TV Trivia: Star Marg Helgenberger got her TV start as a weather girl in Nebraska. The producer didn't like her name so made her change it to Margi McCarty.

WAR AND THE ARMED FORCES

WORLD WAR II COMEDIES STAND ALONGSIDE CIVIL WAR COS-
TUME DRAMAS, SOLDIER ROMANCES AND NUCLEAR FANTASIES
IN THIS SECTION. FOR MORE SERIES FEATURING WAR, SEE ALSO
COSTUME DRAMA, P.375.

THE CIVIL WAR (1990)

An Emmy-award winning documentary mini-series from acclaimed director
Ken Burns, who also made 1996's *The West* (see p.205), this was titled simply
'Civil War' when it was shown in the US (thus once again proving Americans
don't realise there are other countries, and other wars, outside of their own).
Beginning with the rise of the abolitionist movement, the series charts all the
major events and battles that shaped the civil war using photographs and
illustrations from the period, written documents and diaries, while modern-
day historians give insight on the various events that changed the course of
American history.

   Burns, who not only directed but also wrote, produced, photographed the
series, directed the music and presumably made the tea, too, delivered a new
style of documentary that has been much copied since: his use of narrators
reading letters, his mixture of old photographs and present-day footage of
the same places featured all add to the feeling that you are there with these
people as they bravely fought for what they believed in, on both sides of the
war. It's a fascinating story, both dramatic and moving, and, thanks to Burns'
skilled touch, an atmospheric and thought-provoking one, too.

 **TV Trivia: The series took six years to make – which is two
years longer than the war itself.**

BAND OF BROTHERS (2001)

*Starring Damian Lewis, Donnie Wahlberg, Ron Livingston, Matthew Settle, David
Schwimmer*

Filmed on a disused aerodrome in Hatfield, Hertfordshire, which was also
utilised for *Saving Private Ryan*, *Band of Brothers* was a project Tom Hanks very
much wanted to make after he read the book by Stephen E Ambrose. Enlisting
the help of his *Saving Private Ryan* director, Steven Spielberg, the two went to

US TV company HBO to pitch the idea and came away with a budget of $120 million to make the series (making it the most expensive TV series ever made). The 10-hour series followed the epic journey taken by a group of paratroopers, from their training days in Georgia right through to their involvement in the D-Day landings and up to and beyond VE Day.

Unlike many World War II dramas, there are no romances thrown in, nor melodramas, nor war movie cliches. Instead, this is a thoroughly researched, occasionally difficult to penetrate depiction of war, as the Easy Company (a real company of paratroopers) endure horrific conditions and tasks such as the liberation of a concentration camp and the storming of Hitler's 'Eagle's Nest' at Berchtesgaden. While sometimes it's difficult to tell the soldiers apart, this doesn't detract from the sheer power of any episode in which the horror of war is the real star, all of which begin with a real member of Easy Company being interviewed on camera, prefacing what is to come.

The excellent cast includes British actor Lewis (with flawless American accent), *Friends'* star Schwimmer and Ron Livingston, while the directors of episodes include Hanks himself, *Field of Dreams* director Phil Alden Robinson, *Wish You Were Here*'s David Leland and *Brimstone & Treacle* director Richard Loncraine. A testament to soldiers' bravery during a terrible war, this series should be shown in every school the world over.

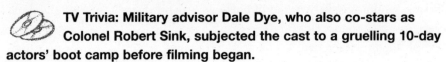 **TV Trivia: Military advisor Dale Dye, who also co-stars as Colonel Robert Sink, subjected the cast to a gruelling 10-day actors' boot camp before filming began.**

BATTLEFIELD (1995)

An acclaimed documentary series narrated by Tim Pigott-Smith that focuses on some of the momentous battles of World War II, including The Battle of France, The Battle of Britain, the siege of Stalingrad and The Battle of Midway in the first series and The Battle for North Africa, The Battle of the Rhine and The Battle of the Atlantic in the second series. Each mini-film describes the events leading up to a specific battle, explaining the commanders, troops, weapons and strategies involved in the planning. A third series of 12 episodes focused on the battles fought by Americans during the Vietnam War.

Aimed at lovers of military strategy and history, these are all well-researched documentaries. If you like these, also check out *Battlefield Britain*, a similarly named BBC series from 2004, presented by Peter Snow and his son Dan Snow, that uses computer imagery and re-enactments to provide historical insight into historical battles such as Boudicca's Revolt, The Battle of Hastings in 1066 and 1940's The Battle of Britain.

TV Trivia: One of the series' directors is Justin McCarthy, an actor who is the brother of Brat Packer Andrew McCarthy.

BY THE SWORD DIVIDED (1983–1985)

Starring Julian Glover, Jeremy Clyde, Peter Jeffrey

Buckle your swashes for this period romp set during the English Civil War. The battle between the Cavaliers and the Roundheads is seen through the eyes of two families – the Fletchers, who are loyal to Oliver Cromwell (Jeffrey), and the royalists the Laceys, who are loyal to King Charles I (Clyde). The families come together – much to the horror of patriarch Sir Martin Lacey (Glover) – when his daughter Anne (Sharon Maughan) marries a leading supporter of Cromwell's government.

As you'd expect from a BBC production, the costumes are gorgeous, the performances crisp and the scripts well-researched (the trial of Charles I is taken from the historical transcripts of the trial). The problem is, it's just not flashy and trashy and dastardly enough, and in places when it should be like a 17th-century episode of *Dynasty*, it instead comes across as a bit too po-faced. Two series were made, ending as the families gather when order is restored to the country and King Charles II comes to the throne.

 TV Trivia: The theme tune for the series was also used for *Miss Marple*.

COLDITZ (2005)

Starring Damian Lewis, Sophia Myles, Laurence Fox, James Fox, Tom Hardy, Timothy West

The classic seventies TV series of *Colditz*, with David McCallum, is sadly unavailable on DVD so we'll have to make do with this flashier 21st-century version, a two-part mini-series that owes more to Mills & Boon romances than it does to gritty wartime drama. Tom (Laurence Fox), Jack (Hardy) and Nick (Lewis) escape from a WWII prisoner of war camp together, but only Nick makes it across the border into Switzerland, while the other two are recaptured. Before they are separated, injured Jack asks Nick to promise to track down his love, Lizzie (Myles) – unfortunately when Nick finds her, he falls in love with her, too. So while Nick is enjoying a nice bit of romance, poor Jack and Tom are sent to Colditz, the notorious castle prison. Tom's determined to escape, and when Jack discovers what his treacherous pal Nick is up to with his girl, he decides to make a bid for freedom, too.

Originally titled *From Colditz With Love* (ick), this enraged historians and ex-POWs for its historical inaccuracies, and should probably be viewed as a period romp rather than anything remotely factual (certainly, the horrors the prisoners faced at the castle are glossed over quickly). Lewis is fun to watch as the man who becomes more dastardly as the story progresses, while Jason Priestley – playing an improbably named character called Rhett Barker – deserves kudos for his performance as a morphine-addicted prisoner.

 TV Trivia: Both Hardy and Lewis also starred together in the war series *Band of Brothers*.

DANGER UXB (1979)

Starring Anthony Andrews, Maurice Roeves, Judy Geeson, Iain Cuthbertson

Thirteen episodes were made of this drama that followed the exploits of a bomb disposal squad during World War II (the 'UXB' of the title stands for UneXploded Bomb). It was fairly watchable stuff but never as exciting as you'd expect (except the final episode, when one of the main characters was blasted off a pier) as Lt Brian Ash (Andrews), Sgt James (Roeves) and the team scuttled around London diffusing bombs (there were over 2,000 in London by summer 1940) while retaining that legendary English stiff upper lip in even the most nail-chewing moments.

There's romance, too: to begin with, Ash has the occasional tumble with his landlady's daughter Norma (Deborah Watling), who hilariously becomes frisky during air raids, but he then becomes involved with nice girl Susan (Geeson), who just happens to be the daughter of his bomb disposal expert boss, Dr David Gillespie (Cuthbertson). What is most interesting about this series, however, is the factual information that comes in between the drama – such as the fact that members of the disposal team had a life expectancy of just over two months, and very little training before they started trying to diffuse highly explosive materials. Yikes.

 TV Trivia: The series was loosely based on the real-life exploits of Major Bill Hartley, which he detailed in his book *Unexploded Bomb*.

DAS BOOT (1981)

Starring Jurgen Prochnow, Herbert Gronemeyer, Klaus Wennemann

Although it was released at the cinema in the UK in a shortened version, *Das Boot* (The Boat) was originally made for German TV and broadcast as a six-hour mini-series that told the harrowing story of a U-boat crew and their captain (Prochnow) in 1941. The most expensive German screen production since World War II (at a cost of over 25 million deutschmarks at the time), the series was based on the bestseller by Lothar-Gunther Buchheim, and follows this one boat on a single mission, from its departure in occupied France, through some early encounters with Allied forces, to an order for the crew to enter the Straits of Gibraltar to engage the enemy.

Filmed mainly in the cramped submarine by director Wolfgang Petersen, this series focuses on various members of the crew but really is about the boat itself, a small, claustrophobic place filled with men, equipment, dangling hammocks and small dark spaces. It's very slow to get going, but once the attack on an Allied convoy begins, this becomes a breathtaking, scary, harrowing look at war, most memorably in a scene in which the sub surfaces and attacks an enemy ship. The crew of the sub sees men leaping from the stricken tanker into the water, their cries for help ignored by the German captain as he moves his own craft away from them. It's very long and at times feels it, but this astonishing drama is worth the effort.

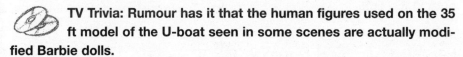 **TV Trivia: Rumour has it that the human figures used on the 35 ft model of the U-boat seen in some scenes are actually modified Barbie dolls.**

FAiR STooD THE WiND FoR FRANCE (1980)

Starring David Beames, Cecile Paoli, Bernard Kay

HE Bates' novel gets the BBC Drama treatment here – and it's a whole-box-of-tissues tale about the crew of an RAF plane that crash in France during World War II. Pilot John Franklin (Beames) is injured and he needs to keep his crew safe until they can escape. Luckily, they are taken in by a local mill-owning family, but things get rather complicated when John falls for the mill owner's daughter Francoise (Paoli), just as those darned Germans close in on his hiding place.

Nicely played by the cast, and set during a balmy summer in the luscious French countryside, this is more a love story than a war story (the war is just a pesky distraction whenever John tries to get up close and personal with Francoise), but it looks lovely and should cause a few snuffles from even the manliest of viewers.

 TV Trivia: HE Bates was a flight lieutenant in the Royal Air Force who used his experiences in many of his novels.

A FAMILY AT WAR (1970–1972)

Starring Colin Douglas, Barbara Flynn, Leslie Nunnerly

Over 25 million people tuned into this drama that ran for 52 episodes and told the story of how one Liverpudlian family was affected by World War II. Spanning the years from 1938 to 1945, the series followed the Ashtons – Edwin and wife Jean, and their children, including daughter Margaret and their son David and his wife Sheila – as they made their way through five tempestuous years, beginning with David's enlistment in the RAF, and covering such events as the 1938 fighting in the Spanish Pyrenees and bombing raids on Liverpool.

Of course, the main focus is family and relationships, and in the seven years the series captures, the family endures bad marriages, unfaithfulness, separation, love, betrayal and pain. A delicious slice of classic British telly.

 TV Trivia: Eight of the later episodes in this series were made in black and white instead of colour, due to a trade union dispute at the time.

FORTUNES OF WAR (1987)

Starring Kenneth Branagh, Emma Thompson, Rupert Graves

An adaptation of the autobiographical novels by Olivia Manning, this period drama follows the travails of newlyweds Guy (Branagh) and Harriet Pringle (Thompson), from their days as British ex-pats residing in Bucharest before World War II, to their flight from the advancing Nazi forces that leads them to Athens and then Cairo.

A mini-series of seven hour-long episodes, this initially shows the events from Harriet's point of view as she comes to terms with the foibles of her idealistic, left-wing spouse and her realisation that he believes she should be happy in his shadow, but we later gain more insight into Guy's life and thoughts when he learns (mistakenly) that his wife has been killed (anyone who doubts Branagh's talents as an actor should watch the scene in which he learns of her death – superb). Beautifully made, and featuring a clutch of subtle, moving performances from a cast that also includes Alan Bennett, Ronald Fraser and Robert Stephens, this is one of the better and classier mini-series to come out of the 1980s.

 TV Trivia: Kenneth Branagh and Emma Thompson became a couple during the filming of this series and married in 1989 (they divorced in 1995).

FOYLE'S WAR (2002–)

Starring Michael Kitchen, Honeysuckle Weeks, Anthony Howell

A sort-of wartime *Inspector Morse* that is almost as popular with British viewers, *Foyle's War* follows dogged Detective Chief Inspector Christopher Foyle (Kitchen), a man solving crime on the home front while England prepares itself for World War II. Of course, he'd rather be fighting on the beaches, but Foyle's superiors think he would better serve the war by staying put solving murders and uncovering spies with the help of his female driver, Sam Stewart (Weeks) and the wounded Detective Sergeant Paul Milner (Howell).

If you like *Morse*, *A Touch Of Frost* and Agatha Christie's novels, this 1940s-set murder mystery series is quite entertaining (although some of the whodunnits are wrapped up a little abruptly) and interesting, especially when the plots touch on the moral ambiguity of war and raise such questions as whether we should hate a whole nation just because their leaders are corrupt and evil. Kitchen is persuasive as Foyle and, with its mix of mystery and war, it's easy to see how *Foyle's War* successfully filled the space fans were left with in their TV viewing schedules when *Inspector Morse* came to an end.

 TV Trivia: The series was created by Anthony Horowitz, who writes the Alex Rider schoolboy spy novels (*Stormbreaker*, etc).

HITLER: THE RISE OF EVIL (2003)

Starring Robert Carlyle, Stockard Channing, Jena Malone, Julianna Margulies

An all-star cast appears in this four-hour mini-series that charts the rise to power of Adolf Hitler during the years before World War II. Beginning in 1899, when Hitler was just 10 years old and already showing signs of isolation and lack of emotion, the series follows him as he fails to win a place at the Academy of Visual Arts in Vienna, and ends up homeless on the streets – the first in a chain of events that leads Hitler to join the German army and later attempt to take over the German government.

Carlyle certainly gives a passionate performance as the man who would become Fuhrer, but it is a little over the top in places as he screams out Hitler's speeches and goes from shabby young man with scary views to the polished, moustachioed orator who would drive many people to do atrocious things in the name of Germany. Better are Liev Schreiber and Margulies as sympathiser Ernst Hanfstaengl and his wife Helene, whose marriage cracks as Helene is enraptured by Hitler's cause, Matthew Modine as reporter Fritz

Gerlich and Jena Malone as Hitler's niece, Geli Raubal, who committed suicide, perhaps due to her rumoured incestuous relationship with her uncle.

 TV Trivia: Ewan McGregor was reportedly originally considered for the role of Hitler.

HORNBLOWER (1998–2003)

Starring Ioan Gruffud, Robert Lindsay, Paul McGann

Loosely based on the novels by CS Forester, this British drama series follows the adventures of naval officer Horatio Hornblower (Gruffud) during the French Revolution and Napoleonic wars. Made up of eight feature-length episodes made over five years, the stories find our hero overcoming seasickness and the abuse from a fellow shipmate, quarantining his men due to a possible outbreak of bubonic plague, doing battle with various nasty foes, rescuing the occasional damsel in distress and even organising a mutiny against his captain.

In a similar vein to *Sharpe* (but, obviously, set at sea) with some equally impressive production values (the recreations of 18th-century ships are stunning, as are the battles at sea), this rollicking series was jointly funded by ITV and the American cable channel A&E, but the expense of the production eventually meant the series' cancellation. Gruffud, who is both dashing and daring as the old-fashioned hero, has suggested he would be available for a film version of the stories should the opportunity arise, though.

 TV Trivia: Gruffud's first TV role was at the age of 14 in the Welsh soap *Pobol Y Cwm*.

JERICHO (2006–2008)

Starring Skeet Ulrich, Gerald McRaney, Lennie James, Pamela Reed

This cracking, if rather implausible, series proves that sometimes fans can save the day. Following dismal ratings in the US for its first season, CBS Television announced that *Jericho* was cancelled and a second season would not be made. Incensed fans started sending nuts (referring to a scene in the final episode of the first season) to CBS's offices, and within a few weeks the TV company had received over eight million nuts, weighing over 40,000 lbs. Realising there was quite a dedicated audience out there, CBS renewed the series in the summer of 2007, if only for a final eight episodes that wrap up a few storylines.

Watch the first few episodes of *Jericho* and it's easy to see why fans became so hooked. Just as black sheep Jake (Ulrich) is returning to his home town of Jericho after five years away (where has he been? why did he leave?), a giant mushroom cloud is seen off in the distance and the residents of the small Kansas town discover there is a complete radio and TV blackout. What just happened? Is it nuclear war? Is America under attack? And are they the only survivors? While Jake's dad, town mayor Johnston Green (McRaney) tries to maintain order, the town panics and also begins to question the arrival of new resident Mr Hawkins (James) and his family. He says he is a St. Louis cop, but how come he knows so much about nuclear fallout procedures?

Many more questions are raised – some answered, some not – as the series progresses and the townsfolk have to deal with dwindling food, water and power supplies, the breakdown of authority and even escaped convicts and mercenaries. It's intriguing, if occasionally frustrating, stuff, packed with neat twists and turns as the Jericho residents deal with a possible Armageddon as well as more soapy plot points like exposed marital affairs and a life-threatening birth.

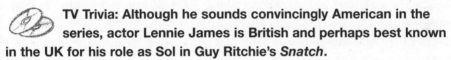 **TV Trivia: Although he sounds convincingly American in the series, actor Lennie James is British and perhaps best known in the UK for his role as Sol in Guy Ritchie's *Snatch*.**

THE DAY AFTER (1983)

Starring Jason Robards, JoBeth Williams, Steve Guttenberg

In the eighties, Brits were scared stiff by the gritty nuclear drama *Threads*, while Americans got this glossier TV movie that also focused on the lead-up and aftermath of a nuclear holocaust. Set mainly in the small town of Lawrence, Kansas, the film follows a group of residents as they try to survive following the attack (an attack that the end credits admit is less devastating than a real one has been predicted to be).

Filmed like a disaster movie, setting up the characters in the first half and then killing some of them off in the second, it introduces us to Dr Russell Oakes (Robards), a young medical student named Stephen (Guttenberg) who has just arrived in town, and an airman (William Allen Young) who leaves his wife and child to return to his unit once things start looking icky. There's also a university professor (John Lithgow) who survives in a shelter with some of his students, a bride-to-be (Lori Lethin), and a pregnant woman (Amy Madigan) to add to the list of potential victims.

Despite the soapy aspects of the plot – and the fact that the film was originally planned to be four hours' long, shown over two nights, but was then edited down to two – this still has some powerful moments, such as the scenes of 'nearly dead' crammed into a high school gym waiting to die, and, with an estimated 100 million viewers, it remains the most watched TV movie in US television history.

TV Trivia: Following the broadcast in the US, a political debate was shown in which scientist Carl Sagan made his famous comment that the arms race was like 'two sworn enemies standing waist-deep in gasoline. One with three matches, the other with five.'

THE MARK OF CAIN (2007)

Starring Matthew McNulty, Gerard Kerns

BAFTA-winning writer Tony Marchant (*The Canterbury Tales*) delivered this one-off drama portraying the experiences of a group of British soldiers stationed in Iraq, based on testimonies from soldiers who have served there. The drama follows lifelong friends Shane (Matthew McNulty) and Mark (Gerard Kerns), two 18-year old privates in Basra, 2003. It's their first tour of duty, and they want to be able to go home saying they have done something, but instead they find themselves in complex situations they never imagined in a highly charged and dangerous environment. At the end of their tour they return home with trophy photos, but those pictures will change their lives forever.

This realistic, sometimes shocking, story makes for harrowing viewing while the men are stationed in Iraq (the scenes were actually filmed in Tunisia), but becomes slightly less gripping when they return to England. Throughout, however, McNulty and especially Kerns, give superb performances in this realistic depiction of a dirty, uncertain war that is still being fought.

 TV Trivia: The drama won Amnesty International's 'Movies That Matter' award in 2007.

NCIS (2003–)

Starring Mark Harmon, Michael Weatherly, David McCallum

Or *Navy NCIS: Naval Criminal Investigative Service* to give it its full title. This series – which spun off from an episode of *JAG* – follows a group of investigators whose job it is to investigate any crimes committed that involve the US Navy or Marine Corps. Special Agent Jethro Gibbs (Harmon) leads the team that comprises of ex-homicide detective Anthony DiNozzo (Weatherly), computer nerd Timothy McGee (Sean Murray), former Secret Service agent Kate Todd (Sasha Alexander), forensics scientist Abby Scuito (Pauley Perrette) and medical examiner Donald 'Ducky' Mallard (McCallum). In later seasons, Lauren Holly joins the team as Gibb's former lover and new boss.

Created by Donald P. Bellasario, the man behind *Magnum PI*, *Quantum Leap* and *Airwolf*, this is similar in style to the *CSI* series as the group use legwork, forensics and scientific techniques to get their man (despite being naval investigators, there is very little action at sea, one presumes because that would be budget-busting). It's stylish to look at, with slick direction, quirky camera angles and fast-paced editing to keep the tension mounting, and it features a nice strand of humour as the members of the team bicker amongst themselves. There are some shocks, too – including the death of a much-liked character at the end of Season 2 – and coupled with good performances from the cast (Harmon giving his best performance since *St Elsewhere*), this is a very likeable whodunnit that has been a ratings winner in the States although sadly underrated in the UK.

 TV Trivia: Mark Harmon's wife is Pam Dawber, of *Mork and Mindy* fame.

NORTH AND SOUTH (1985); NORTH AND SOUTH BOOK II (1986)

Starring Patrick Swayze, James Read, Lesley Anne Down

A yummy bodice-ripper of a historical novel (part of a trilogy: *North and South*; *Love and War*; *Heaven and Hell*) by John Jakes was turned into an even more juicy mini-series that launched the heartthrob career of Patrick Swayze. He stars as Orry Main, a young Southern gentleman who befriends Northerner George Hazard (Read) when they both train to be soldiers at the prestigious West Point academy. Little do they know that their friendship will soon be tested, however, as events build towards the American Civil War and they find themselves on opposite sides.

Of course, this isn't just about soldiering and battles (though the fighting scenes are pretty impressive), this is also about love, betrayal, family, obsession and duels at dawn – while George finds love with a general's (Robert Mitchum) daughter (Wendy Kilbourne), poor Orry falls for the beautiful Madeleine (Down), whose father has promised her to the dastardly plantation owner Justin LaMotte (David Carradine). There are also the machinations of George's ambitious brother Stanley (Jonathan Frakes) for them to deal with, George's outspoken sister (Kirstie Alley), and Orry's rather trampy one (Terri Garber), as well as the mean, vengeful Elkanah Bent (Philip Casnoff), who has it in for our two heroes.

The first mini-series takes the action up to the start of the war, while the second follows the men as they rise through the ranks of opposing armies. In between, the episodes are packed with elaborate costumes, delicious dialogue and performances from well-known actors including Elizabeth Taylor, Jean Simmons, Morgan Fairchild, Forest Whitaker, Gene Kelly,

Johnny Cash, Olivia De Havilland and James Stewart. A third mini-series in which many of the cast return (except Swayze, whose character is killed off), based on Jakes' final book *Heaven and Hell*, was made in 1994 but is only available on US DVD.

TV Trivia: *North and South* was something of a romantic set – James Read and screen wife Wendy Kilbourne are now married in real life, as are Jonathan Frakes and Genie Francis (who played Stanley's wife in the series). Kirstie Alley and Parker Stevenson (who played George's brother Billy in Book II) were also a couple but have since divorced.

NUREMBERG (2000)

Starring Alec Baldwin, Brian Cox, Christopher Plummer, Jill Hennessey

A three-hour dramatisation of the war crime trials that followed the end of World War II, this mini-series won two Emmy awards, one for actor Cox's gripping portrayal of Nazi Reichsmarschall Hermann Göring. Based on Joseph Persico's book *Nuremberg: Infamy On Trial*, the drama follows American prosecuting lawyer Robert Jackson (Baldwin, who also executive produced) as he questions key Nazi figures about their involvement in such atrocities as the concentration camps, while a US army psychologist (Matt Craven) attempts to understand how the men committed these crimes and were able to live with themselves.

Behind the scenes, Jackson is having an affair with his secretary, and the jailer (Michael Ironside) is barely hiding his contempt for his Nazi prisoners, but the best moments are when Jackson is storming around the courtroom, being forceful yet honourable as he brings these evil men to justice. While Cox undoubtably steals the show from everyone as the chilling, manipulative Göring, there are also some other notable courtroom performances from Plummer as British prosecutor Sir David Maxwell-Fyfe, Colm Feore as the commandant of Auschwitz, and Herbert Knaup as Albert Speer.

Ultimately, the script ends up moralising far too much and the Jackson affair is a bit too soapy for such a serious setting, but this is nonetheless an interesting drama about a fascinating piece of history.

TV Trivia: In real life, Maxwell-Fyfe was eight years younger than Jackson, while during filming of the series, Plummer (who plays Maxwell-Fyfe) was 70 to Alec Baldwin's 42.

OVER THERE (2005)

Starring Josh Henderson, Erik Palladino

Steven Bochco, best known for *NYPD Blue* and *LA Law*, produced this dramatic series set during the war in Iraq. Only 13 episodes were made before the series was cancelled due to low ratings, but each was controversial for its depiction of young men fighting in a war that was still taking place, and the grisly outcome of their battles on the streets. (Faint-hearted viewers should note there is a stomach-turning scene in the first episode in which an Iraqi soldier's upper body is blown up but his legs continue to walk for a few seconds).

Among the soldiers we get to know are Bo (Henderson), Chris 'Sgt Scream' Silas (Palladino), Dim (Luke Macfarlane), Smoke (Kirk Jones) and Tariq (Omid Abtahi), as well as some of the families at home, including Dim's hideous wife and their adorable son, while the plots focus on the horrors of the Gulf War, from dubious interrogations to booby traps, pointless and dangerous missions (in one episode, the team are assigned to protect a block of toilets), bloody firefights to the aftermath of suicide bombs.

Modelled on Ridley Scott's movie *Black Hawk Down*, this is often effective – and affecting – stuff, but some of the more soapy aspects of the soldiers' personal lives do spoil what could otherwise (given half a chance) been a powerful series. Sadly, two series that got the balance of war and personal lives right – the Vietnam-set *Tour Of Duty* (1987–1990) with Terence Knox and the 1987 mini-series *Vietnam* with a young Nicole Kidman – are not available on DVD in the UK.

 TV Trivia: Despite the authentic-looking surroundings, the series was filmed entirely in and around Los Angeles.

SECRET ARMY (1977–1979)

Starring Bernard Hepton, Clifford Rose

A superbly well-researched and gripping series set during World War II, *Secret Army* was created by Gerald Glaister, a former RAF pilot who had already produced the acclaimed *Colditz*. Historically accurate and based on real events (sometimes so accurate that the BBC stepped in and rejected episodes they felt would be upsetting to viewers), the series focused on the brave resistance fighters in Belgium who defied their Nazi occupiers by blocking roads, blowing up weapons silos and, most importantly, helping downed British airmen hide and then escape through Scandinavia or down to Spain, even though if discovered they faced torture or death.

The series focused on cafe owner Albert (Hepton), who helped resistance worker Lisa (codename 'Yvette') (Jan Francis) guide airmen to safehouses and out of the country, and the Luftwaffe officers charged with breaking the 'lifeline' and capturing the people responsible for helping the Brits. There were romantic subplots – married Albert has an affair with one of his cafe's waitresses – but in the main the show focused on the characters' war efforts. (If the above sounds a bit familiar, it's probably because the plot was spoofed for the comedy series 'Allo 'Allo). A final episode, 'What Did You Do In The War, Daddy?', set in 1969, was filmed but never shown – rumour has it that the episode's anti-Communist sentiment and suggestion that the war efforts were all in vain was the reason it was deemed unfit to broadcast. There was, however, a sequel of sorts, *Kessler* (1981), that followed the exploits of ruthless Luftwaffe officer Kessler (Rose), now posing as a respected businessman, after the war. It is available on DVD.

TV Trivia: Legend has it that series creator Gerald Glaister pitched the idea for the series to a BBC controller he shared a lift with – and by the time the lift ride was over, the deal was done.

SHARPE (1993–1997, 2006)

Starring Sean Bean, Brian Cox

Sheffield boy Sean Bean became something of a sex symbol as well as a star following his appearances as dashing army officer Richard Sharpe, the character from a series of novels by Bernard Cornwell. Set during the Napoleonic Wars, the feature-length episodes began with Sharpe as a sergeant in the 95th Rifles, serving in Portugal in 1809. After he saves the life of General Arthur Wellesley (David Troughton), Sharpe is promoted to Lieutenant and put in charge of a group of elite riflemen, and – despite being a commoner among titled men – our hero rises through the ranks (making both friends and enemies along the way).

Packed with acts of bravery, romps with pretty women, dastardly deeds and battles, the various *Sharpe* series became a hit with both men and women and also gave sales of the Cornwell novels a healthy boost. Over the years, the supporting cast has included Brian Cox, Pete Postlethwaite, Elizabeth Hurley, Emily Mortimer and James Purefoy, but we know most people (or women at least) don't tune in for the stars, but instead for the sight of Sharpe engaging in some manly sword-play. Two more *Sharpe* series are rumoured for 2009 if movie star Bean can squeeze them into his packed filming schedule.

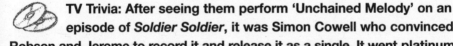

TV Trivia: Paul McGann was actually cast as Sharpe, but following an injury he had to pull out of the production and Bean was called in as his replacement.

SOLDIER SOLDIER (1991–1997)

Starring Robson Green, Jerome Flynn

Soldier Soldier wasn't a bad show, but the inexplicably successful series will forever be remembered for two great sins: not only did it foist the combined acting 'talents' of Green and Flynn on us, but also their eye-wateringly awful crooning as 'pop stars' Robson And Jerome (sorry to bring up that scary memory of 'Unchained Melody').

Beginning in 1991, the drama followed the lives of the officers and soldiers serving in the fictional King's Fusiliers regiment of the British Army, especially Fusilier Dave Tucker (Green) and pal Sergeant Paddy Garvey (Flynn). Tucker has a stormy marriage to moaning Donna (Rosie Rowell), who hates the army life, while Garvey's true love is Colonel Nancy Thorpe (Holly Aird), a member of the military police who isn't quite ready to settle down and give up her own dreams in the armed forces.

Often credited with giving a realistic portrayal of army life, the seven seasons followed the boys (and later, newer characters, including Dougray Scott's Major Rory Taylor, who joined shortly before Green and Flynn left the show in 1995) at training camps, and when they were stationed in Germany and later in Australia. The action is well done, the scripts do give an insight into the lives of soldiers and their wives… but no matter how good it was, we just can't get past the grim spectre that is Robson and Jerome. Sorry.

TV Trivia: After seeing them perform 'Unchained Melody' on an episode of *Soldier Soldier*, it was Simon Cowell who convinced Robson and Jerome to record it and release it as a single. It went platinum in one week and was number one in the UK for seven weeks.

TENKO (1981–1984)

Starring Stephanie Cole, Claire Oberman, Stephanie Beacham

A different side of World War II was depicted in this award-winning BBC drama, which follows the experiences of a group of women who are captured during the fall of Singapore in 1941, and interned in a Japanese prisoner of war camp. (Creator Lavinia Warner had been researching the internment of nursing corps officer Margot Turner for an episode of the chat show *This Is*

Your Life when she realised the potential for a fictional series about women who survived the camps.)

Among the characters that viewers grew to know and love were Beatrice (Cole), a brusque doctor; Australian nurse Kate (Oberman); colonel's wife Marion (Ann Bell), and vain Dutchwoman Domenica Van Meyer (Elizabeth Chambers), as well as camp commander Yamauchi (Burt Kwouk). In the three years they were on screen, the series dealt with personal dramas such as lesbianism, abortion, suicide and rape, as well as the various rivalries in the camp. The first series of 10 episodes chronicled their capture and the first year in captivity, while the second series began with the prisoners being moved to a new camp. Following a season-ending episode in which the Allies bomb the camp, the third series focused on the women's liberation and their adjustment to civilian life. A two-hour special, *Tenko Reunion* (currently unavailable on DVD) was made in 1985, and followed the women as they met again, five years later.

 TV Trivia: Due to budget constraints, only early scenes were filmed in Singapore. The scenes at the camp were filmed on a specially made set in Dorset.

THREADS (1984)

Starring Karen Meagher, Reece Dinsdale, David Brierly

If you were a kid but old enough to watch *Threads* when it was first broadcast, chances are you've had at least one sweat-soaked nightmare about it in the years since. An account of how England would cope and react following a nuclear attack, this is filmed in documentary style by director Mick Jackson (*The Bodyguard*) and focuses on the everyday people of Sheffield. Using government data gathered at the time that predicted 29 million people would die and 19 million would survive for a short time following a nuclear holocaust (and that's the good news), this shows how monumentally screwed we would all be if any nations decided to drop the big one on us, and how useless the nuclear shelters people were keen on in the eighties would actually be if we couldn't leave them for decades because of the fallout.

The plot is this: aware that the war of words between the US and the then-Soviet Union is escalating, residents of Britain have been stocking up on supplies and moving into shelters as the government tells them to, expecting everything to be alright soon. Of course, it's not okay, and those that survive the blast get radiation sickness if they manage to crawl out from under the burning rubble, or are killed as Britain's desperate residents fight over the remaining scraps of food and shelter. While this dark, unsettling drama has dated quite a bit since its ground-breaking first broadcast, it's still shocking, and the central story about young couple Jim (Dinsdale) and pregnant Ruth (Meagher) is still moving. Ruth has her baby, but with nuclear winter on the way, viewers should be prepared for even nastier things to come.

 TV Trivia: *Threads* was broadcast in 1985 to coincide with a week of programmes marking the 40th anniversary of the bombings of Hiroshima and Nagasaki. It was not broadcast again until 2003.

ULTIMATE FORCE (2002–2006)

Starring Ross Kemp, Jamie Draven

When Ross Kemp (aka Grant Mitchell) left *EastEnders* and was given shed-loads of money to go to ITV, he turned up in a few dodgy projects (such as Eddie Scrooge in a modern day version of *A Christmas Carol*) before finding his niche in this gung-ho series that follows the exploits of his character, Sergeant Henno Garvie, and his fellow SAS men who make up the crack team Red Troop. Co-created by Chris Ryan, the former SAS member of the Bravo Two Zero patrol (he also appears in a few first season episodes), the show has the men taking on a bank siege, rescuing kidnapped colleagues, infiltrating a gang of suicide bombers and stopping a plane hijacking, in between the occasional accidental shooting of a superior officer.

Unfortunately, some of the cast (including Draven's lead character, Jamie Dow) and Ryan left after the second series, and took the authenticity of the show with them. Things got more violent and also a bit sillier, and the format changed from one-hour episodes to feature-length mini-movies before it was cancelled during Series 4.

TV Trivia: A female SAS officer joins the group in Series 3, yet in real life, women are not eligible to join the SAS.

WAR AND PEACE (1972)

Starring Anthony Hopkins, Morag Hood, Alan Dobie

There have been numerous screen versions of Tolstoy's classic novel, but the only TV one that is currently available on DVD is the 1972 series that starred a young Anthony Hopkins. He plays the central role of Pierre Bezuhov, the illegitimate son of a wealthy count who becomes embroiled in a fight for his father's inheritance. Once he receives it, he is burdened by his new-found wealth and responsibility, and stifled by a marriage to an unfaithful wife against the backdrop of the Napoleonic Wars.

Of course, the novel is a dense, sprawling epic of love, war, death, hope and betrayal in Russia, and the 20 episodes capture much of the story, featuring many of the minor characters who often get lost in adaptations of the book, as well as giving fascinating life to the major ones, such as the heroic Andrei Bolonsky (Dobie), beautiful Natasha Rostova (Hood) and Napoleon Bonaparte (David Swift) himself.

Filmed in the former Yugoslavia, it is one of the most faithful adaptations of Tolstoy's magnificent tome, both enjoyable viewing to fans of period dramas, and a useful study guide for literature students. Hopkins deservedly won a BAFTA for his performance.

 TV Trivia: Sir Anthony Hopkins is now a US citizen, but he has been allowed to keep his British knighthood.

THE WAR GAME (1965)

Starring Michael Aspel, Peter Graham

Made in 1965 for the BBC's Wednesday Play slot but not aired until 1985 (after viewing it pre-broadcast, the BBC announced 'the effect of the film has been judged by the BBC to be too horrifying for the medium of broadcasting'), *The War Game* was the first British drama/documentary to tackle the aftermath of a nuclear attack in Britain, and was a clear influence on the later TV drama *Threads*. Filmed in black and white documentary style, while also featuring contemporary 'interviews' with the man on the street and fictional interviews with key political figures, the 50-minute play shows the chaos in the run-up to the attack and the effects of a nuclear strike on the residents of a Kent town, from the collapse of society to the psychologically and physically damaged population.

The BBC asked for scenes from the drama – including those of the police shooting civilians – to be cut before it would broadcast the play in 1965, and when that request was refused, it was screened for a select group of politicians and reporters so the BBC could show why it was not suitable for broadcast. Some who saw it came out in defence of the programme (Kenneth Tynan commented it may be 'the most important film ever made'), and eventually it was given a small cinema release in 1966. Those who have seen it never forget the film's compelling images – the wedding rings used to identify the dead piling up in a bucket; the blank-faced children who have survived the horror – and this remains one of the most important, unforgettable television depictions of war ever made.

TV Trivia: Following his battle with the BBC about the broadcast, writer/director Peter Watkins left the UK and for more than 30 years worked mainly in Scandinavia.

WE'LL MEET AGAIN (1982)

Starring Susannah York, Michael J. Shannon

Get out the hankies for this sweet, old-fashioned ITV series that followed a group of American GIs as they 'invaded' a quaint English village in 1942 and got to know the local womensfolk (nothing too steamy happens, though, as this was made in the early eighties). Over 13 episodes, the brash young airmen get involved with the wary Suffolk community who have endured rations, blackouts and food shortages for three years. There's Major Jim Kiley (Shannon), who is drawn to the luminous Helen (York), whose husband has been shipped to Africa, and airman Chuck (Joris Stucyk), who begins a romance with publican's daughter Vi (Kathryn Pogson), but he then goes missing during a mission over Germany and she has to wait anxiously for news. Meanwhile local dad Albert Munday (Ray Smith) is determined his own family won't be affected by the Yank invasion, and young local Sally (Carolyn Pickles), whose husband has been reported killed in action, begins a friendship with American mechanic Joe (Christopher Malcolm), but discovers a knock on the door one night changes everything.

Hugely popular at the time it was broadcast, fans were surprised when a second series was not made. Instead, to satisfy those who wanted to know what happened to all the characters after the war, a follow-up story was written and serialised in the *Daily Mail*.

TV Trivia: Gavan O'Herily, who plays GI Captain Red Berwash, also played Richie's brother Chuck in early episodes of *Happy Days*.

THE WINDS OF WAR (1983)

Starring Robert Mitchum, Polly Bergen, Ali McGraw, Jan-Michael Vincent.

One of the biggest budget mini-series of all time, this epic story of one family's experiences of the early stages of World War II — based on the heavyweight tome by Herman Wouk — boasted lavish locations, and a who's who of stars in the cast list, from Robert Mitchum to Ralph Bellamy (as Roosevelt, no less), and Topol to Wouk himself (in a cameo as the Archbishop of Sienna).

Beginning before the outbreak of the war and ending in 1941, the 15-hour series follows the experiences of Pug Henry (Mitchum), a career Navy man who finds himself (luckily for the show's narrative, though a teeny bit unbelievably) in a position of history – along with brash wife Rhoda (Bergen), he is sent to Berlin to act as US Naval Attaché there in 1938 as the Third Reich gained power. While a bored Rhoda begins an affair, Pug mixes with the rich, powerful and dangerous of both German and American politics. And the family's involvement in such a key piece of world history doesn't end there: daughter Madeline (Lisa Eilbacher) has a front seat working for CBS News in New York, eldest don Warren (Ben Murphy) is a pilot who is stationed at *Pearl Harbor* (uh-oh), while younger, slacker son Byron (Vincent), heads to Italy to work for a renowned Jewish author (John Houseman) and falls for his niece, the headstrong Natalie (McGraw), before returning to America to sign up as a submarine officer in training.

Many events of the war, from the bombing of Berlin to the horror of the Warsaw ghetto and the fear of Jews escaping the Nazis, are shown in a personal way in this gripping drama, that features news footage alongside the drama. Mitchum, Vincent and supporting cast members such as Topol and Houseman are superb in this sprawling tale and, while McGraw lets the side down (she's too old at 45 to play Natalie, and can't make the character remotely sympathetic although she has a tough job as Natalie is a stubborn, selfish cow, even on the page), this remains a storming piece of entertainment packed with romance, politics and edge-of-the-seat drama. They certainly don't make them like this anymore. The follow-up, *War And Remembrance* (in which Jane Seymour took over the McGraw role and Hart Bochner took over from Vincent) is only available as a US DVD box set.

TV Trivia: Logan Ramsey, who has a small part in the series as Senator Lacouture, is the son of Logan Ramsey Sr, who delivered the fatal radio message "Air Raid, Pearl Harbor. This is no drill" on December 7th, 1941.

WiSH ME LUCK (1987–1990)

Starring Kate Buffery, Suzanna Hamilton, Julian Glover, Jane Asher

A well-made ITV drama about the people who risked their lives to spy on the enemy during World War II – in this case, two British women, fluent in French, who are recruited because they have local knowledge of Normandy. Liz Grainger (Buffery) is a young wife and mother from Devon whose husband is fighting overseas, while Matty Firman (Hamilton) has a French mother and is first recruited to work as a wireless operator. Both go to work for the Special Operations Executive, which is run by Colonel James Cadogan (Julian Glover) and the woman they dub 'Snow Queen', Faith Ashley (Asher). They are accompanied by other 'spies', including Kit Vanston (Michael J. Jackson), Colin Beale (Jeremy Northam) and Claudine de Valois (Shelagh McLeod).

A mix of romance, adventure and intrigue, this is an enjoyable wartime affair that focuses on the heroics and personal lives of a group of people. Created by Lavinia Warner and Jill Hyem, who had previously worked on *Tenko*, it boasts strong, well-written female characters, and a nice mix of historical fact and dramatic fiction. A total of 23 episodes were made.

 TV Trivia: Jane Asher was famously engaged to Paul McCartney in the 1960s. She later went on to marry cartoonist/illustrator Gerald Scarfe.

THE WORLD AT WAR (1974)

Narrated by Laurence Olivier

An astonishing television achievement, *The World at War* remains the most comprehensive visual history of World War II ever made. As narrated by Laurence Olivier, it's a collection of documentaries charting the war from beginning to end, focusing on the human achievements and reactions to major events, as well as recording the events themselves. Ambitious, expensive and four years in the making, it features interviews with both ordinary people and recognisable figures such as Lord Mountbatten and Anthony Eden, as well as high-ranking Germans such as Albert Speer and, in one of her first interviews, Hitler's secretary Traudl Junge.

Twenty-six episodes were made, each focusing on a different aspect of the war such as the USA's involvement, the activities on the home front, and the Burma campaign. Archival footage is put to excellent use, be it footage of battle preparations, Londoners during the air raids, children at Hitler Youth rallies or concentration camps, and in between there are surprising touches, such as the inclusion of footage of Hitler at his Bavarian hideaway as filmed by mistress Eva Braun. Fascinating.

TV Trivia: The work of Britain's codebreakers at Bletchley Park could not be included when the series was made, as their involvement in the war was still classified at that time.

DOCTORS, NURSES AND VETS

MEDICAL DRAMAS, HOSPITAL COMEDIES... AND A MAN WITH HIS HAND UP A COW.

ALL CREATURES GREAT AND SMALL (1978–1990)

Starring Christopher Timothy, Robert Hardy, Carol Drinkwater

Based on the books about the life of a country veterinarian by James Herriot, *All Creatures Great and Small* was originally made into a 1975 film with Simon Ward in the lead role. Then in 1978 the idea was adapted for TV and fresh-faced Christopher Timothy was cast as James, the vet running a practice with the more experienced (but rather odd) Siegfried Farnon (Hardy) and his brother Tristan (Peter Davison) in 1930s and 1940s rural Yorkshire. As English as cream teas with extra jam, this was an endearing tale of country life, complete with hands being thrust up cow's posteriors, the occasional tumble into manure and other rural jollities as Herriot learnt about his trade with the help and sometimes hindrance of his new wife Helen (Drinkwater) and the Farnons.

While the biggest drama tended to involve Mrs Bond and her hissing cat Boris (whom she believed was a reincarnation of a Roman gladiator), this was a light-hearted treat for sentimental animal lovers nostalgic for a slice of the country that hadn't got Barratt Homes built on it. Three series were made, followed by specials in 1983 and 1985, then the series was fully revived in 1988, picking up after World War II had ended, for four more series. Drinkwater did not return, and the role of Helen was taken over by Lynda Bellingham.

TV Trivia: During the second series, Christopher Timothy was injured in a car accident, so many of his scenes that year were in the surgery rather than in the field as he had difficulty walking.

BRAMWELL (1995–1997)

Starring Jemma Redgrave, Michele Dotrice, Andrew Connolly

It's 1895 and nice young women aren't expected to have careers. But Eleanor Bramwell (Redgrave) thinks differently, and is determined to be a doctor, despite the objections of just about everyone including her own father (David Calder). Working under the supervision of Sir Herbert Hamilton, she watches a healthy young woman die, and decides that she should leave her medical studies and set up a free clinic for the poor of East London on her own (with the help of Lady Cora Peters, who kindly donates a building to house it). Golly gosh, do you think she will make a go of it?

Each episode followed Eleanor as she tackled a case – from a patient who refuses treatment for TB to a train crash victim who needs his leg amputated – while also focusing on her private struggles as she attempts to keep her clinic from being taken over or closed down. In later episodes (there are four episodes in each mini-season), she gets a bit of romance, too, in the form of suave doctor Finn O'Neill (Connolly), while other male acquaintances Dr Quarry (David Bark-Jones) and Dr Marsham (Kevin McMonagle) also show an interest in what's under her corsets.

Historically, the medical stuff is pretty accurate, and Redgrave gives a good central performance as Eleanor, backed by a classy cast that includes Robert Hardy, Ian Carmichael, Timothy West and Shirley Ann Field. The plots, however, are a bit thin in places, and this would most likely appeal to fans of historical dramas rather than medical ones.

 TV Trivia: Jemma Redgrave is the daughter of actor Corin, and the niece of Lynn and Vanessa Redgrave.

CASUALTY (1986–)

Starring Derek Thompson, Ian Bleasdale, Simon MacCorkindale

Before the Americans had *ER*, the Brits had – and still, after 22 years, have – *Casualty*, a drama about the doctors and nurses working in the busy accident and emergency department of the fictional *Holby City* hospital (Holby being a city that bears a striking resemblance to Bristol). Now a staple of Saturday night TV on BBC1, the series was originally seen as something quite controversial as the overworked and underpaid staff struggled to keep the place open with the help of charge nurse Charlie (Thompson, the only actor to be in every series of the show). A mix of soap opera and medicine, the show focused not only on the often gruesome (and graphically portrayed) cases that were stretchered into the hospital, but also on the complicated lives and loves of the staff with plotlines that included rape, abortion and alcoholism. Cheery stuff, then.

In fact, it's a pretty dangerous hospital to work in, as over the years major characters have been stabbed to death, mugged, burnt to death in an explosion, poisoned, shot by patients and committed suicide – yet despite this, the show somehow manages to never feel very exciting. A spin-off series, *Holby City*, began in 1999, and follows doctors and nurses in other parts of the hospital. At present, it is not available on DVD. A second spin-off, *Holby Blue*, about police in the area, was made in 2007 and is available on DVD.

 TV Trivia: Orlando Bloom, Kate Winslet, Pete Postlethwaite and Minnie Driver have all guest-starred in episodes, while Oscar-winning actress Brenda Fricker starred as nurse Megan in the earlier series.

Doc MARTiN (2004–)

Starring Martin Clunes, Caroline Catz

Doc Martin is the story of Dr Martin Ellingham (Clunes), who leaves his cushy London obstetrician job and retrains as a GP after developing a phobia for blood, and who finds an odd solace in a quirky Cornish seaside village full of interesting characters. Developed from a one-off drama into a popular TV series, this is an enjoyable fish-out-of-water story as Martin gets used to the residents of Port Wenn, who see themselves as one big family, while he prefers to be impersonal and unaffected by his surroundings.

Various characters are much more endearing than Doc Martin himself (a name he hates being called) – the local headmistress, Louisa (Catz), the jolly gossipy plumber Bert (Ian McNeice), the police constable, Martin's own Aunt Joan (Stephanie Cole) – and their stories are revealed as the episodes affectionately plod on by. Thanks to Clunes's sarcastic performance, this is never as naff as *Heartbeat* and is often as funny as *All Creatures Great and Small*.

 TV Trivia: Port Isaac is the stunning location doubling for Port Wenn in the series.

DocToR iN THE HouSE (1969–1970); DocToR AT LARGE (1971); DocToR iN CHARGE (1972–1973)

Starring Barry Evans, Robin Nedwell, George Layton, Ernest Clark

Based on the cheeky 1954 movie of the same name and Richard Gordon's books, *Doctor in the House* was the comedy that followed the antics of a group of junior doctors at St Swithins Hospital in London as they attempted to chat up the nurses. There was Michael (Evans), the rather earnest and anxious doc following in his father's footsteps, Duncan (Nedwell), the intelligent goof-off, their friends Paul (Layton) and Dick (Geoffrey Davies), arrogant Lawrence (Richard O'Sullivan) and their grumpy mentor, Professor Loftus (Clark), who frowned on the various antics the boys got up to.

The likeable comedy (which, with its 'swinging sixties' backdrop, has dated somewhat) was very much in the *Carry On* vein of things, with many of the scripts written by Pythons Graham Chapman and John Cleese and also Goodies Graeme Garden and Bill Oddie. The 1971 series *Doctor at Large* followed Michael as he tried various medical jobs before returning to St Swithins, while *Doctor in Charge* focused on the comic adventures of Duncan and Paul. The other spin-offs to *Doctor in the House* – *Doctor at Sea*, *Doctor on the Go* and *Doctor Down Under* – are currently unavailable on DVD.

 TV Trivia: Both Graeme Garden and Graham Chapman were qualified medical doctors before they became writers and comedians.

DR QUINN. MEDICINE WOMAN (1993–1998)

Starring Jane Seymour, Joe Lando, Chad Allen

A total of 150 episodes and two TV movies were made of this award-winning series, telling the story of Dr Michaela 'Mike' Quinn (Seymour), a doctor in Boston in 1867 who heads out to the wild west of Colorado following her father's death to start up her own practice. The townspeople are shocked on her arrival – having expected a man – but, as Mike makes the adjustment to life in the rugged countryside, the people slowly warm to her, especially mountain man Sully (Lando), a hunky slice of outdoorsy manhood who is soon smouldering in her direction. But it's not all rolls in the hay – after Mike fails to save poor midwife Charlotte from a deadly snakebite, she ends up adopting Charlotte's three orphaned kids, Matthew (Allen), Colleen (Erika Flores, and later Jessica Bowman) and Brian (Shawn Toovey).

Dr Quinn merged real historical events of the time with the fictional characters, so it wasn't unusual to have Custer or Walt Whitman popping up in the town while Mike went about her medical business. A hugely successful series with a devoted fan following (there are numerous fan sites on the web featuring fan fiction about the lives of Mike and Sully), the location used for filming – the Paramount ranch in Agoura Hills, California – has become something of a fan mecca, despite many of the Western sets being dismantled.

TV Trivia: Jane Wyman, Johnny Cash and his wife June Carter Cash, David Carradine and Kenny Rogers are among the guest stars who appeared in *Dr Quinn*.

DON'T WAIT UP (1983–1990)

Starring Nigel Havers, Tony Britton, Dinah Sheridan

George Layton, one of the stars and writers of TV's *Doctor in Charge* in the seventies, wrote this inoffensive, old-fashioned British sitcom about an upper-class doctor, Toby Latimer (Britton), who leaves his wife Angela (Sheridan) and moves in with his divorced son Tom (Havers) who is also a GP. Gosh, will they get along in the pokey flat they have to share?

It's not exactly ground-breaking comedy, but certainly appealed to middle England audiences wanting to watch something 'nice' and inoffensive about nice and inoffensive people. Havers does fine as the weary, put-upon son arguing with Dad about medical matters and why he's left his lovely wife of 30 years, but Britton steals the show as the father refusing to grow up. Jane How costarred as Tom's ex-wife Helen, while Susan Skipper starred as Toby's secretary Madeleine, whom Tom falls for.

 TV Trivia: Tony Britton is TV presenter Fern Britton's dad.

ER (1994–)

Starring George Clooney, Anthony Edwards, Julianna Margulies

In 1994, two series set in hospitals began on US TV: the often whimsical *Chicago Hope* (as yet not available on DVD) and the grittier *ER*, which boasted *Andromeda Strain* author Michael Crichton as one of its creators. Beginning with the attempted suicide of one of the nurses, Carol (Margulies, who was originally only scheduled to appear in that first episode), the show introduced us to the doctors and nurses in the emergency department at cash-strapped County General in Chicago. Each episode featured new patients they were treating (often played by well-known actors, including Forest Whitaker, Ray Liotta, Ewan McGregor and Kirsten Dunst), while the staff's personal lives were the thread holding the show together.

With tough topics (drug abuse, terminal illness, mental illness, gun crime) and occasionally gruesome hospital scenes, *ER* worked both as a medical drama and a relationship one, thanks to the casting.

Of course, it is best known as the TV series that turned George Clooney from jobbing actor to major heartthrob as paediatric doctor Doug Ross, but the series didn't suffer that much from his departure in Season 5, thanks to a solid ensemble that included Margulies (her Carol, finally reunited with Doug, in a weepie episode, 'Such Sweet Sorrow' in Season 6), Anthony Edwards (as dependable Mark), Noah Wyle (as new intern Carter) and

Sherry Stringfield (as Susan). As these characters left/were killed off, new ones have skilfully replaced them, including Goran Visnjic (as hunky Kovac), Maura Tierney (as nurse turned doc Abby), British actresses Parminder Nagra (as Neela), Alex Kingston (as Elizabeth), and Shane West (Ray). In fact, after a couple of wobbly years, *ER* was back on form for 2006/7's Season 13, and looks set to continue for at least another season or two.

 TV Trivia: *ER* was originally planned as a film, with Steven Spielberg directing. Instead he went on to direct another Michael Crichton creation, *Jurassic Park*.

FRASIER (1993–2004)

Starring Kelsey Grammer, David Hyde-Pierce, John Mahoney

Originally a character on the hit series *Cheers*, psychiatrist Dr Frasier Crane (Grammer) left the Boston bar in 1993 and returned to his home town of Seattle to take up a radio psychiatrist job at KACL and to care for his ageing father, Martin (Mahoney) in this hugely successful spin-off sitcom. Part of the reason it worked so well was that the comedy didn't just rely on Grammer's skilled comic timing and deliciously mannered performance as Frasier. It's actually a very well-scripted ensemble piece, thanks to the casting of Mahoney as the gruff, working-class dad at odds with his son, David Hyde Pierce as Frasier's equally effete brother Niles, Peri Gilpen as Frasier's man-hungry producer, Roz, and British actress Jane Leeves as Martin's plain-speaking live-in physical careworker Daphne. Oh, and Eddie the dog (played by Moose), Martin's pet.

In almost every episode, Frasier doles out advice on his radio show (with many of the call-in voices provided by celebrities ranging from Cindy Crawford to Ben Stiller), while dealing with the problems in his life (usually caused by his family) and potential relationships. Meanwhile Niles has a fraught marriage to Maris (who is never seen, though her thinness is often described) and a secret yearning for Daphne, which was finally revealed to her in the seventh season (many fans believe that bringing Niles and Daphne together was the death knell for the series, but it was sweet).

The early series do remain the best, but each of the eleven seasons has its own charms, including the guest performances of Anthony LaPaglia as Daphne's brother Simon (sporting a cockney accent, despite Daphne saying her family is from Manchester), Desperate Housewife Felicity Huffman as tetchy business expert Julia, Harriet Sansom Harris as Bebe, Frasier's barracuda of an agent, and Jane Adams as Niles' second wife Mel.

TV Trivia: Daphne and Niles' baby, who is born in the final episode, is named David after David Angell, one of the show's producers who was aboard one of the planes that crashed into the World Trade Center on 11 September, 2001.

GREEN WING (2004–2006)

Starring Tamsin Greig, Stephen Mangan, Mark Heap, Pippa Heywood

Produced by the team behind *Smack The Pony*, this is a sitcom mixed with a sketch show that perplexed and thrilled viewers in equal measure. Ostensibly, it's the story of a group of doctors at a British general hospital – newcomer Caroline Todd (Greig), irritating Angela Hunter, egomaniacal ladies man Dr Secretan, Mac McCartney (who thinks nothing of riding his motorbike through the corridors naked), and various other staff members including staff liaison officer Susan White and senior doctor Alan Statham, who is having a not-very-secret affair with human relations manager Joanna Clore.

Filled with camera trickery and moments of improvisation, this is akin to a Brit version of *Scrubs*, but with less appealing characters and more risk-taking in terms of comedy style and production (also, unusually for a comedy, each of the 17 episodes is an hour long). Original it certainly was, and often funny in a grotesque sort of way (incest, and even eating a patient's organs were among the subject matters covered), thanks to the comic quirkiness of the cast. Two series were made, plus a special that ended the series.

TV Trivia: Much of the filming was done at two real hospitals, North Hampshire and Northwick Park. This proved problematic when one actor, Stephen Manghan, was hitting squash balls in a scene for Series 1 and accidentally hit a real patient.

GREY'S ANATOMY (2005–)

Starring Ellen Pompeo, Patrick Dempsey, Sandra Oh, TR Knight, Katherine Heigl

With *ER*'s (see review, on p. 314) ratings slipping in the US in 2004, no one expected another medical drama to come along and be as – or maybe even more – successful. But come along it did, in the form of award-winning *Grey's Anatomy*. Focusing on the lives of five surgical interns at Seattle Grace Hospital, the story started off concentrating on Meredith Grey (Pompeo), a student with an Alzheimer's-stricken mother (who used to be a revered surgeon herself), and Meredith's relationship with suave new-to-town doctor Derek Shepherd (Dempsey), whom she dubs 'McDreamy'. Unfortunately he's not as dreamy as he seems on first appearance – he's married – but by the time Meredith finds out she has pals Cristina (Oh), George (Knight), Izzie (Heigl) and Alex (Justin Chambers) to help her through it. In fact, although the series is named after Meredith's character (it's also a play on the medical bible all students use, *Gray's Anatomy*), she's the least interesting of the characters as they all dive into complicated love lives. In Season 1, Cristina begins a secret sexual relationship with one of the senior doctors, Preston Burke (Isaiah Washington), while George nurses a major crush on Meredith and her lover's wife joins the staff, while in Season 2, Izzie falls for one of her patients, a man waiting for a heart transplant (the adorable Denny, as played by Jeffrey Dean Morgan).

At times very funny (just check out the episode in which scary resident doctor Bailey – the terrific actress Chandra Wilson – goes into labour and tells a bewildered George to stop looking at her 'va-jay-jay'), but often moving (the whole-box-of-tissues Season 2 finale) and even tense (Season 2's 'It's The End Of The World', in which a patient arrives with an unexploded bomb embedded in his chest), *Grey's Anatomy* had already established itself as one of the most popular shows on American TV by the end of its first series. By 2007 it had been nominated for 14 Emmys and won one for best cast, and also won Screen Actors Guild and Golden Globe awards.

 TV Trivia: Each episode's title is the name of a song, with Beatles and REM titles used the most frequently.

HoUSE MD (2004–)

Starring Hugh Laurie, Robert Sean Leonard, Lisa Edelstein

He's mean, gruff, insensitive, addicted to painkillers (following a disease that ravaged his leg, causing his limp), manipulative… and incredibly good at diagnosing the undiagnosible in patients who are admitted to the Princeton-Plainsboro hospital where he works. Meet Dr Gregory House (Laurie), – part Grinch, part Sherlock Holmes (the producers often pay homage to Conan Doyle's inspiration, even having House's apartment number as 221B to reflect Holmes' Baker Street address). With his team of crack investigative doctors – eager to please Chase (Jesse Spencer), doe-eyed Cameron (Jennifer Morrison) and argumentative Foreman (Omar Epps) – House attempts each week to cure a patient with strange, unexplainable symptoms, while also running amok in the hospital with his unusual methods that annoy his long-suffering best friend Wilson (Leonard) and boss Cuddy (Edelstein).

While the format: patient comes in, House and team gets diagnosis wrong, then get it right just in time for the end credits, could become monotonous, it doesn't, thanks to Laurie's superb central turn as House. Best known, of course, in the UK as the posh comic actor who appeared with Stephen Fry in *A Bit Of Fry And Laurie* and *Jeeves and Wooster*, and as a upper-class buffoon in *Blackadder III* and *Blackadder Goes Forth*, here he turns in a deliciously spiteful portrayal of a doctor spouting pithy dialogue that one can't imagine any American actor having the nerve to tackle. Bizarrely, even with House's personality flaws, Laurie has also created something of a sex symbol role for himself, leaving fans to debate which female character in the show House should end up with (current popular choice is his boss, Cuddy).

The best episodes include 'No Reason' in Season 2, in which House is shot and 'Airborne' in Season 3, in which House and Cuddy are on a flight facing a possible disease outbreak. Not one episode has been bad, but the ones to avoid are those co-starring Sela Ward as House's ex-love Stacy (big snore) in Season 2.

 TV Trivia: Executive producer Bryan Singer (the director of the X-Men movies) hired Hugh Laurie thinking he was really an American.

HUFF (2004–2006)

Starring Hank Azaria, Blythe Danner, Oliver Pratt

We first meet psychiatrist Craig 'Huff' Huffstodt (Azaria) as a gay teenage patient commits suicide in his office. Not a great start to anyone's day, and Huff's life seems to go downhill from here as he descends into a mid-life crisis. He's got a mentally ill brother (Andy Comeau), an overbearing, alcoholic mother, Izzy (Danner), a teenage son just discovering sex, and a bonkers lawyer pal named Russell (the always delicious Platt), who may be having a fling with Huff's mum. Into this mix come some of Huff's oddball patients and Russell's even quirkier clients – including in Season 1, Lara Flynn Boyle as an unstable woman with designs on Huff, and in the second season (not yet available on DVD), Sharon Stone as a man-eater – and the audience starts to wonder whether it should really be Huff who needs the services of a psychiatrist.

Through it all, Huff receives advice from a homeless Hungarian (Jack Laufer), he continually crosses paths with. Is he real or a figment of Huff's imagination? Both dramatic and funny, this series never really mastered a balance between the two, and despite terrific performances from the cast, and guest appearances from actors including Anjelica Huston, Tom Skerritt and Swoosie Kurtz, it was cancelled after two seasons.

TV Trivia: Comic actor Azaria has performed voices for *The Simpsons* since he was 22, including Moe, Chief Wiggum, Apu and Comic Book guy.

M*A*S*H (1972–1983)

Starring Alan Alda, Wayne Rogers, McLean Stevenson, Loretta Swit

A follow-up to Robert Altman's critically acclaimed 1970 movie *MASH*, this comedy drama had Alan Alda taking on the role of Captain 'Hawkeye' Pierce (made famous in the movie by Donald Sutherland), one of the doctors stationed at an army hospital during the Korean War. Truly believing laughter is the best medicine, Hawkeye and his best friend, Trapper John (Rogers), spent their time away from the operating theatre in their army tent, romancing the nurses and plying them with martinis, much to the annoyance of senior nurse, Major Margaret 'Hotlips' Houlihan (Swit) and bumbling, rule-enforcing killjoy Major Frank Burns (Larry Linville). Other memorable characters attending to the war wounds included cross-dressing (because he wants to be discharged on mental health grounds) Corporal Klinger (Jamie Farr), put-upon Lt Col Henry Blake (McLean Stevenson) and sweet radio controller Radar (Gary Burghoff).

Among the most noteworthy episodes of this very funny and at times melancholy series are 'Dear Dad', in which Hawkeye writes to his father about life at the 4077th, 'Divided We Stand' in which a psychologist examines the doctors in a bid to decide whether the camp should be kept open, and the hilarious 'The Colonel's Horse' from Season 5. Unfortunately, although popular, Rogers's character was replaced in later series (the plot had Trapper being sent home at the beginning of Season 4) by Mike Farrell's B.J. Hunnicutt, while the funny Linville left in Season 6, to be replaced by David Ogden Stiers's Charles Emerson Winchester.

A spin-off series, *Trapper John MD*, that followed the 'Trapper John' character from MASH to his new job at a San Francisco hospital, is not available on DVD.

 TV Trivia: The series lasted eleven years, whereas the Korean War itself only lasted three.

MEDIC (1954–1956)

Starring Richard Boone

Remembered as one of the first TV shows that paid attention to medical detail – and featured acted-out operations shown on camera – *Medic* ran for

59 episodes, each filmed in black and white, and 30 minutes long. Each episode was narrated and introduced by Boone as Dr Konrad Steiner (who sometimes appeared in the stories themselves) and featured an anthology of medical cases, all filmed at a Los Angeles hospital.

The series, which launched with an episode in which a birth was televised, was seen as somewhat controversial, due to an episode in which a caesarean birth was depicted: a Catholic organisation complained before the episode was aired and the offending scene was removed, while an episode in which a black doctor had to decide whether to remain practising medicine in the city or to return to his small Southern home town was seen as potentially racially dangerous in Southern states of the US, who refused to show it, so the television company decided not to broadcast it at all.

 TV Trivia: Richard Boone was a cousin of crooner Pat Boone and is also believed to be a descendant of pioneer Daniel Boone.

NiP/TUCK (2003-)

Starring Dylan Walsh, Julian McMahon, Joely Richardson

Ryan Murphy, who also produced the 1999 teen series *Popular*, is the man behind this love-it or hate-it drama that mixes medicine with excess in every form. Sean McNamara (Walsh) and Christian Troy (McMahon) run a successful plastic surgery office in Florida, and they are best friends despite being polar opposites – Sean is a family man with a depressed wife, Julia (Richardson), rebellious teenage son Matt (John Hensley) and daughter Annie, while bachelor Christian uses his good looks to full advantage, bedding every woman in sight (including some of his patients).

Almost every episode focuses on a patient having surgery performed by the pair, and their controversial cases have included a woman with apparent stigmata, twin sisters who no longer want to look like each other and a man wanting breast implants, all usually graphically depicted (the surgeons play music while they operate so faint-hearted viewers can just hide their eyes until the song is over). But the main reason for tuning in is the regular cast members' complicated love lives: early on, we learn Christian and Sean's wife Julia once had a fling, while Christian's conquests range from threesomes to the cosmetic surgery-enhanced beauty Kimber (Kelly Carlson), who becomes wealthy by designing a blow-up sex doll in her own image (it's not just the surgery scenes that are graphic – both Walsh, and more regularly McMahon, have let the camera size up their buttocks during the show's numerous sex scenes, perhaps making this one of the few shows where male actors get their kit off as often – or more often – than the actresses).

Seasons 1 and 2 are a treat – and quite unlike anything else you'll find on TV, but Season 3 lost its way with an ongoing plot about a murderer/slasher named the Carver (Sean and Christian become targets after they cosmetically treat some of his victims), and the show's 'shocking' mix of sex and surgery seemed somewhat tired by Season 4.

 TV Trivia: Former model Julian McMahon (formerly best known for his role as Cole in *Charmed* and as Ben in the Aussie soap *Home and Away*) is the son of former Australian Prime Minister Sir William McMahon.

NO ANGELS (2004–2006)

Starring Kate Wragg, Louise Delamere, James Frost

A comedy drama from Channel 4 about four nurses and the various lunacies they put up with while working on the wards of St Margaret's Hospital in Leeds, this deals with life within the NHS as well as the various entanglements the girls get themselves into when they are not at work. Anji (Sunetra Sarker) has had numerous sexual encounters, yet is preparing for an arranged marriage, Lia (Delamere) has to deal with the problems of being a mother as well as an overworked nurse, Beth (Jo Joyner) is determined to find a wealthy patient whether it's the new hospital boss or an unwitting patient, and overeager Kate (Wragg) is hoping to work her way up and become management.

Think *Sex and the City* meets *Casualty* and you have some idea of this show's agenda – to be funny, sexy, and occasionally be about medicine. The four lead actresses give suitably raunchy performances – the show was criticised in its first year for portraying the nursing profession as a group of sex-mad drunken maniacs – and this is a fun diversion, along the lines of a 21st-century *Carry On Nurse*, rather than a serious evening's entertainment.

 TV Trivia: Creator Toby Whitehouse wrote the *Doctor Who* episode 'School Reunion' in 2006, that brought back robotic dog K-9 and former Time Lord companion Sarah Jane Smith (Elisabeth Sladen).

ONLY WHEN I LAUGH (1979–1982)

Starring James Bolam, Peter Bowles, Christopher Strauli

An old fashioned British sitcom set on a hospital ward, where working-class patient Roy Figgis (Bolam), posh hypochondriac Archie Glover (Bowles) and young mummy's boy Norman Binns (Strauli) run amok, much to the annoyance of the irritable doctor, Gordon Thorpe (Richard Wilson), the harrassed nurses and hospital orderly Gupte (Derrick Branche).

Set almost entirely on the hospital ward – where, it has to be said, the men don't seem that sick to have been there for a considerable length of time – this is chirpy stuff, boasting terrific comic performances from Bowles, Wilson, Strauli and especially Bolam. It's dated, of course (nowadays the cast would be worrying about MRSA), but thanks to writer Eric Chappell (*Duty Free*, *Rising Damp*), it's good-humoured, warm and fuzzy fun that will still make you giggle three decades after it was made.

 TV Trivia: James Bolam was room-mated with Marc Bolan in the 1960s and has been credited with inspiring Bolan's surname (his real name was Feld).

PEAK PRACTICE (1993–2002)

Starring Kevin Whately, Amanda Burton, Simon Shepherd

Popular, if rather twee, series featuring a team of country doctors who run a medical practice in the pretty Peak District. Fresh from working in Africa, Dr Jack Kerruish (Whately) joins the clinic run by Beth Glover (Burton) and Will Preston (Shepherd), who would rather be playing golf than tending to the sick. It's not long before Beth and Jack are getting friendly with each other's stethoscopes, while poor Will has marital problems, and the trio deal with the problems of the locals, too. A new GP joined the practice in Series Three, Andrew Atwood (Gary Mavers), and remains when Jack and Beth head off to Africa for a sabbatical, while Dr David Shearer (Adrian Lukis) was added to the cast for Series Five.

It's all very nice, packed with picturesque locations (it's clearly aimed at people who have a second home in the country) and sweet storylines, but – aside from the final episode, which ended with a huge cliffhanger that was never resolved, nothing much happens and it all feels bland and a bit wishy-washy. Watch out for Samantha Morton and Minnie Driver in early performances.

 TV Trivia: The house used as David Shearer and wife Clare's house actually belonged to the show's medical adviser, Dr Tim Parkin.

QUINCY. ME (1976–1983)

Starring Jack Klugman, Robert Ito

Loosely based on real-life medical examiner Dr Thomas Noguchi, who acted as a technical advisor for the series, *Quincy ME* – something of a forebear to the *CSI* series – starred Klugman as the coroner who doesn't just cut dead bodies open, he solves the mystery of how they got into his morgue in the first place. With the assistance of Sam (Ito), Quincy follows up many of his cases to see that justice is served, often clashing with the detective who should be doing the legwork, Lieutenant Monahan (Garry Walberg).

The series began as part of a collection of 90-minute long detective shows broadcast as 'NBC Mystery Movies of the Week' in the US (four of these movies were about Quincy) before it was given its own slot of one-hour episodes. The best episodes include 'Snake Eyes' (a two-parter in which Quincy investigates a disease outbreak in a Lake Tahoe hotel) and Season 3's 'Tissue Of Truth', in which Quincy has a race against time to find a boy in an underground prison whose kidnapper has been killed, but all are enjoyable if you take to Klugman's gruff charm as he blusters about, never taking no for an answer. A similarly themed series, *Diagnosis Murder* (1993–2001), in which Dick Van Dyke solves crimes when he isn't operating as a doctor, is also available on DVD.

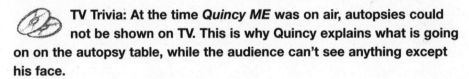 **TV Trivia: At the time *Quincy ME* was on air, autopsies could not be shown on TV. This is why Quincy explains what is going on on the autopsy table, while the audience can't see anything except his face.**

SCRUBS (2001–)

Starring Zach Braff, Sarah Chalke, Donald Faison, John C McGinley

A surreal comedy from Bill Lawrence (*Spin City*) set at the Sacred Heart Hospital, *Scrubs* is packed with fantasy sequences, sly jokes and funny performances as the bonkers doctors and nurses tend to the occasional patient. Doctor John 'JD' Dorian (Braff) is the main focus of the show (and he narrates the events) as he pals around with Turk (Faison), shares sexual innuendo with Elliot (Chalke) and gets on the nerves of abrasive senior doctor Perry Cox (McGinley). At times wistful, at times bizarre, and both sad and funny, the show is loved and hated in equal measures, but no one could accuse it of not being unique – in fact, the best way to describe this show is as a sitcom for people who hate sitcoms.

The ensemble cast is terrific, especially Braff and McGinley, and while this is a comedy, it does deal with ongoing dramatic storylines as well as funny ones, both well written and performed. While both *St Elsewhere* and *Chicago Hope* had done the rare fantasy sequence, here they are almost the norm as JD's daydreams are acted out in full (including a scene in which Dr Cox and senior Dr Kelso duel it out like Darth Vader and Obi Wan Kenobi), and there is also an entirely musical episode in the sixth season called, not surprisingly 'My Musical'. The series makes great use of guest stars, too, including Michael J. Fox, Colin Farrell, Brendan Fraser and Matthew Perry.

 TV Trivia: An abandoned hospital was purchased and refitted for filming the series – it is the old North Hollywood Hospital in the San Fernando Valley, California.

SiLENT WiTNESS (1996–)

Starring Amanda Burton, Emilia Fox, William Ganimara

A BBC drama series following three forensic pathologists who try to uncover the truth behind murders, this began with Amanda Burton in the lead role of Sam Ryan, but has proved so popular that her exit in 2004 and the arrival of Emilia Fox as Nikki in her place hasn't affected ratings at all. Effectively a detective show without detectives (and with more gore), the stories first focused on Sam, a pathologist (later promoted to professor) regularly called to assist homicide crime scenes and to perform graphic autopsies on murder victims. Somehow she manages to solve most of the cases without bothering the police much, aided by her assistants Leo (Ganimara) and Harry (Tom Ward), both of whom joined the show in 2002.

It's not for the weak-stomached, and many fans of crime procedural dramas will be incensed that it seems Ryan (and later Nikki and her team) unrealistically gets to do the detective work herself when she should be sharpening her scalpel, but like the similar *Quincy ME* and the *CSI* series (see Cop Shows, p8), it's well-paced stuff with strong performances.

TV Trivia: Amanda Burton's first TV role was as posh Heather in the first episodes of *Brookside*.

ST ELSEWHERE (1982–1988)

Starring Ed Flanders, William Daniels, Denzel Washington

Possibly TV's best medical drama, *St Elsewhere* not only laid the groundwork for realistic medical series like *ER* and *Grey's Anatomy*, it also launched or boosted the careers of a host of actors, including Denzel Washington, David Morse, Howie Mandel, Eric Laneuville (who now directs, including episodes of *ER* and *Lost*), Alfre Woodard, Mark Harmon, Bruce Greenwood and Helen Hunt. Set at the crumbling – and fictional – Boston hospital St Eligius, the programme ran for six years and 137 episodes, telling the stories of the staff and patients with a blackly humorous style.

The doctors here weren't always life-savers, they were fallible, and sometimes even unlikeable (especially David Birney's Dr Samuels, whose womanising may have given one of the female staff a STD). Led by Chief of Staff Donald Westphall (Flanders), gruff heart surgeon Mark Craig (Daniels) and wise Daniel Auschlander (Norman Lloyd), the student doctors were a motley crew, too, especially goofy Fiscus (played by comic Mandel), ambitious Victor Erlich (Ed Begley Jr) and sweet Jack Morrison (Morse).

No topic was considered too controversial to be explored, from rape and AIDS (at a time when it was rare for the disease to be featured on TV, one of the main characters, Mark Harmon's Dr Caldwell, was diagnosed with it), to a mental patient who is impregnated by another patient or a couple deciding whether to abort a Down's Syndrome baby. And no main character was safe from being heartbroken, imprisoned or killed off, making the series an often edge-of-your-seat affair (the revelation of who the hospital rapist was being a particular jaw-dropper) or so heartrending you were snuffling into a box of tissues.

Among the notable episodes were 1986's two-parter 'Time Heals', that revealed things from staff members' pasts as they celebrated the hospital's 50th anniversary and the first season's 'Cora And Annie', featuring Doris Roberts and James Coco as a homeless couple. The series ended with a controversial plot twist in 1988 (see p.417, TV Endings, for more details).

TV Trivia: A 1985 episode 'crossed-over' with *Cheers*, as doctors Westphall, Auschlander and Craig stopped at the Cheers bar for a drink and were served by Carla (Rhea Perlman).

THIRD WATCH (1999–2005)

Starring Coby Bell, Jason Wiles, Michael Beach

All of the emergency services – police, firemen, paramedics – are covered in this series that follows a group of men and women who work for those departments and are attached to the (fictional) 55th precinct in New York City. At a time when medical dramas such as *ER* (one of the creators of *Third Watch* was *ER*'s creator, John Wells) and police dramas such as *Law and Order* were huge hits, it made sense to combine the two genres, even though the premise was slightly unbelievable: all the cops, paramedics and firefighters work the same shift, the 'third watch' (between 3 pm and 11 pm), and it seems that particular time of day is when everything happens in the city.

A slick ensemble drama, this worked best when handling real events – notably, an episode in 2002 entitled 'In Their Own Words' that told true stories from real-life paramedics, firemen and policemen who worked the streets on 11 September 2001, introduced by members of the cast.

In later years, *ThirdWatch* was criticised for increasing violence, and for the departure of some of the most-loved cast members, including Bobby Canavale, Michael Beach, Kim Raver and Eddie Cibrian.

 TV Trivia: Derek Kelly, who played fireman DK Kitson, and Bill Walsh, who played Billy Walsh, are both firefighters in real life.

A VERY PECULIAR PRACTICE (1986–1988)

Starring Peter Davison, Amanda Hillwood, Barbara Flynn, Graham Crowden

Andrew Davies – now best known for his magic scriptwriting touch on costume dramas such as the BBC's *Pride and Prejudice* and *Bleak House* – wrote this quirky series about the doctors working at the cash-strapped medical practice of a British university. Blackly humorous in tone and a sharp satire on Thatcherite Britain, the series features an odd cast of characters: drunken radical Jock McCannon (Crowden), scheming feminist Dr Rose Marie (Flynn), the well-intentioned but out of his league doctor Steven Daker (Davison), and a host of students finding their way in life (if they can get out of bed/sober up in time to do so).

Beautifully written and smartly played (a special award should go to David Troughton's bonkers performance as Bob Buzzard, who measures his success by the size of BMW he can afford to buy), this is an often surreal but hugely enjoyable series packed with darkness and intelligence.

The series ran for a total of 14 episodes, and was followed by a disappointing TV movie, *A Very Polish Practice*, in 1992, which is unavailable on DVD.

 TV Trivia: The series was inspired by Andrew Davies' own experiences as a lecturer at the University Of Warwick.

VITAL SIGNS (2006)

Starring Tamzin Outhwaite, Steven Waddington

Former EastEnder Outhwaite starred in this six-part series for ITV as Rhoda Bradley, a 34-year-old woman working in a supermarket who decides to train as a doctor. While her husband Tony (Waddington) and three kids support her, going to medical school is a tough decision that will impact on Rhoda's family life – from how often she sees them all, to how much money they will all have to live on.

As well as dealing with Rhoda's struggle to get into medical school, the series touches on her sister's jealousy (she's a nurse), her husband's rather bad reaction to seeing Rhoda kiss a fellow student, and her clashes with Dr Lindsay (Anton Lesser). It's not massively original, but Outhwaite gives a good performance in the lead and the scripts from Chris Lang – who has also written for *Casualty* and *Primeval* – are sharp.

 TV Trivia: Watch out for Outhwaite's EastEnder castmate Brooke Kinsella (aka Kelly in the soap) in a small role.

WiLD AT HEART (2006–)

Starring Amanda Holden, Stephen Tompkinson, Hayley Mills, Jessie Wallace

A family drama that's like a 21st-century TV update of *Born Free*. British vet Danny Trevanion (Tompkinson) and his wife Sarah (Holden) and daughter Rosie (Lucy-Jo Hudson) have left England for a new life in South Africa. There they have set up a veterinary practice and wildlife park, but tending to wild animals is a little different to what they have been used to back home.

With the addition of Mills as Sarah's interfering mother, and ex-EastEnder Wallace in Season 3 as an Essex girl who arrives to be with her husband on the competing Mara Reserve, this series boasted some strong roles for women, and great performances from the trio who play them.

Featuring stunning locations, it's worth a look for the surroundings alone, and the various dramas – from a devastating fire to a deadly strain of anthrax – featured in the series are engaging and interesting, too.

 TV Trivia: In real life, the family's house is actually a museum in the Pilanesburg game reserve.

LAWYERS, JUDGES AND TEACHERS

LEGAL DRAMAS, SCHOOL SET COMEDIES.... BUT ALAS, NO *LA LAW*

ALLY MCBEAL (1997–2002)

Starring Calista Flockhart, Greg Germann, Peter MacNichol

There are many reasons to hate *Ally McBeal*. The David E. Kelley law series made a star of annoying warbler Vonda Shephard, who not only sang the theme song but also appeared in the bar, thumping on the piano and screeching through a classic old tune in many of the episodes. The show also gave us the world's thinnest and whiniest leading character in the form of Ally herself (Flockhart, who is *so* much better in her forties as one of the stars of *Brothers and Sisters*), a character who defined herself by the men in her life, yet could never quite settle on which one she damn well wanted. And let's not forget the dancing baby, that freakish figment of Ally's imagination that popped up just when she (and we) didn't want it to. But, those annoyances aside, this series also gave us John 'The Biscuit' Cage (MacNichol), a lawyer who is a bundle of neuroses, ticks and, somehow, superb wisdom; deliciously arrogant slimeball Richard Fish (Greg Germann); and legal secretary/mad inventor Elaine (Jane Krakowski).

The story, of course, centered around lawyer Ally McBeal. Taking a job at Fish's law firm, Ally discovers the love of her life, Billy (Gil Bellows) works there, as does his wife Georgia (Courtney Thorne Smith). Never mind, she has plenty of quirky cases to focus on, weird fantasies to have (usually during court appearances) and inappropriate men to date. The Billy/Ally/Georgia triangle did wear a bit thin, but the introduction of new characters Nell (Portia De Rossi) and the bitchily blunt Ling Wu (Lucy Liu) spiced things up, as did the arrival in 2000 of (finally!) a decent love interest for Ally in the form of Larry Paul (Robert Downey Jr). We'll gloss over the repeat appearances of Dame Edna Everage/Barry Humphries as Claire Otoms, though.

TV Trivia: Larry and Ally were originally scripted to marry, but Robert Downey Jr's arrest on a drug-related offence and subsequent firing from the show meant the storyline had to be abandoned.

THE BEIDERBECKE AFFAIR (1985)

Starring James Bolam, Barbara Flynn, Terence Rigby

The Beiderbecke Affair is an oddity – it's a comedy, a mystery, an ode to jazz and a drama that touches on education and the environment. Blimey. Made, and set, in the mid-eighties, it concerns teachers Trevor Chaplin (Bolam) and Jill Swinburne (Flynn). He's into obscure jazz, she's into the environment, and they are also into each other. But when Trevor orders some records of obscure jazz artist Bix Beiderbecke from a blonde door-to-door saleswoman, things take a strange turn. First he gets the wrong records delivered, and then he discovers a fellow teacher ordered a hedge trimmer from the same woman that turned out to be rather lethal. So Trevor and Jill decide to track down the mysterious lady and find the Beiderbecke LPs, an adventure that takes them to the heart of British bureaucracy and corruption.

Backed by a soundtrack of Beiderbecke's jazz, this is a quirky British comedy drama packed with pithy dialogue and strange characters, including local shady tradesmen Big Al and Little Norm, and the world's most incompetent police officer. Bolam, as always, is a treat in this sly depiction of Thatcherite Britain. The series was followed by the less enjoyable *The Beiderbecke Tapes* in 1987 and *The Beiderbecke Connection* in 1988 – all are available on DVD but the original series is far and away the best.

 TV Trivia: Bix Beiderbecke is considered the first great white cornet player. He died of pneuomia, aged 28, in 1931.

BOSTON LEGAL (2004–)

Starring James Spader, William Shatner, Candice Bergen

He's travelled through distant galaxies armed with just a phaser and his alien-friendly charisma, patrolled the streets of LA in a too-tight policeman's uniform on *TJ Hooker*, murdered classic songs like 'Lucy In The Sky With Diamonds' by reciting them on record, deadpan – and yet, with all those impressive credits behind him, William Shatner's greatest achievement will probably be his unforgettable turn in *Boston Legal* as the obnoxious, arrogant, pig-headed Denny Crane (a role which won him an Emmy in 2005). Chewing the scenery with gusto and spitting it out with verve, Shatner finally got the role he was born to play, and boy, does it look like he is loving it. (Trek fans will notice the classic sci-fi series is often alluded to in this show).

Created by David E. Kelley, who had already dipped his toe in the lawyer pool with the series *Ally McBeal* and *The Practice* (which *Boston Legal* is spun off from), *Boston Legal* is set at the legal practice of Crane, Poole and Schmidt in Boston. Led by Denny, the team – which includes smarmy Alan Shore (Spader, doing sleaze as only he can), Shirley Schmidt (Bergen) and pouty Tara (Rhona Mitra) – tackle quirky and sometimes utterly ludicrous cases, such as a battle over a professor's collection of Victorian erotica, or the defense of an attorney who is arrested after driving in the carpool lane of the freeway with a blow-up doll in the passenger seat of his car. Surprisingly thought-provoking when it isn't being completely bonkers, this series is a must for those who like weird lawyer shows without a whining woman as the central character (yes, you, Ally McBeal).

 TV Trivia: Bill Clinton is a fan of the series, even though they made fun of him in a Season 2 episode.

BROMWELL HIGH (2005)

Voices by Jo Wyatt, Gina Yashere, Nina Conti

An animated adult comedy from Channel 4, this series ran for 13 episodes (only six were shown in the UK) and depicted life at a fictional South London comprehensive. Three of the students there that we meet are Natella (Wyatt), an Asian prodigy born in London who was sent to live in a tiny, poor and remote village in India before coming to Bromwell High (which perhaps explains her superior intellect, since she avoided the British education system until now), Keisha (Yashere), who had been expelled from every school in South London by the age of eight, including a canine obedience class, and Latrina (Conti), so named because her mother gave birth to her on the toilet. And if you think they sound bad, wait till you meet their teachers, including Iqbal the headmaster, who won the school in a poker game, Mr Bibby (voiced by Graeme Garden), who has links with the slave trade, and Martin Jackson, who took five years to be appointed to the role of head of mathematics, despite being the school's only maths teacher.

A joint British/Canadian production, this is certainly jam-packed with politically incorrect humour in the *South Park* vein, and if you surrender yourself to its subversive madness, it's a truly eye-wateringly funny blast of rudeness.

 TV Trivia: The series was originally to be called *Streatham Hill*, but the name was changed following complaints from schools in the real Streatham, South London.

DAMAGES (2007–)

Starring Glenn Close, Rose Byrne

It seems all the best movie actors are doing TV now, from Alec Baldwin in *30 Rock* to Kiefer Sutherland in *24*. In this gripping series it is Glenn Close who gets to shine as a tough, win-at-all-costs lawyer Patty who is breaking in (or maybe just breaking) a new protégé (Byrne as Ellen Parsons) while also taking on a high-profile case against the powerful Arthur Frobisher (Ted Danson). What makes this different from many legal shows is that nothing here is what it seems – good guys are bad, bad guys may be nicer than you first think – and just as you think you have it all figured out, the show twists in another direction, flashing forward a few months to show Ellen in prison for murder, her boyfriend dead, lying in the bath at her apartment, while everyone else acts suspiciously.

Sharply written, and with a strong supporting cast that includes Tate Donovan and Peter Riegert, this is a must for fans of law/thriller/drama series, and before the end of the first episode is over you'll see why Close has already won a Golden Globe for her performance.

 TV Trivia: Glenn Close was not first choice for her memorable role in *Fatal Attraction* – Debra Winger, Barbara Hershey and Miranda Richardson were all considered for the part.

HOPE AND GLORY (1999–2000)

Starring Lenny Henry, Amanda Redman, Gillian Kearney, Phyllis Logan

Comedian Lenny Henry showed his more serious side for this BBC drama set in a run-down comprehensive school. Based on a real man – acclaimed head teacher William Atkinson – Henry's character Ian George leaves his job as head of a well-funded, exclusive school to take on the thankless task of turning Hope Park Comprehensive around. And it's not an easy task – the sixth-form room is derelict following an arson attack, the previous head teacher (Peter Davison) delivers a farewell speech in which he comments on how worthless his students are, and George is faced with staffing, funding and disciplinary problems from his first day.

Running for three series, the show portrayed the gritty side of British schooling, mixed with melodrama and even the occasional romance. Henry is terrific in his first long-running dramatic TV role, but plot-wise there is nothing here that you wouldn't expect to find in an average 1980s episode of *Grange Hill*.

TV Trivia: *Hope and Glory* **was filmed at Langleybury School in Three Rivers, Hertfordshire.**

JAG (1995–2005)

Starring David James Elliott, Catherine Bell, Patrick Labyourteaux

Top Gun meets *A Few Good Men* (except without Tom Cruise, obviously) for this series set in the Judge Advocate General's office – the place for lawyers whose job it is to prosecute or defend US Marines and Naval Officers who have got themselves into sticky legal situations. Focusing on fighter pilot turned lawyer Harmon Rabb (chisel-jawed Elliott), the show has our hero defending good honest soldiers' honours, flying through the skies ready to bomb anyone threatening America's supremacy, and kicking the occasional bad guy butt.

Made by NBC in the US, the series initially flopped, but then another TV channel (CBS) stepped in, revived it, and went on to make the show for another nine seasons (confusingly, some of the actors were dumped during the transition, with new ones brought on board to play the same roles). It's hard to see why the show lasted so long or gained such a cult following, as it's very formulaic and quite dull stuff that seems to coast by on the appeal of men in uniform, some macho posturing and a few tense flying scenes and battle footage, some of which were apparently taken from the cutting room floors of *Top Gun* and other action movies.

For non-Americans, it's also a bit overly patriotic – if the good old US of A isn't trumpeted loudly in an episode, you can be sure there'll be a prominent Stars And Stripes flag flickering in the breeze before the episode is over.

 TV Trivia: Series creator Donald P. Bellisario served in the marines himself – and one of the marines he served closely with was Lee Harvey Oswald.

JUDGE JOHN DEED (2001–2007)

Starring Martin Shaw, Jenny Seagrove, Barbara Thorn, Donald Sinden

Who knew that under those robes and ridiculous white wigs judges could be sexy? As Judge John Deed, Martin Shaw certainly adds a bit of raunch to the revered career as he has a fumble with his daughter's friend, an affair with fellow judge Sir Ian Rochester's wife, and an on-off relationship with colleague Jo Mills (Seagrove). Where he finds the energy to seduce all these women, trade quips with his 'ice queen' ex-wife (Caroline Langrishe), *and* rule on complex cases is anyone's guess.

Shaw gets his best role since Doyle in *The Professionals* in this drama that mixes Deed's private life with such interesting legal cases as a doctor accused of killing an elderly cancer patient, an MP accused of murdering his boyfriend with a frying pan, a reality show contestant who killed another competitor on camera, and a doctor who wants to be able to cease resuscitating a young child with a very weak heart if the toddler's heart stops again, against the wishes of the parents.

The series has been criticised for upping the drama and ignoring the accuracy of the British legal system – in just about every episode, Deeds seems to be presiding over a case involving his ex-wife or his lover/colleague, leaving us to wonder where all the other lawyers are – and also complaints were made about the episode 'Heart Of Darkness', which portrayed a case that featured a link between the MMR jab and autism, which has not been proved by the medical establishment (the original version of this episode has not been repeated on TV). But, as legal dramas go, this is entertaining stuff that should appeal to fans of lawyerly entertainment in the vein of *LA Law*.

 TV Trivia: Martin Shaw's gown and wig are authentic and cost the production £7,600 from a legal outfitter.

KAVANAGH QC (1995–2001)

Starring John Thaw, Anna Chancellor, Lisa Harrow

The last series Thaw made (he died of cancer in 2002) remains an enjoyable slice of legal life, as James Kavanagh, QC, oversees various criminal cases. Unlike Thaw's other famous TV character, Inspector Morse, Kavanagh doesn't have a posh background – he's a working-class boy from Bolton – and he's prepared to take on the legal establishment (of course) if it will win him a case.

While the cases are formulaic – his client usually looks like he'll be convicted until Kavanagh uncovers a twist in the case – the scenes away from the court chambers are far more interesting (and even moving) as they deal with the barrister's family life. His wife, Lizzie (Harrow), is diagnosed with cancer and his daughter Kate (Daisy Bates) has various boyfriend problems, which includes her having an affair with her tutor at Cambridge University, so it's surprising Kavanagh is rarely distracted during his cases. A well performed, solid legal drama.

 TV Trivia: Daisy Bates is the daughter of actor Ralph Bates, and also a distant descendant of Louis Pasteur.

KiNGDOM (2007–)

Starring Stephen Fry, Karl Davies, Hermione Norris, Celia Imrie

Stephen Fry executive produces and stars in this drama as Peter Kingdom, a solicitor with a small practice in the fictional town of Market Shipborough, Norfolk. When he's not dealing with the quirky local characters who seek his legal advice, Kingdom returns home to the house he shares with his annoying sister, Beatrice (a rather miscast Norris, but perhaps the fact that she is the wife of series creator Simon Wheeler explains her presence), and the pair try to muddle through life while dealing with the mysterious disappearance of their brother, Simon, who vanished at sea but may not have died as they previously assumed.

Fry's first TV series since *Jeeves and Wooster* ended in 1993, this is a cosy affair rather than a ground-breaking one, and is a perfect example of inoffensive, mildly amusing Sunday night telly (it was shown in the same time slot that the equally affable *Foyle's War* had been shown previously). Fry's character is likeable and kind (much like Fry himself), and what wit there is comes courtesy of Tony Slattery as Sidney Snell, a man whose main purpose in life seems to be to sue the local council for various infractions and the always wonderful Phyllida Law as Peter's aunt Auriel. It's a bit smug in places, and as predictable as a wet English June, but Fry is still one of the best living British actors and any TV show with him deserves a chance.

 TV Trivia: When the series began, numerous Norfolk residents wrote and phoned ITV to complain that the actors' Norfolk accents were inaccurate and offensive.

MiND YOUR LANGUAGE (1977–1979. 1986)

Starring Barry Evans, George Camiller, Jacki Harding

A series that couldn't possibly be broadcast now due to its racial stereotypes, *Mind Your Language* was a sitcom set in an adult education college where often-bewildered teacher Jeremy Brown (Evans) attempted to teach a group of immigrants the English language. Proving that quite a lot of TV-watching Brits do view everyone from overseas as Johnny Bloody Foreigner, the successful show (both here and, surprisingly, abroad) was packed with character clichés, from efficient German Anna Schmidt (Harding) to voluptuous French tease Danielle Favre (Françoise Pascal), anti-Sikh Muslim Ali (Dino Shafeek) to anti-Muslim Sikh Ranjeet (Albert Moses). And there's even a lovable cockney, caretaker Sid (Tommy Godfrey), who supplies much of the humour as he tries to teach some of the students to speak like him.

A prime example of unsophisticated British comedy, the series ran for 42 episodes – 29 from 1977 to 1979 and then a final 13 in 1986 with some of the original cast returning – and was remade in the US as *What A Country!*

 TV Trivia: Françoise Pascal was originally a dancer on *Top of the Pops*.

MURDER ONE (1995–1997)

Starring Daniel Benzali, Anthony LaPaglia, Mary McCormack

This law drama from Steven Bochco was based on a clever idea – it followed just one case over the entire first season. Theodore 'Teddy' Hoffman (Benzali) and his legal team are hired to defend Neil Avedon (Jason Gedrick), a young, drug and alcohol-addicted actor who is accused of the murder of 15-year-old Jessica Costello. As the series unfolds, so does the case, which has links to the richest man in town, Richard Cross (the marvellously sleazy Stanley Tucci), a man with many secrets and a penchant for kinky sex.

Covering just one case over 23 episodes would seem like a stretch, but this worked really well thanks to interesting characters, a gripping central story, a great supporting cast (including Patricia Clarkson as Hoffman's wife and Barbara Bosson as DA Miriam Grasso) and two simmering performances from Benzali and Tucci. Unfortunately, it wasn't a huge ratings success, so the series was revamped for the second (and final) season. The gruff Benzali was out (his character trying to work out marital problems caused by the murder trial, we were told) and Anthony LaPaglia was brought in to play former prosecuting lawyer Jimmy Wyler, while the one-case-per-season idea was dumped and Wyler got to tackle three cases while also dealing with ditching his morality now he was working for the defence. One of the best American legal dramas of recent years.

TV Trivia: Co-star Barbara Bosson was married to creator Bochco when this series was made – she also appeared in his show *Hill Street Blues* (see p.12) and *LA Law* (currently unavailable on DVD in the UK).

NEW STREET LAW (2006–2007)

Starring John Hannah, John Thomson, Lisa Faulkner, Paul Freeman

A dull but earnest BBC drama about rival barristers chambers in Manchester: one is headed by working-class lawyer Jack Roper (Hannah) and the other by his former mentor, Laurence Scammel (Freeman). As you'd expect, various 'interesting' characters populate their two chambers: Jack has Charlie Darling (Thomson) on his team, as well as Laurence's daughter Laura (Faulkner), while Laurence has his determined wife Honor (Penny Downie) behind him.

Written by co-creator Matthew Hall, who has a legal background, this is mainly set in the courts and focuses on issues as much as it does character. It is, therefore, quite dry, although a cliffhanger ending to both seasons of the show spiced things up a little. Unfortunately, in July 2007 it was announced that the BBC would not be making any more episodes, leaving audiences to forever wonder what had happened to their favourite characters.

 TV Trivia: John Hannah was rumoured to be the first choice for the role of Charlie in *Lost* (the role went to Dominic Monaghan).

PLEASE, SiR! (1968–1972)

Starring John Alderton, Deryck Guyler, Joan Sanderson

A fun sitcom set in a South London comprehensive, *Please, Sir!* ran for four years (only the first two seasons are funny, though, as cast members began to change in Season 3), and starred John Alderton as Bernard Hedges (nicknamed 'Privet' by his class), the newly qualified teacher of class 5C. While most of his fellow teachers have abandoned all hope in their students, Hedges is determined to find the good in his pupils, often to the annoyance of headmaster Mr Cromwell (Noel Howlett) and Deputy Head Doris Ewell (Sanderson).

Fenn Street School certainly has an interesting cast of characters, from former Desert Rat/caretaker Norman (Guyler) to well-past-retirement-age teacher Mr Smith (who regularly nods off in lessons), but it is the out of control pupils who steal the show, including Catholic girl Maureen (Liz Gebhardt), who has a crush on Hedges, hard nut Eric (Peter Cleall) and lovely Dennis (Peter Denyer), whose father beats him and his mother. Fifty-five episodes were made, plus a movie, and there was a spin-off series, *The Fenn Street Gang*, that followed the kids as they left school and tried to make it in the world (the series is available on DVD).

TV Trivia: Most of the actors playing the pupils were well past their teenage years – Gebhardt was 23, Denyer was 21 and Cleall was 24 when the series began – and John Alderton was only a few years older, at 28!

THE PRACTICE (1997–2004)

Starring Dylan McDermott, Camryn Manheim, Lara Flynn Boyle

A big success in the US but something of a flop in the UK (mainly due to ITV scheduling it to be shown in the early hours), *The Practice* not only ran for eight seasons but also produced a very successful spin-off series, *Boston Legal* (see review, p.329). As the series begins, Bobby Donnell (McDermott) has just three attorneys working with him – Ellenor Frutt (Manheim), Lindsay Dole (Kelli Williams) and Eugene Young (Steve Harris) – alongside receptionist Rebecca (Lisa Gay Hamilton). Donnell's dream was to have a law practice that helped the innocent, but financial struggles mean he has compromised a little, and now he takes on the cases of drug dealers and other obvious criminals to pay the bills.

With a quirky cast of characters added along the way, including Michael Badalucco as Jimmy and Boyle as Assistant District Attorney Helen Gamble, this had occasional moments of humour but – unlike *Legal* and creator David E. Kelly's other law show, *Ally McBeal* – in the main it was all pretty serious, with the criminal cases the lawyers worked on often mirroring serious real-life news stories.

At the end of the seventh season, the show's ratings had slumped and the series was expected to be cancelled. Instead, the production company drastically slashed the show's budget – meaning the main six cast members, including McDermott and Boyle – were fired and James Spader (as Alan Shore) and Rhona Mitra (as Tara Wilson) were added to the cast. One final season was made, and then the two actors (and their characters) made the transition to *Boston Legal*.

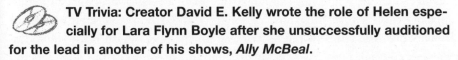 **TV Trivia: Creator David E. Kelly wrote the role of Helen especially for Lara Flynn Boyle after she unsuccessfully auditioned for the lead in another of his shows, *Ally McBeal*.**

RUMPOLE OF THE BAILEY (1978–1992)

Starring Leo McKern, Peter Bowles, Peggy Thorpe-Bates

Based on a character created by John Mortimer, *Rumpole of The Bailey* introduced the world to the grumpy, self-righteous, dogged anti-hero that was Horace Rumpole (McKern), a criminal defence barrister who thunders along the historical corridors and court rooms of the Old Bailey. A connoisseur of cheap red wine who has a fascination for crime, Rumpole confuses his colleagues – including head of chambers Guthrie Featherstone (Bowles) – who don't understand why he enjoys defending low-lifes when he could aspire to much more. His wife, Hilda (Thorpe-Bates for the first three seasons, then Marion Mathie), whom he thinks of as 'She Who Must Be Obeyed' is equally puzzled by Rumpole's career choices, and conspires with their son, Nick, to convince her husband that retirement is the answer.

One of the most enjoyable characters to emerge from seventies TV, Rumpole has a love of literature, a sharp wit and a healthy disregard for his peers that makes him somehow both infuriating and utterly lovable. McKern is simply marvellous in the role of the barrister who likes a good whodunnit in between trips to the Pommeroy wine bar. So utterly, deliciously English, the DVDs should come with their own slice of steak and kidney pudding.

 TV Trivia: Although he sounds convincingly British in the series, Leo McKern was actually Australian. He moved to England, aged 26, in 1946.

SHARK (2006–)

Starring James Woods, Danielle Panabaker, Sophina Brown

Any series that has James Woods grumping, growling and stomping across our TV screens can't be too bad, even if this show is essentially *House MD*, but with a lawyer instead of a doctor at its centre. Sebastian Stark (Woods) is the sarcastic, brilliant attorney who makes a lot of money defending bad guys – until the day a wife-beater he got acquitted goes home and murders her. Luckily, at just the same time the LA mayor (Carlos Gomez) offers him the chance to lead a unit that will handle high-profile cases from the prosecutor's office.

Unfortunately, while this show boasted Spike Lee as a director of the first episode, there's very little new or exciting about it. We've seen numerous lawyers over the years switch to working for the good guys to ease their consciences (though here, there is surprisingly no mention of the huge pay cut Shark will have to endure) on TV and film, and many more featuring gruff, win-at-any-cost lawyers. And while Woods is his usual intense, watchable self (plus there's the nice addition of Panabaker as his daughter), the other lawyers in the show are so dull you'll forget them before they have left the scene. Disappointing.

 TV Trivia: James Woods is a reserve officer in the LA Police Department.

TEACHERS (2001–2004)

Starring Andrew Lincoln, Gillian Bevan, Tamzin Malleson

Any parent with a child at secondary school watched this comedy drama with a mixture of horror and hands-over-eyes amusement. Following a group of school staff inside and outside the classrooms, the show depicted a collection of hapless teachers no sensible parent would want within a million miles of their child, from sex kitten Penny (Malleson), mid-life crisis-suffering Bob (Lloyd McGuire) and atheist Religious Studies teacher Ben (Mathew Horne) to lazy biology teacher Lindsay (Vicky Hall) and childish new games teacher Simon (Lincoln).

Unfortunately, by the fourth (and final) season, most of the more entertaining cast members, including Lincoln, had left the series, and the series limped along to its conclusion. The first two series are the best (the first has Simon as the central character, but it became more of an ensemble piece by series two), with smart scripts, nice performances and a good mix of comedy, drama and the occasional supporting performance by a donkey (don't ask).

 TV Trivia: An American version of the series was made in 2006 but was cancelled after six episodes.

TO SERVE THEM ALL MY DAYS (1980)

Starring John Duttine, Frank Middlemass, Belinda Lang

A simply lovely slice of stiff-upper-lipped drama, based on the RF Delderfield novel of the same name. Wounded and shell-shocked soldier David Powlett-Jones (Duttine) returns from the trenches of World War I and decides to take up teaching, applying for a position as history master at Bamflyde boys' boarding school in Devon. While David has no formal education, the headmaster, Algy Herries (Middlemass) believes he is the right man for the job, and David soon settles into his new position.

There's some humour supplied by one of David's fellow teachers, Howarth (Alan MacNaughton) and the pupils, but this series that spans over two decades also has a big dollop of personal tragedy for David that will have most viewers reaching for the tissues. A moving depiction of Britain between the two world wars that touches on class, education and the horrors of battles as well as romance and friendship, this is a classic tale, beautifully adapted by Andrew Davies (*Bleak House*, *Daniel Deronda*).

 TV Trivia: John Duttine also starred in another adaptation of a RF Delderfield, *People Like Us* (based on the novels *The*

Dreaming Suburb and *The Avenue Goes To War*), but it isn't available on DVD.

WATERLOO ROAD (2006–)

Starring Jill Halfpenny, Jamie Glover, Jason Merrells, Angela Griffin

Footballers' Wives and *Bad Girls* creator Ann McManus is a former English teacher, so drew from experience for this drama set in the fictional Waterloo Road Comprehensive. Beginning when the headmaster has a nervous break-down, leaving his deputy Jack Rimmer (Merrells), to take on the role, the series follows the staff and pupils of a failing school as attempts are made to turn it into a decently performing one. This includes Rimmer's hiring of private school teacher Andrew Treneman (Glover), who wants the opportunity to instruct the disadvantaged kids and use strict discipline to bring them into line. Meanwhile, two engaged teachers – Tom (Jason Done) and Lorna (Camilla Power) – split up, only for Tom to reveal he loves another member of staff, drama teacher Izzie (Halfpenny), who has problems of her own with an irresponsible ex-husband and two kids. And then there are the pupils, including a pregnant teen and the school bully...

A sometimes gritty but often soap-like look at life at an English compre-hensive that angered some headmasters for allegedly damaging the reputation of British schools, *Waterloo Road* has enough betrayals, nasty pupils and over-sexed teachers to make any parent of a school-age child fall faint. It's riveting viewing, however, with a solid cast – new cast members including Christine Tremarco arrived for Series 2, and a major cast member left at the end of that series, while Neil Morrissey and Chris Geere were among those joining for Series 3.

 TV Trivia: The school used for the series is Hilltop Primary School in Rochdale, Greater Manchester.

TV'S MOST MEMORABLE BIRTHS, MARRIAGES AND DEATHS...

BIRTHS

BABY DAMIEN. SON OF RAQUEL AND DEL-BOY TROTTER(1991) – ONLY FOOLS AND HORSES.

Del's brother Rodney suggested the name Damien – from the *Omen* movies – as a joke, but Del took it seriously.

BABY DAVID. SON OF DENISE AND DAVE BEST (1999) – THE ROYLE FAMILY

Denise went into labour in the Royle family bathroom, and gave birth during the Christmas special.

ROBIN'S GREEN ALIEN BABY (1984) – 'V'

After a one-night stand with an alien, Robin gives birth to a normal baby girl and then a green lizard, that growls...

SONIA HAS MARTIN FOWLER'S BABY (2000) – EASTENDERS

Teenager Sonia doesn't even know she is pregnant till she has stomach pains, which surprises boyfriend Jamie as they haven't had sex yet...

PHOEBE AND HER BROTHER'S TRIPLETS (1998) – FRIENDS

On the 100th episode, Phoebe gives birth as a surrogate to her brother's three babies...

MARRIAGES

SCOTT AND CHARLENE GET HITCHED (1987) – NEIGHBOURS

And British schoolkids bunked off school to see them go down the aisle to the tune of Angry Anderson's 'Suddenly'.

NILES AND DAPHNE (2003) – FRASIER

For 10 years everyone wondered whether Niles' love for Daphne would be requited, and in a Reno ceremony they finally got hitched. Then got hitched twice more for the benefit of their relatives.

SONNY CROCKETT AND CAITLIN DAVIES (1988) – MIAMI VICE

Sockless Sonny marries rockstar Caitlin (played by Sheena Easton) and then bad guys shoot her!

MICHAELA AND SULLY (1995) – DR QUINN. MEDICINE WOMAN

A double episode showing Dr Mike and hunky Sully get married made fans happy.

AMANDA AND THE PRINCE OF MOLDAVIA (1985) – DYNASTY

Amanda Carrington marries but then war breaks out in her new hubby's principality and all the guests are gunned down.

DEATHS

CHARLIE (2007) – LOST

Having been told he would die by future-seeing Desmond, Charlie dives down to the underwater station and, when an explosion floods it, shuts himself in and drowns to save his friend.

BRIAN TILSLEY (1989) – CORONATION STREET

Corrie bad boy came to the aid of a woman being hassled and was shockingly stabbed outside a nightclub.

NATE (2005) – SIX FEET UNDER

We knew he had a brain tumour, but the doctors said he would be fine. Then Nate dies suddenly while brother David snoozes at his bedside.

RALPHIE (2002) – THE SOPRANOS

He wasn't the first to die violently in the series (remember Janice shooting Richie Aprile, or Big Pussy being thrown overboard), but Ralphie's was the most shocking – choked to death by Tony Soprano, then dismembered, with his head and hands buried in a field and his body in a quarry.

TERI BAUER (2002) – '24'

On Jack Bauer's first longest day, his missus was kidnapped, raped, suffered amnesia and then tied up by nasty Nina, before being fatally shot in the stomach.

AND FIVE UNINTENTIONALLY FUNNY DEMISES

Den walking along the canal and being shot by a man hiding a gun in a bunch of daffodils – *EastEnders*, 1991.

Dawson's dad Mitch, crashing his car while holding an ice cream – *Dawson's Creek*, 2001.

Rosalind steps into an empty lift shaft and plummets to her death – *LA Law*, 1991

Ken Barlow's wife Valerie being electrocuted by her hairdryer – *Coronation Street*, 1971.

Tiffany being hit by Frank Butcher in the world's slowest moving car (New Year's Eve, 1998), only equalled by Jamie being hit by Martin while buying some flowers (Christmas Day, 2002) – *EastEnders*.

CONTEMPORARY DRAMA

ALAS, MANY OF THE OLDER CLASSIC AND POPULAR DRAMAS, SUCH AS *CATHY COME HOME*, *BOYS FROM THE BLACKSTUFF* AND THE GROUNDBREAKING *TRAFFIK*, ARE UNAVAILABLE (OR VERY HARD TO FIND) ON DVD...

ABIGAIL'S PARTY (1977)

Starring Alison Steadman, John Salthouse

Shown as part of the 'Play For Today' strand on the BBC, this one-off drama was written and directed by filmmaker Mike Leigh and starred his then-wife Alison Steadman. She's utterly, horrendously marvellous as Beverly, the pretentious middle-class housewife who has invited new neighbours Angela and Tony over for drinks, along with divorcée Sue, whose daughter Abigail is throwing a party at her house two doors down.

A look at just how appalling people can be, this evening of suburban entertaining is almost excruciating to watch as all the characters are so unlikeable – but that's what also makes it so riveting. There's Beverly's husband, Lawrence (Tim Stern), who suffers numerous taunts from his wife, while visitor Tony (Salthouse) suffers her flirtations and the whole group endures Lawrence's choice of music (Demis Roussos). Everyone gets drunk, wonders what is happening at Abigail's party, and the evening gets worse and worse before it finally ends. You'd never want to actually spend time in a room with these people, but thanks to the cast's improvisations and Mike Leigh's script and direction, it's still fascinating to watch them from a safe distance.

 TV Trivia: Alison Steadman was pregnant during filming but her voluminous seventies evening dress hid her bump.

AUF WIEDERSEHEN, PET (1983–1986, 2002–2004)

Starring Tim Healy, Kevin Whately, Jimmy Nail, Timothy Spall

Hugely successful series that ran for two seasons on ITV in the 1980s, and was then resurrected over a decade later by the BBC for two more seasons. It is, of course, the comedy drama about a handful of labourers who, in the first series, head off to Germany looking for work where they are thrown together sharing a run-down wooden hut. The magnificent seven who make up the group are reluctant leader Dennis (Healy), henpecked Neville (Whately), bolshy Oz (Nail), bumbling electrician Barry (Spall), jack the lad carpenter Wayne (Gary Holton), plasterer Moxey (Christopher Fairbank) and easygoing Bomber (Pat Roach).

Packed with choice dialogue – much of it xenophobic! – from comedy writers Ian La Frenais and Dick Clement, and likeable performances, the series made stars of its cast. The second series had the lads trying to head to Spain for work while the third, set 15 years later, has the gang reunited for a scheme dreamt up by a disgraced MP (Bill Nighy). The final series, and a Christmas special, had the lads travelling to Cuba and Thailand before ending up back where they started in Germany.

TV Trivia: Gary Holton died during the filming of the second series. Many of his scenes had been filmed, but for others his absence was explained by having his character Wayne being down the pub.

BALLYKISSANGEL (1996–2001)

Starring Stephen Tompkinson, Dervla Kirwin

Young English priest Peter Clifford (Tompkinson) gets more than he bargained for when he takes a position as curate of the church at Ballykissangel, a small rural Irish village. The local townsfolk include stroppy Assumpta (Kirwin), who runs the local pub and is firmly agnostic, slightly dodgy businessman Brian Quigley (Tony Doyle), his daughter Niamh, who wants to marry local garda Ambrose, and Father MacAnally (Niall Toibin).

Anyone nostalgic for a country life from the past (that was probably never as idyllic as depicted here) will love this series set amongst the rolling hills of Ireland. Although modern ways have seeped in – there's even an episode dealing with domestic violence – there's something old-fashioned, warm and cuddly about the series that makes you want to either curl up on the sofa with a warm Guinness or sell up and buy a cottage in the Irish countryside. As much about the locals as central character Peter, the series didn't suffer too much when both Kirwin and Tompkinson departed the show as new, equally interesting characters were added, including a young Colin Farrell as wannabe farmer Danny. Often funny, always lovely stuff.

Farrell fans should note that although he features prominently on the DVD cover for Series 4 and 5, he actually wasn't in the series that much.

TV Trivia: The creator of the series was Kieran Prendiville, one of Esther Rantzen's former *That's Life's* co-presenters.

Big Love (2006–)

Starring Bill Paxton, Jeanne Tripplehorn, Chloe Sevigny, Ginnifer Goodwin

The trend for movie actors to make the switch to TV continued with this series that boasts both Bill Paxton (*Aliens*) and Chloe Sevigny (*Boys Don't Cry*) in the cast. He plays polygamist Bill Henrickson who has three wives – old hand Barb (Tripplehorn), who is the most in control of the unusual situation; selfish spender Nicolette (Sevigny) and the more traditional, girly Margene (Goodwin), who isn't so keen on sharing her husband with two other women. Bill, meanwhile, has his own headaches – as you would, with three demanding wives (he pops Viagra pills as if they were Smarties), seven children and three mortgages (the three houses adjoin each other and share the same backyard).

Set in a suburb of Salt Lake City – the series is at pains to point out that the Mormon church based in this region officially banned polygamy in 1890, although it is believed over 40,000 people still practice multiple marriages in Arizona and Utah – the series focuses on Bill, who clearly got what he wished for yet now isn't so sure, but also shows the daily lives and traumas of his wives and kids, and the people around them. They're not blatant about their arrangement for fear of being arrested (some Mormons despise the practice and will turn followers in) and are also hounded by those who embrace polygamy, like the sinister Roman (Harry Dean Stanton), too.

For a show about such a controversial subject, this isn't as raunchy as you'd expect, and is in fact quite a slow-burning drama. But if you give it a chance, it's interesting stuff, mainly thanks to Paxton's performance, and sharp writing that doesn't sensationalise from a team led by Mark V Olsen and Will Scheffer.

 TV Trivia: Many of the episodes' directors have a background in independent movies, including Michael Lehmann (*Heathers*), Mary Harron (*American Psycho*) and Burr Steers (*Igby Goes Down*).

Bouquet of Barbed Wire (1976)

Starring Frank Finlay, Susan Penhaligon, Sheila Allen

Andrea Newman's steamy novel became an equally eyebrow-raising TV series when it was first broadcast in 1976. Focusing on the naughty middle classes – specifically the Manson family – the story unfolds during one hot summer as neurotic (and, dare we say it, really annoying) daughter Sue (Penhaligon) gets pregnant and marries American Gavin Sorensen (James Aubrey), much to the horror of her father Peter, whose obsessive love for his daughter borders on incest. Meanwhile, Gavin wants to get into the knickers of his new mother-in-law, Cassie (Allen) who has a penchant for sado-masochistic sex – no wonder this show was considered risque!

Just about every character shags every other character – it's almost hard to keep up – and unsurprisingly the saucy series became the topic of everyone's conversation when it was first shown. ITV quickly commissioned Newman to write a follow-up, *Another Bouquet* (which was a TV screenplay before it became a novel), which tied up all the loose ends before it finished (it's also on DVD). It all looks a bit trashy now, and the seventies fashions (check out Finlay's ties, you can't miss them) are a bit distracting, but watch one episode of this romp and you'll be hooked.

 TV Trivia: Andrea Newman also wrote 1990's equally raunchy *A Sense Of Guilt*, in which a middle-aged man (Trevor Eve) has an affair with his best friend's daughter. Tsk tsk.

THE BROTHERS (1972–1976)

Starring Jean Anderson, Richard Easton, Robin Chadwick, Patrick O'Connell

Following the death of their father Robert Hammond, who died whilst having sex with his secretary, Jennifer, brothers Edward (O'Connell), Brian (Easton) and David (Chadwick) inherit the family trucking company in this drama that ran for seven seasons in the UK. The series was a huge success at the time, a soap about family and business as the trio, plus their formidable mother (Anderson), bicker and fight and try to prevent the company from falling into the hands of various characters including slippery Paul Merrony (Colin Baker) and an Australian businessman (Mark McManus).

More about the family's inner turmoils than the business (thank goodness), this was as soapy as *Dallas* but without the glamorous clothes or Texas sunshine. It was filled with glamorous (at least to British audiences) ladies, though, including actresses Gabrielle Drake, Liza Goddard and Kate O'Mara. Tame by today's standards, only the first series is available on DVD.

TV Trivia: For the first few episodes, the role of Edward was played by Glyn Owen before he was replaced for the rest of the show's run by O'Connell.

BROTHERS AND SISTERS (2006–)

Starring Sally Field, Calista Flockhart, Rachel Griffiths, Rob Lowe

Most people missed this terrific US series, co-created by Greg Berlanti (*Everwood*, *Dawson's Creek*) when it was on TV since Channel 4 and E4 kept moving it around the schedules. It's well worth catching up with the humour and dramas of the Californian Walker family that begin when the head of the household, William Walker (Tom Skerritt) dies, and his wife Nora (Sally Field) and grown-up children discover he wasn't exactly a model dad – he'd been defrauding the family business and had a mistress (Patricia Wettig) on the side, too. Not only does this mean there's an illegitimate daughter to deal with (Emily VanCamp), but William's children have to step in and save the business when they have problems of their own. Tommy (Balthazar Getty) doesn't like the fact his sister Sarah (Griffiths) is his boss, Sarah has to deal with leaving her husband Joe (John Pyper-Ferguson) to look after their kids while she works, brother Kevin (Matthew Rhys) is the family lawyer having relationship problems of his own, sibling Justin (Dave Annable) hasn't recovered from serving in the Gulf, while sister Kitty (Flockhart), an acclaimed journalist, moves back home from New York despite not getting on very well with her mother Nora.

Similar in tone to *thirtysomething* (which, surprisingly, isn't on DVD), this show works well because, just as it looks like it is getting too serious, a nice sprinkling of humour (often deliciously black) is thrown in – after all, in real families, it is often in the darkest moments when laughter comes. Flockhart finally casts off the shadow of Ally McBeal, and shares the screen with a host of great actors – Wettig, Annable and Griffiths especially shine, while Sally Field delivers one of her best screen performances as the woman who not only loses a husband but has to share her grief with another woman (an episode in which she and Wettig get into a food fight is particularly funny).

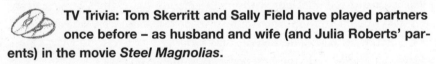 **TV Trivia: Tom Skerritt and Sally Field have played partners once before – as husband and wife (and Julia Roberts' parents) in the movie *Steel Magnolias*.**

THE BUDDHA OF SUBURBIA (1993)

Starring Naveen Andrews, David Bamber, Harish Patel, Brenda Blethyn

Naveen Andrews – now better known as Sayid in *Lost* – gave a strong performance in the title role of this drama based on Hanif Kureshi's novel. Directed by Roger Michell (*The Mother*, *Notting Hill*), the mini-series itself doesn't quite live up to the book from which it is taken (despite Kureshi also writing the script), but it's interesting nonetheless.

Teenager Karim (Andrews) has a Pakistani father, Haroon (Roshan Seth), and an English mother, Margaret (Blethyn). Haroon has become something of a guru to people in their South London suburb, but Karim discovers he is also having sex with one of the attendees of his meditation sessions. Meanwhile, Karim tries to understand his own sexuality while also coming to terms with the way English-born Indians like himself are treated by their middle-class neighbours.

A well-played series set during the seventies and eighties, filled with strong characters and performances, especially from Andrews, Seth, Harish Patel and Nisha Nayar (as Karim's friend who is being forced into an arranged marriage). David Bowie composed the theme song and released an album of music inspired by the series.

 TV Trivia: Andrews' first screen role was in another Hanif Kureshi adaptation, 1991's *London Kills Me*.

CALiFORNiCATiON (2007–)

Starring David Duchovny, Natasha McElhone, Evan Handler

Great title (though the Red Hot Chili Peppers had it first) and a nice return to the small screen for *The X-Files'* David Duchovny. He plays Hank, a Los Angeles-based writer with writer's block, who is trying (and usually failing) to juggle a disapproving ex-girlfriend (McElhone), a daughter (Madeleine Martin), and an appetite for beautiful women. While Hank seems to have it all – his previous book has been made into a movie with 'Tom and Katie', no less – he mopes about, pining for his ex and, truth be told, comes across as a whiny, lecherous fortysomething who needs a good smack round the head.

And that's really the problem with this series – despite Duchovny's charm, Hank is just too sulky to be likeable, even when he finds himself in funny situations (such as when he vomits on an expensive painting belonging to his ex's new beau). Unlike Larry David in *Curb Your Enthusiasm*, Hank isn't jaw-droppingly annoying, he's just miserable, and unless he cheers up a bit, it's unlikely you'll want to stick around to see whether his life brightens up in the California sunshine.

 TV Trivia: Duchovny's screen debut was in 1988's *Working Girl*, as one of the guests hiding in the bathroom at Tess's (Melanie Griffith) surprise party.

CHANCER (1990–1991)

Starring Clive Owen, Simon Shepherd, Leslie Phillips

Only 20 episodes of this series were made but they were enough to establish star Clive Owen as a heartthrob in his role as wide-boy wheeler-dealer Derek Love (known in the first series as Stephen Crane before his past is revealed). The series begins with Stephen/Derek trying to help out the ailing car company Douglas Motors by tricking his own boss, while also trying to keep his love life on track (girlfriend Jo, played by Susannah Harker, isn't too impressed that Victoria Douglas, played by Lynsey Baxter, has taken a shine to him).

By the second series, things had got more gritty and gripping (it is far better than the first series) – Stephen had just been released from jail as the series begins – and Owen is certainly charming and watchable as the lovable rogue. And while it has dated terribly in terms of the socio-political comment in the show and the technology (check out the brick-sized mobile phones), it remains a satisfying drama that mixes Shakespearian-style tragedy and drama with a pithy script. And yes, Clive Owen never looked so yummy.

 TV Trivia: Clive Owen is married to actress Sarah Jane Fenton, who played Juliet to his Romeo in a theatre production.

COLD FEET (1997–2003)

Starring Helen Baxendale, James Nesbitt, Hermione Norris, Fay Ripley, John Thomson

Adam (Nesbitt) suffers from cold feet when it comes to relationships but when he literally crashes into Rachel (Baxendale) – he backs into her car – it looks like he may have finally found a woman he can commit to. If she can get over her old boyfriend, and divorce her husband. Meanwhile Adam's best friend Peter (Thomson) and his wife Jenny (Ripley) are trying for a baby even though he secretly doesn't feel ready to be a dad, and Rachel's friend Karen (Norris) has a child and a husband (Robert Bathurst) who is always at work.

Often compared to *Friends*, this is actually more similar to *thirtysomething* as the characters grapple with impending middle age and the fear of commitment rather than the problems of the young. It's also far more serious than the American sitcom (although there is humour to be had) and there are moving moments and even tragedy mixed in with the more light-hearted ones. In fact, the only real similarity to *Friends* is that there are six main cast members and they all have great chemistry together on screen, and that Helen Baxendale popped up briefly to play Ross' annoying British girlfriend on *Friends*. The series ran for five series and 32 episodes, ending with a death that left viewers in shock and a subsequent well-played and scripted but terribly depressing funeral.

TV Trivia: Apparently, Portmeiron, where a scene from the funeral episode was filmed, saw an increase in the number of people who wanted to marry there after the episode was shown.

CUTTING IT (2002–2005)

Starring Sarah Parish, Angela Griffin, Jason Merrells, Amanda Holden

A drama set in a hair salon named Henshall Ferraday, run by Allie Henshall (Parish) and her lover/business partner Gavin Ferraday (Merrells). Together with Darcey (Griffin) and Sydney (Sian Reeves), the pair cut hair and plan on expanding – until they discover the shop that they were going to buy has been snapped up by Allie's ex, Finn (Ben Daniels), and his wife Mia (Holden). And to complicate things further, Finn wants Allie back.

There are numerous soapy twists and turns in the lives of the snippers, as hidden pregnancies come to lights as well as secret affairs, arson, and life-threatening diseases (do these people ever actually have time to cut anyone's hair?) It's silly indeed, and as frothy as a cappuccino with extra foam, but Parish and the cast are watchable enough if there's nothing else on.

TV Trivia: As research, Merrells received intensive training with hairdresser John Neale, who works with celebrity hairdresser Nicky Clarke.

THE DARLING BUDS OF MAY (1991–1993)

Starring David Jason, Pam Ferris, Catherine Zeta Jones

The series that made Catherine Zeta Jones a star as Mariette, the daughter of Ma (Ferris) and Pop Larkin (Jason), in this series based on the stories of HE Bates. Set in fifties Britain, the series was a light-hearted look at happy, eccentric farm folk, the Larkins – and also included a handful of other kids, former city boy Charlie (Philip Franks), who comes to get Pop Larkin to pay his taxes then never leaves, and a gaggle of animals. Surprisingly for such a simple premise, the show managed to beat just about everything else in the ratings, including long-established soaps. Perhaps we all need a little glimpse at simpler times to cheer us up.

It all looks very sun-drenched and picturesque (they must have been very lucky with the weather while filming in Kent) – even the Rolls Royce the family buy is a sunny yellow – and everyone is cheery and cheeky (Pop's catchphrase is 'perfick!'). However, while to many people that is the show's charm (it's so relentlessly *nice*), it can get a bit grating when you've heard Jason say the p-word for the 10,000th time in one episode. Twenty episodes were made.

 TV Trivia: One of Catherine Zeta Jones' best friends is gravel-voiced Bonnie Tyler, who sang at her wedding to Michael Douglas.

DESPERATE HOUSEWIVES (2004–)

Starring Marcia Cross, Teri Hatcher, Felicity Huffman, Eva Longoria, Nicolette Sheridan

Part comedy, part dark drama and part soap, *Desperate Housewives* became an instant hit as it followed the lives, loves and betrayals – and a few stranger secrets – of a group of women and their spouses who live in the suburban street Wisteria Lane. Narrated by the dead Mary Alice Young (Brenda Strong), one of the housewives who has shocked her friends with her mysterious suicide, the first season had her death as a running theme – why did she do it? Was she murdered? And what did her husband Paul dig up in the garden? – but also focused on the relationships of her friends. There's Bree (Cross), whose home is immaculate but whose marriage and children are less easy to control; the scatty divorcee Susan (Hatcher) and her teenage daughter Julie (Andrea Bowen); truly desperate housewife Lynette, who is trying to raise her unruly brood when she would rather be at work like her husband Tom (Doug Savant); ex-model Gabrielle (Longoria), who is having an affair with young gardener John under the nose of her hot-headed Latin husband Carlos (Ricardo Chavira); and busty blonde neighbour Edie (Sheridan), who is not the sort of woman you'd ever leave alone in a room with your spouse. Oh, and there's also new-to-the-neighbourhood Mike Delfino (James Denton), who catches both Edie's and Susan's eye, but may have the scariest secrets of all of them.

The first season of this guilty pleasure (it's about as intellectually stimulating as jelly) mixed fun – usually the pratfalls of Susan, Lynette's haphazard life and adventures of Gabrielle – with serious stuff, all wrapped up in designer clothing (no one is allowed to move into Wisteria Lane, it seems, without being exceedingly attractive). The mystery of Mary Alice's death was wrapped up by the end of Season 1, so a new, less successful mystery was introduced for Season 2 (just what have new neighbours the Applewhites got in their basement), along with plot twists such as an obsessive admirer for

Bree, and a surrogacy arrangement for Carlos and Gabrielle. It's a disappointing offering, but things picked up in Season 3 thanks to the introduction of Kyle Maclachlan as the possibly sinister Orson (he first appears at the end of Season 2), while Dana Delaney and *Firefly*'s Nathan Fillion were welcome additions for Season 4.

 TV Trivia: All the episodes are named after songs by Broadway composers such as Irving Berlin, Stephen Sondheim and Cole Porter.

EDGE OF DARKNESS (1985)

Starring Bob Peck, Joe Don Baker, Joanne Whalley

A thriller that held you in its grip from the first scene and didn't let you go until the end credits, *Edge of Darkness* was deservedly lavished with praise and a few awards (including four BAFTAs) when it was first shown in 1985. Directed by Martin Campbell, who went on to make the James Bond movies *GoldenEye* and *Casino Royale*, and written by Kennedy Martin (*Z Cars*, *The Sweeney*), the six-part drama followed Yorkshire CID detective Ronald Craven as he investigated the murder of his anti-nuclear campaigner daughter (Whalley), who was killed in front of him. His bosses believe the bullet was meant for Craven, but as he begins to investigate on his own, he discovers a world of intrigue mixed in with environmental politics and governmental secrets and soon becomes sceptical about the powers that be.

Made at a time when membership of the CND was at an all-time high and everyone from students to the elderly were questioning the government involvement in nuclear armament, the series had Craven uncovering the illegal manufacture of plutonium at a nuclear waste disposal plant and links to supplying the US with weapons. It's an engrossing political drama that hasn't lost any of its punch, possibly because it also has the human element of Craven mourning his daughter as well as the threat of nuclear devastation at its core. Still relevant today, and still an edge-of-the-seat must-see.

 TV Trivia: Eric Clapton and Michael Kamen composed the score for the series.

GBH (1991)

Starring Michael Palin, Robert Lindsay, Lindsay Duncan, Julie Walters

Alan Bleasdale (*Boys From The Blackstuff*) wrote this powerful seven-episode series that was broadcast by Channel 4 in 1991 and tells the story of Michael Murray (Lindsay). He's the leader of a Labour council in the north, and seems in charge of all he surveys, but the first hint that something is wrong appears when he storms into the headmaster's office of his old junior school, throws the ageing head teacher Mr Weller (David Ross) out and frantically searches for his old school files. Then he sends Weller to work at a school for special needs children run by Jim Nelson (Palin).

The series focuses on the two men who seem polar opposites – Murray continually has affairs while Nelson is a devoted family man – but the two come head to head as Murray tries to engineer a fragile Nelson's dismissal, but there are many more layers to the story involving racial tension, political machinations, the far-left strands of the Labour party, secrets and lies. Farcical, funny, satirical, gritty and clever, the series also starred Julie Walters as Murray's mother, Lindsay Duncan and Daniel Massey.

 TV Trivia: It is believed the character of Murray was based on Derek Hatton, the former deputy leader of Liverpool City Council.

HOTEL BABYLON (2006–)

Starring Max Beesley, Tamzin Outhwaite

Based on Imogen Edwards-Jones's novel about what goes on behind closed hotel doors, *Hotel Babylon* is a soap in the same vein as *Footballers' Wives* – it's tacky in a guilty pleasure sort of way, and packed with pretty people, scandals, bedroom romps and even the occasional hail of gunfire. Set in a swish London hotel, much of what goes on is seen by Charlie (Beesley, who narrates), the deputy manager, and his boss, the uptight Rebecca (Outhwaite, who appears in the first two seasons). Also working in the stylish lodgings are beautiful head of housekeeping Jackie (Natalie Mendoza), concierge Tony (Dexter Fletcher) and receptionist Anna (Emma Pierson).

A sort of UK version of *Las Vegas*, the flimsy but fun series follows some of the customers, from a reformed rock band who just want a quiet night or a suicidal guest to the prostitutes the staff are trying to remove from the premises. It's all in good fun, and so peppered with guest stars including Anthony Head, Joan Collins, Jerry Hall, Russ Abbot, David Walliams, Kelly Brook, Jennifer Ellison and Paula Abdul you'll feel like you're watching a TV version of the celebrity magazine *OK!*

 TV Trivia: Edward-Jones's novel was based on the true stories told to her by an (anonymous) manager of a five-star London hotel.

HOUSE OF CARDS (1990)

Starring Ian Richardson, Susannah Harker, Miles Anderson

Delicious British drama set in the corridors of political power, *House of Cards* remains one of the most acclaimed political dramas made for TV. Ian Richardson is a mixture of sneers and deviousness as Francis Urquhart, the Chief Whip of the Conservative Party whose job is to maintain party discipline. This means he knows about everyone's skeletons hidden in their closets, a knowledge he uses to further his own ambitions and rise up the political career ladder. With the help of his equally calculating wife, he decides to challenge the party leadership by discrediting his opponents, although he has a secret of his own – an affair with young journalist Mattie (Harker).

Superbly written by Andrew Davies from Michael Dobbs's novel, this series is packed with sharp lines, clever twists and general nastiness, but in the hands of Richardson, the character of Urquhart luckily never quite becomes a pantomime villain – instead his portrayal makes Urquhart someone you could well believe is manipulating our own government from the inside. Riveting stuff, the drama ran for four episodes and was followed by two sequels, *To Play The King* (1993) and *The Final Cut* (1995).

 TV Trivia: Ian Richardson has been reported as saying he based his performance on Shakespeare's Richard III.

JONATHAN CREEK (1997–2004)

Starring Alan Davies, Caroline Quentin

A crime-solving drama with a twist, this series began as investigative journalist Maddy Magellan (Quentin) tried to find the flaw in a seemingly solid alibi by enlisting the help of Jonathan Creek (stand-up comic Davies in his acting debut), a designer of illusions for stage magician Adam Klaus. From then on, the pair become an odd-couple team (she's streetwise, he lives in a windmill), solving mysteries and riddles when Creek isn't helping Klaus out of yet another comic mishap. In 2001, Quentin left the series and was replaced by Julia Sawalha as Carla.

More comedy than drama, especially when you consider some of the guest actors on the show have included comedians such as the late Bob Monkhouse, and Rik Mayall, Adrian Edmondson and Nigel Planer, this zipped along thanks to Davies' affable charm, mixed with Quentin's more brittle manner. Twenty-five episodes were made, and the best are those pre-2000, when the will-they-won't-they tension between Jonathan and Maddy was at its peak.

While Sawalha is a talented actress, her episodes just don't have the sparkle of the earlier seasons.

 TV Trivia: Anthony Stewart Head played the role of Adam Klaus in the pilot, but due to his commitment to *Buffy The Vampire Slayer*, the part was played by Stuart Milligan in subsequent episodes.

LAS VEGAS (2003–2008)

Starring James Caan, Josh Duhamel, Nikki Cox

Action drama set in the famous gambling town and focusing on the staff of the (fictional) Montecito Resort & Casino. It's there that Ed Deline (Caan) keeps an eye on the running of the hotel, especially the security, with the help of Danny McCoy (the model-pretty Duhamel) and techno whizz Mike Cannon (James Lesure). When the show isn't focusing on the various security scams, robberies and other crimes they solve, it's casting an eye on the relationships between the staff: Danny works alongside long-time friend Mary (Cox), who has always had a crush on him, but he's romancing Ed's beautiful daughter Delinda (Molly Sims). Meanwhile top casino hostess Sam Marquez (Vanessa Marcil), seems to spend all her time hooking in big gambling clients and no time on her personal life – until her millionaire husband Casey (Dean Cain) shows up to everyone's surprise.

It's silly, glossy, slick and partnered by a thumping soundtrack – just like Vegas itself. Nothing here goes too deep, and it's really just an excuse for a lot of pretty people to wander around a resort and casino looking, well, pretty – sort of like *Baywatch* with more desert and less water. Punctuated by shots of bathing beauties around the hotel pool, this isn't brain-straining stuff, just guiltily enjoyable tosh that at least makes Vegas look more glamorous than it does in *CSI*. Caan left the cast in 2007, and was replaced by Tom Selleck as the new owner of the hotel, but the series was cancelled in early 2008 before he had a chance to make his mark.

 TV Trivia: Don Johnson was one of the actors considered for the role of Ed Deline.

THE L WORD (2004–)

Sarring Jennifer Beals, Mia Kirshner, Pam Grier

The 'L' word in question is lesbianism or possibly love, as this drama follows a group of Los Angeles women who love women as they fall in love, break up, make up, and bitch about their relationships with their friends (think *Sex and The City* without the testosterone, silly moments and expensive shoes). Created by Ilene Chaiken, this does feature lesbian sex scenes and female nudity that probably has straight men tuning in, but the well-thought out dramas, issue-heavy (yet not overbearing) plots and well-drawn characters are what make this worth watching.

The series focuses on a handful of women – Bette (Beals) and her partner Tina (Laurel Holloman), who are trying to have a baby; Jenny (Kirshner), who moves in next door to be with her boyfriend Tim (*Ugly Betty's* Eric Mabius) but then falls for the exotic Marina (Karina Lombard); Bette's half-sister Kit; the raunchy Shane (Katherine Moenning); bisexual Alice (Leisha Hailey) and closeted Dana (Erin Daniels). Happily none of them are stereo-types, and each actress brings a nice depth to her role that makes you want to tune in again to see what happens to her character. A fun drama.

 TV Trivia: Although set in trendy West Hollywood, California, the series is actually filmed in Vancouver, Canada.

THE LAKES (1997–1999)

Starring John Simm, Kaye Wragg

Created by writer Jimmy McGovern (*Hillsborough*, *Cracker*), *The Lakes* is the story of Danny Kavanagh, a compulsive gambler who leaves a life on the dole in Liverpool to start anew in the Lake District. He marries local girl Emma (Emma Cuniffe) and the pair eventually settle with Danny getting a job renting out rowing boats on the lake. However, when he rejects the advances of Lucy Archer (Wragg) and she decides to get back at him, Danny finds himself blamed for the deaths of three schoolgirls in a boating accident – Lucy lies to implicate him, and his alibi is that he was on the phone to his bookies at the time, which he doesn't want to admit as he had promised to stop gambling.

That's just one of the plots in this series that also features the twists and turns in the lives of the locals Danny gets to know – there's a cuckolded man who bludgeons his wife to death, a forbidden affair between a priest and a married parishioner, and a young woman's rape – that show life in the country isn't peaceful at all. Controversial thanks to its explicit depictions of sex and violence, the series ran for two series, and featured strong performances from Simm and Wragg. It's a bit heavy-handed in its treatment of religion (specifically Catholicism) and the town/country divide, but it's interesting nonetheless.

TV Trivia: This was one of John Simm's first leading roles – he had made his TV debut five years before in an episode of *Rumpole of The Bailey*.

LoST (2004–)

Starring Matthew Fox, Naveen Andrews, Josh Holloway, Terry O'Quinn, Dominic Monaghan

One of the most discussed shows on TV, *Lost* gripped from the first episode back in 2004 and has had fans discussing, guessing, debating, scratching their heads and obsessing about it ever since. On the surface, it is the story of a group of survivors of a plane crash. Oceanic flight 815 took off from Sydney, Australia, bound for the US, but the pilot flew off course and the plane crashed on a remote island. Among the survivors are Jack (Fox), a doctor; British former rock musician Charlie (Monaghan), who is a drug addict; former Iraqi soldier Sayid (Andrews); pregnant young woman Claire (Emilie de Ravin); chubby lottery winner Hurley (Jorge Garcia); con artist Sawyer (Holloway) and the mysterious Kate (Evangeline Lily), who boarded the plane shackled to a police officer who was transporting her back to the US to stand trial for a crime.

Of course, as anyone will tell you, *Lost* is about so much more than just the survivors and the superb actors who play them. The island they are on seems to be uninhabited, but it soon emerges that the plane crash survivors are not alone. There's a strange black smoke, a sighting of a polar bear (on a tropical island?), a sinister hatch they can't open, and references to a group called the Dharma Initiative and a collection of inhabitants dubbed 'the Others'. Then there's the computer, the six numbers that keep cropping up (4, 8, 15, 16, 23, 42), and a man who can occasionally see future events. Confused? You will be, as each episode mixes adventures on the island with flashback revelations of a survivor's past (and later, flash-forwards hinting what happens next), weird coincidences occur, people discover the island's bizarre phenomena (wheelchair-bound Locke, played by O'Quinn, finds he can walk again after the crash) and nasty things go bump in the day and night. Is it a mystery, a sci-fi series, a drama, or a thriller? It's all those and more, slickly packaged by producers J.J. Abrams (*Cloverfield*, *Alias*) and Damon Lindelof, and cleverly promoted by the TV company who waged a masterful internet campaign so ardent fans can log on to related websites (there's one for the doomed airline, for example) and try and solve the mystery themselves.

In 2007, it was announced that a finite number of episodes would be made and all the loose ends would be tied up… by 2010. The question is, can you hold your breath that long without passing out?

 TV Trivia: *Lost* **is filmed in Oahu, Hawaii, with the majority of the beach scenes on a remote north shore beach that the public would find hard to spot.**

MAD MEN (2007–)

Starring Jon Hamm, Elisabeth Moss, Vincent Kartheiser

A slick American drama, this is based around the employees of an advertising agency in the New York of the early 1960s. Back then, of course, a woman's place was in the home, so the few female employees are sexually harassed and accepting of it, the men think nothing of swigging a few drinks during office hours, smoking is almost obligatory and gay men in the office are so firmly in the closet that they boast about the women they 'nailed' over the weekend. Those were the days, eh?

The series focuses on creative mastermind Don Draper (Hamm), his new secretary Peggy (Moss) and protégé Pete (Kartheiser), who wants to be as successful as his mentor. But it's not just the home life and office politics that make this so watchable, it's the pitch-perfect sixties setting, as the agency decides whether to represent Nixon in the upcoming Nixon/Kennedy race for the White House, or how to deal with marketing cigarettes just as the first health concerns are raised about the product. Luscious to look at – check out the fashions – and filled with interesting characters, this is one of 2007's TV gems and won a well-deserved Emmy for Best Drama in 2008.

 TV Trivia: Series creator Matthew Weiner was previously a writer/producer on *The Sopranos***.**

LOVEJOY (1986–1994)

Starring Ian McShane, Dudley Sutton, Phyllis Logan

A hugely successful British comedy/drama series that ran for six seasons, this follows the antics of cheeky antiques dealer/lovable rogue *Lovejoy* (McShane). He's an expert at sniffing out the genuine article, so he uses his talents to fleece unscrupulous dealers, and refund money they have taken from ordinary people (at a small fee, of course). With the help of posh totty Lady Jane Felsham (Logan) and his pals, the permanently pissed Tinker (Sutton) and the sweet but dim Eric (Chris Jury), *Lovejoy* is like a latter day Robin Hood of sorts, a talent that often has him falling foul of nasty antiques dealer Charles Gimbert (Malcolm Tierney).

Playing it with tongue firmly in cheek, McShane became something of a housewives' heartthrob with his five o'clock shadow, twinkly eyes, shaggy mullet hairdo (!) and the series' trademark of having his character talk directly to the audience on occasion. Adapted from the Jonathan Gash novels by comic writer Ian La Frenais, this is an enjoyable if not exactly taxing show that expertly mixes sleuthing with comedy and swindling with sharp dialogue. Fans of the series prefer the first four series, as Logan left at the beginning of the fifth series, and Chris Jury later in that series.

 TV Trivia: In the books, Lovejoy's first name is never mentioned, and in the series McShane's character always asks to be referred to as just 'Lovejoy'.

MADE IN BRITAIN (1982)

Starring Tim Roth, Eric Richard

David Leland (*Wish You Were Here*) wrote this storming drama that was originally broadcast as part of the ITV season *Tales Out Of School* in 1982. A young Tim Roth is astonishing and raw as 16-year-old Trevor, a white-power skinhead who has been charged with throwing a brick through a Pakistani man's window, as well as shoplifting (at Harrods!) and other crimes. His social worker, Harry (Richard), believes there is hope for the teenager, and Trevor is sent to an assessment centre for punishment to be decided. But Trevor, who is bright but refusing to co-operate, seems to want a life in prison rather than a second chance.

Directed by Alan Clarke, who also made *Scum* and *The Firm*, which both looked at the dark underbelly of the British class system, this gritty, no-holds-barred drama is shocking because Trevor is not depicted as a mindless thug, as you would expect, but as an intelligent, angry boy battling authority (as he sees it) who is proud of his heritage and wants to fight for it – although, of course, his reasoning is racist rather than patriotic. Stunning stuff that is still relevant today, unfortunately.

 TV Trivia: Legend has it that Tim Roth walked into the audition for this film by mistake. En route to somewhere else, his bicycle tyre got a puncture and he popped into a building to see if anyone had a pump he could borrow. He then learnt there were auditions being held there and asked to try out.

MILE HIGH (2003–2005)

Starring Tom Wisdom, Sarah Manners, James Redmond, Emma Ferguson

Anyone complaining about the crass shows that sometimes pop up on cable/satellite TV has probably seen this tacky series about the antics of the cabin crew of a budget airline called Fresh! that operates out of Stansted Airport. Think *Airline* mixed with *Baywatch*, then subtract 100 IQ points and you'll have a rough idea of what goes on here. It's a 'saucy' series that mixes humour, drama and lots of semi-nakedness as naive Marco (Wisdom) begins his job as a flight attendant and discovers his fellow crew members spend most of their time in the sky talking about sex, and most of their time on the ground having it.

A show so dumb and frothy it makes *Footballers' Wives* look like *Citizen Kane*, this featured a gaggle of actors who looked like their day job was modelling for the *Sun* and boasted scripts that sounded like they had been penned by someone still hungover from a week at a Club 18–30 holiday. So bad it's too awful to even be a guilty pleasure.

 TV Trivia: Made by the creators of *Dream Team*, the show has featured some of that series' cast while a TV advert for the fictional airline was shown on a TV in *Dream Team*.

THE NAKED CIVIL SERVANT (1975)

Starring John Hurt

Based on Quentin Crisp's book of the same name (the first instalment of his autobiography), *The Naked Civil Servant* deservedly won John Hurt a BAFTA award. He stars as Crisp, the man born as Denis Pratt in 1908 who was openly gay at a time when it was frowned upon, and who has been credited with helping to make British society understand/accept homosexuality.

Crisp himself introduces the film, and it begins in the late 1920s as Quentin is becoming aware he is attracted to men and not women. His middle-class parents don't understand and seek medical advice to find a cure, and are relieved when he befriends a female student at art college, unaware the relationship is platonic. It's a transvestite prostitute who opens Crisp's eyes to an alternative lifestyle, and it is not long before he has dyed his hair a striking red and developed his own sense of style that leads to a great deal of abuse from the outside world. His is a fascinating story with many interesting and often funny twists – Crisp is rejected by the army in 1939 on the grounds of sexual perversion, for example – and his own sense of sharp humour (he refers to himself as one of the 'stately homos' of England) comes through in Hurt's expressive, memorable performance. Simply fascinating.

 TV Trivia: After seeing the drama, Crisp described Hurt as his 'representative on Earth'.

NORTHERN EXPOSURE (1990–1995)
Starring Rob Morrow, Janine Turner, Barry Corbin

A quirky drama series that became a cult favourite, *Northern Exposure* followed young doctor Noel Fleischman (Morrow) from his arrival in the remote Alaskan mountain town of Cicely, where it seems every local is a tad eccentric. There's former astronaut Maurice Minnifield, pilot Maggie O'Connell, film buff Ed Chigliak, mayor/bar owner Holling Vincoeur and his very young girlfriend Shelly, and philosophical ex-con/DJ Chris Stevens (*Sex And The City*'s John Corbett) among them.

Although it began as a fish-out-of-water story (Fleischman was a New York city boy unused to small town ways, and this town is small with a population of just over 200), soon it became apparent that the residents of Cicely were far more interesting than the newcomer. As well as the series regulars, there were some enjoyable recurring characters, including Adam Arkin's Adam, who may have a secretive CIA past, hyper-allergic lawyer Mike (Anthony Edwards), who has to live in an airtight house due to his allergies, and One-Who-Waits (Floyd Westerman), a long-dead Native American chief who is Ed's spirit guide. Dark and often funny, the series puzzled many but enchanted those who have embraced its quirkiness.

The first three seasons are the best, as Morrow's dissatisfaction with the show (it became more of an ensemble piece and his role was reduced) in the fourth season caused him to appear less (leaving plot lines dangling) and eventually leave the show one season before it ended for good.

 TV Trivia: Eighties pop star Adam Ant appeared in an episode as Brad, the lead singer in a heavy metal band, who arrives in Cicely when he should have ended up in Sicily, in the Mediterranean.

OUR FRIENDS IN THE NORTH (1996)
Starring Christopher Eccleston, Daniel Craig, Gina McKee, Mark Strong

Based on a play by Peter Flannery, this nine-part series focused on the lives of four friends between the years 1964 to 1995. Beginning as idealistic teens,

Nicky Hutchinson (Eccleston), Geordie Peacock (Craig), Mary Soulsby (McKee), and Terry 'Tosker' Cox (Strong) take very different paths in life, as each episode shows their situation in a specific year, whether it be 1974, (the infamous Winter of Discontent), 1979 (Thatcher comes to power) or 1984 (the miners strike).

A social comment of the times featured as well as a drama, the plot has Nicky becoming involved with the Labour Party before seeking more radical ways of expressing his politics, Geordie heading for London where he gets a job with porn baron Bennie Barratt (the always deliciously nasty Malcolm McDowell), Tosker cheating on Mary but staying with her because they have children, and each of the friends dealing with successes and setbacks over the time period when Britain went through many changes. It's a fascinating depiction of the time, and features four riveting central performances from a cast who were, at the time, relatively unknown.

 TV Trivia: The original play only went up to 1979, but Flannery decided to bring the story up to date for TV.

THE PRISONER (1967–1968)

Starring Patrick McGoohan

Is this a drama, science fiction, a mystery or a thriller? This legendary series that only ran for 17 episodes is all of those and much more, thanks to creators George Markstein and Patrick McGoohan, who was also the show's star. He is, of course the British secret agent who resigns and then is kidnapped and taken to a strange village where he is known as Number Six. There, the people in charge subject him to psychological tests, drugs and hypnosis – are they trying to break him or train him? Where is this village, and who are the people in charge?

Because the final episode, 'Fall Out', never completely solved the mystery and, in fact, added even more puzzles to the mix, this cult series has remained a firm favourite with anyone drawn into the head-scratching plot. Dialogue such as 'I am not a number, I am a free man!' is recognisable even to people who have never seen the show, while McGoohan's enigmatic performance adds to the tension. A masterpiece of complex drama, littered with symbolism, trippiness and words that have you dissecting them for hidden meanings while watching, this remains one of the best shows ever made for British TV.

TV Trivia: A film version of *The Prisoner* has often been mooted, with actors ranging from Mel Gibson to Russell Crowe in the lead role, but nothing has been made as yet.

QUEER AS FOLK (1999)

Starring Aiden Gillen, Craig Kelly, Charlie Hunnam

Daily Mail readers must have fainted in front of their TVs if they caught a glimpse of this controversial Channel 4 show that ran for two seasons. First off, it was a series about gay men and second, it actually featured them *shagging* (and often quite explicitly, too). Created by Russell T. Davies, the man who went on to revamp *DoctorWho* for the 21st century, *Queer As Folk* followed the horizontal antics of Manchester gay friends Vince (Kelly) and Stuart (Gillen), who seem to spend their time clubbing, doing drugs or having sex. Vince is the shy one, while Stuart is always bringing home one night stands, and it is he who picks up 15-year-old Nathan (Hunnam), who wants more than Stuart is prepared to offer.

Such storylines caused numerous shocked newspaper headlines, but beneath the furore it caused this is actually an extremely well-written comedy drama that believably depicts the men's relationships, both with their lovers and their families and friends. Gillen is superb as the seemingly thoughtless lothario, but Kelly is equally good as his sweet friend and Hunnam is convincing as Stuart's young, often annoying conquest who just won't go away.

Two series were made and the show was also remade for American TV. (It's not available in the UK on DVD, though.)

 TV Trivia: Christopher Eccleston was offered the role of Stuart but turned it down, suggesting Gillen in his place.

RESCUE ME (2004–)

Starring Denis Leary, Mike Lombardi, Steven Pasquale

Described by some as a soap opera for men, *Rescue Me* was conceived as a homage to the brave firefighters who lost their lives on 11 September 2001 in New York. It's not reverential or too sombre, however, as it deals with both the humorous and dangerous situations the firemen of Truck Company 62 face every day. The crew is still mourning the loss of four of their number who died on that horrendous day, and one suffering more than most is Tommy, whose cousin died and who is now facing a divorce from his wife and animosity from his kids. Oh, and he has started seeing the ghosts of former firefighters and fire victims he was unable to save as he goes about his work. And he's not the only one with problems: boss Jerry (Jack McGee) is repressing his anger and hiding a gambling problem, Lou (John Scurti) is secretly writing poetry to cope with his grief and co-workers Sean, Mike, Franco and Billy aren't doing too great, either.

A show that sets out to show that firefighters are both heroes and ordinary guys – and sometimes complete misogynistic assholes, truth be told – this details rescue and emergency scenes that depict their bravery, then switches to shine a light on their often muddled personal lives (Tommy's being particularly messy, as he lies to his kids, sleeps around and yet wants to make up with his missus). While the entire cast are good, it is Leary's show as the real-life stand-up comic delivers his sharp dialogue with the viciousness and sarcasm (and bad language) he was known for on stage ('Let me tell you something, sister, you serve two purposes in this house – you can give me a blow job or make me a sandwich. I'm not in the mood for head and I had a late breakfast, so you're shit out of luck'), so if you hate his stand-up style it's likely you won't like *Rescue Me*, whereas if you like him, this is the show for you. The easily offended should note there is a *lot* to be offended about here – the firemen often make anti-gay, anti-female, and anti-anything-else-you-can-think-of comments.

TV Trivia: Many of the extras in the show are retired and active New York firemen.

THE RICHES (2007–)

Starring Eddie Izzard, Minnie Driver, Noel Fisher

Wayne Malloy (Izzard), his fresh-out-of-jail wife Dahlia (Driver) and their kids are grifters, con artists and thieves whom we first meet scamming their way into a high school reunion party at a school none of them went to, so they can rob the attendees. But a true opportunity comes their way when they spot a crashed car – when the Malloys go over to help, they discover the occupants are dead, and inside the car is a house key and a letter. The deceased couple, a lawyer named Doug Rich and his wife Cherien, were on their way to Louisiana from Florida, to move into a big house in a gated community. Doug bought the house over the internet, so no one knows what he looks like. Which means Wayne and Dahlia can move right in and pretend to be... the Riches.

A mix of comedy and drama, this is a fish-out-of-water tale that also tips a hat to the importance of family and raises a smile with its look at the oddities of life in suburbia. While Izzard, best known for his expressive stand-up comedy, seems a bit reined in here, he's nonetheless convincing as the conman who is considering going straight, and Shannon Woodward, Noel Fisher and Aidan Mitchell give nice support as his kids who seem to miss the travellers' lifestyle much more than he does. Best of all, though, is Driver, as an angry ex-con with a cough syrup habit who finds her criminal ways being stifled by the family's new lifestyle. While the mix of drama and comedy in the series doesn't always work, it's well worth catching for her spitfire performance.

 TV Trivia: John Cleese once described Eddie Izzard as 'the lost Python'.

SECRET DIARY OF A CALL GIRL (2007–)

Starring Billie Piper, Iddo Goldberg, Cherie Lunghi

Based on the popular blog and book written by the mysterious Belle De Jour, this is a rather risqué (for ITV) series about a high-class London call girl, as played by former pop moppet/Doctor Who assistant Billie Piper. By day she is Hannah, but at night she is seductive Belle, whom the series follows from novice to experienced sex seller, as she learns to please her clients while keeping her personal and professional lives separate (even her best friend, Ben, doesn't know what she does).

Unsurprisingly a hit (a second season has already been made) as well as a controversy – much of the language and situations are pretty explicit – this is basically a thinly plotted tale written around various scenes of Piper in her scanties. In the style of the movie *Alfie*, Belle often talks to camera, which can be quite irritating, but otherwise Piper gives a strong performance despite little material (in both the writing and clothing sense!) and is ably supported by Lunghi as her 'manager'.

 TV Trivia: Susan Tully, better known as Michelle in *EastEnders*, directed four episodes of the series.

SIX FEET UNDER (2001–2005)

Starring Peter Krause, Michael C. Hall, Frances Conroy, Lauren Ambrose

Another gem from HBO, this darkly comic series set in a family run funeral home was an instant hit. After his father is killed in a car crash, David Fisher (Hall) becomes the new director of Fisher and Sons funeral home. His carefree, absentee younger brother Nate (Krause) returns for the funeral and reluctantly agrees to join his sibling as a partner in the family business. While dealing with their grief, each member of the family has their own personal issues to cope with as well – David is in denial about his homosexuality, commitment-phobe Nate struggles with his relationships, troubled teen Claire

(Ambrose) is moodiness personified while their mother (Conroy) attempts to rebuild her life.

Each episode begins with the demise of some unfortunate soul – usually in a delightfully inventive way. The next time we see them is on the slab at the funeral home having fluids replaced and wounds repaired. An interesting device the show uses is to feature the dead, in various states of preparation, awake and in casual conversation with the living. This manifestation of their conscience shows clearly what they are thinking and highlights the issues being addressed in particular episodes or story arcs.

Six Feet Under is a drama that pulls no punches dealing with topics such as drug taking, sex and, of course, death. The writing is sharp and clever but never pretentious. Die-hard action fans, pun intended, may not appreciate the subtleties of the show, as characters slowly develop, storylines gradually unwind and then right in the middle of the most heart rending moment there'll be something to make you laugh. If you are offended by foul language, mangled corpses or seeing two men snog, *The Waltons* might be a more palatable depiction of family life.

 TV trivia: Frances Conroy plays Peter Krause's mother despite the fact that she is only 12 years older than him.

SPARKHOUSE (2002)

Starring Sarah Smart, Joseph McFadden, Alun Armstrong

Emily Bronte's *Wuthering Heights* gets the 21st-century update treatment (basically that means less big frocks and more steaminess) in this drama from Sally Wainwright, who also wrote *At Home With The Braithwaites*. Carol Bolton (Smart) lives with her drunken father (Armstrong) at the poverty-stricken Sparkhouse Farm, along with her younger sister Lisa (Abigail James). Throughout her life, Carol has had a soul-mate in the form of brooding Andrew Lawton (McFadden) and they share an animal passion that, as any fan of the Bronte book will know, is destined to be tortuous.

One of those dramas in which everything looks grey and the protagonists only seem to want to snog in pouring rain, this is surprisingly affecting, mainly due to Smart's tough and vulnerable central performance. McFadden is less successful – his Yorkshire accent is all over the place – but with support from a cast that includes Celia Imrie and the always reliable Armstrong, this is an interesting twist on a classic well-known tale.

 TV Trivia: In the 1990s, writer Sally Wainwright wrote over 50 episodes of *Coronation Street*.

STATE OF PLAY (2003)

Starring David Morrissey, John Simm, Kelly Macdonald, Bill Nighy

Enthralling drama which is being remade into a 2009 movie starring Helen Mirren, Russell Crowe and Ben Affleck, *State of Play* is a complex thriller about government and big business that begins when a young political researcher, Sonia Baker, is killed by a London tube train. Her Labour MP boss, Stephen Collins, (Morrissey) is devastated, while newspaper reporter Cal McCaffrey (Simm) and his boss Cameron Foster (Nighy) start to dig into whether Stephen and Sonia had more than a working relationship. Things take a sinister turn when a black teenager named Kelvin Stagg is found murdered, and it turns out he had stolen a briefcase that contained photos of Stephen and Sonia... and a gun.

The plot twists and turns as the police (led by DCI Bell, played by Philip Glenister) get involved, Cal's colleague Della (Macdonald) is drawn into the investigation, and secrets are revealed. With a cast that also includes Polly Walker, Marc Warren and James McAvoy all giving strong performances, a script from *Cracker*'s Paul Abbott and taut direction from David Yates (*Harry Potter and The Order Of The Phoenix*), it's nail-biting stuff – and one of the best British TV thriller/dramas we've had in the past few years (we'll be very impressed if the Hollywood movie is even half as good).

 TV Trivia: The BBC wanted to make a second series but writer Abbott couldn't think how it would work. He went on to become the creator of *Shameless*.

STUDIO 60 ON THE SUNSET STRIP (2007)

Starring Matthew Perry, Bradley Whitford, Amanda Peet, Sarah Paulson, Steven Weber

A comedy drama series created by *The West Wing*'s Aaron Sorkin and Thomas Schlamme, and starring *Friends*' Matthew Perry and *West Wing*'s Bradley Whitford was destined to be a hit, right? Well, er, no. Despite rave reviews from critics, this sharp series, set behind the scenes of a live comedy sketch show, never gained much of an audience and was cancelled after just 22 episodes (luckily, the producers knew the end was nigh, so all the plot loose-ends are tied up by the finale). It's a shame, because the show had a lot to offer in its smart mix of drama, politics and humour – but perhaps that was the problem, as some reviewers decided the show failed because it was too clever for the average viewer. Boo.

Perry and Whitford starred as Matt Albie and Danny Tripp, a comedy writing and producing duo who are tempted back to work for a TV show they had quit years before by hot new TV executive Jordan McDeere (Peet). Their job isn't going to be easy, though, as Jordan's boss Jack Rudolph (Weber) is hovering in the background making sure they don't put anything too controversial on air, while Matt is frequently distracted by his ex-girlfriend Harriet (Paulson), the lead comedienne on the show. In the single season, *Studio 60* touched on religion (Harriet's devout beliefs and Matt's cynicism was one of the reasons they split), the war in Iraq (one of the comics has a brother stationed there), racism and other hot-potato subjects. Sometimes their treatment of such was a bit trite, but all in all, this was a well-written, slickly performed series that should have lasted longer than it did.

TV Trivia: Many of the characters are alleged to have been based on people Aaron Sorkin knew or worked with – the character of Harriet is supposed to be based on his ex-girlfriend, the comedienne Kristin Chenoweth (Pushing Daisies).

TALKiNG HEADS (1987. 1998)

Starring Thora Hird, Julie Walters, Maggie Smith

Not the rock band led by David Byrne, but a series of thought-provoking, often moving one-person plays written by Alan Bennett. In each, an actor delivers a monologue to camera, and in each, their story unravels slowly and elegantly as they tell their tale. Six episodes were originally made, followed by a further six almost a decade later, and each is available. Among the most memorable stories are those of a woman (Eileen Atkins) struggling to run her antiques shop ('The Hand Of God'); a middle-aged man dominated by his mother (Bennett himself in 'A Chip In The Sugar'); an alcoholic vicar's wife having an affair (Maggie Smith in 'Bed Amongst The Lentils'); an aspiring actress who seems unaware her big break is in a soft porn movie (Julie Walters in 'Her Big Chance'); an elderly woman contemplating going to a care home (Thora Hird in 'A Cream Cracker Under The Settee'); and a man with a dark secret about his past (David Haig in 'Playing Sandwiches').

Perhaps the best, and certainly the most moving, is Thora Hird's second performance in a Bennett Talking Head – as Violet in 'Waiting For The Telegram'. Playing a confused, elderly woman in a nursing home who has been told she will soon be getting a telegram from the Queen as she's going to be 100 years old, the news reminds her of when telegrams meant news of death on a battlefield, and one particular telegram she waited for from a long lost love.

Each play has moments of sadness and laughter, but this one encapsulates the best of Bennett – a sad, riveting soliloquy about life and love, loneliness, irony and what could have been. Just lovely.

 TV Trivia: Although the episodes all seem to be set in Leeds, Bennett has commented it is the Leeds of his memory, rather than the real place.

THiS LiFE (1996–1997)

Starring Jack Davenport, Andrew Lincoln, Daniela Nardini

If you were white, middle class and in your twenties in the mid-nineties, chances are you watched this series about a group of annoying – sorry, fascinating – young professionals that ran for two series (32 episodes). The soapy drama followed the relationships and traumas of five housemates: arrogant Miles (Davenport), control freak Milly (Amita Dhiri), in-therapy Warren (Jason Hughes), lazy Egg (Lincoln) and smart-mouthed Anna (Nardini), as they attempted to find their footing in the world in between delivering pithy one-liners.

Hated by the *Daily Mail* for its depiction of booze-drinking, drug-taking, shagging urban professionals (shock horror!), and especially for some homosexual sex scenes (steady on!), and described as a British version of *Friends* by other papers (it's not – it's franker, meaner and the characters aren't as glossily pretty or perfect, thank god), this became a cult hit thanks to a pithy script and the raunchy talk (and situations) of the characters. It's dated a bit – these pals are products of Thatcher's Britain – but the antics of the group are still enjoyable if you don't find the protagonists grating. A follow-up, *This Life + 10*, was made in 2007, in which the friends reunite for a pal's funeral a decade on. It's awful.

 TV Trivia: Jack Davenport is the son of actors Maria Aitken and Nigel Davenport.

UGLY BETTY (2006–)

Starring America Ferrara, Eric Mabius, Alan Dale, Vanessa Williams

Based on the Colombian soap opera *Yo Soy Betty La Fea*, this soap operatic comedy drama set around a fashion magazine is wildly unrealistic, which is somehow part of its charm. Betty Suarez (Ferrara) is a serious wannabe journalist who gets a job on the one magazine she has no interest in – fashion title

Mode. While Betty is, well, homely (and cursed with braces and glasses) and fond of garish outfits, everyone from the editor to the receptionist on the magazine are dressed head to toe in high fashion, and don't take too kindly to frumpy Betty's presence. But she's been hired by the head of the company, Bradford Meade (Dale), whose son Daniel is editor-in-chief but easily distracted by pretty assistants (Bradford thinks hiring Betty as Daniel's PA will keep his son's mind on the job). So Betty enters the backstabbing, bitchy world of fashion, where fashion director Wilhelmena Slater (Williams) rules the day – with the help of flunkies such as her flamboyant assistant Marc (Michael Urie) and bitchy receptionist Amanda (Becki Newton).

Silly in the extreme – plot twists include Daniel's brother Alex coming back as a woman (Rebecca Romijn) following a sex change operation, and their mother Claire (Judith Light) being accused of murder – this could be incredibly annoying and over-the-top but works thanks to the warm central characters of Betty and her family, including sister Hilda (Ana Ortiz) and her son Justin (Mark Indelicato), and the often sharp scripts, delivered with glee by Newton, Williams, Urie and Britain's own Ashley Jensen (as stylist Christina).

Produced by Salma Hayek, who appears as magazine editor Sofia in some of the early episodes, this is often hilarious but even managed to pull off a truly moving episode at the beginning of Season 2: make sure you have a strong heart and tissues at the ready while watching Ana Ortiz at her best in 'How Betty Got Her Grieve Back'.

TV Trivia: Vanessa Williams was the first African-American to win the beauty contest Miss America. She had to resign her crown, however, when nude photos of her taken years before were published in *Penthouse* magazine.

A VERY BRITISH COUP (1988)

Starring Ray McAnally, Keith Allen, Alan MacNaughtan

A British political drama, based on Labour MP Chris Mullin's novel (written in the 1970s), this was made shortly after Labour had lost to the Conservatives in the third general election in a row. At the time very politically current, touching on nuclear issues and secrecy in power, it remains interesting from a 21st-century perspective, especially when you consider that Alistair Campbell, Tony Blair's spin doctor, was one of the drama's advisors.

The story follows a fictional Labour government, led by Prime Minister Perkins (McAnally), which is envisioning radical change for Britain, including the removal of American nuclear weapons from British soil. However, not everyone is keen on these plans and it is soon revealed that an American woman is taping Perkins' private conversations, and there are powerful people who expect to be able to manipulate the new head of the state and his government. A fascinating political drama that boasts a thundering central performance from McAnally as the Sheffield-born steel worker-turned-leader, this also boasts strong support from a cast that includes Tim McInerney and Keith Allen as Perkins' press secretary.

 TV Trivia: The series was directed by Mick Jackson, who also made the nuclear drama *Threads*... and the Kevin Costner/Whitney Houston movie *The Bodyguard*.

WEEDS (2005–)

Starring Mary-Louise Parker, Elizabeth Perkins, Hunter Parrish

Nancy Botwin (Parker) looks like your average suburban mum – she's the mother of two sons, struggling to pay the bills after the sudden death of her husband. However, her way of making ends meet is a little unique – she's dealing pot. So when the kids are at school, she's picking up marijuana from her source, an African American family led by matriarch Heylia (Tonye Pantano), and selling it on to affluent white people such as the local city councillor (Kevin Nealon). Meanwhile, she does all her daily motherly duties, while hiding her secret and lending an ear to best friend Celia (Perkins), who in turn spends her time nagging her overweight daughter (she even takes her to a boot camp to thin her up enough so she won't be embarrassingly chubby when she goes to fat camp) and unfaithful husband.

A mixture of comedy and drama, this series took a while to get going – the first few episodes are a bit forced – but things perked up with the addition of Justin Kirk as Nancy's roguish brother-in-law Andy. He provides many of the laughs, whether advising his pubescent nephew on the etiquette of masturbation ('There's no such thing as polishing the raised sceptre of love too much') or sparring with his weary sister-in-law.

While not quite as hilarious/gripping as it wants to be, thanks to nice performances this is still a sharp-witted, enjoyable show (those of a sensitive nature should note it also has more bad language than a Quentin Tarantino movie).

 TV Trivia: The theme song for the show is 'Little Boxes', recorded by Malvina Reynolds in 1962.

THE WEST WING (1999–2006)

Starring Martin Sheen, Bradley Whitford, Allison Janney, Richard Schiff

A drama about the inner sanctum of the Oval Office doesn't sound like it would be one the most riveting show to hit the airwaves but *The West Wing* was compulsive viewing. The series followed President Jed Bartlett (Sheen) and his White House staff as they attempt to resolve all manner of political, legislative and personal issues. A large ensemble cast portrays the president's advisors and support team including press secretary C.J Cregg (Janney), deputy chief of staff, Josh Lyman (Whitford) and Stockard Channing as the first lady. This glossy, intelligent show first aired towards the end of the tarnished Clinton administration so American viewers embraced this moral, fictional president as the one they wished they had.

An in-depth knowledge of the American political system is not necessary to fully appreciate *The West Wing*, in fact, the less you know about it the better. There are many inaccuracies regarding the machinations of federal government but a few factual errors do not detract from the nail biting drama. The show focuses on the human side of the political process making it more engaging than the reality could ever be, and if real life White House advisors are fans, then who are we to complain. The show has also received some criticism for being too left wing with Bartlett's liberal administration emerging from conflicts as heroes while conservatives were often depicted as bad guys. Certainly, *The West Wing* presents an idealised, optimistic insight into the privileged world of the White House, although things took a darker tone in Season 3 after 9/11. However, throughout its run, the show remained challenging and witty with enough intrigue and rapid fire banter to keep you on your toes.

 TV trivia: At the end of its run in 2006, *The West Wing* had amassed a grand total of 26 Emmys, the most in history for a drama series, tied with *Hill Street Blues*.

A YEAR IN PROVENCE (1993)

Starring John Thaw, Lindsay Duncan, Jean-Pierre Delage

Peter Mayle's books about his family's experiences living in France were winningly translated to the screen with John Thaw starring as Mayle and Duncan as his wife Annie. They decide to leave the London rat race behind and head to the south of France, tempted by the picturesque countryside, simple rural life, great food, fine wine and sunshine. Of course, it's not that simple, and the Mayles soon find themselves in various comic situations as they meet colourful locals, endure mistral winds and even discover the Mafia are involved in the regional truffle season.

It's a charming series, more comedy than drama, which boasts luscious locations and sweet performances from Thaw, Duncan and the supporting cast. And while the couple may have numerous trials and tribulations in their year abroad, it can't have been all bad, as Provence property agents noticed a marked increase in Brits looking for homes in the region following the series being shown on TV.

 TV Trivia: Peter Mayle was awarded a Knight of the French Legion of Honour in 2002.

COSTUME DRAMA

BIG SKIRTS, STUFFED SHIRTS AND LITERARY ADAPTATIONS FOR
ALL AGES...

ANNE OF GREEN GABLES (1985)

Starring Megan Follows, Colleen Dewhurst, Richard Farnsworth

Lucy Maud Montgomery's classic novel about a red-headed orphan girl at the
turn of the century was lovingly translated for TV in this 1985 series. On
Prince Edward Island, elderly siblings Matthew and Marilla Cuthbert have
decided to take on an orphan boy to help them on their run down farm.
Thanks to a mistake, they get an orphan girl instead – the dreamy, cheeky,
headstrong Anne Shirley (Follows).

Made for Canadian TV, this is a yummy adaptation that stays close to the
much-loved children's book as red-headed Anne grows up on the Cuthbert
farm, makes friends with the pretty Diana (Schuyler Grant) and has adventures with nemesis-turned pal Gilbert Blythe (Jonathan Crombie), all the
while saying what she thinks ('Mrs. Hammond told me that God made my
hair red on purpose and I've never cared for Him since'), no matter what the
consequences.

A sequel in 1987 that followed Anne as she took on a teaching position at a
girls' boarding school – it is partly based on the next three Anne books by
Montgomery, and a final mini-series, *Anne: The Continuing Story* (2000), that
followed Anne to New York and France during World War I.

**TV Trivia: *Anne of Green Gables* director Kevin Sullivan is
producing a new TV movie based on the characters – *A New
Beginning* – for 2009, in which Shirley Maclaine is expected to star.**

THE BARCHESTER CHRONICLES (1982)

Starring Donald Pleasance, Alan Rickman, Nigel Hawthorne

If you thought Alan Rickman's sinister bad guy roles in *Die Hard* and *Robin
Hood: Prince of Thieves* were deliciously nasty, wait till you see him almost slith-
er across the screen as slimy Reverend Obadiah Slope in this adaptation of the
first two of Anthony Trollope's Barchester novels (there are seven in all). Set

in the town of Barchester, this series focuses on the machinations of the local clergy, as the sweet warden of the parish, Reverend Harding (Pleasance), a beacon of goodness surrounded by ambition and weak-willed men in the form of Bishop Proudie (Clive Swift) and Slope.

Pleasance is superb in his central role, and is equally matched by Rickman and a cast that also includes David Gwilim, Joseph O'Conor, Phyllidia Law, Susan Hampshire and Geraldine McEwan. Adapted by Alan Plater, it's a clever, often witty drama, and a superb TV version of Trollope's stories and characters.

 TV Trivia: Harding's daughter Susan is played by Donald Pleasance's real-life daughter, Angela Pleasance.

BLEAK HOUSE (2005)

Starring Gillian Anderson, Charles Dance, Denis Lawson, Anna Maxwell Martin

Charles Dickens' novel had been tackled on TV twice before (in a 1959 BBC series and a 1985 production with Diana Rigg and Denholm Elliott), but the version that has deservedly had praise heaped upon it is Andrew Davies' BBC series, broadcast in 2005. It was a challenging task to take on, as *Bleak House* is widely regarded as one of Dickens' greatest literary achievements, especially in its depiction of Victorian London. The story was first published in 19 monthly instalments (many with cliffhanger endings), and so the decision was made to pace the TV version in the same way: following an hour-long introductory episode were fourteen half-hour ones, shown twice a week to keep viewers hooked.

It's the tale of the icy Lady Dedlock (Anderson), who is harbouring a dark secret about her past, and the lawyer, Tulkinghorn (Dance) who is determined to uncover it. Lady Dedlock is caught up in an infamous law case, Jarndyce vs. Jarndyce, as is John Jarndyce (Lawson) and his young wards Richard (Patrick Kennedy) and Ada (Carey Mulligan). John also takes the lovely Esther (Martin) under his wing, but she is unaware that she has ties to Lady Dedlock that could ruin them all.

Packed with entertaining characters such as Pauline Collins' Miss Flite, Johnny Vegas' Krook and police inspector Bucket (Alun Armstrong), this is a cracking adaptation that boasts over 80 speaking roles and 2,000 extras in the cast. One of the best adaptations of any Dickens novel you're likely to see.

 TV Trivia. The first day of filming was 7 February, which was Charles Dickens' birthday.

BLUE REMEMBERED HILLS (1979)

Starring Colin Welland, Michael Elphick, Robin Ellis, Helen Mirren

Part of BBC's Play For Today series, *Blue Remembered Hills* was written by Dennis Potter and remains one of his most successful plays. A group of seven year olds – all played by adult actors – are playing in the Forest of Dean on a summer afternoon in 1943, but things are about to take a dark turn. A look at childhood imagination and the loss of innocence, the play shows the children play acting, then bullying each other, and jokes turn to tragedy.

It's thought-provoking stuff – a sort of simpler version of *Lord of the Flies* – that stays in the memory thanks to Potter's script and the device of grown men and women playing the children. Elphick and Welland, especially, are convincing, while Colin Jeavons is moving as the disturbed Donald. The Play For Today strand also featured work by writers such as Willy Russell, Alan Bennett, David Hare, Jack Rosenthal, John Mortimer and Mike Leigh, as well as Potter's own controversial *Brimstone and Treacle* with Michael Kitchen and Denholm Elliot that was made in 1976 but banned from being shown on TV until 1987. It's available on DVD, as are a few of the Play For Todays.

 TV Trivia: The film's title comes from AE Houseman's poem 'XL' from the collection *A Shropshire Lad*, which Potter reads at the end of the play.

BRIDESHEAD REVISITED (1981)

Starring Jeremy Irons, Anthony Andrews

Widely regarding as the best British TV period drama ever made, this 13-hour series became the show to watch and talk about in winter 1981 when it was first broadcast. Boasting a who's who of acclaimed British actors – Diana Quick, John Gielgud, Claire Bloom, Laurence Olivier – the series had an impressive pedigree as it was based on the Evelyn Waugh novel and adapted for TV by John Mortimer.

Charles Ryder (the always impeccable Irons) narrates the story of his relationship with the foppish Sebastian Flyte (Andrews, in a career-best performance) and his sister Julia (Quick), a tale that spans two decades from the men's first meeting at Oxford University in the 1920s to Ryder's service as a Captain during the latter part of World War II. Sebastian is the son of an aristocratic family, and he takes Charles home to the family stately home, Brideshead Castle, where Charles meets the rest of the family, including the beautiful Julia.

A tale of an England that is long gone – or perhaps never existed except in novels and period dramas like this – *Brideshead Revisited* is filled with luscious scenes of Oxford's dreamy spires, the stunning Brideshead (actually Castle Howard) and iconic images such as Sebastian clutching his much-loved teddy, Aloysius. Touching on class issues (Ryder is definitely not to the manor born but is seduced by the Flytes' lifestyle), religion (Sebastian's family is Catholic), family relationships, duty, love, war and societal obligation, this is a very British drama, one that is beautifully filmed and played and a must-see for everyone.

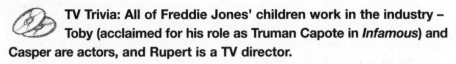 **TV Trivia: In 2003, producer Douglas Rae announced he was going to remake *Brideshead* for the big screen, with Colin Farrell and Jude Law in the lead roles. It never happened, but a 2008 movie, with Ben Whishaw, Matthew Goode, Emma Thompson and Michael Gambon was made.**

THE CAESARS (1968)

Starring Roland Culver, Andre Morell, Ralph Bates, Freddy Jones

'An everyday story of sex, madness and regicide' is how this Granada TV series was described. It is not as well known as *I, Claudius*, but is just as fascinating. Filmed in black and white, the series ran for six one-hour episodes, each focusing on a particular character in Roman history, beginning with Augustus (Culver) as he wonders who will succeed him on his death. There's Germanicus (Eric Flynn), who debates whether he should march on Rome and claim the throne; ruthless Tiberius (Morell), who sees Germanicus as his main (and deadly) rival; and, as Tiberius weakens, the threat of Caligula (Bates) and Claudius (Jones) as potential leaders – the scariest of which is, of course, the utterly bonkers Caligula, who goes on to declare himself a god.

While not quite as debauched as *I, Claudius*, this is nonetheless a terrific drama showing the murderous, treacherous power struggles of Rome. Jones, especially, is superb, and there is winning support from Caroline Blakiston as the scheming Agrippina.

TV Trivia: All of Freddie Jones' children work in the industry – Toby (acclaimed for his role as Truman Capote in *Infamous*) and Casper are actors, and Rupert is a TV director.

CHURCHILL: THE WILDERNESS YEARS (1981)

Starring Robert Hardy, Sian Phillips, Nigel Havers

While everyone remembers Churchill as the prime minister who led Britain to victory during World War II, it's often forgotten that he was completely out of favour for over a decade before the war, and politically ostracised for his views (one of which was that a man named Hitler was a potential threat to our nation).

The Wilderness Years chronicles the period from 1929 to 1939 in which he became estranged from the Conservatives, some who were none too pleased with his opinions on India and his relationships with various Americans, including press baron William Randolph Hearst, and is a fascinating look at the years leading up to the war. But the star, throughout, is not the meaningful history, the often fascinating facts or the impressive script – it is Robert Hardy, who does more than 'play' Churchill, his performance is so gripping it is as if he is channelling the great man himself. Although the cast also includes talent such as Sian Phillips, Tim Pigott-Smith, Paul Freeman, Eric Porter (as Chamberlain) and Edward Woodward, it is Hardy's bullish, gruff, powerhouse performance that makes this such riveting viewing.

TV Trivia: Since this series, Robert Hardy has played Winston Churchill in four other series: *The Woman He Loved*; *War and Remembrance*; *Bomber Harris*; and even in an episode of *Miss Marple*.

CRANFORD (2007)

Starring Judi Dench, Eileen Atkins, Imelda Staunton

The most talked about series on TV in winter 2007, *Cranford* was remarkably successful when you consider it is a drama that centres around a group of both middle-aged and older women in the 19th century. Based on Elizabeth Gaskell's series of novels (three of them), the series of five episodes from producer Sue Birtwhistle (who also made the acclaimed 1995 TV version of *Pride and Prejudice*) became as addictive as a soap and boasted the cream of British actresses.

Set in the market town of Cranford in 1842 (and based on Gaskell's own growing-up in the Cheshire town of Knutsford), the series focuses on one year of upheaval as a new railway, built by migrant workers, is constructed, sending the local townspeople into a tizzy as they fear the breakdown of law and order it will bring. Among the community shocked by the railway's impeachment on their lives – and the arrival of a young, forward-thinking doctor, Frank Harrison (Simon Woods) – is spinster Matty Jenkyns (Dench), who has never recovered from giving up the man she loved and her sister Deborah (Atkins), who has appointed herself the town's moral guardian.

While a series featuring two of Britain's greatest living actresses together on screen is impressive enough (and Atkins, especially, truly shines), this funny, smart drama also boasts Staunton, Julia McKenzie, Philip Glenister,

Lesley Manville, Julia Sawalha, Jim Carter, Francesca Annis, Greg Wise and Michael Gambon amongst the cast. Truly brilliant.

 TV Trivia: The weather during the summer *Cranford* was filmed was so awful that the cast had to wear polythene sheets between scenes to protect their period costumes from the rain.

A DANCE TO THE MUSIC OF TIME (1997)

Starring James Purefoy, Simon Russell Beale

Anthony Powell's 12-volume tome, considered a literary classic, attracted some of Britain's most impressive actors when it was made for television in 1997. John Gielgud, Alan Bennett, Edward Fox, James Purefoy, Miranda Richardson and Eileen Atkins are just some of the weighty names appearing in the lavish production that spans more than half a century from the 1920s to the 1970s and features luscious settings such as Berkeley Castle, the city of Venice, the Café Royal and stately homes including Luton Hoo.

The plot is twisting, complex and packed with characters, although the narrator of the story is Nick Jenkins (played by James D'Arcy, Purefoy and John Standing), who relates the successes, failures, infidelities and even deaths of the people he befriends as he makes his way through private school, World War II and beyond, including Peter (Bobby Webster, Jonathan Cake), the odious Kenneth Widmerpool (Beale) and the alcoholic Charles (Luke De Lacey, Paul Rhys).

Many more characters come and go in this ambitious production, to the point that it all gets a bit confusing, especially when some characters have up to three actors playing the role, while other characters are played by just one. In the end, it doesn't quite work, but the filmmakers, including directors Christopher Morahan (*The Jewel in the Crown*) and Alvin Rakoff (ITV Playhouse), have a very decent stab at an almost impossible project.

 TV Trivia: Various screenwriters had attempted to adapt Powell's books for the screen before and never finished the project, including Dennis Potter.

DAVID COPPERFIELD (1999)

Starring Bob Hoskins, Maggie Smith, Daniel Radcliffe, Nicholas Lyndhurst

One of the best adaptations – for film or TV – of Charles Dickens' *David Copperfield*, this BBC version manages to take the author's very weighty tome and turn it into a less-than-four-hour mini-series without losing the feel of the novel, even when some of the secondary characters and their sub-plots have been cut out in favour of the main story. A very young, pre-Harry Potter Daniel Radcliffe plays the young David, who doesn't get on with the stern Edward Murdstone (Trevor Eve), the man his mother married following the death of his father. Eventually David is sent away to boarding school Salem House, where he meets James Steerforth, and the series follows David after he leaves the school and, following the death of his mother, is sent to work at a factory, and the story then follows him to adulthood.

Packed with memorable characters such as Micawber (Hoskins), Aunt Betsy Trotwood (Smith), housekeeper Peggotty (Pauline Quirke), Little Em'ly (Laura Harling) and Uriah Heep (Lyndhurst), this adaptation is brimming over with top performances from an impressive cast that also includes Emilia Fox, Michael Elphick, Zoe Wanamaker, Ian McKellen, Imelda Staunton, Dawn French, Paul Whitehouse and Ian McNeice, while Tom Wilkinson narrates. (Apparently even a young Colin Farrell is in it, as a milkman, though his scenes were left on the cutting room floor).

Other TV versions available on DVD include 1969's two-hour film with Laurence Olivier, Ron Moody and Richard Attenborough and a 2000 three-hour series from the US with Sally Field, Hugh Dancy and Michael Richards (of *Seinfeld* fame).

 TV Trivia: Harry Lloyd, who plays young Steerforth, is actually a descendant of Charles Dickens.

THE DUCHESS OF DUKE STREET (1976)

Starring Gemma Jones, Christopher Cazenove

Widely believed to have been put into production by the BBC following the success of rival ITV's *Upstairs Downstairs* (it was actually created by John Hawkesworth, who produced that series), this was the rags-to-riches saga of Louisa Trotter (Jones), a Cockney scullery maid who rises through the ranks to become the best chef in London, running her own hotel (where the fashionable clientele dub her 'Duchess'). Loosely based on the real-life story of Rosa Lewis, who ran the Cavendish Hotel in Jermyn Street, the series follows Louisa through numerous tragedies at the turn of the century as she has an affair with the Prince of Wales (never a good idea), goes bankrupt, has a bad marriage and then an illegitimate child.

Thirty-one episodes were made (shown in two series), and Jones shines throughout. It's a little soapy in places, but the Edwardian era is nicely captured and there are good supporting performances from Cazenove, as the one love of Louisa's life, Donald Burton as Louisa's errant husband Gus, John Cater as hotel porter Starr and June Brown (best known now as Dot in *EastEnders*) as Louisa's brittle, selfish mother.

 TV Trivia: Gemma Jones has the distinction of playing the first-ever character to die in the series *Inspector Morse*.

EDWARD AND MRS SIMPSON (1978)

Starring Edward Fox, Cynthia Harris, Peggy Ashcroft

One of the most shocking events in royal history – until, of course the Diana/Charles/Camilla tragedy and subsequent regal tabloid headliners – was translated into a guilty TV pleasure that raised many an eyebrow when it was first broadcast for its no-holds-barred depiction of an infamous British scandal. It is, of course, the story of how Edward, Prince of Wales (Fox, in a role he will always be associated with) fell in love with American divorcée Wallis Simpson (Harris) and, in 1936 – after he had become King Edward VIII – how he abdicated the throne so he could marry her.

'The people must take me as I am,' Edward decides, and certainly in Fox's portrayal that means a man who lived an extravagant life, a man who visited depressed areas of England and was loved for it, but also a man who admired Mussolini and infuriated his own government, and someone who perhaps saw a brash American woman as a way of escaping the obligations he had been born into. Wallis, meanwhile, is depicted as something of a gold-digger who naively thought she would end up marrying a king – she was perhaps more sympathetically portrayed in the 2005 drama (available on DVD) *Wallis & Edward*, in which Joely Richardson played the divorcée and Stephen Campbell Moore played Edward.

 TV Trivia: The real Wallis Simpson hated the series depiction of herself so much she attempted to get the series banned in France, where she was living.

EDWARD THE SEVENTH (1974)

Starring Timothy West, Annette Crosbie, Robert Hardy, John Gielgud

An impressively performed ITV series that told the life story of Edward VII from his birth in 1840 to his death in 1910, this was apparently a big hit with the current royal family (possibly because the scandalous Edward was depicted quite kindly). For the first 59 years of his life, Edward (played as an adult by

West) was simply heir to the throne – son of Queen Victoria (Crosbie) and Prince Albert (Hardy) – and, frustrated that he wasn't able to participate in government, he spent his time philandering with numerous mistresses, gambling and drinking, despite being married to the long-suffering Alexandra.

Titled *Edward The King* in the US (because Americans think anything with a number in the title must be a sequel, apparently), the series looks a bit shabby around the edges compared to today's epic period dramas (some of it looks very stage-bound and there are very few outside location shots) but the performances remain powerful. West is commanding as the older Edward (Charles Sturridge equally good as the younger man), and there is strong support from Gielgud as Disraeli, Deborah Grant and Helen Ryan as the young and older Alexandra, as well as Michael Hordern (as Gladstone) and upcoming stars Felicity Kendal (as Princess Vicky), Charles Dance (as Edward's son, played as a child by West's own son, Samuel) and Francesca Annis, whose performance as Edward's mistress Lillie Langtry was so good that series writer David Butler created a series about Langtry's life, *Lillie* (see review, p.395) for her.

 TV Trivia: Timothy West's father, Lockwood West, played Edward VII in an episode of *Upstairs Downstairs*.

ELizABETH R (1971)

Starring Glenda Jackson, Robert Hardy, Ronald Hines

For many years (until Cate Blanchett, Helen Mirren and Anne Marie Duff's recent interpretations for film and TV), there was only one woman associated with the role of Queen Elizabeth I – Glenda Jackson. At the age of 35, she played the Virgin Queen from the young princess who reluctantly inherits the throne to the elderly woman who had seen off suitors, plots against her and the Spanish Armada during her lengthy rule that ended with her death in 1603.

Following in detail the events of Elizabeth's life (and being pretty historically accurate about them, too), the six-part series focuses on court politics, the execution of Elizabeth's cousin Mary, Queen of Scots, her relationship with Dudley (Hardy) and the other men in her court. Throughout, Jackson is majestic and regal, giving a tour de force performance of a defiant, yet conflicted queen. Over 30 years on, it's still impressive.

 TV Trivia: More than 200 costumes were made for Jackson alone, including some so elaborate and heavy she could only sit in them.

FALL OF EAGLES (1974)

Starring Patrick Stewart, Michael Kitchen, Charles Kay

A BBC dramatisation of the decline and subsequent collapse of three European dynasties – the Hapsburgs, Romanovs and Hohenzollerns – between the mid-19th century and the end of World War I, this was an interesting, if somewhat downbeat tale of fortune lost, that also featured such historical events as the reign of Tsar Nicholas II of Russia (Kay) and the rise of Lenin (Stewart).

While soap operatic in places (especially as most of the plot developments take place on indoor sets), the drama relies on good acting and the cast delivers throughout, from Stewart's Lenin to Gayle Hunnicutt as Tsarina Alexandra, Curd Jurgen as Otto Von Bismarck and Kitchen as Trotsky. Although some of the events have to be mentioned rather than depicted due to budget constraints, this is still worth a look just to catch some renowned British performers acting their socks off, and to spot early turns from actors including John Rhys-Davies, Miriam Margolyes and Jan Francis.

 TV Trivia: Patrick Stewart has a human rights scholarship named after him from Amnesty International.

THE FAR PAVILIONS (1984)

Starring Ben Cross, Amy Irving

In 1984 there were two epic mini-series focusing on the British Empire in India – the serious *The Jewel in the Crown* (see review, p.393) and the more Mills-and-Boon-style *The Far Pavillions*. Set during the 19th century, this series encompassed forbidden love, betrayal, intrigue and war in colonial India as British Cavalry officer Ash Pelham-Martyn (Cross, looking like he has been basted in gravy) falls for beautiful Indian Princess Anjuli (the very American Amy Irving), who has been promised in marriage to the nasty Rajah of Bithor (Rossano Brazzi).

Based on the book by M.M. Kaye, this lavish production follows Ash – who, orphaned as a child, was raised in the palace of Anjuli before having to flee to England – and his former childhood playmate as they fall in love en route to her marriage, as part of a grand procession of elephants, wealth, camels, jewels and horses. Overflowing with an impressive cast that includes Omar Sharif, Sir John Gielgud, Christopher Lee, Robert Hardy and Rupert Everett, it all looks sumptuous and yummy, but much of the feel of Indian culture and simmering political problems that feature in Kaye's book are glossed over in favour of shots of Irving looking panic-stricken or lovelorn, depending on the most recent plot twist.

 TV Trivia: A stage musical production of the book/series opened in London's West End in April 2005, but closed just five months later.

FLAMBARDS (1979)

Starring Christine McKenna, Steven Grives, Alan Parnaby

Girls who were young in the seventies fondly remember this lovely series based on the popular books by K.M. Peyton – after all, it had everything a gal could desire: a plain Jane heroine, dashing men, unrequited – and very chaste – love, men bravely going off to war and lots and lots of horses.

In the years before World War I, young orphan Christina Parsons (McKenna) is sent to live with her bitter and beastly paralysed uncle William Russell (Edward Judd), and his two sons, the arrogant horseman Mark (Grives) and the more timid and caring Will (Parnaby), who has a secret passion for those magnificent new flying machines and a fear of horses since one threw him, leaving him lame. They live at a crumbling estate and Christina is soon working hard to keep the place going while also learning to ride, experiencing the rituals of the hunt, and falling in love with one of her cousins (that's about as raunchy as it gets).

Featuring a memorable and haunting theme – 'The Song of Christina' – the series captured all the events of Peyton's first three books – *Flambards*, the weepy *The Edge of the Cloud* and *Flambards in Summer* – over 13 hour-long episodes. (The final book, *Flambards Divided*, wasn't finished by Peyton until 1981, and many fans don't like it anyway, as it spoiled the romantic ending of the previous book). Like *Anne of Green Gables*, sobbing through this sweet series – and the books on which it was based – should be a rite of passage for every girl.

 TV Trivia: K.M. Peyton began writing at the age of nine, and won the prestigious Carneigie Medal in 1969 for the Flambards novel *The Edge of the Cloud*.

THE FLAME TREES OF THIKA (1981)

Starring Hayley Mills, David Robb

A sort of TV equivalent to *Out Of Africa*, *The Flame Trees of Thika* was based on Elspeth Huxley's own experiences when she went with her Scottish parents to Kenya, and they began a coffee plantation at the beginning of the 20th century. As Elspeth (Holly Aird) learns about the beauty and cruelty of the nature around her, she also makes friends with ex-pats and Africans, while observing the struggles her parents Robin (Robb) and Tilly (Mills) go through and the various traumas that affect the British striving to build a little corner of society in a different culture.

A seven-episode mini-series from producer Verity Lambert, this was filmed on location in Kenya and the country looks breathtaking. Mills is simply luminous, but the current politics of the country, and the way the series waxes nostalgic about a society where the British took advantage of the Kenyans makes this retrospectively uncomfortable viewing. While Huxley did mention the growing tensions in her memoirs, they're glossed over here for a more romantic story that now looks very dated.

 TV Trivia: Elspeth Huxley was a friend of Joy Adamson, author of the famous *Born Free*.

THE FLASHING BLADE (1967)

Starring Robert Etcheverry, Jacques Balutin

Or *Le Chevalier Tempête*, to give this series its proper title. Made in France and dubbed into English, this was made up of 12 half-hour episodes that were broadcast to an unsuspecting British public on Saturday mornings in the early seventies. Unintentionally hilarious (we think), this boasted dashing heroes, thundering horses, sword-fights, castle dungeons and exploding cannons – but ask any kids who watched it back then and they probably couldn't explain the plot! That was because it was re-edited for the UK, making the wobbly plots even more confusing than they already were in their native tongue.

What we can say is that the series was set in the early 17th century, it centred on the war between France and Spain and was mainly set in Casal, and particularly a castle under siege from the Spanish and the two Frenchmen – Francois, Chevalier de Recci (Etcheverry) and his servant Guillot (Balutin) – who do their best to infuriate the Spanish forces in the name of France. Badly dubbed, truly dreadful stuff, in an utterly compelling and fun way.

TV Trivia: When it was first broadcast in Britain, part of the final episode was shown with sound but no picture due to a problem with the film. The final few minutes had to be rebroadcast for kids on the show 'Ask Aspel' after the show was inundated with requests.

THE FORSYTE SAGA (1967. 2002)

Starring Eric Porter, Kenneth More (1967)
Starring Damian Lewis, Rupert Graves, Gina McKee (2002)

Two TV versions of John Galsworthy's novels have been made for television, the first being a deservedly much revered 1967 Emmy award-winning series, made in black and white. Over 26 episodes, it followed the tempestuous lives of the aristocratic Forsyte family from the 1870s until the 1920s. It's gripping stuff – the writers of the series ensured each episode ended on something of a cliffhanger to keep people viewing – as the family feuds, schemes and implodes, most memorably in a scene in which Soames Forsyte (Porter, who became something of a bizarre heartthrob in the utter-bastard role) rapes his wife Irene (Nyree Dawn Porter) after discovering she has had an affair. Meanwhile Soames' cousin Jolyon (the wonderful More) is cheating on his own wife with their daughter's governess (whom he eventually runs away with).

While that series flagged a little in the middle episodes, the 2002 version, in which the story is condensed into six parts, romps along at a faster pace. It's even more like *Dynasty* in period costume as the family machinations are played out once more – secret affairs, doomed marriages, tragic death, family dysfunctions. Damian Lewis is a perfect mix of scheming and needy and mean as Soames, while Rupert Graves is winning as Jolyon and Ioan Gruffud suitably hunky as the architect whose romantic overtures cause problems in the family. Only McKee as Irene isn't quite right – she's a little too aloof as the woman Soames is obsessed with and other men are in love with – but that's a small criticism about what is otherwise, in both versions, a thoroughly enjoyable, often riveting period drama.

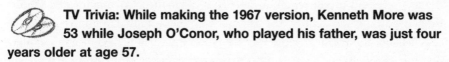 **TV Trivia: While making the 1967 version, Kenneth More was 53 while Joseph O'Conor, who played his father, was just four years older at age 57.**

GORMENGHAST (2000)

Starring Jonathan Rhys Meyers, Cameron Powrie, Ian Richardson

A fantasy series that looks and feels like period drama, *Gormenghast* is based on Mervyn Peake's eccentric *Gormenghast* trilogy (*Titus Groan*, *Gormenghast* and *Titus Alone*) and follows the fortunes and misfortunes of the inhabitants of Gormenghast castle, who have lived there for over 70 generations. However, in their midst is someone who wants to change all that – kitchen boy Steerpike (Meyers), a conniving but attractive young man who wants to rise from his menial servant's position and take control of the castle himself.

It's a dastardly treat that features such plot twists as death-by-owls, arson and banishment, plus the occasional murder-by-starvation, and at its centre is a deliciously evil performance from Meyers. He's surrounded by a superb supporting cast, too, including Ian Richardson as mad Lord Groan, Zoe Wanamaker and Lynsey Baxter as doomed twins Clarice and Cora, and Christopher Lee as Fray.

 TV Trivia: Rhys-Meyers's real name is Jonathan O'Keefe – he changed his surname to his mother's maiden name when he took up acting.

HEiMAT (1984)

Starring Marita Breuer,Willli Burger, Gertrud Bredel

An epic undertaking for German television, *Heimat: Eine Deutsche Chronik* was a 15-hour series that followed the lives of the Simon family in the fictional village of Schabbach from 1919 to 1982, depicting how they were affected by the many traumatic events in German history during that time period. The story begins by introducing us to Paul Simon, who returns from World War I and marries Maria (Breuer), the mayor's daughter. However, the war has left him ill at ease, and one day he goes out for a drink and never comes back, leaving Maria with their two sons. For many years, no one in the village knows his whereabouts – dissatisfied with Germany, Paul has emigrated alone to America.

Beautifully filmed in colour and black and white, the series was shown on TV and released at the cinema, and is a fascinating chronicle of a family affected both by war and by the advances in technology and communication that changed the world over the following decades. Well played by an ensemble cast, this also features a stunning central performance from Breuer, who has to age from 19 to old age over the course of the series, and does so incredibly convincingly. It's a big task to take on, watching such a lengthy series, but it's worth the effort. Two further *Heimat* series were made – the 25-hour long *Die Zweite Heimat* followed Maria's son Hermann to Munich during the 1960s, while *Heimat 3* follows Hermann's story from 1989 until 2000.

 TV Trivia: *Heimat* took over five years to make, and is loosely based on director Edgar Reitz's family's own remembrances.

HENRY VIII (2002)

Starring Ray Winstone, Helena Bonham Carter, David Suchet, Sean Bean

If you're looking for scandal, adultery, executions and banishment, you can't do much better than a series based on the reign of King Henry VIII. And this mini-series boasts all that – in graphic detail, no less – and more, as Ray Winstone's growling, thuggish Henry storms about shagging wives, divorcing wives, beheading others, pissing off the Catholic Church and ruling his kingdom. Spanning Henry's life from the time he inherited the throne as a teenager to his death, portly and riddled with disease, this is a blood-splattered romp through the infamous king's reign.

Winstone, while a great actor, is a bit too rough-and-ready as the strong-minded king who was equally as renowned for his learned ways as for his enthusiastic bed-hopping – his loutish manner means you expect Henry to suddenly head-butt anyone who disagrees with him. The supporting cast is better suited to their roles – Bonham Carter as the ill-fated Anne Boleyn, Suchet as Cardinal Wolsey, Bean as Robert Aske – but all are bogged down by a rather trite script and clichéd plotting. Faint-hearted viewers should note that this series is quite violent (Henry rapes one wife, a jouster is speared through the head with a lance, that sort of thing), and that's even before you consider all the beheadings.

 TV Trivia: Over 10 gallons of fake blood were used in this production.

A HORSEMAN RIDING BY (1978)

Starring Nigel Havers, Prunella Ransome, Glyn Houston

A TV adaptation of RF Delderfield's (*To Serve Them All My Days*) novel about a former soldier, invalided in the Boer War, who accepts the invitation to become squire of a very rundown manor in Devon. Beginning in 1902, the series follows Paul Craddock (Havers) as he takes on the dilapidated estate, and tries to renovate it and also win the trust of suspicious locals.

It's all terribly, terribly English, packed with stiff upper lips, a sense of duty and that annoying English habit of leaving things unspoken as Craddock eventually finds a bride and has a family only for things to sour as World War I approaches. The series has dated quite badly and the plot moves very slowly, while the performances border on hammy. While Delderfield's three 'Horseman' books took the story of the Craddocks up to the 1960s; this mercifully ended after 13 episodes, ending the TV story in 1919.

TV Trivia: Paul Craddock was Havers' first major leading role on TV.

HOTEL DU LAC (1986)

Starring Anna Massey, Denholm Elliott, Julia McKenzie, Patricia Hodge

A bittersweet drama based on Anita Brookner's Booker Prize-winning novel about a woman named Edith (Massey) who retreats to the Hotel Du Lac, on the shores of Lake Geneva in Switzerland, following an affair with a married man. Desperately lonely and reflecting on the life that brought her to this point, she observes the guests around her – Mrs Pusey (Googie Withers) and her vulgar daughter, Jennifer (McKenzie); gentleman Mr Neville (Elliott); Madame de Bonneiul (Irene Handl) and the sad Monica (Hodge).

Wih a beautiful score from Carl Davis and a taut script, adapted for the screen by Christopher Hampton (*Dangerous Liaisons*), this is a sumptuous, melancholy BBC drama that showcases the terrific talents of Massey, Elliott and Hodge especially and also features a classy supporting cast, including Barry Foster and Jean-Marc Barr. Rather beautiful but also terribly sad.

 TV Trivia: Anna Massey won a Best Actress BAFTA for her performance.

THE HOUSE OF ELIOTT (1991–1993)

Starring Stella Gonet, Louise Lombard

Deliciously parodied by French and Saunders in their sketch shows, *The House of Eliott* was created by actresses Eileen Atkins and Jean Marsh, who had previously developed the acclaimed series *Upstairs Downstairs*. The 1920s-set series begins by introducing us to sisters Beatrice (Gonet) and Evangeline Eliott (Lombard), whose respected father has recently died. Hoping for a nice inheritance, the gals are in for a bit of a shock when they discover all they have been left is a mountain of debt and the family house, and there are more shocks to come, including the existence of their father's mistress and illegitimate son. When the sisters find their homemade clothes are being praised by everyone who sees them, they decide to set up their own fashion house – the House of Eliott – as a way of earning money and keeping their places in society.

It's all terribly terribly posh and packed with lovely twenties fashion, eager gals, wonderful parties and dashing men (as well as a few dastardly ones) and over three series, the plucky ladies encounter enough scandal, deception, jealousy and betrayal to give *Dallas* or *Dynasty* a run for its money. It is a bit *too* soapy in places, and the second and third series aren't as good as the first (the second particularly lacks any new ideas), but as a drama about independent young women doing it for themselves, it's entertaining enough.

 TV Trivia: The exterior of the House of Eliott was actually a house in Berkeley Square, Bristol.

I. CLAUDIUS (1976)

Starring Derek Jacobi, John Hurt, Sian Phillips

A jaw-droppingly impressive cast brought this lavish, yet studio-bound drama to the screen. Based on Robert Graves' *I Claudius* and *Claudius The God*, the series introduced us to the stammering Roman Emperor of the title (Jacobi, convincing both as an 18-year-old youth and a 64-year-old man) as he writes a secret history of his family in 54 AD. And what a family it is – from his nefarious, murdering grandmother Livia (Phillips, brilliantly nasty) to her utterly bonkers and debauched descendant Caligula (Hurt) who thinks nothing of making his favourite horse a senator. Both deeply serious and sometimes joyfully comic – you'll laugh as Augustus (Brian Blessed) tells off all the men, standing in a line, who have slept with his married daughter – this also became renowned for various shocking scenes, the most discussed being Caligula murdering his pregnant sister (to whom he is married), and then cutting the foetus from her womb and eating it. Definitely not for sensitive viewers (or stomachs).

While some of the Roman history is a bit ropey – one character appears at an event that took place more than a decade after his recorded death – the performances are stunning, from the leads to cast members including Patrick Stewart – with hair! – as Sejanus, George Baker as Tiberius and Christopher Biggins as Nero. The script, too, is a treat, packed with machinations, wit, kinkiness, murder and betrayal, and, over 30 years on, it is easy to see why this series is still deserving of the title of one of the best period dramas ever made. A true classic.

 TV Trivia: In his memoirs, Ronnie Barker wrote that he was originally offered the role of Claudius.

JANE EYRE (2006)

Starring Ruth Wilson, Toby Stephens

Charlotte Bronte's classic novel has been adapted for the screen (big and small) on numerous occasions, with everyone from Joan Fontaine to

Charlotte Gainsbourg taking on the role of the eponymous heroine. There have been six main television versions: three of them – 1970s series with Susannah York as Jane and George C. Scott as Rochester; 1997's adaptation with Samantha Morton and Ciaran Hinds and 1956's drama with Daphne Slater and Stanley Baker – are currently unavailable on DVD. Of the three that are available, 1973's lengthy production with Sorcha Cusack and Michael Jayston probably stays closest to the original text, while 1983's mini-series with Timothy Dalton as Rochester is an enjoyable romp. But best of all the versions is the most recent, 2006's BBC four-part series starring newcomer Wilson as Jane Eyre.

The story is, of course, about orphaned Jane, who grows up first in the miserable household of her aunt, Mrs Reed, and then at Lowood School, where she lives until she gains a job as a governess to a child who lives at Thornfield Hall, the home of Mr Rochester (Stephens). As fans of the novel will know, his house holds many secrets, including the presence of someone who cackles madly in the night. It's gripping stuff, even if you know the source material well, and Wilson and Stephens fit well into their roles of young, vulnerable woman and grumpy older man. At the same time the BBC broadcast this, they also showed an adaptation of *Wide Sargasso Sea* (author Jean Rhys' 'prequel' to Jane Eyre, about Rochester and his first wife) starring Rebecca Hall and Rafe Spall – unfortunately it's not available on DVD.

 TV Trivia: Renishaw Hall in Derbyshire was used as the location for Thornfield Hall.

JESUS OF NAZARETH (1977)

Starring Robert Powell, Anne Bancroft, Ernest Borgnine, James Earl Jones, James Mason

As Martin Scorsese (*The Last Temptation of Christ*) or Mel Gibson (*The Passion of the Christ*) would probably tell you, it's very tricky translating the story of Jesus to the screen – however you depict Him, you're going to offend someone. This star-studded mini-series was no exception – it was banned in Egypt – although it later got the thumbs up from the Vatican as one of the movies/TV series they regarded as suitable viewing for the faithful. Praise indeed. And while everyone from Christian Bale to Ralph Fiennes to Donald Sutherland has portrayed the son of God, it is Powell's performance here that remains one of the most memorable depictions of Christ committed to screen.

Directed by Franco Zeffirelli, this mini-series is an accessible, reverent look at the life of Jesus that features in-depth passages from the Bible as part of the script, and delivers the story in immense detail, beginning with his birth and spending time on some of the key events including the Last Supper, Jesus's first meeting with John the Baptist (Michael York), the crucifixion and resurrection.

It's beautifully made and an involving watch – though parents should note that some scenes are surprisingly graphic for a seventies TV series (the baby boys snatched from mothers' arms is particularly upsetting, while the crucifixion does show the nails being driven into hands and feet). Powell is simply mesmerising in the lead role, an impressive feat when you consider the cast also includes Bancroft as Mary Magdalane, Ian McShane as Judas, Ralph Richardson as Simeon, Laurence Olivier as Nicodemus, and James Earl Jones as Balthazar.

 TV Trivia: Zeffirelli has stated that his main motivation to make the film was to put an end to the belief that the Jews killed Jesus.

THE JEWEL IN THE CROWN (1984)

Starring Susan Wooldridge, Geraldine James, Art Malik, Tim Pigott-Smith, Charles Dance

A lavish production, based on the four novels of *The Raj Quartet* by Paul Scott, this hugely successful series brilliantly captured the last days of the Raj in 1940s India. Daphne Manners (Wooldridge) is newly arrived from England when she falls for English-educated Hari Kumar (Malik). Their romance turns to tragedy, however, when one night the couple are attacked, Daphne is raped and a British officer named Ronald Merrick (Pigott-Smith, who should be commended for taking a thoroughly unlikeable character and making him human), who once proposed to Daphne, accuses Hari of the crime.

Shown in 14 parts, this prestigious series featured some great performances from the cast that also included Dame Peggy Ashcroft, Rachel Kempson, Charles Dance and Geraldine James, and created an image of the British Empire as being something rather glorious at a time in the eighties when there was mass unemployment and strikes often mentioned on the news. Scott's novels weren't as linear as the series, but the dramatisation of his stories (which originally featured multiple narrators and twisting storylines) made for challenging, intellectual viewing and also made stars of Malik and Dance. A classic.

 TV Trivia: One of Tim Pigott-Smith's earliest TV roles was in an episode of *Doctor Who* in 1971 for which he was reportedly paid £60.

LADY CHATTERLEY (1993)

Starring Joely Richardson, Sean Bean

D.H. Lawrence's infamous novel about infidelity has been adapted for the screen more than once (including one raunchy version with *Emmanuelle* star Sylvia Kristel), but this is the version most people remember (especially women transfixed by star Sean Bean's sweaty torso). Directed by Ken Russell, this is decidedly tamer than his cinematic efforts like *The Devils* and *Women in Love*, but nonetheless gets a bit steamy as mistress of the house Joely Richardson gets a bit of rough from hunky Bean.

When her husband returns from the war, Lady Chatterley (Richardson) discovers he has changed – wounded in battle, Lord Chatterley (James Wilby) is paralysed from the waist down and unable to produce an heir to his estate. It's not long before his pretty wife is off to find a baby-maker elsewhere, which leads her into the grubby arms of estate gamekeeper Mellors (Bean). Their affair, if discovered, would be social suicide, and they have little in common, but one look at Mellors in his wellies and Lady Chatterley throws caution to the wind. Surprisingly steamy for TV, this was the enjoyably Mills-and-Boon-like series that really turned Bean from an up-and-coming actor (he had already appeared in the first few *Sharpe* adaptations) into a thinking woman's crumpet.

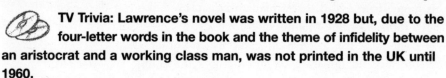 **TV Trivia: Lawrence's novel was written in 1928 but, due to the four-letter words in the book and the theme of infidelity between an aristocrat and a working class man, was not printed in the UK until 1960.**

LILIES (2007)

Starring Catherine Tyldesley, Leanne Rowe, Kerrie Hayes

Interesting costume drama from the BBC that only ran for eight episodes. It follows the fortunes and misfortunes of three Catholic sisters growing up in the Liverpool of the 1920s – Iris (Tyldesley), May (Rowe) and Ruby (Hayes) – as they cope with the return of their brother Billy (Daniel Rigby) from World War I and try to make their way as working-class women, struggling against the restrictive options open to them at the time. Ruby is a corsetiere when she isn't training for the Olympic swimming team, May works as a raunchy (for the time) performer at a gentlemen's club, while Iris holds the family together following the death of their mother. Complicating matters is life with their Dadda (Brian McArdie), an Orangeman who allowed his wife to raise their daughters as Catholic so long as he could raise his son as a Protestant.

Oddly scheduled by the Beeb to air on Friday nights, this was cancelled after one season because, apparently, it did not appeal to younger audiences. One of the few period dramas to be based on original material, rather than a classic novel, the series was written by Heidi Thomas (*Cranford*) and inspired by her own family, so has a feel of truth about it that is often missing from costume drama stories. It was filmed on location in Liverpool, too, although the street the family's house is in had to be recreated on set, as there were no terraced streets in the Liverpool area that weren't blighted by double-glazing or other modern additions.

 TV Trivia: McArdie's mother, a Catholic, told him she couldn't face watching him play an Orangeman.

LiLLiE (1978)

Starring Francesca Annis, Anton Rodgers, Denis Lil, Peter Egan

After appearing as renowned royal mistress Lillie Langtry in the series *Edward the Seventh*, Francesca Annis was given her own series, once again portraying the woman who took many lovers while trapped in a loveless marriage to Edward Langtry (Rodgers). Among the lucky men were Edward, the Prince Of Wales (later Edward VII), and the 13-episode series followed this game gal as she rose through society, befriending notable names such as Oscar Wilde and James Whistler, while also becoming a well-known actress in England and America and many an artist's muse.

Francesca Annis had the difficult task of portraying Lillie from the age of 15 to her death, aged 75 – although most of the story focuses on the period between the 1870s and 1890s, capturing her from her twenties to her forties – and also bringing some warmth to the role of a woman who could be accused of being ambitious, calculating and manipulative. Annis, who looks stunning throughout, manages to make Lillie fascinating and enjoyable company, but the script never really takes a guess at why Lillie went about life the way she did, which is a shame. Nevertheless, if you enjoy watching a royal romp packed with gorgeous costumes, this is still entertaining stuff.

 TV Trivia: Annis was actually pregnant during filming.

LORNA DOONE (2000)

Starring Richard Coyle, Aidan Gillen, Amelia Warner, Martin Clunes

A delicious adaptation of R.D. Blackmore's 17th century-set novel of heroes, feuds, murder and romance that focuses on the family of fallen nobility, the

Doones. Years before, young John Ridd saw his father murdered by the Doones, who rampage through the countryside, killing and stealing whenever they see fit. Now an adult, Ridd (Coyle) has vowed revenge, but he falls for the beautiful Lorna (Warner), unaware that she is a Doone herself, who is promised to Carver Doone (a nasty turn from Gillen), a man who will kill her if he can't have her.

Luscious to look at – every outdoor scene seems to take place amidst a lush green landscape – this is a good, old-fashioned tale of family grudges and forbidden romance (think *Romeo and Juliet* but with more mud) that is nicely played by the leads. It's a little long at three hours (especially as the end is quite guessable), but definitely worth a look. A 1990 TV version of the novel, with Sean Bean, Clive Owen and Polly Walker, is also available on DVD.

 TV Trivia: Amelia Warner was briefly married to Colin Farrell in 2001.

THE LOST PRINCE (2003)

Starring Miranda Richardson, Gina McKee, Michael Gambon, Tom Hollander

One of the sadder episodes in British history, this drama – written and directed by Stephen Poliakoff – tells the story of Prince John, the youngest child of King George V (Hollander) and Queen Mary (Richardson). While his parents are caught up in the tumultuous events of the time, including the build-up to World War I, John is kept hidden away after being diagnosed with epilepsy and learning difficulties, isolated from his family and raised by devoted nanny Lalla (McKee).

It's a terribly moving tale, as John – played first by Daniel Williams and as a teen by Matthew Thomas — is sheltered from the world and his family, and both children playing the role are achingly superb. Kudos should also go to McKee, lovely as the one person who cares about John, and Richardson, who has the tough task of portraying John's duty-bound mother, while Poliakoff's script deftly shows major events in British history as seen through the eyes of this graceful, tragic child. Simply heartbreaking.

 TV Trivia: Matthew Thomas beat over 600 young actors to win the role of the young prince.

MADAME BOVARY (2000)

Starring Frances O'Connor, Hugh Bonneville, Eileen Atkins, Hugh Dancy, Greg Wise

More than 10 adaptations of Gustave Flaubert's notorious novel have been made, including six for TV (one of them, a 1975 mini-series with Francesca Annis, is available on DVD), but perhaps the most lavish is this 2000 BBC version with Frances O'Connor in the lead role of Emma Bovary. The story is, of course, about a 19th-century country doctor's wife who longs for a more passionate existence than the one she has with her steadfast husband, Charles (Bonneville), so she embarks on a series of affairs that begin with an intense relationship with Rodolphe (Wise), followed by a romp with a young student (Dancy). It's all going to end in tears, you know.

Far raunchier than other adaptations – this also features a rather cringe-making shag against a tree – this tragic story is slickly made by director Tim Fywell and features a strong central turn from O'Connor. Bonneville is spot on as the nice but dim Charles, while Wise and Dancy are perfectly cast as the rakish Rodolphe and idealistic Leon, respectively.

 TV Trivia: Both Bonneville and Dancy are fluent French speakers in real life.

MANSFIELD PARK (2007)

Starring Billie Piper, Blake Ritson, Michelle Ryan, James D'Arcy

In 2007, ITV decided to make a handful of costume dramas (traditionally tackled by the BBC) – including *Northanger Abbey*, reviewed below – and this Billie Piper-starring version of Jane Austen's *Mansfield Park*. Unfortunately, this one's a bit of a misfire. The story of Fanny Price (*Doctor Who* star Piper), who grows up with her rich relatives, the Bertrams, at Mansfield Park, is Austen's least enjoyable novel, and the treatment here is incredibly dull (the only bright thing being Piper's 21st-century hair highlights).

Thanks to a plodding script and uninspired direction, you won't really care whether Fanny's secret love for her cousin Edmond (the bland Ritson) will be requited, or about the various other romantic entanglements that involve cousins Maria (Ryan), Julia (Catherine Steadman) and Tom Bertram (D'Arcy) and newcomers Henry (Joseph Beattie) and Mary Crawford (Hayley Atwell). Snore.

 TV Trivia: Newby Hall in North Yorkshire was used as the setting for *Mansfield Park*.

MASADA (1981)

Starring Peter Strauss, Peter O'Toole, Barbara Carrera, Anthony Quayle

Based on the historic novel *The Antagonists*, *Masada* is the fictionalised version of what happened at the siege of Masada in 73AD. O'Toole stars as Lucius Flavius Silva, the Roman commander ordered to lay siege to the fortress citadel of Masada, where hundreds of Jewish Zealots, led by Eleazar ben Ya'ir (Strauss), defended their stronghold only for the standoff to end in tragedy.

It's a moving tale – filmed at the site of Masada itself – that focuses on the two men on opposing sides who try to reach agreement, unaware the might of Rome will never allow such a thing. O'Toole, as you would expect, is almost regal in his performance as Silva, while Strauss gives his usual gruff and tough (and often storming) performance as the leader of the inhabitants of Masada. Historians will quibble that there are factual inaccuracies compared to what is widely believed to be historical truth – for example, the series has the two adversaries meeting on a few occasions for dramatic impact, which in all likelihood never happened – and Carerra as Silva's Jewish mistress is pretty but rather vacant, but all in all this is a fascinating drama packed with a superb cast that also includes Anthony Quayle, David Warner, Timothy West and, erm, Christopher Biggins.

 TV Trivia: When he isn't acting, Peter Strauss runs a citrus farm in Ojai, California.

THE MAYOR OF CASTERBRIDGE (1978)

Starring Alan Bates, Janet Maw, Jack Galloway, Anna Massey

Thomas Hardy's classic novel was turned into one of the BBC's best-ever costume dramas, in part due to the fact that the screenplay was written by Dennis Potter. Over seven 50-minute episodes he tells the story of itinerant worker Michael Henchard (Bates), who drunkenly sells his wife (Anne Stallybrass) and baby daughter to sailor Mr Newsom (Richard Owens) at a fair. Filled with remorse, he determines to change his ways and slowly improves himself, eventually becoming the town mayor. Eighteen years later, his wife and daughter come looking for him, just as Henchard is about to marry again.

Bates, unsurprisingly, is a powerhouse in the role of Henchard, whose rise and fall involves much storming around, brutishness and stubbornness as he forms difficult relationships with his daughter Elizabeth-Jane (Maw), his mistress Lucetta (Massey) and his business rival Donald Farfrae (Galloway).

It's a difficult (and depressing) novel to capture on screen – a movie version, re-sited to the American West, called *The Claim*, was uneven, while another TV series, starring Ciaran Hinds and James Purefoy was solid but forgettable – but, thanks to Potter and Bates, this is a storming adaptation.

 TV Trivia: In 1969, Bates became one of the first actors (along with his co-star Oliver Reed) to do full frontal male nudity in a mainstream movie (*Women in Love*).

MiDDLEMARCH (1994)

Starring Juliet Aubrey, Patrick Malahide, Douglas Hodge, Rufus Sewell, Robert Hardy

George Eliot's tome is regarded as one of the greatest novels of the Victorian era, but as any English literature student will tell you, it's quite a slow, heavyweight read. In the hands of the BBC and screenwriter Andrew Davies, though, it's gripping stuff that successfully mixes stories of the 19th-century people of fictional town Middlemarch with social and political comment, against a backdrop of the looming Industrial Revolution.

It's the story of Dorothea Brooke (Aubrey), who wants to be educated and socially aware, but isn't taken seriously because she is a woman. Wanting to improve her education, she marries aging Reverend Casaubon (Malahide) so she can help him in his scholarly work. Casaubon has a dashing cousin, Will Ladislaw (Sewell), who takes a shine to Dorothea, and the town is also distracted by the arrival of Doctor Lydgate (Hodge), who wants to find a cure for cholera and change the working practices of the local hospital. There are many other characters whose stories we are introduced to, each one as fascinating as the next, in this complex, romantic epic. Unfortunately, the 2002 adaptation of Eliot's final novel, *Daniel Deronda*, is not currently available on DVD.

 TV Trivia: The town of Stamford in Lincolnshire was used for many of the *Middlemarch* locations.

THE MiLL ON THE FLOSS (1996)

Starring Emily Watson, Bernard Hill, James Frain

Originally made into a TV series in 1978 (no longer available on DVD), George Eliot's classic novel got the TV treatment again in 1996 with Emily Watson in the starring role of young Maggie Tulliver. The original novel is quite weighty, beginning by focusing on mill owner Edward Tulliver (Hill) and his children Maggie and Tom (Ifan Meredith), then following Maggie as she falls for the man who betrayed her father (which incurs the wrath of her brother), and ending up as Maggie is torn between two men, Philip (Frain) and Stephen (James Weber Brown), but this adaptation charges through all that at a fair old pace (it's under two hours long), sacrificing some of Eliot's characterisations in the process.

It all looks rather yummy, though, with the River Floss itself almost as much of a character as the people whose lives revolve around it (it was mostly filmed in the wilds of Norfolk). Watson is perfect as the strong-willed Maggie, and it is her performance that really makes this BBC production worth a look.

 TV Trivia: The Mill on the Floss exteriors were filmed at the Bintree Mill in Bintree, Norfolk.

MOLL FLANDERS (1996)

Starring Alex Kingston, Daniel Craig

Made the same year as a dull cinema version with Robin Wright Penn and Morgan Freeman, this ITV production of Daniel Defoe's novel is much more of a colourful romp, and far more enjoyable for it. Flame-haired Alex Kingston shot to fame as Moll, a poor young woman who has a series of fortunes and misfortunes, usually due to a man. Determined to make a better life for herself (usually by using her feminine charms), Moll began life born in prison and tells her story from another prison cell, relating the events that led her there that include taking five husbands – among them her own brother, and the dashing adventurer, Jemmy (Craig) who is her one true love.

The mini-series, adapted from the novel by acclaimed screenwriter Andrew Davies, sticks pretty close to the original story as Moll seduces her way through a series of men, marries into wealth, loses it all, and becomes a clever thief with her own gang, all the while commenting directly to the camera when she makes a good or bad decision, a trick that works quite well. The supporting cast is enjoyable, too, including Diana Rigg, James Fleet and Christopher Fulford.

 TV Trivia: In the US, the mini-series was titled *The Fortunes and Misfortunes Of Moll Flanders*, which is the true title of Defoe's book.

THE MONOCLED MUTINEER (1986)

Starring Paul McGann, Cherie Lunghi, Jane Wood

The series that made a star of Paul McGann, this drama arrived somewhat controversially to TV, advertised as a true story. Critics were soon to point out it was historically inaccurate in places and rather left-wing (frowned upon in Thatcher's England), and numerous newspaper column inches were devoted to the 'scandal' – shame it wasn't just advertised as a historical drama, saving everyone involved in the production a big headache (the *Daily Mail*, for example, called it 'a tissue of lies'). Written by Alan Bleasdale, it focused on the 1917 mutiny at Bull Ring, a British Army training ground in Etaples, France, and the conditions the army endured during World War I. McGann stars as the monocled mutineer of the title, Percy Toplis, who history has portrayed either as some sort of hero or a deserter, coward, thief and even rapist and murderer.

Best watched with a very large pinch of salt by your side, this rather clichéd drama (all the officers are snooty toffs, for example) is nonetheless quite fascinating, although possibly not quite as riveting on screen as the furore caused by its broadcast (the controversy was considered one of the nails in the coffin of BBC Director General Alasdair Milne's career at the Beeb).

 TV Trivia: Toplis's regiment was actually en route to India at the time of the Etaples mutiny, but it has never been proved whether he was with them or not.

NANNY (1981–1983)

Starring Wendy Craig, David Burke, Colin Douglas

The brainchild of star Wendy Craig (who submitted the idea to the BBC under a pseudonym as she was worried the idea would be rejected if producers realised it was from 'an actress who thinks she can write'), this was a nostalgic series about a nanny looking after children in the 1930s. Craig apparently got the idea after seeing advertisements for children's nurses in the old-fashioned society magazine *The Lady*, and from that came up with the story of Nanny Barbara Gray (Craig), a newly qualified carer who is quite enlightened in her approach to child-rearing, and the relationships she builds with both the children in her charge and their often dysfunctional (and usually very wealthy) parents.

It was often weepy fare, especially as the plot moved towards World War II and Nanny cared for evacuees and then took a job in London as a nurse, but there are some funny moments too, and romance in the form of Sam Tavener

(Bourke), whom Nanny Barbara marries before he goes off to war.

Craig is lovely throughout, and the mix of cute but sometimes cheeky children, along with Craig's mumsy charm make this enjoyably old-fashioned family entertainment.

 TV Trivia: Following the popularity of the series, a marked increase in the number of young women choosing nannying as a career was reported.

NORTH AND SOUTH (2004)

Starring Daniela Denby-Ashe, Richard Armitage, Tim Pigott-Smith, Sinead Cusack

Not the Patrick Swayze American civil war bodice-ripper (that's reviewed in War and the Armed Forces, p.299) but a BBC production based on Elizabeth Gaskell's 19th-century love story of the same name. Margaret Hale (ex-EastEnder Denby-Ashe) is the rather forthright daughter of a vicar who has grown up in a nice village in the south of England. Unfortunately dad Richard (Pigott-Smith) decides to relocate the family from this picturesque place to the slightly less lovely northern factory town of Milton, a town where many of the residents are illiterate and suffering from great poverty. Local cotton mill owner John Thornton (Armitage) befriends Richard Hale but offends Margaret with his seemingly brutish ways towards his workers. Oh, can you guess who's going to fall in love despite themselves?

It's all brooding looks and simmering passions (especially from the superb Armitage) between the pair, when they're not puzzling over each other's misunderstandings and insults. Director Brian Percival depicts a grim up-north world of smoking chimney stacks, grime and grimness without going over the top, so it is easy to understand how Margaret goes from hating the place to embracing it as she befriends the working people she meets. Solid romantic stuff.

 TV Trivia: A version of the story was made in 1975, with Tim Pigott-Smith playing the son of the character he plays in this adaptation.

NORTHANGER ABBEY (2007)

Starring Felicity Jones, J.J. Feild, William Beck

Jane Austen's gentle parody of gothic fiction was translated for the screen by Andrew Davies and is an enjoyable version of one of the author's lesser known books. Catherine Morland (Jones) has quite an active imagination, fuelled by the gothic novels she loves, and when she is invited to stay in Bath for the season, she finds herself in a world of elaborate balls and handsome men, including the arrogant John Thorpe (Beck). But when one suitor, Henry Tilney (Feild), takes her to his family estate of Northanger Abbey, Catherine's imagination goes into overdrive and she is entralled by both her beau and his home. Is there a dark mystery behind the house's closed doors? Was Henry's mother murdered?

Davies skilfully blends Catherine's imaginings with the realities around her, and delivers an amusing drama that keeps to the spirit of the original book. He is ably assisted by the cast, which also includes Geraldine James as the voice of Jane Austen herself, Carey Mulligan as John's sister Isabella, Hugh O'Conor as Catherine's brother James, Catherine Walker as Eleanor Tilney and Liam Cunningham as Henry's father. A terrific production from ITV.

 TV Trivia: *Northanger Abbey* **was the first novel Jane Austen completed but the last one to actually be published.**

THE ONEDIN LINE (1971–1980)

Starring Peter Gilmore, Anne Stallybrass, Jessica Benton

A long-running saga about James Onedin, who enters into a marriage of convenience with Anna Webster so he can gain control of her father's ship and eventually run his own shipping line in the Liverpool of the 1860s. The series focused on James's ruthless methods to keep his line running in competition with bigger companies, and also featured the lives of his family, including brother Robert, who runs a shop, and sister Elizabeth, who becomes pregnant by a local sailor but marries steamship designer Albert Frazer.

Perfect entertainment for anyone who has ever dreamed of abandoning life on land and heading for the high seas, this was a watery soap opera that featured early performances from Jill Gascoine, Kate Nelligan and Jane Seymour. Gilmore became something of a heartthrob in his role as Onedin, despite some rather interesting facial hair, and this remains an enjoyable nautical drama, even if it has dated somewhat. The scenes at sea, especially, are worth a look – among the tall ships that were used were the *Sagres*, *Christian Radich* and *Stratsraad Lehmkuhl*.

 TV Trivia: Series creator Cyril Abraham came up with the distinctive name Onedin after he saw the word Ondine, which is a mythological sea creature.

THE OTHER BOLEYN GIRL (2003)

Starring Natascha McElhone, Jodhi May, Jared Harris

Anyone who studied history at school will remember King Henry VIII (played here by Harris) and his six wives – and, in particular, his first two spouses, Catherine of Aragon and her successor, young Anne Boleyn, whose presence caused Henry to divorce his first wife and break away from the Catholic Church (not that he stayed interested in Anne for long – when she didn't bear him a son, he had her head chopped off). This drama, based on Philippa Gregory's novel of the same name, supposes Anne wasn't the only Boleyn woman to catch the corpulent king's eye – there was also Mary, who was first to have an affair with him before her sister came to the court.

Like Gregory's book, the series has been rightly criticised for being historically inaccurate in places, and it's also portrayed on screen as a soapy adventure rather than a historical drama. Fans of traditional period series will find the hand-held cameras and the characters-talking-to-camera devices irritating – it feels more like it's set in the *Big Brother* house rather than Tudor court – but this is worth a look for May's striking performance as Anne (McElhone's as Mary is less successful).

Since this series was made, Gregory's novel has been adapted once more, this time for the big screen, with Natalie Portman as Anne, Scarlett Johansson as Mary and Eric Bana as Henry VIII.

 TV Trivia: While director Philippa Lowthorpe wrote a script for the series, she also spent weeks with the cast prior to filming, improvising dialogue.

OUR MUTUAL FRIEND (1976: 1998)

Starring Jane Seymour, Nicholas Jones, Patrick Troughton (1976);
Anna Friel, Paul McGann, Steven Mackintosh (1998)

Two versions of Dickens' novel have been made for TV – a 1998 mini-series and a 1976 drama. Considered Charles Dickens' most complex and dark novel, the tale begins as John Harmon's body is pulled from the River Thames. He had been expected to marry the mercenary Bella Wilfer, but his death means his estate goes to his former employees, the poor Boffin family, who take Bella in and begin to rise through London society. Meanwhile, a man who was present when Harmon's body was found, Julius Handford, tells the Boffins his name is Rokesmith and offers his services, free of charge, as their secretary. Also featuring in the tale are Gaffer Hexam, who found Harmon's body, his son Charley, devoted daughter Lizzie and barrister Eugene Wrayburn, who falls for her.

There are many other characters featured in both versions of the story as twists and turns take place, many revolving around the characters' obsessions with money and power. The 1998 version is an absolute corker, capturing the essence of Dickens' intricate book perfectly, and featuring strong performances from Anna Friel as Bella, Steven Mackintosh as Rokesmith and Paul McGann as Wrayburn, while Keeley Hawes, David Morrissey, Pam Ferris, Kenneth Cranham, and Timothy Spall are part of the classy supporting cast. The 1976 adaptation isn't quite on a par with the later one, but it's equally as interesting. Jane Seymour makes for a fascinating Bella, and she is joined by Patrick Troughton and his real-life son David Troughton, Warren Clarke, Leo McKern and Ronald Lacey. Both versions are worth a look, but the 1998 one isn't just a little better, it's also one of the best TV adaptations of any Dickens novel.

 TV Trivia: *Our Mutual Friend* was Dickens's last completed novel, finished in 1865. He died five years later of a stroke.

THE PALLISERS (1974)

Starring Susan Hampshire, Philip Latham, Donald Pickering

The BBC adaptation of Anthony Trollope's six Palliser novels could easily be included in the Soap Opera section of this book. There's political scandal, lecherous men, money and power struggles, betrayal, murder and passion amongst the posh Victorians in this period romp. The 26-episode saga begins as Lady Glencora (Hampshire) reluctantly marries the older Plantagenet Palliser (Latham), despite being in love with the rather less financially reliable Burgo Fitzgerald.

Spanning more than a decade of family affairs and politics, this series doesn't stand up as well as the better-known *The Forsyte Saga* – the acting is good while the script unfortunately borders on the hysterical. There's a nice central performance from Hampshire, though, and the cast also includes Penelope Keith, Derek Jacobi, Donal McCann and Anna Carteret.

 TV Trivia: Sudeley Castle in Gloucester was used to represent the Pallisers' family home.

PERSUASION (2007)

Starring Sally Hawkins, Rupert Penry-Jones, Anthony Head

A sumptuous, if rather truncated version of Jane Austen's novel, featuring another one of Austen's trademark plucky heroines. Anne (Hawkins) was once in love, but her parents persuaded her it was an ill-advised marriage, mainly because her father (Head) wanted her to marry into money. Her former beau, Captain Wentworth (Penry-Jones) is now an eligible bachelor, surrounded by swooning young ladies while Anne contemplates a life as an old maid.

It charges along at a fair old pace – the TV film is only an hour and a half – so many of the nuances of Austen's novel are lost along the way. Penry-Jones and Head, along with Julia Davis and Alice Krige, are enjoyable to watch, but Hawkins isn't right (too twitchy) as Anne. There is another TV version worth seeking out on DVD: made in 1995, it stars Ciaran Hinds as Wentworth, Amanda Root as Anne and Corin Redgrave as her father. It's less grand and slower going, but well worth the journey, especially if you are a fan of the novel.

 TV Trivia: Some of the footage of Wentworth's ship in the 1995 version was actually left over film from the 1984 movie *The Bounty*.

POLDARK (1975–1977)

Starring Robin Ellis, Angharad Rees, Judy Geeson, Jill Townsend

A hugely popular series that was broadcast all over the world, *Poldark* was based on the novels of Winston Graham, and has often been described as a Cornish *Gone With The Wind*. Beginning as Ross Poldark (Ellis) rides across the Cornish countryside having returned from the American War of Independence, the series follows Poldark as he discovers his true love is engaged to his cousin and his father's estate ruined. He marries Demelza (Rees) and starts a mining company that brings him up against businessman George Warleggan (Ralph Bates), who becomes his bitter rival, and the story follows their feud, which is complicated by their families' lives becoming entwined with each other.

The series has dated a bit – if it was made nowadays, the fights would be bloodier and the horizontal romps more explicit, for starters – but it's still a fun costume soap opera, with bad guys and good guys, love lost and won, death by drowning, lifelong feuds and tragic misunderstandings. The series ran for 29 episodes. A remake (available on DVD) was made in 1995 with John Bowe as Poldark and Mel Martin as Demelza, but it's not a patch on the original.

TV Trivia: Winston Graham has said that Demelza is loosely based on his own wife, Jean.

PRiDE AND PREJUDiCE (1995)

Starring Colin Firth, Jennifer Ehle, Susannah Harker

There have been numerous film and TV adaptations of Jane Austen's best-loved novel, including a Bollywood version and a 1952 TV series with Peter Cushing as Darcy, but the one that fans of Austen hold dear is this 1995 BBC production that turned Colin Firth from jobbing actor into a screen heart-throb in just one scene. That scene, of course, has Firth – as the brooding Mr Darcy – emerging dripping from a lake with his shirt clinging to his chest (steady on, girls), but there is much more to this TV drama than a bit of watery frolicking.

At almost six hours long, it keeps faithfully to many of Austen's words while also giving more depth to Darcy's character than in previous versions where he's often come off as just a sulky old bore. The story, of course, is of feisty young Elizabeth Bennett (Ehle), who, along with her sisters, is of marrying age. While sister Jane (Harker) has her sights set on Mr Bingley (Crispin Bonham-Carter), Elizabeth finds herself in the company of Bingley's friend, wealthy Darcy, only for him to think she is beneath him and for her to consider him completely awful in every respect.

It's all utterly charming and gorgeous to look at throughout, and peppered with delicious performances – both from the leading cast members and supporting performers such as Alison Steadman (as the overbearing Mrs Bennett), Anna Chancellor (as Caroline Bingley) and Barbara Leigh-Hunt (as Lady Catherine De Bourgh). A yummy adaptation (from literary adaptation maestro Andrew Davies and director Simon Langton) that is the only screen version of the classic novel you will ever need to see.

 TV Trivia: Colin Firth originally turned the role of Darcy down.

ROME (2005–2007)

Starring Kevin McKidd, Polly Walker, James Purefoy, Ray Stevenson

A co-production between the BBC and American cable channel HBO, this lavish drama set in ancient Rome (Season 1 spanning the years 52 BC to 44 BC, Season 2 covering 44 BC to 31 BC) not only followed the political intrigue of the time but also viewed the Roman Empire through the eyes of two ordinary people and their families: soldiers Titus Pullo (Stevenson) and

Lucius Vorenus (McKidd). It's also positively bubbling over with lust, although there's quite a lot of characters to get acquainted with and plot machinations to scratch your head over before anyone gets their togas off.

In 52 BC Julius Caesar (Ciaran Hinds), who has been off conquering nations for almost a decade, and Pompey Magnus (Kenneth Cranham) have an uneasy agreement to share the power in Rome. Meanwhile Caesar's niece Atia (Walker) is sleeping with many of the state's most powerful men – including Mark Antony (Purefoy) – and happily pushing her own daughter to follow in her mother's devious footsteps. Such steamy and political machinations are mixed with the story of the two soldiers who play their own part in Rome's history as time goes by. Packed with a talented British and Italian cast, including Lindsay Duncan, Camilla Rutherford and Indira Varma, and direction from acclaimed directors Michael Apted and Allen Coulter, among others.

The series only ran for two years as its stunning sets and lush locations (it was filmed in and around Rome) became too expensive, but it was definitely raunchy, bloody, complicated fun while it lasted.

 TV Trivia: Five acres of sets were built to replicate ancient Rome, the biggest standing set in the world at the time. Unfortunately in 2007, a fire at Rome's Cinecitta Studios destroyed most of the sets.

Roots (1977)

Starring LeVar Burton, Leslie Uggams, Ben Vereen

One of the best and most ambitious historical mini-series ever made, *Roots* – based on the Alex Haley book of the same name – was watched by over 80 million Americans when it was first broadcast in the US. Originally broadcast over eight nights, it is the epic 12-hours-long fictionalised story of Hailey's own family and heritage that begins with young Kunta Kinte (LeVar Burton, who went on to star in *Star Trek: The Next Generation*), who is snatched from his home in 18th-century Africa and taken to America as a slave. Sent to work on a tobacco plantation under the watchful eye of Fiddler (Louis Gossett Jr), Kunta attempts to escape but is brutally beaten and returned to the plantation. The story follows his life, and that of his daughter, Kizzy (Uggams) who is raped by her master and bears a son, 'Chicken' George (Vereen), and ends as Kunta Kinte's great grandson Tom (Georg Stanford Brown) gains emancipation from slavery at last.

Featuring brutal scenes of rape, beatings and whippings and upsetting moments as families are separated and victimised, this gripping, harrowing drama was expected to be a flop when it was first broadcast in the US – TV companies aimed their programming at white middle-class viewers, who they imagined would not want to watch a drama that vividly showed their ancestors' abuse of African-Americans. Instead, people tuned in to such a degree that it was estimated over 85 per cent of American homes saw at least part of the series.

A worthy sequel, *Roots: The Next Generations*, was made in 1979 and picked up the story of Haley's search for his roots from post-Civil War America onwards. Brown returned for his role as Tom, and was joined by a cast that included Olivia De Havilland, Henry Fonda, Marc Singer, Ruby Dee, Ossie Davis, Debbie Allen and Marlon Brando, while James Earl Jones took on the role of Alex Haley. There was also a TV movie, *Roots: The Gift* (only available on DVD as part of a complete Roots boxset) that told the story of a Christmas with Kunta Kinte and Fiddler, but it is very disappointing compared to what went before.

 TV Trivia: Look out for the now-infamous O.J. Simpson as an African tribesman.

THE SALLY LOCKHART MYSTERIES (THE RUBY IN THE SMOKE. 2006; THE SHADOW IN THE NORTH. 2007)

Starring Billie Piper, Julie Walters, Matt Smith

Author Philip Pullman has written four mystery novels featuring the Victorian heroine Sally Lockhart, and so far the BBC have adapted two – *The Ruby In The Smoke* and *The Shadow In The North* – into enjoyable dramas, adapted by BAFTA-winning writer Adrian Hodges. Set at the turn of the century in a London filled with opium dens, seedy boarding houses and dank alleyways, the first story begins as Sally receives a message from her father telling her to beware of the Seven Blessings. She has no idea what this means or why people seem to drop down dead when she mentions it, so she decides to investigate with the help of wannabe detective, Jim Taylor (Smith).

Both Sherlock Holmes-in-a-frock dramas – the second is set a few years later – are fun, thanks to good stories and nice performances from a cast that includes Julie Walters as mean Mrs Holland, and Sian Thomas as Mrs Rees. In fact, it is only the rather modern Piper who seems a little out of place – while Pullman's character is supposed to be a strong, feisty young woman, the actress seems just a bit too 21st-century ballsy to fit in here.

TV Trivia: Piper's real first name is Lianne.

SHOGUN (1980)

Starring Richard Chamberlain, Toshiro Mifune

What would seventies and eighties mini-series have been without Richard Chamberlain? He outfoxed dastardly Tony Curtis by changing his identity in *The Count of Monte Cristo*, was a naughty, naughty priest in *The Thorn Birds* (see p.412), and even romped around as the ultimate 18th-century seducer Casanova. Chamberlain's most serious – and best played – role in this genre was, however, as Major John Blackthorne in *Shogun*, the lavish adaptation of James Clavell's bestselling 17th century-set novel.

Blackthorne is the English commander of a Dutch ship that crashes off the coast of Japan. The beautiful land is caught up in feudal wars led by warlords Toranaga (Mifune) and Ishido, who both wish to be the ruler, 'Shogun'. At first captured and threatened with execution by Samurai warriors, Blackthorne (who is given the name Anjin-san) eventually embraces the strange, mythical culture around him, becoming a trusted aide to Toranaga, learning the Japanese ways of fighting and codes of honour, and falling for the beautiful interpreter Mariko (Yoko Shimada).

With stunning costumes, breathtaking scenery (aside from some interior shots, it was all filmed on location in Japan) and captivating performances from the cast that also includes John Rhys-Davies, Michael Hordern and narration by Orson Welles (which is not present in all version of this series), this is a fascinating look at a piece of Japanese history. It's also a groundbreaking one in TV terms – the series was allegedly the first to show a person urinating on screen, and the first prime-time mini-series to feature explicit nudity, and the series was so popular that restaurants and cinemas in the US noticed a marked drop in custom on the nights the mini-series was first broadcast.

 TV Trivia: Rumour has it that James Clavell wanted Sean Connery for the lead role but he turned it down.

THE SIX WIVES OF HENRY VIII (1970)

Starring Keith Michell, Annette Crosbie, Dorothy Tutin

Although numerous actors, from Richard Burton and Charles Laughton to Jonathan Rhys Meyers, have played him, the one actor who will always be associated with the role of King Henry VIII is Keith Michell. He was the undoubted star of this 1970 BBC series made up of six episodes – each one an individual play devoted to one of Henry's wives. So we have Annette Crosbie as Katherine of Aragon, whom Henry divorced to marry Anne

Boleyn (Tutin). She, as all history students know, was beheaded, and her role of royal missus was taken over by Jane Seymour (Anne Stallybrass), the only one of Henry's wives to bear him a son, Edward. After Jane died, Henry married Anne of Cleves (Elvi Hale having the unenviable role of the woman who Henry decided to marry on the basis of her portrait, a pretty picture she did not live up to in real life), followed by Catherine Howard (Angela Pleasance) and lastly, Catherine Parr (Rosalie Crutchley), who was lucky enough to survive him.

It's a quality costume drama of the highest order, thanks to the superb cast – that also included Anthony Quayle and Patrick Troughton – and especially the commanding central performance from Michell, who has to portray a king from a young man to the obese 56-year-old he was on his deathbed. Unlike previous adaptations, Henry is seen as more than just a portly fellow with an eye for the ladies of the court – Michell depicts him as the learned man he was, a clever politician who had been quite an athlete in his younger days.

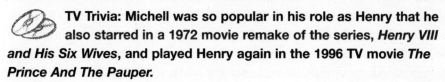 **TV Trivia: Michell was so popular in his role as Henry that he also starred in a 1972 movie remake of the series, *Henry VIII and His Six Wives*, and played Henry again in the 1996 TV movie *The Prince And The Pauper*.**

SWEENEY TODD (2006)

Starring Ray Winstone, Essie Davis, David Warner, Tom Hardy

There have, of course, been numerous versions of the Sweeney Todd tale, including Stephen Sondheim's stage musical, Tim Burton's 2008 film version of that, with Johnny Depp, and TV adaptations including 1982's *Sweeney Todd: The Demon Barber Of Fleet Street* with Angela Lansbury and George Hearn, and 1998's *The Tale Of Sweeney Todd*, with Ben Kingsley and Joanna Lumley (both of these TV versions aren't currently on DVD in the UK). The most gruesome TV adaptation, however, is probably the most recent – director David Moore's version of the story for the BBC, as based on former *Peak Practice* writer Joshua St Johnston's screenplay.

Gruff Ray Winstone stars as Sweeney Todd, a damaged man who was mistreated in jail as a child and discovers his inner murderer when he is shaving a boastful jailer who reminds Sweeney of his past. Quick as a flash, Sweeney's blade slashes the man's throat, and the barber gets such a taste for murder that he's soon slicing and dicing numerous London residents and delivering their flesh to his amour, Mrs Nellie Lovett, who unwittingly serves up the evidence in her sought-after pies. Yum. Winstone's portrayal of Sweeney is of a man tortured by his past, torn between hatred and love, someone both sexually repressed and perverted who is kind to Nellie, considered an honorable man by all around him, but who hides an extremely barbaric secret. In another actor's hands such a split personality could have come across as almost comic, but Winstone delivers such a chill you'll think twice before you have another short back and sides...

 TV Trivia: It may be about the demon barber of London's Fleet Street, but this drama was filmed entirely in Romania...

THE THORN BIRDS (1983)

Starring Richard Chamberlain, Rachel Ward, Jean Simmons, Barbara Stanwyck, Bryan Brown

There's nothing quite like a good old-fashioned bodice ripper, and Colleen McCullough's novel *The Thorn Birds* has all the usual cleavage-heaving ingredients and more – not only does the story span an epic 42 years of family loves, lives and betrayal, and feature a ballsy heroine, but the love interest is the most unattainable of men: a priest. Not much chance of their love being consummated, you would think, but of course, if you remember this eighties romp you'll know not everything that goes on in it is holy and pure.

Ignored by her mother Fee Cleary (Simmons), young Meggie (as a child played by Sydney Penny) idolises her older brothers and watches them run their aunt Mary Carson's (Stanwyck) ranch in the Australian outback. When tragedies strike (and there are many, including one involving a hungry wild boar), Meggie seeks solace in the company of the local ambitious priest, Father Ralph de Bricassart (Chamberlain), and as she becomes a woman (and turns into Rachel Ward), her interest in him becomes more romantic, despite (or perhaps because of) his celibate priestly status. Of course, their love is not to be, so Meggie runs off with the nearest unsuitable man, Luke O'Neill (Brown), but it is not long before Ralph's trembling under his cassocks becomes too much for him and he is torn between his duty to the church, his ambitions of rising through the ranks at the Vatican, and his love/lust for Meggie.

One of the most watched mini-series of all time, this is packed with sin, misunderstanding, romance and stomping performances. Chamberlain is perfect as the arrogant but appealing Ralph, while Ward does well with a character that on screen and on the page is pretty darned selfish and unlikeable. Stanwyck, as you would expect, steals the show as calculating Mary Carson, and this luscious, campy delight also features supporting performances from Christopher Plummer, Piper Laurie, Mare Winningham and Richard Kiley.

A follow-up, *The Thorn Birds: The Missing Years* (1996), with Richard Chamberlain returning as Ralph and Amanda Donohoe taking on the role of Meggie, focused on a period that was featured in the original book but skipped in the 1983 mini-series, in which Ralph lets Meggie under his cassock once more during the Second World War. It's available on DVD but not worth the bother.

 TV Trivia: Rachel Ward and Bryan Brown fell in love during filming – they have been married since 1983 and have three children.

TiPPiNG THE VELVET (2002)

Starring Rachael Stirling, Keeley Hawes, Anna Chancellor

The BBC raised a few eyebrows with Andrew Davies' adaptation of Sarah Waters' novel set during the music hall days of the 1890s – partly because of the subject matter ('tipping the velvet' is Victorian slang for oral sex on a woman, and the story is about a lesbian love affair). Everything you can imagine would get the readers of the *Daily Mail* in a tizzy is here – lesbian sex, cross-dressing, prostitution, sex slavery – as young Nancy (Stirling) leaves her seaside town for the bright lights of the big city, and for the arms of male-impersonating music hall star Kitty (Hawes). When Kitty dumps Nan for a man, the young girl ends up as a sort-of rent-boy, dressing up as a man and selling herself on the streets, before she becomes the kept woman of a high society lady (Chancellor).

It's not as shocking as tabloid newspapers led audiences to believe at the time it was first shown, although some of the language and situations aren't what you'd expect in most period dramas. Both Hawes and Stirling add class to the proceedings, and while some may tune in for the sauciness, what they'll actually discover is a well-made and even moving drama about love and betrayal.

 TV Trivia: Rachael Stirling is Dame Diana Rigg's daughter.

THE TUDORS (2007–)

Starring Jonathan Rhys Meyers, Natalie Dormer, Jeremy Northam, Sam Neill

Forget all those 16th century portraits of a portly, bearded, rather unattractive king – in this drama about the life of King Henry VIII, the Tudor king (Meyers) is muscular, sexy and sporting a trendy buzz cut as he deals with matters of state and beds the ladies of the court. Written and created by Michael Hirst – who wrote the acclaimed feature film *Elizabeth*, starring Cate

Blanchett – this does take some liberties with the facts, but if you can ignore some historical inaccuracies, it's an enjoyable romp that follows Henry after he gained the crown of England at the age of 18, and married Katherine of Aragon (Maria Doyle Kennedy). Of course, he decides to divorce her when she doesn't provide him with a son and heir.

Meyers' Henry VIII is petulant, moody, angry, sexually rampant and a joy to behold as he charges up and down Royal corridors in his tight trousers and flowing shirts, falling for temptress Anne Boleyn (Dormer) and leading his courtiers, including Sir Thomas More (Northam) and Cardinal Wolsey (Neill), a merry dance. The political machinations of the time are slickly mixed in with Henry's personal dealings, but there's also quite a lot of shirtless-ness on Meyers' part for those who would rather focus on the raunch rather than the serious stately matters. The costumes – when they are being worn – are beautiful, and the locations (mainly in County Dublin, Ireland) are luscious in this fun serial.

A second season includes the addition of Peter O'Toole to the cast, as Pope Paul III, who clashed with Henry over his divorce from Katherine, which eventually led to England separating from the Vatican and the Roman Catholic Church. Parents – and those of a sensitive disposition – should note this has some gore (an ambassador is brutally murdered at the beginning of Episode 1) and lots and lots of shagging.

 TV Trivia: Meyers has won a Golden Globe for playing another 'king': he starred as Elvis Presley in 2005's *Elvis*.

UPSTAIRS DOWNSTAIRS (1971–1975)

Starring Jean Marsh, Gordon Jackson, David Langton, Angela Baddeley, Christopher Beeny, Pauline Collins

An absolutely yummy TV series, devised by actresses Eileen Atkins and Jean Marsh, this show ran for five years and followed the fortunes and misfortunes of the Bellamy family, and their servants below stairs who resided at 165 Eaton Place. Spanning the years 1903 to 1930, the series introduced us to such memorable characters as Hudson (Jackson), the sometimes pompous butler, Mrs Bridges (Baddeley), the jolly cook, tragedy-magnet maid Rose (Marsh), mentally disabled maid Ruby (Jenny Tomasin), and the Bellamy's children – Elizabeth (Nicola Pagett) and James (Simon Williams), who had an affair with parlourmaid Sarah (Collins).

Over the years the family and their below-stairs servants endured numerous trials and tribulations, ranging from affairs to stillborn children, suicide, homosexual revelations, the death of a major character on the *Titanic*, another being injured at the Front during World War I, shell shock, financial ruin and other tragedies. Beautifully played by the cast – especially Jackson, Marsh, Baddeley and Langton, the series is comfortingly English, like a cup of tea with jam and scones, and deservedly ranks as one of our best British period serials.

The final series, when many loved characters had left or died, is less enjoyable, but the first three series especially capture a period of time when Britain and its families went through massive social change. And the final ever episode is a must, if just to see maid Rose, remembering the past and realising times have changed, leaving the house (now sold) for the last time and using the front door for the first time, instead of the servants' entrance she had always used before. A spin-off series, *Thomas and Sarah*, following Pauline Collins and John Alderton's characters, was made in 1979 and is available on DVD, but is rather dull and disappointing.

 TV Trivia: The outside shots of the house were actually filmed at 65 Eaton Place, with the missing '1' painted on for the series.

THE VIRGIN QUEEN (2005)

Starring Anne-Marie Duff, Dexter Fletcher, Ian Hart, Joanne Whalley

Following Cate Blancett's superlative performance in the movie *Elizabeth*, and even Miranda Richardson's deliciously cheeky one in *Blackadder II*, it is a brave actress who would take on the role of Queen Elizabeth I in any adaptation. Anne-Marie Duff does just that in this mini-series, and her performance isn't just brave, it's simply stunning. She first portrays the daughter of King Henry VIII and Anne Boleyn as a teenager imprisoned in the Tower Of London by her half sister, Queen Mary (Whalley), and the role spans Elizabeth's life from her inheritance of the throne, through various political crises during her reign (including the Spanish Armada) to her death in 1601.

Packed with passion – despite, of course, Elizabeth being the virgin queen of the title – intrigue and drama, the series expertly captures how the Queen was caught between her desire to serve her country and her own, more personal, desires. It's riveting stuff, with Tom Hardy making a convincing object of the ruler's affections (he plays Robert Dudley, the man she always loved) and Hans Matheson is enjoyable as the Queen's young protege, the Earl of Essex. Tara Fitzgerald, Ian Hart and Emilia Fox also star, and the sumptuous locations include Warwick Castle, Broughton Castle in Oxfordshire and Bamburgh Castle in Northumberland.

 TV Trivia: Screenwriter Paula Milne's first televised script was for an episode of *Crossroads*.

THE END iS (ALMOST) NIGH . . .

EVERY TV SERIES (EXCEPT, PERHAPS, *CORONATION STREET*) COMES TO AN END AT SOME POINT. HERE ARE SOME OF THE WAYS TV'S BEST-LOVED CHARACTERS SAID FAREWELL...

M*A*S*H

On 28 February 1983, 60 per cent of all TVs in the United States were tuned to CBS as nearly 106 million people said a sad goodbye to Hawkeye, Klinger and the rest of the 4077th medics when the long-running hit series *M*A*S*H* came to an end. The last episode, 'Goodbye, Farewell and Amen', in which the characters finally left their army hospital in Korea, was so riveting that New York's water companies reported an extra 320 million gallons of water were used as people rushed to the loo once the show finished.

THE SOPRANOS

Fans and critics were equally disappointed when the final episode of the acclaimed mob drama was aired in June 2007. After months of speculation as to whether lead mobster Tony Soprano (James Gandolfini) would be murdered, the series instead ended rather ambiguously, with Tony in a restaurant with his family sitting down to dinner, and then looking up as someone arrived (a gunman, maybe, or his daughter Meadow?) as the screen faded to black. Did he live? Did he die? We'll never know...

SEINFELD

Critics and fans were divided as to whether the final episode of *Seinfeld* was good or bad as Jerry, George, Elaine and Kramer finally got their comeup-pance for nine years of bad behaviour by being arrested for witnessing a crime and failing to help the victim. 'Hilarious... everything *Seinfeld* was at its best,' said the *New York Times*, while *USA Today* disagreed, declaring it was 'a slow, smug exercise in self-congratulation'

THE COLBYS

This spin-off of *Dynasty* took any logic the show ever had (which, granted, was little) and dumped it by the roadside as Fallon (Emma Samms) was abducted from her car by aliens. Miraculously, she then turned up in the next season of *Dynasty* seemingly unscathed. Sadly, but perhaps not surprisingly, it's not available on DVD.

ST ELSEWHERE

The award for the Most Head-Scratching Ending of all goes to the 1980s hospital drama that launched the career of Denzel Washington. After six years of medical traumas and surgical romance, the final scene implied that the entire show was all in the mind of an autistic child, whom we see staring into a snow globe housing a model of the fictitious hospital. This ending has far-reaching consequences – since characters from *St Elsewhere* appeared in an episode of *Cheers* and have also been mentioned in *Homicide: Life On The Street*, does that mean those shows were a figment of the boy's imagination, too? Writer/producer Tom Fontana admits that since the show ended he has met fans 'who think I should be tarred and feathered.' Note that only the early seasons are currently available on DVD in the UK, with more to be released soon.

MOONLIGHTING

In the last episode of *Moonlighting*, the writers apologised to anyone who suffered through the final interminable series of the previously superb detective drama that had lost the plot from the moment its two leads, David (Bruce Willis) and Maddie (Cybill Shepherd), found romance on screen. The pair beg a producer to save the show from being cancelled, but he replies, voicing the thoughts of viewers, 'Even I can't get people to tune in to watch what they don't want to watch anymore. You two were a great love story. People fell in love with you two falling in love, but you couldn't keep falling forever. It's over.' Indeed.

ROSEANNE

One way of saving face when a series is well past its sell-by date is to end with the 'oops, sorry, it was all a dream' chestnut. After two terrible seasons of the sitcom, *Roseanne*, in which the blue-collar family won the lottery and the writers presumably took a holiday, we discovered it was all a figment of Roseanne's imagination, part of a book she had started to write after husband Dan's death. Currently, the later seasons of *Roseanne* are only available on US DVD.

CROSSROADS

When the new, improved version of *Crossroads* was sent to the old soaps' graveyard, it turned out the sexploits and machinations at the Crossroads motel were actually just a dream Angel (Jane Asher) was having. While the original 'classic' *Crossroads* is on DVD, the newer version is not.

MAGNUM PI

When the series about the hunky Hawaii-based detective was cancelled, the final episode had Magnum (Tom Selleck) popping off to that big luau in the sky (we even got to see him go to heaven). However, the TV company then decided to renew the series after all, so when it came back the next year, producers backtracked and Magnum was alive and well, having dreamt his death following a shooting.

LIFE ON MARS

The hit BBC show about a cop, Sam (John Simms), who is hit by a car in 2006 and then bizarrely wakes up in 1973, ran for two series as fans scratched their heads wondering whether his experiences could be explained as time travel, a dream while Sam was in a coma in 2006, or that he is really from 1973 and mentally unstable. All was revealed in the final episode: Sam was being operated on for a tumour in the present day, and when it was removed he woke up in 2006. However, realising life was better in '73, he then throws himself off a building to return to the time he likes best. So does that mean 1973 is the afterlife, and we'll all be wearing flares and listening to Bowie in heaven? Cool, man...

QUANTUM LEAP

For 95 episodes, scientist Sam (Scott Bakula) was trapped in a time-travelling past, jumping into characters who lived in his lifetime, switching into the next body each time he changed history for the better. The hope was that one day he would leap back into his own life, but at the end of the final episode – which featured numerous characters from previous episodes popping up – audiences were told that 'Dr Sam Beckett never returned home'.

SOAPS AND MINI-SERIES

BETRAYALS, LOVE AFFAIRS, WARM PINTS OF BEER AND
EXPLOSIVE CLIFFHANGERS...

BROOKSIDE (1982–2003)

Starring Sue Johnston, Dean Sullivan, John McArdle, Paul Usher, Ricky Tomlinson

Created by Phil Redmond, whose previous successes included *Grange Hill*, this was the flagship soap for the new British TV station, Channel Four, with the first episode airing on the night the channel was launched in November 1982.

Set in a Liverpool cul de sac, the series was groundbreaking due to the fact it was filmed in a 'real' street, featuring real houses rather than sets to add to the programme's realism. Originally criticised for poor scripts, bad language and dodgy acting, the series improved as it focused on the different families who moved into the close – the Grants, who moved in from a council house; the posh Collins family who had downgraded to the street from a big house in the Wirral; yuppies Heather (Amanda Burton) and Roger; working-class petty criminals Gavin and Petra; and later the Cross family, the loudmouthed Jacksons and the 'scally' Corkhills.

While the original premise was that the series would be very much like real life, it wasn't long before more outlandish and sometimes shocking plot elements were introduced, including a siege situation; incest; a religious cult leader going psycho; the very well-handled but disturbing rape of Sheila Grant (Johnston); the heroin overdose of Heather's second husband; the death of a mother and baby, pushed off scaffolding; and British TV's first pre-watershed lesbian kiss between young resident Beth Jordache (Anna Friel) and Margaret (Nicola Stephenson). Most infamous of all, of course was the 'body under the patio' plot, in which Beth stabbed her abusive dad Trevor and, with the help of window cleaner Sinbad, buried him under the patio (where he would remain for over a year before being discovered).

The first few years of *Brookside* remain the grittiest and most interesting episodes of any British soap, but by the mid-nineties the series had taken a serious downturn as explosions and fires seemed to take place on the previously quiet close nearly every episode. Following drastically falling ratings, the show was cancelled in 2003.

At present, only a feature length spin-off DVD, *Brookside: Unfinished Business* is available, although rumour has it that the siege episodes and the body under the patio ones will make it onto DVD in the future.

TV Trivia: Jason Hope, who played Rod Corkhill (Billy's son) is now a hairdresser in Bermuda.

CORONATION STREET (1960–)

Starring William Roache, Anne Kirkbride

Britain's longest running and most consistently successful soap began in December 1960 two nights a week and focused on the lives and loves of the residents of Weatherfield, a fictional town in the Manchester area. Concentrating on the neighbours of one street, who all seem to frequent the pub on the corner, the Rovers Return, the often comic drama series created by Tony Warren became a staple of ITV's programming and has remained one of its most popular shows for over 40 years.

In those years, memorable characters have come and gone, including the wonderful busybody Ena Sharples (Violet Carson) and blowsy Elsie Tanner (Pat Phoenix), who were both members of the original cast, and from 1964, the curlers-and-hairnet-wearing Hilda Ogden (Jean Alexander) and her layabout husband Stan (Bernard Youens). Brassy barmaid Bet Lynch (Julie Goodyear) first appeared in 1966, while other unforgettable residents include former singer Rita (Barbara Knox), who got her best storyline when her abusive husband Alan tried to kill her and ended up being squashed by a Blackpool tram, and Jack and Vera Duckworth (William Tarmey and Elizabeth Dawn), who first appeared as two of life's losers in 1974. There have been some terrific stories, too, including the 1971 death of Valerie Barlow (electrocuted by a dodgy hairdryer), the wedding of Ken Barlow (William Roache, the programme's only surviving original cast member) to Deirdre Langton (Anne Kirkbride) in 1981 and her subsequent affair with cockney businessman Mike Baldwin, the murder of Brian Tilsley in 1989 and the 'Free Deirdre' storyline in 1998, when 19 million people tuned in to see her wrongly sent to prison (Prime Minister Tony Blair even commented on the story in parliament).

A love it or loathe it show about ordinary folk 'oop north', *Coronation Street* is available in special DVD box sets – each focusing on the most memorable events of a particular decade, and also as individual DVDs, featuring the high-lights of one particular year in the soap's storylines.

 TV Trivia: HRH The Prince Of Wales made a cameo appearance in 2000 to celebrate Corrie's 40th anniversary.

CROSSROADS (1964–1988)

Starring Noele Gordon, Jane Rossington, Ronald Allen, Sue Lloyd

Infamous for its wobbly sets and even wobblier acting, *Crossroads* first appeared on ITV in 1964 and was shown early evening five days a week to begin with (by 1979 it had been reduced to three showings a week). Set at a motel in a fictitious town near Birmingham, the series focused on the motel's owner, Meg Richardson (Gordon), her children Jill (Rossington) and Sandy (Roger Tonge) and various staff members including waitress Diane (Susan Hanson), manager David Hunter (Allen) and his wife Barbara (Lloyd), chef Shughie McFee (Angus Lennie) and the incredibly popular character Benny (Paul Henry), who appeared to be mildly mentally disabled and is best remembered for the woolly hat he wore in every episode, rain or shine.

Despite the bad acting – some of it due, perhaps, to the fact that early episodes were filmed in one take with no chance to redo fluffed scenes – the series developed a large following and something of a cult one in later years as memorable episodes included the fire at the motel (it was assumed poor Meg had perished in it, but she later popped up on the QE2, sailing off for a new life), Sandy's car accident (which left him in a wheelchair – the first paraplegic role in a major soap), and Meg's wedding in 1975. Among the actors who briefly checked into the Crossroads motel and managed to check out with their careers intact were Stephen Rea, John Rhys-Davies, Elaine Page, Sue Nicholls and Johnny Briggs (who both went on to appear in *Coronation Street*), Malcolm McDowell and Adrian Lester.

An ill-advised revival of the series began in 2001, with former cast members Kathy Staff, Tony Adams and Jane Rossington returning, but the series, which featured guest appearances from light entertainers Lionel Blair and Les Dennis, was killed off for good in 2003. The DVDs currently available contain 'classic' episodes from the show's early years (and thankfully none from the revamped series).

 TV Trivia: TV husband and wife Ronald Allen and Sue Lloyd were also married in real life in 1991, but Allen died a few months later.

DALLAS (1978–1991)

Starring Larry Hagman, Patrick Duffy, Linda Gray, Victoria Principal

Terry Wogan discussed it on his radio show (dubbing the character Lucy 'the poison dwarf'), Ceausescu's Romanian government allegedly showed episodes on TV to prove how corrupt the West was, and two plot twists – who shot JR and the whole Bobby 'it was all a dream' sequence – remain some of the most talked about pieces of television ever made. Welcome to the wealthy, wacky, wonderful world of *Dallas*.

In 357 episodes, the story unfolded of the Ewing family, a wealthy brood in the oil business who all lived (most of the time) in the same house, Southfork Ranch, despite their immense wealth. Jock (Jim Davis) was the gruff patriarch, Miss Ellie (Barbara Bel Geddes) the kind but firm mother, while the 'Ewing boys' were brothers Gary (the blond, wussy one, as played by Ted Shackleford, who left the series for the spin-off *Knots Landing*), conniving JR (Hagman) and the pretty, moralistic one, Bobby (Duffy) – although a later plot twist also added the ranch's handyman Ray Krebbs (Steve Kanaly) to the list when it turned out he was Jock's illegitimate son. Added to the mix were Cliff Barnes (Ken Kercheval) as the family's arch rival in business (he believes the Ewings double-crossed his daddy, Digger, and vowed revenge) and his sister Pamela (the pneumatic Principal), who marries Bobby in an early episode, to both the Ewings' and Barnes' disgust. Over the years, the Ewings loved, swindled, lost their riches, won them back, cheated, lied, drove wives to drink (notably JR's missus, Sue Ellen), spawned children, raised horses, got shot at and drilled for oil in what was one of the most successful mixes of sex, power and intrigue on TV.

Some cast members stayed with the series for many of its years, including Hagman, Gray and Kercheval, while others left and returned (including Duffy, who quit the series, was killed off, then after a year of bad ratings was tempted back, bringing about the aforementioned plot twist 'where the whole previous series in which he was dead turned out to be wife Pam's dream; he then magically reappeared alive in her shower). Following a pay dispute, Bel Geddes left, only to find herself replaced by Donna Reed for a season before she renegotiated and came back (poor Reed was unceremoniously sacked), while characters introduced later on in the show included Miss Ellie's beau Clayton Farlow (Howard Keel), Bobby's first love Jenna (Priscilla Presley) and Ray's wife Donna (Susan Howard).

The final episode had JR being shown by the devil what life would have been like for everyone without him (somewhat nicer, it could be assumed). Three unsuccessful spin-off TV movies have been made – *Dallas: The Early Years* (1986), set in the 1930s; *Dallas: JR Returns* (1996) and *Dallas: Return Of The Ewings* (1998), but none are available on DVD.

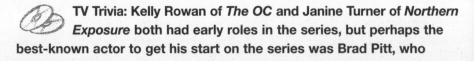 **TV Trivia: Kelly Rowan of *The OC* and Janine Turner of *Northern Exposure* both had early roles in the series, but perhaps the best-known actor to get his start on the series was Brad Pitt, who**

played Randy, the boyfriend of Jenna's daughter Charlie, in the eleventh season.

DYNASTY (1981–1989)

Starring John Forsythe, Linda Evans, Joan Collins

Along with *Falcon Crest* (unavailable on DVD), *Dynasty* was conceived as a direct competitor to the huge success that was *Dallas*. Like its rival, it was focused on the loves, feuds and battles of one family – the Carringtons – who resided in an impressive Denver mansion. The story began as patriarch Blake (Forsythe) settled in with his new wife and ex-secretary, Krystal (Evans), much to the annoyance of his spoilt brat daughter Fallon (Pamela Sue Martin). Adding to the tension was Blake's son, Steven (Al Corey), whose homosexuality his dad chose to ignore, and Fallon's husband Jeff Colby (John James), the rather clueless son of Blake's business rival Cecil (Lloyd Bochner).

The first season of the show was not as successful as expected, but a cliffhanger ending ensured viewers tuned in: Blake was on trial for the murder of Stephen's lover, Ted, when a mysterious witness was called… Blake's ex-wife, Alexis. Her face hidden by a hat and sunglasses, she wouldn't be revealed to the world until the start of Season 2, by which time Joan Collins had been cast in a role that she will always be known for. Wanting to destroy Blake and ruin his marriage to Krystal, Alexis's scheming – and the fantastically bitchy chemistry between her and Evans – turned *Dynasty* from a mediocre success into a phenomenon, and by 1985 it was the number one show around the world.

Plotlines often became silly – Stephen was disfigured in an accident so a new actor (Jack Coleman) could be brought in to play him (he also forgot he was gay and married tarty Sammy Jo, as played by Heather Locklear) – and each series ended with cliffhangers involving shockers like Alexis and Krystal trapped inside a burning building, but nothing came close to the infamous 'Moldavian Massacre', in which just about every character was gunned down during a royal wedding leaving viewers to wonder who would survive to return the next series. None of the major characters were killed, leaving fans disappointed, and viewers fell away as actors were replaced (Emma Samms appeared as Fallon in later years) and plotlines got even dafter (including a hostage situation involving a character from the first season and some South American guerillas).

A 1985 spin-off, involving Jeff and Fallon and his family, entitled *The Colbys* and also starring Charlton Heston, ran for two years but is unavailable on DVD.

TV Trivia: The mansion used for the Carrington house is called Filoli, and is in Woodside, California. It was also the location for *The Wedding Planner*, *George of the Jungle* and *Heaven Can Wait*.

EASTENDERS (1985–)

Starring Adam Woodyatt, Wendy Richard, Barbara Windsor, Steve McFadden

Conceived by the BBC as a challenger to ITV's *Coronation Street*, and created by Julia Smith and Tony Holland, *EastEnders* has a grittier, and you could say bleaker, take on life than its northern-set rival. Set in the fictitious Albert Square, Walford, in East London – a square boasting its own tube station, a few shops, and the Queen Vic pub – the series began in 1985 as three neighbours crashed into one of the local flats to find its elderly resident slumped in a chair, dead. Cheery stuff.

Originally broadcast twice a week (it's now up to four episodes per week and the quality has subsequently dipped), the show quickly introduced us to memorable characters such as pub landlords (and bickering spouses) Den and Angie (Leslie Grantham and Anita Dobson) and their adopted, pouting daughter Sharon (Letitia Dean); grumpy middle-aged couple Pauline (Richard) and Arthur (Bill Treacher) and their kids Mark (Todd Carty), Michelle (Susan Tully) and late addition Martin; and the Beale family, led by salt of the earth stallholder Pete (Peter Dean) and his younger wife Kathy (Gillian Taylforth).

With plots such as teen Michelle's secret affair with middle-aged Den and her subsequent pregnancy, a neighbour's baby's cot death, Mark having a drug problem and later learning he is HIV-positive, and later ones including the domestic abuse of Little Mo (Kacey Ainsworth) and her almost fatal retaliation on her husband, and sister Kat's sexual abuse by an uncle – this isn't exactly big on laughs, but it is certainly high on drama.

Characters and families have come and gone over the years – later additions include the petty criminals that are the Mitchell family, led by brassy mum Peggy (Windsor) and her no-good sons Grant (Ross Kemp) and Phil (McFadden); the brassy Slater girls, including Jessie Wallace's memorable Kat; loveable rogue Alfie (Shane Ritchie); and misunderstood brooding hunk Dennis (Nigel Harman), while numerous people have left the series in memorable fashion. Who can forget poor Tiffany (Martine McCutcheon), squashed under Frank's (Mike Reid) taxi cab? Or Phil's nephew Jamie (Jack Ryder), killed on the way to buy flowers for his young love Sonia? And, of course, Den's demise – shot by a gun hidden in a bunch of daffodils as he walked along the canal – which turned out to be fake when he popped back up a few years later to boost ratings. Ah, the fickle world of soap opera showbiz.

At present, only a spin-off feature about the Slater sisters – *EastEnders: The Slaters In Detention* – is available on DVD.

 TV Trivia: On Christmas Day 1986, over 30 million viewers tuned in to watch Den serve Angie with divorce papers – it remains the highest-rated episode of a soap in British TV history.

ECHO BEACH/MOVING WALLPAPER (2008)

Starring Ben Miller, Martine McCutcheon, Jason Donovan

An interesting experiment by ITV – *Echo Beach* is a peak-time soap, set in a fictional Cornish town, and *Moving Wallpaper* is a mockumentary comedy set behind the scenes of the production of that soap. So you have Martine McCutcheon, Hugo Speer, and Jason Donovan, among others, playing characters having relationships, fights and affairs on *Echo Beach*, and then appearing as over-the-top versions of themselves in *Moving Wallpaper*, alongside Ben Miller as the show's ambitious (fictional) producer Jonathan Pope and his team of harassed writers.

Confused? The problem here is that the kind of audience who would tune into a rather naff, flashy, soap like *Echo Beach* (which has wooden dialogue and performances that make *Crossroads* sound like Kafka) aren't the same audience who would tune into the often funny, sarcastic spoof documentary that is *Moving Wallpaper*. While you don't need to watch one show to understand the other, it does help, as in MW they refer to scenes they have filmed which viewers will then see spool out in front of them on EB. Avoid *Echo Beach* at all costs, but – for Miller's performance alone – *Moving Wallpaper* is worth a look. Bizarrely, while *Echo Beach* was cancelled in 2008, a new series of *Moving Wallpaper* was made with the characters working on a new TV series.

 TV Trivia: Both series are created by Tony Jordan, one of the creators of *EastEnders* and Life on *Mars*.

EMMERDALE (1972–)

Starring Clive Hornby, Richard Thorp, Frazer Hines

Originally known as *Emmerdale Farm* (until 1989), this country-set soap plodded along for years as a lighter, simpler, rather boring alternative to *Coronation Street*. Set in a fictional Yorkshire village – it was known as Beckindale, but in later years the village was referred to as *Emmerdale* – and focusing on the residents who congregate at the Woolpack pub, the series began as a daytime soap but was later moved to an evening time slot. Among the families to grace the rolling hills and farmland were the Sugdens – including Jack (Hornby), who returns from London to help run the family farm after the death of his dad; the posher Wilks family; and later the Tates, the Dingles and the Kings.

While fans always loved the rural idyll that *Emmerdale* offered, it wasn't until 1993 that a bigger audience tuned in. It was then that a Lockerbie-style plane crash brought *Emmerdale* to the attention of the TV viewing masses: the aircraft smashed into the village, fireballs rained down and characters including Leonard Kempinski, Elizabeth Pollard and Mark Hughes lost their lives while another, Chris Tate (Peter Amory), was trapped under rubble and paralysed for life. Ten years later, another 'big' storyline, a violent storm, once again brought in big ratings, as did the fire of 2006, in which the King family's new show home exploded, and the 'Tom King kidnapping' later the same year, that saw Cain Dingle (Jeff Hordley) and Sadie King (Patsy Kensit) plot to kidnap the millionaire (Kenneth Farrington). He was later killed, spawning a 'who killed Tom King' storyline that marked a first for British TV – a fully interactive storyline in which fans could view clues on the *Emmerdale* website.

Currently, an interactive *Emmerdale* DVD game, and highlights from more recent episodes are available on DVD.

 TV Trivia: Anna Friel, Joanne Whalley, Angela Griffin and Ross Kemp all had minor roles in *Emmerdale* early on in their careers.

HOWARD'S WAY (1985–1990)

Starring Maurice Colbourne, Jan Harvey, Stephen Yardley, Glyn Owen, Susan Gilmore

Surprisingly successful BBC soap that ran for six series (each 13 episodes long, and each episode was 50 minutes in length) about a redundant aircraft designer named Tom Howard (Colbourne) who decides to invest in a boat-building business that's nearing bankruptcy. Working with his pal Jack (Owen), things look rosy to Tom, but little does he know that his wife (Harvey) – used to a very nice, middle-class existence that is now threatened – is hitting the bottle, and there are choppy waters ahead thanks to shark-like businessman Ken Masters (Yardley). Over five years, affairs are had, business deals are brokered, trouble brews and the producers try and make it all look glamorous, even though the main locations were windswept coastal areas of Hampshire (the 'exotic' locales of Gibraltar and Malta were featured in the final two series).

It's all rather like a toned-down, grey-skied version of *Dallas* (the Ken

Masters character being the JR Ewing of the piece) that worked best when the characters were bed-hopping rather than talking business. Worth a look, though, for the ill-advised eighties fashion.

 TV Trivia: The working title for the series was the rather unimaginative 'The Boatbuilders'.

KNOTS LANDING (1980–1993)

Starring Joan Van Ark, Michele Lee, Donna Mills

A spin-off of *Dallas* (see above), *Knots Landing* followed Gary Ewing (aka, the boring blond brother of Bobby and JR) and his wife Valene (Ted Shackleford and Van Ark) as they relocated to a middle-class cul-de-sac in California. Sharing the sunshine with them were neighbours Sid (Don Murray) and Karen Fairgate (Lee) and their kids, bickering couple Laura (Constance McCashin) and Richard Avery (John Pleshette), newlyweds Ginger (Kim Lankford) and Kenny Ward (James Houghton) and conniving divorcée Abby Cunningham (Mills). These guys may not have been brokering million-dollar oil deals, but there was certainly enough sex, betrayal, secrets and lies to keep audiences watching – in just the first two seasons, alcoholic Gary hit the booze and got caught up with mobsters, Ginger discovered her record producer husband was cheating on her, Abby slept with most of the men in the street, and the women were held hostage during a baby shower. Phew.

During the early seasons, the show wasn't as successful as *Dallas* and some characters left (including Don Murray's Sid), while new ones were introduced, including federal prosecutor 'Mack' McKenzie (Kevin Dobson), singer CJ (Lisa Hartman), reporter Ben Gibson (Douglas Sheehan) and senator Greg Sumner (William Devane). Ratings rose, even when some of the plots got terribly daft – Hartman played a second role as Cathy, a new girl in town who looked remarkably like the (now deceased) CJ, characters were shot and/or kidnapped, a long lost brother of Valene's, named Joshua (Alec Baldwin) showed up, and to top it off, Valene lost her memory and lived life as a character from the book she had been writing for almost a season.

All in all, it was glossy, mindless stuff that lasted even longer than *Dallas*, possibly because the characters were more everyday (as opposed to 'rich') folk, yet still tanned, beautiful and unfaithful!

 TV Trivia: Oscar winners Halle Berry, Helen Hunt and Billy Bob Thornton, and *Desperate Housewives*' Marcia Cross and Nicolette Sheridan all had early roles in the series.

MELROSE PLACE (1992–1999)

Starring Heather Locklear, Andrew Shue, Courtney Thorne-Smith, Grant Show, Marica Cross

Created by Darren Star, who went on to make *Sex and the City*, this was produced by Aaron Spelling as a grown-up version of *Beverly Hills 90210* – character Jake Hanson (Show) appeared in a few episodes of the teen soap as a link to the new series, and *90210* stars Jennie Garth, Ian Zierling and Brian Austin Green then popped up briefly in the first three episodes of *Melrose Place*. The series followed the lives, loves and scheming of a group of young, good-looking people living in and around an apartment building (the Melrose Place of the title) in West Hollywood, including wannabe writer Billy (Shue), gay social worker Matt (Doug Savant), Dr Michael Mancini (Thomas Calabro), handyman Jake and photographer Jo (Daphne Zuniga). Laura Leighton, Rob Estes, Alyssa Milano, Kristin Davis and Vanessa Williams were among the other attractive cast members. To begin with, the ratings were low, so a few characters with less appealing personalities were thrown into the mix – most notably Heather Locklear's backstabbing, conniving Amanda.

As the ratings grew, storylines became more ridiculous: one character, Richard (Patrick Muldoon), is buried alive; Kimberley (Cross) decides to rig up the complex's pool with explosives (Season 3, Episode 31); various characters are run over by cars; and one even rises from the dead (Season 2, Episode 28).

Glossy, silly, overacted and deliciously trashy, *Melrose Place* became a *Dynasty* for the nineties that was fun rather than thought-provoking. The series was eventually cancelled in 1999 due to growing production costs (and, rumour has it, a few hefty cast salaries), with two characters faking their own deaths, and one on her way to a mental asylum. Similarly themed (and short-lived) fantastical nineties soaps *Central Park West*, *Models Inc* (which was intended as a spin-off to *Melrose Place*), *Savannah* and *Pacific Palisades* are not available on DVD.

 TV Trivia: Courteney Cox, Calista Flockhart and *ER*'s Noah Wyle all unsuccessfully auditioned for roles on the series.

TRIANGLE (1981–1983)

Starring Kate O'Mara, Michael Craig, Larry Lamb

How's this for a glamorous idea – a soap set on a North Sea ferry that runs between Felixstowe, Gothenberg and Amsterdam (not exactly the exotic Caribbean, is it?). With such an idea, this soap was sinking before it even left port, and the memorable image of lovely Kate O'Mara sunbathing topless on the ship's deck under threatening grey British skies did nothing to help the series' reputation. Maybe the BBC thought they were making a Brit version of *The Love Boat*, but instead this was about as attractive as a seat on the *Titanic*, thanks to leaden scripts, wooden performances, and the lack of excitement as viewers got to know the snoresome crew and the various passengers who boarded for each 'thrilling' episode.

Created by Bill Mears, who produced the seventies drama *The Brothers*, this was actually a bit of landmark TV at the time, as the majority of filming was done on the ferry, making it one of the first series to be filmed almost entirely on location (apparently, the camera crew regularly suffered sea-sickness during filming). Along with ill-fated Spanish-set soap *Eldorado* (alas, unavailable on DVD), *Triangle* has been voted one of the worst British TV series ever made (it was re-screened on the BBC during a 1992 evening of programming called 'TV Hell'), and unbelievably it ran for three whole series (78 episodes) before it was finally sunk for good.

 TV Trivia: The ferry used for the series was *Tor Scandanavia* (renamed *Dana Anglia* for the series).

For teen-oriented soaps such as *Hollyoaks*, see Teenagers, p.149.

Soapy Mini-Series

Those trashy romantic dramas aimed at women who wanted to watch the characters face betrayal, heartbreak and the odd broken nail on the way to true happiness. Unfortunately, two of the best known, *Hollywood Wives* (based on Jackie Collins's novel) and Shirley Conran's *Lace* (the one with the goldfish scene that got Radio 2 DJ Terry Wogan in a tizzy) are currently unavailable on both UK and US DVD. For more serious mini-series dramas, see Contemporary Drama, p.344 and Costume Drama, p.375.

Act of Will (1989)

Starring Elizabeth Hurley, Victoria Tennant, Peter Coyote

Anyone who has ever wondered whether celebrity/model/actress Liz Hurley can actually act should watch this mini-series as it's proof that she really can't. Unfortunately, that's a big problem as she's one of the leads in this adaptation of Barbara Taylor Bradford's novel. The mini-series spans five decades, beginning with the story of Audra (Tennant), who is determined to give her own daughter a better life than the one she had following the death of her mother and her marriage to a workman. However, the grown Christina (Hurley), follows her own path, rising through London's elite and then risking everything for an affair with a married MP (Coyote).

It's utterly preposterous stuff that's definitely best left on the shelf as your DVD player will never forgive you if you actually put it on.

 TV Trivia: Author Bradford sold her first short story to a children's magazine at the age of 10.

Mistral's Daughter (1984)

Starring Stacy Keach, Stefanie Powers

A trashy eighties mini-series based on an excruciatingly tacky romance novel by Judith Krantz. Keach is Julian Mistral, a Picasso-style painter who somehow can get the sanest woman to drop her knickers – from Stefanie Powers's artist's model Maggy (try not to laugh when she is playing her as a 17-year-old) to Maggy's own daughter Teddy (Stephanie Dunnam). Spanning the decades from the 1920s, this romp follows Mistral's various love affairs, the women in his life and such unsavoury things as his collaboration with the Nazis during World War II, while Maggy goes off and becomes successful without him. Then zipping forward, Mistral has to come to terms with an illegitimate daughter he soon adores, only to find she's going to marry the son of a Jewish art dealer whom Mistral turned his back on during the war. Oops.

Mix in *'Allo 'Allo*-style French accents, a gouge-your-own-eyes-out-it's-so-bad theme song from Nana Mouskouri, and the hilarity of watching fortysomething Powers pretending to be a teenager and you have some idea how bad this all is. Trust me, it's even worse. Robert Urich, Joanna Lumley and Lee Remick are among the co-stars who should have known better.

 TV Trivia: Star Stacy Keach spent six months in prison for smuggling cocaine in a hollowed-out can of shaving cream into the UK.

PRINCESS DAISY (1983)

Starring Merete Van Kamp, Stacy Keach, Robert Urich

One of the raunchier mini-series of the 1980s (not counting the infamous *Lace*, of course), this daft but addictive drama is based on the bestselling romance novel from Judith Krantz. It's the story of Daisy (ex-model Van Kamp), the daughter of a Russian prince (Keach) and an American movie star (Lindsay Wagner). Sent to live with her father after her mother's death, Daisy discovers he won't accept her mentally disabled twin sister, and also has to deal with a half-brother, Ram (Rupert Everett) who has a rather unhealthy interest in her. Following her father's death, her stepmother sends Daisy away from Ram to college as an ordinary girl in America, but when Daisy's inheritance disappears, she is forced to use her royal title as a way of earning money. Oh dear, poor girl. And could that be a hunky man (Urich) on the horizon to make her feel better?

It's very silly stuff (aside from a rather realistic rape scene) in which Van Kamp wanders around looking pretty while a cast that includes Paul Michael Glaser, Claudia Cardinale and Lysette Antony pretend they are in a serious drama rather than a steamy romance. Most enjoyable of all is Ringo Starr, hilarious as camp millionaire Robin Valerian and Starr's real-life wife Barbara Bach as Valerian's bisexual missus. Fans of author Krantz should note that the TV mini-series of her novels *Till We Meet Again*, *I'll Take Manhattan*, *Scruples*, *Dazzle* and *Secrets* are not available on DVD in the UK.

 TV Trivia: Shari Lewis, of *Lamb Chop* fame, was married to Judith Krantz's brother.

QUEENIE (1987)

Starring Mia Sara, Kirk Douglas, Joss Ackland, Claire Bloom

Michael Korda's bestselling novel got the full glossy treatment here, with a cast that includes Kirk Douglas, Martin Balsam, Joel Grey, Topol and Sarah Miles. Loosely based on the story of *Wuthering Heights* actress Merle Oberon, it's the story of beautiful Queenie Kelley (Sara), a poor, half-caste girl from Calcutta who finds success in Hollywood amongst the film world and the jet set under the pseudonym Dawn Avalon. Will her rich friends and the hunky men in her life discover her secret?

Thanks to some horrendous overacting, you won't really care, but the Indian locations are luscious and it's fun guessing which bits of this fictional story relate to the facts of Merle Oberon's real life (she did marry a director, Alexander Korda, and in this version his name is David Konig, as played by Douglas, for example).

 TV Trivia: Michael Korda, who wrote this series and the novel before it, was Alexander Korda's nephew.

RETURN TO EDEN (1983)

Starring Rebecca Gilling, James Reyne, Wendy Hughes

If you thought only Americans could make ridiculous soap mini-series, then you've never seen this choice offering from Australia. So bad it's actually laughably good, it's the story of Stephanie Harper (Gilling), a rich, happily married woman (and a bit of a frump) with an apparently loving husband (Reyne). All is peachy until he falls in love with her best friend Jilly (Hughes) and decides that the best way to get his hands on Stephanie's money is to toss her off their boat into the waiting jaws of a crocodile. What he doesn't know is that plucky Steph survives the attack, washes up at a plastic surgery clinic and spends months plotting revenge while surgeons give her a beautiful but different face. Armed with a new name and new looks, she arrives back in town all glamorous and soon becomes an international model (!) as part of her quest to bring down the people who wronged her and served her up as monster munchies...

Utterly hilarious in its awfulness, this features a deliciously over the top performance from Hughes as the villainess of the piece, tongue-in-cheek ones from the rest of the cast and the worst performance from a rubber crocodile ever. A series was spun-off from this mini in 1986, with some of the cast returning, but it is unavailable on DVD at present.

TV Trivia: James Reyne is better known in his native Australia as a musician rather than an actor, as lead singer for the eighties band Australian Crawl.

RICH MAN, POOR MAN (1976)

Starring Peter Strauss, Nick Nolte, Susan Blakely

Irwin Shaw's bestselling novel became one of the first mega-rated mini-series on TV, spending a whopping 720 minutes (it was originally shown in 12 one-hour installments) covering the trials and tribulations of the Jordache family from post-war America to the late 1960s. Nominated for an impressive 20-odd Emmys (it won four of them), it is the story of two brothers, Tom (Nolte) and Rudy (Strauss) Jordache. Tom is the reckless, hot-headed one, while Rudy is the good boy – the perfect student who becomes a big success. With backdrops such as the Korean War, campus riots, and the rise of McCarthyism, the boys' jealousy played out as affairs were had, resentments were aired and they battled alcoholism, adultery and betrayal.

It's a gripping series, based on a page-turner of a book, and it rightly made stars of its two leads, Nolte and Strauss, who were backed by an impressive cast that included Ray Milland, Edward Asner, Van Johnson and Dorothy McGuire. A sequel (also on DVD), entitled *Rich Man, Poor Man: Book II*, was made after the success of the first, but Nolte and co-star Susan Blakely declined to appear. Fans of Shaw's novels should note that Book II is not based on his written sequel to *Rich Man, Poor Man* that was entitled *Beggar Man, Thief*. And the TV version of Jeffrey Archer's rip-off, *Kane and Abel*, is not available on DVD.

TV Trivia: One of the directors of this mini-series was Bill Bixby, better known as mild-mannered David Banner in the seventies series *The Incredible Hulk*.

SINS (1986)

Starring Joan Collins, Steven Berkoff, Timothy Dalton

Collins stars as Helene Junot, who sees her mother killed by Nazis and is separated from her brother Edmund. After the war, she goes to work for a Count and falls in love with his son, but when that goes horribly wrong, she heads to Paris to become first a fashion model and later the head of a fashion empire. Of course, Helene has stamped on quite a few toes along the way, so there are many people who would like to bring her down.

With more ham than a sty full of pigs, this is a decidedly silly version of Judith Gould's already melodramatic bestselling potboiler. Collins, hot following the success of *Dynasty*, was – to be very polite – a little old to play this role, but she does the later bitchy scenes to perfection and looks fab in the many clothes she has to parade about in. Adding to the sniggers are Berkoff as Helene's former Nazi tormentor and Dalton as her brother. The series also featured Gene Kelly in sadly what was to be his final screen role.

 TV Trivia: There is no real author named Judith Gould – it is the pseudonym of Nick Bienes and Rhea Gallaher.

WiLD PALMS (1993)

Starring James Belushi, Robert Loggia, Dana Delaney.

Based on a comic strip that appeared in the US men's magazine *Details*, *Wild Palms* was almost as quirky as *Twin Peaks* and boasted an equally famous director as one of its creators – Oliver Stone (*JFK*, *Platoon*). Set in the near-future (2007!) the twisting plot that focused on Harry Wykoff (Belushi), an attorney with a wife and family… and a recurring nightmare about a rhino appearing in his LA swimming pool. Harry doesn't know it, but others have the same dream – including bonkers senator Tony Kreutzer (Loggia), who is head of a religion called Synthiotics and also runs a media company with plans to project holographic images into people's homes that they can interact with (and that boast the side effect of brainwashing the viewers).

There are two organisations controlling the politics that Harry uncovers, and he also discovers many of his friends and family have ties with one or the other faction. Throw in oodles of surreal images, mind-control drugs, cults, some eye-gouging, women in swimsuits looking stylish by the side of Californian swimming pools for no apparent reason and frankly head-scratching plotlines, and this is something of a muddle – albeit a very watchable one. Belushi is fine in the lead role, but even better are some of the supporting cast that includes Angie Dickinson, Dana Delaney, Kim Cattrall, Brad Dourif, Ned Beatty and Bebe Neuwirth. The directors who made the series – *Near Dark*'s Kathryn Bigelow and Phil Joanou (*U2: Rattle And Hum*) among them – add a sense of atmosphere to the proceedings, so even if you don't understand what the hell is going on, it's still great to look at.

 TV Trivia: James Belushi apparently admitted in interviews he had no idea what the show was about – he just turned up and read his lines each day.

A WOMAN OF SUBSTANCE/HOLD THE DREAM/TO BE THE BEST (1984, 1986, 1992)

Starring Jenny Seagrove, Deborah Kerr, Barry Bostwick

Barbara Taylor Bradford's trilogy of novels was turned into three mini-series, with the first, *A Woman of Substance*, being the most enjoyable. In it, Emma Harte (Kerr), a successful department store owner (the shop is called 'Hartes' and is a blatant copy of Harrods), looks back on her life – beginning when she was a poor kitchen maid (the young Emma played by Seagrove) to a pompous Yorkshire family. Left destitute by their schemings, she becomes determined to have revenge on the Fairley family who wronged her and become successful herself, which she does by building a textile business empire with the help of her lifelong friend Blackie (Liam Neeson), while falling in love with various men (usually doomed to failure) and having a few bitter children along the way.

The first book, and series, deals with Emma's history from the turn of the century to the 1980s as her now-grown-up children fight for control of her empire, while the second series, *Hold The Dream*, has Seagrove playing Emma's granddaughter Paula, the new head of the Harte business. Paula has her own set of problems: an incredibly annoying husband (Nigel Havers), a creepy business associate (James Brolin) and secret feelings for Blackie's son, Shane (Stephen Collins), not to mention more machinations from her own power-hungry family. It waffles on too much about big business and lacks the charm of the first series, perhaps because it is set entirely in the present day.

A third series has Lindsay Wagner taking over the role of Paula (erm, did anyone notice Paula is supposed to be English?) as she fights to save her grandmother's business (expect a ridiculous espionage subplot) and her own failing marriage (Shane is now played by David Robb). It closes the story, but that's about all that recommends it. Anthony Hopkins co-stars as Paula's chief of security – one can only assume he agreed to appear in return for a very large cheque.

Fans should note that Bradford has written three more novels: *Emma's Secret*, *Unexpected Blessings* and *Just Rewards* – about the Harte family, but these have not been filmed.

 TV Trivia: *A Woman of Substance* remains the most watched series ever to be shown on Channel Four.

DANIELLE STEEL, ROMANCE QUEEN

JUST ABOUT EVERY NOVEL BY ROMANCE WRITER DANIELLE
STEEL HAS BEEN TURNED INTO A TV MOVIE OR MINI-SERIES, AND
AS THE BOOKS/FILMS OFTEN TREAD SIMILAR GROUND – NICE
GIRL SUFFERS TRAGEDY BUT EVENTUALLY FINDS TRUE LOVE –
HERE ARE BRIEF SUMMARIES OF THE ONES CURRENTLY AVAIL-
ABLE ON DVD:

CHANGES (1991)

Cheryl Ladd is the news reporter who falls for hunky surgeon Michael
Nouri, but the children from their previous marriages threaten to spoil their
newfound happiness. Watch out for *Third Rock from the Sun*'s Joseph Gordon
Levitt as one of the spoiled brats.

DADDY (1991)

Kate Mulgrew is the wife who decides to go and find herself, leaving bewildered husband Patrick Duffy behind to raise (and get to know) his children
(watch out for a young Ben Affleck as one of them). And to complicate matters, he then falls for glamorous Lynda Carter... Worth a look just to see
Wonder Woman and the Man From Atlantis smooching!

FAMILY ALBUM (1994)

As the title hints, this film focuses on the troubles and strifes of one family,
led by mom Jaclyn Smith and dad Michael Ontkean. There's a war-related
death, a closeted relative, and much sobbing before the end credits. Brian
Krause and Kristin Minter co-star.

FINE THINGS (1990)

Nice guy Bernie (D.W. Moffat) finds true love with Liz (Tracy Pollan) and
her stepdaughter Jane, but when Liz dies of leukemia he has to battle Jane's
no-good dad for custody of the little girl he has come to love. Cloris
Leachman also stars.

FULL CIRCLE (1996)

A woman looks back on her life – from a college rape to her relationship with her best friend, from a romance with a married man to her high-flying career. It's as dull as it sounds. Corbin Bernsen, Jennifer Barker and Teri Polo star.

HEARTBEAT (1993)

Husky-voiced Polly Draper is the woman whose husband (Kevin Kilner) leaves her when she becomes pregnant, while John Ritter stars as the really nice man who befriends and then falls in love with her. Of course, just about then, hubby decides he may want her back...

KALEIDOSCOPE (1990)

Following the deaths of their parents, three sisters are sent to separate foster homes. Thirty years later, private detective Perry King is hired to reunite them – but will family secrets eventually drive them apart? Jaclyn Smith, Patricia Kalember and Claudia Christian are the siblings.

MESSAGE FROM NAM (1993)

After her boyfriend is killed in Vietnam, young journalism student Paxton (Jenny Robertson) travels to the country to find out why the war is happening, not just for herself but also for everyone back home. Once there, she has an affair with an army captain, but their relationship is threatened when she begins a search for her lost love, who may not be dead after all.

MIXED BLESSINGS (1995)

Three newly married couples want to have a baby. Brad and Pilar are worried they are too old (he already has a grown-up daughter who is pregnant), Andy and Diana are looking into surrogacy as she can't conceive, and while Charlie wants to be a dad, his partner Beth isn't so sure she's ready. Scott Baio, Gabrielle Carteris, Bruce Greenwood, Bess Armstrong, James Naughton and Alexandra Paul star.

NO GREATER LOVE (1996)

Ooh, a historical one. Edwina (Kelly Rutherford) loses her fiancé and parents in the *Titanic* disaster and has to raise her surviving siblings and take on managing her late father's newspaper. Can she hold her family together, beat off competitors and find true love? Chris Sarandon, Daniel Hugh Kelly, Michael Landes and Simon MacCorkindale also star.

ONCE IN A LIFETIME (1994)

Can you find love more than once in a lifetime? Lindsay Wagner has a fair old try in this weepie. She plays a woman whose husband and daughter die in a house fire while her unborn son is deafened in the disaster. First she has an affair with an egocentric actor, but then it looks like true love could happen with the understanding deaf school teacher (Barry Bostwick). Oh, but watch out for that speeding car....

PALOMINO (1991)

After the break-up of her marriage, Samantha (Lindsay Frost) stays at a friend's ranch and falls in love with ranch hand Tate (Lee Horsley). He leaves her when he discovers her ex was smarter than him, she has a riding accident and doesn't let Tate know... gosh, what do you think may happen?

A PERFECT STRANGER (1994)

A fan favourite, this adaptation of Steel's novel is the story of a nice man named Alex (Robert Urich) who falls for the lovely Raphaella (Stacy Haiduk), only to discover she is the wife of a very rich, invalid man and their love may never be. *Charmed*'s Holly Marie Combs co-stars as Urich's teenage daughter.

REMEMBRANCE (1996)

Italian royal Serena (Eva La Rue) leaves her tiaras behind to marry her true love (Jeffrey Nording), but he dies and she is left to raise their child and battle her late love's unforgiving family. Angie Dickinson costars as the bitchy matriarch.

THE RING (1996)

Nastassja Kinski is the young woman separated from her family and imprisoned by the Nazis in World War II. After the war she falls in love with a German officer, but when he is killed, she flees to America in the hope that one day she will be reunited with her lost family. Michael York, Rupert Penry Jones, Alessandro Nivola and Jon Tenney star.

SAFE HARBOUR (2007)

Melissa Gilbert is the mourning mother whose daughter befriends an artist, beginning a relationship that could help a lonely child and woman confront their grief. Brad Johnson co-stars.

SECRETS (1992)

A truly soapy drama set behind the scenes of... a soap. Each actor has a problem, while Christopher Plummer is the poor producer trying to keep it all together. The cast includes Stephanie Beacham, Nicole Eggert, John Bennett Perry and Linda Purl.

STAR (1993)

Crystal (Jennie Garth) falls for Spencer (Craig Bierko), a soldier just back from Vietnam, but the path of true love really doesn't run smooth. She is badly treated by her stepmother, raped by the man who also kills her brother, and then she runs away to San Francisco to become a singer only to discover Spencer has married someone else. The bastard.

VANiSHED (1995)

In 1930s New York, Marielle (Lisa Rinna) and Malcolm (George Hamilton) live a privileged life with their young son Teddy. But when Teddy (Alex D Linz) is kidnapped, the family's secrets are unearthed and Marielle's old love, Charles, is suspected of the crime. But where is Teddy?

ZOYA (1995)

Melissa Gilbert is the young Russian countess who escapes the 1917 revolution and tries to make a new life for herself in America in this drama. There's tragedy galore along the way, of course, including a husband who snuffs it and a daughter who resents her mother having to go to work. Gilbert's real-life husband Bruce Boxleitner co-stars, along with a young Jennifer Garner as Zoya's daughter.

10 OF THE MOST MEMORABLE CLIFFHANGERS ON TV...

THEY KEEP US GRIPPED UNTIL THE NEXT SEASON OF THE SHOW, AND SERIES LIKE *24* AND *LOST* HAVE TURNED THE CLIFFHANGER INTO A FINE ART, KEEPING US ON THE EDGE OF OUR SEATS FROM EPISODE TO EPISODE AND SEASON TO SEASON. HERE ARE 10 OF THE MOST MEMORABLE TV CLIFFHANGERS...

WHO SHOT JR? (DALLAS)

The end of the second season of soap *Dallas* ended on the most famous cliffhanger of all time. Nasty JR Ewing (Larry Hagman), having pissed off his alcoholic wife Sue Ellen, do-gooder brother Bobby, pneumatic sister-in-law Pam and just about everyone else in a 100 mile radius, is shot at his desk. Is he dead? And more importantly, who shot him? The cliffhanger made the cover of *Time* magazine, and 76 per cent of American viewers tuned in for the first episode of Season 3 to find out whodunnit. (it was Kristin, Sue Ellen's sister, who was pregnant with the tycoon's baby).

IT WAS JUST A DREAM... (DALLAS)

Another *Dallas* cliffhanger – and possibly the silliest. In 1985, Patrick Duffy, who played Bobby, decided to leave the series and his character was killed off, on camera. But then, after a year away, he decided to come back. What were the producers to do? At the end of an already preposterous 1985/1986 season, they had Bobby's bereaved wife, Pam, wake up, and see Bobby emerging from the shower! His return was explained the following season – apparently the entire previous year, with all its intricate plot developments, had been a dream of Pam's that she had just woken up from... and Bobby had never really died.

WHAT'S IN THE HATCH? (LOST)

Just about every episode of the twisting, turning, head-scratching *Lost* ends on a cliffhanger, but one of the best must be the end of Season 1, when Jack, Kate, Locke and Hurley blow open the mysterious hatch they have found on the island they are stranded on and peer down. All we see – until the next season – is a deep hole and a ladder. Who, or what, is down there? (It turns out to be a Scottish bloke named Desmond and a computer needs numbers entered into it every 108 minutes...)

WHO SHOT MR BURNS? (THE SIMPSONS)

A clever homage to *Dallas*'s Who Shot JR? cliffhanger had the animated Simpson clan, and most of Springfield, under suspicion for the shooting of nasty nuclear businessman Mr Burns in the show's only two-part episode so far. The second part was first shown in September 1995, and the case was resolved – Burns had tried to snatch candy from baby Maggie Simpson, dropped his gun, and it accidentally fired, shooting him.

"I AM LOCUTUS OF BORG. RESISTANCE IS FUTILE..." (STAR TREK: THE NEXT GENERATION)

The third season finale of *Star Trek: The Next Generation* – 'The Best Of Both Worlds: Part I' – delivered a shocker: Captain Jean-Luc Picard (Patrick Stewart) of the starship *Enterprise* is abducted by Trek's scariest villains, the Borg, and taken aboard one of their ships. The Enterprise crew are in hot pursuit, however, but when they board the vessel, they discover an 'assimilated' Picard – he has been taken over by the Borg and is now part man, part creepy alien. 'I am Locutus of Borg', he tells the *Enterprise*, and fans had to wait six months until Season 4 to discover whether the crew would be able to rescue him and make him human again...

THE MOLDAVIAN MASSACRE (DYNASTY)

If the 'it was all a dream' ending from *Dallas* seems silly, check out the daftest cliffhanger of all-time in *Dynasty*. In 1985, Blake Carrington's youngest daughter Amanda marries Prince Michael of Moldavia – just as a military revolution breaks out in his country. The wedding turns into a massacre as revolutionaries storm in and send bullets in every direction, and the people in the chapel (most of the cast) fall to the ground. Who would survive, if anyone? Unfortunately, there were no big shockers, and when the series returned revealing just about everyone was still alive, fans began to desert the show, and the conclusion to the massacre is often cited as the series' downfall.

THE BLACK LODGE (TWIN PEAKS)

David Lynch's spooky series had weird and wonderful cliffhangers throughout, but most memorable is the cliffhanger at the end of the second and final season. Agent Cooper heads to the mysterious and dangerous Black Lodge in the woods, to find the missing Annie. Does he escape? We next see him wake up at the hotel and head to the bathroom. He looks in the mirror and uncharacteristically smiles, then smashes his head into the glass. The face that stares back is no longer Cooper, but the otherworldly entity that is Bob...

SAM'S PROPOSAL (CHEERS)

At the end of the fourth season of *Cheers*, viewers had seen bar owner Sam and prissy waitress Diane fight, make up, fall in love, and fight again. Now, Sam has a new girlfriend named Janet, just as Diane comes back on the scene. The series ends with Sam picking up the phone and proposing marriage – but to whom? (The first episode of Season 5 revealed it was Diane – wearing a face mask and eating a drumstick at the time – who received the proposal).

THE ONE WHERE ROSS SAID RACHEL (FRIENDS)

It's not easy for a sitcom to do a cliffhanger but *Friends* has managed it memorably twice – the episode in which Monica marries Chandler, and we're left guessing which of the three girls are pregnant, following a discovered pregnancy test (it's Rachel), and the episode set in London in which Ross marries English girl Emily. Except, at the altar, he says Rachel's name by mistake, and fans were left waiting to see what would happen in his complicated love life next.

BUFFY'S GIFT (BUFFY THE VAMPIRE SLAYER)

The first four seasons of *Buffy* ended with bad guys defeated and even some happy endings, but then Season 5 ended with a jaw-dropping episode called 'The Gift'. The evil Glory uses Buffy's sister to open the door between dimensions and unleash hell on earth, and Buffy realises only she can save the world – by throwing herself into the void and dying. Fans had to wait until Season 6 to discover how the writers were going to resolve that one (Buffy's mystical friends bring her back from the dead but it turns out she liked it there).

DOCUMENTARY AND REALITY

EVERY WEEK, A NEW DOCUMENTARY OR REALITY SHOW MAKES ITS WAY ONTO DVD (SADLY NEITHER MICHAEL MOORE'S *TV NATION*, MORGAN SPURLOCK'S *30 DAYS* OR THE SHOCKING *DEATH ON THE ROCK* IS AMONG THEM), SO HERE ARE JUST SOME OF THE MOST MEMORABLE AND BEST-SELLING. SEE ALSO WAR AND THE ARMED FORCES, P.289; WESTERNS, P.195 AND MUSIC, P.458.

ALISTAIR COOKE'S AMERICA (1972–1973)

A personal history of the United States, from broadcaster and journalist Alistair Cooke, this remains a satisfying look at the country from the man made famous by his *Letters From America* broadcasts on BBC radio that began in 1946 and ran for nearly six decades. Distinctive, personal and mesmerising when dealing with subjects such as the American Civil War and the impact of slavery, this guide to the USA may have dated but it has never been bettered.

 TV Trivia: Cooke's *Letters From America* was the world's longest-running speech-radio show.

AROUND THE WORLD IN 80 DAYS (1989)

Former Monty Python member Michael Palin turned travel journalist for this series in which he attempted to recreate the journey of fictional character Phineas Fogg, who travelled around the world (without using an airplane) in 80 days for a bet. Palin's an amiable guide as he experiences the frustrations of land travel and discovers hidden places along the way. This first remains the best of his subsequent adventures – it was followed by the enjoyable *Pole to Pole* in 1992, *Full Circle* in 1997, *Sahara* in 2002, *Himalaya* in 2004 and *New Europe* in 2007.

 TV Trivia: Palin has a Virgin train named after him.

THE ASCENT OF MAN (1973)

Jacob Bronowski wrote and presented this history of man's endeavours, from prehistory to the modern age. Four years in the making, the series focused on such themes as chemistry, Darwinism and the Industrial Revolution. Ground-breaking in its scope and personal feel, the series is often best remembered for the moving, unscripted scene in which Bronowski visits Auschwitz (where some of his family died) and holds the ashes of the dead in his hands.

 TV Trivia: Bronowski sadly died a year after the series was broadcast.

BEAR GRYLLS: BORN SURVIVOR (2006–)

Whether you're stranded in the Sahara or Panama, Bear Grylls is the man you want with you. The mountaineer, adventurer and ex-SAS man (real name Edward Grylls) is happily dropped into inhospitable places around the globe (with a camera) and then shows viewers how to survive, whether it means putting a urine-soaked t-shirt around your head in the desert sun or eating a tree frog when your food has run out. There was some controversy that Grylls was never actually alone during these adventures (and sometimes was staying in the nearest motel!) but Channel 4 admitted the series was more of a guide to survival than a documentary. So that's okay then.

 TV Trivia: In June 2005, Grylls hosted a dinner party at a table suspended from a hot air balloon, at over 24,000ft.

BIG BROTHER (2000–)

At first, it was an amusing novelty to watch a group of regular people butt heads as they adjusted to life inside Big Brother house, without contact with the outside world. The first series (won by Craig the builder, but ruled by Nasty Nick) was a treat, but in recent years it has become almost an insane asylum of social misfits and wannabe glamour models vying for the chance of fame. Highlights of most years are available should you wish to observe people at their very worst. Yuck.

 TV Trivia: Invented by John De Mol for Netherlands TV, the series has been a success in 19 countries. The USA is one of the few territories where it hasn't been a ratings winner.

THE BLUE PLANET (2001)

David Attenborough narrates this epic documentary that was five years in the making and looks at the varying types of species living in the world's seas and oceans. The underwater world looks almost alien, thanks to the superb camerawork and footage of creatures including spinner dolphins, emperor penguins and never-seen-before-on-camera hairy angler fish. Eight programmes were made. The *Planet Earth* series followed in 2006.

 TV Trivia: Attenborough was the first controller of BBC2 and has been credited with bringing *Monty Python's Flying Circus* to TV.

BRITISH ISLES: A NATURAL HISTORY (2004)

Housewives' favourite Alan Titchmarsh – perhaps better known as a gardener and writer of country-set romantic novels – chats away about the geological history of Britain that can be seen in plants, rocks and even weeds. Whether he's swigging malt whisky to demonstrate how water permeates through rock or standing on a cliff-edge narrating to camera while the helicopter holding it flies perilously near, Titchmarsh delivers a jolly view of our island home.

 TV Trivia: Before his TV career, Titchmarsh worked at the Royal Botanic Gardens in Kew and was an assistant editor of gardening books.

CHANGING ROOMS (1997–2004)

Would you let a group of eccentric designers, armed with little more than sticky-backed plastic, some cheap lampshades and violent-pink paint loose in your house? And would you also let your neighbours decide what you wanted, while you're wreaking havoc on their home? It's surprising how many people did, especially when some of the end results shown on TV (usually compliments of foppish designer Lawrence Llewellyn Bowen or ditzy Linda Barker) looked like the emulsion ravings of a mad man. Do the British public never learn?

 TV Trivia: Laurence Llewellyn Bowen originally trained as a fine artist.

CIVILISATION (1969)

A series in which art historian Sir Kenneth Clark examined how 2,000 years of creativeness moulded Western civilisation into what it is today. Made for a then whopping £500,000 and filmed over three years, the series has long been regarded as a benchmark for quality documentaries, even though at the time, only one million British viewers tuned in.

 TV Trivia: Clark was the father of Alan Clark, MP.

COAST (2005–)

Neil Oliver has become something of a housewives' heartthrob following his enthusiastic appearances in this British series. Since 2005 he has travelled the British coastline (for the first series as the archaeological and social history expert, from Series 2 as the main presenter), enthusing about our dramatic coastline and the history behind it and the people who live by it. If you don't feel patriotic about our green and pleasant land after watching this, you never will.

 TV Trivia: In most of the first series' episodes, then-presenter Nicholas Crane stated that Britons should remember they are only ever 72 miles away from the sea while in Britain.

CROCODILE HUNTER (1996–2004)

Bursting with enthusiasm and perhaps a little recklessness, adventurer Steve Irwin introduced viewers to the wildlife refuge he and his wife Terri ran in Australia that houses some of the world's most dangerous, toothy creatures. There's some fascinating interaction with the crocodiles Irwin captures from populated areas and relocates to the wilds, and his bounciness ('Crikey!') is infectious. Sadly, of course, Steve Irwin was killed off the coast of Queensland by a stingray to his heart in 2006, but his wife and young daughter Bindi continue his work.

 TV Trivia: By the time he was nine, Steve – taught by his dad – could jump in and catch crocodiles in the rivers of north Queensland.

DEAD FAMOUS (2004–2006)

Supposedly sceptical TV presenter Gail Porter (who jumps every time someone opens a door) and the paranormally 'sensitive' Chris Fleming take a ride across America in this series to track down the spirits of famous dead people. Yes, it is as bad and ridiculous as it sounds, especially when they decide the best place to channel John Lennon is Shea Stadium, where The Beatles played (rather than, say, the apartment building where he died in New York) or hold a seance for possible suicide victim Marilyn Monroe and conclude she seems a bit sad. So bad it's almost unwatchable.

 TV Trivia: Gail Porter is probably best known for the naked photograph of her that was projected onto the side of the Houses of Parliament by *FHM* magazine.

THE ED SULLIVAN SHOW (1948–1971)

As music fans will know, Ed Sullivan was the grumpy-faced old geezer whose variety show was one of the highest rated in America during the 1950s and 1960s. Elvis shocked the nation by swizzling his hips to Ed's audience, The Doors were asked to remove a drug-recommending lyric from 'Light My Fire' (they didn't), and the Beatles made a bouncy debut in February 1964 (one of four appearances), but the show is also remembered for non-musical stars, too – from Jackie Mason to Bob Hope and Milton Berle.

 TV Trivia: Ed Sullivan's nickname was 'the great stone face'.

FROM THE EARTH TO THE MOON (1998)

Apollo 13 star Tom Hanks and the film's director, Ron Howard, were the men behind this fascinating 12-part drama-documentary that details the legendary Apollo missions into space in the 1960s and 1970s. Episodes include one devoted to the media's handling of the 'failed' Apollo 13 mission, the Apollo 1 fire and investigation, and one that sees the Apollo adventures from the point of view of the wives involved in the missions, with all the major players played by actors including Adam Baldwin, Gary Cole, Sally Field and Blythe Danner.

 TV Trivia: Several of the actors playing NASA flight controllers were reprising their roles from *Apollo 13*.

GORDON RAMSAY (THE F-WORD. 2005– ; KITCHEN NIGHTMARES. 2004–)

Brash, argumentative, foul-mouthed and award-winning chef Ramsay certainly made a change from sweet Delia Smith and cheeky Jamie Oliver when he blasted onto our TV screens. The former footballer first appeared in the riveting *Kitchen Nightmares*, in which he goes to a failing restaurant, figures out what is wrong (usually it's run by idiots or a twit of a chef who thinks prawns in chocolate is a good idea), yells at the staff a lot, and then turns the place around. The slightly less explosive *The F Word* has Ramsay raising livestock, cooking and taking up challenges such as an onion-chopping contest between him and a prisoner at Marshgate jail (Ramsay lost and offered the prisoner a job once he was released).

 TV Trivia: In the first series of *The F-Word*, Ramsay named the turkeys he raised after fellow chefs Antony Worrall-Thompson,

Ainsley Harriott, Jamie Oliver, Delia Smith, Gary Rhodes and Nigella Lawson.

GRAND DESIGNS (2001–)

Sadly, *Property Ladder* and *Location Location Location* aren't available on DVD, so those of us who enjoy property porn will have to make do with this duller series about people who design their own homes and attempt to build them. Hosted by Kevin McCloud, it is sometimes entertaining to watch people build their dream houses, no matter how impractical they are, and have him comment on their folly, but ultimately they're never homes you would actually want to live in so you end up shouting at the TV about how narrow-minded these people are.

 TV Trivia: McCloud has a good background for the show – he grew up in a house his parents built.

GROUND FORCE (1998–2002)

While the 'experts' on *Changing Rooms* tended to ruin people's houses, this more horticultural makeover show was far nicer – as a viewer you knew the lucky homeowner would end up with a lovely garden courtesy of presenter/gardener Alan Titchmarsh, the infamously bra-less female gardener/posh totty Charlie Dimmock, and handyman Tommy Walsh. There would usually be some catastrophe along the way (burst water pipes, bad weather flooding their masterpieces etc), but what was so lovely was that, even when tempers flared, everyone was so bloody nice about it…

 TV Trivia: When transforming an African garden, Nelson Mandela told Charlie he thought she looked like a Spice Girl.

THE HUMAN BODY (1998)

BAFTA award-winning documentary series presented by Professor Robert Winston. This series covered everything you could possibly think of with regards to our human form – conception and childbirth, puberty, ageing and even death. Using terrific techniques, like seeing the birth of a baby from inside the mother, and following fibre-optic cameras along the intestines – this was fascinating stuff, if occasionally stomach-churning!

 TV Trivia: Winston is one of the foremost pioneers of reproductive surgery and fertility treatment.

JACQUES COUSTEAU'S ODYSSEY (1977)

The master of underwater filming known for his red woolly hat made many documentaries about life in the oceans, but the only one that is easily available on DVD is this *Odyssey* series in which he and his crew explore the possible source of the legendary Atlantis, and search the Aegean sea for the *Titanic*'s sister ship, the *Britannic*. Fascinating stuff.

TV Trivia: The character played by Bill Murray in Wes Anderson's *The Life Aquatic with Steve Zissou* is reportedly based on Cousteau.

JAMIE OLIVER (THE NAKED CHEF. 1999; JAMIE'S KITCHEN. 2002; SCHOOL DINNERS. 2005; CHRISTMAS. 2006; AT HOME. 2007)

Cheekie chappie Jamie Oliver brought his own brand of cooking to TV with the *Naked Chef* series back in 1999, in which he – to many a woman's dismay – kept his clothes on but offered simple recipes delivered in his own chirpy style. Later series are more sophisticated, while *School Dinners* followed an often emotional Oliver as he attempted to change the hideous school dinners served to our kids (the infamous turkey twizzlers among them) for healthier food. Give that man a knighthood!

TV Trivia: In 2005, Jamie Oliver was criticised for killing a conscious lamb on his TV show.

LIFE ON EARTH (1979)

Legendary David Attenborough series in which he travelled the globe to trace the story of the evolution of life on the planet. Numerous special filming techniques were devised to show animals' movements and life (including filming bats in a wind tunnel in slow motion to show how their wings moved) but the most memorable sequence will always be Attenborough's hushed meeting with an adult female gorilla, who even groomed and played with him. The series launched a succession of 'Life' documentary series, including *Life in the Undergrowth*, *The Life of Mammals*, *The Trials of Life* and *The Living Planet*. All are available on DVD.

TV Trivia: Channel 4 viewers, voting for the most memorable TV moments of all time, rated Attenborough's gorilla meeting

above the wedding of Prince Charles and Diana Spencer, and the Queen's coronation.

LONG WAY ROUND (2004)/LONG WAY DOWN (2007)

Actor Ewan McGregor and his best pal Charley Boorman decided to take a motorcycle trip around the world back in 2004. Leaving family at home and followed by just a small camera crew, they rode through hazardous places (for weather and/or political reasons) such as Siberia, Kazakhstan and Mongolia, before deciding they loved it so much they'd do another jaunt, from Scotland down to the tip of South Africa three years later. Fascinating stuff, made all the more watchable by the pair's seemingly boundless enthusiasm for life and bikes.

 TV Trivia: Charley Boorman is the son of director John Boorman and appeared in the lead role in his dad's film *The Emerald Forest*.

LOUIS THEROUX'S WEIRD WEEKENDS (1999–2001)

Even if you don't like the rather opinionated (and, slightly obnoxious) Theroux, you have to admire his nerve as he worms his way into people's homes or lives and then proceeds to look down his nose at them. This US-set series had the intrepid reporter hanging out with televangelists, survivalists, porn stars, body-builders and swingers (thankfully, not all at the same time), while the DVD collection also includes Theroux's bizarre interactions with UK celebrities, including Jimmy Saville and Neil and Christine Hamilton.

 TV Trivia: Louis is the son of *Mosquito Coast* author Paul Theroux.

MONARCHY (2004–)

An in-depth look at England's rulers from historian and academic Dr David Starkey, this Channel Four series has, over four seasons so far, covered some of the most turbulent events in British history, from the Norman conquest to the execution of Charles I, all retold in Starkey's incredibly well-informed, gripping style. In fact, the series aims to cover over 1,500 years of murder, betrayal, religious persecution and bloody battles, with the first series beginning in 400AD as the Romans leave Britain. Great stuff.

 TV Trivia: Starkey's salary from Channel Four made him the highest paid performer on British TV at the time.

MOST HAUNTED (2002–)

Inexplicably successful 'reality' TV series, in which paranormal 'investigator' Yvette Fielding (an ex-*Blue Peter* presenter) and a guest medium (often the theatrical Derek Acorah) and a para-psychologist investigate supposed paranormal activity, which usually means numerous shots of Fielding looking petrified at the camera in the dark (illuminated by green light) as something wobbles in the background. The series was accused of faking some of the 'events' (no, really?!) but so far only one accusation of faking has been proven, that involved Acorah who has since left the show. Watch and see for yourself if you dare…

 TV Trivia: Yvette Fielding was, aged 19, the youngest presenter *Blue Peter* had ever had.

NIGELLA BITES (2001)

Delia Smith may have been the queen of recipes on TV for a time (her stern directions no longer available on DVD), but posh, raven-haired Nigella Lawson stole her crown with a series of fun TV shows in which she cooked without strictly following recipes (you can almost hear Delia tutting), dunked her finger in things to taste them, and became almost orgasmic over chocolate desserts and other sinful treats. You won't learn much about cooking, but Ms Lawson manages to make a visit to the cooker seem almost appealing.

 TV Trivia: Nigella Lawson declined the offer of an OBE for services to journalism and cookery in 2001.

THE OPRAH WINFREY SHOW (1986–)

A US TV phenomenon, Oprah Winfrey has flattered Hollywood stars, explored social issues, discussed her personal weight loss and gain (and loss, and gain), and become a multi-millionairess in the process. Much imitated, but never bettered, the series is a great balance between heart-rending stories and fun guests, and a 20th anniversary DVD of her finest moments on air was released in 2006.

 TV Trivia: Oprah was the first African–American woman to be featured on *Forbes* Billionaire List in 2003.

A PICTURE OF BRITAIN (2005)

David Dimbleby wrote and presented this documentary series about the British landscape and the art it has inspired over the years. Each of the six episodes focused on a different area of the country – The Romantic North, The Flatlands, Highlands and Glens, The Heart of England, The Home Front and The Mystical West – and how it has influenced poets, painters and composers. Dull in places, but with some simply stunning scenery to keep you enthralled.

 TV Trivia: The series was produced in association with the Tate Gallery and the Tate Modern.

PREHISTORIC PARK (2006)

Hot on the heels of BBC's phenomenally successful *Walking With Dinosaurs* and its sequels came this ITV documentary-drama in which Nigel Marven travels back in time to collect various creatures such as a T-Rex and a woolly mammoth before they became extinct so he can bring them back to a preservation park in the present day. One for kids more than grown-ups, its special effects aren't on a par with the *Walking With Dinosaurs* series or *Jurassic Park*, but Marven is an enjoyable host.

 TV Trivia: Marven collaborated for 12 years with David Attenborough as a documentary producer.

THE QUEEN'S CASTLE (2005)

A revealing look behind the scenes at life at Windsor Castle over the course of a year. As well as being one of the queen's favourite homes, the castle has also played host to many important royal occasions, including the Order of the Garter Ceremony. But what is most fascinating here are the unguarded moments as HRH Prince Philip, The Duke of Edinburgh, guides the cameras around the land that he obviously holds very dear.

 TV Trivia: The 1992 fire at Windsor Castle destroyed over 20 per cent of the building and took five years to restore.

RIVER COTTAGE (1999-2006)

Beginning with 1999's *Escape To River Cottage* (which was followed by *Return To...* in 2000, *River Cottage Forever* in 2002, *Beyond River Cottage* in 2004, etc), city dweller Hugh Fearnley-Whittingstall attempts to simplify his life by moving to a smallholding in rural Dorset. It's sort of like a serious version of *The Good Life* as Hugh turns a pretty garden into a vegetable patch, and starts raising livestock to provide for his family, while offering up some yummy recipes along the way. Hugh F-W's series *A Cook on the Wild Side* is also on DVD.

 TV Trivia: River Cottage was originally a weekend and holiday home you could rent out before the series were made.

SIMON SCHAMA: A HISTORY OF BRITAIN (2000-2002)

Historian Schama joined forces with the BBC for this history of Britain, beginning with the Roman conquest and romping through various events using reconstructions, his always thought-provoking opinions, and even pop songs to illustrate his points. Covering over 5,000 years of British history in 15 hours, he draws you in, fascinates you and leaves you with a sense that you have been very lucky to be in the presence of such a very clever and likeable man. Schama followed this series with *The Power of Art* (2006) and *Rough Crossings* (2007). Both are available on DVD.

 TV Trivia: Although it is called *A History of Britain*, the series was criticised for mainly focusing on England and glossing over the history of Scotland, Wales and Ireland.

TIME TEAM (1994-)

Tony Robinson – best known, perhaps, as Baldrick in the *Blackadder* series – is the presenter of this long-running, hugely enjoyable archaeology show. With a team of archaeologists, he visits a site ripe for investigation and the team describe why it is of historical interest and what they might find buried beneath the soil. Over the years, their finds have included coins from the reign of Henry V, the remains of a burnt-down Tudor mansion and the rather creepy 'bone cave' in Gloucestershire.

TV Trivia: Robinson received an honorary doctorate from Exeter University to acknowledge his contribution towards raising awareness of archaeology in Britain.

TWO FAT LADIES (1997)

Former barrister Clarissa Dickson-Wright and Jennifer Paterson (who died in 1999) were the two no-nonsense cooks who hopped on their motorcycle and sidecar to travel through the English countryside and cook a meal that usually involved heart-attack-inducing ingredients like cheese, cream or red meat. Packed with gossip, laughter and even songs, this was a great programme, thanks to two jolly women who loved both cooking food and eating it.

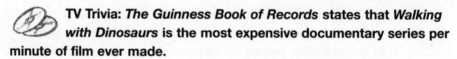 **TV Trivia: Because Paterson's uncle was an aide to the Archbishop of Westminster, the ladies were allowed to cook and be filmed at Westminster Cathedral.**

WALKING WITH DINOSAURS (1999)

Stunning BBC documentary series narrated by Kenneth Branagh about these fascinating prehistoric creatures, this incorporated the latest CGI effects to depict dinosaurs walking the earth. If you think *Jurassic Park* was impressive, this will blow you away as it vividly tells the tale of the epic creatures who roamed the planet during the Triassic, Jurassic and Cretaceous periods. If you only ever own one documentary, make it this one. *Walking with Beasts* followed in 2001, then *Walking with Cavemen* (2003) and *Walking with Monsters* (2005). .

TV Trivia: *The Guinness Book of Records* **states that** *Walking with Dinosaurs* **is the most expensive documentary series per minute of film ever made.**

EiGHT SERiES WE WiSH WERE AVAiLABLE ON DVD iN THE UK...

EVERWOOD (2002–2006)

Utterly lovely family drama, starring Treat Williams as New York brain surgeon Andy Brown, who is so absorbed in his work he barely knows his children. That changes when his wife dies, and he follows her wishes to take their kids, brooding teen Ephram (Gregory Smith) and young Delia (Vivien Cardone) to the Colorado mountain town of Everwood for a new start. Over four seasons, we got to know the residents of the town – including fussy town doctor Harold Abbott – and came to love all of them. Shown in the middle of the day and later the middle of the night by ITV (as *Our New Life in Everwood*), only the first season is available in the US, too.

FREAKS AND GEEKS

Fans of Judd Apatow (writer/director of *Knocked Up* and *The 40-Year Old Virgin*) would love this terrific teen series that made his name. Set in the 1980s at McKinley High, the comedy drama follows two sets of teens – the Freaks, with cool Daniel (James Franco) and tomboy Lindsay (Linda Cardinelli) and the nerdy Geeks, with Lindsay's younger brother Sam (John Francis Daley) among them. Sharply written, brilliantly played, this only lasted one season but it's a true gem. Watch out for *Knocked Up* star (and Apatow pal) Seth Rogen in a supporting role if you get your hands on a US DVD copy.

TOUR OF DUTY (1987–1990)

Well-written, well-played, award-winning drama set during the Vietnam War, *Tour Of Duty* followed the fortunes and tragedies of one US army platoon, led by Lieutenant Goldman (Stephen Caffrey) and his brusque sergeant, Zeke Anderson (Terence Knox), and the problems they suffered while 'in country'. Inspired by the success at the cinemas of *Platoon*, this gritty drama boasts a similarly memorable soundtrack, including the show's theme song, the Rolling Stones' classic 'Paint It Black'.

GUNSMOKE (1955–1975)

Marshal Dillon is the lawman for Dodge City in this classic Western series set in the 1870s that ran for two decades – his job is to keep those in line who have no respect for the law, prevent cattle rustling, stop gunfights and bar brawls and other crimes that blight frontier life. A thigh-slapping adventure series that ran for over 600 episodes, the series starred James Arness as Dillon, Milburn Stone as Doc Adams, and also featured young actors including Dennis Weaver and Burt Reynolds in recurring roles. Classic westerns *Rawhide* and *Maverick* aren't currently on DVD either.

SOAP (1977–1981)

Yes, it has dated terribly, but there is something classic and also hysterically funny about this comedy series that spoofed soaps and drama serials. Following the antics of two families – the Campbells and the Tates – the show featured a host of quirky characters including ditzy Jessica Tate (Katherine Helmond); Chuck, who thinks his ventriloquist's dummy is a real person and Burt, who was abducted by aliens, and is also notable for being one of the first mainstream US shows to feature a gay character (Jodie, as played by Billy Crystal).

DUCKMAN: PRIVATE DICK/FAMILY MAN (1994–1997)

Warped, wicked and wildly funny adult animation from Klasky/Csupo, the creators of *Rugrats*. Duckman (voiced by Jason Alexander of *Seinfeld* fame) is a wise-ass, foul-mouthed, lazy and crude duck who is also a private detective, though if he does actually manage to solve a crime it is usually thanks to the help of his porcine pal, Cornfed Pig (voiced by Gregg Berger). The series ran for four seasons and currently only seasons 1 and 2 are available on DVD in the US.

PICKET FENCES (1992–1996)

Quirky American TV series about small town life – made a decade before *Desperate Housewives* came along – *Picket Fences* was set in Rome, Wisconsin, and focused on the Brock family. Jimmy Brock (Tom Skerritt) is the sheriff, his wife Jill (Kathy Baker) the local doctor, and with their kids they mingle with the many eccentric people of the town. Utterly bonkers and surreal stuff that's very addictive – in this town, there is murder, kidnapping and even spontaneous human combustion around every corner. Created by David E Kelley, who also devised *Ally McBeal*, the series also starred Lauren Holly,

Costas Mandylor, and *Charmed*'s Holly Marie Combs.

VERONICA MARS (2004–2007)

Superb teen series from creator Rob Thomas that ran for just three seasons. Veronica (Kristin Bell) used to be one of the popular girls at school, with a hunky rich boyfriend named Duncan Kane (Teddy Dunn), and his sister Lily as a best friend. But Lily was murdered and Veronica's dad — then the local sheriff — accused Duncan and Lily's father of the crime. Now Veronica is a social outcast, helping her dad on the occasional case (he was fired due to the Kane accusation and is now a private detective) while trying to find out who really killed Lily. The first season dealt with the Kane crime, while new puzzles needed to be solved in the later seasons. Witty and smart stuff — think *Buffy* without the vampires.

MUSIC

HERE ARE THE CLASSIC MUSIC SHOWS AND POP-RELATED REALITY SERIES AVAILABLE ON DVD. FOR MORE MUSIC-THEMED SERIES, SEE TEENAGERS, P.149.

AMERICAN IDOL (2002–)

Starring Ryan Seacrest, Simon Cowell, Paula Abdul, Randy Jackson

Following on from the success of *Pop Stars* and *Pop Idol* in Britain (neither of which are on DVD), creator Simon Fuller and music executive-turned television producer and judge Simon Cowell took their product stateside and developed it into an international phenomenon. Essentially a talent show, *American Idol* became the biggest success on US television and made megastars of presenter Ryan Seacrest and judges Cowell, Randy Jackson and Paula Abdul.

The format is simple but fiendishly brilliant: each summer, there are auditions at cities around the US, where Cowell, Jackson and Abdul decide (in front of the cameras, of course), which members of the public are talented enough singers to move onto the next round. These auditions attracted some very talented singers, but also some of the weirdest, most disillusioned people you are likely to come across, which adds to the interest. Once the numbers have been whittled down, the lucky few go to Hollywood where they try out once more, with many being eliminated before a group of finalists is selected to compete each week against each other on live TV. While some of the winners haven't done as well post-Idol as you would expect (Taylor Hicks, Ruben Studdard, we mean you), some have gone on to mega success, including country singer Carrie Underwood, pop star Kelly Clarkson and Fantasia Barrino, who has won rave reviews on Broadway.

People tune in to see the bad as well as the good, but this has become must-see TV thanks to the bitching/teasing (you decide) between Seacrest and Cowell, the scathing comments Cowell comes up with each week, and the bizarre love/hate relationship between Cowell and Abdul. Utterly compelling viewing. At present, highlights of the best and worst of the first four seasons are available on DVD.

TV Trivia: There was actually a second presenter, Brian Dunkleman, as well as Seacrest, for Season 1. A comedian, he was not asked back for Season 2.

THE ANDY WILLIAMS SHOW (1962–1967. 1969–1971)

Starring Andy Williams

With Val Doonican's TV specials currently unavailable on DVD, those who enjoy their music with a hot cup of cocoa, fuzzy slippers and a nice warm cardi could do worse than settle down with crooner Andy Williams, whose show provided a mix of soothing tunes (rock and pop not allowed) and entertainment on a weekly basis in the sixties.

Over the years, his show featured guests including Peggy Lee, comedian Bob Newhart, Bobby Darin, Eddie Fisher, Pat Boone, Tony Bennett, Sammy Davis Jr, Liberace and Woody Allen, though many will remember Williams' other claim to fame – his was the first show to feature a family group of singers from Utah called The Osmonds.

A slice of what variety TV was like in the sixties, and a way of seeing some very famous people at the peak of their careers, this is TV to doze off to, in the nicest possible way.

 TV Trivia: Williams was discovered by that ultimate crooner, Bing Crosby, who heard him sing with his siblings as part of the Williams Brothers Quartet.

DANCING ON ICE (2006–)

Starring Jayne Torvill, Christopher Dean, Philip Schofield, Holly Willoughby

First there was the BBC's *Strictly Come Dancing* (in which celebrities competed in a ballroom dancing competition with often hilarious results), which, surprisingly, isn't available on DVD – and then came ITV's maliciously genius twist on the idea. Instead of getting celebrities to compete on the dance floor, why not set them an even bigger challenge: to make complete prats of themselves on the ice as ice dance skaters, paired with professional skaters?

Under the tutelage of Olympic gold medal winners Torvill and Dean, stars including former child actor Bonnie Langford, footballer David Seaman, professional celeb Ulrika Jonsson and boyband member Duncan James squeezed themselves into spangly outfits, strapped on their skates and trained like crazy in an attempt to go from stumbling buffoons on ice to slick skaters in a matter of weeks.

While some may pretend they tune in for the ice dance (some of which is actually pretty good), deep down we all know the real reason for watching is to see a D-list celebrity take a tumble onto their tushies. (Unfortunately for Seaman's professional partner, Pam O'Connor, it was she rather than him who took a memorable fall in rehearsals and hurt herself). Hilarious stuff if you enjoy luminous yellow, tight sparkly lycra ensembles and watching other people in pain.

 TV Trivia: Former royal butler Paul Burrell was due to compete in the first season but pulled out just a week before due to concerns about his skating ability.

DONNY & MARIE (1976–1979)

Starring Donny Osmond, Marie Osmond

She was a little bit country and he was a little bit rock and roll – together siblings Donny and Marie Osmond grinned their way through four years as hosts of possibly the world's most inoffensive variety show. Cheesier than a Stilton factory, the show featured the pair singing/butchering popular tunes (watching them murder 'Jive Talkin' is truly awesome), performing eye-wincingly bad comedy sketches and, most dreadful of all, joining in an ice skating routine (below their stage was an ice rink, you see).

A big hit in the US – meaning millions of children there were blinded by the Osmonds' dazzling teeth, and hypnotised by their shiny jumpsuits and too-good-to-be-true niceness – the show suffered a dip in ratings when it was revealed (shock, horror!) that Donny was dating Debbie Glenn, whom he later married. The show was expanded to include the entire Osmond brood and retitled *The Osmond Family Show* before it was cancelled. Donny, of course, went on to star on stage in *Joseph and His Technicolor Dreamcoat* while Marie launched her own line of Victorian-style dolls which she sells on American TV. (The pair also reunited to present a US chat show in 1998 that ran for two years.)

 TV Trivia: At the show's height, you could buy a toy TV studio with accompanying Donny and Marie dolls.

EUROVISION SONG CONTEST (1956–)

Starring Johnny Logan, Bucks Fizz, Celine Dion etc

One of the longest-running TV events in the world, the Eurovision Song Contest was devised back in 1956 as a way of bringing Europe together in song. While the format has changed over the years – and new countries have joined the 'Eurovision' family – the idea remains the same: each competing country submits a song sung by an artist or group and all the member countries vote to decide which is the best (a country is not allowed to vote for its own song). The main rule is that the song must be original and should not have been commercially released prior to the competition. But forget the rules – as anyone who has ever watched the show knows, the Eurovision Song Contest, especially in recent years, is more comedy than serious competition. While some artists who have competed in the past have had international success – ABBA, who won in 1974 for 'Waterloo'; Celine Dion, representing Switzerland with 'Ne Partez Pas Sons Moi' in 1988; and Britain's Bucks Fizz, who won with 'Making Your Mind Up' in 1981 – the main reason we all tune in is to see the bad acts, the ones we're hoping will score absolutely nothing (or 'nil points') at all, and Terry Wogan's sarcastic commentary.

Recent competitions are available on DVD in their entirety, but since much of Eastern Europe has joined in, it is just a dull exercise in strategic voting as they all vote for their neighbouring countries. Instead, track down *Eurovision's Greatest Hits* to once again enjoy the naff vocal stylings of such middle of the road artists as Johnny Logan, Cliff Richard and the Brotherhood of Man. So bad it's (almost) good.

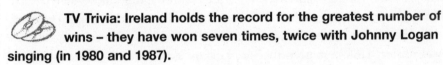 **TV Trivia: Ireland holds the record for the greatest number of wins – they have won seven times, twice with Johnny Logan singing (in 1980 and 1987).**

FAME ACADEMY (2002–2003)

Starring Cat Deeley, Patrick Kielty

The BBC's answer to *Pop Idol*, this had a *Big Brother* element to it that added a nice slice of tension but was less flashy and generally a bit duller and more earnest than its ITV counterpart. A group of wannabe musicians compete each week for the chance to win a £1 million recording contract and, based on their performances in front of judges, they would either be declared 'safe' or in the 'danger' zone. Each week, one person in the danger zone would be voted out by his/her fellow contestants. And that wasn't all – the 'students', as they were known, all had to live together in a house in north London that was wired up with cameras so viewers could see their fights and sobbing fests online, as well as watch the competitors be trained in singing techniques and performing skills during the week.

Two series were made featuring unknowns competing, but in 2003, 2005 and 2007 the series was relaunched as *Celebrity Fame Academy*, with celebs (many of whom couldn't hold a tune at best, and screeched at worst – Ruby Wax earning special praise in that department) living under the same roof and getting their chance to warble for the public. Far more entertaining than the original show due to the varying levels of talent and amusement of seeing celebs in their pjs, the three celebrity competitions were won by Will Mellor, Edith Bowman and Tara Palmer-Tomkinson. Unfortunately only the non-celeb series are available on DVD.

TV Trivia: The house used for the series was Witanhurst, a Georgian-style mansion in Highgate that boasts 25 bedrooms and a grand ballroom. It is the second-largest privately owned house in London, the first being Buckingham Palace.

THE FRANK SiNATRA SHOW (1950–1952; 1957–1958)
Starring Frank Sinatra

In 1950, 'Ol Blue Eyes had been a chart-topper and a movie star, but his career was on the wane (due to problems with his voice and his well-publicised affair with Ava Gardner) when he gained his own TV series. In viewing terms, it wasn't a huge success, and critics weren't too kind either (*Variety* said the show had 'bad pacing, bad scripting, bad tempo, poor camera work and an overall jerky presentation') but the show improved every time Sinatra began to sing. Unfortunately, the variety skits in between – including a New Year's episode in which Frank hired the Three Stooges to be butlers for his party – were dire, and the show was cancelled after two series. However, by the late fifties, Sinatra's star had soared following his role in *From Here to Eternity* and a string of successful albums, so he returned to TV in 1957 and took more control of the proceedings. Again, the series was a mix of comedy, variety and song, with guests including Sammy Davis Jr, Dean Martin, Bob Hope and Frank's daughter Nancy.

Sinatra went on to make a series of TV specials, the best remembered of which is *Welcome Home Elvis*, a tribute to Elvis Presley that featured the King in his first TV appearance following his return from army service in May 1960. Although Sinatra reportedly didn't like Presley or his music, it became the most successful episode of Frank's TV show.

 TV Trivia: In 1957 Sinatra described Elvis as a 'rancid-smelling aphrodisiac'.

LATER WiTH JooLS HOLLAND (1992–)
Starring Jools Holland

Former Squeeze keyboard player Jools Holland brought music to a cozy setting for this long-running series. Each week, he has a handful of musical guests performing in the studio, and sometimes joins in with them himself. It's mellow rather than rocking – possibly because the artists form a circle so are effectively performing to each other and the camera, rather than to the live audience which amounts to a few people (possibly BBC employees) scattered about in between.

Because Holland has such varied musical knowledge, and a clear enthusiasm for it, the performers on the show have been a superbly eclectic mix, from jazzy chanteuses Amy Winehouse and Ruby Turner to popsters Paul Weller and Jarvis Cocker to old hands Tom Jones, Dr John and Elvis Costello. Each act gets to perform at least twice during the show, which has often led to some cracking performances of both their own material (Dido singing 'Thank You') and cover versions (Patti Smith singing Nirvana's 'Smells Like Teen Spirit').

 TV Trivia: In 2003 Jools Holland was awarded an OBE for services to music.

MARC (1977)

Starring Marc Bolan

He was the king of glam rock, the pin-up of teenage girls everywhere and, at the height of his fame, Marc Bolan also had his own hit TV show, called *Marc*. Made by Granada TV and shown during children's TV time, the series was presented by the former T-Rex frontman and featured his electric performances and those of a host of musical guests. Of course, now all the sparkly sets look terribly dated (and Bolan wasn't the best at miming), but the series captured a fun, silly and infectious slice of British pop history. One series was made, with a second due to start production in 1978.

Sadly, Marc was killed in a car accident on 16 September 1977, aged just 29 and the last few episodes of the first series were broadcast after his death. Unfortunately the only DVD of *Marc* the series is a compilation of Bolan's performances for the show, including 'Jeepster', 'Get It On' and 'I Love To Boogie', which, while great to watch, misses out the other acts who performed with him, including Billy Idol, Thin Lizzy and The Damned.

 TV Trivia: Although Marc loved cars, he never learnt to drive (his girlfriend, Gloria Jones, was at the wheel when he died).

THE OLD GREY WHISTLE TEST (1971–1987)

Starring Bob Harris, Mark Ellen, David Hepworth, Andy Kershaw

While *Top of the Pops* was a music show for people who liked their tunesmiths poppy and chirpy, *The Old Grey Whistle Test* on BBC2 was a music programme for more serious music lovers, who wanted stripped-down performances (none of those flashy strobe lights and all that techno nonsense) – bands and artists performing live on a bare stage.

On air for 16 years, the show has become a time capsule of raw, memorable performances from artists (both known and up and coming when they appeared on the show) including Roxy Music, The Who (disappointingly miming), New York Dolls, Tim Buckley, Hall And Oates, Joan Armatrading, Suzanne Vega, Janis Ian, Supertramp, Japan and Lone Justice. For rock fans, the compilations available of these performances are a rare treat, although the commentaries from former presenters slow down proceedings somewhat. Just sit back and let the music play...

TV Trivia: The show's title refers to an old record company trick: when they got the first pressing of a new record they would play it to the 'old greys', the office cleaners. The tunes they remembered and could whistle after only hearing the song a few times were the ones that had passed the old grey whistle test...

PENNIES FROM HEAVEN (1978)

Starring Bob Hoskins, Cheryl Campbell, Gemma Craven

Screenwriter Dennis Potter's first big TV series (he was best known for one-off dramas) was a lengthy mini-series, punctuated with 1930s melodies, which the characters in the story step out of the drama to mime and dance to. Such light, fluffy songs are in contrast with the dark central story about cockney songsheet salesman Arthur Parker (Hoskins). Trapped in an affectionless marriage to Joan (Craven) during the Depression, he falls for teacher Eileen (Campbell) but they are parted when she is dismissed from her teaching position and ends up in London, supporting herself as a prostitute. Later reunited, the pair find their happiness thwarted when Arthur is falsely accused of the rape and murder of a blind girl.

As you'd expect from Potter, this is a mix of extremely traumatic moments, alongside witty ones, poignant and sometimes sentimental songs (that reflect Arthur's own naive belief that the world can be a lovely place, as it is in the songs he peddles). It works wonderfully well, and features superb performances from the cast that also includes Freddie Jones, Nigel Havers and Kenneth Colley. A film version was attempted in 1981, with Steve Martin in the lead role, but it didn't manage to capture the uniqueness of the original.

TV Trivia: In the British Film Institute's list of the best British Television Programmes of the 20th Century, *Pennies From Heaven* came 21st (Potter's *The Singing Detective* was 20th).

POP IDOL (2001–2003)

Starring Ant and Dec, Simon Cowell

Remember *New Faces* and *Opportunity Knocks*? Well, *Pop Idol* was effectively a 21st-century version of those shows, a talent contest in which members of the public could become stars. Following on from the success of *Popstars* (no longer on DVD), the reality show that had launched the careers of groups Hear'Say and Liberty X, *Pop Idol* creator Simon Fuller took the format and applied it to individual performers. After hundreds of wannabe singers were eliminated in early auditions in front of judges Simon Cowell, Nicki Chapman, Pete Waterman and DJ Neil Fox, the remaining performers then sang each week for a live audience, with viewers' phone votes deciding who should stay another week and who should go home, back to obscurity and pub karaoke nights.

From this, the phenomenon that is *American Idol* was launched, and due to his acerbic comments on both, judge Simon Cowell became an international star, while presenters Ant McPartlin and Declan Donnelly secured their places as ITV's best light entertainment hosts. The winners and runners-up of the show haven't been so lucky: Michelle McManus, Gareth Gates (now best known for his liaison with a very pregnant Jordan) and Darius Danesh (who, with a bit of a makeover went from looking like a serial killer to becoming quite a pin-up, apparently) have slipped out of the public view, and only Will Young has a continuing career. Oh well.

TV Trivia: Ant and Dec received the Lifetime Achievement Award at the National Television Awards in 2002. They were both just 27 years old.

ROCK FOLLIES (1976–1977)

Starring Rula Lenska, Julie Covington, Charlotte Cornwell

This camp ITV series followed the rise and inevitable fall of The Little Ladies, a fictional pop band featuring three singers: Dee (Covington), Anna

(Cornwell) and 'Q' (Lenska). Struggling to make it big, the girls take on the good and the bad of the music industry, while the drama itself broke new ground for evening telly, depicting the fast world of rock 'n' roll, drug use and (gasp!) homosexuals.

With music written by Andy Mackay (Roxy Music), this was considered cutting edge at the time, and boasted some sharp scripts and fun acting from the three leads. Aside from Julie Covington's vocals, the singing wasn't up to much, but the gals were popular enough that two hit albums were made. Unintentionally funny now, thanks to the hideous seventies fashions and the 'scandalous' plot points that now seem rather tame.

 TV Trivia: Charlotte Cornwell is now a professor at an USC university in Southern California.

THE SONNY AND CHER COMEDY HOUR (1971–1974): THE SONNY AND CHER SHOW (1976–1977)

Starring Sonny Bono, Cher

Husband and wife Sonny and Cher traded on their personalities – he was a goof, she was a more serious performer, with a storming singing voice – for two series that became popular on American TV during the seventies. A mixture of performance and some of the daftest comedy skits you're ever likely to witness, their show attracted big names – Glenn Campbell, Carol Burnett, Jerry Lewis, George Burns – and made the couple (who weren't quite as happy off stage as they seemed on it) into megastars.

Together, in their sheepskin waistcoats, bell-bottoms and increasingly revealing outfits (for Cher, at least), the pair sung songs, told jokes, exchanged off-the-cuff banter and even brought their young daughter Chastity on to the stage. It's all pretty naff now, but still fun to watch the pair bicker and sing songs like their popular 'I Got You Babe'. The show was cancelled in 1974 as the pair divorced in real life, but was revived in 1976 (after both Sonny and Cher tried their hands at solo TV shows that both failed) as *The Sonny and Cher Show*, with a young Steve Martin among the writing staff, but it only lasted two seasons until low ratings forced the show's cancellation.

 TV Trivia: The couple had originally toured the clubs as a serious singing act (Cher being too nervous to perform solo) as Caesar and Cleo.

TOP OF THE POPS (1964–2006)

Starring Jimmy Saville, Tony Blackburn, Pan's People

BBC1's landmark music show for over four decades began in 1964, with DJ Jimmy Saville introducing a collection of pop acts (beginning with The Rolling Stones and then Dusty Springfield) performing in the studio. In the early years, if an artist couldn't be at BBC Manchester's studios or BBC Television Centre to perform, their hit song was played while the resident dancers (Pan's People and later Ruby Flipper, Legs & Co and Zoo) danced along, often interpreting the music hilariously (one example being the canine-influenced dancing to Gilbert O'Sullivan's 'Get Down'). In later years, these dances were replaced by pop music videos, and the show often had very few 'live' performances in between the flashy video clips, though the BBC eventually tried to remedy this by requesting every band/artist with a chart hit must perform live.

There have been some hilarious moments over the years – Dexy's Midnight Runners singing 'Jackie Wilson Said', a tribute to the soul legend, while some berk at the Beeb projected a photo of darts player *Jocky* Wilson behind them; Noel and Liam Gallagher switching roles (Noel miming to Liam, Liam pretending to play guitar) while Oasis performed 'Roll With It' to name just two – and some memorable ones, such as Rod Stewart's rendition of 'Maggie May' with DJ/presenter John Peel faking playing the mandolin behind him.

A national institution and essential viewing for teens wanting to know the chart hits and misses over the years, the show couldn't perhaps keep up with the times but remains sorely missed.

TV Trivia: When told he had just 15 seconds to interview Debbie Harry, John Peel asked an extra long question so she wouldn't have time to answer. Harry was reportedly greatly amused by this.

THE TUBE (1982–1987)

Starring Paula Yates, Jools Holland

It always looked like something was about to go terribly wrong and the presenters – ex-groupie Paula Yates and former Squeeze keyboardist Jools Holland – weren't exactly slick, but this Channel Four rock show was addictive. It was partly due to Holland and Yates' irreverent style and screen chemistry (and Yates' flirting with guests that made for compulsive viewing) but also due to the calibre of acts they attracted – from established artists like

U2, Madonna and Bowie to up-and-coming acts like INXS and Frankie Goes To Hollywood.

The cameras were hand-held (and often shaky), the interviewing style rough to say the least, and the whole thing was live, fresh and fun (especially when a celebrity or presenter decided to start swearing – you wouldn't get that on *Top of the Pops*). Currently, highlights of the first series are available on DVD, which includes The Jam's last TV appearance, and performances from Soft Cell, Iggy Pop, Depeche Mode, Yazoo and Heaven 17, to name a few.

 TV Trivia: The series was cancelled in 1987 after Jools Holland accidentally said a very choice swearword during a live trailer for the show, broadcast during children's TV time. Oops.

THE X-FACTOR (2004–)

Starring Simon Cowell, Sharon Osbourne, Louis Walsh

A similar idea to *Pop Idol* (so similar that *Pop Idol* creator Simon Fuller sued *X-Factor*'s Simon Cowell for copyright infringement), *The X-Factor* is another British talent competition that lures thousands of wannabe singers to audition each year and then face elimination before a live audience every Saturday night. The difference is that the competition is divided into categories: the under-25s, over-25s and groups (in 2007 this was changed to girls, boys, over-25s and groups) and once the numbers of performers have been whittled down, each of these categories is assigned a 'mentor' in the form of Cowell, music producer Louis Walsh or former rock manager Sharon Osbourne (pop singer Dannii Minogue was added to the line-up in 2007 and Cheryl Cole in 2008).

The novel formula works better for viewers than contestants as Cowell and his fellow mentors have their acts competing against each other, so entertainingly bitter wars of words usually break out (often between a preening Cowell and childish Walsh, although Osbourne has been known to throw the odd glass of water). Thus it turns into a fun but utterly pointless competition between the judges/mentors rather than their acts, and becomes even more frustrating when novelty acts such as Chico (2005) stay in the competition longer than their talent should allow.

A DVD of the best/worst auditions is available as well as behind-the-scenes footage of the competition itself.

 TV Trivia: Simon Cowell began his music career as a mailroom boy at the offices of EMI Music.

STARS SINGING THEIR OWN THEME SONGS...

Little Britain parodied Dennis Waterman writing the theme tune and singing the theme tune to his TV shows – but he's not the only actor to have warbled over a TV series' opening credits:

Paul Nicholas sang the theme song (written by John Sullivan) to the romantic comedy series *Just Good Friends* (1983–1986).

Judi Dench sang the theme song to *A Fine Romance* (1981–1984) in which she starred with husband Michael Williams.

Cybill Shepherd, once the girlfriend of Elvis Presley, sang the theme song 'Nice Work If You Can Get It' to her sitcom *Cybill* (1995–1998).

Kelsey Grammer sings 'Tossed Salad And Scrambled Eggs', the theme song to his long-running comedy *Frasier* (1993–2004).

Lee Majors sang the theme 'The Unknown Stuntman' for his series *The Fall Guy* (1981–1986).

David Hasselhoff sang the music 'I Believe' (a duet with Laura Branigan) over the end credits from the third season of *Baywatch* (1989–2001).

Greg Evigan sang 'BJ McKay', the theme song to *BJ And The Bear* (1979–1981).

Will Smith – as the Fresh Prince – and music partner DJ Jazzy Jeff sang the theme tune to *The Fresh Prince of Bel Air* (1990–1996).

The entire cast, including Johnny Depp, sang the theme to *21 Jump Street* (1987–1991).

And, saving the best till last...
Dennis Waterman sang the theme song to not one but *four* of his shows: *Minder* ('I Could Be So Good For You'), *Stay Lucky* ('Stay Lucky And Free'), *On The Up* and *New Tricks* ('It's Alright').

SPORT

MANY FOOTBALL MATCHES, CRICKET TESTS, SNOOKER GAMES AND GRAND PRIX RACES – CLASSIC AND OTHERWISE – THAT HAVE BEEN SHOWN ON TV ARE AVAILABLE ON DVD, BUT THEY BELONG IN A BOOK ON THEIR OWN. BELOW ARE THE TV DRAMAS, COMEDIES, QUIZZES AND FACTUAL SHOWS INVOLVING SPORT THAT YOU CAN BUY ON DISC (SADLY, THE FUNNY *MY SUMMER WITH DES* ISN'T ONE OF THEM…)

ALL IN THE GAME (2006)

Starring Ray Winstone, Danny Dyer, Roy Marsden

Not to be confused with the 1993 mini-series of the same name that was co-created by footballer Gary Lineker, this drama has Ray Winstone chewing the scenery as gruff, sheepskin coat-wearing manager Frankie. Intended to show the ugly side of the beautiful game, the TV film has Frankie signing a new young player with the help of agent Martin (Dyer), who isn't just corrupt… he's Frankie's son.

Unfortunately, this drama is as packed with stereotypes as it is with enjoyably ripe bad language. Frankie is the archetypal grumpy, cussing manager, and he shares the screen with slimy football agents, bling-wearing players and brassy wives. It's all a bit miserable to watch, as none of the characters except club chairman George (Marsden) are remotely sympathetic as they connive, twist and turn everything to their advantage just so they can have a bigger house or car.

 TV Trivia: In a Sky Movies' Sexiest British Actor poll, Winstone came seventh, beating Paul Bettany and Jonny Lee Miller among others.

BODYLINE (1984)

Starring Gary Sweet, Hugo Weaving, John Doyle

A mini-series about cricket doesn't necessarily sound riveting, but this period drama was quite fascinating stuff, focusing as it did on the 1932–33 Test cricket series between England and Australia that changed cricketing history. During the matches played in Australia, the English team, led by ambitious captain Douglas Jardine (Weaving), used a controversial technique called 'leg theory' or 'bodyline', which basically allowed bowlers to aim the ball directly at the poor batsman's body rather than the stumps, resulting in injuries and and some very pissed-off Australians. (One player, Bert Oldfield, ended up with a cracked skull, but in real life this wasn't due to the English bowling – the ball glanced off his bat and conked him).

Made in Oz by Australians, this doesn't exactly paint the English in a great light and plays a little fast and loose with the facts, which may annoy cricket fans familiar with the story. For example, a scene in which Australian fans burn the English flag is fictional. However, as a drama about ego, pride and national spirit (both English and Australian), this is interesting (though if you don't know a thing about cricket, it will remain a mystery to you once this is over), and for fans of the game, there are good portrayals of famous players Don Bradman (considered the greatest batsman ever) by Gary Sweet and English bowler Harold Larwood (Jim Holt), who was often blamed for the injuries the Aussies sustained.

 TV Trivia: Harold Larwood emigrated to Australia in 1950, and when this series was first aired he received threatening letters and phone calls.

FANTASY FOOTBALL (2004)

Starring David Baddiel, Frank Skinner

Comedians (and footy fans) Baddiel and Skinner scored a hit TV show when they mixed their love of the game with comic sketches, football statistics and their own wry observations (usually broadcast from their comfy sofa). While the series proper ran for three years (1994–1996), only highlights of the 2004 special are available on DVD but they contain the duo's witticisms about the Euro 2004 championship, including 'The Adventures Of Cristiano Ronaldo' and fan favourites such as 'Phoenix From The Flames' (where Baddiel and Skinner recreate an historic goal with one of the players involved) and 'Homo Erotic Moments in Football'.

It's all cheeky fun, with Statto providing the football trivia and various celebrity guests joining the comics on the couch to discuss the finer points of the game.

 TV Trivia: In the 1998 special (unavailable on DVD), guest Johnny Rotten was thrown out during a commercial break for being overly aggressive.

FOOTBALLERS' WIVES (2002–2006)

Starring Zoe Lucker, Gillian Taylforth, Gary Lucy, Susie Amy

With more scandal, backstabbing, designer fashion and jewels than an entire series of *Dynasty*, *Footballers' Wives* exploded onto TV screens in 2002, depicting (with a liberal dose of humour, sex and exaggeration) the glamorous lives of a group of fictional British footballers and their shopping, shagging and bitching-loving wives. Packed with betrayals and outrageous plot points such as kidnappings, suspicious deaths (usually the unfortunate husbands of queen bitch Tanya Tucker, as played with relish by Zoe Lucker), comas and surprise pregnancies, the show sizzled with silliness and sharp dialogue ('You go anywhere near my husband again and it'll take more than Botox to sort your face out') and sex scenes so raunchy that one (in which one of the footballers is having sex with a male prostitute) was cut due to an outcry before it was even broadcast.

Of the various Earls Park players and their wives, the most memorable by far were the trashy, scheming Tanya, pretty mummy's boy Kyle (Lucy) and his amour, model Chardonnay (their wedding is a hilarious spoof of the excesses of Posh and David Beckham's – she lies in state as Sleeping Beauty while the groom, dressed as Prince Charming has to kiss her to 'wake' her at the beginning of the ceremony) and Kyle's mother Jackie (Taylforth). Sadly, they didn't all stay for the entire five seasons of the show and some new, less interesting characters were added, but the addition of Joan Collins as magazine editor Eva De Wolffe in the final season spiced things up a bit.

Utterly ridiculous, over the top and as shallow as a puddle, this soap was steamy, preposterous and thoroughly addictive.

 TV Trivia: One episode of an American version of the series was made in 2007, with Lucy Lawless, James Van Der Beek and Ving Rhames.

FRIDAY NIGHT LIGHTS (2006–)

Starring Kyle Chandler, Connie Britton

A spin-off loosely based on the 2004 Billy Bob Thornton-starring movie about a Texan high school football team, this US drama follows the kids, parents, supporters and coach of the Dillon High School Panthers. Eric Taylor (Chandler) has recently been hired as the new head coach of the town's team, and he soon learns the pressure the residents put on their kids to win at all costs (even his wife is questioned about football strategy during her book club meeting).

To non-Americans, this obsession with the heavily padded, seemingly non-sensical game of American football may seem a bit bizarre, but while the town's drive for their team to win takes up some of the plot, there is other stuff going on, from Taylor's own strained relationship with his wife (Britton) and daughter to teen traumas such as the cheerleader dating both the star quarterback and a local troublemaker, and the smart-mouthed Landry (Jesse Plemons) beginning a relationship with Tyra (Adrianne Palicki) after helping her when she has been attacked. In fact it is more of a relationship/family drama than a sporting one, and performance-wise, not a bad one at that. Forget the football, a nd enjoy the drama.

 TV Trivia: *The Friday Night Lights* movie was based on a book, *Friday Night Lights: A Town A Team A Dream*, about a real-life Texas high school football team.

MiKE BASSETT: MANAGER (2005)

Starring Ricky Tomlinson, Amanda Redman

Ricky Tomlinson first played the character of Mike Bassett in the 2001 movie of the same name, and here he returns to the role of football manager Mike, now managing struggling club Wirral County FC after being fired from his England manager role (his team lost to Lichtenstein).

Only six 30-minute episodes of this comedy were made, and when you watch it, it's not a surprise that the series was not renewed for another year. The jokes are very broad but not that funny, and the humorous moments are more likely to make you smile than laugh out loud. Tomlinson is engaging as the worn-out manager and there's nice support from Amanda Redman, but this never really rises above second-division fare.

 TV Trivia: The series was actually made in 2003, but not broadcast until two years later.

PLAYiNG THE FiELD (1998–2002)

Starring James Nesbitt, Lesley Sharp, Gaynor Faye

A drama about a local football club doesn't sound like much fun but this series was surprisingly enjoyable – partly because the club in question was a women's footie club, and partly because it was scripted by Kay Mellor, of

Band of Gold fame. She focused on the fictional Castlefield Blues, a badly managed, under-funded team in South Yorkshire and the lives and loves of the women on the team, as well as their antics on the field.

For the first few seasons, the series boasted a cast that included James Nesbitt, John Thomson and Lesley Sharpe, but as they left, the show became rather forgettable, and it was cancelled in 2002. Other cast members included Gaynor Faye (Mellor's real-life daughter), Sean Bean's ex-wife Melanie Hill, Brigit Forsyth and Marsha Thomason, who went on to co-star in the American TV series *Las Vegas*.

 TV Trivia: After the series was cancelled in 2002, the BBC reportedly wanted to bring it back as a half-hour long soap opera.

SUPERSTARS (1976–1983)

Presented by David Vine, Ron Pickering

Sadly, those staples of naff seventies telly, *We Are The Champions* (in which schools competed against each other in various silly sporting contests) and *It's a Knockout* (even more absurd competitiveness) aren't on DVD but – hurrah! – we can still laugh ourselves silly at sportspeople of the era making utter prats of themselves on *Superstars*.

Various sport stars, including judo star Brian Jacks, footballer Kevin Keegan, racing driver James Hunt, strongman Geoff Capes and squash player Jonah Barrington competed in a decathlon of events ranging from cycling (Keegan memorably injuring himself when he fell after much wobbling on his bike) to clay pigeon shooting, with Jacks and boxer John Conteh among the series winners.

Terrific stuff if you like to watch sportsmen and women completely out of their comfort zone. Other versions of the series were also broadcast throughout Europe and in the US and a new British version was made in 2008.

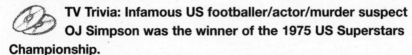 **TV Trivia: Infamous US footballer/actor/murder suspect OJ Simpson was the winner of the 1975 US Superstars Championship.**

THEY THINK IT'S ALL OVER (1995–2007)

Starring Nick Hancock, Gary Lineker, Ian Wright

A long-running quiz show that mixed comedy with sport. Nick Hancock hosted the quiz as two celebrity teams competed against each other to answer a series of daft sporting questions as accurately/daftly/wittily as possible.

And, er, that's about it. The show ranged from mildly amusing to rib-ticklingly funny, depending on the guests (regular Jonathan Ross always provides a few sniggers) but while some parts of the show were enjoyable, the round where the contestants have to 'feel the sportsman' while blindfolded (basically, grope some poor individual to guess who it is) wore out its welcome in the first series. Not bad overall, but the similar (music-themed) *Never Mind The Buzzcocks* is much better. Note that the other famous British sporting quiz show, the rather more serious *A Question of Sport*, is only available as an interactive DVD game.

 TV Trivia: Panellist Jonathan Ross was voted the sexiest male voice on UK radio in a poll by Trojan Condoms!

TOP GEAR (1978–)

Starring Jeremy Clarkson, Richard Hammond, James May

Originally a conventional motoring show on the BBC with presenters that included Angela Rippon, Noel Edmonds and Jeremy Clarkson, *Top Gear* went from being a reasonably straight-laced half-hour show, reviewing cars and running features on car safety, to something entirely more enjoyably bonkers following a revamp in 2002. (Some of *Top Gear*'s presenters and crew had defected to Channel Five's similar *Fifth Gear* in 2001, giving the BBC a good reason to give their flagship show a new look). Now with Clarkson (who had departed from old *Top Gear* in 1999), James May and Richard Hammond at the wheel, this series has become BBC2's highest-rated show – and one of its most fun.

Whether the guys are trying to drive converted cars into the English Channel, launching caravans off a clifftop to see which one hit the 'bullseye' below, or racing across Europe to see whether Clarkson in a car can beat the other presenters in anything but a car, this show works incredibly well, thanks to the enthusiasm the trio have for the cars and their sheer joy when they get to test drive a good one. All three share a nice repartee, and features such as 'star in a reasonably priced car' (in which a celebrity – and everyone from

Simon Cowell to Helen Mirren has done it – races around the *Top Gear* track) and the various nutty challenges help to make this one of the funniest programmes on TV. They are joined each week by 'The Stig', a white-jumpsuit and helmet-clad racer who tests the cars on the *Top Gear* track – his identity is unknown but believed to have been, at times, Damon Hill, Julian Bailey and the late Colin McRae.

TV Trivia: In September 2006, Hammond received a severe brain injury following a high-speed crash during a sequence he was filming for the series. When he returned to the show, he was greeted by showgirls after telling Clarkson he didn't want any fuss made.

INDEX OF ENTRIES